Our
LIVING LANGUAGE

SECOND EDITION

KELLOGG W. HUNT · PAUL STOAKES
THE FLORIDA STATE UNIVERSITY

Houghton Mifflin Company · Boston

NEW YORK · ATLANTA · GENEVA, ILL. · DALLAS · PALO ALTO

PRINTED IN THE U. S. A.

❧ PREFACE

Freshman English should direct the student to our language in its most vital forms. It should impel him to an awareness that language pungently alive can add conviction to message and enchantment to fact. It should inform him about language, explicitly through those who write about it and implicitly through those who use it well. It should encourage him to examine curiously and scrupulously the way language functions at its most intense — in literature. It should make him sensitive to the procedures of those who manipulate language in advertising, motion pictures, television, magazines, newspapers, and books.

Part of the frustration felt by many teachers of Freshman English results from the fact that the course, though usually concerned with freshmen, is not always concerned with the most important aspects of English. Pursuing unruly commas, libelous misspellings, and criminal solecisms is no more rewarding than other forms of police work — and a lot less fun. Training freshmen to avoid misdemeanors without giving them a motive for doing so is a waste of their time and the teacher's. It can't be done that way, any more than a boy can learn to swim without going near the water. Even if freshmen learn to proofread, they learn at best a negative virtue — one they should have mastered before they got to college, and won't learn in college either, if they are not given better reasons for learning it than they apparently got in high school.

There are better things to spend time on in a college course in written communication. Developing a style is one of them. And the student who begins to glimpse the meaning of style and who, however falteringly, gropes toward a style of his own will acquire along the way an increasingly firm control of the mechanics he couldn't master until he was given a reason to.

So this book is undeviatingly concerned with language — which after all ought to be the subject of an English course. We do not ask the teacher of English to become expert on everything from anthropology to zoology and to struggle alongside his students to grasp Heisenberg on the atom and Schweitzer on ethics. Those are important matters, but the nature of language and of the English language in particular is an important matter too, and far more nearly within the English teacher's competence.

The selections in this volume are all concerned with writing well — with talking about it and exemplifying it. Part One offers discussions of language by writers of both scholarship and skill. One effect of seeing what they say and how they say it should be to banish the notion that excellence in writing, like purity, is the automatic reward for avoiding "errors."

In Part Two, the intensity of the writing rises above the experience of daily life — in short, it is literature. Nobody expects freshmen to produce literature. But there is no better place than Freshman English to examine with some care the functions of language as language in producing it. Courses in literature seldom get around to this consideration. They are often concerned with subject matter instead of language form, and they often assume on the student's part a sensitiveness to language unjustified by anything in his experience. The stories, poems, and plays provided here may well be studied with particular attention to the qualities in the language itself that help them to be literature.

In Part Three, sensitive and articulate critics grapple with literature in general and with specific works and the men behind them. If poetry, as someone has said, is language at its most efficient, in what does its efficiency consist? In maximum effect from minimum cause? In spiraling emotions from little black marks on white paper? In connotations that spread, like ripples from a dropped pebble? In some reverberating quality in the thought itself so that, language aside, nobility shines through? These are vast questions, and there are but sparse answers. Yet awareness of questions may be one of modern man's most pressing needs.

If the selections in this book help us to raise fruitful questions about our language and its most vital use, they will have done the thing we wanted most to have them do.

KELLOGG W. HUNT

PAUL STOAKES

❧ CONTENTS

PART TWO • LANGUAGE IN LITERATURE

The Short Story

MYSTERY AND SURPRISE

SELF-REVELATION OF CHARACTER

POINT OF VIEW

FANTASY

SYMBOLISM

viii · *Contents*

PART THREE • LANGUAGE ABOUT LITERATURE

What Literature Is

How Writers Mean

PART ONE

❦

THE LANGUAGE WE USE

Writing Our Language

Standards in Language

What Language Is

WRITING

OUR LANGUAGE

How to Say Nothing in Five Hundred Words

PAUL ROBERTS

Nothing About Something

It's Friday afternoon, and you have almost survived another week of classes. You are just looking forward dreamily to the week end when the English instructor says: "For Monday you will turn in a five-hundred word composition on college football."

Well, that puts a good big hole in the week end. You don't have any strong views on college football one way or the other. You get rather excited during the season and go to all the home games and find it rather more fun than not. On the other hand, the class has been reading Robert

Hutchins in the anthology and perhaps Shaw's "Eighty-Yard Run," and from the class discussion you have got the idea that the instructor thinks college football is for the birds. You are no fool, you. You can figure out what side to take.

After dinner you get out the portable typewriter that you got for high school graduation. You might as well get it over with and enjoy Saturday and Sunday. Five hundred words is about two double-spaced pages with normal margins. You put in a sheet of paper, think up a title, and you're off:

WHY COLLEGE FOOTBALL SHOULD BE ABOLISHED

College football should be abolished because it's bad for the school and also bad for the players. The players are so busy practicing that they don't have any time for their studies.

This, you feel, is a mighty good start. The only trouble is that it's only thirty-two words. You still have four hundred and sixty-eight to go, and you've pretty well exhausted the subject. It comes to you that you do your best thinking in the morning, so you put away the typewriter and go to the movies. But the next morning you have to do your washing and some math problems, and in the afternoon you go to the game. The English instructor turns up too, and you wonder if you've taken the right side after all. Saturday night you have a date, and Sunday morning you have to go to church. (You shouldn't let English assignments interfere with your religion.) What with one thing and another, it's ten o'clock Sunday night before you get out the typewriter again. You make a pot of coffee and start to fill out your views on college football. Put a little meat on the bones.

WHY COLLEGE FOOTBALL SHOULD BE ABOLISHED

In my opinion, it seems to me that college football should be abolished. The reason why I think this to be true is because I feel that football is bad for the colleges in nearly every respect. As Robert Hutchins says in his article in our anthology in which he discusses college football, it would be better if the colleges had race horses and had races with one another, because then the horses would not have to attend classes. I firmly agree with Mr. Hutchins on this point, and I am sure that many other students would agree too.

One reason why it seems to me that college football is bad is that it has become too commercial. In the olden times when people played football just for the fun of it, maybe college football was all right, but they do not play football just for the fun of it now as they used to in the old days. Nowadays college football is what you might call a big business. Maybe this is not true at all schools, and I don't think it is especially true here at State, but certainly this is the case at most colleges and universities in America nowadays, as Mr. Hutchins points out in his very interesting article. Actually the coaches and alumni go around to the high schools and offer the high school stars large salaries to come to their colleges and play football for them. There was one case where a high school star was offered a convertible if he would play football for a certain college.

Another reason for abolishing college football is that it is bad for the players. They do not have time to get a college education, because they are so busy playing football. A football player has to practice every afternoon from three to six, and then he is so tired that he can't concentrate on his studies. He just feels like dropping off to sleep after dinner, and then the next day he goes to his classes without having studied and maybe he fails the test.

(Good ripe stuff so far, but you're still a hundred and fifty-one words from home. One more push.)

Also I think college football is bad for the colleges and the universities because not very many students get to participate in it. Out of a college of ten thousand students only seventy-five or a hundred play football, if that many. Football is what you might call a spectator sport. That means that most people go to watch it but do not play it themselves.

(Four hundred and fifteen. Well, you still have the conclusion, and when you retype it, you can make the margins a little wider.)

These are the reasons why I agree with Mr. Hutchins that college football should be abolished in American colleges and universities.

On Monday you turn it in, moderately hopeful, and on Friday it comes back marked "weak in content" and sporting a big "D."

This essay is exaggerated a little, not much. The English instructor will recognize it as reasonably typical of what an assignment on college football will bring in. He knows that nearly half of the class will contrive in five hundred words to say that college football is too commercial and bad for the players. Most of the other half will inform him that college football builds character and prepares one for life and brings prestige to the school. As he reads paper after paper all saying the same thing in almost the same words, all bloodless, five hundred words dripping out of nothing, he wonders how he allowed himself to get trapped into teaching English when he might have had a happy and interesting life as an electrician or a confidence man.

Well, you may ask, what can you do about it? The subject is one on which you have few convictions and little information. Can you be expected to make a dull subject interesting? As a matter of fact, this is precisely what you are expected to do. This is the writer's essential task. All subjects, except sex, are dull until somebody makes them interesting. The writer's job is to find the argument, the approach, the angle, the wording that will take the reader with him. This is seldom easy, and it is particularly hard in subjects that have been much discussed: College Football, Fraternities, Popular Music, Is Chivalry Dead?, and the like. You will feel that there is nothing you can do with such subjects except repeat the old bromides. But there are some things you can do which will make your papers, if not throbbingly alive, at least less insufferably tedious than they might otherwise be.

Avoid the Obvious Content

Say the assignment is college football. Say that you've decided to be against it. Begin by putting down the arguments that come to your mind: it is too commercial, it takes the students' minds off their studies, it is hard on the players, it makes the university a kind of circus instead of an intellectual center, for most schools it is financially ruinous. Can you think of any more arguments just off hand? All right. Now when you write your paper, *make sure that you don't use any of the material on this list.* If these are the points that leap to your mind, they will leap to everyone else's too, and whether you get a "C" or a "D" may depend on whether the instructor reads your paper early when he is fresh and tolerant or late, when the sentence "In my opinion, college football has become too commercial," inexorably repeated, has brought him to the brink of lunacy.

Be against college football for some reason or reasons of your own. If they are keen and perceptive ones, that's splendid. But even if they are trivial or foolish or indefensible, you are still ahead so long as they are not everybody else's reasons too. Be against it because the colleges don't spend enough money on it to make it worth while, because it is bad for the characters of the spectators, because the players are forced to attend classes, because the football stars hog all the beautiful women, because it competes with baseball and is therefore un-American and possibly Communist inspired. There are lots of more or less unused reasons for being against college football.

Sometimes it is a good idea to sum up and dispose of the trite and conventional points before going on to your own. This has the advantage of indicating to the reader that you are going to be neither trite nor conventional. Something like this:

> We are often told that college football should be abolished because it has become too commercial or because it is bad for the players. These arguments are no doubt very cogent, but they don't really go to the heart of the matter.

Then you go to the heart of the matter.

Take the Less Usual Side

One rather simple way of getting interest into your paper is to take the side of the argument most of the citizens will want to avoid. If the assignment is an essay on dogs, you can, if you choose, explain that dogs are faithful and lovable companions, intelligent, useful as guardians of the house and protectors of children, indispensable in police work — in short, when all is said and done, man's best friends. Or you can suggest that those big brown eyes conceal, more often than not, a vacuity of mind and an inconstancy of purpose; that the dogs you have known most intimately have been mangy, ill-tempered brutes, incapable of instruction; and that only your nobility of mind and fear of arrest prevent you from kicking the flea-ridden animals when you pass them on the street.

Naturally, personal convictions will sometimes dictate your approach. If the assigned subject is "Is Methodism Rewarding to the Individual?" and you are a pious Methodist, you have really no choice. But few assigned subjects, if any, will fall in this category. Most of them will lie in broad areas of discussion with much to be said on both sides. They are intellectual exercises, and it is legitimate to argue now one way and now another, as debaters do in similar circumstances. Always take the side that looks to you hardest, least defensible. It will almost always turn out to be easier to write interestingly on that side.

This general advice applies where you have a choice of subjects. If you are to choose among "The Value of Fraternities" and "My Favorite High School Teacher" and "What I Think About Beetles," by all means plump for the beetles. By the time the instructor gets to your paper, he will be up to his ears in tedious tales about the French teacher at Bloombury High and assertions about how fraternities build character and prepare one for life. Your views on beetles, whatever they are, are bound to be a refreshing change.

Don't worry too much about figuring out what the instructor thinks about the subject so that you can cuddle up with him. Chances are his views are no stronger than yours. If he does have convictions and you oppose them, his problem is to keep from grading you higher than you deserve in order to show he is not biased. This doesn't mean that you should always cantankerously dissent from what the instructor says; that gets tiresome too. And if the subject assigned is "My Pet Peeve," do not begin, "My pet peeve is the English instructor who assigns papers on 'my pet peeve.'" This was still funny during the War of 1812, but it has sort of lost its edge since then. It is in general good manners to avoid personalities.

Slip Out of Abstraction

If you will study the essay on college football printed above, you will perceive that one reason for its appalling dullness is that it never gets down to particulars. It is just a series of not very glittering generalities: "football is bad for the colleges," "it has become too commercial," "football is a big business," "it is bad for the players," and so on. Such round phrases thudding against the reader's brain are unlikely to convince him, though they may well render him unconscious.

If you want the reader to believe that college football is bad for the players, you have to do more than say so. You have to display the evil. Take your roommate, Alfred Simkins, the second-string center. Picture poor old Alfy coming home from football practice every evening, bruised and aching, agonizingly tired, scarcely able to shovel the mashed potatoes into his mouth. Let us see him staggering up to the room, getting out his econ textbook, peering desperately at it with his good eye, falling asleep and failing the test in the morning. Let us share his unbearable tension as Saturday draws near. Will he fail, be demoted, lose his monthly allowance, be forced to return to the coal mines? And if he succeeds, what will be his reward? Perhaps a slight ripple of applause when the third-string center replaces him, a moment of elation in the locker room if the team wins, of despair if it loses. What will he look back on when he graduates from college? Toil and torn ligaments. And what will be his future? He is not good enough for pro football, and he is too obscure and weak in econ to succeed in stocks and bonds. College football is tearing the heart from Alfy Simkins and, when it finishes with him, will callously toss aside the shattered hulk.

This is no doubt a weak enough argument for the abolition of college football, but it is a sight better than saying, in three or four variations, that college football (in your opinion) is bad for the players.

Look at the work of any professional writer and notice how constantly he is moving from the generality, the abstract statement, to the concrete example, the facts and figures, the illustration. If he is writing on juvenile delinquency, he does not just tell you that juveniles are (it seems to him) delinquent and that (in his opinion) something should be done about it. He shows you juveniles being delinquent, tearing up movie theatres in Buffalo, stabbing high school principals in Dallas, smoking marijuana in Palo Alto. And more than likely he is moving toward some specific remedy, not just a general wringing of the hands.

It is no doubt possible to be *too* concrete, too illustrative or anecdotal, but few inexperienced writers err this way. For most the soundest advice is to be seeking always for the picture, to be always turning general remarks into seeable examples. Don't say, "Sororities teach girls the social graces." Say, "Sorority life teaches a girl how to carry on a conversation while pouring tea, without sloshing the tea into the saucer." Don't say, "I like certain kinds of popular music very much." Say, "Whenever I hear Gerber Spinklittle play 'Mississippi Man' on the trombone, my socks creep up my ankles."

With pen and with pencil we're learning to say
Nothing, more cleverly, every day.

WILLIAM ALLINGHAM

Get Rid of Obvious Padding

The student toiling away at his weekly English theme is too often tormented by a figure: five hundred words. How, he asks himself, is he to achieve this staggering total? Obviously by never using one word when he can somehow work in ten.

He is therefore seldom content with a plain statement like "Fast driving is dangerous." This has only four words in it. He takes thought, and the sentence becomes:

In my opinion, fast driving is dangerous.

Better, but he can do better still:

In my opinion, fast driving would seem to be rather dangerous.

If he is really adept, it may come out:

In my humble opinion, though I do not claim to be an expert on this complicated subject, fast driving, in most circumstances, would seem to be rather dangerous in many respects, or at least so it would seem to me.

Thus four words have been turned into forty, and not an iota of content has been added.

Now this is a way to go about reaching five hundred words, and if you are content with a "D" grade, it is as good a way as any. But if you aim higher, you must work differently. Instead of stuffing your sentences with straw, you must try steadily to get rid of the padding, to make your sentences lean and tough. If you are really working at it, your first draft will greatly exceed the required total, and then you will work it down, thus:

It is thought in some quarters that fraternities do not contribute as much as might be expected to campus life.
Some people think that fraternities contribute little to campus life.

The average doctor who practices in small towns or in the country must toil night and day to heal the sick.
Most country doctors work long hours.

When I was a little girl, I suffered from shyness and embarrassment in the presence of others.
I was a shy little girl.

It is absolutely necessary for the person employed as a marine fireman to give the matter of steam pressure his undivided attention at all times.
The fireman has to keep his eye on the steam gauge.

You may ask how you can arrive at five hundred words at this rate. Simply. You dig up more real content. Instead of taking a couple of obvious points off the surface of the topic and then circling warily around them for six paragraphs, you work in and explore, figure out the details. You illustrate. You say that fast driving is dangerous, and then you prove it. How long does it take to stop a car at forty and at eighty? How far can you see at night? What happens when a tire blows? What happens in a head-on collision at fifty miles an hour? Pretty soon your paper will be full of broken glass and blood and headless torsos, and reaching five hundred words will not really be a problem.

Call a Fool a Fool

Some of the padding in freshman themes is to be blamed not on anxiety about the word minimum but on excessive timidity. The student writes, "In my opinion, the principal of my high school acted in ways that I believe every unbiased person would have to call foolish." This isn't exactly what he means. What he means is, "My high school principal was a fool." If he was a fool, call him a fool. Hedging the thing about with "in-my-opinion's" and "it-seems-to-me's" and "as-I-see-it's" and "at-least-from-my-point-of-view's" gains you nothing. Delete these phrases whenever they creep into your paper.

The student's tendency to hedge stems from a modesty that in other circumstances would be commendable. He is, he realizes, young and inexperienced, and he half suspects that he is dopey and fuzzy-minded beyond the average. Probably only too true. But it doesn't help to announce your incompetence six times in every paragraph. Decide what you want to say and say it as vigorously as possible, without apology and in plain words.

Linguistic diffidence can take various forms. One is what we call *euphemism.* This is the tendency to call a spade "a certain garden implement" or women's underwear "unmentionables." It is stronger in some eras than others and in some people than others but it always operates more or less in subjects that are touchy or taboo: death, sex, madness, and so on. Thus we shrink from saying "He died last night" but say instead "passed away," "left us," "joined his Maker," "went to his reward." Or we try to take off the tension with a lighter cliché: "kicked the bucket," "cashed in his chips," "handed in his dinner pail." We have found all sorts of ways to avoid saying *mad:* "mentally ill," "touched," "not quite right upstairs," "feeble-minded," "innocent," "simple," "off his trolley," "not in his right mind." Even such a now plain word as *insane* began as a euphemism with the meaning "not healthy."

Modern science, particularly psychology, contributes many polysyllables in which we can wrap our thoughts and blunt their force. To many writers there is no such thing as a bad schoolboy. Schoolboys are maladjusted or unoriented or misunderstood or in need of guidance or lacking in continued success toward satisfactory integration of the personality as a social unit, but they are never bad. Psychology no doubt makes us better men or women, more sympathetic and tolerant, but it doesn't make writing any easier. Had Shakespeare been confronted with psychology, "To be or not to be" might have come out, "To continue as a social unit or not to do so. That is the personality problem. Whether 'tis a better sign of integration at the conscious level to display a psychic tolerance toward the maladjustments and repressions induced by one's lack of orientation in one's environment or —" But Hamlet would never have finished the soliloquy.

Writing in the modern world, you cannot altogether avoid modern jargon. Nor, in an effort to get away from euphemism, should you salt your paper with four-letter words. But you can do much if you will mount guard against those roundabout phrases, those echoing polysyllables that tend to slip into your writing to rob it of its crispness and force.

Beware of the Pat Expression

Other things being equal, avoid phrases like "other things being equal." Those sentences that come to you whole, or in two or three doughy lumps, are sure to be bad sentences. They are no creation of yours but pieces of common thought floating in the community soup.

Pat expressions are hard, often impossible, to avoid, because they come too easily to be noticed and seem too necessary to be dispensed with. No writer avoids them altogether, but good writers avoid them more often than poor writers.

By "pat expressions" we mean such tags as "to all practical intents and purposes," "the pure and simple truth," "from where I sit," "the time of his life," "to the ends of the earth," "in the twinkling of an eye," "as sure as you're born," "over my dead body," "under cover of darkness," "took the easy way out," "when all is said and done," "told him time and time again," "parted the best of friends," "stand up and be counted," "gave him the best years of her life," "worked her fingers to the bone." Like other clichés, these expressions were once forceful. Now we should use them only when we can't possibly think of anything else.

Some pat expressions stand like a wall between the writer and thought. Such a one is "the American way of life." Many student writers feel that when they have said that something accords with the American way of life or does not they have exhausted the subject. Actually, they have stopped at the highest level of abstraction. The American way of life is the complicated set of bonds between a hundred and eighty million ways. All of us know this when we think about it, but the tag phrase too often keeps us from thinking about it.

So with many another phrase dear to the politician: "this great land of ours," "the man in the street," "our national heritage." These may prove our patriotism or give a clue to our political beliefs, but otherwise they add nothing to the paper except words.

Colorful Words

The writer builds with words, and no builder uses a raw material more slippery and elusive and treacherous. A writer's work is a constant struggle to get the right word in the right place, to find that particular word that will convey his meaning exactly, that will persuade the reader or soothe him or startle or amuse him. He never succeeds altogether — sometimes he feels that he scarcely succeeds at all — but such successes as he has are what make the thing worth doing.

There is no book of rules for this game. One progresses through everlasting experiment on the basis of ever-widening experience. There are few useful generalizations that one can make about words as words, but there are perhaps a few.

Some words are what we call "colorful." By this we mean that they are calculated to produce a picture or induce an emotion. They are dressy instead of plain, specific instead of general, loud instead of soft. Thus, in place of "Her heart beat," we may write "Her heart *pounded, throbbed, fluttered, danced.*" Instead of "He sat in his chair," we may say, "He *lounged, sprawled, coiled.*" Instead of "It was hot," we may say, "It was *blistering, sultry, muggy, suffocating, steamy, wilting.*"

However, it should not be supposed that the fancy word is always better. Often it is as well to write "Her heart beat" or "It was hot" if that is all it did or all it was. Ages differ in how they like their prose. The nineteenth century liked it rich and smoky. The twentieth has usually preferred it lean and cool. The twentieth century writer, like all writers, is forever seeking the exact word, but he is wary of sounding feverish. He tends to pitch it low, to understate it, to throw it away. He knows that if he gets too colorful, the audience is likely to giggle.

See how this strikes you: "As the rich, golden glow of the sunset died away along the eternal western hills, Angela's limpid blue eyes looked softly and trustingly into Montague's flashing brown ones, and her heart pounded like a drum in time with the joyous song surging in her soul." Some people like that sort of thing, but most modern readers would say, "Good grief," and turn on the television.

Colored Words

Some words we would call not so much colorful as colored — that is, loaded with associations, good or bad. All words — except perhaps structure words — have associations of some sort. We have said that the meaning of a word is the sum of the contexts in which it occurs. When we hear a word, we hear with it an echo of all the situations in which we have heard it before.

In some words, these echoes are obvious and discussable. The word *mother,* for example, has, for most people, agreeable associations. When you hear *mother* you probably think of home, safety, love, food, and various other pleasant things. If one writes, "She was like a mother to me," he gets an effect which he would not get in "She was like an aunt to me." The advertiser makes use of the associations of *mother* by working it in when he talks about his product. The politician works it in when he talks about himself.

So also with such words as *home, liberty, fireside, contentment, patriot, tenderness, sacrifice, childlike, manly, bluff, limpid.* All of these words are loaded with favorable associations that would be rather hard to indicate in a straightforward definition. There is more than a literal difference between "They sat around the fireside" and "They sat around the stove." They might have been equally warm and happy around the stove, but *fireside* suggests leisure, grace, quiet tradition, congenial company, and *stove* does not.

Conversely, some words have bad associations. *Mother* suggests pleasant things, but *mother-in-law* does not. Many mothers-in-law are heroically lovable and some mothers drink gin all day and beat their children insensible, but these facts of life are beside the point. The thing is that *mother* sounds good and *mother-in-law* does not.

Or consider the word *intellectual.* This would seem to be a complimentary term, but in point of fact it is not, for it has picked up associations of impracticality and ineffectuality and general dopiness. So also with such words as *liberal, reactionary, Communist, socialist, capitalist, radical, schoolteacher, truck driver, undertaker, operator, salesman, huckster, speculator.* These convey meanings on the literal level, but beyond that — sometimes, in some places — they convey contempt on the part of the speaker.

The question of whether to use loaded words or not depends on what is being written. The scientist, the scholar, try to avoid them; for the poet, the advertising writer, the public speaker, they are standard equipment. But every writer should take care that they do not substitute for thought. If you write, "Anyone who thinks that is nothing but a Socialist (or Communist or capitalist)" you have said nothing except that you don't like people who think that, and such remarks are effective only with the most naïve readers. It is always a bad mistake to think your readers more naïve than they really are.

Colorless Words

But probably most student writers come to grief not with words that are colorful or those that are colored but with those that have no color at all. A pet example is *nice*, a word we would find it hard to dispense with in casual conversation but which is no longer capable of adding much to a description. Colorless words are those of such general meaning that in a particular sentence they mean nothing. Slang adjectives, like *cool* ("That's real cool") tend to explode all over the language. They are applied to everything, lose their original force, and quickly die.

Beware also of nouns of very general meaning, like *circumstances, cases, instances, aspects, factors, relationships, attitudes, eventualities,* etc. In most circumstances you will find that those cases of writing which contain too many instances of words like these will in this and other aspects have factors leading to unsatisfactory relationships with the reader resulting in unfavorable attitudes on his part and perhaps other eventualities, like a grade of "D." Notice also what "etc." means. It means "I'd like to make this list longer, but I can't think of any more examples."

FOR DISCUSSION

1. Roberts makes nine specific suggestions for adding life to your writing. Have you copied them out and posted them above your desk to guide you in your next writing assignment? If not, why not?

2. Does Roberts follow his own suggestions? Can you find examples of each?

3. Do you agree that a tedious theme with no errors in it should get a grade of "D"?

THEME TOPICS: *Try to figure out a fresh approach for the following hackneyed subjects:* The value of fraternities. Campus politics. Christmas. An ideal holiday. *Try a theme on one of the following unpopular subjects:* I hate dogs. Too many people go to college. Why all students should study Greek. Cars are useless luxuries. Why people shouldn't have hobbies.

Grammar and Style

HUGH SYKES DAVIES

The main problems of style centre round the gap which exists between the spoken and written versions of the same language. This gap is not always of the same size. Written English, for example, is now much more different from spoken English than it was in Shakespeare's time, and critics are generally agreed that our literature is the worse for it. Ever since Wordsworth urged that poetry should be written in a "selection of the language really used by men" it has been generally agreed that the gap should be narrowed again, and the best modern writers and authorities on style repeat the Wordsworthian view in one form or another, generally without acknowledgement.

Reprinted from *Grammar Without Tears* by Hugh Sykes Davies by permission of The John Day Company, Inc., publisher.

But while it is certainly true that written English would be all the better if it approached spoken English more closely than it does, it would be impossible to close the gap completely, and foolish even to try. The fact is that a speaker commands resources of expression far richer than those of a writer. He can reinforce particular points by giving special emphasis of voice and intonation to them; he can make use of facial gesture, "Nods and Becks and wreathed Smiles," or their opposites. He can play tricks with his hands and fingers, opening and shutting them, waving them up and down and sideways. If he is near enough to his victim, he can even nudge him to drive home a specially important sally, although modern ideas of good manners tend to look on this practice as low-bred.

Sometimes these oratorical and conversational tricks are more than mere adornments and graces of style. The first especially, vocal emphasis, is often a part of the meaning itself; if it is altered, the meaning alters with it. Victorian church-goers seem to have solaced themselves largely for the rigours of their religious duties by collecting examples of this kind of emphasis, the more misplaced the better. For example, a passage from *Samuel*, describing how Saul was finally persuaded to eat after long fasting, was once rendered like this: "And the woman had a fat calf in the house; and she hasted, and killed it, and took the flour, and kneaded it, and did bake unleavened bread thereof; and she brought it before Saul, and before his servants; and they *did eat*." On another occasion, a passage in the first *Book of Kings* was spoken thus: "He spake to his sons, saying, 'Saddle me the ass.' And they saddled *him*."

The same kind of modulation of meaning is very common in ordinary social intercourse. A hostess, for example, welcoming some guests might say "I'm very glad you've come" in at least three different ways. First, with a fairly even accent throughout, she would imply nothing more than a conventional greeting. Second, she might accent the sentence like this: "I'm very glad *you've* come," and so indicate that she was particularly pleased with the arrival of these guests rather than any of the others. And thirdly, she might accent it thus: "I'm very glad you've *come*," which would mean that there had been some doubt of their ability to be at the party, and that she was relieved to know that the obstacles had been overcome.

A very rich example of the same kind of phrase "It's no use asking her to change her mind," which can be given at least five quite different meanings by means of vocal accent:

> It's *no use* asking her to change her mind.
> It's no use *asking* her to change her mind.
> It's no use asking *her* to change her mind.
> It's no use asking her to *change* her mind.
> It's no use asking her to change her *mind*.[1]

[1] I owe this admirable example to Mr. Walter de la Mare, who gave it in a lecture some years ago.

Compared with this luxuriance of variation and modulation, the resources at the command of the writer are indeed limited. The words on the page are as dead as butterflies in a museum case; they have no life and glitter and movement; and one cannot be made to spring to notice before the others, or more than the others, by being uttered more loudly. Many of the special qualities of a written as opposed to a spoken version of the same language arise from the necessity to overcome this deadness in the word on the page, and to give life and emphasis to it by other means.

The simplest and most direct of these other means is the use of italics in print or underlining in manuscript. But for some reason not clearly explained by its exponents, modern taste is against these devices. Underlining is generally described as "feminine," by which it is to be inferred that no real man would make use of it, for fear of being thought womanly, while no real woman would use it either, because it is unmanly. Italics have suffered a similar discouragement, and it is likely that printers have reinforced it because they feel that their art is best displayed in an entirely uniform, ultra-tidy page. It is true, of course, that both underlining and italics are liable to abuse, especially in the hands of the young, who are inclined to make use of them for escaping from linguistic tight corners they never should have got into. But the danger of abuse is no good reason for avoiding the use of these devices altogether, and it would probably be a means of enlivening modern English style if they were more freely allowed. Coleridge and De Quincey would afford good models of their effective use.

But a revival of italics alone would go only a short way to solving the special problems of the writer. It is the simplest resource for pointing emphasis in writing or print; and for that reason, one of the least effective and most quickly exhausted of its full force by frequent use. Other resources must be understood and used as well, and the more of them the better. The most obvious and important is to bring into play a far wider vocabulary than is generally used in speaking. This enables the writer to make his most emphatic words do their own shouting, as it were — to impinge sharply on the consciousness of his readers by their unfamiliarity and inherent force. The first variation of the last sentence quoted above, for example, "It's *no use* asking her to change her mind," might be rendered in writing by doing away with the commonplace phrase *no use,* and putting in its place some word such as *futile* or *otiose.* But since this is not a book on the use of the English vocabulary, it is enough to observe the existence of this second way of marking emphasis, without illustrating it further.

A third way of doing the same thing, not so generally known, at any rate consciously, but hardly less important, is the proper management of word-order. A good deal has been said about this already, in its relation to various grammatical problems. But it fully deserves further consideration here, because it is the main contribution that grammatical studies can make to good style in the positive sense — to liveliness and force of language.

We have seen that in an ordinary English sentence (excluding questions and certain other special orders of words) the positions of greatest emphasis will be found at the end and at the beginning. There is, of course, nothing absolute about this rule, and in particular instances the fall of the emphasis will be altered greatly by the shape of the sentences that have come before, or those that come after. But as a rough general guide it can probably be accepted. Here are two examples of it:

> The true aspect of the place, especially of the house in which he lived as a child, the fashion of its doors, its hearths, its windows, the very scent upon the air of it, was with him in sleep for a season; only, with tints more musically blent on wall and floor, and some finer light and shadow running in and out, along its curves and angles, and with all its little carvings daintier (Walter Pater, *Emerald Uthwart*).

> Patrons are respectfully requested not to use the plates and saucers as ashtrays, as not being of china these will burn.

No other order of words would have given Pater just this degree of emphasis on "daintier," or the proprietor of the cafe where the second sentence hangs such an effective advertisement of the inflammable nature of his crockery.

Very neatly the same force of emphasis can be gained by making good use of the beginning of a sentence, and this is particularly effective when there is some approach to an inversion, or obvious departure from the normal order. There is in English a special device for bringing about this type of emphasis, in the use of the phrase "It is . . ." For example, "Man shall not live by bread alone" can be made substantially more emphatic by being written: "It is not by bread alone that man shall live."

But these examples of variation of emphasis by means of word-order are only the simplest part of the writer's special problem. Except for a few specialists in epigrams and apothegms, literary composition does not consist of the construction of single sentences; it is made up of the far more difficult process of stringing sentences together in such a way that they link up with one another naturally and easily, carrying the attention of the reader along with them in a sequence that corresponds as closely as possible with the development of the meaning itself. This process has been well described, and its importance rightly estimated, by one of the greatest masters of it, De Quincey:

> The two capital secrets of prose are these: first, the philosophy of transition and connexion, or the art by which one step in the evolution of thoughts is made to arise out of another; all fluent and effective composition depends on the connexions; secondly, the way in which sentences are made to modify each other; for the most powerful effects in written eloquence arise out of this reverberation, as it were, from each other in a rapid succession of sentences . . .

Although De Quincey did not say it himself, it is obvious that one of the most important ways of securing ease of transition and connection, and of enabling sentences to "reverberate," is by arranging the words in them in suitable orders.

One of the most obvious ways of securing these benefits is by the various forms of parallelism in word-order. Mrs. Micawber, for example, shows a real grasp of the principles of prose, as well as of her husband's character, when she says: "Talent, Mr. Micawber has; capital, Mr. Micawber has not." On a much more elaborate scale, Dr. Johnson was a regular employer of the same device, and one of his choicest examples of it is his comment on Pope's famous grotto at Twickenham: "Pope's excavation was requisite as an entrance to his garden, and as some men try to be proud of their defects, he extracted an ornament from an inconvenience, and vanity created a grotto where necessity enforced a passage." Another variant of the same device is Peacock's account of a young nobleman whose hobbies included breaking-in wild horses and designing patent safety-carriages: "The grooms said they wouldn't drive any horse in that carriage, nor that horse in any carriage."

But parallelism, though very useful for special effects of this kind, and for witty and ironic expression generally, is perhaps too sparkling and conscious a device for the ordinary, day-to-day business of plain prose. For this, a less obtrusive way of linking sentences together is needed: one which allows the thoughts to "arise out of one another" naturally and easily, without obtruding itself on the reader's conscious attention. A very good and workmanlike example of this type of connection is this set of sentences from Dr. Johnson again:

> The metaphysical poets were men of *learning*, and to *show* their *learning* was their whole endeavour; but unluckily resolving to *show* it in *rhyme*, instead of writing poetry, they only wrote *verses*, and very often such *verses* as stood the trial of the finger better than of the ear; for the modulation was so imperfect, that they were only found to be *verses* by counting the syllables. (*Life of Cowley.* The italics are mine.)

Here the thought is carried on by a careful and very skilful repetition of words, and even more by ensuring that the order of the words in each sentence provides, as it were, a hook at the beginning and an eye at the end, so that they make an unbroken, closely linked chain. How aptly the hooks and eyes fit together can best be seen by disturbing their order, so that hooks are next to hooks and eyes to eyes, in this way:

> The metaphysical poets were men of *learning*, and their whole endeavour was to show their *learning*; but unluckily, instead of *writing* poetry, they only *wrote* verses, having resolved to *show* it in rhyme; and very often it was rather by the trial of the finger than by the ear that they were *verses* at all.

Perhaps to the average modern taste, there is something a little cumbrous in Dr. Johnson's repetition of the nouns and verbs intact, instead of putting pronouns and "pro-verbs" in their places. But the fundamental soundness of his word-placing allows this substitution to be made very easily:

> The metaphysical poets were men of learning, and their whole endeavour was to show it; but unluckily resolving to do so in rhyme, instead of writing poetry, they only wrote verses, which very often stood the trial of the finger better than the ear, for the modulation was so imperfect that they were only found to be verses by counting the syllables.

This runs more naturally, at any rate to the modern eye; but the trick of repeating the words entire, as in the original, is well worth the notice of the modern prose-writer. If it is used with tact, and not too constantly, it can be of great help in securing firm connections between one sentence and another. And if a warning is needed of the results of its abuse, it is ready to hand in the works of Matthew Arnold.

A somewhat more elaborate and subtle method of linking thoughts and sentences together is often found in Burke, who was generally regarded by Coleridge and De Quincey as the greatest exponent of "reverberation" and the mutual modification of sentences. Here is the content of one of his admirably constructed periods, expressed in hack-English:

> Opinions exert a strong influence on men's actions, because they are often combined with strong feelings. Sometimes they even produce strong feelings. It is the duty of government, in its own interest, to pay much attention to opinions. And therefore a government has the right to do so.

This is logical enough in the order of presentation, but in the actual manner of expression, flat, feebly orchestrated, unlikely to seize upon the attention of any but the most willing listener. This is what Burke makes of it:

> It is the interest, and it is the duty, and because it is the interest and the duty, it is the right, of government to attend much to opinions; because, as opinions soon combine with passions, even when they do not produce them, they have much influence on actions.

There is a richly varied and significant order of words and structure of sentences, presenting the thoughts with the greatest possible impact and interweaving of their necessary connections. It is essentially clearer than the other version, not because it is more logical, but because it treats its reader as a human being, liable to be weary or blunted in his faculties and capacity for attention; it does far more work for him, in the psychological sense, and is far more likely to be understood. And it depends ultimately upon the good management of word-order, on a highly developed sense of the possible varieties of one and the same expression.

The possibility of variation in word-order, then, is the greatest single contribution that grammar, as distinct from vocabulary, can make to solving the fundamental problems of written English, and to supplying resources for the variation of emphasis to take the place of those which are restricted to the spoken language. And therefore the real English grammarian will make it his business to preserve these possibilities of variation so far as possible, and to avoid making rules about word-order for purely grammatical purposes unless they are absolutely unavoidable. He should not, for example, make rules for the order and placing of words such as those which have been made in the past for the placing of prepositions and adverbs with the infinitive. They are unnecessary from the point of view of pure grammar. And they are far better left to the general guidance of the over-all rule that the words should be placed in the order which makes the meaning most clearly and forcibly.

The teacher of grammar — not necessarily quite the same person as the grammarian — should pay careful attention to developing in his pupils a sense of the possibilities of variation in sentence structure. This would be a far more direct contribution to the formation of a good, lively style than any amount of parsing and analysis, and it is not very difficult to devise interesting exercises for the purpose. One such exercise, indeed, often used to appear in the older books of grammar, and is still retained, on a small scale, in some modern ones. It was thus described, very sensibly, in one of the later supplements to that grammar by Lindley Murray that was one of the great forgotten formative books of the Victorian age:

> The practice of transposing the members of sentences, is an exercise so useful to young persons, that it requires a more particular explanation, than could have been properly given in the preceding work. A few of the various modes in which the parts of a sentence may be arranged, have, therefore, been collected. By examining them attentively, the student will perceive, in some degree, the nature and effect of transposition: and, by being frequently exercised in showing its variety in other sentences, he will obtain a facility in the operation; and a dexterity in discovering and applying, on all occasions, the clearest and most forcible arrangement. By this practice, he will also be able more readily to penetrate the meaning of such sentences, as are rendered obscure and perplexing to most readers, by the irregular disposition of their parts.

These remarks, sensible in themselves as they are pawky in expression, are followed by a series of examples in the same tradition of English prose. This is one of them:

> That greatness of mind which shows itself in dangers and labours, if it wants justice, is blamable.
> If that greatness of mind, which shows itself in dangers and labours, is void of justice, it is blamable.
> That greatness of mind is blamable, which shows itself in dangers and labours, if it wants justice.
> If that greatness of mind is void of justice, which shows itself in dangers and labours, it is blamable.
> That greatness of mind is blamable, if it is void of justice, which shows itself in dangers and labours.
> If it wants justice, that greatness of mind, which shows itself in dangers and labours, is blamable.

This example, like all the others in the same book, would be altogether unsuitable for modern use. Indeed, if we bear in mind the fruit that it bore in so much Victorian prose, we can hardly escape the conclusion that it was very unsuitable for use a century and a half ago. But although this particular sentence is intolerably heavy and cumbrous, the principle that it illustrates is a sound one. It ought not to be difficult to devise sentences on the same grammatical principle, but much lighter in tone, and more interesting in matter, upon which modern learners of English could exercise themselves with real profit, and with at any rate a little amusement. Certainly with more amusement (and therefore generally more profit too) than they can ever be expected to derive from most of the grammatical exercises now in use. It would open a path to the teaching of grammar, not in the abstract, as a business of formal classifications of words and phrases (subject, predicate, and so forth), but concretely, in the process of moulding and remoulding meaningful sentences in such a way as to explore and modify their meaning. It would, incidentally, provide a basis for a more realistic education in the use of the comma; for it would be a rough working rule that commas should come before and after the blocks of words that could be transferred from one place to another in such a sentence, but never in the middle of a block. And this, rough though it may be, would be preferable to the seventeen or eighteen different rules that are generally necessary to cover its use. The whole problem of punctuation, in fact, would be greatly simplified by this kind of training, for most errors of punctuation arise from ill-designed, badly shaped sentences, and from the attempt to make them work by means of violent tricks with commas and colons and such like. If sentence structure were more malleable, most difficulties over punctuation would disappear of themselves.

Above all, this kind of exercise would come a little nearer to the modern conception of an education based on activity and construction, rather than on static memory work or supine submission to rules laid down in a vacuum. It would give children some encouragement to feel that language is something which can be manipulated with as much pleasure as plasticine or bricks, with something to show at the end of the exercise, something created, if not wholly original. It would go some way towards abolishing the idea that English is merely something that you generally get wrong and that gives you no fun even if you get it right.

FOR DISCUSSION

1. "Written English, for example, is now much more different from spoken English than it was in Shakespeare's time, and critics are generally agreed that our literature is the worse for it." What are some of the differences between written English and spoken English? Sentence length? Vocabulary? Intensity of meaning? Rhetorical features? Figures of speech? Others?

2. Would everyday writing — of the business letter, for instance, — be better if it approached spoken English more closely? Would it be a good criterion for a business letter that it should sound natural if spoken over the telephone?

3. What are some communication devices available to the speaker that are not available to the writer?

4. What three devices can be used to overcome the "deadness of the word on the page"?

5. Select some sentence and see how many ways you can rewrite it. Try, for example, "These are the times that try men's souls."

VOCABULARY: sally, infer, ultra-tidy, inherent, otiose, epigram, apothegm, obtrude, malleable, supine.

THEME TOPICS: Why it is easier to speak than to write. Writing symbolizes speech — but not all of it. Good writing is more than the right words; it is the right arrangement. Good writing is edited speech.

A Note on Style and the Limits of Language

WALKER GIBSON

Questions about style can most usefully be approached if we think of a style as the expression of a personality. I do not mean at all that our words necessarily reveal what we are "really like." I do mean that every writer and talker, more or less consciously, chooses a role which he thinks appropriate to express for a given time and situation. The personality I am expressing in this written sentence is not the same as the one I orally express to my three-year-old who at this moment is bent on climbing onto my typewriter. For each of these two situations, I choose a different "voice," a different mask, in order to accomplish what I want accomplished. There is no point in asking here which of these voices is closer to the Real Me. What may be worth asking is this: what kinds of voices, in written prose, may be said to respond most sensitively and efficiently to the sort of contemporary world that this book [1] has been describing?

From *The Limits of Language* edited by Walker Gibson, © 1962 by Walker Gibson. Reprinted by permission of Hill and Wang, Inc.

[1] In this essay, references to "this book" refer, of course, to Mr. Gibson's book.

First, let's be logical about it. Given the kind of dilemma with respect to knowledge and language that this book defines, what sort of style might we *expect* in our own time? What sort of speaking voice adopted by the writer, what mask, would be appropriate in a world where, as we have seen, the very nature of nature may be inexpressible? If we live in a pluralistic and fluxlike universe, what manner of word-man should we become in order to talk about it? Well, we might at least expect a man who knows his limits, who admits the inevitably subjective character of his wisdom. We might expect a man who knows that he has no right in a final sense to consider himself any wiser than the next fellow, including the one he is talking to. The appropriate tone, therefore, might be informal, a little tense and self-conscious perhaps, but genial as between equals. With our modern relativistic ideas about the impossibility of determining any "standard dialect" for expressing Truth in all its forms, we might expect the cautious writer to employ many dialects, to shift from formal to colloquial diction, to avoid the slightest hint of authoritarianism. The rhythm of his words will be an irregular, conversational rhythm — not the symmetrical periods of formal Victorian prose. Short sentences alternating erratically with longer sentences. Occasional sentence fragments. In sum we might expect a style rather like *this!* [2]

This style, indeed, is easily recognizable and can be discovered all around us in modern prose. Thirty years ago in a book called *Modern Prose Style,* Bonamy Dobrée described it much as we have done here. "Most of us have ceased to believe, except provisionally, in truths," he wrote, "and we feel that what is important is not so much truth as the way our minds move toward truth." The consequence is a kind of self-searching need for frankness and humility on the part of the writer. "The modern prose-writer, in returning to the rhythms of everyday speech, is trying to be more honest with himself than if he used, as is too wreckingly easy, the forms and terms already published as the expression of other people's minds." Finally, in a touching sentence, "In our present confusion our only hope is to be scrupulously honest with ourselves." That was written in 1933: since then the confusion has multiplied spectacularly, while our hopes of ever being "scrupulously honest" about anything look pretty dim. Still, the relation Dobrée made, between an intellectual difficulty and a style, is essentially the relation we are making here.

The trouble with it — and a reminder of the awful complexity of our subject — is that sometimes this proposition simply doesn't work. Some con-

---

[2] A few of the writer's obvious attempts to echo a conversational tone in that paragraph can be quickly summarized. Contractions (let's). Colloquialisms (well . . . , the next fellow). Some very short sentences. Capitalization in an effort to place an ironical turn on a Big Fat Abstraction (Truth) — an effort that is of course much easier to accomplish with the actual voice. Italics (*expect*, like *this!*), again in mimicry of the way one speaks in conversation. And so on. The purpose of such devices, to compensate for the loss of oral intonation, is strictly speaking impossible to achieve. If only you were here I could *say* all this to you!

temporary writers, sensitively aware of the limits of language, indeed conceding them explicitly, nevertheless write in a *style* that sounds like the wisdom of Moses, or like Winston Churchill. Far from echoing the rhythms of ordinary speech, they pontificate or chant in authoritarian rhythms the assertion that one cannot be authoritarian. We have a fine example of this paradox in the paragraph by Oppenheimer that I have so much admired.[3] Oppenheimer uses a vocabulary, sentence structure, tone, and rhythm all highly structured and formalized; there is no unbending there. The theme of his discourse — that style is "the deference that action pays to uncertainty" — seems at odds with the *personality* we hear uttering this theme. That personality, because of the way the words are chosen and arranged, appears curiously self-confident, even dictatorial, with echoes perhaps of Johnsonian prose, or Macaulay's elegant sentences. Thus the first sentence is built around a handsome triplet of alliterative abstractions ("the implicit, the imponderable, and the unknown"); the second sentence is built out of another triplet of nicely balanced clauses. The extraordinary final sentence approaches incantation in its parallel repetitions of structure. The "voice" we hear, remote indeed from ordinary conversation, seems to *know* even as it asserts its own humility. Different readers will explain all this in different ways: some will argue that the traditional manner lends sincerity and persuasiveness to the message, while others will be set off by what they consider a real discrepancy between matter and manner. We recall that the passage was taken from an address delivered at a formal occasion. I have heard Mr. Oppenheimer's platform manner described as "arrogant"; our stylistic observations might well account in part for such an impression. In any case it is clear that no easy formula — Dobrée's or anyone else's — is going to account for all the vagaries of modern prose.

Other writers in this collection will illustrate Dobrée's thesis with less embarrassment — that is, will show clear evidence of a "conversational" voice. Thus [Herbert J.] Muller:

> Emerson remarked that it is a good thing, now and then, to take a look at the landscape from between one's legs. Although this stunt might seem pointless when things are already topsy-turvy, it can be the more helpful then. One may

[3] The paragraph, from J. Robert Oppenheimer's "The Open Mind," reads as follows:

The problem of doing justice to the implicit, the imponderable, and the unknown is of course not unique to politics. It is always with us in science, it is with us in the most trivial of personal affairs, and it is one of the great problems of writing and of all forms of art. The means by which it is solved is sometimes called style. It is style which complements affirmation with limitation and with humility; it is style which makes it possible to act effectively, but not absolutely; it is style which, in the domain of foreign policy, enables us to find a harmony between the pursuit of ends essential to us and the regard for the views, the sensibilities, the aspirations of those to whom the problem may appear in another light; it is style which is the deference that action plays to uncertainty; it is above all style through which power defers to reason.

say that what this chaotic world needs first of all is *dis*sociation; by breaking up factitious alliances and oppositions, one may get at the deep uniform-
ities. Or. . .

The simplicity of the diction in that first sentence, and the absurdity of the
described action, support a familiar relation of equality between the speaking
voice and the reader. There is no talking down; we all know who Emerson
is. (Not "That great American Transcendentalist, Ralph Waldo Emerson.
. . .") "Now and then," "stunt," "topsy-turvy" contribute the colloquial touch.
The slightly awkward "then" at the end of the second sentence suggests that
in this particular communication formal grace would be inappropriate. But
with the third sentence the writer boldly shifts his tone as his diction becomes
more polysyllabic and his sentence structure more complex. "Enough of
geniality," he seems to say, "you must now follow me into a serious tangle."
With this abruptness, Muller is perhaps "breaking up factitious alliances"
in his style, so that his own prose both expresses and dramatizes the point he
is making.

The trick, if that is what it is, of mingling formal and colloquial vocabulary can convey a kind of ironical thrust by the writer at his own pretensions.
Thus he can have it both ways — make his great assertion and kid himself
for his own gall. It is a device much employed in circles that are verbally
sophisticated, including academic circles. Consider an extreme example,
from a professor of law at Chicago, here discussing a flexible approach to
problems of judicial interpretation:

> But it leads to *good* rules of law and in the main towards flexible ones, so that
> most cases of a given type can come to be handled not only well but easily,
> and so that the odd case can normally come in also for a smidgeon of relief.
> The whole setup leads above all — a recognition of imperfection in language
> and in officer — to *on-going and unceasing judicial review of prior judicial
> decision* on the side of rule, tool, and technique. That, plus freedom and duty
> to do justice *with* the rules but *within* both them and their whole temper, that
> is the freedom, the leeway for own-contribution, the scope for the person,
> which the system offers.[4]

Here style and message work with a degree of co-operation: a call for
unceasing flexibility in the operations of judicial review is expressed in an
idiom that is itself almost wildly flexible. The speaker in this passage betrays
the strains of an impassioned conversationalist, with his heavy reliance on
italics and his interrupted sentence structures. We are buttonholed. This is
a technical discussion, and most of the vocabulary has to be fairly heavy, but
we have "smidgeon" and "whole setup" to cut across the formality. We have
even a jazzy bit of alliteration and rhyme — "rule, tool, and technique." The
"recognition of imperfection in language," therefore, which is explicitly

[4] From Karl N. Llewellyn, *The Common Law Tradition: Deciding Appeals,* Little,
Brown, 1960.

granted by the text, is implicitly conveyed as well by the unorthodox scram-
blings of language. Nobody has to like this style (many are simply irritated),
but at least one can see what is going on, and why.

Or consider another extreme example, from a professor of English at Wis-
consin, here discussing problems of usage:

> Bad, fair, good, better, best. Only the best is Correct. No busy man can be
> Correct. But his wife can. That's what women are for. That's why we have
> women to teach English and type our letters and go to church for us and
> discover for us that the English say "Aren't I?" while we sinfully hunt golf-
> balls in the rough on Sunday and, when our partner finds two of them, ask
> "Which is me?" (Webster: *colloq.* — Professor K of Harvard: I speak colloq
> myself, and some times I write it.) . . . Only a few of us today are aware of the
> other scales of English usage. It is our business to consciously know about
> their social unity.[5]

These sentences from a treatise on language admirably demonstrate that self-
consciously unbuttoned informality which the subject nowadays seems to
demand. To some, again, it will appear offensively "cute," idiosyncratic.
Short sentences, some without predicates, surround one almost endless ram-
bling sentence. The ironical capital in Correct (cf. Truth *supra*). Indifference to the rule that pronouns should have specific antecedents ("That's what
women are for. That's why . . ."). Muddled number in using personal pronouns (we hunt golf-balls, our partner [sing.] finds, [we] ask "Which is
me?"). Deliberately split infinitive in the last sentence quoted, at a point in
the utterance when a conventionally formal tone has begun to enter. We may
anticipate, I am sure, a time when writers will endeavor to carefully split their
infinitives, at whatever cost in awkwardness, just as writers of a former generation endeavored so elaborately to avoid the "error." All this should prove
to at least be amusing.

To many readers, the style displayed by a Professor Llewellyn or a Professor Joos will seem undisciplined, vulgar, and chaotic. A sign of academic
deterioration. A result of wild "permissiveness" in education and in society
generally. But such readers will be missing the point. There is nothing indiscriminately permissive in this style, but the writers do accept and reject
different kinds of language from those accepted and rejected by traditional
stylists. They express different personalities. Without insisting on the merits
of these particular passages, which are certainly debatable, it ought nevertheless to be clear that you do not write in this way simply by saying anything
that occurs to you. The process of selection can be, indeed, *more* discriminating because the available supply of language and experience is larger. As this
is being written, in the autumn of 1961, a mild flurry about such extensions of
language is going on in the press, relating to the publication of a new edition
of *Webster's New International Dictionary. The New York Times* has edi-
torialized as follows:

---

[5] From Martin Joos, *The Five Clocks.* Copyright 1961 by Martin Joos.

A passel of double-domes at the G. & C. Merriam Company joint in Springfield, Mass., have been confabbing and yakking for twenty-seven years — which is not intended to infer that they have not been doing plenty work — and now they have finalized Webster's Third New International Dictionary, Unabridged, a new edition of that swell and esteemed word book.

Those who regard the foregoing paragraph as acceptable English prose will find that the new Webster's is just the dictionary for them. The words in that paragraph all are listed in the new work with no suggestion that they are anything but standard.

Webster's has, it is apparent, surrendered to the permissive school that has been busily extending its beachhead on English instruction in the schools. This development is disastrous. . . .

The *Times* goes on to acknowledge "the lexical explosion that has showered us with so many words in recent years," and to congratulate the Dictionary for including 100,000 new words or new definitions. "These are improvements, but they cannot outweigh the fundamental fault." Webster's has always been a "peerless authority on American English," and therefore its editors have "to some degree a public responsibility." "A new start is needed."

There is, I think, something wrong about all this. If you are acknowledging a "lexical explosion," a language changing with accelerating rapidity, then it seems rather difficult to insist at the same time on a "peerless authority." The editors of the Dictionary may have fulfilled their public responsibility by taking the only wise course — by including as many new words and definitions as they could without making "authoritative" judgments about "standard," "colloquial," and "slang." This is not to say that the modern writer ignores such distinctions; on the contrary he is sensitively aware of them as never before. But he knows, and the dictionary editors know, that no such label is good for long in a culture as volatile as this one. Yesterday's slang is today's standard, and the writer who remains resonant to these shifts has at his disposal a huge and varicolored vocabulary for his art.

The reason we call that opening paragraph in the *Times* editorial "unacceptable English" is not that it contains slang. The reason is that it contains too many kinds of slang at once, without any awareness of their differences. You do not say "passel of double-domes" unless you have some good reason for juxtaposing terms from utterly distinct language worlds. "Passel" is presumably of western-frontier origin and now has a kind of weary whimsy about it, while "double-domes" is recent, cheaply anti-intellectual, with a history something like "egghead" but without the popular acceptance of "egghead." It is conceivable that these words could be included in one sentence, but it would take more skill than the *Times* man has employed. Of course the appearance of clumsiness was just what served his purpose.

Meanwhile the writer who looks backward to "authority," who takes a static view of Standard Language, is likely to sound like the "straight" paragraphs of that editorial. The voice there is closer to a chiding or dictatorial professor than were the voices of the actual professors quoted. And when such a writer uses "modern" terms, he uses them in ways that are long overused before he gets to them — ways like "extending its beachhead on English instruction" or "lexical explosion that has showered us with so many words." It is this sort of thing that is the true vulgarity in our time.

Nevertheless our society remains generous with half-conscious concessions to the imperfections of its language. It may be, for example, that the language of the beatniks, especially their oral conventions, could be looked at in the light of such concessions. Consider just one curious symptom of jive-talk (now dated) — the suffix-plus-prefix *like*. "We came to this big town like and all the streets were like crazy, man." This attempt at rendering beat dialect is doubtless inaccurate but it should serve to make the point. That point is that the beats have (deliberately?) modified or qualified their nouns and adjectives by suggesting that they are not quite accurate, not quite the way things are. "This big town like" — it is a one-ended metaphor. Like what? We have a tenor but no vehicle, or is it a vehicle without a tenor? I have been told that many beats are determinedly antiverbal, preferring to listen to jazz while lying on beaches in Zenlike silence. It fits. The skepticism about the validity of words that "like" implies is a peculiarly twentieth-century skepticism, it seems to me, though there may be analogies with other ages such as the seventeenth century, when scientific developments encouraged similar self-scrutinies and self-doubts. In any event the beats, in their crude and sloppy way of course, have surrounded much of their language with a metaphorical blur by using (among other things) the simple device of "like." They suggest, with this blur, their conviction of the impossibility of anybody else's doing any better with words. Only squares believe you can speak "precisely."

The complexities of experience do occasionally get faced one way or another — if not with the beats' pose of inarticulateness, then with some other pose that will serve to avoid the charge of *really knowing*. Modern novelists adopt a "point of view" which is often no point of view at all, but several points of view from which to indicate various inadequate interpretations of various fictitious characters. It is a technique that will show how two novels as apparently unlike as *The Waves* and Faulkner's *As I Lay Dying* belong after all to the same age. There is no narrator, no one of whom the reader might conceivably say, "There! That's the author talking." The technique is not new; there is *The Ring and the Book,* to mention one example. But the difference is that when you read *The Ring and the Book,* you feel how firmly and finally Browning is on Pompilia's "side," in spite of his wonderful multiplicity throughout that great poem. Whereas in many modern novels you scarcely know who is on anybody's side — you must simply flow in the flux. Sometimes it is so lifelike you can hardly stand it.

And of course that road — the road of chaos chaotically expressing chaos — is a dead end of imitative form where we end with a grunt, or maybe a whimper. The very point is that language will never *say* our experience "as is," and recognizing this truth, we have immense freedom of possibility to make, create, form what we can out of words or out of anything else. The most elaborate of villanelles is not much further removed from Real Life than the latest Allen Ginsburg poem, or a slice of Mr. Bloom's day. So write a villanelle if that will meet your need. But whatever it is, there remains this simple blasphemy to be avoided, and that is the blasphemy of ignoring the limits, of assuming that one's words do indeed tell the reader what is going on. There is an important sense in which nobody knows what he is talking about.

I hope I do not except myself and everything uttered here.

FOR DISCUSSION

1. "Every writer and talker, more or less consciously, chooses a role which he thinks appropriate to express for a given time and situation." Are you aware of choosing a "role" or "voice" or "mask" when you write a theme? What is the difference in voice of the following utterances? (a) "The immediate implementation of this directive is urgently requested." (b) "I suggest we put this into effect at once." (c) "Let's start the ball rolling right away." (d) "Illumination is required to be extinguished when these premises are closed to business." (e) "Put out the lights when you leave."

2. By what means does Gibson "dramatize" his meaning in the following passage? "We may anticipate, I am sure, a time when writers will endeavor to carefully split their infinitives, at whatever cost in awkwardness, just as writers of a former generation endeavored so elaborately to avoid the 'error.' All this should prove to at least be amusing."

3. Gibson seems to believe that the style of the first paragraph of the editorial quoted from *The New York Times* is "indiscriminately permissive" but that the paragraphs quoted from Professors Llewellyn and Joos are not. Can you summarize, and perhaps expand, his argument?

4. The voice in the last two quoted paragraphs of the *Times* editorial, says Gibson, "is closer to a chiding or dictatorial professor than were the voices of the actual professors quoted." Can you illustrate this statement? What is the voice of the first paragraph of the editorial?

VOCABULARY: pluralistic, fluxlike, subjective, relativistic, symmetrical, erratic, incantation, discrepancy, factitious, ironical, sophisticated, judicial review, unorthodox, idiosyncratic, *supra*, volatile, resonant, juxtapose, concession, antiverbal, metaphorical, inarticulate, villanelle.

THEME TOPICS: The voices of Charlie Brown, Linus, Lucy, and Snoopy. The voice of Ann Landers. The voice of newspaper editorials. Professorial voices.

At the Fringe of Language

C. S. LEWIS

Language exists to communicate whatever it can communicate. Some things it communicates so badly that we never attempt to communicate them by words if any other medium is available. Those who think they are testing a boy's "elementary" command of English by asking him to describe in words how one ties one's tie or what a pair of scissors is like, are far astray. For precisely what language can hardly do at all, and never does well, is to inform us about complex physical shapes and movements. Hence descriptions of such things in the ancient writers are nearly always unintelligible. Hence we never in real life voluntarily use language for this purpose; we draw a diagram or go through pantomimic gestures. The exercises which such examiners set are no more a test of "elementary" linguistic competence than the most difficult bit of trick-riding from the circus ring is a test of elementary horsemanship.

Another grave limitation of language is that it cannot, like music or gesture, do more than one thing at once. However the words in a great poet's phrase interanimate one another and strike the mind as a quasi-instantaneous chord, yet strictly speaking, each word must be read or heard before the next. That way, language is as unilinear as time. Hence, in narrative, the great difficulty of presenting a very complicated change which happens suddenly. If we do justice to the complexity, the time the reader must take over the passage will destroy the feeling of suddenness. If we get in the suddenness we shall not be able to get in the complexity. I am not saying that genius will not find its own ways of palliating this defect in the instrument; only that the instrument is in this way defective.

One of the most important and effective uses of language is the emotional. It is also, of course, wholly legitimate. We do not talk only in order to reason or to inform. We have to make love and quarrel, to propitiate and pardon, to rebuke, console, intercede, and arouse. "He that complains," said Johnson, "acts like a man, like a social being." The real objection lies not against the language of emotion as such, but against language which, being in reality

From *Studies in Words* by C. S. Lewis, New York: Cambridge University Press, 1960. Reprinted by permission of Cambridge University Press.

emotional, masquerades — whether by plain hypocrisy or subtler self-deceit — as being something else.

All my generation are much indebted to Dr. I. A. Richards for having fully called our attention to the emotional functions of language. But I am hardly less indebted to Professor Empson for having pointed out that the conception of emotional language can be very easily extended too far. It was time to call a halt.

We must obviously not call any utterance "emotional" language because it in fact arouses, even because it must arouse, emotion. "It is not cancer after all," "The Germans have surrendered," "I love you" — may all be true statements about matter of fact. And of course it is the facts, not the language, that arouse the emotion. In the last the fact communicated is itself the existence of an emotion but that makes no difference. Statements about crime are not criminal language; nor are statements about emotions necessarily emotional language. Nor, in my opinion, are value-judgements ("this is good," "this is bad") emotional language. Approval and disapproval do not seem to me to be emotions. If we felt at all times about the things we judge good the emotion which is appropriate, our lives would be easier. It would also be an error to treat "I am washed in the blood of the Lamb" as emotional language. It is of course metaphorical language. But by his metaphor the speaker is trying to communicate what he believes to be a fact. You may of course think the belief false in his particular case. You may think the real universe is such that no fact which corresponded to such a statement could possibly occur. You may say that the real cause which prompts a man to say things like that is a state of emotion. But if so, an emotion has produced erroneous belief about an impossible fact, and it is the fact erroneously believed in which the man is stating. A man's hasty belief that the Germans had surrendered (before they did) might well be caused by his emotions. That would not make "The Germans have surrendered" a specimen of emotional language. If you could find a man nowadays capable of believing, and saying, "The Russians have all been annihilated by magic," even this would not be emotional language, though his belief in magic might be a belief engendered by emotion.

All this is fairly plain sailing. We reach something harder in the things said by poets. For these the purpose of utterance would be frustrated if no emotion were aroused. They do not merely, like the sentences cited above, arouse emotion in fact; it is their purpose — at any rate, part of their purpose — to do so. But we must be very careful here. Having observed that a poetical utterance in fact arouses emotion, and is intended to arouse emotion, and that if taken as a statement about reality — or even about the make-believe "realities" of the fictitious narrative — it would be nonsensical or at least false, can we conclude that it communicates nothing but emotion? I think not.

Nothing will convince me that "My soul is an enchanted boat" [Shelley, *Prometheus Unbound*] is simply a better way — however much better — of doing what might be done by some exclamation like "Gee!" Asia has risen from the dark cave of Demogorgon. She is floating upwards. She is saluted as "Life of Life!" The reversed temporal process in ll. 97-103 ("We have passed Age's icy caves" etc.), borrowed from Plato's *Politicus* (269ᶜ *sq.*), marks the fact that at this moment the whole cycle is reversed and cosmos begins anew. She is undergoing apotheosis. What did it feel like? The poet says to us in effect "Think of going in a boat. But quite effortless" ("Like a sleeping swan gliding with the current," he adds in the next line), "Like a boat without sail or oar; the motive power undiscoverable. Like a magic boat — you must have read or dreamed of such things — a boat drawn on, drawn swiftly on, irresistibly, smoothly, by enchantment." Exactly. I know now how it felt for Asia. The phrase has communicated emotion. But notice how. By addressing in the first instance my imagination. He makes me imagine a boat rushing over waves, which are also identified with sounds. After that he need do no more; my emotion will follow of itself. Poetry most often communicates emotions, not directly, but by creating imaginatively the grounds for those emotions. It therefore communicates something more than emotion; only by means of that something more does it communicate the emotion at all.

Burns compares his mistress to " a red, red rose"; Wordsworth his to "a violet by a mossy stone Half hidden from the eye." These expressions do communicate to me the emotion each poet felt. But it seems to me that they do so solely by forcing me to imagine two (very different) women. I see the rose-like, overpowering, midsummer sweetness of the one; the reticent, elusive freshness, the beauty easily overlooked in the other. After that my emotions may be left to themselves. The poets have done their part.

This, which is eminently true of poetry, is true of all imaginative writing. One of the first things we have to say to a beginner who has brought us his MS. is, "Avoid all epithets which are merely emotional. It is no use *telling* us that something was 'mysterious' or 'loathsome' or 'awe-inspiring' or 'voluptuous.' Do you think your readers will believe you just because you say so? You must go quite a different way to work. By direct description, by metaphor and simile, by secretly evoking powerful associations, by offering the right stimuli to our nerves (in the right degree and the right order), and by the very beat and vowel-melody and length and brevity of your sentences, you must bring it about that we, we readers, not you, exclaim 'how mysterious!' or 'loathsome' or whatever it is. Let me taste for myself, and you'll have no need to *tell* me how I should react to the flavor."

In Donne's couplet

> *Your gown going off, such beautious state reveals*
> *As when from flowery meads th'hills shadow steales*

beautious is the only word of the whole seventeen which is doing no work.

There are exceptions to this principle. By very successful placing, a great author may sometimes raise such words to poetic life. Wordsworth's lines are a specimen:

> *Which, to the boundaries of space and time,*
> *Of melancholy space and doleful time,*
> *Superior —*

Here we have almost the reverse of the process I have been describing. The object (space and time) is in one way so familiar to our imaginations and in another so unimaginable — we have read so many tedious attempts to exalt or over-awe us with mere superlatives or even with simple arithmetic — that nothing can be made of it. This time, therefore, the poet withdraws the object (the ground for emotion) altogether and appeals directly to our emotions; and not to the quite obvious ones. Another exception is naturally to be found in drama or very dramatic lyric, where the poet — with discretion and a proper use of illusion — imitates the speech of people in some highly emotional situation — even, at need, their inarticulate cries. This in its purity, which purity a good poet never sustains for long, belongs to poetry not in so far as poetry is a special use of language but in so far as poetry is *mimesis*. In themselves the "Ah! Ah!" or "Otototoi" or "Iou! Iou!" of characters in a Greek tragedy are not specimens of poetry any more than the "Bé, bé" of the lamb or the "Au! Au!" of the dog in Aristophanes.

In general, however, the poet's route to our emotion lies through our imaginations.

We must also exclude from the category "emotional language" words such as I have taken *supernatural* to be. The class of things which they refer to may be bound together chiefly by a common emotion; but the purpose of using the words is to assign something to that class, not merely to communicate the emotion which led to the classification.

Having thus narrowed the field, we can now make a new start. It will be noticed that I have throughout used the word *emotional* rather than *emotive*. This is because I think the latter word applicable to only one aspect of emotional language. For an "emotive word" ought to mean one whose function is to arouse emotion. But surely we ought to distinguish utterances which arouse, from those which express, emotion? The first is directed towards producing some effect on a (real or imagined) hearer; the second discharges our own emotion, cleanses our stuffed bosom of some perilous stuff.

The distinction will seem straw-splitting if we have in mind the language of love. For, as Samson says, "love seeks to have love," and it would be hard to say whether endearments serve more as expressions of love in the speaker or incitements to it in the beloved. But that tells us more about the nature of love than about the nature of language. One of my old headmasters once wisely said it was a pity that *amare* was the first Latin verb we all learn. He thought this led to an imperfect grasp of the difference between the active and the passive voice. It might be better to begin with *flagellare.* The difference between flogging and being flogged would come home to the business and bosoms of schoolboys far more effectively than that of loving and being loved. On the same principle, we can best see the distinction between the stimulant and the expressive functions of emotional language in a quarrel; and best of all where the same word performs both. The man who calls me a low hound both expresses and (actually or intentionally) stimulates emotion. But not the same emotion. He expresses contempt; he stimulates, or hopes to stimulate, the almost opposite emotion of humiliation.

Again, in the language of complaint we often find the expressive without the stimulant. When two people who have missed the last train stand on the silent platform saying "Damn" or "Bloody" or "Sickening," they neither intend nor need to stimulate each other's disappointment. They are just "getting it off their chests."

The vocabulary of endearment, complaint, and abuse, provides, I think, almost the only specimens of words that are purely emotional, words from which all imaginative or conceptual content has vanished, so that they have no function at all but to express or stimulate emotion, or both. And an examination of them soon convinces us that in them we see language at its least linguistic. We have come to the frontier between language and inarticulate vocal sounds. And at that frontier we find a two-way traffic going on.

On the one hand we find inarticulate sounds becoming words with a fixed spelling and a niche in the dictionary. Thus English *heigh-ho* and Latin *eheu* are clearly formalised imitations of the sigh; *ah,* of the gasp; *tut-tut,* of the tongue clicked against the hard palate. These are general. In particular situations the "verbification" of the inarticulate may occur *ad hoc.* A voluntary scream may become a cry for mercy. A voluntary groan, from a wounded man, uttered to attract the attention of the stretcher-bearers, may be the equivalent of a sentence ("There is a wounded man in this ditch").

But we also see the frontier being crossed in the opposite direction. In the vocabulary of abuse and complaint we see things that once were words passing out of the realm of language (properly so called) and becoming the equivalents of inarticulate sounds or even of actions; of sighs, moans, whimperings, growls, or blows.

The "swear-words" — *damn* for complaint and *damn you* for abuse — are a good example. Historically the whole Christian eschatology lies behind them. If no one had ever consigned his enemy to the eternal fires and believed that there were eternal fires to receive him, these ejaculations would never have existed. But inflation, the spontaneous hyperboles of ill temper, and the decay of religion, have long since emptied them of that lurid content. Those who have no belief in damnation — and some who have — now damn inanimate objects which would on any view be ineligible for it. The word is no longer an imprecation. It is hardly, in the full sense, a word at all when so used. Its popularity probably owes as much to its resounding phonetic virtues as to any, even fanciful, association with hell. It has ceased to be profane. It has also become very much less forceful. You may say the same of *sickening* in its popular, ejaculatory, use. There are alarms and disappointments which can actually produce nausea, or, at least, emotions which we feel to be somehow similar to it. But the man who says *sickening!* when he has missed the train is not thinking about that. The word is simply an alternative to *damn* or *bloody*. And of course far weaker than it would be if it still carried any suggestion of vomiting.

So with abusive terms. No one would now call his schoolfellow or next door neighbour a *swine* unless someone has once used this word to make a real comparison between his enemy and a pig. It is now a mere alternative to *beast* or *brute* or various popular unprintable words. They are all interchangeable. *Villain*, as we know, once really compared your enemy to a *villein*. Once, to call a man *cad* or *knave* assigned to him the status of a servant. And it did so because, earlier still, these words meant "boy" or "junior" (you address a slave as "boy" in Greek and a waiter as *garçon* in French).

Thus all these words have come down in the world. None of them started by being *merely* abusive, few of them by being abusive at all. They once stimulated emotion by suggesting an image. They made the enemy odious or contemptible by asserting he was like somebody or something we already disliked or looked down on. Their use was a sort of passionate parody of the syllogism: pigs (or servants or my juniors) are contemptible — John is like a pig (or servant or adolescent) — therefore John is contemptible. That was why they really hurt; because hurting was not the whole of what they did. They stimulated emotion because they also stimulated something else; imagination. They stimulated emotion in the particular case because they exploited emotions which already existed towards whole classes of things or persons. Now that they are nothing whatever but emotional stimulants, they are weak emotional stimulants. They make no particular accusation. They tell us nothing except that the speaker has lost his temper.

And even this they do not tell us linguistically, but symptomatically; as a red face, a loud voice, or a clenched fist, might do equally well. The fact of the other person's anger may hurt or frighten us; hurt us if we love him, or frighten us if he is larger and younger than ourselves and threatens violence. But his language as such has very little power to do the only thing it is intended to do. It would have been far more wounding to be called *swine* when the word still carried some whiff of the sty and some echo of a grunt; far more wounding to be called a *villain* when this still conjured up an image of the unwashed, malodorous, ineducable, gross, belching, close-fisted, and surly boor. Now, who cares? Language meant solely to hurt hurts strangely little.

This can be seen clearly when we catch a word "just on the turn." *Bitch* is one. Till recently — and still in the proper contexts — this accused a woman of one particular fault and appealed, with some success, to our contempt by calling up an image of the she-dog's comical and indecorous behavior when she is in heat. But it is now increasingly used of any woman whom the speaker, for whatever reason, is annoyed with — the female driver who is in front of him, or a female magistrate whom he thinks unjust. Clearly, the word is far more wounding in its narrower usage. If that usage is ever totally lost — as I think it will be — the word will sink to the level of *damn her*. Notice, too, how *cat* (of a woman) is still strong and useful because the image is still alive in it.

An important principle thus emerges. In general, emotional words, to be effective, must not be solely emotional. What expresses or stimulates emotion directly, without the intervention of an image or concept, expresses or stimulates it feebly. And in particular, when words of abuse have hurting the enemy as their direct and only object, they do not hurt him much. In the field of language, however it may be in that of action, hatred cuts its own throat, and those who are too "willing to wound" become thereby impotent to strike. And all this is only another way of saying that as words become exclusively emotional they cease to be words and therefore of course cease to perform any strictly linguistic function. They operate as growls or barks or tears. "Exclusively" is an important adverb here. They die as words not because there is too much emotion in them but because there is too little — and finally nothing at all — of anything else.

In this there is not much to be lamented. If a mother with a baby, or lovers in each other's arms, use language so emotional that it is really not language at all, I see no ground for shame or offence; and if men in an orgy of resentment, though (in the physical sense) they articulate, are no more speaking — are saying no more — than a snarling animal, this is perhaps all for the best. The real corruption comes when men whose purpose in speaking is in fact purely emotional conceal this from others, and perhaps from themselves, by words that seem to be, but are not, charged with a conceptual content.

We have all heard *bolshevist, fascist, Jew,* and *capitalist,* used not to describe but merely to insult. Rose Macaulay noticed a tendency to prefix "so called" to almost any adjective when it was used of those the speaker hated; the final absurdity being reached when people referred to the Germans as "these so-called Germans." *Bourgeois* and *middle class* often suffer the same fate.

A literary man of my acquaintance, on reading an unfavourable reference to his own words, called it *vulgar*. The charge brought against him was one that only highly educated people ever bring; the tone of the passage not otherwise offensive than by being unfavourable; the phrasing perfectly good English. If he had called it false, unintelligent, or malicious, I could have understood, though I might have disagreed. But why *vulgar?* Clearly, this word was selected solely because the speaker thought it was the one that the enemy, if he could hear it, would most dislike. It was the equivalent of an oath or a growl. But that was concealed from the speaker because "This is vulgar" sounds like a judgement.

When we write criticism we have to be continually on our guard against this sort of thing. If we honestly believe a work to be very bad we cannot help hating it. The function of criticism, however, is "to get ourselves out of the way and let humanity decide"; not to discharge our hatred but to expose the grounds for it; not to vilify faults but to diagnose and exhibit them. Unfortunately to express our hatred and to revenge ourselves is easier and more agreeable. Hence there is a tendency to select our pejorative epithets with a view not to their accuracy but to their power of hurting. If writing which was intended to be comic has set our teeth on edge, how easily the adjectives *arch* or *facetious* trickle out of the pen! But if we do not know exactly what we mean by them, if we are not prepared to say how comic work which errs by *archness* and *facetiousness* differs from comic work which errs in any other way, it is to be feared that we are really using them not to inform the reader but to annoy the author — *arch* or *facetious* being among the most effective "smear-words" of our period. In the same way work which obviously aspires and claims to be mature, if the critic dislikes it, will be called *adolescent;* not because the critic has really seen that its faults are those of adolescence but because he has seen that adolescence is the last thing the author wishes or expects to be accused of.

The best protection against this is to remind ourselves again and again what the proper function of pejorative words is. The ultimate, simplest and most abstract, is *bad* itself. The only good purpose for ever departing from that monosyllable when we condemn anything is to be more specific, to answer the question "Bad in what way?" Pejorative words are rightly used only when they do this. *Swine*, as a term of abuse is now a bad pejorative word, because it brings no one accusation rather than another against the person it vilifies; *coward* and *liar* are good ones because they charge a man with a particular fault — of which he might be proved guilty or innocent. As applied to literature, *dull, hackneyed, incoherent, monotonous, pornographic, cacophonous*, are good pejoratives; they tell people in what particular way we think a book faulty. *Adolescent* or *provincial* are not so good. For even when they are honestly used, to define, not merely to hurt, they really suggest a cause for the book's badness instead of describing the badness itself. We are saying in effect "He was led into his faults by being immature" or "by living in Lancashire." But would it not be more interesting to indicate the faults themselves and leave out our historical theory about their causes? If we find words like these — and *vulgar*, and others — indispensable to our criticism, if we find ourselves applying them to more and more different kinds of things, there is grave reason to suspect that—whether we know it or not — we are really using them not to diagnose but to hurt. If so, we are assisting in verbicide. For this is the downward path which leads to the graveyard of murdered words. First they are purely descriptive; *adolescent* tells us a man's age, *villain*, his status. Then they are specifically pejorative; *adolescent* tells us that a man's work displays "mawkishness and all the thousand bitters" confessed by Keats, and *villain* tells a man has a churl's mind and manners. Then they become *mere* pejoratives, useless synonyms for *bad*, as *villain* did and as *adolescent* may do if we aren't careful. Finally they become terms of abuse and cease to be language in the full sense at all.

．　．　．　．　．　．　．

FOR DISCUSSION

1. What are some limitations of language?

2. "We must obviously not call any utterance 'emotional' language because it in fact arouses, even because it must arouse, emotion." Why not?

3. Why does Lewis say that in the couplet quoted from John Donne only the word *beautious* is doing no work?

4. Explain the statement, "The vocabulary of endearment, complaint, and abuse provides . . . almost the only specimens of words that are purely emotional . . ."

5. "In general, emotional words, to be effective, must not be solely emotional." Why not?

VOCABULARY: interanimate, unilinear, palliate, propitiate, engender, apotheosis, mimesis, *ad hoc*, eschatology, hyperbole, imprecation, malodorous, vilify, pejorative, archness, facetious, cacophonous, verbicide, mawkish.

THEME TOPICS: How words arouse emotions. Language that is really emotional. Emotional language is poetry. The limitations of language.

Three Aims for Writers

W. SOMERSET MAUGHAM

I knew that I should never write as well as I could wish, but I thought with pains I could arrive at writing as well as my natural defects allowed. On taking thought it seemed to me that I must aim at lucidity, simplicity and euphony. I have put these three qualities in the order of the importance I assigned to them.

I have never had much patience with the writers who claim from the reader an effort to understand their meaning. You have only to go to the great philosophers to see that it is possible to express with lucidity the most subtle reflections. You may find it difficult to understand the thought of Hume, and if you have no philosophical training its implications will doubtless escape you; but no one with any education at all can fail to understand exactly what the meaning of each sentence is. Few people have written English with more grace than Berkeley. There are two sorts of obscurity that you find in writers. One is due to negligence and the other to wilfulness. People often write obscurely because they have never taken the trouble to learn to write clearly. This sort of obscurity you find too often in modern philosophers, in men of science, and even in literary critics. Here it is indeed strange. You would have thought that men who passed their lives in the study of the great masters of literature would be sufficiently sensitive to the beauty of language to write if not beautifully at least with perspicuity. Yet you will find in their works sentence after sentence that you must read twice to discover the sense. Often you can only guess at it, for the writers have evidently not said what they intended.

Another cause of obscurity is that the writer is himself not quite sure of his meaning. He has a vague impression of what he wants to say, but has not, either from lack of mental power or from laziness, exactly formulated it in his mind and it is natural enough that he should not find a precise expression for a confused idea. This is due largely to the fact that many writers think, not before, but as they write. The pen originates the thought. The disadvantage of this, and indeed it is a danger against which the author must be always on his guard, is that there is a sort of magic in the written word. The idea acquires substance by taking on a visible nature, and then stands in the way of its own clarification. But this sort of obscurity merges very easily into the wilful. Some writers who do not think clearly are inclined to suppose that their thoughts have a significance greater than at first sight appears. It is flattering to believe that they are too profound to be expressed so clearly that all who run may read, and very naturally it does not occur to such writers that the fault is with their own minds which have not the faculty of precise reflection. Here again the magic of the written word obtains. It is very easy to persuade oneself that a phrase that one does not quite understand may mean a great deal more than one realizes. From this there is only a little way to go to fall into the habit of setting down one's impressions in all their original vagueness. Fools can always be found to discover a hidden sense in them. There is another form of wilful obscurity that masquerades as aristocratic exclusiveness. The author wraps his meaning in mystery so that the vulgar shall not participate in it. His soul is a secret garden into which the elect may penetrate only after overcoming a number of perilous obstacles. But this kind of obscurity is not only pretentious; it is short-sighted. For time plays it an old trick. If the sense is meagre time reduces it to a meaningless verbiage that no one thinks of reading. This is the fate that has befallen the lucubrations of those French writers who were seduced by the example of Guillaume Apollinaire. But occasionally it throws a sharp cold light on what had seemed profound and thus discloses the fact that these contortions of language disguised very commonplace notions. There are few of Mallarmé's poems now that are not clear; one cannot fail to notice that his thought singularly lacked originality. Some of his phrases were beautiful; the materials of his verse were the poetic platitudes of his day.

Simplicity is not such an obvious merit as lucidity. I have aimed at it because I have no gift for richness. Within limits I admire richness in others, though I find it difficult to digest in quantity. I can read one page of Ruskin with delight, but twenty only with weariness. The rolling period, the stately epithet, the noun rich in poetic associations, the subordinate clauses that give the sentence weight and magnificence, the grandeur like that of wave following wave in the open sea; there is no doubt that in all this there is something inspiring. Words thus strung together fall on the ear like music. The appeal is sensuous rather than intellectual, and the beauty of the sound leads you easily to conclude that you need not bother about the meaning. But words are tyrannical things, they exist for their meanings, and if you will not pay attention to these, you cannot pay attention at all. Your mind wanders. This kind of writing demands a subject that will suit it. It is surely out of place to write in the grand style of inconsiderable things. No one wrote in this manner with greater success than Sir Thomas Browne, but even he did not always escape this pitfall. In the last chapter of *Hydriotaphia* the matter, which is the destiny of man, wonderfully fits the baroque splendour of the language, and here the Norwich doctor produced a piece of prose that has never been surpassed in our literature; but when he describes the finding of his urns in the same splendid manner the effect (at least to my taste) is less happy. When a modern writer is grandiloquent to tell you whether or no a little trollop shall hop into bed with a commonplace young man you are right to be disgusted.

But if richness needs gifts with which everyone is not endowed, simplicity by no means comes by nature. To achieve it needs rigid discipline. So far as I know ours is the only language in which it has been found necessary to give a name to the piece of prose which is described as the purple patch; it would not have been necessary to do so unless it were characteristic. English prose is elaborate rather than simple. It was not always so. Nothing could be more racy, straightforward and alive than the prose of Shakespeare; but it must be remembered that this was dialogue written to be spoken. We do not know how he would have written if like Corneille he had composed prefaces to his plays. It may be that they would have been as euphuistic as the letters of Queen Elizabeth. But earlier prose, the prose of Sir Thomas More, for instance, is neither ponderous, flowery nor oratorical. It smacks of the English soil. To my mind King James's Bible has been a very harmful influence on English prose. I am not so stupid as to deny its great beauty. It is majestical. But the Bible is an oriental book. Its alien imagery has nothing to do with us. Those hyperboles, those luscious metaphors, are foreign to our genius. I cannot but think that not the least of the misfortunes that the Secession from Rome brought upon the spiritual life of our country is that this work for so long a period became the daily, and with many the only, reading of our people. Those rhythms, that powerful vocabulary, that grandiloquence, became part and parcel of the national sensibility. The plain, honest English speech was overwhelmed with ornament. Blunt Englishmen twisted their tongues to speak like Hebrew prophets. There was evidently something in the English temper to which this was congenial, perhaps a native lack of precision in thought, perhaps a naïve delight in fine words for their own sake, an innate eccentricity and love of embroidery. I do not know; but the fact remains that ever since, English prose has had to struggle against the tendency to luxuriance. When from time to time the spirit of the language has reasserted itself, as it did with Dryden and the writers of Queen Anne, it was only to be submerged once more by the pomposities of Gibbon and Dr. Johnson. When English prose recovered simplicity with Hazlitt, the Shelley of the letters and Charles Lamb at his best, it lost it again with De Quincey, Carlyle, Meredith and Walter Pater. It is obvious that the grand style is more striking than the plain. Indeed many people think that a style that does not attract notice is not style. They will admire Walter Pater's, but will read an essay by Matthew Arnold without giving a moment's attention to the elegance, distinction and sobriety with which he set down what he had to say.

The dictum that the style is the man is well known. It is one of those aphorisms that say too much to mean a great deal. Where is the man in Goethe, in his bird-like lyrics or in his clumsy prose? And Hazlitt? But I suppose that if a man has a confused mind he will write in a confused way, if his temper is capricious his prose will be fantastical, and if he has a quick, darting intelligence that is reminded by the matter in hand of a hundred things he will, unless he has great self-control, load his pages with metaphor and simile. There is a great difference between the magnificence of the Jacobean writers, who were intoxicated with the new wealth that had lately been brought into the language, and the turgidity of Gibbon and Dr. Johnson, who were the victims of bad theories. I can read every word that Dr. Johnson wrote with delight, for he had good sense, charm and wit. No one could have written better if he had not wilfully set himself to write in the grand style. He knew good English when he saw it. No critic has praised Dryden's prose more aptly. He said of him that he appeared to have no art other than that of expressing with clearness what he thought with vigour. And one of his Lives he finished with the words: "Whoever wishes to attain an English style, familiar but not coarse, and elegant but not ostentatious, must give his days and nights to the volumes of Addison." But when he himself sat down to write it was with a very different aim. He mistook the orotund for the dignified. He had not the good breeding to see that simplicity and naturalness are the truest marks of distinction.

For to write good prose is an affair of good manners. It is, unlike verse, a civil art. Poetry is baroque. Baroque is tragic, massive and mystical. It is elemental. It demands depth and insight. I cannot but feel that the prose writers of the baroque period, the authors of King James's Bible, Sir Thomas Browne, Glanville, were poets who had lost their way. Prose is a rococo art. It needs taste rather than power, decorum rather than inspiration and vigour rather than grandeur. Form for the poet is the bit and the bridle without which (unless you are an acrobat) you cannot ride your horse; but for the writer of prose it is the chassis without which your car does not exist. It is not an accident that the best prose was written when rococo with its elegance and moderation, at its birth attained its greatest excellence. For rococo was evolved when baroque had become declamatory and the world, tired of the stupendous, asked for restraint. It was the natural expression of persons who valued a civilized life. Humour, tolerance and horse sense made the great tragic issues that had preoccupied the first half of the seventeenth century seem excessive. The world was a more comfortable place to live in and perhaps for the first time in centuries the cultivated classes could sit back and enjoy their leisure. It has been said that good prose should resemble the conversation of a well-bred man. Conversation is only possible when men's minds are free from pressing anxieties. Their lives must be reasonably secure and they must have no grave concern about their souls. They must attach importance to the refinements of civilization. They must value courtesy, they must pay attention to their persons (and have we not also been told that good prose should be like the clothes of a well-dressed man, appropriate but un-obtrusive?), they must fear to bore, they must be neither flippant nor solemn, but always apt; and they must look upon "enthusiasm" with a critical glance. This is a soil very suitable for prose. It is not to be wondered at that it gave a fitting opportunity for the appearance of the best writer of prose that our modern world has seen, Voltaire. The writers of English, perhaps owing to the poetic nature of the language, have seldom reached the excellence that seems to have come so naturally to him. It is in so far as they have ap-proached the ease, sobriety and precision of the great French masters that they are admirable.

Whether you ascribe importance to euphony, the last of the three character-istics that I mentioned, must depend on the sensitiveness of your ear. A great many readers, and many admirable writers, are devoid of this quality. Poets as we know have always made a great use of alliteration. They are persuaded that the repetition of a sound gives an effect of beauty. I do not think it does so in prose. It seems to me that in prose alliteration should be used only for a special reason; when used by accident it falls on the ear very disagreeably. But its accidental use is so common that one can only suppose that the sound of it is not universally offensive. Many writers without distress will put two rhyming words together, join a monstrous long adjective to a monstrous long noun, or between the end of one word and the beginning of another have a conjunction of consonants that almost breaks your jaw. These are trivial and obvious instances. I mention them only to prove that if careful writers can do such things it is only because they have no ear. Words have weight, sound and appearance; it is only by considering these that you can write a sentence that is good to look at and good to listen to.

I have read many books on English prose, but have found it hard to profit by them; for the most part they are vague, unduly theoretical, and often scolding. But you cannot say this of Fowler's Dictionary of Modern English Usage. It is a valuable work. I do not think anyone writes so well that he cannot learn much from it. It is lively reading. Fowler liked simplicity, straightforwardness and common sense. He had no patience with preten-tiousness. He had a sound feeling that idiom was the backbone of a language and he was all for the racy phrase. He was no slavish admirer of logic and was willing enough to give usage right of way through the exact demesnes of grammar. English grammar is very difficult and few writers have avoided making mistakes in it. So heedful a writer as Henry James, for instance, on occasion wrote so ungrammatically that a schoolmaster, finding such errors in a schoolboy's essay, would be justly indignant. It is necessary to know grammar, and it is better to write grammatically than not, but it is well to remember that grammar is common speech formulated. Usage is the only test. I would prefer a phrase that was easy and unaffected to a phrase that was grammatical. One of the differences between French and English is that in French you can be grammatical with complete naturalness, but in English not invariably. It is a difficulty in writing English that the sound of the living voice dominates the look of the printed word. I have given the matter of style a great deal of thought and have taken great pains. I have written few pages that I feel I could not improve and far too many that I have left with dissatisfaction because, try as I would, I could do no better. I cannot say of myself what Johnson said of Pope: "He never passed a fault unamended by indifference, nor quitted it by despair." I do not write as I want to; I write as I can.

Ropes more than any other subject are a test of a man's power of exposition in prose. If you can describe clearly without a diagram the proper way of making this or that knot, then you are a master of the English tongue.

HILAIRE BELLOC

But Fowler had no ear. He did not see that simplicity may sometimes make concessions to euphony. I do not think a far-fetched, an archaic or even an affected word is out of place when it sounds better than the blunt, obvious one or when it gives a sentence a better balance. But, I hasten to add, though I think you may without misgiving make this concession to pleasant sound, I think you should make none to what may obscure your meaning. Anything is better than not to write clearly. There is nothing to be said against lucidity, and against simplicity only the possibility of dryness. This is a risk that is well worth taking when you reflect how much better it is to be bald than to wear a curly wig. But there is in euphony a danger that must be considered. It is very likely to be monotonous. When George Moore began to write, his style was poor; it gave you the impression that he wrote on wrapping paper with a blunt pencil. But he developed gradually a very musical English. He learnt to write sentences that fall away on the ear with a misty languor and it delighted him so much that he could never have enough of it. He did not escape monotony. It is like the sound of water lapping a shingly beach, so soothing that you presently cease to be sensible of it. It is so mellifluous that you hanker for some harshness, for an abrupt dissonance, that will interrupt the silky concord. I do not know how one can guard against this. I suppose the best chance is to have a more lively faculty of boredom than one's readers so that one is wearied before they are. One must always be on the watch for mannerisms and when certain cadences come too easily to the pen ask oneself whether they have not become mechanical. It is very hard to discover the exact point where the idiom one has formed to express oneself has lost its tang. As Dr. Johnson said: "He that has once studiously formed a style, rarely writes afterwards with complete ease." Admirably as I think Matthew Arnold's style was suited to his particular purposes, I must admit that his mannerisms are often irritating. His style was an instrument that he had forged once for all; it was not like the human hand capable of performing a variety of actions.

If you could write lucidly, simply, euphoniously and yet with liveliness you would write perfectly; you would write like Voltaire. And yet we know how fatal the pursuit of liveliness may be; it may result in the tiresome acrobatics of Meredith. Macaulay and Carlyle were in their different ways arresting; but at the heavy cost of naturalness. Their flashy effects distract the mind. They destroy their persuasiveness; you would not believe a man was very intent on ploughing a furrow if he carried a hoop with him and jumped through it at every other step. A good style should show no sign of effort. What is written should seem a happy accident. I think no one in France now writes more admirably than Colette, and such is the ease of her expression that you cannot bring yourself to believe that she takes any trouble over it. I am told that there are pianists who have a natural technique so that they can play in a manner that most executants can achieve only as the result of unremitting toil, and I am willing to believe that there are writers who are equally fortunate. Among them I was much inclined to place Colette. I asked her. I was exceedingly surprised to hear that she wrote everything over and over again. She told me that she would often spend a whole morning working upon a single page. But it does not matter how one gets the effect of ease. For my part, if I get it at all, it is only by strenuous effort. Nature seldom provides me with the word, the turn of phrase, that is appropriate without being far-fetched or commonplace.

FOR DISCUSSION

1. Make a list of Maugham's most illuminating comments (such as "A good style should show no sign of effort") and be prepared to discuss the implications of each.

2. What does Maugham think of the influence of the Bible on English prose?

3. Maugham gives qualified praise to Fowler's *Modern English Usage*. This was published in 1926 but has been reissued by Margaret Nicholson as *A Dictionary of American-English Usage* (1957) and is now available in paperback. Some experts feel that for Americans a more useful work is *A Dictionary of Contemporary American Usage* (1957) edited by Bergen and Cornelia Evans. You should compare the two works by examining their treatments of similar points of usage.

VOCABULARY: perspicuity, verbiage, lucubrations, sensuous, grandiloquent, purple patch, aphorism, rococo, baroque, sobriety, demesne, mellifluous.

THEME TOPICS: Select a passage of 100-200 words from some writer you admire, and analyze the way it is written: sentence length, number of words per hundred with three or more syllables, choice of words, figures of speech, striking phrases, parallelism, rhythm, kinds of sentences (simple, compound, complex).

You, Too, Can Write the Casual Style

WILLIAM H. WHYTE, JR.

A revolution has taken place in American prose. No longer the short huffs and puffs, the unqualified word, the crude gusto of the declarative sentence. Today the fashion is to write casually.

The Casual Style is not exactly new. Originated in the early Twenties, it has been refined and improved and refined again by a relatively small band of writers, principally for the *New Yorker*, until now their mannerisms have become standards of sophistication. Everybody is trying to join the club. Newspaper columnists have forsaken the beloved metaphors of the sports page for the Casual Style, and one of the quickest ways for an ad man to snag an award from other ad men is to give his copy the low-key, casual pitch; the copy shouldn't sing these days — it should whisper. Even Dr. Rudolf Flesch, who has been doing so much to teach people how to write like other people, is counseling his followers to use the Casual Style. Everywhere the ideal seems the same: be casual.

But how? There is very little down-to-earth advice. We hear about the rapier-like handling of the bromide, the keen eye for sham and pretension, the exquisite sense of nuance, the unerring ear for the vulgate. But not much about actual technique. The layman, as a consequence, is apt to look on the Casual Style as a mandarin dialect which he fears he could never master.

Nonsense. The Casual Style is within everyone's grasp. It has now become so perfected by constant polishing that its devices may readily be identified, and they change so little that their use need be no more difficult for the novice than for the expert. (That's not quite all there is to it, of course. Some apparently casual writers, Thurber and E. B. White, among others, rarely use the devices.)

The subject matter, in the first place, is not to be ignored. Generally speaking, the more uneventful it is, or the more pallid the writer's reaction to it, the better do form and content marry. Take, for example, the cocktail party at which the writer can show how bored everyone is with everyone else, and how utterly fatuous they all are anyhow. Since a non-casual statement — *e.g.*, "The party was a bore" — would destroy the reason for writing about it at all, the Casual Style here is not only desirable but mandatory.

From *Harper's Magazine*, October, 1953. Reprinted by permission of the author.

Whatever the subject, however, twelve devices are the rock on which all else is built. I will present them one by one, illustrating them with examples from such leading casual stylists as Wolcott Gibbs, John Crosby, John McCarten, and (on occasion) this magazine's "Mr. Harper." If the reader will digest what follows, he should be able to dash off a paragraph indistinguishable from the best casual writing being done today.

1. *Heightened Understatement.* Where the old-style writer would say, "I don't like it," "It is not good," or something equally banal, the casual writer says it is *"something less than* good." He avoids direct statement and strong words — except, we will note, where he is setting them up to have something to knock down. In any event, he qualifies. "Somewhat" and "rather," the bread-and-butter words of the casual writer, should become habitual with you; similarly with such phrases as "I suppose," "it seems to me," "I guess," or "I'm afraid." "Elusive" or "elude" are good, too, and if you see the word "charm" in a casual sentence you can be pretty sure that "eludes me," or "I find elusive," will not be far behind.

2. *The Multiple Hedge.* Set up an ostensibly strong statement, and then, with your qualifiers, shoot a series of alternately negative and positive charges into the sentence until finally you neutralize the whole thing. Let's take, for example, the clause, "certain names have a guaranteed nostalgic magic." Challenge enough here; the names not only have magic, they have guaranteed magic. A double hedge reverses the charge. "Names which have, *I suppose* [hedge 1], a guaranteed nostalgic magic, *though there are times that I doubt it* [hedge 2]. . . ."

We didn't have to say they were guaranteed in the first place, of course, but without such straw phrases we wouldn't have anything to construct a hedge on and, frequently, nothing to write at all. The virtue of the hedge is that by its very negating effect it makes any sentence infinitely expansible. Even if you have so torn down your original statement with one or two hedges that you seem to have come to the end of the line, you have only to slip in an anti-hedge, a strengthening word (*e.g.*, "definitely," "unqualified," etc.), and begin the process all over again. Witness the following quadruple hedge: "I found Mr. Home entertaining *from time to time* [hedge 1] on the ground, *I guess* [hedge 2], that the singular idiom and unearthly detachment of the British upper classes have *always* [anti-hedge] seemed *reasonably* [hedge 3] droll to me, *at least in moderation* [hedge 4]." The art of plain talk, as has been pointed out, does not entail undue brevity.

If you've pulled hedge on hedge and the effect still remains too vigorous, simply wipe the slate clean with a cancellation clause at the end. "It was all exactly as foolish as it sounds," says Wolcott Gibbs, winding up some 570 casual words on a subject, "and I wouldn't give it another thought."

3. *Narcissizing Your Prose.* The casual style is nothing if not personal; indeed, you will usually find in it as many references to the writer as to what he's supposed to be talking about. For you do not talk about the

subject; you talk about its impact on you. With the reader peering over your shoulder, you look into the mirror and observe your own responses as you run the entire range of the casual writer's emotions. You may reveal yourself as, in turn, listless ("the audience seemed not to share my boredom"); insouciant ("I was really quite happy with it"); irritated ("The whole thing left me tired and cross"); comparatively gracious ("Being in a comparatively gracious mood, I won't go into the details I didn't like"); or hesitant ("I wish I could say that I could accept his hypothesis").

4. *Preparation for the Witticism.* When the casual writer hits upon a clever turn of phrase or a nice conceit, he uses this device to insure that his conceit will not pass unnoticed. Suppose, for example, you have thought of something to say that is pretty damn good if you say so yourself. The device, in effect, is to say so yourself. If you want to devastate a certain work as "a study of vulgarity in high places," don't say this flat out. Earlier in the sentence prepare the reader for the drollery ahead with something like "what I am tempted to call" or "what could best be described as" or "If it had to be defined in a sentence, it might well be called. . . ."

Every writer his own claque.

5. *Deciphered Notes Device; or Cute-Things-I-Have-Said.* In this one you are your own stooge as well. You feed yourself lines. By means of the slender fiction that you have written something on the back of an envelope or the margin of a program, you catch yourself good-humoredly trying to decipher these shrewd, if cryptic, little jottings. *Viz.:* "Their diagnoses are not nearly as crisp as those I find in my notes"; ". . . sounds like an inadequate description, but it's all I have in my notes, and it may conceivably be a very high compliment."

6. *The Kicker.* An echo effect. "My reactions [included] an irritable feeling that eleven o'clock was past Miss Klein's bedtime," — and now the Kicker — *"not to mention my own."* This type of thing practically writes itself. "She returns home. She should never have left home in the first place. ⸻ ⸻ ⸻ ⸻." [1]

7. *Wit of Omission.* By calling attention to the fact that you are not going to say it, you suggest that there is something very funny you could say if only you wanted to. "A thought occurred to me at this point," you may say, when otherwise stymied, "but I think we had better not go into *that.*"

8. *The Planned Colloquialism.* The casual writer savors colloquialisms. This is not ordinary colloquial talk — nobody is more quickly provoked than the casual writer by ordinary usage. It is, rather, a playful descent into the vulgate. Phrases like "darn," "awfully," "as all getout," "mighty," and other folksy idioms are ideal. The less you would be likely to use the word normally yourself the more pointed the effect. Contrast is what you are after, for it is the facetious interplay of language levels — a blending, as

---

[1] "And neither should I."

it were, of the East Fifties and the Sticks — that gives the Casual Style its off-hand charm.

In the way of writing, no great thing was ever, or will ever be done with ease, but with difficulty!

THOMAS CARLYLE

9. *Feigned Forgetfulness.* Conversation gropes; it is full of "what I really meant was" and "maybe I should have added," backings and fillings and second thoughts of one kind or another. Writing is different; theoretically, ironing out second thoughts beforehand is one of the things writers are paid to do. In the Casual Style, however, it is exactly this exposure of the writer composing in public that makes it so casual. For the professional touch, then, ramble, rebuke yourself in print ("what I really meant, I guess"), and if you have something you feel you should have said earlier, don't say it earlier, but say later that you guess you should have said it earlier.

10. *The Subject-Apologizer, or Pardon-Me-for-Living.* The Casual Stylist must always allow for the possibility that his subject is just as boring to the reader as it is to him. He may forestall this by seeming to have stumbled on it by accident, or by using phrases like: "If this is as much news to you as it is to me," or "This, in case you've been living in a cave lately, is. . . ."

11. *The Omitted Word.* This all began modestly enough the day a *New Yorker* writer dropped the articles "the" and "a" from the initial sentence of an anecdote (*e.g.*, "Man we know told us"; "Fellow name of Brown"). Now even such resolutely lowbrow writers as Robert Ruark affect it, and they are applying it to any part of speech anywhere in the sentence. You can drop a pronoun ("Says they're shaped like pyramids"; verb ("You been away from soap opera the last couple of weeks?"); or preposition ("Far as glamour goes . . .").

12. *The Right Word.* In the lexicon of the casual writer there are a dozen or so adjectives which in any context have, to borrow a phrase, a guaranteed charm. Attrition is high — "brittle," "febrile," "confected," for example, are at the end of the run. Ten, however, defy obsolescence: *antic, arch, blurred, chaste, chill, crisp, churlish, disheveled, dim, disembodied.*

They are good singly, but they are even better when used in tandem, *c.f.*, "In an arch, antic sort of way"; "In an arch, blurred sort of way"; "In an arch, crisp sort of way." And so on.

Finally, the most multi-purpose word of them all: "altogether." Frequently it is the companion of "charming" and "delightful," and in this coupling is indispensable to any kind of drama criticism. It can also modify the writer himself (*e.g.*, "Altogether, I think . . ."). Used best, however, it just floats, unbeholden to any other part of the sentence.

Once you have mastered these twelve devices, you too should be able to write as casually as all getout. At least it seems to me, though I may be wrong, that they convey an elusive archness which the crisp literary craftsman, in his own dim sort of way, should altogether cultivate these days. Come to think of it, the charm of the Casual Style is something less than clear to me, but we needn't go into *that*. Fellow I know from another magazine says this point of view best described as churlish. Not, of course, that it matters.

FOR DISCUSSION

1. How many of the twelve characteristics of the casual style can you find in the final paragraph?

2. Is there any particular writer — a newspaper columnist, perhaps, or a sports writer — whose work you enjoy? Can you find elements of the casual style in his writing?

3. Exactly what is wrong with the casual style? Is it too faddish? Silly? Obvious?

4. Can you find examples of it in the *New Yorker,* where Whyte says it originated?

VOCABULARY: gusto, sophistication, metaphor, mandarin dialect, fatuous, mandatory, nostalgic.

THEME TOPICS: Style on the sports page. Casual writing is not easy. Better a casual style than none at all. I, too, can write the casual style.

On the Teaching of Writing

ARCHIBALD MacLEISH

Everybody knows that "creative writing" — which means the use of words as material of art — can't be taught. Nevertheless hundreds of professors in hundreds of colleges go on teaching it. Which is absurd but not as absurd as it sounds.

Everybody knows, too, that you can't teach a horse to race but Kentucky is full of racing stables with neat oval tracks and miles of expensive, white-washed fencing which costs as much to maintain as a presentable professor. Even more.

There is one difference, of course. In Kentucky they begin with the horse's sire and dam whereas the professor of writing rarely breeds his own students and wouldn't know where to begin if he tried. Who would have picked that pair from the livery stable to beget and bear John Keats?

But otherwise the situation in Cambridge is much like the situation in Kentucky. You have to have a horse that can race before you can teach it racing. You have to have a writer who can write before you can teach him how.

Which means, of course, that you aren't really teaching in Cambridge. To teach you have to have a subject: Elementary German or Physics A or The Novel Since Henry James. But there is no subject in "creative writing": there is merely an object: that boy (that horse). I say *that* boy because there isn't apt to be more than one in a year or maybe in five or even ten. Indeed a man would be spectacularly lucky, even by Kentucky standards, to have one distinct and distinguishable writer of real power in a professorial lifetime.

There are those, I know, who have tried to concoct a subject for "creative writing" courses by combining the best elements of the best writers in a kind of appetizer paste, a *mélange adultère de tous,* which their students are expected to consume. The young critics who make up the majority of any college writing course — the lads who have mistaken an interest in writing for writing itself — will thrive on such a diet but the young writers, if there are any, will gag on the surfeit. They know instinctively that there is no such thing as Best Writing. There are merely a number of different writers writing well and the successes of one would be the failures of

From *Harper's Magazine,* October, 1959. Reprinted by permission of the author.

51

another. You can't borrow and you can't mix. If anyone had tried to solve D. H. Lawrence's writing problems by teaching him Flaubert's solutions there would have been a suicide in the family attic — or more likely a murder in the local school. Exposition has rules and can be taught, as generations of British state papers demonstrate. The "art of writing" has graces and can be taught as armies of belletrists prove. But writing *as* an art cannot be taught because writing as an art is the unique achievement of *an* artist. Which is to say, of one unique and different man solving his unique and different problems for himself. When a student tells me that I haven't taugh him *how,* I take it as a compliment — but not to him.

I am not saying, of course, that a young writer should not read. He should, quite literally, read his head off. But he should do his reading for himself, following the leads that are meaningful for him, not for someone else, and least of all for an older professor-writer who did his own essential reading a generation ago and by a different light. To do an older writer's reading over again in a time like ours is to submit to that process, already so destructive in our fashion-following super-civilization, by which everything is turned into a vogue — even art which should be the great destroyer of all fashions, not their pimp. Everyone reads James. Then everyone reads Joyce. Then everyone switches to Eliot, to Proust, to Kafka — to the Communists in one decade — to the homosexuals in another — until the new writing begins to sound like the advertising patter in the smart magazines which echoes the changing chatter of the chic. It sometimes seems as though only Robert Frost were old enough and cantankerous enough and magnificent enough to be himself and remain himself and thus be disrespectfully and entirely new in this age of stylish novelties.

A real writer learns from earlier writers the way a boy learns from an apple orchard — by stealing what he has a taste for and can carry off. He will imitate his elders as every good writer has since the world began — even an original, even a Rimbaud — but the hunger and the pants pocket will be his own. Some of his apples will make him sick, but it will be *his* sickness. Others will shape his hand for life — because *he* picked them. When I set myself, after college and after law school, to try to find my way to a place where I could begin, I taught myself Italian enough to read *The Divine Comedy* because Tom Eliot had read it to his great profit and because I was — as I remain — his devoted admirer. It did me, I am sure, no harm. But neither did it do me Eliot's good, for it was not my need that took me to it.

The truth is that the whole situation in a writing course is a reversal of the usual academic pattern. Not only is there no subject, there is no content either. Or, more precisely, the content is the work produced by students in the course. And the relation of the teacher to his students is thus the opposite of the relation one would expect to find. Ordinarily it is the teacher who knows, the student who learns. Here it is the student who knows, or should, and the teacher who learns or tries to. The student writes. The teacher reads. And the object of the teacher's reading is to learn if he can how closely the knowing of the words approximates the knowing of their writer. It may be less. It may be far, far more, for such is the nature of the struggle between a writer and the obdurate material of words in which he works. But whether less or more, the only question the man who undertakes to teach can ask, is the question of the adequacy of the writing to its own intent. As a writer himself he may call it "good" or "bad." As a man he may have his human opinion of the mind which conceived it. But as a teacher of writing it is not his task to tell his students what they should try to write or to judge their work by the standards he would apply to his own or his betters'.

A student's poem does not fail because it is not Yeats's "Byzantium" or even "Sailing to . . ." It fails only if it is not itself. And the labor of the reader who calls himself teacher is the difficult labor of discerning, if he can, what "itself" would be. For only then can he bring his own experience and skill to bear upon it. Only then can he say to the student across the corner of his desk: "Well, if *I* had tried to write this poem . . ."

The real relationship, in other words — the only relationship in which anything in this paradoxical undertaking can be accomplished — is a relationship between two writers. Which is why it is essential that at least one writer should enroll in a writing course if it is to get anywhere. The problems which arise, young as the students are, are problems all writers face, whatever their age or experience. They are problems which cannot be discussed in a class, any more than in a bar in Paris, without a text to relate them to, and a writer's human experience to give them perspective. And they involve, as such problems always do involve, a writer's conception of the world: a conception different in every way from a critic's or a scholar's because a writer never gets *outside*. He works as Tolstoy works in *Anna Karenina* — at Levin's heart and Kitty's and Anna's. Techniques without works are as empty to a practicing writer as faith without works to a practicing clergyman: only amateurs would waste time talking about them.

But difficult as it is to describe the relationships of a writing course, it is even more difficult to justify one, either from the point of view of the student who takes it or from the point of view of the college which pays for it. (I defer, for a moment, the point of view of the poor devil of a poet or a novelist who tries to do the teaching.) Why, if all there is is a couple of writers, should any young writer send himself to a college writing course instead of to a park bench in Washington Square or a jazz session in San Francisco or any other spot where he might find an older writer willing to help him to help himself? And why, even with academic salaries what they are, should a college pay for the ten or twelve necessary hours of a professor's time every week if only one student a year or one student every five is going to profit?

I don't know the answer to the second question. You could probably justify a course in commercial fiction from the purely budgetary point of view if enough of its graduates sold stories to magazines with commercial prestige, but there is no way of adding up the justifications of a course devoted to the art of writing. Undoubtedly it is helpful to a college to be able to list a respectable number of writers as graduates but the trouble is that not all the proven writers come out of the writing courses. Harvard's poets from Robinson through Frost and Stevens to Aiken and Eliot and Cummings constitute an unequaled galaxy but I have never heard it said that any of them got their start in a writing course.

What justification there is must be academic rather than economic and there too one runs into trouble. One can argue that it is desirable to dilute the critical and scholarly atmosphere of a college community with a few artists but you won't get all the critics and scholars to agree. And if you remark that a good writing course will at least prevent English from becoming a dead language you might as well eat your lunches somewhere else than the faculty club. The plain truth is that these courses are eleemosynary enterprises so far as the college budget is concerned — opportunities provided to a small minority of students to investigate their artistic possibilities at the college's expense. The students who take them should be grateful. Sometimes, improbably enough, they are.

As for the first question, however, the answer is obvious. The young writer who graduates straight from high school into San Francisco, or wherever the people who used to congregate in Paris now hang out in the innocent hope that he will thus combine his initiation into art with his initiation into life, is deluding himself. If we are to judge by its works there can scarcely be a worse place to get admitted to life than San Francisco. In comparison a great university or even a competent college is liveliness itself. There are more people of more kinds in a college than in a cult — particularly a cult in which Bohemianism itself is stereotyped and you can't even be a bum without bad liquor, boring sexuality, and the regulation beard. Indeed the American university — the American university I know best in any case — is almost the only place left in America where the infinite variety of the kind of life a writer wants to live can still be found.

In addition to which there is the highly pertinent fact that universities and colleges have books. Life is not all on the sidewalks or even in the bedrooms. The nine-tenths of it a writer needs under him to keep the rest afloat is in the books in which other men have put their living down. And there is one other consideration which bears upon those long conversations with older and sympathetic writers of which the young so understandably dream: most of the older writers are now employed by universities and colleges and the rest put limits on the number of young strangers they will entertain. Also the rest aren't as constantly available as the prisoners of the academic offices. They have a way of traveling to Africa or Spain.

As for the point of view of the poor devil who does the teaching, it can be given as briefly and simply as the annals of the poor. The rewards depend on the students. If they are uninteresting he will be bored to death. If they are exciting there will not be hours enough in the week. But it is not as simple as that, either. For if the students are dull the fault is his whereas if they are good *they* get the credit.

Mine have been good more often than I deserved.

FOR DISCUSSION

1. What is the difference between writing as a tool of communication and writing as an art? Can an art be "taught"?

2. Why should a young reader follow his own interests in reading rather than the interests of an older person?

3. How is the situation in a writing course a reversal of the usual academic pattern?

4. Why is a university campus an excellent environment for a young writer?

VOCABULARY: surfeit, belletrist, chic, defer, galaxy, eleemosynary, cult, stereotype.

THEME TOPIC: Write an analysis of the paragraph beginning, "The truth is that the whole situation in a writing course . . ." (page 52). Note some of the following points in your analysis: average sentence length; number of words per hundred with three or more syllables; sentences beginning with conjunctions; parallelism; number of sentences with "is" as verb; kinds of sentences (simple, compound, complex). What evaluative judgment would you make of this paragraph? Is it lucid, simple, and euphonious, as Maugham believes good writing should be? Is it easy to understand?

The Principles of Poor Writing

PAUL W. MERRILL

Books and articles on good writing are numerous, but where can you find sound, practical advice on how to write poorly? Poor writing is so common that every educated person ought to know something about it. Many scientists actually do write poorly, but they probably perform by ear without perceiving clearly how their results are achieved. An article on the principles of poor writing might help. The author considers himself well qualified to prepare such an article; he can write poorly without half trying.

The average student finds it surprisingly easy to acquire the usual tricks of poor writing. To do a consistently poor job, however, one must grasp a few essential principles:

1. Ignore the reader.
2. Be verbose, vague, and pompous.
3. Do not revise.

Ignore the Reader

The world is divided into two great camps: yourself and others. A little obscurity or indirection in writing will keep the others at a safe distance; if they get close, they may see too much.

Write as if for a diary. Keep your mind on a direct course between yourself and the subject; don't think of the reader — he makes a bad triangle. This is fundamental. Constant and alert consideration of the probable reaction of the reader is a serious menace to poor writing; moreover, it requires mental effort. A logical argument is that if you write poorly enough, your readers will be too few to merit any attention whatever.

Ignore the reader wherever possible. If the proposed title, for example, means something to you, stop right there; think no further. If the title baffles or misleads the reader, you have won the first round. Similarly, all the way through you must write for yourself, not for the reader. Practice a dead-pan technique, keeping all facts and ideas on the same level

From *The Scientific Monthly*, January, 1947. Copyright 1947 by the American Association for the Advancement of Science. Reprinted by permission of the author.

of emphasis with no telltale hints of relative importance or logical sequence. Use long sentences containing many ideas loosely strung together. *And* is the connective most frequently employed in poor writing because it does not indicate cause and effect, nor does it distinguish major ideas from subordinate ones. *Because* seldom appears in poor writing, nor does the semicolon — both are replaced by *and.*

Camouflage transitions in thought. Avoid such connectives as *moreover, nevertheless, on the other hand.* If unable to resist the temptation to give some signal for a change in thought, use *however.* A poor sentence may well begin with *however* because to the reader, with no idea what comes next, *however* is too vague to be useful. A good sentence begins with the subject or with a phrase that needs emphasis.

The "hidden antecedent" is a common trick of poor writing. Use a pronoun to refer to a noun a long way back, or to one decidedly subordinate in thought or syntax; or the pronoun may refer to something not directly expressed. If you wish to play a little game with the reader, offer him the wrong antecedent as bait; you may be astonished how easy it is to catch the poor fish.

In ignoring the reader avoid parallel constructions which give the thought away too easily. I need not elaborate, for you probably employ inversion frequently. It must have been a naive soul who said, "When the thought is parallel, let the phrases be parallel."

In every technical paper omit a few items that most readers need to know. You had to discover these things the hard way; why make it easy for the reader? Avoid defining symbols; never specify the units in which data are presented. Of course it will be beneath your dignity to give numerical values of constants in formulae. With these omissions, some papers may be too short; lengthen them by explaining things that do not need explaining. In describing tables, give special attention to self-explanatory headings; let the reader hunt for the meaning of P^1r_0.

Be Verbose, Vague, and Pompous

The cardinal sin of poor writing is to be concise and simple. Avoid being specific; it ties you down. Use plenty of deadwood: include many superfluous words and phrases. Wishful thinking suggests to a writer that verbosity somehow serves as a cloak or even as a mystic halo by which an idea may be glorified. A cloud of words may conceal defects in observation or analysis, either by opacity or by diverting the reader's attention. Introduce abstract nouns at the drop of a hat — even in those *cases* where the *magnitude* of the *motion* in a downward *direction* is inconsiderable. Make frequent use of the words *case, character, condition, former* and *latter, nature, such, very.*

Poor writing, like good football, is strong on razzle-dazzle, weak on information. Adjectives are frequently used to bewilder the reader. It isn't much trouble to make them gaudy or hyperbolic; at least they can be flowery and inexact.

DEADWOOD

Bible: Render to Caesar the things that are Caesar's.

Poor: In the case of Caesar it might well be considered appropriate from a moral or ethical point of view to render to that potentate all of those goods and materials of whatever character or quality which can be shown to have had their original source in any portion of the domain of the latter.

Shakespeare: I am no orator as Brutus is.

Poor: The speaker is not what might be termed an adept in the profession of public speaking, as might be properly stated of Mr. Brutus. (Example from P. W. Swain. *Amer. J. Physics*, 13, 318, 1945.)

Concise: The dates of several observations are in doubt.

Poor: It should be mentioned that in the case of several observations there is room for considerable doubt concerning the correctness of the dates on which they were made.

Reasonable: Exceptionally rapid changes occur in the spectrum.

Poor: There occur in the spectrum changes which are quite exceptional in respect to the rapidity of their advent.

Reasonable: Formidable difficulties, both mathematical and observational, stand in the way.

Poor: There are formidable difficulties of both a mathematical and an observational nature that stand in the way.

CASE

Reasonable: Two sunspots changed rapidly.

Poor: There are two cases where sunspots changed with considerable rapidity.

Reasonable: Three stars are red.

Poor: In three cases the stars are red in color.

RAZZLE-DAZZLE

Immaculate precision of observation and extremely delicate calculations. . . .

It would prove at once a world imponderable, etherealized. Our actions would grow grandific.

Well for us that the pulsing energy of the great life-giving dynamo in the sky never ceases. Well, too, that we are at a safe distance from the flame-licked whirlpools into which our earth might drop like a pellet of waste fluff shaken into the live coals of a grate fire.

Do Not Revise

Write hurriedly, preferably when tired. Have no plan; write down items as they occur to you. The article will thus be spontaneous and poor. Hand in your manuscript the moment it is finished. Rereading a few days later might lead to revision — which seldom, if ever, makes the writing worse. If you submit your manuscript to colleagues (a bad practice), pay no attention to their criticisms or comments. Later resist firmly any editorial suggestions. Be strong and infallible; don't let anyone break down your personality. The critic may be trying to help you or he may have an ulterior motive, but the chance of his causing improvement in your writing is so great that you must be on guard.

Final Suggestion for Poor Writing

Do not read:

Allbutt, Clifford. *Notes on the Composition of Scientific Papers.* Macmillan, 1923.

Flesch, Rudolf. *The Art of Plain Talk.* Harper, 1946.

Graves and Hodge. *The Reader Over Your Shoulder.* Macmillan, 1943.

Quiller-Couch, Arthur. *On the Art of Writing.* [V]. Putnam, 1928.

Suggestions to Authors of Papers Submitted for Publication by the United States Geological Survey. U. S. Gov. Ptg. Off., 1935.

FOR DISCUSSION

You could type out on a single sheet the three main principles of poor writing with the sub-principles under each. You could post this sheet over your desk beside the list you have already drawn up from Roberts's "How to Say Nothing in Five Hundred Words." Do you think these two check lists would actually help you write the way you want to?

VOCABULARY: sequence, subordinate, transition, antecedent, naive, verbosity, infallible, ulterior.

THEME TOPICS: I've been using the principles of poor writing without knowing it. You, too, can write poorly. It isn't how you say it, it's what you say.

STANDARDS

IN LANGUAGE

Grammar for Today

BERGEN EVANS

In 1747 Samuel Johnson issued a plan for a new dictionary of the English language. It was supported by the most distinguished printers of the day and was dedicated to the model of all correctness, Philip Dormer Stanhope, Fourth Earl of Chesterfield. Such a book, it was felt, was urgently needed to "fix" the language, to arrest its "corruption" and "decay," a degenerative process which, then as now, was attributed to the influence of "the vulgar" and which, then as now, it was a mark of superiority and elegance to decry. And Mr. Johnson seemed the man to write it. He had an enormous knowledge of Latin, deep piety, and dogmatic convictions. He was also honest and intelligent, but the effect of these lesser qualifications was not to show until later.

Oblig'd by hunger and request of friends, Mr. Johnson was willing to assume the role of linguistic dictator. He was prepared to "fix" the pro-

From *The Atlantic Monthly*, March, 1960. Reprinted by permission of the author.

nunciation of the language, "preserve the purity" of its idiom, brand "impure" words with a "note of infamy," and secure the whole "from being overrun by . . . low terms."

There were, however, a few reservations. Mr. Johnson felt it necessary to warn the oversanguine that "Language is the work of man, a being from whom permanence and stability cannot be derived." English "was not formed from heaven . . . but was produced by necessity and enlarged by accident." It had, indeed, been merely "thrown together by negligence" and was in such a state of confusion that its very syntax could no longer "be taught by general rules, but [only] by special precedents."

In 1755 the *Dictionary* appeared. The noble patron had been given a great deal more immortality than he had bargained for by the vigor of the kick Johnson had applied to his backside as he booted him overboard. And the *Plan* had been replaced by the *Preface,* a sadder but very much wiser document.

Eight years of "sluggishly treading the track of the alphabet" had taught Johnson that the hopes of "fixing" the language and preserving its "purity" were but "the dreams of a poet doomed at last to wake a lexicographer." In "the boundless chaos of living speech," so copious and energetic in its disorder, he had found no guides except "experience and analogy." Irregularities were "inherent in the tongue" and could not be "dismissed or reformed" but must be permitted "to remain untouched." "Uniformity must be sacrificed to custom . . . in compliance with a numberless majority" and "general agreement." One of the pet projects of the age had been the establishment of an academy to regulate and improve style. "I hope," Johnson wrote in the *Preface,* that if "it should be established . . . the spirit of English liberty will hinder or destroy [it]."

At the outset of the work he had flattered himself, he confessed, that he would reform abuses and put a stop to alterations. But he had soon discovered that "sounds are too volatile and subtle for legal restraints" and that "to enchain syllables and to lash the wind are equally undertakings of pride unwilling to measure its desires by its strength." For "the causes of change in language are as much superior to human resistance as the revolutions of the sky or the intumescence of the tide."

There had been an even more profound discovery: that the grammarians and lexicographers "do not form, but register the language; do not teach men how they should think, but relate how they have hitherto expressed their thoughts." And with this statement Johnson ushered in the rational study of linguistics. He had entered on his task a medieval pedant. He emerged from it a modern scientist.

Of course his discoveries were not strikingly original. Horace had observed that use was the sole arbiter and norm of speech and Montaigne had said that he who would fight custom with grammar was a fool. Doubtless thousands of other people had at one time or another perceived and said the same thing. But Johnson introduced a new principle. Finding that he could not lay down rules, he gave actual examples to show meaning and form. He offered as authority illustrative quotations, and in so doing established that language is what usage makes it and that custom, in the long run, is the ultimate and only court of appeal in linguistic matters.

This principle, axiomatic today in grammar and lexicography, seems to exasperate a great many laymen who, apparently, find two hundred and five years too short a period in which to grasp a basic idea. They insist that there are absolute standards of correctness in speech and that these standards may be set forth in a few simple rules. To a man, they believe, of course, that they speak and write "correctly" and they are loud in their insistence that others imitate them.

It is useless to argue with such people because they are not, really, interested in language at all. They are interested solely in demonstrating their own superiority. Point out to them — as has been done hundreds of times — that forms which they regard as "corrupt," "incorrect," and "vulgar" have been used by Shakespeare, Milton, and the Bible and are used daily by 180 million Americans and accepted by the best linguists and lexicographers, and they will coolly say, "Well, if they differ from me, they're wrong."

But if usage is not the final determinant of speech, what is? Do the inhabitants of Italy, for example, speak corrupt Latin or good Italian? Is Spanish superior to French? Would the Breton fisherman speak better if he spoke Parisian French? Can one be more fluent in Outer Mongolian than in Inner Mongolian? One has only to ask such questions in relation to languages other than one's own, languages within which our particular snobberies and struggles for prestige have no stake, to see the absurdity of them.

The language that we do speak, if we are to accept the idea of "corruption" and "decay" in language, is a horribly decayed Anglo-Saxon, grotesquely corrupted by Norman French. Furthermore, since Standard English is a development of the London dialect of the fourteenth century, our speech, by true aristocratic standards, is woefully middle-class, commercial, and vulgar. And American speech is lower middle-class, reeking of counter and till. Where else on earth, for instance, would one find crime condemned because it didn't *pay!*

In more innocent days a great deal of time was spent in wondering what was the "original" language of mankind, the one spoken in Eden, the language of which all modern tongues were merely degenerate remnants. Hector Boethius tells us that James I of Scotland was so interested in this problem that he had two children reared with a deaf and dumb nurse on an island in order to see what language they would "naturally" speak. James thought it would be Hebrew, and in time, to his great satisfaction, it was reported that the children were speaking Hebrew!

Despite this experiment, however, few people today regard English as a corruption of Hebrew. But many seem to think it is a corruption of Latin and labor mightily to make it conform to this illusion. It is they and their confused followers who tell us that we can't say "I am mistaken" because translated into Latin this would mean "I am misunderstood," and we can't say "I have enjoyed myself" unless we are egotistical or worse.

It is largely to this group — most of whom couldn't read a line of Latin at sight if their lives depended on it — that we owe our widespread bewilderment concerning *who* and *whom*. In Latin the accusative or dative form would always be used, regardless of the word's position in the sentence, when the pronoun was the object of a verb or a preposition. But in English, for at least four hundred years, this simply hasn't been so. When the pronoun occurs at the beginning of a question, people who speak natural, fluent, literary English use the nominative, regardless. They say "Who did you give it to?" not "Whom did you give it to?" But the semiliterate, intimidated and bewildered, are mouthing such ghastly utterances as a recent headline in a Chicago newspaper: WHOM'S HE KIDDING?

Another group seems to think that in its pure state English was a Laputan tongue, with logic as its guiding principle. Early members of this sect insisted that *unloose* could only mean "to tie up," and present members have compelled the gasoline industry to label its trucks *Flammable* under the disastrous insistence, apparently, that the old *Inflammable* could only mean "not burnable."

It is to them, in league with the Latinists, that we owe the bogy of the double negative. In all Teutonic languages a doubling of the negative merely emphasizes the negation. But we have been told for a century now that two negatives make a positive, though if they do and it's merely a matter of logic, then three negatives should make a negative again. So that if "It doesn't make no difference" is wrong merely because it includes two negatives, then "It doesn't never make no difference" ought to be right again.

Both of these groups, in their theories at least, ignore our idiom. Yet idiom — those expressions which defy all logic but are the very essence of a tongue — plays a large part in English. We go to school and college, but we go to *the* university. We buy two dozen eggs but a couple *of* dozen. *Good and* can mean *very* ("I am good and mad!") and "a hot cup of coffee" means that the coffee, not the cup, is to be hot. It makes a world of difference to a condemned man whether his reprieve is *upheld* or *held up*.

There are thousands of such expressions in English. They are the "irregularities" which Johnson found "inherent in the tongue" and which his wisdom perceived could not and should not be removed. Indeed, it is in the recognition and use of these idioms that skillful use of English lies.

Many words in the form that is now mandatory were originally just mistakes, and many of these mistakes were forced into the language by eager ignoramuses determined to make it conform to some notion of their own. The *s* was put in *island,* for instance, in sheer pedantic ignorance. The second *r* doesn't belong in *trousers,* nor the *g* in *arraign,* nor the *t* in *deviltry,* nor the *n* in *passenger* and *messenger.* Nor, so far as English is concerned, does that first *c* in *arctic* which so many people twist their mouths so strenuously to pronounce.

And grammar is as "corrupted" as spelling or pronunciation. "You are" is as gross a solecism as "me am." It's recent, too; you won't find it in the Authorized Version of the Bible. *Lesser, nearer,* and *more* are grammatically on a par with *gooder. Crowed* is the equivalent of *knowed* or *growed,* and *caught* and *dug* (for *catched* and *digged*) are as "corrupt" as *squoze* for *squeezed* or *snoze* for *sneezed.*

Fortunately for our peace of mind most people are quite content to let English conform to English, and they are supported in their sanity by modern grammarians and linguists.

Scholars agree with Puttenham (1589) that a language is simply speech "fashioned to the common understanding and accepted by consent." They believe that the only "rules" that can be stated for a language are codified observations. They hold, that is, that language is the basis of grammar, not the other way round. They do not believe that any language can become "corrupted" by the linguistic habits of those who speak it. They do not believe that anyone who is a native speaker of a standard language will get into any linguistic trouble unless he is misled by snobbishness or timidity or vanity.

He may, of course, if his native language is English, speak a form of English that marks him as coming from a rural or an unread group. But if he doesn't mind being so marked, there's no reason why he should change. Johnson retained a Staffordshire burr in his speech all his life. And surely no one will deny that Robert Burns's rustic dialect was just as good as a form of speech as, and in his mouth infinitely better as a means of expression than, the "correct" English spoken by ten million of his southern contemporaries.

The trouble is that people are no longer willing to be rustic or provincial. They all want to speak like educated people, though they don't want to go to the trouble of becoming truly educated. They want to believe that a special form of socially acceptable and financially valuable speech can be mastered by following a few simple rules. And there is no lack of little books that offer to supply the rules and promise "correctness" if the rules are adhered to. But, of course, these offers are specious because you don't speak like an educated person unless you are an educated person, and the little books, if taken seriously, will not only leave the lack of education showing but will expose the pitiful yearning and the basic vulgarity as well, in such sentences as "Whom are you taking about?"

As a matter of fact, the educated man uses at least three languages. With his family and his close friends, on the ordinary, unimportant occasions of daily life, he speaks, much of the time, a monosyllabic sort of shorthand. On more important occasions and when dealing with strangers in his official or business relations, he has a more formal speech, more complete, less allusive, politely qualified, wisely reserved. In addition he has some acquaintance with the literary speech of his language. He understands this when he reads it, and often enjoys it, but he hesitates to use it. In times of emotional stress hot fragments of it may come out of him like lava, and in times of feigned emotion, as when giving a commencement address, cold, greasy gobbets of it will ooze forth.

The linguist differs from the amateur grammarian in recognizng all of these variations and gradations in the language. And he differs from the snob in doubting that the speech of any one small group among the language's more than 300 million daily users constitutes a model for all the rest to imitate.

The methods of the modern linguist can be illustrated by the question of the grammatical number of *none*. Is it singular or plural? Should one say "None of them is ready" or "None of them are ready"?

The prescriptive grammarians are emphatic that it should be singular. The Latinists point out that *nemo*, the Latin equivalent, is singular. The logicians triumphantly point out that *none* can't be more than one and hence can't be plural.

Dictionaries are like watches; the worst is better than none, and the best cannot be expected to go quite true.

SAMUEL JOHNSON

The linguist knows that he hears "None of them are ready" every day, from people of all social positions, geographical areas, and degrees of education. He also hears "None is." Furthermore, literature informs him that both forms were used in the past. From Malory (1450) to Milton (1650) he finds that *none* was treated as a singular three times for every once that it was treated as a plural. That is, up to three hundred years ago men usually said *None is*. From Milton to 1917, *none* was used as a plural seven times for every four times it was used as a singular. That is, in the past three hundred years men often said *None is*, but they said *None are* almost twice as often. Since 1917, however, there has been a noticeable increase in the use of the plural, so much so that today *None are* is the preferred form.

The descriptive grammarian, therefore, says that while *None is* may still be used, it is becoming increasingly peculiar. This, of course, will not be as useful to one who wants to be cultured in a hurry as a short, emphatic permission or prohibition. But it has the advantage of describing English as it is spoken and written here and now and not as it ought to be spoken in some Cloud-Cuckoo-Land.

The descriptive grammarian believes that a child should be taught English, but he would like to see the child taught the English actually used by his educated contemporaries, not some pedantic, theoretical English designed chiefly to mark the imagined superiority of the designer.

He believes that a child should be taught the parts of speech, for example. But the child should be told the truth — that these are functions of use, not some quality, immutably inherent in this or that word. Anyone, for instance, who tells a child — or anyone else — that *like* is used in English only as a preposition has grossly misinformed him. And anyone who complains that its use as a conjunction is a corruption introduced by Winston cigarettes ought, in all fairness, to explain how Shakespeare, Keats, and the translators of the Authorized Version of the Bible came to be in the employ of the R. J. Reynolds Tobacco Company.

Whether formal grammar can be taught to advantage before the senior year of high school is doubtful; most studies — and many have been made — indicate that it can't. But when it is taught, it should be the grammar of today's English, not the obsolete grammar of yesterday's prescriptive grammarians. By that grammar, for instance, *please* in the sentence "Please reply" is the verb and *reply* its object. But by modern meaning *reply* is the verb, in the imperative, and *please* is merely a qualifying word meaning "no discourtesy intended," a mollifying or de-imperatival adverb, or whatever you will, but not the verb.

This is a long way from saying "Anything goes," which is the charge that, with all the idiot repetition of a needle stuck in a groove, the uninformed ceaselessly chant against modern grammarians. But to assert that usage is the sole determinant in grammar, pronunciation, and meaning is *not* to say that anything goes. Custom is illogical and unreasonable, but it is also tyrannical. The least deviation from its dictates is usually punished with severity. And because this is so, children should be taught what the current and local customs in English are. They should not be taught that we speak a bastard Latin or a vocalized logic. And they should certainly be disabused of the stultifying illusion that after God had given Moses the Commandments He called him back and pressed on him a copy of Woolley's *Handbook of English Grammar*.

The grammarian does not see it as his function to "raise the standards" set by Franklin, Lincoln, Melville, Mark Twain, and hundreds of millions of other Americans. He is content to record what they said and say.

Insofar as he serves as a teacher, it is his business to point out the limits of the permissible, to indicate the confines within which the writer may exercise his choice, to report that which custom and practice have made acceptable. It is certainly not the business of the grammarian to impose his personal taste as the only norm of good English, to set forth his prejudices as the ideal standard which everyone should copy. That would be fatal. No one person's standards are broad enough for that.

FOR DISCUSSION

1. What did Samuel Johnson learn about language during the eight years he spent preparing his dictionary?

2. Is there any basis for believing that the English used today is a corruption of some earlier form, or of some other language?

3. Do you naturally use *who* or *whom* when it stands first in a sentence? Do you regard *whom* as a better form in such a sentence? (Who[m] did you meet?)

4. Why do many people want to rid themselves of the rustic or provincial forms of language they grew up with?

5. How would you explain the difference between a prescriptive grammarian and a modern linguist?

6. Does a modern linguist believe that "anything goes"?

VOCABULARY: dogmatic, idiom, oversanguine, inherent, linguistics, axiomatic, intimidate, mandatory, codified, prescriptive, mollify.

THEME TOPICS: Why we should use a dictionary of usage. What correct English is. When is English bad? What dictionaries say about *who-whom, can-may, farther-further,* etc. Gobbledegook is worse than slang.

Our National Mania for Correctness

DONALD J. LLOYD

Every now and then the editors of the university presses let out a disgruntled bleat about the miserable writing done by scholars, even those who are expert in literary fields; and from time to time there are letters and editorials in our national reviews bewailing some current academic malpractice with the English language. At present, even *PMLA* (the Publications of the Modern Language Association), traditionally the repository of some of the worst writing done by researchers, is trying to herd its au-

From *The American Scholar,* Volume XXI, Number 3, Summer 1952, © copyright 1952, by the United Chapters of Phi Beta Kappa. Reprinted by permission of the publishers.

thors toward more lucid exposition. And at two recent meetings of the august Mediaeval Academy, one at Boston and one at Dumbarton Oaks, bitter remarks were passed about the failure of specialists in the Middle Ages to present their findings in some form palatable to the general reader, so that he can at least understand what they are writing about.

Even admitting that a really compelling style is the result of years of cultivation, much scholarly writing is certainly worse than it needs to be. But it is not alone in this. Generally speaking, the writing of literate Americans whose primary business is not writing but something else is pretty bad. It is muddy, backward, convoluted and self-strangled; it is only too obviously the product of a task approached unwillingly and accomplished without satisfaction or zeal. Except for the professionals among us, we Americans are hell on the English language. I am not in touch with the general run of British writing by non-professionals, but I suspect that it is nothing to make those islanders smug, either.

Furthermore, almost any college professor, turning the spotlight with some relief from himself and his colleagues to his students, will agree that their writing stinks to high heaven, too. It is a rare student who can write what he has to write with simplicity, lucidity and euphony, those qualities singled out by Somerset Maugham; far more graduating seniors are candidates for a remedial clinic than can pass a writing test with honors. And freshman writing is forever the nightmare of the teachers of composition, as it would be of their colleagues if the latter could not escape to the simple inanities of their objective tests.

Yet it was not always so. I have on my desk a little manuscript from the fourteenth century written by an unknown author, which I am in the process of editing. When I read it to one of my classes, as I occasionally do, with no more modernization than my own Great Lakes pronunciation and the substitution of a word for one which has become obsolete, it is a simple, clear and engaging document. "Where is any man nowadays that asketh how I shall love God and my fellow-Christians," it begins. "How I shall flee sin and serve God truly as a true Christian man should, What man is there that will learn the true law of God, which he biddeth every Christian man to keep upon pain of damnation to hell without end? . . . Unnethe (scarcely) is there any lewd man or lewd woman that can rightly well say his Pater Noster, his Ave Maria, and his Creed, and sound the words out readily as they should. But when they play Christmas games about the fire, therein will they not fail. Those must be said out without stumbling for dread of smiting. But if a lewd man should be smited now for each failing that he maketh in saying of his Pater Noster, his Ave Maria, and his Creed, I trowe he should be smited at the full." And so on, to the beautiful poetic line, "Then think it not heavy to dwell with thy mother in her wide house, thou that laist in the strait chamber of her womb." The spelling in the original is hectic, and the capitalization and punctuation sporadic, to say the least.

Yet there was a man who knew what he had to say and set out about saying it, with no nonsense and no fumbling. He aimed for his audience and, judging by the dog-ears and sweat-marks on the book, which is about the size of one of our pocket books, he hit it. Why cannot we do as well in our time? Indeed, the eighteenth century was about the last age in which almost any man, if he was literate at all, could set down his thoughts — such as they were — so that they did not have to be excavated by the reader. We have an abundance of letters, diaries, pamphlets, and other papers from that period, and they are well written. It was the age, we may recall, not only of Boswell and Johnson, but of Pepys and Franklin as well, and of a host of other men whose main legacy to us was a simple, direct, work-manlike style, sufficient to the man and to the occasion, which said what it had to say and said it well. With the end of that century we go into the foggy, foggy darkness, and God knows whether we shall ever find our way out of it — as a people, that is, as a nation of thinking men and women with something to say.

Nevertheless, there is no question what makes our writing bad, or what we shall have to do to better it. We shall simply have to isolate and root out a monomania which now possesses us, which impedes all language study and inhibits all mastery of our native tongue — all mastery, that is, on paper; for as speakers of English, we Americans are loving and effective cultivators of our expression. I recall the gas station attendant who was filling my car. The gasoline foamed to the top of the tank, and he shut off the pump. "Whew!" I said, "that nearly went over." "When you see white-caps," he replied, "you better stop." "You better had," I said, lost in admiration. But if you had given him a pencil, he would have chewed the end off before he got one word on paper.

The demon which possesses us is our mania for correctness. It dominates our minds from the first grade to the graduate school; it is the first and often the only thing we think of when we think of our language. Our spelling must be "correct," — even if the words are ill-chosen; our "usage," must be "correct" — even though any possible substitute expression, however crude, would be perfectly clear; our punctuation must be "correct" — even though practices surge and change with the passing of years, and differ from book to book, periodical to periodical. Correct! That's what we've got to be, and the idea that we've got to be correct rests like a soggy blanket on our brains and our hands whenever we try to write.

This mania for correctness is another legacy from the eighteenth century, but it did not get a real grip on us until well into the nineteenth. Its power over us today is appalling. Among my other tasks, I teach advanced courses in English language to students preparing to teach. Most of these are seniors and graduate students, and in the summer especially, there is a sprinkling of older men and women, experienced teachers, who are sweating out a master's degree. They have had courses in "English" throughout their schooling. But of the nature and structure of the English language, the nature of language habits, the relation of speech to writing, and the differences in usage which arise from dialect and from differing occupational and educational demands — of all these, they know nothing at all. Nor do they come to me expecting to learn about these. They want to know two things: what correct usage is and how you beat it into the kids' heads. That there are other considerations important to an English teacher is news to many of them. What they get from me is a good long look at their language.

To trace this monolithic concentration on usage is to pursue a vicious circle, with the linguists on the outside. The literate public seems to get it from the English teachers, and the teachers get it from the public. The attitudes and pronouncements on language of a Jacques Barzun, a Wilson Follett, a Bernard De Voto or a Norman Lewis ("How Correct Must Correct English Be?") mean more to English teachers than anything said by the most distinguished professional students of language — such as Leonard Bloomfield, Robert Hall or Charles Carpenter Fries. Correct usage is pursued and discussed, furthermore, without much reference to the actual writing of literary men. Now and again I amuse myself by blue-penciling a current magazine such as the *Saturday Review* or *Collier's* against the rules. I have to report that error is rampant, if variation is to be considered error. The boys just don't seem to pay attention to the rules. Moreover, having seen some of their first drafts, I am pretty sure that what conformity they do display is the work of their wives, secretaries, editors, proofreaders and typesetters, rather than their own. It takes a determined effort to beat the old Adam out of a readable manscript.

Thus it is only the determined, consciously creative professional who can build his work on the actual language of men. In a recent issue of the *Saturday Review*, I stumbled on a quotation from Wólfgang Langewiesche. "Well, it isn't crowned by no castle, that's for sure," he wrote, "and by no cathedral either." My eyes popped, and I read it again. I liked it. It looked right; it sounded right; it had a fine Chaucerian swing to it. But I bet it cost him some blood and a fifth of Scotch to get it into print. In my own limited publication, I find "a historical" changed to "an historical," all my "further's" changed to "farther" and all my "farther's" to "further," "than us" watered down to "than we," and many, many more. How E. M. Forster got by with "the author he thinks," and got it reprinted in a freshman handbook a few pages along from the prohibition of such locutions baffles me. A phony standardization of usage appears in print, the work of editors unconscious of the ultimate meaning of what they do.

Syllables govern the world.

JOHN SELDEN

The result of all this is that a wet hand of fear rests on the heart of every nonprofessional writer who merely has a lot of important knowledge to communicate. He writes every sentence with a self-conscious horror of doing something wrong. It is always a comfort to him if he can fit himself into some system, such as that of a business or governmental office which provides him with a model. It is thus that gobbledegook comes into being. I once braced a distinguished sociologist, a student of occupational myths and attitudes, about the convoluted, mainly nominal turgidity of his writing. He apparently admitted verbs into sentences the way we admit DP's into the United States, reluctantly and with pain. In speech he was racy, confident and compelling, a brilliant lecturer. "It's the only way I can get my work into the periodicals," he told me blandly. "If it's clear and simple, they don't think it's scholarly." With what relief the pedagogues subside into pedagese!

If we really want to get good writing from people who know things, so that we can come to learn what they know as easily as we learn from their talk, we can do it in a generation or so. In school and out, in print and out, we can leave usage to its natural nurse, the unforced imitation of the practices which are actually current among educated people. We can use our English courses in school and college, not to give drill on questionable choices among common alternatives, demanding that one be taken as right and the others as wrong, but to give practice in reading and writing. We can learn to read and write for the idea, and go for the idea without regard for anything else. Then our young people will come to maturity confidently using their pencils to find out what they think and get it down on paper; then our scholars will come to write simply, clearly and brilliantly what they brilliantly know.

In our speech we have arrived, I think, at a decency of discourse which is conducive to effective expression. We listen, with a grave courteous attention, to massive patterns of speaking different from our own because they come from differences in dialect and social status; we listen without carping and without a mean contempt. Furthermore, we participate; we go with a speaker through halts and starts, over abysses of construction, filling in the lacunae without hesitation; we discount inadvertencies and disregard wrong words, and we arrive in genial good will with the speaker at his meaning. In this atmosphere, our speech has thrived, and the ordinary American is in conversation a confident, competent expressive being. In writing he is something else again.

No one flourishes in an atmosphere of repression. It is possible, of course, for a person with special aptitudes and a special drive to bull his way past the prohibitions and achieve an individual style. But with the negative attitude that attends all our writing, those whose main interest lies elsewhere are inhibited by fear of "error" and the nagging it stirs up from setting pen to paper, until the sight of a blank white page gives them the shakes. It is no wonder that their expression is halting and ineffective. They cannot fulfill the demands of a prissy propriety and trace the form of an idea at the same time. They thus arrive at adulthood victims of the steely eye of Mr. Sherwin Cody, whose bearded face stares at them from the countless ads for his correspondence school, demanding, "Do YOU make these mistakes in English?" The locutions he lists are not mistakes, and Mr. Cody knows they are not; but his readers do not know it, and they do not know that they don't matter anyway.

For usage doesn't matter. What matters is that we get done what we have to do, and get said what we have to say. Sufficient conformity is imposed upon us by the patterns of our language and by the general practices of its users so that we do not have to run the idea of conformity into the ground by carping about trivial erratics in expression. Why in this matter of language alone complete conformity should be considered a virtue — except to typists, printers and typesetters — it is difficult to see (unless, perhaps, we are using it as a covert and pusillanimous means of establishing our own superiority). In our other concerns in life, we prize individuality; why in this one matter we should depart from a principle that otherwise serves us well is a puzzle for fools and wise men to ponder, especially since there is no general agreement on what to conform to, and one man's correctness is another's error. Not until we come to our senses — teachers, editors, writers, and readers together — and stop riding each other's backs, will the casual, brisk, colorful, amused, ironic and entertaining talk of Americans find its way into print. We should all be happy to see it there.

FOR DISCUSSION

1. Lloyd seems to believe that if you'll stop worrying about correctness you'll write easier and better. Try it the next time you write. Are there any other reasons why writing is harder than speaking?

2. Is it true that most English teaching is concerned with usage, that is, with choices between "correct" and "incorrect" forms?

3. Many considerations besides correct usage are important to an English teacher, Lloyd says. Have you any notion what they are?

4. Do you agree that nonprofessional writers are more concerned about correctness than professional writers are? Can you explain why?

5. At what precise point in the essay does Lloyd state his thesis? What is his thesis?

6. What do you think of Lloyd's own writing? Do you object to expressions like "beat it into the kids' heads" and "The boys just don't seem to pay attention to the rules"? Can you find other examples? Does the fact that this article first appeared in *The American Scholar* imply anything about usage?

VOCABULARY: palatable, convoluted, inanity, rampant, gobbledegook, turgidity, pedagese, locution, pusillanimous.

THEME TOPICS: Good writing is edited speech. Relax — and write! It's what you say, not how you say it. One can say "you" occasionally, can't he?

Right *vs.* Wrong

ROBERT A. HALL, JR.

"How many of these frequent errors in English do YOU make?"

"Do YOU say KEW-pon for KOO-pon, ad-ver-TISE-ment for ad-VER-tise-ment, or AD-ult for ad-ULT?"

"Almost everybody makes these blunders in English: *between you and I it's me, those kind of books.*"

"Even the greatest writers sin against the laws of grammar."

We have all seen advertisements in newspapers or magazines, with messages like those just quoted, implying to the reader "Shame on you if you are one of those who sin!" — and, of course, offering to teach him better. It is easy, on the one hand, to see that those who talk or advertise in this way and offer to cure our errors in pronunciation or grammar are simply appealing to our sense of insecurity with regard to our own speech. On the other hand, we must also admit that this sense of insecurity does exist, in almost all except those who are hardened against criticism and disapproval, and renders us easily susceptible to appeals of this kind. Our problem now is, to look at some of the ways in which we are supposed to be speaking wrongly, and to see whether there really exists a choice between "right" and "wrong," and, if so, what "right" and "wrong" consist of.

Our first approach may be made through very ordinary, everyday instances of "mistakes" like *I ain't, he don't, we seen him, you done it* or *hisn.* Most of us know that these are pretty widely condemned as "errors," when used instead of the corresponding *I am not* or *I'm not, he doesn't, we saw him, you did it, his.* But what is it that makes them "mistakes" or "errors"? If we drive through a traffic light, steal somebody's property, or kill someone, we know exactly what provides sanctions against these actions: the law of the land; and we know what will punish us if we disobey the law: the government. Is there any law of the land to set up rules about our speech, or any branch of the government that will enforce them? Obviously not. There are books that contain rules for speaking and writing, and there are people who will raise objections and criticise us if we fail to follow these rules; but those books and those people have no legal authority over us (outside of the rather special and limited situation in the schoolroom, where of course the teacher

From *Linguistics and Your Language* (Anchor Books, 1960). Copyright, 1960, by Robert A. Hall, Jr. Reprinted by permission of the author.

can give us a bad mark for not obeying the rules). Not only have they no legal authority, they have no authority whatsoever conferred on them by any power. Some countries, it is true, have had regulators of language with a kind of authority, such as the national Academies of France and Spain, which were set up by the king with the specific duty of "regulating and preserving the purity of the language." Even in those countries, very few people ever took the Academies' authority over language too seriously; but, technically speaking, their authority did exist in a way. But no such authority has ever existed in any English-speaking country, nor does it seem likely that speakers of English would ever be willing to accept the decrees of an Academy or similar institution, or of a Ministry of Education.

And yet, if we say *I ain't, you done it,* or *hisn,* we *are* likely to run into trouble. Trouble with whom? — with everybody? No. A foreigner using some completely abnormal turn of phrase, such as *this must we first do,* will confuse the ordinary speaker of English considerably, and will run no chance of finding anybody who would accept that as normal English. He would have trouble with everybody. But with *I ain't* and the like, some people would not be in the slightest upset; in fact, more than a few would find those "incorrect" forms more normal than the supposedly "correct" usage that they "ought" to be following themselves and insisting on in others. With some other people, however, our use of *he don't* and similar expressions may get us into more or less serious trouble. Our hearers may correct us on the spot, and tell us "Don't say *I ain't,* say *I'm not;* not *hisn,* but *his*"; or, even though they may not correct our usage then and there, they are nevertheless likely to hold it against us, and to allow it to determine their attitude toward us in one way or another. They may, perhaps, not consider us their social equals; they may not invite us to their home again; they may object to our marrying into their family; they may pick someone else, who says *I'm not* and *his,* to give a job or a promotion to; or some other form of unfavorable reaction may result from our using a form or word which is the wrong one for the given situation.

Usually, we are told and we believe that "correctness" is a characteristic of educated, intelligent people, whereas "incorrectness" is the special quality of uneducated, ignorant, or stupid people. But notice that exactly the type of situation we described above, where someone arouses an unfavorable reaction because of his language, can arise from the use of "correct" speech where the hearer does not use that kind of speech, or has a prejudice or other objection against it. It can be just as much of a *faux pas* to say *I saw him,* where your hearer expects and wants *I seen him,* as the other way around. One friend of mine found that, when he went to work in a Houston shipyard during the second World War, he was regarded as a snob for saying *those things* instead of *them things,* and he did not get full cooperation from his fellow-workers until he started to say *them things.* There are even some ways of speaking, some turns of expression, such as *am I not?,* which, no matter how "correct" they may be in theory, are just too artificial for almost any situation.

Notice also that the forms themselves are of equal worth as expressions of the ideas you are trying to communicate. *You done it* is just as good an expression of "doing" something, in past time, as *you did it,* and no present-day speaker of English will ever be confused as to what you mean. The same is true for *he don't* instead of *he doesn't;* for *we seen him* instead of *we saw him;* and for a host of others. In some cases, one might even argue that the "incorrect" form is actually somewhat preferable from the point of view of clarity or simplicity. The form *his,* in "correct" speech, is both an adjective (*his book*) and a pronoun (*that's his*); whereas the "incorrect" form *hisn* and the others parallel to it ending in *-n* (*hern, ourn, yourn, theirn*) are clearly marked, by their ending, as being possessive pronouns and nothing else. The argument runs similarly for *ain't.* To make the present-tense forms of the verb *be* negative, we must use, in "correct" speech, three different forms: *I'm not, he isn't, we (you, they) aren't;* whereas the "incorrect" *ain't* offers us one single form, exactly parallel to *can't, won't* or *don't* and equally convenient. *He doesn't* instead of *he don't* is also an extra complication, seen to be needless when compared with *can't* or *won't.* We might make similar arguments in favor of other "incorrect" forms as well.

What is it, then, that makes some forms "incorrect" and others not? This is not a matter of legal or quasi-legal authority, as we have seen. It is not a matter of universal condemnation, nor yet of incomprehensibility; in fact, some "incorrect" forms, as we have just pointed out, would be clearer or simpler than the corresponding "correct" forms. It all boils down, really, to a question of acceptability in certain classes of our society, in those classes which are socially dominant and which set the tone for others. Whether a form is accepted or rejected does not depend on its inherent merit nor yet on any official approval given it, but purely on whether its hearers like it or not — on whether they will react favorably or unfavorably towards a person they hear using it. "Correct" can only mean "socially acceptable," and apart from this has no meaning as applied to language.

The social acceptability, and hence "correctness," of any form or word is determined, not by reason or logic or merit, but solely by the hearer's emotional attitude towards it — and emotional attitudes naturally differ from person to person, from group to group, from social class to social class. Forms and words also change in social acceptability in the course of time: in the early seventeenth century, conservative speakers and purists objected violently to *ye* and *you,* used in speaking to one person, instead of the earlier *thou* and *thee;* and there must have been a time when *cows,* instead of the order plural *kine,* seemed an objectionable innovation.

Nevertheless, the difference in social acceptability between *I ain't* and *I am not,* between *hern* and *hers,* and so forth, is a real fact. If my child is likely to run into trouble later on for saying *I done it* or *hisn,* I will try to keep him from getting into the habit of using those forms which are actually not acceptable socially and which may cause others to react unfavorably towards him. But, if I am sensible about it, I will realize that the reason I want him to avoid these "incorrect" forms is not any inherent badness or evil character that they may have, but a purely practical consideration, that of their social acceptability. His choice of language will be used by others as a purely arbitrary means of classifying him socially among the sheep or the goats. All we need to do in the case of *I ain't*, etc., is to re-word the traditional instructions, and say that we avoid using such turns of speech, not because they are "bad" or "wrong" or "ungrammatical," but because they are socially unacceptable. Of course, as soon as people in any given group stop treating, say, *he don't* as socially unacceptable, it automatically becomes "correct."

There is a close parallel between acceptable usage in language and "correct" behavior in other social customs, such as personal garb or table manners. What is it that makes it perfectly good manners to eat some things, such as bread-and-jam, with the fingers, and not others, like meat or vegetables? Certainly not the decree of any official or self-appointed authority; and certainly not any inherent feature or characteristic of what we eat or do not eat with the fingers. Some things that we eat with our fingers are much more messy than others that we would always take up with knife and fork. Here again, it is social acceptability that determines whether we may or may not eat a given item of food with our fingers, or wear a four-in-hand tie with a tuxedo. This acceptability varies from place to place, and from one period of time to another. Thus, in England it is perfectly good manners to pile your peas up on the back of your fork, using your knife as a pusher, and to eat the peas from the back of the fork; but it is very much frowned upon to keep changing the fork from the left hand to the right and back again, as Americans normally do. And the permissibility of, say, table behavior is constantly changing; for instance, I was brought up always to eat bacon with knife and fork or in a sandwich, whereas by now it has become much more widely "correct" to eat it with the fingers.

For cases like those we have been discussing up to now, the situation is clear: we will avoid forms like *I seen him, he don't* because they are used as shibboleths, disregard of which may lead to unfortunate results for us in our living and relations with others. There are many instances, however, where reality and what we are taught do not correspond as to the actual "correctness," the actual acceptability, of what we are told to avoid. Take the case of *it's me*. Grammarians tell us that a rule exists that "the verb *to be* never takes a direct object," and that hence we must always say *it is I* and never *it's me*. The rule itself is found in plenty of grammar books, but that is no guarantee of its accuracy or relevance; in reality, this rule is meaningless as a statement of the facts of English usage. It was taken over by English grammarians from Latin grammar, where it is an accurate statement of the facts of Latin usage: in Latin, you said *sum egō* "[it] am I," never *sum mē* "[it] am me."

The facts of actual acceptable usage in English are quite different: we normally say, and have said for hundreds of years, *it's me, it's us,* and so forth.

This is not merely an unsupported assertion on my part; statistical studies have been made which show *it's me* to be by far the most frequent and normal usage in current English, as compared with *it is I.* Professor Charles C. Fries made a detailed study of many such points that are often the objects of dispute and condemnation, in his *American English Grammar,* by analyzing thousands of letters which had been written to the War Department by people of all levels of education and social standing. He found very clear documentary proof that many forms and many constructions that are often condemned are actually in perfectly good standing in the usage of educated persons, and hence by definition acceptable or "correct." He found, for instance, that it is normal to say *it's me, these kind of things, none of the children are here, everybody should take off their hat,* in standard English, and that there is no real difference in such respects between standard and vulgar speech. The story is told of a certain very puristic lady — let's call her Miss Fidditch — who was teaching her class very strictly to avoid *it's me:*

> Miss Fidditch: You must always say *it is I.* The inflexible rule of grammar is that the verb *to be* never takes a direct object.
> (*A few minutes later:*)
> Principal: (outside the door, knocking): Who's there?
> Miss Fidditch: It's me — Miss Fidditch.

Miss Fidditch was right when she said *it's me,* naturally and normally, in a give-and-take conversational situation and without reflecting; she was wrong when she tried to force on her class an artificial, unrealistic rule that applied to no one's, not even her own, usage in actual fact. And we all know the old story about the grammarian who said "Never use a preposition to end a sentence with."

We are often told that such-and-such a form or combination of forms is "in accordance with the rules of logic," which make other competing forms or combinations "illogical" and hence inadmissible. Such a rule as "*everyone* or *everybody* is singular and hence a word referring to it must be in the singular" in an instance of this, or the rule that "a double negative makes a positive" and that hence we mustn't say *I didn't see nobody* except when we really did see somebody. It is perfectly true that, in strictly ordered systems like mathematics or symbolic logic, a violation of the rules of discourse will introduce confusion and make a statement into its opposite or into something else from what was intended. The purists' error here lies in identifying language and logic, and expecting normal linguistic usage to be strictly logical. As a matter of fact, no language ever was strictly logical, nor can we make it so by preaching at its speakers. To begin with, we should have to define what "logical" meant — and we would find that each different language would, from the outset, give its speakers different ideas as to what "logic" is. To us, for instance, it seems logical, and, in fact, inescapable to say *one book*, but *two books, three books, five books*, using the form *books* when we refer to more than one of them, and thus distinguishing between "one" and "more than one" or (to use the traditional grammatical terms) singular and plural. To someone brought up speaking Hungarian, that difference seems useful in general — a Hungarian will say *könyv* for "book" and *könyvek* for "books," with *-ek* indicating the plural for him just as *-s* does for us — but when he has a numeral to tell him how many books there are, he uses, not the plural, but the singular form of the word for "book." The Hungarian says *egy könyv* "one book," *két könyv* "two book," and likewise *három könyv* "three book," *öt könyv* "five book" and so forth. To him it seems silly, needless and illogical to say "five books" where the indication of plurality is already given by the number, so that "five book" will do just as well. Which is more logical, English or Hungarian, in this respect? One could argue both ways, and perhaps the Hungarian way of saying "two book, three book" might prove to be more strictly logical. It all depends on what you are brought up to say.

The same thing holds for such points as the "double negative," which many persons condemn violently — *I didn't see nobody* instead of *I didn't see anybody*. They tell us that "logically" a double negative makes a positive, and that therefore *I didn't see nobody* "really" means *I did see somebody*. Here again, our traditional grammar rule is based on Latin, as it is in so many other instances — as if the rules of Latin could be applied to English. In Latin, those who spoke it about the time of Caesar, Cicero and Augustus normally took a double negative to mean a positive. So for them, *nōn nihil* "not nothing" meant "something," and *nōn vīdī nēminem* "I didn't see nobody" could only have meant "I saw somebody." That was right, logical and natural *for them*, because that was the way they used Latin. But later, in the course of the centuries, those who spoke Latin and the Romance languages which developed out of Latin, got in the habit of using a double negative with *negative* meaning. In Spanish, for instance, it is downright incorrect (because nobody will accept it) to say such a thing as *vi a nadie* in the meaning of "I saw nobody." You *must* say *no vi a nadie*, literally "I didn't see nobody," with the two negatives *no* "not" and *nadie* "nobody," whenever *nadie* "nobody" follows the verb; otherwise what you say is meaningless. It may be "illogical," and it may be "incorrect" from the point of view of Latin grammar; but in Spanish, French and Italian, for instance, the requirement of a double negative is so absolute that no one would be able to get away with condemning it on the grounds of logic. The reason that the point can be raised at all in modern English is that we have a divided usage: in actual current speech, when there is no emphasis, a double negative and a single negative both have a negative meaning, and everybody will understand what we mean whether we say *I didn't see nobody* or *I saw nobody* or *I didn't see anybody*. But when we are putting emphasis on the verb or the pronoun, then *I DIDN'T see NObody* does have positive meaning, and would be normal as an answer, say, in contradiction to *You saw nobody.* The drift of our language is inevitably toward the use of the double negative; this is as normal and natural as anything else in English, and as logical in English as it is in Spanish and French.

Now with regard to this second group of "wrong" usages, the situation is essentially different from that of *ain't* and *hisn.* Such forms as *ain't* are both socially unacceptable and condemned by purists; whereas *it's me* and *those kind of things,* although grammarians may condemn them, are nevertheless in normal, everyday use by socially accepted people and hence are socially acceptable and by definition "correct." And when it comes to such pronunciations as KEW-pon, ad-ver-TISE-ment, AD-ult, the purists' condemnations are absolutely fanciful, without any rhyme or reason whatsoever. Both KEW-pon and KOO-pon, both ad-ver-TISE-ment and ad-VER-tise-ment, both AD-ult and ad-ULT are normal, regular, and acceptable variants; to call either member of these pairs "correct" and the other "incorrect" is quite arbitrary. Language is not an either-or proposition, in which no variation, no deviation from a strictly maintained party line is permissible; in many instances, such as those of *coupon* and *advertisement,* more than one alternative exists and both are equally acceptable or "correct." . . .

Another objection that we often hear made against such a usage as *it's me* (instead of *it is I*) or *none of the boys are here* (instead of *none of the boys is here*) is that it is "ungrammatical" or that it does not "conform to the rules of grammar." The assumption involved here, whether we state it openly or not, is that there is such a thing as a body of rules, which are as fixed and unchangeable as the laws of the Medes and the Persians, which are called "grammar" and to which all language must conform or else be condemned as "ungrammatical." As a matter of fact, no such body of rules exist, or ever could exist. What passes for "grammar" in the usual textbook is really a conglomeration of rules, most of them taken from Latin grammars, some of them not, but often misstating the facts about English. We have already seen that the rule "the verb *to be* never takes a direct object" is a very good statement of the actual facts of Latin, but has no relation to the actual facts of English; and likewise for the double negative. Nor is there any reason why Latin should be taken as a model for all other languages, whether related or not. People used to think, and some still do, that Latin should be a universal model for language; the reason for this is that all during the Middle Ages in Western Europe, the language of learning and religion happened, through a historical accident, to be Latin. Educated people, just because they happened to get their education through Latin rather than through their native language, came to the conclusion that high intellectual activity and use or imitation of Latin were inseparable. We can easily see that such an idea was rather naive, and based on a false identification of two unrelated factors in the situation. Actually, Latin is just a language like any other, with its faults and shortcomings as well as its virtues, and its rules are far from being universally applicable. How would a speaker of Hungarian react to being told that he must say *három könyvek* "Three books" just because that is the way they say it in Latin or English or some other language?

Many other "grammar rules," although not derived from Latin grammar, are still quite inaccurate and unfounded: the best example of this is the "shall" and "will" rules that we are taught with regard to the future of English verbs. Most of us can never remember those rules, and are always uneasy about whether we are or are not making a mistake in their application: is it *I shall go* or *I will go, he should go* or *he would go?* We have been told that there is some difference in the meaning of each member of these pairs, that one of them indicates "determination" and the other "simple futurity" — but which? As a matter of fact, there is no wonder that we can't remember — because such a distinction does not really exist: in normal speech we would usually say *I'll go, he'd go, we'll go.* Even with the full forms, there is no distinction in meaning, except the artificial distinction that we may have been taught to make. Where did the grammar books get this rule? A seventeenth-century English grammarian, one John Wallis, sitting in his study, dreamed the rule up, manufactured it out of whole cloth, and put it in his book; and later grammarians have copied and re-copied it, each from his predecessor. Its relation to the facts of the English language is completely null, and its origin classifies it among works of fiction rather than of science.

And even with rules that do state normal, current usage accurately — have they any authority beyond that of simple statements of fact? We have already seen that there is no legal sanction, not even any semi-legal academic backing, for any claim to "authority" in language and its use. Suppose that usage should change, and that what we now say universally (such as *he goes, she sings*) should go out of fashion and be replaced by some other usage which we now wouldn't accept (like *he go, she sing*). Would the old be "right" and the new be "wrong"? By no means; if people's habits and usage change, then there is no "authority," no law that can keep them from doing so, and the new is just as good as the old. Not necessarily better, of course: neither better nor worse, but just different. Some of us are inclined to think that because a habit, a custom, or a thing is old, it must necessarily be better than something new. This was the prevailing attitude all through ancient times and the Middle Ages, and has lasted even up to now in some matters like those of language; it is the only reason some grammarians have for preferring one usage to another.

Another norm that is often set up for deciding disputed points is the usage of great writers: do we find *it ain't, he don't* or split infinitives in great writers, men who must have had great knowledge of their own language in order to write their great books? First of all, though, we must ask *which* great writers — those of the present, or those of the past? Our choice is difficult here; if we go too far back, the literary language is obviously archaic, and nobody nowadays, not even the most conservative grammarian, would recommend every feature of Milton's or Dr. Johnson's prose for our modern usage. If we come too close to the present, it is hard to tell just who is a really great writer and who is not; and even if we have our great writers picked out, we find that very often they use freely the very forms we want to condemn, especially the more "realistic" writers like Steinbeck and Farrell. Then let's restrict our choice of great writers to, say, the late nineteenth and early twentieth century, so that they will fit what we want to prescribe. Even so, we find that their actual usage was considerably freer than we want to think. Hence the defensive accusations we often hear dogmatic purists make, that "even the greatest writers" make this, that or the other "mistake."

Furthermore, just how much bearing does great literature and its language have on normal everyday usage? That great literature gives us examples of the *artistic* use of language, we can easily grant; and that studying the way a Thomas Hardy or a Henry James has manipulated his language will be of use to us if we want to write literature — likewise granted. But such men as Hardy or James (to say nothing of authors like Carlyle or Meredith) are not typical, they are exceptional, in their language as in their content; and the very fact that they are exceptional disqualifies them as examples for everyday, normal, non-literary usage. Wouldn't it be nice if we all tried to talk like great literature in our daily contacts? It would be almost like trying to handle everyday affairs in the style of grand opera.

The entire attempt to set up absolute standards, rigid norms, for regulating people's language is destined to failure from the outset, because, as we have seen in this chapter, (1) there is no authority that has either the right or the ability to govern people's usage; and (2) such an authority, even when it has been set officially (as were the French and Spanish academies), can never find valid standards by which to govern usage. Logic, Latin grammar, the usage of literature, appeals to authority as such — none have any applicability. In our country, especially, attempts to prescribe rules, to set up a normative grammar, have been very widespread, and have battened on our insecurities, on our fears for our social standing in the face of linguistic shibboleths. But all such attempts have been, and will continue to be, failures.

Is there any definition at all that we can give for "good language? Only, I think, something like this: "good" language is language which gets the desired effect with the least friction and difficulty for its user. That means, of course, that "good" language is going to vary with the situation it is used in. In elegant or puristically inclined society, "good" usage will include *it isn't he, he doesn't,* and also *this kind of people, it is I,* since those forms will get the best results in favor and compliance with what we desire. In normal everyday situations with normal everyday people, *it isn't him, he don't, these kind of people, it's me* will be good usage, since ordinary people speak that way normally; and we won't be too worried about saying *damn!* unless our hearers have specific objections. With people who customarily say *it ain't him, he don't, we have seen them, hisn,* those forms will be good usage, provided they serve to get results most effectively.

One type of confusion which often crops up at this point, and which we should be on our guard against, is that between language and style. We are often inclined to think that "correctness" is the same thing as good style, particularly in writing. Actually, the two are not the same, though the situation is parallel for both. "Good" style is simply that style of speaking or writing which is most effective under any given set of circumstances. When we speak of "good style," what we usually mean is clarity, absence of ambiguity, orderly structure, and the like — and these are, indeed, important in most situations. But they are not the same thing as type of language, and "good style" is possible in any dialect. Aesthetic considerations — whether a given way of expressing ourselves is pleasing or not to our listeners or readers — of course enter into the picture, too, with regard to "good" style. But all matters of aesthetics depend so much on individual preference, and differ so much not only from one language to another but from one speaker to another, that no one can presume to set up objective standards for them, nor legislate or make authoritative pronouncements on what is or is not pleasing to the ear or to the eye.

"Right" and "wrong," then, have no meaning, as applied to language, apart from the situations in which language is used. That is, by definition, we can never be wrong in our own language, when we use it as we have grown up speaking it, among our own family and friends. The ditch-digger who says *him and me ain't got none* and who uses swear-words and "four-letter" words freely is absolutely right — in his own language. His type of speech is not necessarily right for the language of other groups, just through the very fact that they speak differently. But when we condemn the ditch-digger's speech, we do so, not because of any inherent demerit of the way he talks, but because we take his speech as being characteristic of his social class. This factor in our speech attitudes is a relic from earlier, antidemocratic times, which accords very poorly with other aspects of our modern aspirations to true democracy.

When a person who has grown up using *him and me ain't got none* speaks in his normal, natural way and is told he is "wrong," therefore, all that this really means is that he is using these forms in a situation where his usage would make things harder rather than easier for him. But most often — in fact, we can say usually — neither the person making the "error" nor the one criticizing him understands this. As a result, speakers who have not been brought up speaking "correctly" are made to feel inferior, and either have to make a strong (and often poorly guided) effort to change their habits of speech, or else take shelter behind defensive feelings of hostility, mockery, etc., towards the approved type of speech. Current prescriptions of "right" and "wrong" thus serve only to divide our society, and to increase further the split between upper and lower, favored and unfavored classes — just at the time when greater unity, not greater division, is our crying need.

In short: the entire structure of our notions about "correctness" and "right" *vs.* "wrong" in language is not only inaccurate, erroneous and useless; it is definitely harmful, and we would do well to outgrow it. When purists tell us that we are using "bad" or "incorrect" or "ungrammatical" language, they are simply telling us that what we say would not be acceptable in the upper social levels; sometimes they are right as to the facts of the case, and sometimes they are just talking through their hats. What our purists give us in the way of rules and laws to observe has no authority, no validity aside from their own preference, and is often based on specious pseudo-logic or on the structure of a distantly related language, Latin, which has no relevance to English. If an "error" or "mistake" is frequent, if almost everybody makes it, if it is found in even the greatest writers, then it is no error: as the great Byzantine emperor and lawcodifier Justinian put it, *commūnis error facit iūs* — a mistake that everybody makes is no longer a mistake. We need to look at our language realistically, not feeling "inferior" about it and taking nobody's word as to its being "right" or "wrong." Often enough, we may find we need to change our usage, simply because social and financial success depends on some norm, and our speech is one of the things that will be used as a norm. In a situation like this, it is advisable to make the adjustment; but let's do so on the basis of the actual social acceptability of our speech, not because of the fanciful prescriptions of some normative grammarian or other pseudo-authority.

FOR DISCUSSION

1. "It can be just as much of a *faux pas* to say *I saw him*, where your hearer expects and wants *I seen him*, as the other way around." Does this statement imply that the only measure of effectiveness in language is the audience? Do you believe this statement should be qualified?

2. " 'Correct' can only mean 'socially acceptable,' and apart from this has no meaning as applied to language." This concept may help us choose between forms like *seen* and *saw*, *dragged* and *drug*, but what about *who-whom, can-may, farther-further, fewer-less,* etc.? When alternative word-forms convey identical meanings, how do we know which to use? Can you suggest some alternative word-forms either of which might be acceptable under any circumstances?

3. In Early Modern English (i.e., before Shakespeare), these were forms of the second-person pronoun:

Nominative singular	*Nominative plural*
thou	ye
Accusative singular	*Accusative plural*
thee	you

In Modern English *you* has replaced the other three forms. Is a similar tendency at work today with regard to *who-whom*? What should be our attitude toward such a tendency?

4. " 'Good' language is language which gets the desired effect with the least friction and difficulty for its user." " 'Good' style is simply that style of speaking or writing which is most effective under any given set of circumstances." If you accept these statements, how would you describe the problem that faces all of us as speakers and writers?

5. "The entire structure of our notions about 'correctness' and 'right' *vs.* 'wrong' in language is not only inaccurate, erroneous and useless; it is definitely harmful, and we would do well to outgrow it." In what ways is the "structure of our notions" harmful?

VOCABULARY: sanction, *faux pas*, quasi-legal, purist, inherent, arbitrary, shibboleth, documentary proof, predecessor, split infinitive, dogmatic, ambiguity, specious.

THEME TOPICS: Dialect *vs.* language. What good English really is. Is one kind of English enough? Change in language is inevitable. Word forms we could do without. Why don't we simplify our language?

Social Aspects of Language: Class, Taboos, Politics

MARGARET SCHLAUCH

Language Like Clothing

Speculating on the function of clothes in society, and what they have done to us, Carlyle at one point of *Sartor Resartus* asks us to imagine the functioning of "government, legislation, property, police, and civilized society" if all persons were abruptly forced to appear in public without any clothing whatsoever. We are so accustomed to reliance on badges, buttons, styles, and materials in judging our fellow-men, he argues, that august institutions would dissolve in "wails and howls" without them. These are the signs of rank and class; we deplore their artificiality, but we need them. "Lives the man," he asks, "that can figure a naked Duke of Windlestraw addressing a naked House of Lords? Imagination, choked as in mephitic air, recoils on itself, and will not forward with the picture. . . ." It is the wig, squirrel-skins, and plush gown that announce the judge; without them he would be no more by day than he is by night, only "a forked Radish with a head fantastically carved."

But Carlyle is wrong. Even with the badges and uniforms stripped away, something would remain as a guide, as sure if less ponderable, to the social position of each forked radish. Even a naked Duke of Windlestraw, upon opening his mouth, would speak the English language with a certain air, an accent and intonation inextricably associated with his rank and authority. An untrained impostor from the lower levels of society would be detected by his speech, although appearing as one nude radish among many. Of course, his speech could be faked for this occasion; but so could his clothes, for other occasions. Both types of deception have been practiced. It is a pity that Carlyle did not turn his attention to language as a metaphorical clothing of man in society.

Class Dialects

The existence of different manners of speech for persons in various ranks is a familiar fact. We are constantly sorting and classifying people according to them. A variation of any national language according to social levels is called a *class dialect*. Even within the class dialect there may be many variations and minor divisions. For instance, the younger members of a privileged class who attend special schools sometimes develop a special jargon among themselves which is almost incomprehensible to outsiders. Yet it is clearly an offshoot of the general "upper-class" dialect of their parents. Poorer youngsters also develop a kind of tribal school jargon as local and esoteric as the other. Even families and other restricted groups develop special jargons mystifying to an outsider. But these are even more clearly recognized and assigned to the general class dialects to which they belong.

When we talk, then, we tell much more about ourselves than the factual statements we are making. The sum total of small nuances will indicate much about our training, environment, economic position, and even profession. In conversation we are unconsciously providing a rich commentary about ourselves which supplements the clothing and outward possessions we gather.

Cockney English

Not all European languages offer the same number of levels contrasted with equal sharpness. Within the English-speaking world the sharpest contrast is probably to be found between Cockney London dialect on the one hand and "upper-class" speech on the other. Londoners are not skittish about admitting this contrast; they are very frank about the existence of class levels in speech. The attitude of most observers is that Cockney is intrinsically humorous, and can be appreciated — at best — only by a condescending tolerance. Of course this is a result of the social connotations of the speech. In an early play, *Captain Brassbound's Conversion* (written before his better known *Pygmalion*), George Bernard Shaw experimented with the use of Cockney for dramatic purposes involving class distinctions. One of his problems was the difficult task of recording the vowel sounds of his low-class character, Drinkwater. This is what the attempt looked like on the printed page. Drinkwater, an engaging ne'er-do-well, finds himself entertaining Sir Howard Hallam, a judge before whom he once appeared as defendant:

> Drinkwater (*placing the chair for Sir Howard*). Awskink yr pawdn for the libbety, Sr Ahrd.
> Sir Howard (*looking at him*). I have seen you before somewhere.
> Drinkwater. You ev, Sr Ahrd. But aw do assure yer it were hall a mistike.
> Sir Howard. As usual. (*He sits down.*) Wrongfully convicted, of course.
> Drinkwater (*with sly delight*). Naow, gavner. (*Half whispering, with an ineffable grin.*) Wrongfully hacquittid!
> Sir Howard. Indeed! That's the first case of the kind I have ever met.
> Drinkwater: Lawd, Sr Ahrd, wot jagginses them jurymen was! You an me knaowed it too, didn't we?
> Sir Howard. I daresay we did. I am sorry to say I forget the exact nature of the difficulty you were in. Can you refresh my memory?
> Drinkwater. Owny the aw [high] sperrits o youth, y'lawdship. Worterloo Rowd kice. Wot they calls Ooliganism. . . . Nime [name] giv huz pore thortless leds baw, a gent on the Dily Chrorncile. . . . Awll eng [hang] abaht within ile [hail], gavner, hin kice aw should be wornted.

In this conversation, it will be observed, the only attempts at phonetic writing are limited to the speech of the Cockney. Sir Howard Hallam's speech is given in conventional (that is, highly unphonetic) spelling. As Shaw admits, this procedure is quite inconsistent, but it has the merit of convenience. When educated persons, for instance professional people, read a printed page each assumes that the unreal orthography stands for his own special form of "acceptable" English. It would be too complicated for a dramatist to indicate every shading (even if he could) within that very inclusive territory. Shaw finds many attractive features in the Cockney dialect, and is particularly impatient with the snobbish contempt of outsiders for the so-called "misplaced aitch" which is one of its characteristics. "Roughly speaking, I should say that in England he who bothers about his *h*'s is a fool, and he who ridicules a dropped *h* a snob."

Yet persons with social ambitions have spent much time and suffered real distress in an effort to achieve conformity with their "betters" in details such as this. The matter has been treated with solemnity in a novel by May Sinclair, *The Divine Fire*, which was widely read about a generation ago. The hero was supposed to be a gifted poet born with the soul of ancient Greece lodged in a Cockney bosom: "The child of 'Ellas and 'Ollywell Street — innocent of — er — the rough breathing,"[1] as one of the London literati puts it. Later his "innocence" of that minor phoneme when under emotional stress causes him the most excruciating social agonies. It is amusing to remember that at a certain time in ancient Rome it was considered very *chic* to insert unhistorical *h*-sounds before words normally beginning with vowels. It gave a fashionable Greekish flavor to ordinary everyday Latin. Catullus tells us in one of his poems that the fops of his day were saying *hinsidiae* for *insidiae* ("hambushes" for "ambushes"). It was the obverse of the Cockney poet's failing. So relative are the social connotations of a single sound!

Levels of Speech

The existence of an accepted upper-class dialect associated with those who govern a country and man its professions has some amusing consequences. The sociological implications have never been adequately explored. For one thing, the levels will not be clearly preserved if historical change is moving rapidly, as at the time of the French Revolution. And even where change has been slow and barriers are clearly marked, the rise and fall of individuals brings about incongruities — a lack of harmony, let us say, between the physical clothing and the garment of speech.

It is only human for people in a stratified society to want to appear more smart and elegant than they are by birth and training. This is true if the society does leave some opportunities for personal advancement from the lower ranks. When people are over-eager to climb, they adopt a speech of uneasy and self-conscious gentility. One of its obvious characteristics is an excess of zeal for correctness: zeal to "talk good grammar," as it is sometimes called. This solicitude produces what we call hypercorrect forms.

Hypercorrectness

For instance, a person may have been drilled in school to correct his native speech in the matter of present participles: to "pronounce the final *g*," as the unscientific saying is, in words like "ringing, singing, eating." The drill em-

---

[1] This is the term used in Greek grammars to designate initial [h].

barrasses him into self-consciousnss, and he tends, for safety's sake, to substitute the syllable [ɪŋ] for *all* final [m]'s in his speech. So he says "curting," "garding," "ruing" for "curtain," "garden," "ruin." Or it may be that in triumph at having corrected errors like 'Him and me get along fine" into "He and I get along well," the rising individual produces sentences like "It's a secret between him (he) and I."

The *arriviste* in language is also apt to gloat in the use of perfect tenses and to overdo them. "It was a great pleasure *to have met you.*" Excessive self-consciousness about adverbial endings produces "finely" or "fastly" if the speaker has recently learned to avoid "He works good." A preposition is doubled in sentences like "It's the man for whom I was waiting for" when the speaker is just unlearning "who I was waiting for."

Another more refined vice of the self-consciously correct person is the refusal to use unstressed forms of articles or prepositions, as if they were always vulgar. He pronounces "the man and the girl" with painful distinctness, as if he were still in first grade struggling over individual words under a teacher's strict eye. He says [ði: mæn ænd ði: gəɹl], pedantically; and yet it is the best speakers, those at home in cultured English, who say: [ðə mæn ən ðə gəːl]. In accepted English, too, there is a clear difference between "to" [tə] and "too" [tuː]. The man at ease in society says: "I'm about to come too" as [aɪm ə'baut tə 'kʌm 'tuː] not the hypercorrect [aɪ 'æm ə'baut 'tu: 'kʌm 'tuː], which is in fact a bad self-betrayal. A mistaken snobbishness prompts this schoolroom isolation of words. Yet the most snobbish of snobs, the man poised with inherited confidence, is the one who freely permits slurred forms — provided, of course, they are the "right" slurred forms, hallowed by general usage in his "set."

Underworld Speech

There is another type of class dialect more baffling to the uninitiated: the argot of the underworld of great cities. Here the normal substandard speech is deliberately and frequently modified by slang periphrases to keep outsiders from understanding. Thus it is that jewels become "ice," and stolen jewels, the object of police questioning, become, quaintly enough, "hot ice." Drugs like heroin and cocaine become "snow." A whole vocabulary has developed around the use of the forbidden "reefers' of marihuana by "vipers" (addicts). It is interesting to note that American argot has had its influence on the underworld of foreign cities. Paris, rich in its own special language, shows in addition some loans from American gangster speech. In fact the word "gangster" has been taken over unchanged save for accent. Collaborated robbery is called "American robbery" or *vol à l'américaine.* If three work together they are called *le leveur* ("lifter"), *l'Américain* and *l'utilité* ("utility-man"). If there are two, one is designated by an American-English phrase, *le contact-man,* and the other is *le banquier* ("the banker"). Professions more or less related to a robber's life are also designated by picturesque English loans. The woman who works for a *souteneur* is called by many words, including an English one: *biftek* ("beefsteak"). A prostitute's work is called by another English term: *le bizness.* The underworld shows a certain measure of internationalism in its vocabulary. For the most part, however, it relies on metaphor and semantic shifts in native words.

Courtly and Polite Forms

In English we show our social levels primarily by choice of words and general style. One method used by other languages is unknown to us: the multiplication of personal pronouns to express various social attitudes towards the person addressed. We say "you" when talking to someone, whether he is a haughty superior, a friendly equal, or a subservient inferior. In this one pronominal respect English may be said to be classless. Other European languages make differences which seem formal or exclusive or arrogant or groveling to us users of the simple "you." In addressing a child or an intimate or (strangely enough) one for whom he feels contempt, a German says *du.* In addressing a stranger, he uses *Sie,* which is identical in form as well as origin with the word for "they" — a tribute to the distance and importance (plurality) of the person addressed. If he wishes to be deferential he uses a third-person noun while he looks straight at the person addressed. Thus, "Did the lady (or the gracious lady) sleep well? Has the gentleman finished his coffee?" Other languages use the third person similarly for cautious and reserved address. A Dane will say *"Har Fruen tabt sin Bog?"* and a Frenchman *"Est-ce que Madame a perdu son livre?"* ("Has madam lost her book?") But both use such forms more sparingly, I think, than the polite German.

In courtly circles it was formerly quite customary to use (usually feminine) astract nouns like "Excellency" or "Your Excellency" in speaking directly to a person of rank. The pronoun which might be substituted for this abstract noun, in languages with grammatical gender, was naturally "she." The contemporary Spanish word for "you" comes from a feminine noun with distinctly courtier-like connotations. *Usted* is a contraction of *vuestra merced,* which means "your mercy" or "your graciousness." A touch of the ancient formality of a sixteenth-century Spanish grandee hangs about the word.

Nothing in Europe, however, corresponds to the elaboration of pronominal snobbishness in some Eastern languages. In Malay a whole series of social levels are stratified in the pronouns of address. Nobody can simply and blithely say "you" without further reflection. He must stop to think: "How far is this man above or below me on the social ladder?" And according to the relative positions on that ladder, he will modify not only the "you" but also "I" and "we." The following table will indicate how many forms a Malay speaker must choose among, according to the social positions of the three possible persons to be designated. The choice involves not only words for "you" but *all* pronouns; and there are ten levels:

Person speaking	"I, we"	"thou, you"	"he, she, they"
Peasants to one another	*aku;* pl. *kita*	*ĕngkau*	*ia, dia*
Superior pointedly to inferior	*aku;* pl. *kita*	*ĕngkau*	*ia, dia*
Superior ordinarily to inferior	*sahaya,* pl. *kita*	*kamu, awak* [diff. dialect]	
Superior with affected modesty to equals	*hamba* (*tuan*)	*tuan* (*hamba*)	*tuan* (*hamba*)
All classes to Europeans	*sahaya; kita*	*tuan*	*tuan*
Malay gentry to one another	*kami*	*ĕnche', tuan*	*ĕnche', tuan*
Commoner to chief	*hamba* (*dato'*) *sahaya* (*dato'*)	*dato'*	*dato'*
Commoner to rajah; lesser to greater rajahs	*patek*	*tĕngku; ĕngku*	*tĕngku; ĕngku raja*
Subject to sultan	*patek*	*tuan-ku*	*yam-tuan; tuan-ku*
Literary	*beta*	*sahabat beta*	[name and title]

In Japanese, according to Von der Gabelentz, politeness forbids a speaker to use the simple active voice in referring to high-class people, as if they were obliged to engage in activity themselves. So the speaker chooses the causative voice, giving them the role of persons acting mediately, by command — or the passive voice, as if the action were happening by itself. The Koreans are unequaled in this respect, since they express through the *verbal* form whether a higher personage is talking to a lower, a lower to a higher, or one equal to another; and, moreover, whether this is happening in a comparatively reverential, contemptuous, or indifferent manner. This would, properly speaking, yield 3x3x3 or 27 modal forms. Thus voice and other verbal inflections may also be determined by sociological relations — titles and income, in short. The Algonquin language is said to possess complex stratified forms of polite locution also.

Regional Dialects

It is customary to distinguish class dialects from local or regional dialects. The latter include the ways of speech which mark people off according to the province, village, or region from which they come. "Everyone who does not speak a Regional dialect," says Henry Cecil Wyld, "speaks a Class dialect." Yet the matter is not quite so simple as that. The two dialect types cannot be so completely separated.

In America, for instance, we have several varieties of regional dialect. A citizen of Louisiana is said to speak Southern American; one from Massachusetts, New England American (English). A few tricks of pronunciation of vowels and many niceties of sentence tempo and intonation betray the regional origins of the two. The former will say "po'k" [po:k] for "pork"; the latter, [pɔ:k]. Each one, in fact, may tend to jeer at the other with entire good nature because of these perceptible differences, minor though they may be. But although the educated, traveled, and affluent Southerner may share some of these traits with poor cotton-pickers and mill workers, there are other ways of speech quite as marked which separate the two groups within the confines of the very same regional dialect. Comparative analyses are still lacking. It is probable, however, that the study of the levels *within* such a regional dialect would show two things: that the individual sounds were very much alike throughout the region, regardless of class, but that the syntax (grammatical structure) of sentences was different. In saying "He doesn't like me any more," speakers of all levels would agree on the vowel sounds in "like" [la:k] and "more" [mo:], and they might have the same deliberate and agreeable speech melody; but the mill worker would change the verbal agreement and use a double negative as Chaucer often did. "He don't like me no more." In this he would agree with many persons of the same class in other parts of the country.

Dialect and Governmental Power

Where the governmental and economic power have been associated with one place and one dialect, the use of regional language may be a social or class handicap. The overlapping is clear in England, where the broad Lancashire dialect, for all its venerable history, is a label of class as well as region for a person wishing to rise in the social scale. According to English writers, the speech of the "better class" is heard with practically no variation all over the country: it is "Public School English," and all else — "the vulgar English of the towns, and the English of the Villager who has abandoned his native Regional Dialect" — is Modified Standard. In compiling his *English Pronouncing Dictionary* Daniel Jones tells us that he recorded what is "most usually heard in everyday speech in the families of Southern English persons who have been educated at the great public boarding schools. . . . The pronunciation may also be heard, to an extent which is considerable though difficult to specify, from educated people in the South of England who have not been educated at these schools." It is assumed, however, that the linguistic influence radiates from them. The Lancashire manufacturer may despair of changing his own speech, but he will probably see to it that his children learn Public School English. Even Scots dialect, with its distinguished literary history, has been regarded as a handicap. J. M. Barrie's play, *What Every Woman Knows,* presents the efforts of an ambitious politician who, with his wife's help, is at some pains to smooth out of his speech the local flavor which might hamper his career. In ancient Greece, the Attic dialect became the accepted "superior" language because it was used in the powerful city-state of Athens and particularly was employed in the writings of a splendid galaxy of writers in the fifth and fourth centuries B.C. As a consequence Attic speakers began to look down their noses at "countrymen" who used other local dialects. The only exception was perhaps Ionian, which also represented political power and had an early, distinguished literature. A politician hampered by a "countryman's" dialect has always been a subject of unkind jests by his enemies.

Frontier Life

In the early days of the American republic our ancestors were sensitive about the minor differences of pronunciation and vocabulary which already marked us off perceptibly from British speakers. Political independence seems to have converted the uneasy sense of inferiority into a truculent claim upon "superiority," as might be expected. Ardent patriots hoped that a new day had dawned for the English language in America. They wished to see differences recognized and accelerated. On the other hand, British writers tended to sharpen their attitude of disapproval towards American "provincialisms." Some of the Founding Fathers carried on a lively discussion on the desirability of showing the world by means of our language that we had become an independent, proudly republican state. English was supposed to be "purer" in the land of freedom, at the very time when British critics were making contemptuous remarks about it.

Politics and American "Provincial" Speech

As a matter of fact, some of the very "provincialisms" cited in early dictionaries of American speech, and condemned by British purists, give a lively picture of frontier life and struggles. They make up a colorful creation — an unconscious linguistic record of early American ways of living. Here are a few of them, classified according to the pioneers' occupations:

Farm Life
   to make a bee-line
   to have a long row to hoe
   to fly off the handle
   to sit on the fence
   to have an ax to grind
   to go haywire [origin in doubt]
   to have a chip on the shoulder
   to fork over
   to have the wrong end of the stick
Hunting and Gunmanship
   to make the fur fly
   to knock the spots out of
   to draw a bead [i.e., to take aim]
   to bark up the wrong tree
   to get on one's own hook
   to be up a tree
Warfare (Indian style)
   to scalp
   to walk Indian file
   to bury the hatchet
   to put on war-paint
Pioneering
   to make tracks
   to blaze a trail
   to jump a claim
   to pull up stakes
   to peter out
   to be as easy as rolling off a log
   to clear out
   to spark [to woo a girl]
   to have the latchstring out
   to be stumped
   to swap horses in mid-stream

For all their vividness, however, it may be imagined that these expressions redolent of frontier life would be regarded as low barbarisms in the sophisticated coffee houses and drawing rooms of eighteenth-century London, and would therefore be a social handicap to the user of them.

Lower-class Speech in Earlier Times

The lower ranks of society had a dialect of their own in past ages too. Feudal England gives an especially clear case of linguistic division on class lines. For a certain period of time after 1066, as we have observed, government, courts, and local administration were in the hands of persons speaking a tongue foreign to the native English: French as opposed to Anglo-Saxon. The situation was solved more quickly, it now appears, than earlier historians supposed. But out of the original division came the tendency still noticeable in English to use Anglo-Saxon words for homely, intimate, and even ugly or indecent things, and to use French words for the loftier ideas (or to conceal the ugly ones).

With the development of town life and commerce, lower-class speech was further diversified. It was not merely the language of the peasant as opposed to that of the knight. It included the language of guildsmen and artisans, of retainers, clerks, and hangers-on of the aristocracy; of beggars, thieves, sharpers, and peddlers. Each trade had its own cant. Most diverting was the speech of the last group.

Robert Greene, Shakespeare's contemporary, wrote a series of satirical pamphlets describing the tricks of sharpers and cheats in the London underworld. They give us most valuable material on substandard urban locutions during the reign of Elizabeth. From dictionaries and other sources we can then trace the underworld language through the seventeenth and eighteenth centuries. Thievery created a list of metaphors which were not only esoteric — for trade use — but also poetic. Here are a few, taken from a dictionary compiled in the reign of William and Mary:

> *bacon:* skin; body. "He saved his bacon," meaning "he escaped."
> *bracket-face:* ugly, homely, ill-favored
> *briers:* trouble. "To be in the briers," to be in trouble
> *bess:* an instrument to crack open a door
> *jenny:* "an instrument to lift up a grate, and whip anything out of a shop-window."
> *dead men:* empty bottles
> *dub:* a pick-lock key
> *fork:* a pickpocket. "Let's fork him" is thus glossed: "Let us Pick that man's Pocket, the newest and most dexterous way: It is, to thrust the Fingers, strait, stiff, open and very quick into the Pocket, and so closing them, hook what can be held between them."
> *green-bag:* a lawyer
> *milch-kine:* "a term us'd by Gaolers, when their Prisoners will bleed freely to have some Favor, or be at large."
> *mill:* to rob, steal, break open. "Milling the Gig with a Betty, c[ant for] Breaking open the Door with an Iron-Crow, milling the Glaze, c. Breaking open the Window."
> *queer birds:* "such as having got loose, return to their old Trade of Roguing and Thieving."
> *Spanish-money:* "fair words and Compliments"
> *splitter-of-causes:* a lawyer
> *unrig:* to strip the clothes off someone — whether for stealing or amorous purposes.

Metaphors of Slang

One fact emerges clearly from the study of disreputable slang, both past and present. No one impulse explains its creation and its peculiar qualities

It results from specialization, like any other trade dialect; also from a need for secrecy, for economy of expression; but certainly also from humor, delight in metaphor, and a quite uneconomic playfulness. Both conciseness and a pleasing contempt for conciseness will be found operative in the slang of the more respectable traders as well.

No occupation is more rushed, for example, than quick-lunch counter service at high noon. Hundreds of thousands of busy, nervous Americans besiege these dispensaries of pabulum every noon-time. Above the clamor of dishes and public conversation can be heard the cries of waiters and chefs calling and repeating orders for food in a language as special, mysterious, and playful as any thieves' cant. Surely here, you would suppose, the feverish tempo of service would make economy the paramount virtue of speech. And some expressions, like "B.T." for "bacon and tomato sandwich," are in fact a kind of spoken short-hand designed to clip a second or two off the necessary communication. Others are graphic as well as brief: *fizz* for "carbonated water"; *freezone* for "chocolate frosted milk"; *one-down* (referring to the electric toaster) for "an order of toast"; and *sparkle one* for "an order of Bromo-Seltzer. But what shall we say of the gay wastefulness of the following delightful expressions:

> *Adam's ale:* water
> *clean up the kitchen:* hamburger; *also* hash
> *Coney Island bloodhounds:* frankfurters
> *dough well done with cow to cover:* bread and butter
> *draw one in the dark:* black coffee
> *Hudson River ale:* water
> *Noah's boy with Murphy carrying a wreath:* ham and potatoes with cabbage
> *shot out of the blue bottle:* Bromo-Seltzer
> *slab of moo — let him chew it:* rare rump steak
> *twelve alive in a shell:* a dozen raw oysters
> *yesterday, today, and forever:* hash

They ignore the requirements of economy but provide verbal entertainment.

Taboo on Death

Another social attitude reflected in our language is the existence of all sorts of forbidden subjects which must be avoided or carefully disguised when we speak. The reasons for fear in connection with certain words and names are deep-lying and complicated. The use of such words presumably gives the speaker an exposed and vulnerable feeling, due ultimately to the magic powers originally attributed to language. To name death, disease, and wounds was felt, and indeed, is still felt, to be a way of inviting their presence. Hence elaborate phrases are to be found among many types of people, civilized and uncivilized, to avoid use of the simple words "die" or "be sick." We use them too. The very persons who protest that death is a fortunate release into a happier hereafter, or that disease is a negligible inconvenience easily conquered, are most wary about using the simple straightforward words to describe these aspects of our mortality. They use euphemisms like "passing on" or "passing away" or "being taken away." They also use noncommittal terms about someone who is seriously ill. Of course it is true that another element appears in the situation when politeness impels us to avoid direct reference to topics unpleasing to the listener. This may or may not be true among all peoples, but we certainly pride ourselves on this motive so far as we ourselves are concerned. Nevertheless it is very likely that some of the old fear of spirits and demons lurks within us still. Rational as we may think we are, we can still feel for the peasant of the fairy tales who cries out carelessly: "May the Devil take this stubborn mule of mine" — and at once beholds the Old Man himself at his elbow, smiling and saying "Always ready to oblige!" We still feel in some obscure way that to name is to summon.

Nationalism

Language and politics offer a combination somewhat easier to investigate than language and indecency. Nevertheless we seldom stop to reflect upon the great import of language in political issues such as the conflict of nations. Many bloody struggles have centered about claims and oppressions which used languages as symbols. When people engage in agitation for political independence, one very appealing issue is the demand to use a native tongue for official purposes, and to have it taught in the schools. It is usually felt by the most indifferent of observers that a real grievance is endured by any people when foreign officials, supported by a foreign army, take over a school system and suddenly forbid the use of a language hitherto officially accepted, as well as dear and familiar, to the children. Suppressed patriotism frequently centers about the determination of families to maintain the despised language within the home, no matter what may happen to it in the courts and schools.

A conspicuous example is the faithful preservation of Polish as a national language when the country had been divided by three empires in the eighteenth century. A language is also a rallying point for peoples who have never enjoyed the privileges of nationhood in the modern sense. In Ireland the Gaelic speech was consistently repressed for centuries, and a child who inadvertently slipped into native idiom in the (exclusively English) schools was severely punished, according to nineteenth-century reports. Parallel situations may be found all over the world, especially in colonies and semi-colonial countries. Here the native peoples frequently have no access to any schools except those founded and maintained by an outside group, a linguistic minority who have established themselves by military or commercial invasion.

Today, when conquest succeeds conquest with terrifying rapidity, the shifts in official speech must be confusing in the extreme to young students. If there were time in the midst of world affairs, it would be very enlightening to have a study by trained psychologists on the emotional and mental difficulties engendered in students by some of the recent political shifts of territory. In some Central American countries the situation is very complex for different reasons. The Indian populations have quietly and faithfully retained the indigenous dialects as their primary speech; Spanish, the official language, is still regarded as the imposed dialect of a conquering minority. But Spanish itself now finds competition in English, employed by resident company officials, higher paid employees, wives, children, and teachers connected with the small "colony" of American business enterprises. If Spanish is still resented by many natives, it would be curious to know what attitude is being built up towards English, the super-language of rulers.

So strong is the feeling for language in relation to nationality that it is quite possible to resurrect a language long since dead and reestablish it among the living. Hebrew is an example in point. The tongue of the Bible had become extinct so far as everyday life is concerned, but the zeal of Jewish re-settlers in Palestine has made it once more a living and expanding medium.

In the conflict of nations, enthusiasts for one side or another sometimes claim superiority for their special language. They affirm that their cause must be right because their language is "naturally" better than that of the opponent. Such statements are based rather on emotion than scientific judgment. An over-patriotic German will claim that his language is superior because it has such qualities as *Innerlichkeit* and *Tiefe* — and he will prove this to you triumphantly by pointing to idioms carefully chosen for the purpose. On the other hand the complacent Frenchman, sure that civilization and France are co-extensive, will claim for his language a monopoly of lucidity: *"Tout ce qui est clair est français!"* It should be remembered, however, that the best scholars carefully avoid these extravagant and unscientific claims. The German *Literaturblatt* has frequently reproved linguistic flag-wavers for their excesses, with exemplary scientific honesty, and the French sins of a similar nature have been most devastatingly satirized by French-speaking scholars like Daniel Mornet, Charles Bally, and Ferdinand Brunot.

Undeveloped Languages

But, someone may urge, some languages *are* limited in one way or another. They may at this given moment have an inadequate vocabulary for modern needs, or their traditional syntax may be needlessly elaborate, or they may lack the use of simple common nouns like "tree" or "table" without which one cannot conceive of the philosophical "tree-in-general." Hence they can never rise to the abstractions of lofty Western European philosophy, with its tradition of abstract thought reaching back to Plato. If this is so, perhaps we are justified, after all, in thinking of such languages as really inferior, since they are handicapped by their very structure in comparison with our own.

We have touched on this question before, but it is so important that a bit of repetition is not out of place.

Let us grant that at this particular moment in world history some languages, remote from major currents of events, are less developed than others in the directions required by a dominant civilization based on industry and machines. The grammar may employ cumbersome, repetitious constructions to express simple relations. Nevertheless even these languages are dynamic, not static. Change is always going on, rapidly or slowly according to the stimulus of cultural change. The complex syntax may be simplified; the needed words borrowed or created by compounding. Even sentence structure is modified with the ages. Useless distinctions are sloughed off when the need for them has died. If this has occurred unconsciously, for the most part, in the past, it is increasingly done with conscious direction today.

Under kindly tutelage directed toward the people's cultural advancement, a backward language can be speedily adapted, out of its own potential resources, to meet the requirements of modern civilization. Franz Boas reports how young Indian students can be introduced to the concept of Platonic universals even though their language traditionally lacks unmodified common nouns. They can easily be taught to isolate the term "house" out of expressions meaning "that-house-yonder," "my-house-here," and "the-house-made-of-wood." In the same way medieval scholastics created abstractions like "quiddity" when they felt the need for them. At first the natives may feel that they are doing violence to their language, since traditional syntax demands that every noun must have a modifier; but once they have been made to feel the intellectual need for the bare term "house," they will accept the usage — and thus push the language ahead a thousand years in one generation. A minority may first avail itself of the development, but there is no inherent reason why its use may not become general. The potentiality was always there; all that was needed was to elicit its application in a new situation.

Unfortunately people speaking undeveloped languages have hitherto encountered more developed idioms in a highly unpleasant manner. It was difficult to appreciate the virtues of a more economic speech when fellow-tribesmen had just been massacred in large numbers by those using it. The results may be quite different when a more fraternal spirit prevails. When the emissaries of a modern culture arrive with no intent to exploit or deceive or oppress, and without any arrogant assumption of superiority, they may obtain quite a different reception. There will be no sullen resistance to linguistic instruction, we may assume, when there is no resentment or fear. Under such happy circumstances a backward language can surmount structural handicaps in a very short time. Deficiencies in vocabulary have never presented serious difficulties. There is no reason why such adaptations should be left to slow and bungling processes as in the past. Conscious direction may be desirable in this situation as in others where an interchange occurs between one culture and another. Rarely, in fact, is the debt exclusively on one side when two languages meet on such a basis, even if one is more "advanced" than the other.

Slogans

Of course there is no aspect of man's social life which is not reflected in his language. Politics too offers material for the linguist. He may amuse himself by collecting the metaphors engendered in a lively campaign, or analyzing the special vocabulary of modern war, or tabulating the semantic shifts which accompany a change like the French Revolution. Upsetting movements like that of 1789 create a new terminology, elevating humble terms and hurling ancient ones into the discard, to the perturbation of conservatives. Back in 1799 an irate opponent of *Liberté, Egalité, Fraternité* expressed his disapproval of the new order by publishing anonymously in Venice a satirical Dictionary — really a political tract — called *Nuovo Vocabolario Filosofico-Democratico,* "indispensable," as the title page announces, "for all who wish to understand the new revolutionary language." Among the clichés the author denounced were: "ally, alliance," which, he said, "is used by Democrats only when they plan deceit"; "hypocrisy," a term applied to Napoleon and his followers for flirting with religion after denouncing it; "perfection, to perfect" an optimistic formula of Enlightenment expressing the hope of human progress, here stigmatized by the author as the immoral and irreligious slogan of assassins. Other expressions to be found in the alphabetical index are: "celibate," "civic guard," "gazette," "regeneration," "revolution," and "tribunal." Political slogans that have been cordially loved have also been cordially hated, until in many cases the intellectual content (if any) has been submerged by emotional inundations.

The linguistic aspect of demagogy and political spellbinding deserves more study than it has hitherto received. The Institute of Propaganda Analysis has done useful work in exposing the psychological devices employed. The rhetoric is just as interesting. For instance, archaisms are used, along with iteration, sound effects, epithets, and so forth, to play on the feelings of the listeners. A Biblical flavoring of sevententh-century language will reinforce the appeal. Here it is still possible to use extinct pronouns like "ye, thou, thee" or verbal endings long since discarded, or constructions no longer understood like "Woe worth the day!" Such phrases affect people all the more because they are mysterious and unclear, with sacred connotations. Likewise the figures of speech are kept archaic when appeal is made to feeling rather than reason. Orators will speak of defending the gates or the walls of the city even when none exist, as everyone knows. Certain undefined terms like "free enterprise" or "rugged individualism" are used in a manner to suggest incantations more readily than reasoned exposition. Perhaps no department of human expression justifies more clearly the cynical statement that the chief function of language is to conceal thought.

Social Values of Clarity

Nevertheless we still use it, hopefully, to understand one another. By becoming aware of limitations we begin to circumvent them. Since language is so eminently social there is no end to the problems interrelating society and language. Amateurs may provide themselves with unending diversion if they wish to extend their original observation of language behavior into various special aspects of the subjects here indicated, and to others as well. In a living medium there are always new developments, significantly indicative to the trained listener. You will find that the correlation of social tendencies and language will deepen your understanding of both: what you say and the milieu in which you say it.

In language as in many other things awareness is the first step towards intelligent adaptation and change. Laymen as well as professional linguists can have the fun and also the benefits of awareness. A pencil, a notebook, and an alert ear are all you need. You will learn much about yourself and your fellow man if you jot down striking phenomena connected with social concerns important for all of us: not only those here surveyed, but others. And you may very possibly be ready in a short time to make an original contribution concerning your discoveries. Language is the heritage of all of us, and so there is no reason why all of us may not be critical students of it — or even creators in the use of it.

FOR DISCUSSION

1. Is there in the United States a clearly recognizable "upper-class" dialect? Is there a "lower-class" dialect? When you hear a stranger's voice on the telephone, what features of his speech help you "place" him?

2. What are some features of "hypercorrectness"? What is your reaction to such locutions as the following: (a) Shall you be going to the concert tonight? (b) It's something to be shared between you and I. (c) It was I who found it. (d) To whom do you wish to speak? (e) He ain't never given me nothing.

3. What is the difference between regional dialects and class dialects? Are you aware of any class or regional features in your own dialect?

VOCABULARY: jargon, esoteric, nuance, hypercorrectness, *arriviste,* argot, periphrase, locution, galaxy, truculent, redolent, barbarism, pabulum, euphemism, engender, indigenous, emissary, stigmatize, demagogy, archaism, iteration, epithet.

THEME TOPICS: Your language betrays you. Children and adults do not talk alike. Men and women (boys and girls) do not talk alike. How to speak like a college professor. How to speak like a college student. How to speak like a phony.

British and American English

SIMEON POTTER

The language taken by John Smith to Virginia in 1607 and by the Pilgrim Fathers to Massachusetts in 1620 was the English of Shakespeare and Milton. During the following century and a half most of the colonists who reached the shores of New England were British, but the Dutch founded New Amsterdam and held it until it was seized by the British in 1664 and re-named after the King's brother, the Duke of York. When, in 1790, the thirteen colonies on the Atlantic seaboard ratified the Federal Constitution, they comprised four million English-speaking people, most of whom still dwelt to the east of the Appalachian Mountains. From the linguistic point of view this was the first and decisive stage in the history of United States English, which, by universal consent but less accurately, we call American English for short.

During the period from 1790 to the outbreak of the Civil War in 1860, new States were created west of the Appalachians and the Alleghanies and fresh immigrants arrived in large numbers from Ireland and Germany. The Irish potato famine of 1845 drove one and a half million Irishmen to seek a home in the New World and the European revolution of 1848 caused as many Germans to settle in Pennsylvania and the Middle West.

The third period, from the end of the Civil War in 1865 to the present day, was marked ethnographically by the arrival of Scandinavians, Slavs and Italians. During the closing decades of the nineteenth century one million Scandinavians, or one fifth of the total population of Norway and Sweden, crossed the Atlantic Ocean and settled, for the most part, in Minnesota and in the Upper Mississippi Valley. They were followed by millions of Czechs, Slovaks, Poles, Yugoslavs, and Italians, whose numbers were still further augmented by refugees in flight from the dire political persecutions which degraded Europe in the first half of the twentieth century. As the great American Republic took shape with the attachment of French and Spanish populations, with the addition of native Indian tribes in the Middle West, and with the absorption of Chinese and Japanese who landed on the Pacific Coast, so the cosmopolitan character of the United States became more accentuated. Further, the African Negroes have come to number over ten millions. Never, however, has the language of Washington and Lincoln been in jeopardy. At no time has there threatened any real danger that English might not be cap-

From *Our Language*, Penguin Books, Ltd., Harmondsworth, Middlesex, England, 1950. Reprinted by permission of the publisher.

able of completely assimilating the immigrant tongues or that the children of the French in Louisiana, the Germans in Pennsylvania, the Scandinavians in Minnesota, or the Slavs and Italians in Michigan might not all be able to understand, speak, read, and write English in the third and fourth generations.

The literary language, indeed, has seldom diverged perceptibly from that of the homeland. Washington Irving, Edgar Allen Poe and Nathaniel Hawthorne spared no pains in their day to write impeccable standard English. Henry James, Logan Pearsall Smith and Thomas Stearns Eliot were born in America but found an intellectual home in Europe. Edmund Wilson, Elmer Edgar Stoll, George Sherburn, Douglas Bush, and other eminent American critics wrote not unlike their British models, George Saintsbury, Andrew Cecil Bradley, Oliver Elton, and Sir Herbert Grierson. English literature is now cosmopolitan and worldwide: no sea or ocean bounds can be set to its domain. Henceforth English literature must include all excellent and memorable writing in the English language, regardless of political and geographical boundaries.

In spelling, vocabulary, and pronunciation, and in the syntax of the lower levels of speech, divergences remain. The distinctive features of American spelling are mainly a legacy bequeathed by that energetic little pale-faced man Noah Webster (1758-1843), whose *American Spelling Book* appeared in 1783 and whose *American Dictionary of the English Language,* the ancestor of all later Webster Dictionaries, was published in 1828. Webster would have liked to effect more drastic reforms in spelling, but he was restrained by necessity. 'Common sense and convenience,' he averred, 'would lead me to write *public, favor, nabor, hed, proov, flem, hiz, giv, det, ruf,* and *wel* instead of *publick, favour, neighbour, head, prove, phlegm, his, give, debt, rough,* and *well.*' The practical man of business, however, prevailed over the theoretical reformer. Webster sought a market for his new book on both sides of the Atlantic and he was advised to modify his drastic changes considerably. Today the second unabridged edition (1934) of Webster's *New International Dictionary* is the official spelling guide of the Government Printing Office and the accepted authority in all American courts. It sanctions such spellings as *-or* for *-our* in *favor, honor, humor, labor, odor,* and *valor* for English *favour, honour, humour, labour, odour,* and *valour; -er* for *-re* in *caliber, center, fiber, meter,* and *theater* for English *calibre, centre, fibre, metre,* and *theatre;* one consonant for two in *traveler, traveling, traveled, jewelry,* and *wagon* for English *traveller, travelling, travelled, jewellery,* and *waggon; -s-* for *-c-* in the substantives *defense, offense,* and *practise* for English *defence, offence,* and *practice;* various simplifications such as *ax, catalog, check, forever, jail, mask, medieval, program, story, tho, thoro, thru,* and *today* for English *axe, catalogue, cheque, for ever, gaol, masque, mediaeval, programme, storey* (of a building), *though, thorough, through,* and *to-day.* On the analogy, as he thought, of *affection, collection,* and *direction,* Noah

Webster clung to *connection* and *reflection* and these spellings are still favoured in America instead of the preferable forms *connexion* and *reflexion*. In general, however, the modified spellings of Webster's Dictionary are sound and sensible. Hundreds of American spellings have won acceptance in England, not only *public* for *publick, jail* for *gaol, cider* for *cyder, asphalt* for *asphalte,* and the like, but also the *-or* spellings for all agent substantives — *author, censor, conqueror, donor, juror, tailor, tutor,* and *visitor* — all, in fact, except *paviour* and *saviour.* The schoolchildren of England are no longer penalized for spelling in the American way and in recent years certain American publishers have deliberately restored a more old-fashioned English spelling.

On arriving in the United States for the first time the Englishman is made unduly aware of differences in vocabulary because these differences happen to loom exceptionally large in the language of travel and transport. Let us assume, by way of illustration, that he decides to continue his journey by rail, that is, by *railroad.* He does not register his luggage but he *checks* his *baggage,* which is then placed, not in the luggage van, but in the *baggage car;* perhaps he must first rescue it from the left-luggage office, which, he discovers, is called the *checkroom.* A goods train is referred to as a *freight train* and a brake-van becomes a *caboose.* He looks for the inquiry office in order to corroborate details and he finds that it is called the *information bureau;* or he may decide to consult a *bulletin-board,* in England a notice-board, or a *schedule,* in England a time-table, on his own account. He is surprised to learn that a season ticket is a *commutation ticket* and that a season-ticket holder is a plain *commuter.* The driver of his train is the *engineer* and the guard is the *conductor.* He hears someone refer to a *switch,* which turns out to be a *point,* and he soon discovers that a *grade crossing* is merely a level crossing. When he reaches his destination he finds an *automobile* waiting for him at the *railroad depot.* He cannot help noticing that the windscreen is called the *windshield,* the bonnet the *hood,* and that petrol is alluded to as *gasoline* or plain *gas.* That explains why the filling station is named the *gas station* and why *accelerating* is described as *stepping on the gas.* On his way through the town he passes trams or *street cars* with their trolley-poles or *contact rods.* He observes cyclists, *cyclers* or *wheelmen,* riding near the pavement or *sidewalk.* One of them has just stopped to mend a puncture or *fix a flat.* Not far away a lorry or *truck* is in difficulties and the breakdown gang or *wrecking crew* is getting to work. Having alighted at his hotel, he finds that it has no personal lift or *elevator* to take him up to his room on the *fifth floor* (which, luckily for him, turns out to be only what he calls the fourth), but that a service lift or *dumbwaiter* may be used for luggage or *baggage.*

At no point is the intelligent traveller inconvenienced by these hitherto unfamiliar, but easily assimilable, expressions. The more difficult task is to understand the living and ever-changing idioms of American slang. Much may be learnt about colloquial and slang idioms from the pages of that intermittent journal *Dialect Notes,* which began its career as long ago as 1890; from numerous articles appearing in *American Speech,* which was founded as a monthly in 1925, and which now continues to thrive as a quarterly publication of the Columbia University Press. Much, too, may be learnt from the large fourth edition (1936) of Henry Louis Mencken's *The American Language* and its two copious *Supplements* of 1945 and 1948. From *A Dictionary of American English on Historical Principles* (1938-44), by Sir William Craigie and James R. Hulbert, much may be learnt about the 'more serious and solid elements of American English' and about those 'speech-ways' which mirror the American life of the past. Here, naturally, information may be gleaned about those many trees, shrubs, animals, birds, and reptiles which are rare or unknown in Europe. The countless new arts and techniques of a highly developed civilization figure prominently in its pages, but slang and dialect are restricted to expressions of early date or of special prominence. Twentieth-century neologisms do not appear in it at all, for the editors set the year 1900 as their arbitrary time-limit. Since that date many thousands of new words have become current American and have made their way up from slang to the more respectable levels of colloquial speech. 'Today', wrote the Baltimore journalist H. L. Mencken in 1945 (*The American Language Supplement One,* p. 323), 'it is no longer necessary for an American writer to apologize for writing American. He is not only forgiven if he seeks to set forth his notions in the plainest and least pedantic manner possible; he is also sure of escaping blame (save, of course, by an Old Guard of English reviewers) if he makes liberal dips into the vocabulary of everyday, including its most plausible neologisms. Indeed, he seems a bit stiff and academic if he doesn't make some attempt, however unhappy, to add to the stock of such neologisms himself. How many are launched in this great Republic every year I do not know, but the number must be formidable. . . . So many novelties swarm in that it is quite impossible for the dictionaries to keep up with them; indeed, a large number come and go without the lexicographers so much as hearing of them. At least four-fifths of those which get any sort of toe-hold in the language originate in the United States, and most of the four-fifths remain here. We Americans live in an age and society given over to enormous and perhaps even excessive word-making — the most riotous seen in the world since the break-up of Latin. It is an extremely wasteful process, for with so many newcomers to choose from it is inevitable that large numbers of pungent and useful words and phrases must be discarded and in the end forgotten by all save linguistic paleontologists. But we must not complain about that, for all the great processes of nature are wasteful, and it is by no means assured that the fittest always survive'. Such neologisms are clipped words like *lube* for *lubricating oil* and *co-ed* for *co-educational;* back-formations like to *televise* (1931) from *television* and *to propagand* (1939) from *propaganda;* blends like *cablegram* from *cable* and *telegram, Aframerican* from *African* and *American, radiotrician* from *radio* and *electrician, sportcast* from *sport* and *broadcast,* and *sneet* from *snow* and *sleet;* artificial or made-up formations like *carborundum, cellophane,* and *pianola;* and acronyms or telescoped names like *nabisco* from *National Biscuit Company* or *socony* from *Standard Oil Company.* Hundreds of new expressions have also arisen by a revival and extension of grammatical conversion or the free interchange of function among parts of speech. When we *park* our cars we are using the substantive *park* as a verb in a particular sense. Shakespeare, it is true, used *to park* as a verb in the sense 'to confine or enclose as in a park' in I *Henry the Sixth,* IV. ii. 45: 'How are we park'd and bounded in a pale!' But *to park* in the sense 'to place compactly in a park' was a new conversion made by the British Army in 1812 at the time of the Napoleonic Wars. Nearly one hundred years later, in 1910, it was adopted by British chauffeurs and by American automobilists into their vocabulary. Since then *to park* has come to mean 'to leave or keep other things and persons in a suitable place until required' and Americans park not only their automobiles but also their children, their dogs, and the chewing-gum (P. G. Wodehouse, *The Inimitable Jeeves*). *Stream-line* was first recorded in 1873 in the highly technical language of hydrodynamics. Later, in 1907, it was applied in aerodynamics to the shape given to cars and aircraft offering the minimum resistance to the air. Later still, in 1913, it was converted into the verb *to streamline,* which has recently become a vogue-word in America and has been extended to mean any attempt whatever at simplification. That 'nasty newcomer' *to panic* was used by Thomas Hood in 1827, but apparently by no other writer until it was re-invented in the United States in 1910. To-day Americans no longer hesitate to *loan* (as well as to *lend*), to *audition* (grant a hearing or audition to), to *accession* (new library-books), to *remainder* (unsold and unsalable books), to *service* (a car or an automobile), to *blueprint* (to make any plan of any thing), to *contact* (to get into touch with), to *deadhead* (to admit as a 'deadhead' without payment), to *highlight* (to bring out the brightest parts or chief features of a subject), to *research* (to make researches), to *wastebasket* (to cast as rubbish into the wastepaper-basket), to *air* (to disseminate by radio), to *wax* (to record for the phonograph), and to *brain-trust* (to participate in what we English prefer to call a brains-trust). A bargain is a *good buy,* articles of food are *eats,* and technical skill is the *know-how.*

We refer quite naturally in everyday English to 'children and *grown-ups*' without realizing, perhaps, what an interesting linguistic form the word *grown-ups* is. It is the second or past participle of the intransitive durative verb *grow* (the past participle of which, because durative, has present signification) + the adverb *up;* compounded, converted into a substantive, and given the plural inflexion *-s.* This precise form is not old. It is first recorded in a letter penned by Jane Austen in 1813, although *grown-up* had been used as an epithet adjective in the seventeenth century. When we speak of giving our friends a good *send-off* we are employing an expression first used in this sense of 'a good-will demonstration' by Mark Twain in 1872. Hitherto this verb-adverb substantive had referred to the sending off or starting of contestants in a race. Many other substantives of this type have since found favour in America. A place of concealment is a *hide-out,* a drop in social esteem a *come-down,* a re-organization of staff a *shake-up,* and a free lunch a *hand-out.* Any arrangement or establishment is a *set-up,* a meeting of any kind is a *get-together,* and an escape is a *get-away.* Any action which brings matters to an issue or forces men to disclose their plans is a *show-down* as, at card-games, the players suddenly lay cards on the table. The Americans have a liking, too, for picturesque and vivid verb-phrases, both old and new: *to cut a shine, go the whole hog, shell out, go for, go in for, rope in, go him one better, go it blind, face the music, go it alone, stand from under, do the square thing, knock the spots off, spread it on thick, shinny on one's own side, get away with it,* and *paint the town red.* Journalists, gossip-columnists, makers of film and radio scripts, song writers and advertising agents are busy coining new turns of speech day by day. Some of these are literally ephemeral. They do not 'catch on'; they have their day and they are forgotten. Others live on and eventually, perhaps, they are tacitly adopted by the whole English-speaking world.

Suffixes may be resuscitated and multiplied by analogy. In conformity with *mathematician* and *electrician* the old *undertaker,* itself shortened from *funeral undertaker,* becomes *mortician* (1923), not to mention *beautician.* *Cafeteria* in Spanish is a 'coffee-house': in American English it is extended to mean a 'help-yourself restaurant' and thence proceed *caketeria, fruiteria, groceteria, smoketeria,* and a host of others, some accepted, others transitory, if not merely facetious. On the basis of *sanatorium,* other institutions are named *healthtorium, restatorium,* and *shavatorium.* Thomas Carlyle and others sought to revive the suffix *-dom,* corresponding to German *-tum,* in the nineteenth century and among their creations that survived were *boredom, officialdom,* and *serfdom.* Hundreds of new *-dom* compounds — *filmdom, stardom, crosswordpuzzledom, dictatordom, gangsterdom,* and *slumdom* — are now fashionable in America. The ancient agent suffixes, Greek *-ist* and Germanic *-ster,* have likewise come to life again in *vacationist* (holiday-maker, 1888), *manicurist* (1889), *behaviorist* (coined by John B. Watson in 1913), *receptionist* (1923), *blurbist* (concoctor of blurbs or slip-cover encomiums, 1925), and *editorialist* (1944); *ringster* (1879), *gangster* (1896), *roadster* (1910), and *speedster* (1918).

Among the more outstanding features of American pronunciation a few may here be noted. In words like *for, door, farm,* and *lord* the r is still sounded as a fricative, whereas in English it is silent except in expressions like *far away* and *the door opens* where a linking r is naturally inserted. In most dialects of Southern England the rolled or trilled r sound was weakened in pronunciation in the seventeenth century and lost in the eighteenth. Americans pronounce words like *dance, fast, grass, half,* and *path* with a low front a sound [æ] as in *cat,* which is still heard in the northern counties of England and which persisted in the southern counties until the end of the eighteenth century. Americans pronounce words like *dock, fog, hot,* and *rod* with a low back *a* sound [ɑ] like the vowel sound in *car* and *father* shortened. They pronounce words like *dew, duke, new,* and *steward* with the [ju:] sound reduced to [u:] so that *dew* and *duke* sound like *do* and *dook.* Just as in Spanish, Portuguese and Provençal, the Latin and Italian *armata,* past participle feminine, 'armed (force)', has become *armada,* so in present-day American *-t-* is often voiced, so that *beating* sounds very much like *beading, matter* like *madder,* and *metal* like *medal.* The plosion, however, is softer and less aspirated than in English.

Further, it may be noted that both word-stress and sentence-stress are weaker in American than in British English and intonation is more level. Consequently American speech is more monotonous, but at the same time it is generally more distinct. It is, as Mencken puts it, 'predominantly *staccato* and *marcato*', whereas British English, like Russian, 'tends toward *glissando*'. Unstressed syllables are pronounced with more measured detachment and therefore with greater clarity. There is less variety of tone and the customary tempo is slower. Many speakers have fallen into a habit which they have unconsciously inherited from seventeenth-century East Anglican Puritans. They allow the soft palate or velum to droop while speaking, and as a result part of the breath stream passes through the nose giving a certain nasalized quality or 'nasal twang' to vowel sounds which may vary considerably in degree from individual to individual.

Compare the way in which a New Yorker says *extraordinary, supernumerary, temporary,* and *unexceptionable* with the pronunciation of a Londoner. The American invariably gives to the unstressed syllables in these words greater 'prominence' (to use the technical term in phonetics) and, consequently, greater audibility. In words like *dormitory, monastery, necessary,* and *secretary* he habitually places a not unpleasing secondary stress upon the penult or last syllable but one. Some words he stresses differently from us. He stresses *aristocrat, detail, eczema, frontier, harass, primarily,* and *subaltern* on the second syllable whereas we stress them on the first. Conversely, he stresses *address, alloy, ally, corollary, defect, idea, inquiry, opponent, quinine, recess, recourse, redress, research, resource,* and *romance* on the first syllable, whereas we English stress them on the second. Other words, like *advertisement* and *financier,* are stressed on the second syllable in London but on the third syllable in New York.

Now these observations apply not only to the speech of New York City but also to the so-called General American dialect as a whole, which includes the Middle Atlantic States, that is, New Jersey, Pennsylvania and the whole of New York State west of the Hudson River, as well as all the Middle and Western States. General American thus comprises two-thirds of the whole population and four-fifths of the land surface of the United States reaching from the Atlantic Ocean in the east to the Pacific Ocean in the west.

The other two dialects, New England and Southern, are important and significant, but they are much more limited. The dialect of New England is spoken in Maine, New Hampshire, Vermont, Massachusetts, Rhode Island, Connecticut and the strip of New York State lying to the east of the Hudson River. It is nearer British English in many respects. For example, the rounded vowel is retained in *dock,* the long low back *a* is heard in *dance* and the *r* is dropped in *far* and *farm.* At the same time, it is less homogeneous than General American. Even within its narrower confines the New England dialect has far more social and regional variations. The Southern dialect includes the States of Maryland, Virginia, North and South Carolina, Georgia, Florida, Kentucky, Tennessee, Alabama, Mississippi, Arkansas, and Louisiana, as well as a great part of Missouri, Oklahoma, and Texas. In other words, it is spoken in all the States, except Delaware and West Virginia, lying south of Pennsylvania and the Ohio River and east of a line running from St. Louis to the middle waters of the Colorado River and thence down that river to its mouth in the Gulf of Mexico. Many people in these parts speak with a drawl. They speak with slow enunciation and they frequently drag out and diphthongize stressed vowels, saying [jeɪs], or even [jeɪjəs], for *yes,* and [klæɪs], or even [klæɪjəs], for *class.*

In spite of countless smaller variations in pronunciation, vocabulary, and idiom, the three American dialects do not greatly differ from one another. For two centuries and more American families have been constantly on the move: speech communities have seldom been isolated for more than one generation. It would be no exaggeration to say that greater differences in pronunciation are discernible among the speech-forms of Northern England between Trent and Tweed than among the dialects of the whole of North America.

It is now customary for American and British scholars and scientists to co-operate in the writing of composite books addressed to the whole English-speaking world and the councils of learned societies have taken steps to standardize technical nomenclature. Other potent forces are now at work bringing the two main streams of English more closely together. Future historians of our language, with their longer perspective in looking back, may well record that it was during the century and a quarter from 1800 to 1925 that British and American English showed the greatest divergence and that, after 1925, unifying factors — the ubiquity of radio and the interchange of films, novels, journals, and plays — all worked in one and the same direction to make that divergence narrower and narrower. Films and newspapers bring the latest American slang to England, so that even a trained observer may no longer differentiate with certainty between native and imported neologisms. Such a highly expressive phrase as *It's up to us* sounds so very American. We take it for granted that it *is* American. But who could be really certain about its provenance without looking a little more closely into the matter, without consulting Mencken, Horwill and *American Speech* on the one hand, and Partridge and the Supplement to *The Oxford English Dictionary* on the other? In 1942 the United States War Department furnished men and women serving in Europe with *A Short Guide to Great Britain* which included a long list of American and English variants. It was a painstaking, if over-elaborate, publication: its aim — to obviate every conceivable occasion of misapprehension — was entirely meritorious. This aim was shared by H. W. Horwill in his two careful studies which had appeared a few years previously and which have already acquired historical value: *A Dictionary of Modern American Usage* (1935) and *An Anglo-American Interpreter* (1939). In his Preface to the last mentioned book the author quotes the statement of a 'distinguished journalist' that 'an American, if taken suddenly ill while on a visit to London, might die in the street through being unable to make himself understood. . . . He would naturally ask for the nearest drugstore, and no one would know what he meant.' Everyone would now know the meaning of this and hundreds of other expressions marked American in Horwill's *Interpreter* and in the War Department's *Short Guide*. Indeed, they may now be heard from the lips of English children every day. The most fashionable American locution of the hour may be heard all over England within the space of a few weeks and then, perhaps, heard no more.

FOR DISCUSSION

1. Notice carefully the list of words spelled one way in the United States, a different way in England. Do you spell the following words with *s* or *c*: *defense, offense, practise*? Which spelling does Potter identify as British, which as American? He cites American spellings as *ax, catalog, tho, thoro, thru*. Are these the spellings you would expect or would use? What does your dictionary say about them?

2. Are the differences in British and American vocabulary sufficient to lead to serious misunderstanding? What is Potter's opinion? Here is a contrived and probably rare kind of sentence that may puzzle an average American; check the words in your dictionary to ascertain the British meaning: "Standing on the pavement, I lifted up the bonnet, wiped the paraffin off the dynamo with a napkin and then threw the napkin into the boot."

3. British English probably *sounds* more different from American English than it *looks*. Potter rather specifically indicates the features of pronunciation and intonation that make it sound so different. What are they?

VOCABULARY: ethnographical, augment, cosmopolitan, jeopardy, assimilate, impeccable, neologism, pedantic, lexicographer, paleontologist, back-formation, acronym, durative verb, substantive, literal, ephemeral, tacit, analogy, encomium, nomenclature, ubiquity, provenance.

THEME TOPICS: Is there an American language? How to tell a New Yorker from a Londoner. British expressions in American English. Noah Webster and the spelling of English.

WHAT

LANGUAGE IS

Linguistics

WILLIAM G. MOULTON

How language changes through time, how it varies through space, how it differs from one social group to another, and most of all how it *works* — these things are studied in linguistics. Because modern linguistics has roots which go back to the early nineteenth century and beyond, many people are familiar with some of the things which interested linguists then and still interest them today.

They find it understandable that a linguist should try to find the line which separates those areas in New England where *barn* is *"barrn"* (with *r*) from those areas where it is *"bahn"* (without *r*); and they may even envy him a bit

From *NEA Journal*, January 1965. Reprinted by permission of the author and the publisher.

when he goes to an Indian reservation or South America or Africa to investigate some hitherto undescribed tongue and thus add his little bit to our meager knowledge of the world's 2,000 to 4,000 languages. (No one knows how many there are.)

But when a linguist says that he is doing some research which he hopes will help us understand a little better how it is that "two people are able to talk together," most people shake their heads in puzzlement.

Yet how two people are able to talk together is, of course, the central problem. During the 1930's and 1940's, most American linguists attacked it by trying to work out better techniques of discovering the structure of language — any language — and of analyzing and classifying what they found. Then, in the late 1950's there came a rather dramatic swing in another direction: away from mere classification of data toward a search for universals and a broad, inclusive "theory of language."

In a sense this has been merely a return to some of the prime interests of our nineteenth century predecessors — Wilhelm von Humboldt, for example. It has also brought American linguistics out of the scholarly isolation from which it suffered for a time, and into closer contact with such related disciplines as psychology and philosophy. (The contact with anthropology has always been close.)

How *are* two people able to talk together? Since most of us never ask this question, but take the matter for granted, it is useful to consider just what goes on. Let us assume that we have a speaker A and a hearer B, that A says something to B, and that B understands him without difficulty. Here an act of communication via language has taken place. But *how* did it take place? What went on inside of A? How did the communication move from A to B? And what went on inside of B? The process seems to consist of at least eleven different steps.

1. Semantic Encoding

We assume that A has some sort of "meaning" (or whatever we want to call it) which he wishes to convey to B. His first step is to get this meaning into proper shape for transmission in the language he is using (English, we shall say). Since this is like putting a message in shape to fit the code in which it is to be sent, we can call the process *semantic encoding*.

If A wants to talk to B about some sort of timepiece, his encoding will depend on whether he means the kind that hangs on the wall or stands on a table (a *clock*), or the kind that is carried in the pocket or worn on the wrist (a *watch*). In German the single semantic unit *Uhr* includes both types. If he wants to ask whether B "knows" something, he can use the single semantic unit *know*. Spanish would force him to choose between *conocer* (for a person, place, or thing) and *saber* (for a fact).

As these examples show, each language "slices the pie of reality" in its own capricious way. In English, we group a host of different objects, of many types, colors, sizes, and shapes, into the semantic unit *stool*. If to a stool we add a back, however, it suddenly becomes the semantic unit *chair*. If we widen it so that two or more people can sit on it, it is a *bench*. If to a chair we add upholstery, it is still a *chair*. But if to a bench we add upholstery, it suddenly becomes a *sofa*.

Using a bold and imprecise metaphor, we can think of every language as a vast sieve with thousands of semantic slots in it. Any idea which we want to express in that language first has to be put through this sieve. And every language has a special sieve of its own. The discipline which studies such metaphorical sieves is semantics. (A semanticist would describe his valuable and difficult work more elegantly, but this is a reasonable approximation to part of what he does.)

2. *Grammatical Encoding*

Once speaker A has found the proper semantic units for his message, he must next arrange them in the particular way the grammar of his language requires. If in English he wants to get across the idea of "dog," "man," and "bite" — with the dog and not the man doing the biting — he has to encode it in the order *dog bites man;* the order *man bites dog* gives quite a different message.

The grammatical code of Latin employs totally different devices. For the meaning "dog bites man" it marks the unit "dog" as nominative (*canis*), the unit "man" as accusative (*virum*), and it can then combine these words with *mordet* "bites" in any order whatever. For the opposite message it would mark "dog" as accusative (*canem*), "man" as nominative (*vir*), and it could then again combine these with *mordet* in any order at all.

English grammar signals the difference between subject and object by means of word order; Latin grammar signals it by means of inflectional endings; other languages use still other devices.

The basic units used in grammatical encoding are called morphemes (from Greek *morphē* "form"). Morphemes may be either words: *dog, bite, man,* or parts of words: the *-s* of *bites,* the *-ing* of *biting,* etc. Some clearly correspond to semantic units: *dog, bite, man;* with others, however, the semantic connection is less clear, e.g. *-s, -ing*. Still others seem to have no semantic connection at all, the *to* of *try to come,* for example, or the *-ly* of *quickly.*

Morphemes are then arranged grammatically into such higher level units as words: *bites, biting, quickly* (some morphemes are of course already words: *dog, bite, man, quick*); then phrases of various sorts, e.g. *the dog* (which can function, among other ways, as a "subject"); then clauses of various sorts (in English, such constructions contain a subject and predicate);

and finally sentences, which are marked in some way as not being parts of still larger constructions.

Recent interest in grammar has focused on the following familiar and yet astonishing (and somehow disturbing) fact — any speaker can say, and any hearer can understand, an infinite number of sentences; and, indeed, many of the sentences we say and hear have never been said before.

How does our grammar provide for this enormous variety and flexibility? If we merely want to reach infinity quickly, we need only allow ourselves to use the word *and* over and over again. There are, however, two far more elegant devices. One is that of *embedding:* putting a construction inside a construction inside a construction, etc., like a Chinese puzzle. A classic example is the old nursery tale: "This is the cat that killed the rat that ate the malt (and so on and on and on) . . . that lay in the house that Jack built."

Still more elegant is *transformation,* whereby a basic sentence type may be transformed into a large variety of derived constructions. Thus *the dog bites the man* can be transformed into: *the dog bit (has bitten, had bitten, is biting, was biting, has been biting, can bite, etc.) the man; the man is bitten (was bitten, has been bitten, etc.) by the dog; (the dog) that bites (etc.) the man; (the man) that the dog bites; (the man) that is bitten by the dog; (the dog) that the man is bitten by; etc.*

3. Phonological Encoding

When grammatical encoding has been completed, the message enters the phonological component of the code as a string of morphemes, and these must now be encoded for sound. This is accomplished by encoding each morpheme into one or more basic phonological units or phonemes (from Greek *phōnē* "sound"). The morpheme -*s* of *bites* is converted to the phoneme /s/, *check* to /ček/, *stone* to /stōn/, *thrift* to /θrift/, etc.

(Written symbols for phonemes are customarily placed between slant lines to distinguish them from the letters of regular spelling and from the symbols used in phonetic transcription. Just what symbols are used for phonemes is unimportant; one must merely have a different symbol for each phoneme in the language.)

This device of encoding morphemes into *one or more* phonemes each is an extraordinarily powerful one, and in terms of sheer economy it is hard to overestimate its importance. If a language used only one phoneme per morpheme, it could have only as many morphemes as it has phonemes. But if a language uses from one to five phonemes per morpheme (as in the above English examples), the number of possible morpheme shapes soon becomes astronomical.

For a stock of twenty phonemes, the figure is 3,368,420; for thirty phonemes it is 25,137,930; and for forty phonemes (English has between thirty and forty, depending on just how you figure them) it reaches the fantastic total of 105,025,640 possible morpheme shapes.

We have given these figures to show what an enormous economy is achieved by having in human language this "duality principle," as it has been called: first an encoding into morphemes, and then a separate encoding of morphemes into *one or more* phonemes each.

There is, however, a very bad flaw in our figures. We have assumed that it is possible for phonemes to occur in any mathematically possible sequence, such as (for English) /ppppp/, /fstgk/, etc. But English of course does not do this; like every language, it places very strict limitations on possible sequences of phonemes. Nevertheless, even with the strictest sorts of limits, the duality principle permits every language to form far more morpheme shapes than it will ever use.

If we take English to be a thirty-phoneme language (it has more than thirty, no matter how you figure them), permit no morpheme shape of more than five phonemes (*glimpse*/glimps/ actually has six), and assume that only one out of very 1,000 possible sequences can be used, we still end up with a total of 25,137 possible morpheme shapes (the above 25,137,930 divided by 1,000) — enough to take care of any language.

If we remind ourselves that English words can easily consist of three or more morphemes (e.g. *un-friend-li-ness*), it is clear that we are also provided with an overabundance of possible word shapes — more than enough for Lewis Carroll to invent "slithy toves did gyre and gimble in the wabe," using a few of the thousands of available word shapes which had not previously been claimed.

In the preceding paragraphs we have assumed, for purposes of presentation, that a message is neatly encoded first semantically, then grammatically, and then phonologically. But since normal speech is full of false starts, hesitations, grammatical slips, and the like, it seems clear that we behave a good deal more like the young lady who, when told that she should "think before she spoke," replied with rare honesty: "But I can't do that! How do I know what I'm going to say until I start talking?"

If we do *not* normally plan out our entire message before we start sending it, then we must possess some sort of feedback device which permits us to "monitor" the message as it is sent and to make necessary adjustments as we proceed — adjusting a present tense verb to agree with its singular subject, for example.

4. From Brain to Speech Organs

When phonological encoding has been completed, the message has been changed from a string of morphemes to a string of phonemes. Speaker A must now somehow program and send on down to his speech organs a set of instructions telling them what movements to make so as to turn each phoneme into sound. We can compare this with the way paper tapes are punched to provide instructions to automatic typewriters, telegraph transmitters, computers, and the like. Programmed in this way, the message is sent sequentially from the brain to the speech organs.

5. *Movements of the Speech Organs*

Triggered by successive innervations, the speech organs (vocal cords, tongue, lips, etc.) now perform the proper series of movements. As they do so, an interesting and rather disturbing thing happens. We have assumed that, when the message is sent to the speech organs, it is transmitted in the form of a string of separate instructions, one for each phoneme.

If the message is the word *pin* /pin/. for example, there are first instructions for producing a /p/, then for producing an /i/, and then for producing an /n/. This seems, at least, to be the most reasonable assumption. If the speech organs responded ideally to these instructions, they would first assume the position for /p/, then move jerkily and instantaneously to the position for /i/, then jerkily and instantaneously to the position for /n/.

Common sense tells us that they cannot do this, and X-ray moving pictures of the speech organs in action prove it beyond a doubt. Instead of moving instantaneously from one position to the next, the speech organs bobble back and forth in a constant flow of motion which does not seem to consist of any specific number of segments at all.

A remarkable transformation has taken place. Where the message previously consisted of a string of discrete segments — three, we assume, in the case of /pin/ — it has now been "smeared" into a continuum. As the speech organs move into position to produce the /p/, they already anticipate part of the position for the following /i/. (The reader can test this by whispering the *p*'s of *peer, par, poor;* the sound of each *p* shows clearly which vowel would follow if he went on with the rest of the word.)

As the speech organs then move into the /i/, they carry over part of the position of the /p/ and anticipate part of the position for the following /n/. (We normally "nasalize" such a vowel slightly.) And when the speech organs get to the /n/, they still have a part of the position of the preceding /i/. This drastic change in the shape of the message may seem quite harmless now, but it means that later on this "smeared continuum" of sound will have to be turned back into a string of discrete segments if the message is to be recovered. This is what must take place at stage 3, "phonological decoding."

When the speech organs interact so as to produce a speech sound, they are said to articulate the sound. The study of this aspect of the speech event, *articulatory phonetics,* has long been a highly developed research field.

6. *Vibrations of the Air Molecules*

As the speech organs articulate, they set the air molecules into vibration and produce audible sound. The study of this aspect of the speech event is *acoustic phonetics.* Here again a great deal of research has been done, and some remarkable advances have been achieved, especially since World War II.

7. *Vibrations of the Ear*

When the vibrations of the air molecules reach hearer B's eardrum, they produce corresponding vibrations which are then transmitted via the three bones of the middle ear to the cochlear fluid of the inner ear. The study of this aspect of the speech event is *auditory phonetics.* It is usually combined with study of the ear in general, and with the study of auditory perception (which of course involves also the activity of the brain farther up the line).

8. *From Ear to Brain*

Though this stage is in a sense the mirror image of stage 4, "From brain to speech organs," there are two important differences.

First, when the message went from A's brain to his speech organs, it was transmitted as a string of discrete segments; but since it was then turned into a "smeared continuum" by A's speech organs, this is the shape in which it now reaches B's brain.

Second, speaker A was able to send the message only because, somewhere inside his head, he possessed the proper code; hearer B, however, can receive all the energy in the message whether he knows the code or not — though of course he can do nothing further with it unless he *does* know the same code. We can "hear" all there is to hear in a foreign language message; we can "understand" the message only if we also know the foreign language code.

9, 10, 11. *Phonological, Grammatical, and Semantic Decoding*

Though we surely use these three different types of decoding when we hear and understand a message, the evidence suggests that we do not use them in a step-by-step procedure but rather race back and forth from one to the other, picking up all the information we can get.

Suppose, for example, that we receive a message which we tentatively decode phonologically as, "I hope this'll suture plans." A quick check with the grammatical component of the code reveals that there is indeed a morpheme *suture* marked "transitive verb" (that is to say, we know that one can "suture something"), so all is well for the moment. But a check farther up the line in the semantic component tells us that one just does not "suture plans," so something must be wrong.

Back we race to the phonological component. Again the message (held in the meantime by some sort of storage device) is decoded as having the phonemic structure "I hope this'll suture plans." But a second check in the grammatical component now reveals that the phoneme sequence "suture plans" can be grammatically either one of two different things: *suture plans* or *suit your plans*. So we check this *second* possibility in the semantic component of the code. This now "makes sense" — and we accept it.

Our brain can function so swiftly that all of this happens in a flash. Only rarely does this "searching process" take so long that it interferes with our understanding of the speaker's next sentence.

In addition to the message itself, our decoding brings us information of three other types. First, there is information about the identity of the speaker (the quality of his voice tells us that it is Jones and not Smith who is speaking), his state of health (hoarse voice, stuffed up nose), and the like. Such things are presumably the same in all languages and hence not part of any code.

Second, there is the kind of information we often refer to as "it wasn't what he said but how he said it" — things indicating that the speaker is angry, excited, sarcastic, unctuous, etc. Since such matters are different in English from what they are in French or Vietnamese, they are clearly part of the English language in the wider sense of the term. (They also make a fascinating subject for linguistic study.)

Third, there is information as to where the speaker comes from and what social and educational class he belongs to. If he uses the phonological encoding "thoity-thoid," this will suggest that he comes from Brooklyn or thereabouts; if he says "thihty-thihd" we may suspect that he comes from the vicinity of Boston.

If he uses the grammatical encoding "I seen him when he done it," we will place him at a relatively low social and educational level — even though (and this is an interesting point) the message comes through just as clearly as if he had said "I saw him when he did it." Matters of this third sort are also part of the English language in the wider sense of the term.

In the above description of a speech event, the part which is of most fundamental interest to the linguist is of course the code itself: its phonological component (here great progress was made in the 1930's and 1940's), its grammatical component (again great progress at that time, and a whole new approach opening up since the late 1950's), and its semantic component (long neglected by American linguists, though there has been a recent revival of interest).

When one looks back upon it all, one is perhaps inclined to say: What is it good for? Is it just a game? To the linguist it is more than a game: It is a thing of beauty and wonder, and it needs no more justification than this. At the same time, with a bit of a sigh, he will say that (like such long "useless" fields as astronomy) it *can* be of practical value. It has obvious applications to foreign language teaching and — with great help from the teachers themselves — these applications are now being exploited.

If presented clearly and simply (and this has in general not been the case — nor is it easy) it seems likely that it could also be applied usefully to the teaching of reading and writing, and to the teaching of the English language at all levels. Tentative applications of this sort have already been made; with cooperation on all sides, perhaps they can lead to truly useful results.

Suggested Readings

Carroll, John B. *The Study of Language: A Survey of Linguistics and Related Disciplines in America.* Cambridge: Harvard University Press, 1953.

Hall, Robert A., Jr. *Linguistics and Your Language.* New York: Doubleday (paperback: Anchor Books A-201), 1960.

Gleason, H. A., Jr. *Introduction to Descriptive Linguistics,* rev. ed. New York: Holt, 1961. (College text.)

Hockett, Charles F. *A Course in Modern Linguistics.* New York: Macmillan, 1958. (More advanced.)

Waterman, John T. *Perspectives in Linguistics.* Chicago: University of Chicago Press (paperback: Phoenix Books), 1963. (History of linguistics.)

Fries, Charles C. *Linguistics and Reading.* New York: Holt, 1963. (Applications.)

FOR DISCUSSION

1. Professor Moulton distinguishes three stages of "encoding" — semantic, grammatical, phonetic. Would writing be a fourth stage? What, exactly, is encoded by writing? Could we describe the marks we make on paper as a code that encodes another code?

2. What, in English, is the relation between phonemes (units of the phonetic code) and letters (units of the writing code)? What would the ideal relationship be?

3. Consider the second sound in *so,* i.e., the sound represented by the letter *o.* How many ways do we spell this sound in English? (You should find at least twelve.)

4. How about the letter *o*? How many sounds does it represent? What sound does it represent in *choir,* for instance?

5. To encode a message we must select the appropriate morphemes and arrange them in an appropriate sequence. *Dog bite-s man* has four morphemes. *Dog bites men* has five morphemes (man + plural morpheme). Can you identify the eight morphemes in *Dogs were biting men?*

6. What are the grammatical morphemes in this sentence: *The figgledy oogles wombled the iggles.* Can you identify the nouns in that sentence? How do you know they are nouns?

Vocabulary: linguist, semantics, phoneme, morpheme, encode, phonetic, "duality principle" in linguistics, sequential, transmit, assumption, continuum, discrete segments, articulatory phonetics, tentative, component.

Theme Topics: What the Morse Code encodes. The miracle of language. How we communicate. Grammar — a system for encoding meaning. Theory for a perfect spelling system.

The Coming Revolution in Teaching English

ANDREW SCHILLER

Modern parents complain that they can't help the kids with their home-work anymore. The senile gaffers of forty or fifty have been left far behind by the physical sciences with their arcane particles and space gibberish. The youngsters don't even do long division the way we did it in the 1920s and '30s. For those thus bewildered, it is comforting to return to good old English grammar. In a world where the tables of multiplication shift treacherously underfoot, we touch solid bedrock in the eternal truth that a noun is the name of a person, place, or thing.

And it is true the grammar still taught in most American schools would look perfectly familiar to Bishop Robert Lowth, who published *A Short Introduction to English Grammar* in 1762. Nevertheless, traditional, or Latinical, or Lowthian grammar is under heavy fire from the new grammarians. There are almost as many sects among these innovators as there are in Christendom. But all of them have in common the desire to analyze language with the same rigorous precision with which the chemist analyzes compounds, and all are more or less mathematical in style. Some of their formulations look rather terrifying to the non-initiate.

Here is one example:[1]

Description: NP W + Af as A X as (NPV$_c$) NP Y # Z

$$\underbrace{\hphantom{NP\ W}}_{1\quad 2}\quad \underbrace{\hphantom{+ Af as A X as (NPV_c)}}_{3}\quad 4\quad 5$$

Condition: $2 = 4 + 5$
        If 3 includes NPV$_c$, 4 is not null
Change: $1 + 2 + 3 + 4 + 5 \rightarrow 1 + 2 + 3 + 4$

[1] From Carlota S. Smith, "A Class of Complex Modifiers," *Language,* 37: 3, p. 365.

And now for another[2]:

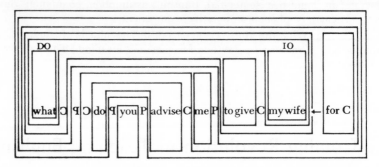

These formulations typify the two leading (and often contending) "schools" of modern linguistic thought. The first is known as transformational grammar. Its essential assumption is that language consists of irreducible kernel utterances, plus transformation laws, plus lexicon. The illustration is an abstract formula for generating sentences of the type, "John is taller than Bill."

The second example is from phrase-structure grammar (which, some of the more condescending transformationalists are already calling "classical linguistics"). The interconnected boxes are a graphic device to show how the sentence, "What do you advise me to give my wife for Christmas?" is analyzed. To do this, you peel the grammatical construction apart by orderly stages, much as a mechanic disassembles an automobile into body, engine, cooling system, exhaust system, and running gear, these in turn into subassemblies, and so on to the ultimate constituents.

Taken undiluted, such grammars are sophisticated and difficult, strong drink for graduate students, not milk for children in the grades. But we do not teach school or college students linguistics; we teach them structural grammar which is based on what we have learned from linguistics. And I can report that youngsters who have been taught structural grammar (diluted, of course), have not only grasped but enjoyed it — an accomplishment comparable to making castor oil palatable. Generally, they are impressed by the ease with which a few principles cover a vast territory.

Formulae of the kind shown above may seem far removed from the primary grades. But so are the equations of Einstein and Bohr. Yet modern grade schoolers prattle easily of orbits and weightlessness, atomic energy and space-time. In a like fashion, the concepts of modern linguistics, on which the new grammars are based, will one day filter down in a general, accessible form to most adults and children. So far this has not happened. But that is an accident of history. Structural linguistics — the exact science of language — is about three or four decades behind the physical sciences in this respect.

Around 1925, for example, physicists were already familiar with the the-

[2] From W. Nelson Francis, *The Structure of American English*, p. 388. Copyright © 1958, The Ronald Press Company.

oretical basis of nuclear fission. No one could then have predicted that in twenty years the equations would be translated into a bomb, ten years later into a power plant — and that the average teen-ager of the 1950s and '60s would be as glib with his physics as his parents had been with Freudian psychology. In the same fashion the new science of language is bound to erupt into the public consciousness. When that happens, much grammatical theory that has been passed from generation to generation in our schools, virtually unchanged for centuries, will be laid quietly in our intellectual attic alongside astrology and alchemy.

What — if any — will be the practical benefits? Will this new information from the linguists help us in our job of teaching reading and writing? I have no doubt that it will.

At present, the teacher of traditional grammar is at a serious disadvantage compared with the science teacher. In a chemistry class, for example, students learn that the electrolysis of water produces hydrogen and oxygen in the proportion of two to one. In the laboratory they verify this for themselves. But when the grammarian asserts that a sentence must consist of a subject and a predicate, and state a complete thought, his students cannot prove this for themselves. To begin with, we cannot precisely define a "complete thought." Take the sentence, "I am going to the concert." According to the grammarians, that is a complete thought. If "complete" has its ordinary meaning, then if we subtract something, what remains should be less than complete. But the statement, "I am going," is, according to the same grammarians, still a complete thought. So is "I am."

Nor does any particular form or shape or length of sentence distinguish a complete thought from an incomplete one.

The other classic criterion of a sentence is that it names a subject and predicates something about it. This is just as slippery. Consider the sentence, "The door is open." Here we have a subject and a predicate — a complete sentence. On the other hand, consider the phrase, "the open door." Have we not given the name of a thing, place, or person? Have we not stated something about that thing? Certainly the student cannot verify this definition for himself.

Now let us take a different approach. I say to someone, "The door is open." He may reply, "I'll close it." However, if I say, "The open door . . ." he simply waits for me to continue. If I fail to go on he will laugh, believing I have fallen asleep with my mouth open. He knew after the first utterance that I was finished, that some reply or action was expected of him. He knew after the second that I was not. This was not because I said less, but because the two utterances had different formal characteristics. Take another example. If I say to you, "This is the best," you know that you can now agree or disagree. But if I say, "This is the best . . ." you will not respond until I add best *what*.

These two utterances were word for word the same but you received two different sets of signals. The difference is not merely a matter of completion and non-completion; in the second utterance you not only knew something else was coming, you knew exactly what sort of thing — namely a noun or some nominal expansion. That is, I could not possibly have completed the utterance with the word "very," but I could have completed it with "piano" or "of all possible worlds." From such examples the linguist concludes that it is not particularly useful to define a noun in terms of meaning. It is more useful to identify a class of words that can be placed at the end of the utterance, "This is the best . . ." He concludes also that the difference between a sentence and a non-sentence must be stated in terms other than meaning.

Stress, Pitch, Juncture

What other criteria are there? Further analysis reveals three phenomena which together differentiate "This is the best . . ." from "This is the best." These phenomena are stress, pitch, and juncture. Understanding how they function gives us an insight into the structural linguists' approach to language.

As to stress, in English speech four distinct degrees can readily be heard in such a phrase as "portable typewriter." The first syllable of each word is marked by a heavy stress, but — and this is the important distinction — not equally heavy. If you ask how I wrote this article, I reply, "I used a portable TYPEwriter." If on the other hand you ask what kind of typewriter I generally use, I say, "I use a PORTable typewriter." So we distinguish primary and secondary stress, marked respectively ′ and ^. Now if we listen to the word "typewriter" we can hear that the stress on the second syllable is lighter than the first but heavier than the third. This gives us the third and fourth degrees (tertiary and minimal) marked respectively ` and ˘ (though in actual transcriptions, minimals are usually left unmarked for simplicity). The two different stress patterns are indicated thus:

Q: How did you write this article?
A: I used a pôrtăblĕ týpewrìtĕr.
Q: What kind of typewriter do you generally use?
A: I use a pórtăblĕ tŷpewrìtĕr.

Note that the shift in stress is not random. Changes in stress affect meaning.

There are also four levels of pitch in English. Our first sentence would look like this on a musical staff:

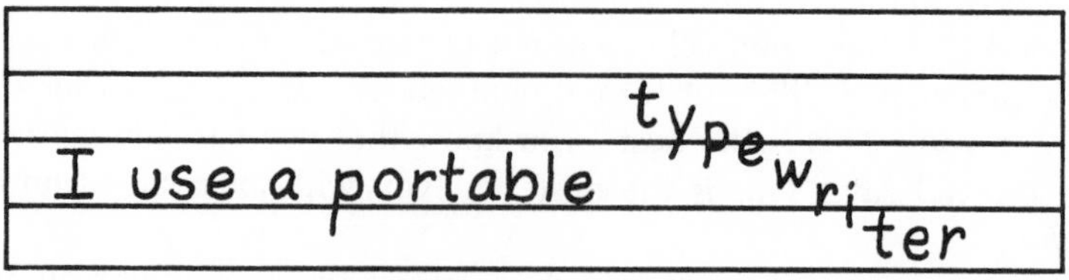

To replace the cumbersome staff, linguists express the pitch pattern in this grammatical notation:

2   3   1

I use a portable typewriter.

Suppose now that I am not going to finish the sentence with the word "typewriter" — perhaps I will continue with the clause, "since I work while I travel." You now hear:

2   3   2

I use a portable typewriter

and you know that I am not finished. If I were dictating, you would use a comma after the word "typewriter." On the other hand, suppose I said:

2   3   3

I use a portable typewriter

the so-called rising inflection would tell you that I was finished and had asked a question.

Pitch four is commonly used *in extremis* to indicate intense emphasis, alarm, indignation, such as:

2   4   1

Come here this instant!

A stream of speech is composed not only of sounds but of breaks in the succession of sounds. These gaps are of specific types and come in specific places. They are part of the grammar of the utterance, like nouns and verbs, and this pitch-pause phenomenon is known as juncture.

One type of juncture enables us to distinguish "announce" from "an ounce." In "announce" the sounds are all hooked together without a break. But in "an ounce" there is a break between the second and third sounds. The same phenomenon occurs in such pairs as "anneal" and "an eel," "nitrates" and "night rates," or in "grade A" and "gray day."

This kind of "open" juncture necessarily occurs between sounds. There are also several other kinds of juncture. Consider the pair:

"Her Ladyship awaits without, Seymour."

"Her Ladyship awaits, without Seymour."

The commas in these sentences indicate level juncture, so-called because the voice usually resumes speech, after the gap, at the same level of pitch at which it broke off. The shift of juncture restructures the entire utterance. The word "without," for example, is an adverb in the first sentence but a preposition in the second.

Falling juncture, characterized by rise and fall of pitch, is most commonly the end-signal in a declarative sentence. We hear it after "Seymour" in both examples. Rising juncture, on the other hand, is commonly an end-signal in an interrogation such as, "Her Ladyship awaits without, Seymour?" Rising juncture inside an utterance usually separates the elements of a series as in counting: "One, two, three, four . . ." or in listing: "Vanilla, chocolate, strawberry, pistachio . . ."

Pitch, stress, and juncture together provide us with an objective way to distinguish between an incomplete utterance ("I am going . . .") and a complete one ("I am going."). The classic criterion of a "complete thought" is, at best, subjective. But the presence of certain stress-pitch-juncture patterns can be verified simply by speaking or listening.

It Accentuates the Positive

The structural approach to language has another great advantage: it is positive. The conventional grammar is negative, analyzing utterances only after they have been made, and stamping them, as the Department of Agriculture stamps meat, as acceptable for various levels of users. The structuralist, by contrast, is not trying to teach students to parse sentences that are put before them, but rather to enable them to devise sentences where none existed before.

To this end the chief teaching method is pattern practice. Nearly all English utterances can be reduced to a half-dozen or so basic patterns. One, for example, is the NVN: The boy loves the girl. The dog bites the man. Mantle hit a homer. Such a sentence consists of three parts, but only two different ones, the noun and the verb. These can be expanded into noun clusters and verb clusters. The expansive devices are finite — indeed, very few — but the permutations are infinite.

The noun, for example, grows by an agglutinative process, fore and aft. Single word modifiers come before, in any number but not in any order. The adjective precedes the modifying noun. Thus we say, "The nervous police dog bit the postman," but we do not say, "The police nervous dog bit the postman." From this we can see that the difference between an adjective and a pre-modifying noun is a real one: they pattern differently. We can verify by the simple test of speaking out loud. We can say, "The dilapidated yellow house," or, "The yellow dilapidated house," indifferently. But we cannot reverse the order of the modifiers in "The yellow ranch house."

In the post-modifying position are the adjective phrase and the adjective clause, commonly in that order. Thus, "The nervous police dog in the yard next door who is a friend of mine . . ." All of it is, essentially, an expansion by modification of the single noun, "dog." It can be schematized thus:

The	nervous		police	dog
Determiner	*Adjective*		*Noun*	*Noun*
in the yard next door			who is a friend of mine	

| *Adjective Phrase* | *Adjective Clause* |

Abbreviating this, and inserting arrows to show the direction of modification, we arrive at the abstraction:

$$D \quad \longrightarrow A \rightarrow \quad \longrightarrow N \rightarrow \quad N \quad \longleftarrow AP \longleftarrow \quad \longleftarrow ACl \longleftarrow$$

In the classroom, we might simply begin with that formula and ask the students to flesh it out in real language. Then we can play around with these elements, making elaborate repetitions, substitutions, and expansions. For example, the noun within the adjective phrase can itself become the head-word of a noun cluster. Take the phrase "in the front yard" and it can be expanded to "in the weedy, toy-littered front yard of that shiftless Kallikak family that's always disgracing the neighborhood." Students enjoy playing this game. Sometimes the sentences that emerge are shapely and admirable, sometimes not. If not, one can always try again, for the resources of the language are infinite. The point is that the student is learning to use these resources.

Thus, in the NVN, the N's may also be phrases or clauses. Double such a pattern into a parallel construction and you get "To err is human; to forgive, divine." The student comes to such things by stages.

Begin with a simple NVN: "You receive your earnings." Now transform the predicate N into a clause: "You receive what you earn." Now transform into parallel clauses, NCl V NCl "What you receive is what you earn." Now modify the verbs in each clause with a phrase so as to make your reference concrete. "What you receive in happiness is what you have earned in suffering."

The verb expands as well, in its own fashion. The point of this technique is that it is concrete and positive, synthetic rather than analytic. The emphasis is on what you do rather than on what you don't do.

Talking Prose All His Life

Thus far I have spoken of the bone-structure of language, which the average child has pretty well under control by the age of five. He will add a good deal of vocabulary. And he has yet to learn to read and write, but these are coding processes for the language he already knows.

In theory, he ought to write as fluently as he speaks, once he learns the code. Many teachers ask the student simply to reproduce his speech on paper. He is told to act as his own stenographer, to write it down as he says it. But this advice the student finds astonishingly hard to put into practice. Why?

For one thing, the student does not write as much as he speaks. Who does? He does not even write enough to make the act commonplace. Ideally, he should approach a blank sheet of paper as casually as he sits at a table to eat. But of course he doesn't.

Our students hate to write. It is hate born of fear, for a composition is a deadly game between them and their teacher. Every time the student commits something to paper he incurs the risk of error. Writing at school is a maze of pitfalls — shall or will? like or as? comma or semicolon? EI or IE? Writing has been taught as an endless series of proscriptions, of things thou shalt *not* do.

The aim of the new grammarians is to convince the student that he has been talking prose all his life, to make him conscious of the linguistic devices he has been using unconsciously. We do not harry him, nag him, and pester him about trivialities of usage.

This does not mean that the linguists have opened the floodgates of illiteracy or have sanctioned the debasement of the tongue of Shakespeare, Milton, and Dwight Macdonald — as has sometimes been charged. This is sheer nonsense derived, I think, from a misunderstanding of the purpose of *descriptive* linguistics, particularly dialect geography. It is a fact that some people say, "He done it. I seen it with my own eyes." Those who chart dialects can tell you who is likely to say this, where, and when. They will not pretend that nobody says it. On the other hand, they will certainly not recommend that if you are given to this kind of speech you apply to NBC for an announcer's job. The linguists supply data, not ethical judgments.

They are aware, too, that "I seen him" is *structurally* no different from "I seed him," "I done seen him," or even, if you insist, "I saw him." None of them can be misunderstood. All of them have the same moral content, which is zero. Once the student realizes that the teacher treats his dialect with the same indifference with which he treats his face, the ground is prepared for learning. The "I seen" speaker attests by his presence in a classroom that he wishes to become an "I saw" speaker. He may not know this, but he can be convinced. Furthermore, you do not attack his problem by picking at his usage errors. Those are the mop-up operations, not the main field of battle. The teacher's basic job is to convince his students that written English is the language he has known all his life; that there is a real relationship, which you can verify and manipulate, between the sounds you make in the air and the marks you put on a paper.

I am all for teaching the dialect of the educated, whatever that may be. But language is different wherever you go, and changing all the time. The material we deal with is alive. As a teacher I advise my student about the current status of linguistic shibboleths, just as the lawyer tells his client where he thinks he may safely chisel on taxes this year. Thus I can tell freshmen that "Who did you see at the party?" is relatively safe by now; but "I seen him" is non-U.

Don't Blame Miss Prouty

To what extent has structural grammar penetrated the curricula of American schools? The answer is, No more than slightly. On the face of it, this fact is amazing, if not un-American. Characteristically, we are enchanted by the new, contemptuous of yesterday (unless it is nostalgically "antique"). And we are automatically convinced that today's fashions represent Progress. Yet, though my children find my old fountain pen as quaint as a quill, they are still being taught the grammar Thomas Jefferson learned.

Is this because modern linguistics has become so arcane that only a small group of specialists in the graduate schools know what is going on? If so, what can you expect of poor old Miss Prouty, who teaches sixth grade? But Miss Prouty is also teaching the New Mathematics, and relatively up-to-date science. She does not, of course, discourse on genetics and nucleonics in terms remotely like those of the scientists working in these fields. And the new grammar would make no more technical demands on her. So don't blame Miss Prouty.

She is — as a practical matter — subject to the educational Establishment which is dominated by the rebellious generation reared in the so-called Progressive movement of the 1920s and '30s. The bias of this group is anti-academic, in fact anti-intellectual. Whatever was rigorous, traditional, impractical was anathematized as undemocratic. "Life adjustment" was the objective. "Democratic" education *had* to be good education. Hence the public shock at Sputnik I. The agonizing reappraisal, however, encompassed only mathematics and the sciences — at least at first. It has taken some time for the public to accept the notion (if it has yet) that an illiterate engineer cannot be a good engineer, that a comic-book culture stifles young physicists no less than young novelists.

It was only after huge sums of money, public and private, had been poured into an effort to make a great leap forward in the sciences that the small scattered voices of the humanities began to be heard. Now such enterprises as the federally supported "Project English" are attempting to do for English what has been done already for mathematics, the creation of a sequential modern curriculum from kindergarten to college. At last there is hope of bringing new vitality into our ancient discipline.

But thus far it is hope more than actuality. What is the outlook for the future? In a general way, textbooks are an indicator of classroom practice. A typical case is the 1964 college catalogue of one of the largest textbook publishers in the United States, Scott, Foresman & Company. Listed here under the heading "English Composition" are no less than eighteen composition texts, some of which are used by scores of thousands of students, year after year. Every one of them is traditional in approach. From the technical as distinct from the pedagogical point of view, there is very little choice among them.

In this same catalogue we find — but under a different heading, "English Language" — *A Short Introduction to English Grammar* by the eminent linguist, James Sledd. The author calls his book a "transitional" text, and says in a note to teachers who use the book that "a number of interim textbooks, not one or two, are needed to prepare for some future text which might enjoy a general success in the English classroom." Sledd's book, as he prophesied, has not swept the college field.

Neither have his predecessors', which make a short list. Among these are Lloyd and Warfel, *American English in its Cultural Setting* (1956); Paul Roberts, *Understanding English* (1958); and the same author's *English Sentences* (1962). Admitting some marginal cases, one could double this catalogue and exhaust it.

For the high school there is Paul Roberts, *Patterns of English,* which is essentially a simpler version of the *Understanding English.* And aimed at the junior high school is Postman, Morine, and Morine, *Discovering Your Language* (1963), a brilliant presentation of modern grammar in a very simple style. It is too soon to know how wide an acceptance this book will have.

When we turn to the lower grades, we find next to nothing. In short, the entry of linguistically oriented grammars into the school system is in the form of an inverted pyramid, with the least where it is needed most.

Like the automobile manufacturers, the textbook houses are Big Business. Both must offer change within continuity. Both must be prepared with some reply to the yearly challenge, "What have you got that's new?" They are too committed to be radical, yet fearful of being left behind. The usual response to this familiar dilemma is compromise. Yet compromise is often impractical, sometimes impossible. You can't design a tight-cornering racing car which is also a gently moving living room for Aunt Tillie. So there is a basic incompatibility between rigorous linguistic analysis and the comfortable old truisms. Nevertheless it is a commonplace now for the publishers to advertise their texts as "structural" or "embodying the best of the new," and so on. The fifth edition of the *Harbrace College Handbook* (1962) — for decades one of the most widely adopted college texts — states in its introduction that "teachers of English composition welcome the new knowledge of grammar that has come from the active linguistic scholarship of the past few decades." For all that, we read in the body of the text that verbs are "indicators of action or a state of being."

The publisher, it seems, is nervously pretending to climb aboard a nonexistent bandwagon without jeopardizing his best-sellers. In short, the fraction of our students which is sent to the bookstore to buy a scientific grammar of English is about the same as the fraction of American automobile buyers which purchases all-out sports cars.

Nonetheless I believe it is inevitable that the new will eventually supplant the old, though the change will not be soon or sudden. Several academic generations will be required to teach enough teachers to teach enough teachers — and for enough of those teachers to rise to positions of administrative power where decisions on curricula are made.

What Makes an Emerson?

And in the meantime there are discouraging difficulties. For instance, the drift of information has been downward, from the graduate school to the grades. Naturally enough, experimental programs and curricular changes have been seeping down in the same direction, despite the fact that the logical way to build a curriculum is from the bottom up.

For three years we conducted a controlled so-called "structural experiment" at the University of Illinois in Chicago. A certain number of sections of freshman rhetoric were taught structural grammar, using the Lloyd-Warfel text, and later the Roberts *Understanding English.* A control group was taught conventionally. Both groups were tested not on their knowledge of grammar, however, but on their improvement in composition. The tests were elaborate and were conducted by disinterested panels of English professors and psychologists. (They of course did not know which group was which.) To the astonishment of some, the two sets of classes came out exactly even. Looked at one way, we didn't do our guinea pigs any harm; from another point of view, we did them no remarkable amount of good.

I was not surprised. I had said at the outset that structural grammar is no panacea; I say it now with authority. If I had it to do over again, I would add a third element to the experiment: a group of students who were taught nothing at all. My prediction is that they would run nose to nose with the others.

We haven't had the nerve to try this experiment, for fear it might put us out of business. My contention is that this has already happened, for we have no more business teaching basic grammar (new or old-fashioned) in colleges than a college mathematics department has teaching the multiplication tables. We never agreed to do it, exactly, but we have taken the job by default. The trouble is that we can't do it. Our students are too old.

We college professors complain that they can't read and write. After a year or more of heroic struggle, we leave them pretty much as we found them. We blame the high schools, the teachers' colleges, our culture — hot rods, TV, comic books, conformity, togetherness — and none of these recriminations teaches a single student how to read and write.

College instructors, at least, have a valid excuse. If they don't teach English composition very well, it is for the excellent reason that they are trying to train the dog after he has grown up. What we have got to do first of all is put grammar back in the grammar school.

At this point I hear the voice of the opposition: "We really taught them in the old days." I agree. A cumbersome and inaccurate system is better than no system at all. In fact, some of those old-fashioned rhetoric teachers did very well indeed.

I am thinking now of Professor Tyrell Channing, who once occupied the chair of Rhetoric at Harvard College. Among his students were R. W. Emerson, Henry Thoreau, James R. Lowell, Edward Everett Hale, Charles Sumner, Oliver Wendell Holmes. . . . He produced some pretty good writers, and he taught them out of Lindley Murray's uncompromisingly Latinical grammar. But Professor Channing did well enough with what he had. Professor Schiller — with all the apparatus of structural linguistics at his disposal — cannot make any comparable claim.

I conclude from this, in all humility, that Professor Channing got a high percentage of Emersons, Thoreaus, and Lowells in his classes, and I do not. Emersons, whether Channing teaches them, or I teach them, turn into Emersons. We can help them sometimes; we probably can't do them too much harm — but we can't make them. They have the language in their bones.

The good student always had sense enough to ignore grammar. His intuition of the language overrode the theory. But what of poor Johnny, who can't read? I'm afraid an occasional reference to a predicate nominative or the subjunctive mood won't help him much. Now that we have undertaken to educate everybody, *we need a grammar that really works.*

Structural linguistics has given us the tools; we have to learn to use them. In the past few years some of us have brought this theoretical information down to the college freshman level. The next step is the high schools — and we have a very thin end of a wedge in there. But the final objective is the grammar schools. When the day comes that we have finally reinstated grammar — a rational grammar — as a body of subject matter in our elementary schools, on that day we college professors will have reconquered our own territory.

FOR DISCUSSION

1. When the "new science of language" erupts into the public consciousness, "much grammatical theory that has been passed from generation to generation in our schools . . . will be laid quietly in our intellectual attic alongside astrology and alchemy." What are some examples of such theory?

2. Is the "new science of language" a new set of facts about language or a new way of looking at the facts that have been there all along?

3. The two "classic" criteria of a sentence: Do you agree that if we subtract something from what is complete, what remains must be less than complete? Professor Schiller says that grammarians would call "I am going to the concert" a complete thought. What would they call "I am going"? Is there a flaw in the logic here?

4. "Pitch, stress, and juncture together provide us with an objective way to distinguish between an incomplete utterance . . . and a complete one. . . ." Explain a possible context in which the expression, "The open door," would have the marks of completeness. Would a sentence in such a context be acceptable in writing?

5. Try creating a short dialogue in which neither speaker uses a "complete" sentence: "Hi, Elsie." "Hi, Tom." "Where to?" "Class." Etc. How far could this exchange be reasonably developed?

6. Professor Schiller suggests that we should become consciously aware of the structural devices by which we expand the half-dozen or so basic sentence patterns. One such pattern is NVN (Dog bites man), in which the first N represents whatever serves as subject, the second N represents whatever serves as the noun complement and V represents whatever serves as predicate. Does NVN describe the structure of the following sentences?

    a. I never saw so many shocking bad hats in my life. (Duke of Wellington)
    b. My idea of heaven is eating pâté de foie gras to the sound of trumpets. (Sydney Smith)
    c. He's simply got the instinct for being unhappy highly developed. (Saki)
    d. Every fool believes what his teachers tell him, and calls his credulity science or morality as confidently as his father called it divine revelation. (Bernard Shaw)
    e. Where there is much desire to learn, there of necessity will be much arguing, much writing, many opinions; for opinion in good men is but knowledge in the making. (John Milton)

7. Professor Schiller suggests that new grammarians do not harry, nag, and pester their students about "trivialities of usage." Are there degrees of triviality? How do you feel about "Who (whom) did you see at the party?" and "I seen (saw) several of my friends there"?

8. Is it true that an "illiterate engineer cannot be a good engineer"?

VOCABULARY: innovator, assumption, criterion, verity, nonsentence, phenomena, bone-structure of language, sanction, moral content, linguistic shibboleths, anathematize, sequential, disinterested panels.

THEME TOPICS: What grammar really is. Trivialities of usage. The new science of language. How to define a sentence. What I know about English. What my textbook didn't tell me about English. Basic criteria for a science of language.

The Speech That Blooms on the Tongue, Tra-La, Has Little to Do with Case

CHARLTON LAIRD

Grammar Is Not a Pigeonhole Desk

The previous chapter has suggested that our traditional grammar and our actual grammar bear little resemblance to each other. Many people to whom this statement may be unwelcome would reply, however, that whatever the theory may be, the practice of modern grammar is sound. They will say that although applying grammatical rules may be a little difficult, because grammar is a difficult and complicated subject, grammatical rules do explain the language. These people are likely to feel that they themselves can explain most of the language, and would be able to explain the remainder if they knew their grammar a little better.

This I have not found to be true. For years I have taught a college course in the nature of language through which have passed a considerable number of persons who were sure that the grammatical rules had been worked out and that they knew these rules. During this time I have maintained a standing challenge to anybody to make the following simple experiment. Pick up a book at random, open to a page at random, and put your finger on a sentence. Then explain the meaning of the sentence by conventional grammar. I have never found anyone who could do so. Some day I will. Some day I will lose because somebody will be lucky enough to put his finger on *Ouch!* He will say "Interjection," and I shall have lost, at least by his rules of the game. In reality, to explain the grammar of *Ouch!* we should need to examine adjacent sentences, but the conventional grammarian would never concede I was being fair in expecting that of him, and accordingly I should lose. As yet, however, this has not happened, and nobody has explained a sentence for me on the basis of Latin grammar.

People who think the conventional grammar makes sense usually do so because they are not examining the grammar at all. They are doing one, and usually all, of the following:

(1) They restrict their examination of language to sentences made up to fit rules, and they do not examine these sentences further than to notice that

they do fit. This of course is nonsense. If grammar will not explain ordinary prose — to say nothing of sentences made up *not* to fit the rules — there is something wrong with the grammatical rules.

(2) They expect to save any rule which gets into trouble by assuming, in any example which will not fit it, that additional words or a different order is "understood." The sentence is accordingly changed so that it does fit. Let us see how this works. Since I have recommended taking a sentence at random from a book, I will take one from a book which happens to be lying open on the table. It is Josephine Tey's *The Daughter of Time* (New York; Macmillan, 1952), opened to page 80. Running my eye down the page — since I am now looking for an example, not trying to explain any piece of prose — I find that one character says "Oh!" unexpectedly, and the hero asks, "What was the 'Oh' for?" Let us endeavor to parse this last sentence. *What* is an interrogative pronoun, subject of the sentence. *Was* is the verb. *Oh* is the complement. What is *for?* The *New International Dictionary,* second edition, which embodies a good compendium of conventional but relatively liberal grammatical opinion, gives *for* as a conjunction or a preposition. (Lest I be accused of treating dictionaries unkindly — and I am very far from wishing to do so — let me say once for all that I am citing dictionaries partly for my own convenience, and partly because the makers of widely used dictionaries have generally been more liberal than the makers of widely used grammars.) But *for* in this sentence cannot be a conjunction; it has nothing to join. It cannot be a preposition; it has no object.

Obviously, *for* must be something. Accordingly a conventional grammarian would be likely to start by changing the sentence to another which is "understood." He might substitute "What was the 'Oh' intended for?" *Intended* can modify *oh,* and if *for* can be an adverb, it can modify the past participle *intended.* This is possible, for although the *New International* does not enter *for* as an adverb, doubtless some other authority does so. Or the grammarian could change the sentence to "For what was the 'Oh intended?" *For* has now become a preposition. Other additions are possible, for instance, "For what remark which you suppressed was the 'Oh' intended to substitute?" and "What does the 'Oh' stand for?" The conventional grammarian also changes the order, although, if order is the basis of English grammar, one wonders what right he has to change it. He might say that the sentence is understood to be "For what was the 'Oh'?" No one would talk such nonsense, but let us pass that. Is *for what* the subject? Obviously not, for whatever a *for what* is, it is not and was not an *Oh.* Nor does the sentence improve if we try to make *for what* the complement and *Oh* the subject. Can *for what* be a modifier of *is?* Surely not; it does not qualify the is-ness of *is.* Unless *is* means *serves, substitutes,* or something else it does not mean, *for what* can scarcely modify it.

This sort of grammatical juggling might warrant several comments, but here are two obvious ones. First, these additions of words and changes of structure are not "understood." If they are understood, how are we to know which of the various possibilities we are to understand? I suspect that Miss Tey would have been outraged were we to suggest that she had meant any of these words or structures to be understood in place of the words and structure she used.

Now for a second comment. If we are to discuss the grammar of this sentence, we must discuss the sentence as it is. Obviously it has grammar. It was written by a reputable writer; it is put into the mouth of a presumably well-educated man and one who is highly intelligent; the man is at the moment discussing a subject seriously. Certainly Miss Tey thought the sentence had grammar when she wrote it. Any competent reader of English would know at once what the sentence was intended to mean. Therefore, Miss Tey is right; the sentence has grammar, and any grammatical statement which will not account for "What was the 'Oh' for?" without changing it in any particular is an inadequate statement. Our grammatical rules, not Miss Tey's grammar, are at fault.

(3) The people who defend conventional grammar are not concerned with understanding the grammar but with putting words into pigeonholes. This is a harmless diversion, but it has little to do with English grammar, particularly since there are no pigeonholes into which grammatical concepts in English can be assorted so as to form anything like a classification. On what basis does the conventionally accepted grammar classify words? Not on form. Most of the so-called parts of speech have no connection with form, and those which do have some have not much. Adverbs end in -*ly*, but *fast* and *well* are adverbs (unless you call them verbs, modifiers, or adjectives, which of course they can be) and *homely* and *family* are supposedly not adverbs, although they end in -*ly*. Neither does traditional grammar classify words on meaning. Supposedly nouns are determined on meaning, and within limits the division is valid, but the presence of nouns determined by meaning among other pigeonholed objects determined on other bases only confuses the classification. And last, the conventional grammarians do not use function as a means of classification, although this is the most commonly supposed basis. Most of the supposed functions do not exist, and those that do, do not fit the categories.

For instance, where does the verb in the following sentence begin and end?

You'd better start doing something about getting the tire blown up. You is the subject. *Had* (contracted to '*d*) is part of the verb, but part of what verb: *had start, had doing, had start doing?* None of these makes any sense. Unless the verb includes *better* the sentence has no meaning, and yet no conventional grammarian can admit, and no conventional authority I have consulted does admit, that *better* in this sense can be part of a verb. Is the verb *better start doing?* This still has no meaning. *Had better start doing some-*

thing has meaning, but not the meaning of the sentence. Clearly the verb must include *doing something about;* it must also include *getting,* and *blown up* if the words in the sentence are to have their meanings. *The tire,* by all conventional statements, is a noun with its article and presumably is a complement. But observe what happens if we remove it: *You'd better start doing something about getting blown up.* Can we say that even a noun is not somehow involved in the verb if the entire meaning of the verb changes when the noun is removed? Pretty clearly we have one idea which develops all the way from *had* to *blown up;* it cannot be broken up into little chunks which can be filed in pigeonholes unless we are willing to ignore the meanings of words and the whole meaning of the sentence.

But perhaps this sentence is exceptional. Suppose we try *Grandma was peeling apples by the window.* This is certainly a simple, ordinary sentence which should fit conventional rules if any sentence will. The conventional statement would be as follows: *Grandma* is a noun, subject of the verb; *was peeling* is a verb made up of present participle *peeling* and auxiliary *was; apples* is a noun, direct object of *peeling; by the window* is an adverbial prepositional phrase, made up of the preposition *by,* which introduces the object of the preposition, *window,* modified by the article *the,* and the whole prepositional phrase modifies the verb, *was peeling.* This sounds objective, learned, even final. But does it make much sense? *By the window* is said to modify *was peeling,* but it must also modify *grandma* and *apples.* They must all have been by the window or grandma could not have been peeling the apples. But to say this is heresy, for *grandma* and *apples* are both nouns, and modifiers of nouns are adjectives, not adverbs. That is, it is completely impossible to decide whether *by the window* is an adjective or an adverb. It is a modifier, but pretty clearly it modifies the whole sentence. Now for *apples;* it is said to be the direct object, because it receives the action of the verb. But it also determines the action of the verb. Remove it, and the action becomes quite different: *Grandma was peeling by the window.* Grandma has now become scrofulitic, or perhaps, like Gypsy Rose Lee, ecdysiastic.

And these, of course, are not the difficult grammatical categories. They are the common ones. Even a concept like *pronoun* will stand no analysis. "A pronoun is a word used in place of a noun." Consider the following:

> Johnny is my nephew.
> He is a brat.

Conventional grammarians would say something like this of the pair of sentences: *He* in the second sentence is a pronoun because it is used in the place of the noun *Johnny.* To simplify:

> *Johnny = he* ∴ *he* is a pronoun because it is used in place of *Johnny,*
>   a noun.

Now substitute another word for *he* in the second sentence.

Johnny is my nephew.
The boy is a brat.

Follow the some procedure with this pair of sentences.

Johnny = *the boy* ∴ *boy* is a pronoun because it is used in place of
Johnny, a noun.

If *boy* is a pronoun, and it must be, by the logic of conventional grammar,
then what has become of the concept of nouns and pronouns? Why cannot
all nouns be pronouns?

For is called a co-ordinating conjunction and *because* a sub-ordinating
conjunction, but are they not identical in use in *I honor Brutus, for he is
an honorable man; I honor Brutus because he is an honorable man?*

And so it goes. Any careful examination of the conventional categories of
the parts of speech will reveal that they mean very little; they do not
include what they should include, they do not exclude all words outside
their category, and they do not reveal the functioning of Modern English.
Usually they are unworkable, and when they can be made to include the
words we use, most of them tell very little about what gives the words
meaning. In short, the conventional grammar is not much more revealing
of the actual grammar of Modern English than one would expect it to be
when we consider what has happened: The grammar of an inflected language, Latin, has been forced upon a distributive language, English, which
has been wrenched in an attempt to make it fit the alien grammar. A large
number of intelligent people have labored for generations to make sense
of this forced wrenching, this set of rules which is fundamentally wrong.
That the conventional grammar makes as much sense as it does is a high
tribute to the patience and intelligence of our grammarians.

The Grammatical System We Do Not Have

According to the traditionalists, the core of our grammar is nouns which
have gender, number, and case, and verbs which occur in certain tenses
and moods. Let us examine these assumptions. Most nouns have number,
expressed in form; except for certain borrowed words and some words which
retain archaic characteristics, the plural is formed by adding -*s*, or -*es*. We
have developed other plurals by distributive means (*many a man, person
after person*), but on the whole, declension provides number in the noun.

Of gender there remain scraps, such fragmentary scraps that most Americans do not know what gender is. With us it has become a synonym for
sex, which it is not, because distinction on the basis of sex is the only bit
of gender we have left, and that appears only in the third person singular
pronoun (*he, she, it*), unless one excepts forms like *comedian, comedienne,
actor, actress.* Gender is a much broader concept, which can include any

sort of classification of objects, and in Indo-European must have included a considerable number, distinguished by different sets of case endings. So in other languages. Certain North American Indian languages have gender which requires with any noun the use of syllables which indicate one of the following: that the object mentioned is in the immediate possession of the speaker; that it is not in his possession, but can be reached by sight, sound, smell, or touch; that it is not within reach of his senses, but is supposedly not far away; that it is at a remote or unknown place.

Of case, also, almost nothing remains. Of the seven cases in Indo-European, only one, the so-called possessive, can now be recognized. It is steadily being replaced by forms with *of*, and of course it often does not indicate possession. Consider the following:

> Please keep *your* seats while I introduce *your* candidate for sheriff. From *his* earliest childhood he has been a staunch supporter of *our* party; he has been a noble servant of *his* constituents in *his* previous offices, promoting *their* best interests in *our* country as, prior to *his* entry into public life, he promoted the interests of *his* company, distributing *their* products in *your* community.

The italicized words are all "possessives," although most of them do not show possession in the capitalistic sense. *Your seats* are yours only because you are sitting in them; they belong to whoever owns the hall. *Your candidate* is yours only in the sense that you are expected to vote for him. *His childhood* is his only in the sense that he experienced it. *Our party* is ours not because it belongs to us but because we belong to it. The candidate did not own *his offices, his constituents,* or *his company;* and the company, although it owns its products, would still call them *their* products after they have sold them.

Such are the remnants of declension in the noun. Most of the relationships within a sentence which involve names for things are now made clear by order or by relationship words. Anybody who tries to talk about nouns on the conventional basis is not talking about much.

With verbs the situation is no better. The following are the commonly recognized tenses:

Present:	I drive
Past:	I drove
Perfect:	I have driven
Pluperfect:	I had driven
Future:	I shall (will) drive
Future Perfect:	I shall (will) have driven

But these are not the tenses they profess to be. *I drive* is not simple present. No one would say, "I drive an automobile," meaning that he is now at this moment in process of operating a vehicle. If he wishes to say that he would probably say "I'm driving an automobile," which is supposedly a progressive form. One says, "I drive to work every morning," thereby implying a past, a present, and a probable future. Similarly, the past is not usually the past, and the perfect is not usually the perfect since it does not represent a "perfected" or completed action. The past is most commonly used for the perfect (I *drove* into the yard and *stopped* at the front door), and the perfect is commonly used for the past (I *have driven* all my life; I *have been driving* all my life). Curiously enough, the pluperfect is actually used for the pluperfect. The future can be the future, but the approved form *I shall drive* is certainly less common than *I'm going to drive*. The future perfect also exists, but is a rare form which might well be removed from a simplified paradigm in favor of some of the common uses of the verb which we do not recognize.

The supposed uses of the verb, then, are not the uses they are supposed to be. But do these forms give us any notion of the English verb, even though the uses are misnamed? They do not. Consider, for instance, the following list, which by no means exhausts the forms which we use constantly as futures:

> I shall (will) drive (I'll drive)
> I am going to drive (I'm going to drive)
> I drive tomorrow
> I am just about to drive
> I am just going to drive
> I am off to drive
> I am on the verge of driving
> I am now in a position to drive
> I expect to drive
> I am considering driving
> I am scheduled to drive
> I am determined (have decided) to drive
> This requires me to drive
> It would seem best to drive
> I am bound to drive
> There will be the drive
> And then there is the drive
> I have to plan on driving

This is only a beginning. One might notice that although the simple present *I drive* is not a simple present, it can be a future. One might notice, also, something about the nature of the future tense. The future is always uncertain, and Modern English, since it builds its verbs mainly by distributive means, is uncommonly rich in devices for expressing degrees of future uncertainty. The list above includes futures which allow for doubt in the speaker's mind and for the unpredictability of events. The following forms provide for a still wider latitude of uncertainty:

If I am able to drive
If I could drive
If I were able to drive
If only I were able to drive
Could I drive
Were I in a position to drive
If I could manage to drive
If it were possible to drive
If the road were drivable
I should like to drive
I should like to be able to drive
I wish I could drive
If I were in a position to drive
If the driving conditions were other than they are

The list omits many of the strongly subjunctive forms, expressing a wish, like *Oh, that I could drive;* the passive forms like *I'm going to be driven, I am about to be driven,* and the imperative and interrogative forms.

Furthermore, we have ignored the concept of aspect, one of the most important qualities of a verb, but one so neglected that until recently it did not even appear in dictionaries as a grammatical term, and it still does not occur in many grammars. It might be called the attitude of the speaker toward time. For instance, *I keep falling into mudholes; I am forever getting into debt* are iterative; they imply a repeated action. *I walk to work whenever it is not raining* and *Rain usually accompanies a moist front of air* imply habitual or routine actions. *I am just going to start making payments* is inceptive, implying beginning and *I have only now finished the inventory* is conclusive, implying ending. By combining aspects with tense and mood, and by combining the resulting verbs with modifiers and complements, verb forms can be devised which permit extremely exact expression: *We used to go to the beach every Sunday, but this summer we haven't felt like bothering except now and then.*

The English verb, and especially the American verb, can become extremely complicated. Early in this chapter we observed a verb which seemed to be so amorphous that it was taking unto itself various supposed nouns, pronouns, and modifiers. But let us not complicate the situation so much. Let us now use a verb which is made of nothing but recognizable verb forms:

I should like to go
I should like to be able to go
I should have liked to be able to go

These are acceptable forms. Furthermore, they represent slight variations in meaning, so that the writer of English can vary his statement with extreme exactitude if he wishes. But what are the names of these forms? Do we have paradigms for them?

On the whole, no. No book which has gained any currency contains anything like a description of the Modern American verb. If anyone has as yet made a genuinely serious effort to collect and classify the forms of the American verb I have not heard of it — although I admit that this may be going on and I do not know about it. There is a good beginning in Harold Whitehall's *The Structural Essentials of Written English* (Indiana University, 1951), and Professor Whitehall would be the first to point out that his paradigms provide only a beginning. Margaret Bryant's *A Functional English Grammar* (Boston, 1945) contains a sound survey of verbs. I say with admiration that much excellent work in the study of modern language including grammar, is now going forward in this country. The fact remains, however, that as yet nothing like a full description of Modern English has been published; and only recently have we begun to become aware of the fantastic depths of our ignorance.

Grammar is Slippery Stuff

Grammar is somewhat like a freshly caught fish. Take it in your hand to wash it in the stream; two wriggles, and it is gone. So with grammar, and I speak as one who has gone through the chastening experience of asking himself quite soberly what our grammar is. I have tried to divest myself of old grammatical prejudices beaten into me at an early age; and acquired later with the profligate expenditure of midnight electricity. I have at times thought I had drawn from the deceptive grammatical waters a fine, trim, grammatical fact. I grasped him firmly by the tail, and meant only to clean him up a bit. Two flips, and he was gone.

> *If language is not correct, then what is said is not what is meant; if what is said is not meant, then what ought to be done remains undone; if this remains undone, morals and arts will deteriorate; if morals and arts deteriorate, justice will go astray; if justice goes astray, the people will stand about in helpless confusion. Hence there must be no arbitrariness in what is said. This matters above everything.*
>
> CONFUCIUS

And thus it is in all humility that I point out that we have not as yet described our grammar. Grammatical concepts are not easy to deal with. Grammatical phenomena are extremely numerous, extremely varied, and bafflingly shifty. Part of our trouble is that we have no precedent. Except English, Chinese is the only great distributive language, and the Chinese have apparently done no more than we to understand their grammar. At least, if there is any adequate Chinese analyses of language it has gained no currency in this country to provide students of English with anything like a pilot job. Apparently, if we are to understand our language we shall have to think, and observe, and argue our way through the exploration ourselves.

We have a start. In fact, we have an excellent start. All grammarians now concede — even those who still think as though Latin grammar is the basis of grammar — that the grammar of any language must be derived from the language itself. All grammarians now concede that the source of English grammar is to be sought in Anglo-Saxon, and in the changes which the English language has undergone since Anglo-Saxon days. They all concede that in studying language we must take account of both written and oral language, and that of the two, oral language is probably the more significant, although the more difficult, to deal with.

It is hard to see how this new understanding of the revealing ways to work with language can be wrong. It is also hard to see how any work on the old basis, a basis that is fundamentally wrong, could produce entirely valid conclusions. But we have now changed our approach to one which seems basically right. We now think we know how to work with English grammar and we are working.

We have acquired this new approach neither easily nor quickly. Apparently the new attitudes grew out of the study of Anglo-Saxon and Middle English. It is interesting to observe that linguistic truth came as a sort of handmaiden of literary love. Early English was not much studied before the last century; *Beowulf* was not known, and nobody knew how to pronounce Chaucer's English. Only a smattering of early writing had been printed, and that smattering mostly in poor editions. Even universities did not teach the study of early English languages; Latin, Greek, and Hebrew were either the marks of a gentleman or the tools of a divine, but relatively few scholars bothered with Anglo-Saxon or Middle English. Partly the change came about through the Romantic Movement, which made old things, especially bizarre, primitive, and "Gothic" things popular. Partly the change is due to German philologists who started studying language, especially all dialects of Germanic language, with patience, competence, and objectivity.

Then love took a hand. Scholars discovered that the ancient and medieval Germanic writings constituted an entrancing body of literature. *Beowulf*, for instance, appeared no longer as the crude product of a barbarous time, but as a highly wrought, powerful, and in some ways sophisticated poem. Chaucer was obviously a literary craftsman of very high order, as well as one of the most engaging human beings who ever harbored a sly smile. Since *Beowulf* and the *Canterbury Tales* had become works of art, their grammar became subjects of scholarly study. Gradually, students who had gone to the older literatures for love of the literatures saw in these works evidence that English grammar was a native thing, that it existed before Anglo-Saxons knew anything about Latin, and that English seemed quite capable of living on its own resources, using a grammar that differed sharply from Latin.

While all this was going on, a philosophical background was growing for a new linguistic approach. Brilliant grammatical thinkers, mostly German and Scandinavian, had broken loose from traditional limitations. The whole concept of language families, which appeared with the knowledge of the relationships of languages like Sanskrit, Gothic, Greek, and Anglo-Saxon, suggested that grammatical notions needed revision, that linguistic truths might be much broader, deeper, and more significant than the older writers upon language had been aware. Men like Bopp and Rask, Max Müller and the Grimm brothers produced most fruitful researches and most pregnant thought, although, as a matter of course, these men were wrong much of the time. Their conclusions have required revision. Nevertheless, they shook Western linguistic study loose from its old classic complacency, and in a general way they laid out the lines which modern thinking about language has followed.

The New Look in Language

This is not the place for a history of modern linguistic thought. Among the results of this growth, however, are bodies of careful linguistic study, and in this century several efforts to approach Modern English grammar objectively. The Danish grammarian, Otto Jespersen, endeavored to salvage the terminology of conventional grammar while superimposing upon it a system of ranks in words. He started with the noun as the name of an object, and a use as subject or complement; this noun became primary, its modifiers secondary, and the modifiers of modifiers tertiary. Thus in the combination, *slightly aching head*, *head* is primary, *aching* is secondary, and *slightly* is tertiary. This ranking he maintained in the face of the older conceptions; *father* would normally be considered a noun, but in the combination *father's aching head*, *father's* would become tertiary. There is much to be said for this system; it certainly has some logic behind it. But it provides us with two schemes of grammar, where one is baffling us already, and it has never received the subsequent careful working over which would be required in a satisfactory grammatical statement — assuming that a statement could be worked out with this system.

Some grammarians, recognizing that speakers of English make themselves understood by naming a subject and then modifying this subject, have tried to reduce the parts of speech to two, subjects and modifiers. This would seem to be simplicity itself, and certainly as far as it goes it is hard to find out what is wrong with it. In the sentence *John runs, runs*, although it is commonly called a verb, certainly modifies our conception of John. Or expand the sentence as follows: *John, being as stubborn as a mule and as conceited as a peacock, runs every four years for President of the United States, having himself nominated by the No-Cigarettes-for-Women Party*. We still have

John, the subject, modified in our minds by all that comes after it. But assuming that this description is valid, does it help much? In effect, this approach provides us with a new term for the old grammatical tenet that a sentence is made up of a subject and a predicate. If we accept this statement, the fact remains that the modifier (or predicate) can be an extremely complicated agglomeration, which would seem to need some breaking down before we can hope to grasp it very well.

I. A. Richards suggested that the study of grammar be based entirely upon meaning, but understandably did not care to spend the remainder of his life trying to do so. No systematic study of English grammar has been founded exclusively upon meaning, but since grammarians have usually assumed that the "use" of a word — that is, its function in composition — was to reveal meaning, the whole idea of function rests upon meaning. Other grammarians have forsaken both meaning and function as a starting point for the study of English grammar, and have tried to study it upon the basis of speech rhythm, upon word patterns, or upon something which can be approached with relative objectivity. Studying meaning objectively has proved very difficult, because meaning is highly varied and shifting.

The most elaborate recent attempt is embodied in *The Structure of English* by Professor Charles Carpenter Fries of the University of Michigan. Professor Fries has long been an independent thinker and indefatigable worker in language. During the late war he was able to acquire some fifty hours of transcribed conversation. By studying the conversation he constructed a theory of grammar which makes but limited use of meaning. He relies upon sentence patterns and accepts as a part of speech any word which can fall into a certain position within the pattern. The results are extremely interesting, and they will certainly be worked over carefully by other grammarians. Obviously Professor Fries is right about many things, and his book will deeply affect our thinking about Modern English grammar. Whether the book will be accepted as the standard statement no one can as yet safely predict — it was published while this manuscript was being written — but it suggests the degree to which modern grammar is at last being studied, in and for itself.

Another interesting recent treatment appears in *The Structural Essentials of Written English* mentioned above. Professor Whitehall employs sentence pattern, as indeed anyone must, for if modern grammar has demonstrated one fact it is that a distributive grammar relies upon patterns of words as an inflected language relies upon forms of words. He also makes use of the phoneme, a relatively recent concept in language, which may be defined as all the sound within a spread of sound which hearers would recognize as part of the same word. For instance, the [l] in *lean* differs from the [l] in *hill,* but the two sounds constitute one phoneme because they convey one meaning. Similarly, some speakers will pronounce the [ɪ] in *hill* lower or farther back than other speakers do, but so long as this vowel does not go so far back or down that the word becomes *hull* or *hell*, all of these sounds of [ɪ] constitute one phoneme. In his use of pattern and the phoneme Professor Whitehall is modern, although not startlingly new; but in resting grammar and grammatical analysis mainly upon the rising and falling tone of the spoken voice, he is pioneering. He asserts (the italics are his): "Remember that *English sentences are not sentences merely by virtue of the kind of constructions they represent or the kind of words they contain; they are sentences because they possess one or other of the final tone patterns characteristic of English.*"

At this writing Modern English grammar is a lively if confusing subject. We do not understand our grammar, but apparently it has become something distinctive enough to intrigue our interest and warrant our understanding. And we may yet solve its mystery.

FOR DISCUSSION

1. What are three procedures of conventional grammarians?

2. Naming the parts of speech in a sentence still does not explain how the sentence conveys its meaning. Why not?

3. Does the possessive case in English always indicate possession?

4. In language "most Americans do not know what gender is." Do you know? What about gender in Spanish, French, German?

5. When we want to express a future action, do we have to use a future tense form? If not, what are some of the forms we could use?

6. What are some of the basic beliefs of modern grammarians?

7. What are some of the concepts in the new look in language?

VOCABULARY: ecdysiastic (Mencken in "Scented Words" alludes to his invention of this word), inflected, traditionalist, distributive, inceptive, amorphous, precedent, bizarre, philologist, complacency, tertiary.

THEME TOPICS: Who knows grammar? English is not Latin. How English expresses plurality. Is the present tense really present? The future tense in English.

The "What" and the "Way"

DWIGHT L. BOLINGER

The primacy of the *spoken* language is one of those re-orientations of thinking comparable to the shift from a geocentric to a heliocentric system, or that from creation to evolution. Once the shift is made, everything takes on a different perspective. The inconsistencies that forced the change of view are automatically solved, and it seems impossible that anyone could have believed in the former error.

Like all views that are grounded in popular belief, however, the ramifications of the error are legion, and have to be rooted out one by one. It was not enough to say, once and for all, that the sun was central; it had to be pointed out, patiently, over whole generations, that the earth was only one of many planets; that the earth rotates; that the year is determined by the earth's revolution about the sun — and a hundred other facts as readily deduced from the one grand thesis but not obvious until separately observed and driven home.

The ramifications of written language as "the" language are just as numerous and may take as long to eradicate. It follows, from the main thesis of the primacy of the spoken language, that the distinction of "correct" language, so far as it depends on most-written forms, is unfounded; that outworn spellings are pernicious; that etymological word-divisions (*all right* versus *altogether*) need to be revised; but each of these and manifold others have to be tackled separately.

One such bit of folk-lore is that which is often expressed in the phrase "What you say is all right, but I don't like the way you say it." It is obvious from the main thesis that in any sound brought forth by the human vocal mechanism there is no part that can be singled out as a "thing" while other parts are merely ways of doing that thing. All is either thing or manner.

What one encounters here is a reflexion, back into the spoken language, of the superstition of the importance of written language: the traditionally *writable* features of the sound are regarded as more substantial than the features for which the letter signs are not used. They may be variously shown on the page, of course; italics, punctuation marks, and even (as in Mark Twain's setting of the elocutionary speech) wavy lines; but the "words themselves" are always conceived of as the firm substratum, with the residue as ephemeral and relatively unimportant ornamentation.

From *Language Learning*, 2.86-88 (July-September, 1949). Reprinted by permission of the author.

This ramification, the false dichotomy of "what" versus "way," has enough basis in fact to keep it going beyond the span of life of the other ramifications of the error. Certain features of sound are more important in most situations, than others. The features that distinguish *wheat* from *oats* are more urgent as a rule than those which distinguish oats-liked from oats-disliked; the features that distinguish *ear* from *year* in some dialects may cause difficulties of communication that compel us to note them, but the variations of resonance that distinguish haughty from humble speech are left to the novelist, and find no place in public documents or courts of law. In addition, the disability of not having all features of the sound writable has been partly overcome by other means: descriptive terms (the *haughty* and *humble* just used), circumlocution, etc., so that we are frequently unaware of the insufficiency of the written formula; there is even a kind of vested interest in these halting substitutes.

It takes little imagination, however, to discover situations in which the supposed unimportance of the "way" becomes damaging. In quoting another's discourse, for example, it becomes possible for a speaker to distort completely the meaning of the original, and still imagine that he is reporting truthfully. A lawyer confronts a defendant with the question: Did you or did you not say to Mr. W. on this occasion, "I could kill you for what you've done"? How many wretches have had to answer "yes" to such a question, and suffered for it, when the words were actually uttered upon an intonation profile that clearly implied (and could never imply anything else) that the action set forth was precisely one which the speaker did not intend to carry out? How pervasive is the error one sees in this very exposition where I fall into the use of *implies* rather than *says;* for *to say* has usually the connotation of that "what," and *to imply* has that of the "way."

So much, too, for the question of truth and falsity. The "yes" of the courtroom scene was a lying answer, though the victim was not clever enough to see it. Truth and falsehood as a moral issue have been made to adhere completely to the "what" of language. Any one of us can recall a dozen anecdotes or episodes in our own lives when we have cleverly "evaded" an embarrassing question, and have thereby saved ourselves an attack of conscience; while few but can recall at least one or two instances when we have been cornered, have said *yes* when the situation demanded *no,* and have gone about with inner gnawings afterward. If language had been completely described, and if our sense of guilt were made to adhere to the whole of it, there would be very few answers that could be regarded as truthful unless they gave the precise information that the questioner wanted; there would still be mistakes, for people can misunderstand, but if the intent of a question were understood the person questioned would have to regard it as adequately symbolized and answer accordingly. Instead, we go childishly about our verbal gymnastics with the "what," and feel no remorse at lying with every element of language except our words. As with *imply* and *say,* the what-way dichotomy is reflected in this sphere as *to evade* and *to lie*.

And what of the language teachers, who ought to know the medium they deal with? I will instance a pet of theirs, the well-known Misplaced Modifier. To use *I just want one* (they say) is wrong, because *just* modifies *one* and accordingly should go next to it. Now this prescriptive argument supposes that the hearer will misunderstand when the *just* is misplaced; the "what," the words, are spatially conceived, and all discriminative elements of speech except those of temporal order are ignored. Actually no such expression, if naturally spoken, would ever be misunderstood, for the intonation, part of the "way," clearly shows that *just* is the companion of *one*.

The importance, socially, of the "unimportant" features may be gauged by the fact that the majority of our emotional misunderstandings as a result of misquoting are probably traceable not to misquoted words but to misquoted "ways." With the "way" the reporter is apt to feel that he may do as he pleases, so that communication features such as gesture and intonation get completely out of control.

In short, the Virginian had the correct measures of the oneness of the communication-complex when he said, "When you call me that, smile."

FOR DISCUSSION

1. Linguists regard speech as primary, writing as secondary. Is this valid? What arguments can you advance to support the linguists?

2. Bolinger says that learning to recognize the primacy of speech is comparable to "the shift from a geocentric to a heliocentric system." Why is it so important?

3. What are some of the ramifications of the erroneous notion that spelling is primary? Would a belief that we should pronounce words as we spell be one of them? What should be our guide to pronunciation, if not spelling? On what basis would you condemn or justify the spelling *alright*? Does your dictionary permit the spelling *alright*? Does the primacy of speech suggest any principles to guide us in choosing (in writing) between such word forms as *who-whom, shall-will, farther-further, less-fewer, can-may*? Consult your dictionary and a usage dictionary on these items.

VOCABULARY: re-orientation, geocentric, heliocentric, perspective, ramification, deduce, one grand thesis, etymological, folk-lore, elocutionary, ephemeral, false dichotomy, dialect, resonance, circumlocution, prescriptive argument, spatially conceived, discriminative elements of speech, intonation.

THEME TOPICS: Speech comes first. The relation of writing to speech. Should we spell as we pronounce or pronounce as we spell? Gestures can qualify meaning. Watch your tone of voice. Writing is two removes from reality — a symbol of a symbol.

How to Talk to a Martian

G. R. SHIPMAN

Of all the stock characters in science fiction that I wish the BEM's[1] would eat alive, number one on my list is the Telepathic Martian.

You know the one I mean. His spaceship lands in an Iowa cornfield one hot July day. The nation panics; a frantic Defense Department throws a cordon around the farm; the yokels take to the woods; reporters and TV cameramen trample on inquisitive scientists; the Chicago *Tribune* gets out an extra to warn us that the whole thing is probably a Fair Deal plot. Then, as the world and his wife sit with their ears glued to the radio, the hatches of the spaceship open and the Martian emerges to tell us he wishes us well and only wants to save our civilization from self-destruction.

In American English, no less. By some miracle the authors never explain, this visitor from outer space can not only project his thoughts into human brains, but can force them to rearrange his extraterrestrial ideas into the patterns of American speech. Every listener in the surrounding throng hears the Martian's off-the-cuff eloquence in the same way, and not even the most ignorant bystander ever translates a Martian thoughtwave by an "ain't" or a "he don't." Given the enormous cultural differences between Martians and ourselves, you'd expect large blank spots where earthly languages have no equivalents for Martian concepts. But no — we always read their signals one hundred per cent.

Of course there are variations of the telepathy theme. Sometimes the Martian has a walkie-talkie translating machine that picks up his native garglings, whirls them around for a few microseconds in its electronic insides, and sends them out of its loudspeaker in pure United States. Sometimes he seems to have learned English by reading our lips with a super-super-telescope. There may be still other gimmicks I haven't read about. But I have yet to see a science-fiction opus that meets this problem of communication across cultural boundaries head-on and tries to solve it by extrapolating from our present techniques.

The fact is, most science-fiction writers don't know such techniques exist.

From *Astounding Science Fiction,* Vol. LII, No. 2, October, 1953. Reprinted by permission of R. M. and Mary Shipman.

[1] [A BEM is a "bug-eyed-monster," science-fiction slang for one of the weird monsters invented by a writer more interested in adventure than in legitimate extrapolation from current theories. *Eds.*]

At that, the writers are no more naive than most of the educated public. In this century descriptive linguistics has made such strides that we can already crack the code of extraterrestrial speech; yet the average intelligent reader has barely heard of the science. People who keep up with modern chemistry and physics can still talk about the study of language in terms handed down from the days when astrology was considered an exact science. They still refer to the study of language as "philology," and have a vague idea that philologists look for "roots" the way a pig looks for truffles. Well, calling the modern science of linguistics "philology" is like calling atomic physics "natural philosophy" — a subject my grandmother studied, without apparatus, when she was a student at a "female seminary."

Fortunately, the linguists haven't waited to be appreciated. They have simply gone on working while the world choked itself in yards and yards of cultural lag, and one of the reasons we won the war was that they knew their business. Thanks to them, GI's in many remote jungles and on lonely atolls learned exotic languages fast — and were really able to talk to the natives. The technique of learning strange tongues that the linguists had worked out with American Indians was equally applicable to Chinese or Russian, and brought results much sooner than traditional methods.

Some of these same linguists are also anthropologists, for language is the indispensable key to an alien culture. When the time comes to establish communication with Martians or any other race from Outside, the linguistic anthropologists will be the ones who forge the link. If beings from another planet use speech or any recognizable analogue, they will be able to decode it with the same techniques they have used to decode Salish or Navaho or Kwakiutl. (Those are American languages, by the way.)

The linguist doesn't need any impressive apparatus — only a pencil and paper, and perhaps a tape recorder. He gets along faster if he has an "informant," a native speaker of the language who has some other language in common with the linguist. There won't be any such informants aboard the spaceship, but, as we'll see later, it's possible to learn Martian without them.

When a linguist works with a human informant, he begins by asking him how to say things like "Good morning," "How do you feel?" "What color is that apple?" and "I'm sure it's going to rain tonight." He writes the answers down in the most exact phonetic transcription possible, with a translation of each phrase. He does this even if the language has an alphabet of its own. Most languages, however, are unwritten, and phonetic script is the only way to record them.

The first few jottings in the linguist's notebook are simply odds and ends, as meaningless as ten answers in a Gallup poll. But as the entries pile up, patterns begin to emerge. By skillful questioning, the linguist wheedles more sentences out of the informant to confirm his hunches about the pattern. After he has filled a good many pages, he has enough material to peel out all the verb-forms, variations of the noun, and relevant categories. He is almost ready to write a grammar.

Not quite ready, though; he first has to be sure of the sound-system. Sounds are usually the first units to be analyzed, because they are the smallest elements into which human speech can be divided, and because all the rest of his work depends on his understanding of how they pattern. Though the number of noises that human tongues, lips, and larynges can make is almost infinite, no one language ever uses more than a small fraction of them. Moreover, no naïve speaker is aware of all the sounds he makes. He is conscious only of *classes of sounds* that are functional in his language.

To show what "functional" means, let's turn the tables and imagine that a Martian linguist is trying to get the hang of certain American English consonants. His ears and sound spectrograph have recorded a rather large variety of noises made by closing the lips. He might arrange some words containing these sounds into a table like this:

	1	2	3
Voiceless	*pat*	*spat*	*tap*
Voiced	*bat*	——	*tab*

All these words contain sounds called *labial stops*, made by closing the lips and checking the breath-stream for an instant. The stops in the first, or "voiceless" row, are made with the vocal cords relaxed. Those in the "voiced" row are made while the vocal cords are tense and vibrating. Our conventional way of writing these sounds is with the letters *p* and *b*.

We write the labial stops in *pat, spat,* and *tap* with the same letter, but to the Martians and their instruments they will not sound exactly alike. The p_1 of *pat* has a puff of breath after the lip-closure that isn't heard after the p_2 of *spat*. If you doubt it, light a match, hold it near your lips, and say the two words, in a low voice but aloud. The flame flickers after the *p* of *pat*, doesn't it? Perhaps it even goes out. In *tap* we have another variety, p_3, which is made by closing the lips and banking up the breath without a following explosion. This is an *imploded* stop.

In the "voiced" row the Martians can find only two words; English has no words beginning with *sb*. The b_1 of *bat* is exploded like p_1, but the vocal cords vibrate while the lips close. The b_3 of *tab* is imploded like p_3, but again the vocal cords vibrate in the process. You can verify all this with another match.

Now let's suppose the Martian linguist does a little experimenting with these sounds. He says to his human informant, "Pat me," using p_1. The informant gently strokes the Martian's fur. The Martian again says "Pat me," using p_2. The informant may notice something strange about the Martian's pronunciation, but again he gives him a gentle pat.

On the next trial, the Martian actuates his vocal cords and says, not "Pat me," but "Bat me." The results are somewhat startling. Instead of being gently stroked, the Martian intercepts a stunning blow over the head from a blunt instrument. Nursing a dented cranium, he retires to his laboratory and records an important discovery: The acoustic difference between p_1 and b_1 is correlated with a striking (pun intended) difference in meaning, but the acoustic difference between p_1 and p_2 does not affect the meaning at all.

Did you realize the three *p*'s were different before you started to experiment? Probably not, unless you have already studied phonetics. The reason is that the little variations are automatic adjustments to other sounds preceding or following. We are no more conscious of making these adjustments than we are of using every individual muscle we employ in walking. Thus p_1 occurs only at the beginning of a syllable, p_2 only after *s*, p_3 only at the end of a word. Since one sound never poaches on another's territory, we say the three *p*'s are in *complementary distribution*.

With b_1 of *bat*, the situation is altogether different. It occurs at the beginning of a syllable in exactly the same relative position as p_1 in *pat*. The two sounds, which are acoustically distinct, are not in complementary distribution but in *contrast*. We are conditioned to respond to their acoustic difference. For us, *pat* and *bat* are two different words, as the growing lump on the Martian's skull attests.

Since a voiceless *p*-sound can contrast with a voiced *b*-sound in at least some positions, linguists sum up the difference by saying that sounds which have some features in common and can contrast with other sounds in the same relative position belong to different classes called *phonemes* — first syllable like "phone." All the different varieties of *p* are members of the /*p*/ phoneme, and all the *b*'s belong to the /*b*/ phoneme. (The slants are the linguist's shorthand sign to show that he is talking about a phoneme, not one of its members. The members are written in square brackets: $[p_1]$, $[p_2]$, $[p_3]$.)

This phonemic contrast of voiced and voiceless sounds is a pervading feature of English. In the following pairs, the first word begins with a voiceless consonant, the second with a voiced consonant. Otherwise the initial consonants are exactly alike; try it and see:

tame	:	dame
came	:	game
fat	:	vat
Chet	:	jet
sell	:	Zell

These remarks hold good for English, but not necessarily for other languages. The distinction between voiced and voiceless consonants which is so meaningful to us may not even be perceptible to speakers of other languages which do not have it. Leonard Bloomfield tells us that the Menomini Indians heard Scandinavian lumberjacks called "Swedes" and translated the word by *sayewenet*, "one who is sweet." In Menomini there is a phoneme that includes sounds like our *t* and *d*. Since these sounds never contrast, the Indians were not aware that to English-speakers *t* and *d* sound quite different. The Chinese, on the other hand, think that our p_1 and p_2 are quite different, because their own language has contrasts between sounds similar to them.

Unless we understand the phonemic structure of a language, we cannot describe it accurately. A good deal of the English grammatical system, for instance, depends on the contrast of voiced and voiceless consonants. The past-tense ending that we write -*ed* is pronounced like *t* after voiceless consonants. Compare *locked, slapped*, with *logged, rigged*. Now imagine a Menomini Indian without phonemic training trying to write a grammar of English for his people. He would make a pretty awful mess of the section on the past tense of verbs.

Another advantage of phonemics is that it cuts down the number of sound-features we need to talk about in a grammar to manageable size. Few languages use more than two or three dozen phonemes, but the number of positional variants may be several times as many. Another advantage is that a phonemic — not phonetic — transcription is the best basis for a system of writing. If we assign a letter to each phoneme, a native speaker will automatically put the variants in the right places. For languages that have never been written, phonemics speeds up the task of making illiterate people literate.

The phonemes of a language are the "bricks" it uses to build up words and sentences. The way these "bricks" are laid together is purely arbitrary. There is no fancy philosophical reason why three English phonemes in one order mean a fish, *shad*, and in reverse order a punctuation mark, *dash*. It just *is* that way, by social custom. But this combination of phonemes in an arbitrary order enables a language to say a good deal with a limited number of basic elements. The thirty phonemes of my Midwestern pronunciation are enough to build up all the words in Webster's dictionary.

If the inhabitants of other planets use speech-sound as we do, their language should yield to analysis by our methods as easily as any Earth language. The same would be true if they use any combination of other types of visual, audible, or tactile signals. A language might be based on musical notes of varying pitch and duration. An idealist named Francois Sudré once invented a language, Solresol, whose entire vocabulary was formed by combining the names of the seven notes of the musical scale, *do, re, mi, fa, sol, la, ti*. Solresol, which the inventor hoped would become the international language, could be spoken, sung, or played on any instrument except a drum. The Mazateco Indians of southern Mexico actually have a "whistle speech" beside their spoken language. Telegraph and blinker codes and the hand alphabets of the deaf-and-dumb substitute electronic impulses or gestures for letters, which in turn represent phonemes more or less exactly. In one of Gilbert K. Chesterton's stories, a professor invented a language of dance steps.

Whatever the "bricks" of Martian language may be, it should be possible to discover them as we discover the sound-patterns of earthly speech. Finding the larger patterns — words and sentences — into which they fit will be the real drudgery. Some languages have grammatical patterns so different from those of European speech that it is quite impossible to draw up a list of word-for-word equivalents. English is a somewhat extreme example of a pattern that is fairly rare. It breaks down its ideas into short units of expression — words — that undergo little change in form to show their relationship. The order of words is much more significant in English than their endings, and changing the order changes the meaning. "The man kicked the boy" is quite different from "The boy kicked the man." Chinese, which has no word-endings at all, is another language where order is supremely important. On the other hand, Latin and many other languages show relationship by changing endings. The three words *Marcus Mariam amat* may be combined in six ways, but in any order they mean "Mark loves Mary." The only way to make the affection mutual is to change the form of two words to *Maria Marcum amat*, "Mary loves Mark."

In still other languages, ideas that we express by separate words are fused into one utterance. Nootka, an Indian language of Vancouver Island, has such a structure. According to the late Benjamin Lee Whorf, Nootka *tlihisma* means "the boat is grounded on the beach" and *lashtskiqistama*, "the boat is manned by picked men." In many languages, the parts of such expressions have no more independent existence than the *-ed* of English *kicked*.

Look at those Nootka examples again, because we are going to use them to expose the Telepathic Martian for the fraud he is. The English translations of the Nootka sentence-words are constructed much alike. Both are statements about a boat, and we could formulate them: "The boat is *x*-ed preposition *y*." Our speech-habits lead us to think that the two situations they describe must be something alike because our verbal descriptions of them are alike. Nootka shows that it isn't necessarily so. The parts of the two utterances mean:

> *tlih:* "moving pointwise"; hence, "traveling as in a canoe"
> *is:* "on the beach"
> *lash:* "pick, choose"
> *tskiq:* "reminder, result"
> *ista:* "in a canoe as crew"
> *ma:* (third person singular ending)

So the first expression means more or less: "It is on the beach pointwise as an event of canoe motion" and the second, "They are in the boat as a crew of picked men" or "The boat has a crew of picked men." Neither of the Nootka expressions contains anything you can dissect out and say, "This means *boat*." The canoe is referred to only by implication.

Now the Indian and the paleface see the same canoe on the same beach. Both could identify it and its picked crew from a photograph and agree that the snapshot recorded the same event. But the two observers, conditioned by totally different linguistic systems, make a totally different set of "abstracts" or "isolates" from the observed event. In our way of looking at it, we have to specify the boat, or canoe, as an explicit element. For the Indian, the fact that a boat is concerned is implied by his choice of certain other elements. *Tlih*, "moving pointwise," has to apply to a canoe, just as "rolled" in English has to apply to a round or cylindrical object. Yet the English and the Nootka formulations are equally clear to another speaker of the same language. To the Indian, our English way of lumping together events that seem totally distinct to him must be perplexing and illogical.

The seventeenth-century philosophers used to speculate about "general grammar." All languages — so they reasoned — are attempts to translate the "reality" of the universe; a single logic underlies all of them. Our increased knowledge makes it seem more likely that the opposite is true. Languages do not depend on universal logic; logic depends on the structure of languages. *For any human being, "reality" is the sum total of the abstracts his language can make from observed events.*

Here is an example, also from Whorf, of two very different ways of regarding time. All human beings are aware that some things happen later than others. European languages express the "passage of time" in terms similar to those used to describe extension in space. We cut time into units of days, months, and years as we cut length into feet, yards, and miles. Nothing seems more natural to us; we speak of "a long day" and "a long pole." But a language like Hopi shows the analogy is not universal. English says "ten days" and "ten houses," but we can never experience ten days at once as we can see ten houses at once. *Houses* is a real plural; *days* is an imaginary plural.

Now Hopi has no imaginary plurals. For a Hopi Indian, the idea "ten days is longer than nine days" becomes "the tenth day is later than the ninth." He does not conceive of "ten days" as a length of time — see our spatial metaphor again? — cut up into shorter "lengths" called days, but as the recurrence of a phenomenon in a cycle. Hence a Hopi cannot multiply ten days by two to get twenty days, and the idea of describing time by words that also refer to space or matter would hardly occur to him. In fact, the idea of time as a continuous flow would be quite strange. No Hopi Einstein, uninfluenced by European ideas, would ever evolve the notion of a four-dimensional space-time continuum. His mathematical picture of the universe would have no more in common with ours than a Greek painting has with a canvas by Picasso.

Now, perhaps, you begin to understand why I want to feed the Telepathic Martian and his universal translating machine to the BEM's. If human languages can be so different as English and Nootka, the grammatical categories of Martian speech must be something completely outside our experience. The Telepathic Martian's thoughtwaves would have to be so powerful that they could make our brain cells aware of logical and grammatical relationships that have no equivalent whatever in our language.

Imagine, for the sake of the argument, that a telepathic English-speaking

American and a telepathic Nootka-speaking American sit down for a chat. The only thoughts they could have in common would be mental pictures. The English-speaker might be able to project an image of his family and his bungalow, and the Nootka might succeed in making the white man visualize his squaw and his canoe. But how does the white man translate into pictures: "I paid off the mortgage on my house last year"? How do you visualize a mortgage to an Indian who barely understands money? Is the mortgage "on" the house the same way the shingles are on it? How do you picture the past-tense notion in "paid" and the concept "last year"?

See what I mean? When the Martians land, we'll have to learn their language in the same laborious way we have learned Nootka and Salish and all the rest. Though there won't be any informants on their spaceship, we can teach them a limited amount of English by the time-honored process of *ostensive definition*. This means pointing at a chair and saying "chair," or dropping a brick and remarking "I just dropped a brick." Simple verbs can be acted out, like *eat, wash, shave, cut, scratch, draw, write*. For more complicated ideas, we might begin by verbalizing arithmetical or mathematical statements, like "two and two make four" or "The square of the hypotenuse of a right triangle is equal to the sum of the squares of the other two sides." Presumably the Martians could teach us some of their language in the same way. It would be slow, but not impossible.

If twentieth-century science can already suggest a way to talk to Martians, science-fiction writers have an obligation to base their fantasies of the future on the knowledge of the present. Science fiction, to be enjoyed by an intelligent reader, has to be plausible. Recently I read a story that was spoiled for me because of one elementary error. An extraterrestrial character in it spoke English with a phony foreign accent in which all the *t*'s became *s*'s. Yet this outlander, who couldn't manage our *t*-sound, had one in his own name! You don't have to be a Ph.D. in linguistics to see the howler.

In the best science fiction, the gadgets of the future are logical developments of those we already have. Good writers send their spacefarers to other planets in ways that are already known to be possible, and devise imaginary civilizations that follow logically from the conditions we know to exist on other worlds. I hope to live long enough to read stories that cope with the problem of interplanetary communication as realistically as we now do with interplanetary travel. As a first step, I move we bury the Telepathic Martian and his walkie-talkie interpreter under six feet of solid mars.

FOR DISCUSSION

1. If you were a Martian trying to learn English — and were linguistically oriented — you might very well begin as Shipman suggests by discriminating English phonemes (*bat* vs. *pat*, etc.). Try it. Take the combination *p - t* or *p - l(l)* and see how many vowel sounds occurring between the consonants will differentiate meanings. Some of the vowel sounds will be combinations of vowels, i.e., diphthongs; and some identical vowel sounds will be spelled in more than one way. But what we

want to identify are sounds, not spellings. You should find twelve or more sounds.

2. Eventually as a Martian you'd want to generalize the way speakers of English form the plural of regular nouns. Our textbooks tell us to add *-s* or *-es*. Try it: *goat+s, cow+s, horse+s*. Can you improve on the textbook statement for the Martian who wants to speak and understand English, rather than read it or write it? Devise "rules" to guide him.

3. To *spell* the past tense of regular verbs in English we add *-d* or *-ed*. What rules would guide pronunciation of the *-d* or *-ed* added to the following words: *pass, push, cease; seal, pull, seize; post, pout, seed?*

4. Shipman speaks of the 30 phonemes of his midwestern pronunciation. Some linguists would distinguish 33 phonemes in midwestern pronunciation, some as many as 40. The precise number depends, in part, on the system of classification used; it's a technical problem, not too important for us at the moment. What does matter is the light the concept of phonemes throws on our spelling system. What would be the ideal relationship between the phonemic system of a language and its spelling system? The 30 (or 33) phonemes of English are spelled, in all, in about 250 ways. What would be the practical difficulties in establishing a thoroughgoing system of phonemic spelling for English?

VOCABULARY: anthropologist, analogue, alien, spectrograph, labial, acoustic difference, poach, complementary distribution, conditioned, attest, phonetic, phonemic, phonemic structure, positional variant.

THEME TOPICS: Traditional textbooks and the English language. *Ghoti* spells fish: *gh* as in *enough, o* as in *women, ti* as in *nation.* Why not phonemic spelling? Three alphabet characters we don't need: *c, q, x* (the sounds they represent can be spelled in other ways). Can English spelling be simplified?

A Review of a Dictionary

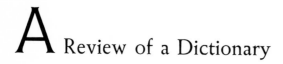

SUMNER IVES

A language is, first of all, a medium of communication. Each living language reflects the total life of some present-day community, and it is the medium through which the social, technical, and intellectual life of this community is carried on. This intimate and necessary connection between a language and a community has several consequences, among them the fact that the language changes as the community changes. It follows, too, that an individual's command of his language is one measure of his ability to participate in community activities, including its business, and that deficiencies in his command of language impose restrictions on this ability. This mutual relationship between language and activity exists whether the subject is baseball, cooking, philosophy, or anything else.

The full social, technical, and intellectual life of the community which includes the speakers of English has become so varied and complex that no one person has a total command of the entire language. Thus everyone whose horizons are expanding — whose contacts occasionally touch unfamiliar territory, whose reading occasionally includes unfamiliar concepts — needs a dictionary, if, in these broader associations, he is to communicate efficiently with others or fully understand their attempts to communicate with him. The constant change resulting from cultural and linguistic interaction makes dictionaries constantly go out of date. The best dictionaries add new words from time to time, but eventually the time comes when a complete revision is in order. G. & C. Merriam Company's *Webster's Third New International Dictionary*, a Merriam-Webster, is such a complete revision.

This sixth in the series of Merriam-Webster unabridged dictionaries is more than just a product of subtracting from and adding to the material in the fifth. It is, in fact, so thorough a revision as to constitute a new dictionary. The details of revision are too many for enumeration, but, in general, this newness results from three major developments. The first, of course, is the evolution of the language itself since the appearance of the 1934 edition. The second is the progress which has been made in linguistics — the systematic study of language as a kind of human behavior. This progress has given us a better understanding of the nature of language, a greater accumulation of details about English pronunciation, grammar, and usage, and a clearer notion of dictionary responsibility in these areas. The third is a very detailed review of lexicography, of the craft of dictionary making, which was made by the editorial staff that produced *Webster's Third New International* and used by it in evolving new dictionary procedures — new refinements in discriminating senses, new precision and grace in wording definitions, and new devices for making entries clearer and more informative.

It is obvious that, for good or ill, we have had a kind of cultural explosion within the twentieth century, not only in technology but also in the arts and in the studies of human behavior. Words such as *carbon 14, impressionism,* and *libido* are encountered by nearly everyone who reads as much as a daily paper. It is less obvious that other influences — the tremendous expansion in mass media, and the greater need for written communication in nearly all undertaking — have had profound effects on the nature of the standard language itself, especially as used in writing. When metropolitan newspapers have circulations running into hundreds of thousands, when a single weekly magazine will be read by millions, when a television program will be seen and heard by even more millions, and when the very existence of large enterprise depends on effective written communication, the language of public use is in the hands of the public; its utilitarian aspect has been expanded.

For these reasons it is likely that English has changed more during the past fifty years than during any similar period in the past, with the possible exceptions of the times just before Shakespeare and just before Chaucer, when profound social and intellectual movements were likewise taking place. Aside from the mere accumulation of new words this change has been evident in two major manifestations: the great increase in open compounds like *traffic island* and *hatchet job;* and a kind of popularization of the language which, apart from some changes in formal writing, has influenced the development of an informative informal style in writing for general readers and the development of special trade styles in writing for special audiences. In both instances the style of writing more closely approximates the style of speech. As a consequence the scope of standard written English has been broadened by the inclusion of words and constructions heretofore associated primarily with conversation and by greater employment of combining facilities already in the language, as in the making of new verbs with *-ize* and the making of new adverbs with *-wise.*

Thus, although we still have an aristocracy of letters, this aristocracy does not arbitrate written English to the extent it formerly did. Parallel to this aristocracy there is something like a middle class of letters. In other words, the use of written English by more people and for a greater variety of purposes has extended its utilitarian character. And the effects of this extension appear in all, or nearly all, uses of the language, spoken or written.

The responsibility of a dictionary regarding these developments is indicated by some present-day conclusions about the nature of linguistic standards. Although these conclusions are becoming better known, they have not yet become part of the general intellectual equipment of educated persons. Underlying this progress, there are a few deceptively simple premises which seem to be self-evident, although logically and experimentally verified conclusions from these premises deny some popular notions about linguistic standards. The premises which are here most relevant follow. First, each language is a system of human conventions rather than a system of natural laws. Therefore all languages are dynamic rather than static, and a valid rule in an individual language can be nothing other than an accurate statement of contemporary practice. Second, each language is unique in pronunciation, grammar, and vocabulary. Consequently, precedents in one language have no force or relevance in ascertaining rules in another or in describing the grammatical characteristics of another, and any attempt to prescribe usage in grammar or vocabulary by reference to "logical" grammar or "real" meaning is simply based on a false premise. These two premises imply the further conclusions that there is no such thing as grammar apart from the individual grammars of individual languages, that the real meaning of a word is nothing more or less than its communicative value in a customary context, and hence there is no such thing as pure English, if *pure* is to be given its common meaning. The third of these basic premises is that an individual's use of his native tongue is a primary index to his position within his community — socially, geographically, and often vocationally. From these premises it follows that a dictionary is reliable only insofar as it is a comprehensive, accurate description of current practices in a language, including community opinion as to the social and regional associations of each practice it describes.

These premises and conclusions are no longer controversial among qualified students of language, including the best lexicographers. They require, however, that books which present information on the proper use of a language, including dictionaries, be ultimately based on observation of how that language is actually used. A statement on the meaning, pronunciation, or status of a word must derive from observation of what meaning it is customarily used to convey, of how it is customarily pronounced (provided the pronunciation has community approval), and of community opinion as to its appropriateness in a variety of contexts. These matters must be observed from actual occurrences in the speech or writing of persons who represent their respective communities. It follows, then, that whoever produces a book on language must himself observe the use of that language — either unsystematically as he encounters speech and writing, or at second hand from statements made in other books, or systematically by gathering and classifying samples of the language in use.

The entries in *Webster's Third New International Dictionary* are based on three major sources. One, which is used by every reputable lexicographer, is the *Oxford English Dictionary*, an historical record of the English language, which occupies about four feet of shelf space. It was compiled from over four million quotations illustrating the use of English words since the language was first written. The second major source is earlier Merriam-Webster dictionaries, especially the *Second Edition*. The third and most important source is a file of several million quotations from recent and contemporary writing and speech, each one illustrating some use of some word. If the word is rare, the collection of citations will be small; but if it is a very common one, the collection of citations may be several inches thick.

Accumulating this enormous file of instances showing the language in use required many years of reading by a great many persons. In making sure that the file contained an adequate sampling of the language in use, the editorial staff has systematically read such publications as the *Dictionary of American Biography*, the books of the American Guide Series, dozens of college catalogs, a comprehensive selection of popular and technical periodicals and of major newspapers, and innumerable government and business reports and journals. This file is the greatest single record of how English has actually been used, the most comprehensive sample of the current, living language. It is not a set of statements about English but a collection of instances of English as it has been used by real individuals in real situations for the primary purpose of saying something to other real individuals. It is, then, the English language itself, the language of the English-speaking peoples, and the profound changes in English which were mentioned earlier are recorded in it. If a dictionary is reliable only insofar as it is a true description of actual practices by actual persons using their native tongue, here is a definitive sample of these practices.

On the authority of this file *Webster's Third New International Dictionary* contains about 50,000 words which have not appeared before in an unabridged Merriam-Webster and about 50,000 new meanings for words which have previously been so recorded.

Such an enormous body of evidence on the present state of English is a fundamental requirement to recording the changing language in a new dictionary according to modern principles of language description. It constitutes a record of practices which reveals the evolution of the language and contains the only kind of raw data from which a truly authoritative description of actual practices can be put together. Although there is general agreement on this basic principle of dictionary responsibility, it can be implemented only if a comprehensive sample of practices is available and only if the editorial staff displays a high degree of professional skill and integrity. Since our intellectual climate includes some notion that dictionaries and handbooks somehow arbitrate usage with some kind of superior wisdom and somehow strive to maintain the "purity" of English against the corrupting influence of popular use, even dictionary editors and handbook writers may be infected to some extent by the virus of this notion. To one who is familiar with the difficulties in this area, the consistency and fidelity with which the editors of *Webster's Third New International* have objectively described rather than arbitrarily prescribed is impressive.

And after all, this is what the average purchaser of a dictionary wants. As a reader he wants to know what meaning an author really intended when he used the word in question (not what, by some theory, he should have intended); and as a writer or speaker he wants to know what meaning his audience is most likely to understand from his use of the word in question (not what, by some theory, they should understand). Thus, his primary concern is what meaning the word has customarily conveyed in a given context — what its semantic value has been in the verbal marketplace.

In addition to the establishment of current meanings, fidelity to the conclusions of modern linguistic study is manifest in the establishment of current status and in the representation of current pronunciation. One of the responsibilities of a dictionary is to indicate when a word or use is nonstandard and to show, by some label or restrictive comment, the kind of limitation there is on its employment. The distinction between standard and nonstandard usage is different from the distinction between formal and informal styles and from that between written and conversational styles. The popular but false notion that standards drop in a series of levels from formal written (high level) to informal conversational (low level) has confused the issue, and a great many persons have taken the label "colloquial" to indicate some departure from the highest standards, contrary to the intention of the editors who affixed this label. Hence, *Webster's Third New International* does not use this label.

A great many persons are properly concerned with whether their English is "good" English, but there is some confusion as to what "good" English actually is. The whole force of what is known about this question by scholars — and incidentally of the intuitive opinion held by most who use the language — indicates that "good" English is that which most effectively accomplishes the purpose of the author (or speaker) without drawing irrelevant attention from the purpose to the words or constructions by which this purpose is accomplished. Thus, for ordinary purposes, "good" English is that which is customary and familiar in a given context and in the pursuit of a given objective. In other words, the language which should be used is that which is currently being used, provided this current use does not bring unwelcome attention. This conclusion throws the issue directly back to the available record of actual practices, the aforementioned citation file.

In *Webster's Third New International Dictionary* usages standard for all purposes are not labeled; nonstandard usages are given some label to indicate the kind of restriction which the evidence implies. An individual word or meaning may be nonstandard because it is restricted as to region, regarded as typical of uneducated speech or writing, out of date either as too old or as not fully established, or considered to be offensive to public decency. A few words or meanings are standard usage only under certain circumstances. For instance, *dolly* to mean "doll" is a child's term but is hardly wrong when used by a child or to a child. A special category of words and usages which stands beside standard English as a kind of facetious extension is slang: for instance, *horse* to mean "heroin," *score* to mean "a successful theft or its proceeds," and *liberate* to mean "steal." On the other hand, some former slang has passed into the standard language, e.g., *hard sell*, and some words which are occasionally regarded as slang really should not be so regarded, for they are the proper terms for the meanings, e.g., *coonjine*. Decisions in this area are especially difficult, for such words do not occur as often in writing as in speech, and no one can have a firsthand speaking acquaintance with everything of this type. At the same time, any speaker of American English is likely to encounter slang, if only in a paperback mystery story, and on occasion may find it useful.

Webster's Third New International represents pronunciation in terms of regional standards. In that respect it follows the conclusions of responsible scholarship in American English — and, in fact, the conclusions of anyone who listens to the voices of national leaders over radio or television. One can hardly pretend that each word has but one pronunciation, or even one preferred pronunciation, when he finds that members of the faculties of the greatest universities, national leaders in business and the professions, and holders of the highest offices speak with a great variety of accents. In order to accommodate this variety, the pronunciation editors have developed an adaptation of the older symbolization. They did not adopt one of the symbolizations used by scholars; rather they modified their own by adding some symbols and dropping others. The objective was a set of symbols which would represent each speech sound which distinguishes one word from another and each difference in sound which is associated with some large region of the country. For example, a word like *foreign* is pronounced with different vowels by persons with equal education and community prestige but from different sections, and the same vowel in *bag* is pronounced differently in different sections. The pronunciations in this dictionary are based on records gathered by members of the pronunciation staff, supplemented somewhat from materials published by certain nationally recognized authorities in American English. In using these pronunciation guides, one selects the representation which fits most naturally into his own pattern of speech. He is thus not encouraged to adopt a pronunciation which will appear to be an affectation. Also, variations which arise from the amount of prominence a word has in different contexts are listed. The usual dictionary practice has been to list pronunciations of words like *he* and *to* as they would be pronounced in a list. Use of such pronunciations in all contexts leads to a kind of pseudocorrectness which is as noticeable, and as revealing, as a substandard pronunciation. This dictionary thus represents the normal pronunciation of English as it is spoken by cultured persons in each major section of the country — the "language of well-bred ease," regionally determined.

The matters which have been discussed so far have importance for everyone who uses a dictionary, but the extent to which this dictionary records current progress in academic fields should be of particular interest to everyone who is engaged in education. The general policy has been to include those terms which are employed in academic fields up to the graduate level. Thus a student on any lower level is likely to find every word that appears in his normal academic pursuits. One who has completed his formal education can expect to find the terms which have come into these fields of study as a result of recent advances. And as progress in scholarship and research is passed into lower academic channels, these terms move further into the public domain, for today we live rather close to the laboratory and the research center.

Since the study of the language and its use is central to the curriculum on practically every level below college, the results of scholarship in this area have a peculiarly broad significance. There is a considerable body of printed material on language in general and English in particular which, for one reason or another, is not widely familiar to teachers, even those in the language arts. Some of this deals with a general understanding of language as a medium of communication, some with the nature of language standards, and some with the details of English pronunciation and their relation to spelling, with the categories and processes in English grammar, and with the relation between vocabulary and meaning. Thus a teacher of English can find the meanings of such terms as *function word, head,* and *nominal,* which are being used in modern descriptions of English grammar. An elementary school teacher can see the true shape of the language more clearly in this dictionary than in any but a small part of the material on English which she is given to teach, and she can find better definitions of basic terms in this dictionary than in the majority of current textbooks. Any educated person who wishes to read the results of qualified scholarship in language can understand it more readily with this dictionary at hand. For *Webster's Third New International* displays a professional knowledge of modern scholarship in language, and, frankly, the greatest part of school textbooks on language do not, although this condition is slowly being corrected.

The preceding remarks have applied to those aspects of this dictionary which reflect two of the major developments mentioned in the introduction — the changing shape of the language, and the progress in the scholarly study of language. What remains now is to consider the application of better lexicographic procedures, including those which are possible only in a dictionary of similar size. These involve, you may recall, refinement in discriminating senses, precision and grace in wording entries, and devices for making entries clear and informative. The preparation of a single entry involves all three matters simultaneously.

As in all Merriam-Webster dictionaries the order of senses is historical. These senses are worked out into classes and subclasses, and the order of listing shows the development of meaning the word has undergone. In this way one sees the flow of semantic evolution which has produced the current meaning or meanings. Often some residue of meaning will remain as a subtle nuance which a very skillful writer will have in mind as he uses the word, even though a word's first recorded meaning is not necessarily permanent. In any event, regardless of the order of listing, anyone using a dictionary must search through the listed definitions until he finds the one which fits most harmoniously into the word's immediate context.

The innovation in dictionary style which is most quickly seen is the sharp distinction between a definition and a synonym. A definition is "a statement of the meaning of a word or word group"; a synonym is a word or word group with nearly equivalent meaning. Thus a definition breaks down a word's meaning into its semantic ingredients. It is analytical in that it reduces a single hard word into a phrase made up of simpler ones, or it expresses a meaning in terms of the components of that meaning. For instance, *courageous* is not defined by associating it with a synonym like *brave,* but it is defined by the phrase "marked by bold resolution in withstanding the dangerous, alarming, or difficult." In this dictionary each synonym in an entry is printed in small capitals to distinguish it as such. Each word in small capitals is also a cross-reference, for it is itself defined where it is listed as an entry.

Each definition and each set of one or more synonyms is marked by a boldface colon, which is used for no other purpose. The material following each boldface colon is a single definition for one sense of the word or a set of one or more synonyms for one sense of the word, with or without a label, explanatory note, illustrative context, or illustrative quotation. In effect, then, each such colon introduces a word or phrase which is one semantic equivalent of the entry word and could be substituted for it in some normal context. This device serves as a prominent mark for the eye to catch in scanning an entry and frees marks of punctuation in the same typeface as the text for ordinary punctuation uses. In consulting a long entry, one looks for the numbers and letters in boldface which break it down into classes and subclasses of senses and picks up definitions or synonyms until he finds a general meaning which he thinks will fit his context. Then he tries each phrasal definition, considering any explanatory material which accompanies it, until he is satisfied.

Of other means of giving the required information about an entry word, the one which is most worthy of mention is the use of quotations. *Webster's Third New International Dictionary* supplies over 200,000 quotations and verbal illustrations from over 14,000 individuals and several hundred publications. Each quotation is followed by a designation of author or source. Sometimes a nuance of meaning is not reducible to a verbal statement, and sometimes an entry word or one of its uses is associated primarily with a particular style. Quotations illustrating the proper use of an entry word demonstrate these matters which are not easily or briefly stated. When, for example, *crash the gate* is illustrated by the quotation "all the kids used to sneak in . . . they had a million ways of crashing the gate," one can see what style it is appropriate to.

Anyone who is familiar with dictionaries knows that their style is frequently cryptic and associative rather than clear and precise. In other words, there seems to be a dictionary jargon as recognizable as a government or business jargon. Entries are often grotesque as writing and merely suggestive as expressions of meaning. Probably the greatest offender in this respect is the phrase "of or pertaining to," in which the participle means little more than "in some general way associated with." The editors of this dictionary have simply eliminated this phrase from their defining vocabulary. Likewise, *or* is sometimes less than clear. In English generally it may be used between elements with similar meanings or, as here, between elements which are mutually excluding alternates. In ordinary writing one depends on the context to indicate which meaning it has, but a dictionary is consulted by someone who is in doubt as to a context. For this reason this dictionary does not use *or* as a divider between synonymous or equivalent words — only when the members of the series are alternatives or when one member adds to another.

The preceding paragraphs discuss a few of the more obvious refinements in lexicography which appear in *Webster's Third New International Dictionary*. It is less easy to display or to describe the quality of professionalism which is likewise evident in it. There is a level of professionalism at which results seem to be both inevitable and effortless. In its best definitions this diction-ary has this quality, and it is generally free of clumsiness resulting from massing word on word without regard for stylistic virtue and of triteness resulting from carelessly employing general formulas rather than specific and individually appropriate phrases. Its style is, in the main, analytic rather than suggestive. In other words, the editors have tried to write as well as to define, and the best definitions are portions of good expository prose rather than mere verbal formulas. There is, in their choice of words, the awareness of semantic values and associations which one expects from thoroughly com-petent writers, and, in their discriminations, the meticulous respect for nuances of meaning which one expects from precise and orderly minds.

One can be completely sincere in saying that this latest dictionary to bear the Merriam-Webster label is an intellectual achievement of the very highest order. It is not easy, in fact it is extraordinarily difficult, to conduct a major intellectual project, involving dozens of persons and requiring many years of effort, in keeping with fundamental principles which are not part of the com-mon intellectual background shared by everyone. To the scholar in language, who knows something of the difficulties in such a project, the consistent skill which has been displayed is more impressive. To one who simply wishes to use a dictionary, it is of primary importance that this dictionary has been pro-duced by a staff of professionals roughly equivalent to the faculty of a small college, that it embodies the best and most thoroughly established principles of current scholarship in language, and that it is based on the largest available collection of evidence showing what current English actually is. Whatever authority these attributes give, it has.

FOR DISCUSSION

1. When *Webster's Third New International Dictionary* appeared in 1961, it was harshly criticized by many reviewers for differing so much from the edition of 1934. Professor Ives says that its newness results from three major developments. What are they?

2. What in your opinion would be some of the characteristics of the "informa-tive informal style in writing" mentioned by Professor Ives? Is such a style found in newspaper editorials? In *Harper's Magazine* and the *Atlantic*? In textbooks?

3. What are three conclusions about linguistic standards that "have not yet be-come part of the general intellectual equipment of educated persons"?

4. Professor Ives speaks of "the popular but false notion that standards drop in a series of levels." Have you been taught this notion? Explain in detail why it is "false."

5. How does Professor Ives define "good" English? According to this definition, could language containing a high percentage of nonstandard expressions ever be regarded as "good" English?

6. A dictionary necessarily indicates the pronunciation of individual words as they are individually pronounced, as in a list. When words are combined into

sentences, should they be pronounced as if they were words in a list? How do you normally pronounce sentences like (a) "I've got to go home now and study my English" (b) "What are you going to do now?" (c) "Where did you eat?" What influences our pronunciation of such sentences? Do we actually pronounce such sentences in various ways?

7. Professor Ives calls the dictionary he is reviewing "an intellectual achievement of the very highest order." Do you agree? What other "intellectual achievements" can you compare it with?

VOCABULARY: unabridged, cultural explosion, libido, utilitarian, open compounds, aristocracy of letters, dynamic, controversial, lexicographer, definitive, raw data, restrictive comment, intuitive, symbolization, pseudocorrectness, public domain, nuance, semantic ingredients, mutually excluding alternates, meticulous.

THEME TOPICS: How to make a dictionary. Dictionaries and "good" English. What dictionaries don't do. Should dictionaries include nonstandard expressions? A word is known by the company it keeps. Do words have "pure" meanings? Slang words that are not slang.

Words and Their Meanings

ALDOUS HUXLEY

For a long time past, thinking men have tended to adopt a somewhat patronizing attitude towards the words they use in communicating with their fellows and formulating their own ideas. "What do you read, my lord?" Polonius asked. And with all the method that was in his madness Hamlet scornfully replied, "Words, words, words." That was at the beginning of the seventeenth century; and from that day to this the people who think themselves realists have gone on talking about words in the same contemptuous strain.

There was a reason for this behaviour—or at least an excuse. Before the development of experimental science, words were too often regarded as having magical significance and power. With the rise of science a reaction set in, and for the last three centuries words have been unduly neglected as

An address delivered at Occidental College in 1938 and printed in a limited edition by The Ward Ritchie Press, Los Angeles, 1940. Reprinted by permission of the author.

things having only the slightest importance. A great deal of attention has been paid, it is true, to the technical languages in which men of science dc their specialized thinking, particularly, of course to mathematics. But the colloquial usages of everyday speech, the literary and philosophical dialects in which men do their thinking about the problems of morals, politics, religion and psychology — these have been strangely neglected. We talk about "mere matters of words" in a tone which implies that we regard words as things beneath the notice of a serious-minded person.

This is a most unfortunate attitude. For the fact is that words play an enormous part in our lives and are therefore deserving of the closest study. The old idea that words possess magical powers is false; but its falsity is the distortion of a very important truth. Words *do* have a magical effect — but not in the way that the magicians supposed, and not on the objects they were trying to influence. Words are magical in the way they affect the minds of those who use them. "A mere matter of words," we say contemptuously, forgetting that words have power to mould men's thinking, to canalize their feeling, to direct their willing and acting. Conduct and character are largely determined by the nature of the words we currently use to discuss ourselves and the world around us. The magician is a man who observes that words have an almost miraculous effect on human behaviour and who thinks that they must therefore be able to exercise an equal power over inanimate nature. This tendency to objectify psychological states and to project them, thus objectified, into the external world is deeply rooted in the human mind. Men have made this mistake in the past, men are making it now; and the results are invariably deplorable. We owe to it not only the tragic fooleries of black magic, but also (and this is even more disastrous) most of the crimes and lunacies committed in the name of religion, in the name of patriotism, in the name of political and economic ideologies. In the age-long process by which men have consistently stultified all their finest aspirations, words have played a major part. It was, I believe, the realization of this fact that prompted the founders of the two great world religions to insist upon the importance of words. In the Christian gospels the reference to this matter is contained in one of those brief and enigmatic sayings which like so many of the *logia*, unfortunately lend themselves to a great variety of interpretations. "But I say unto you, that every idle word that men shall speak, they shall give account thereof in the day of judgment. For by thy words thou shalt be justified, and by thy words thou shalt be condemned." It is possible to interpret this utterance in terms of a merely magical theory of the significance of language. It is equally possible to put another construction on the saying and to suppose that what Jesus was referring to was what may be called the psychological magic of words, their power to affect the thinking, feeling and behaviour of those who use them. That it was the intention of the Buddha to warn men against such psychological magic surviving documents leave us in no doubt whatever. "Right speech" is one of the branches of the Buddhist's Eightfold Path; and the importance of restraint in the use of words for intellectual purposes is constantly stressed in all those passages in the Pali Scriptures, where Gotama warns his followers against entangling themselves in the chains of metaphysical argument.

It is time now to consider a little more closely the mechanism by which words are able to exercise their psychological magic upon the minds of men and women. Human beings are the inhabitants, not of one universe, but of many universes. They are able to move at will from the world, say, of atomic physics to the world of art, from the universe of discourse called "chemistry" to the universe of discourse called "ethics." Between these various universes philosophy and science have not as yet succeeded in constructing any bridges. How, for example, is an electron, or a chemical molecule, or even a living cell related to the G minor quintet of Mozart or the mystical theology of St. John of the Cross? Frankly, we don't know. We have no idea how thought and feeling are related to physical events in a living brain and only the very vaguest notions about the way in which a brain is related to the charges of electrical energy which appear to be its ultimate components. So far as we are concerned, the only connection between various universes consists in the fact that we are able to talk about all of them and in some of them to have direct intuitions and sensuous experiences. The various universes we inhabit all belong to *us;* that is the only thing that unites them. Logical and scientific bridges are non-existent: when we want to pass from one to another, we have to jump.

Now, all these various universes in which we live are members of one or other of two super-universes: the universe of direct experience and the universe of words. When I look at this paper in my hand I have a direct sensuous experience. If I choose to, I can keep my mouth shut and say nothing about this experience. Alternatively, I may open my mouth and, making use of a certain system of signs, called the English language, I may impart the information that my experience consisted of whiteness mitigated by rows of black marks which I recognize as belonging to the alphabetical system by means of which spoken language can be rendered in terms of a visible equivalent.

To discuss the formal mechanism by which the world of immediate human experience is related to the various languages of mankind is a task which, even if I had the time, I should be quite incompetent to perform. And fortunately it is not necessary for our present purposes that it should be performed. It is enough, in this context to point out that, between the world of immediate experience and the world of language, between things and words, between events and speech, certain relations have in fact been established; and that these relations are governed by rules that are in part purely arbitrary, in part dictated by the nature of our common experiences. The form of the rules varies from language to language. We are not, however, concerned with these variations. For our present purposes, the significant fact is that all human societies use some kind of language and have done so from the remotest antiquity.

Human behaviour as we know it, became possible only with the establishment of relatively stable systems of relationships between things and events on the one hand and words on the other. In societies where no such relationship has been established, that is to say, where there is no language, behaviour is nonhuman. Necessarily so; for language makes it possible for men to build up the social heritage of accumulated skill, knowledge and wisdom, thanks to which it is possible for us to profit by the experiences of past generations, as though they were our own. There may be geniuses among the gorillas; but since gorillas have no conceptual language, the thoughts and achievements of these geniuses cannot be recorded and so are lost to simian posterity. In those limited fields of activity where some form of progress is possible, words permit of progress being made.

Nor is this all. The existence of language permits human beings to behave with a degree of purposefulness, perseverance and consistency unknown among the other mammals and comparable only to the purposefulness, perseverance and consistency of insects acting under the compulsive force of instinct. Every instant in the life, say, of a cat or a monkey tends to be irrelevant to every other instant. Such creatures are the victims of their moods. Each impulse as it makes itself felt carries the animal away completely. Thus, the urge to fight will suddenly be interrupted by the urge to eat; the all-absorbing passion of love will be displaced in the twinkling of an eye by a no less absorbing passion to search for fleas. The consistency of human behaviour, such as it is, is due entirely to the fact that men have formulated their desires, and subsequently rationalized them, in terms of words. The verbal formulation of a desire will cause a man to go on pressing forward towards his goal, even when the desire itself lies dormant. Similarly, the rationalization of his desire in terms of some theological or philosophical system will convince him that he does well to persevere in this way. It is thanks to words and to words alone that, as the poet says:

> Tasks in hours of insight willed
> May be in hours of gloom fulfilled.

And let us remember incidentally that by no means all of our tasks are willed in hours of insight. Some are willed in hours of imbecility, some in hours of calculating self-interest; some under the stress of violent emotion, some in mere stupidity and intellectual confusion. If it were not for the descriptive and justificatory words with which we bind our days together, we should live like the animals in a series of discrete and separate spurts of impulse. From the psychological point of view, a theology or a philosophy may be defined as a device for permitting men to perform in cold blood and continuously actions which, otherwise, they could accomplish only by fits and starts and when the impulse was strong and hot within them. It is worth remarking, in this context, that no animals ever make war. They get into individual squabbles over food and sex; but they do not organize themselves in bands for the purpose of exterminating members of their own species in the name of some sacred cause. The emphasis here must be placed on the word "name." For, of course, animals have no lack of sacred causes. What could be more sacred to a tiger than fresh meat or tigresses? What is lacking in the animal's world is the verbal machinery for describing and justifying these sacred causes. Without words, perseverance and consistency of behaviour are, as we have seen, impossible. And without perseverance in slaughter and consistency in hatred there can be no war.

For evil, then, as well as for good, words make us the human beings we actually are. Deprived of language we should be as dogs or monkeys. Possessing language, we are men and women able to persevere in crime no less than in heroic virtue, capable of intellectual achievements beyond the scope of any animal, but at the same time capable of systematic silliness and stupidity such as no dumb beast could ever dream of.

It is time now that I gave a few typical instances of the way in which words have power to modify men's thought, feeling and conduct. But before doing so, I must make a few more remarks of a general nature. For our present purposes, words may be divided into three main classes. The first class consists of words which designate definite and easily recognizable objects or qualities. Table, for example, is an easily recognizable object and brown an easily recognizable quality. Such words are unambiguous. No serious doubts as to their meaning exist. The second class contains words which designate entities and qualities less definite and less easily recognizable. Some of these are highly abstract words, generalizing certain features of many highly complex situations. Such words as "justice," "science," "society," are examples. In the same class we must place the numerous words which designate psychological states — words such as "beauty," "goodness," "personality." I have already mentioned the apparently irresistible human tendency to objectify psychological states and project them, on the wings of their verbal vehicle, into the outer world. Words like those I have just mentioned are typical vehicles of objectification. They are the cause of endless intellectual confusion, endless emotional distress, endless misdirections of voluntary effort.

Our third class contains words which are supposed to refer to objects in the outer world or to psychological states, but which in fact, since observation fails to reveal the existence of such objects or states, refer only to figments of the imagination. Examples of such words are the "dragon" of the Chinese and the "death instinct" of Freudian psychologists.

The most effective, the most psychologically magical words are found in the second category. This is only to be expected. Words found in the second class are more ambiguous than any others and can therefore be used in an almost indefinite number of contexts. A recent American study has shown that the word "nature" has been used by the philosophers of the West in no less than thirty-nine distinct senses. The same philosopher will give it, all unconsciously of course, three or four different meanings in as many paragraphs. Given such ambiguity, any thesis can be defended, any course of action morally justified, by an appeal to nature.

Ambiguity is not the only characteristic which makes these words peculiarly effective in determining conduct. Those which stand for generalizations and those which designate psychological states lend themselves, as we have already seen, to objectification. They take verbal wings and fly from the realm of abstraction into the realm of the concrete, from the realm of psychology into the external universe.

The objectification and even the personification of abstractions is something with which every political speech and newspaper article has made us familiar. Nations are spoken of as though they were persons having thoughts, feelings, a will and even a sex, which, for some curious reason, is always female. This female, personal notion produces certain psychological effects on those who hear it (or rather her) being talked about — effects incomparably more violent than those that would be produced if politicians were to speak about nations as what in fact they are: organized communities inhabiting a certain geographical area and possessing the means to wage war. This last point is crucially important. California is an organized community; but since it does not possess an army and navy, it cannot qualify for a place in the League of Nations.

Another familiar entity in political speeches is the pseudo-person called "Society." Society has a will, thoughts and feelings, but, unlike the Nation, no sex. The most cursory observation suffices to show that there is no such thing as Society with a large S. There are only very large numbers of individual societies, organized in different ways for different purposes. The issue is greatly complicated by the fact that the people who talk about this non-existent Society with a big S, tend to do so in terms of biological analogies which are, in many cases, wholly inapplicable. For example, the so-called philosophical historians insist on talking of a society as though it were an organism. In some aspects, perhaps, a society does resemble an organism. In others, however, it certainly does not. Organisms grow old and die and their component cells break down into inanimate substances. This does not happen to a society, though many historians and publicists loosely talk as though it did. The individuals who compose what is called a decadent or collapsed society do not break down into carbon and water. They remain alive; but the cells of a dead organism are dead and have ceased to be cells and become something else. If we want to talk about the decline and fall of societies in terms of scientific analogies, we had better choose our analogy from physics rather than biology. A given quantity of water, for example, will show least energy, more energy, most energy according to its temperature. It has most energy in the form of superheated steam, least in the from of ice. Similarly, a given society will exhibit much energy or little energy according to the way in which its individual members live their lives. The society of Roman Italy, for example, did not die; it passed from a high state of energy to a lower state of energy. It is for historians to determine the physiological, psychological, economic and religious conditions accompanying respectively a high and a low degree of social energy.

The tendency to objectify and personify abstractions is found not only among politicians and newspaper men, but also among those who belong to the, intellectually speaking, more respectable classes of the community. By way of example, I shall quote a paragraph from the address delivered by Clerk Maxwell to the British Association in 1873. Clerk Maxwell was one of the most brilliantly original workers in the whole history of physics. He was also what many scientists, alas, are not — a highly cultivated man capable of using his intelligence in fields outside his particular specialty. Here is what he could say before a learned society, when at the height of his powers.

"No theory of evolution," he wrote, "can be formed to account for the similarity of molecules." (Throughout this passage, Maxwell is using the word "molecule" in the sense in which we should now use the word "atom.") "For evolution necessarily implies continuous change, and the molecule is incapable of growth or decay, of generation or destruction. None of the processes of Nature, from the time when Nature began, have produced the slightest difference in the properties of any molecule. We are therefore unable to ascribe either the existence of the molecules or the identity of their properties to any of the causes which we call natural. Thus we have been led along a strictly scientific path very near to the point at which Science must stop. . . . In tracing back the history of matter Science is arrested when she assures herself, on the one hand that the molecule has been made and, on the other, that it has not been made by any of the processes which we call natural."

The most interesting point that emerges from these lines is the fact that, like the Nation, but unlike Society, Science has a sex and is a female. Having recorded this item in our text books of natural history, we can go on to study the way in which even a mind of the calibre of Clerk Maxwell's can be led into absurdity by neglecting to analyze the words which it uses to express itself. The word "science" is current in our everyday vocabulary. It can be spelt with a capital S. Therefore it can be thought of as a person; for the names of persons are always spelt with capital letters. A person who is called Science must, *ex hypothesi*, be infallible. This being so, she can pronounce without risk of contradiction, that "none of the processes of Nature, since the time when Nature began," (Nature is also spelt with a capital letter and is of course also a female) "have produced the slightest difference in the properties of any molecule." Twenty-three years after the date of Maxwell's speech, Becquerel observed the radio-activity of uranium. Two years after that Mme. Curie discovered radium. At the turn of the new century Rutherford and Soddy demonstrated the fact that the radium atom was in a process of rapid disintegration and was itself derived from uranium whose atoms were distintegrating at a much slower rate.

This cautionary story shows how fatally easy it is for even the greatest men of science to take the particular ignorance of their own time and place, and raise it to the level of a universal truth of nature. Such errors are particularly easy when words are used in the entirely illegitimate way in which Maxwell employed the word "Science." What Maxwell should have said was something like this, "Most Western scientists in the year 1873 believe that no process has ever modified the internal structure of individual atoms. If this is so (and of course the beliefs of 1873 may have to be modified at any moment in the light of new discoveries), then perhaps it may be legitimate to draw certain inferences of a theological nature regarding the creation of matter."

We should have a great many fewer disputes in the world if words were taken for what they are, the signs of our ideas only, and not for things themselves.

JOHN LOCKE

How was it possible, we may ask ourselves, that a man of Clerk Maxwell's prodigious intellectual powers should have committed a blunder so monstrously ridiculous, so obvious, when attention is called to it, to people of even the most ordinary mental capacities? The question demands a double answer — the first on the purely intellectual level, the second in terms of feeling and will. Let us deal with these in order. Maxwell made his mistake, first of all, out of a genuine intellectual confusion. He had accepted the English language without question or analysis, as a fish accepts the water it lives in. This may seem curious in the light of the fact that he had certainly not accepted the technical language of mathematics without question or analysis. We must remember, however, that non-technical language is picked up in infancy, by imitation, by trial and error, much as the arts of walking and rudimentary cleanliness are acquired. Technical languages are learned at a later period in life, are applied only in special situations where analysis is regarded as creditable and the ordinary habits of daily living are in abeyance. Children and young people must be deliberately taught to analyze the non-technical language of daily life. With very few exceptions, they will never undertake the task on their own initiative. In this respect, Maxwell was not exceptional. He turned his intensely original and powerful mind on to the problems of physics and mathematics, but never on those of everyday, untechnical language. This he took as he found it. And as he found in it such words as "Science" with a capital S and a female sex, he made use of them. The results, as we have seen, were disastrous.

The second reason for Maxwell's error was evidently of an emotional and voluntary nature. He had been piously brought up in the Protestant tradition. He was also, as the few letters to his wife which have been printed seem to indicate, a practising mystic. In announcing that "Science" with the capital S and the female sex had proved that atoms had not evolved, but had been created and kept unchangingly themselves by nonnatural forces, he had a specifically religious purpose in view. He wanted to show that the existence of a demiurge after the pattern of Jehovah, could be demonstrated scientifically. And he wanted also, I suspect, to prove to himself that the psychological states into which he entered during his moments of mystical experience could be objectified and personified in the form of the Hebraic deity, in whose existence he had been taught to believe during childhood.

This brings us to the threshold of a subject, profoundly interesting indeed, but so vast that I must not even attempt to discuss it here; the subject of God and of the relations subsisting between that word and the external world of things, and events, between that word and the inner world of psychological states. Shelley has sketched the nature of the problem in a few memorable sentences. "The thoughts which the word, 'God,' suggests to the human mind are susceptible of as many varieties as human minds themselves. The Stoic, the Platonist and the Epicurean, the Polytheist, the Dualist and the Trinitarian, differ infinitely in their conceptions of its meaning. . . . And not only has every sect distinct conceptions of the application of this name, but scarcely two individuals of the same sect, who exercise in any degree the freedom of their judgment, or yield themselves with any candour of feeling to the influencings of the visible world, find perfect coincidence of opinion to exist between them." Such, I repeat, is the problem. No complete solution of it is possible. But it can at least be very considerably clarified by anyone who is prepared to approach it armed with equipment suitable to deal with it. What is the nature of this suitable equipment? I would assign the first place to an adequate vocabulary. Students of religion have need of a language sufficiently copious and sufficiently analytical to make it possible for them to distinguish between the various types of religious experience, to recognize the difference between things and words, and to realize when they are objectifying psychological states and projecting them into the outside world. Lacking such a language they will find that even a wide knowledge in the fields of theology, of comparative religion and of human behaviour will be of little use to them. It will be of little use for the simple reason that such knowledge has been recorded, up to the present time, in words that lend themselves to the maximum amount of intellectual confusion and the minimum of clarity and distinctness.

Words and their meanings — the subject is an enormous one. "Had we but world enough and time" as the poet says, we could continue our discussion of it almost indefinitely. But unfortunately, or perhaps fortunately, world and time are lacking, and I must draw to a close. I have been able in this place to let fall only a few casual and unsystematic remarks about those particular aspects of the science of signs which Charles Morris has called the semantic and pragmatic dimensions of general semiosis. I hope, however, that I have said enough to arouse an interest in the subject, to evoke in your minds a sense of its profound importance and a realization of the need to incorporate it systematically into the educational curriculum.

Any education that aims at completeness must be at once theoretical and practical, intellectual and moral. Education in the proper use of words is complete in the sense that it is not merely intellectual and theoretical. Those who teach, teach not only the science of signs, but also a universally useful art and a most important moral discipline. The proper use of language is an important moral discipline, for the good reason that, in this field as in all others, most mistakes have a voluntary origin. We commit intellectual blunders because it suits our interests to do so, or because our blunders are of such a nature that we get pleasure or excitement from committing them. I have pointed out that one of the reasons for Maxwell's really monstrous misuse of language must be sought in that great man's desire to reconcile his scientific ideas with the habits of religious belief he had contracted in childhood. There was a genuine confusion of thought; but a not entirely creditable wish was very definitely the father of this confusion. And the same is true, of course, about those who for propagandist purposes, personify such abstractions as "Society" or "the Nation." A wish is father to their mistaken thought — the wish to influence their hearers to act in the way they would like them to act. Similarly, a wish is the father of the mistaken thought of those who allow themselves to be influenced by such preposterous abuses of language — the wish to be excited, to "get a kick," as the phrase goes. Objectified in the form of a person, the idea of a nation can arouse much stronger feelings than it can evoke when it is spoken of in more sober and accurate language. The poor fools who, as we like to think, are helplessly led astray by such machiavellian demagogues as Hitler and Mussolini are led astray because they get a lot of emotional fun out of being bamboozled in this way. We shall find, upon analysis, that very many of the intellectual errors committed by us in our use of words have a similar emotional or voluntary origin. To learn to use words correctly is to learn, among other things, the art of foregoing immediate excitements and immediate personal triumphs. Much self control and great disinterestedness are needed by those who would realize the ideal of never misusing language. Moreover, a man who habitually speaks and writes correctly is one who has cured himself, not merely of conscious and deliberate lying, but also (and the task is much more difficult and at least as important) of unconscious mendacity.

When Gotama insisted on Right Speech, when Jesus stressed the significance of every idle word, they were not lecturing on the theory of semiosis; they were inculcating the practice of the highest virtues. Words and the meanings of words are not matters merely for the academic amusement of linguists and logisticians, or for the aesthetic delight of poets; they are matters of the profoundest ethical significance to every human being.

FOR DISCUSSION

1. "Words make us the human beings we actually are." Could we be human at all without words? What human activities would be impossible without language? Are these the activities that distinguish man from animal?

2. It is easy enough to suggest words that fall into Huxley's first class, but what are some, besides those he suggests, that fall into his second and third classes? What is the difference between the second and third classes?

3. When Huxley speaks of correct writing and speaking, does he mean grammar, spelling, pronunciation, and so on? What does he mean?

4. Can you explain in your own words the "entirely illegitimate way in which Maxwell employed the word 'Science'"? Into what errors did his misuse of the word lead him?

VOCABULARY: ideology, stultify, enigmatic, mitigate, analogy, abeyance, personify, objectify.

THEME TOPICS: Magical words in advertising. Magical words in political discussion. How to protect yourself against word magic.

The Age of the Wordfact

JOHN KENNETH GALBRAITH

After the loss of New York and Long Island to Howe in 1776, General Washington made no effort to picture this misfortune as an important gain for the Continental army. Lincoln was similarly remiss after the de-

From *The Atlantic Monthly,* September, 1960. Reprinted by permission of the author.

bacle at First Manassas. In 1919 Wilson succeeded in persuading a clear majority of the Senate to vote in favor of the Covenant of the League of Nations, although not the necessary two thirds majority. Nothing whatever was made of this moral victory.

Things are different today. In June of 1960 President Eisenhower returned from a trip to the Pacific which would seem, superficially, to have been an unparalleled disaster of its kind. Japan, which was the principal object of his tour, had been beset by violent riots over the visit, and in the end it had been forced to urge him not to come. With the aid of his press secretary, however, the President was able to report on his return that the trip had been a success. A small number of Communists, acting under outside orders, had made things a trifle sour in Japan. But that was because they knew how powerful was the impression Mr. Eisenhower made on his trips to other lands, and they determined, as a result, that no such impression would be made on Japan. This was not the first time this kind of thing had happened. Two years earlier, Communists in South America had been forced to take similar preventive action because of the overwhelming appeal of Mr. Nixon to the Latin populace.

Some will perhaps conclude from this comparison that Mr. Eisenhower (and also Mr. Nixon and Mr. Hagerty) has a deeper and more perceptive insight into the ultimate meaning of events than did Washington, Lincoln, or Wilson. After all, the battles of Long Island, of Bull Run, and over the League all occurred in wars that were eventually won. Such a conclusion would be wrong. The earlier Presidents operated, in fact, without the help and support of one of the most important modern instruments of public administration. Just possibly they would not have used it, but the issue is academic, for it had not been invented. I refer to the institution of the "wordfact."

The wordfact makes words a precise substitute for reality. This is an enormous convenience. It means that to say that something exists is a substitute for its existence. And to say that something will happen is as good as having it happen. The saving in energy is nearly total.

There is a distinct possibility that the inventor of the wordfact was an editor or a newspaperman. But whatever its origins, it has come to have present-day importance less in journalism than in government. A press that fully accepts the institution is essential to its employment, but one of the principal functions of the modern public leader is to find the language which adequately improves the reality. Where once it was said of a statesman that he suited action to the words, now he suits the words to the action. If past action (or inaction) has failed to produce the desired result, then, by resort to wordfact, he quickly establishes that the undesired result was more desirable than the desired result.

Lest any of this seem farfetched or complicated, let us remind ourselves of some of the achievements of wordfact in these last years. We agree, of course, that any manifestation of anti-American sentiment abroad is the work of a misguided minority. And until last summer there was no misunderstanding that could not be cured, no resentment that could not be alleviated, fear that could not be dissipated by a smiling visit of two days to the capital of the country. It would then be stated with appropriate solemnity that the visit was a success; the papers would report that it was a great success; the problems then were presumably gone. Perhaps never before in history had diplomacy become so simple.

But not even traveling has always been necessary. By a bold use of wordfact, we were long able to convert South American dictators into bulwarks of the free world, although on occasion it was thought necessary to drive home the point by decorating them. The recent rise of military regimes in Asia is not a setback for democracy. Rather, it reflects the natural and inevitable difficulty in these countries of basing government on the consent of the governed.

Here at home it is no longer easy to think of unemployment as a misfortune. It reflects the introduction of needed and desirable slack in the system. No properly run economy can be without it. The drastic decline in farm income in recent years has become a manifestation of the vitality of the market system. Though farmers have been leaving their farms at an unprecedented rate, the forces making for this migration have been favorably described by the Secretary of Agriculture in a book with the agreeable title *Freedom to Farm*. Bad television programs were strongly defended early this year by the Federal Communications Commission as a precious manifestation of the freedom of speech. The networks found this a more than satisfactory substitute for any improvement in their programs. They are said, as a result, to be coming up with autumn offerings of unparalleled banality and horror. One hopes that some Sunday afternoon they will have a statesmanlike salute to the principal modern architects of the wordfact.

However, as an indication of what can be done by skillful deployment of the wordfact, with the aid of an acquiescent press, it is unlikely that any recent event matches that of the ill-fated U-2. Until Francis Powers made his unpremeditated landing, the sending of military or paramilitary aircraft by one country over another without the permission of the latter would have been considered a somewhat provocative act. (Even now the appearance of such planes over the United States would not be regarded with any real warmth and enthusiasm.) To have an aircraft shot down in the course of such an excursion into another country would have been regarded as a serious misfortune from which little comfort or reward of any kind could possibly be gleaned.

Yet in the days immediately following the last flight of the U-2, by the massive use of wordfact all of the relevant circumstances were changed. Flying planes over other countries became a kind of fifth freedom, to be justified, not without sanctimony, by the secrecy of the other country. The information gained justified the danger incurred and the mistrust aroused among our friends. Indeed, the flights would have to continue. The loss of the plane had proved, as nothing else, the weakness of the opposing defenses. The flights were then suspended, and this became an act of wise restraint. At this stage, the information being gathered ceased to be important as compared with the danger involved and the discomfort and mistrust created among our allies.

Such is the service of wordfact in transforming misfortune into fortune. But it has at least an equal value in transforming inaction into action. Thus, for a year and half now, a cabinet committee headed by Vice President Nixon has been dealing with the problem of inflation. This it has done all but exclusively by denouncing it, and so great has been the fury of its denunciation that it has not deemed it necessary to propose any concrete remedies of importance. In recent years, medical care for the aged has become a major political issue. As this is written, both parties in Congress are endeavoring to make a record on the issue. Records are made not by enacting legislation but by indicating an all but uncontrollable desire to enact legislation. Yet there is a difference, which is recognizable to those who are old and ill and faced with a terrible medical bill. Strong statements in favor of school integration and voting rights for Negroes are a widely accepted substitute for progress, and much less complicated in practice. To most congressional and campaign strategists, it would be considered little short of eccentric to inquire what might be accomplished. The important thing is to find the form of words that will satisfy, and if possible inspire, the Negro voters. One imagines, incidentally, that the invasion of the lunch counters by Negro students is related to the discovery that much of the civil rights discussion is purely inspirational.

On occasion, as when Republicans opposed slavery and Democrats favored alcohol, political platforms in the past have been a guide to ensuing action. But these, too, have been taken over by wordfact. In those hammered out this summer at Los Angeles and Chicago, little thought was given to whether the good things mentioned in them could or would be done. It would have been a jarring note had anyone on either platform committee asked: "Are we sure we can keep this promise?" (It *was* a jarring note at Los Angeles when Paul Ziffren, the California Democratic national committeeman, said that it was less important to write platforms than to get them enacted.) In the case of the platforms, the people appear to be fully aware of the use of wordfact. As a result, they pay them only the most perfunctory attention. It is unfortunate, but words have value only if they have some nexus, however tenuous, with action.

This truth is well illustrated on a global and tragic basis by the discussion of disarmament. Here it is all but taken for granted that no one means what he says, that proposals are made for their effect on public opinion and not on the arms race. And, as a result, people have ceased to pay any attention to the proposals. Civilized survival may in this instance depend on our ability to redeem this problem from the practitioners of wordfact.

But the redemption had better be general. To some extent, of course, it is automatic. It cannot be supposed that the vast verbal fallout of recent years is intrinsically attractive. It is certain to breed a reaction. Convention viewers doubtless saw the beginning of such a reaction this year in the massive inattention that was accorded these wordy proceedings. One sees it also in the tendency to assume, when the government explains that all is well, that something must be wrong.

In part, the control of wordfact requires only that our leaders be slightly more sensible in their approach to the American people. It would be to their own interest. When President Eisenhower described his trip to the vicinity of Japan as a success, he was fooling no one capable of consecutive thought. He did risk giving the impression that he was susceptible to such nonsensical conclusions. And certainly he revealed an unflattering attitude toward the gullibility of the American people.

This, to some extent, was their — or our — fault. We have come to suffer nonsense gladly, and pompous nonsense far too gladly. Elaborate rationalizations of failure should not be met by bored silence or even by a fishy stare. They should be greeted by loud and vulgar laughter, followed immediately by equally uncouth speeches and letters and, if nothing else is possible, by scribbling on walls. All who proclaim good intentions should be immediately asked for their program as to performance. Speeches of candidates for public office this autumn should be scrupulously clipped and saved — and sent to them at intervals over the next couple of years with a request for a progress report. Four years from now, when the parties meet to write their programs, a large number of articulate citizens must be on hand to inquire what in hell happened to the pious promises of 1960. They should have this year's copies in hand.

Perhaps, having organizations for almost everything else, we should have an organization for enforcing election promises and for fingering the man who imagines that he can make his record with words. At a minimum, however, we must reconstruct our hierarchy of political delinquency. The most serious delinquent, the man now to be marked for extinction even before the Florida free-loader, is the man of any political faith or persuasion whose talk shows any sign of being unmatched by intention. The windy liberal should go, along with the windy conservative, and, as a liberal, I devoutly hope that he will go first. And while dealing kindly with all who confess honest error, we should make a special bipartisan onslaught on any man who defends his mistakes by saying that the unintended was better than the intended and that it was really planned all along.

All words are pegs to hang ideas on.

HENRY WARD BEECHER

FOR DISCUSSION

1. Is "wordfact" a new name for propaganda? Can you distinguish between wordfact and propaganda?

2. Galbraith suggests that wordfact is a recent invention. Do you agree?

3. Was Clerk Maxwell in Huxley's essay an unconscious victim of wordfact?

4. How many specific examples of wordfact does Galbraith cite? Do you accept them all?

5. How much space does the essay devote to examples and how much to abstract discussion of the principle involved? Could you use a similar proportion in the next theme you write?

VOCABULARY: alleviate, banality, deployment, acquiescent, sanctimony, perfunctory, rationalization, articulate.

THEME TOPICS: Wordfact on the campus. Wordfact in courtship. Saving face through wordfact. Wordfact is greater than fact.

On Contexts and Vagueness

MONROE BEARDSLEY

Meaning and Context

One of the fundamental facts about words is that the most useful ones in our language have many meanings. That is partly why they are so useful: they work overtime (but, as we shall see, not for nothing). Think of all the various things we mean by the word "foot" on different occasions: one of the lower extremities of the human body, a measure of verse, the ground about a tree, twelve inches, the floor in front of the stairs. The same is true of nearly every common noun or verb. The editors of *The American College Dictionary*, in their preliminary investigation of words most frequently used, found 55 distinct senses of the word "point" in 1,100 occurrences of the word, and they distinguished 109 different senses of the word "run."

Considering the number of ways of taking a particular word, the task of speaking clearly and being understood would seem pretty hopeless if it

From Monroe Beardsley, *Thinking Straight: Principles of Reasoning for Readers and Writers,* 2d ed., © 1956. Prentice-Hall, Inc., Englewood Cliffs, N.J. Reprinted by permission of the publisher. Pp. 153-159, 167-173.

were not for another very important fact about language. Though a word may have many senses, these senses can be controlled, up to a point, by the *context* in which the word is used. When we find the word in a particular verbal setting — that is, take it with the words that come before it in a discourse — we can usually decide quite definitely which of the many senses of the word is relevant. If a poet says his verse has three feet, it doesn't occur to you that he could mean it's a yard long or is three-legged (unless perhaps you are a critic planning to puncture the poet with a pun about his "limping verse"). The context rules out these maverick senses quite decisively.

We might be puzzled if we read in a newspaper that "in the suicide's pocket the police found a large envelope full of bills." In this sentence, as it stands, the word "bills" can easily be taken in two very different senses. But if the context were expanded so as to read, "The police were surprised to find in the suicide's pocket a large envelope full of bills of various denominations," we should understand that "bills" meant *paper money,* and we might wonder whether it was indeed suicide or accident. Or if the context were expanded differently, so as to read, "The police were surprised to find in the suicide's pocket a large envelope full of unpaid bills," we should understand that "bills" meant *requests for payment of a debt,* and we might wonder whether that explains the suicide.

This is a rather simple illustration of the way in which the context of a word helps to pick out one of its senses and fix that sense. But of course "context" is used broadly here: it may be the rest of a sentence (the *immediate* context), a page, a whole book, or a newspaper file. A "shady street" is one thing; a "shady neighborhood" is something else. The word "strike" means one action on the front page of a paper and another action on the sports page; the words "liberal" and "patriotic" mean certain attitudes in *The New York Times* and mostly different ones in *The Chicago Tribune.* When some time ago a British physicist announced with pleasure that the hydrogen bomb is "safe," his statement caused gasps of surprise; in the technical talk of atomic scientists, "safe" apparently means that it couldn't set off a chain reaction that might destroy the earth itself. This is not the way the man in the street uses the word.

Many common words like "line," "pipe," "base," "stock," and "head," have acquired many serviceable meanings in different occupational contexts — say, in the shoptalk of plumbers, pitchers, or plastic engineers. Think of what the word "wing" means to a birdwatcher, an airman, a stagehand, a general, or an architect. But just because these meanings are so completely distinct — no one can confuse the wing of an airplane with the wing of a house — it is easy to control them by very light contextual pressure. A word or two makes it clear that it is the airman's wing rather than the architect's that is referred to. But when the differences between the senses of a word are slighter and subtler (they may be even more important, however), the most careful management of the context may be required to get and keep one sense in focus. The exact meaning of a word like "middle class" or "evolution" or "justice" may depend upon the whole book in which it appears.

That is why it is often easy to misrepresent what someone has said by quoting some of his remarks out of their context. The words may not, strictly speaking, be *mis*quoted, but their meaning has been changed. The political candidate's promise to obtain peace or balance the budget is echoed and attacked by his opponent — who is careful to leave out the conditions and qualifications that originally surrounded it. Even if a writer is scrupulous enough to put in dots to indicate that something has been left out, he may not be *quite* scrupulous enough to stick to the original meaning. You have seen advertisements of a new play, with a few words from a review. The phrase ". . . emotional subtlety . . . (Bridgeport *Post*)" may be from a sentence that goes: "It has all the emotional subtlety of a barroom brawl." The phrase ". . . great drama . . . (New Haven *Register*)" may be from a sentence that goes: "No doubt it was considered a great drama when it first appeared in 1927, but . . ." And this is nothing to what a professional wiretapper can do if he records a telephone conversation and picks out words to rerecord on a new tape.

Representative Wayne L. Hays, a member of the Special House Committee set up by the 83rd Congress to investigate tax-exempt foundations, frequently argued during the committee's hearings that the "research directors" of the committee were willing to make judgments on passages torn out of contexts that might change their meaning considerably. He finally made a dramatic demonstration of this by producing three paragraphs which the associate research director testified were "closely comparable" with, and parallel to, Communist literature that he had read. They were excerpts from two papal encyclicals.

A loose and sloppy writer lays himself open particularly to accidental misquotation, but any writer would find it very hard to write a paragraph that is proof against a deliberate and skillful excerpt-lifter. Dean Sturges of the Yale Law School perhaps came as close as anyone can when, in 1949, the Harvard Law School *Record* asked him for an appropriate comment on the Harvard Law School's decision to admit women students for the first time. Dean Sturges is reported to have sent the following telegram:

YALE LAW FACULTY AND STUDENT BODY DEEPLY MOVED. FEEL IT QUITE POS-SIBLE HARVARD MAY MAKE CONTRIBUTION TO WOMANHOOD. DOUBT MANY ADVERSE CONSEQUENCES HARVARD FACULTY OR STUDENT BODY. WE HAVE ALWAYS FOLLOWED WITH GENUINE INTEREST LONG STRUGGLE HARVARD LIBERALS IN THIS MATTER. OUR MANY GENERATIONS OF WOMEN GRADUATES ARE OF COURSE A PRIDE AND JOY. BEST WISHES.

Try digging a quotable compliment out of that.

The importance of context in the interpretation of meaning varies from one discourse to another. In a technical article on mathematics or physics, most sentences can stand pretty much on their own feet and be well understood apart from their context. Scientific terms are designed to resist the influence of context so that they can pass from one context to another without changing their meaning. But sentences in ordinary discourse that contain pronouns often lean on other sentences that contain the antecedents of those pronouns. Moreover, some words in our language — and they are among the most useful, but the trickiest, ones — are so adaptable to their context, like chameleons, that they take most of their character from it, and when they are considered apart from any context, they have only the most indefinite meaning. Words like "efficient," "dangerous," "internal," "successful," "free," tell us very little unless we are told, for example, the *purpose* for which it is efficient, or the *standards* in terms of which the success is judged. Contexts like "freehanded," "free lunch," "free love," "free will," "freeborn," "free association," help to limit the word "free" to a somewhat more definite range of meaning, but even in such cases we often feel that we don't know exactly what the word "free" means unless the context provides answers to the questions: "Free *from* what?" "Free *for* what?" "Free *to do* what?"

Another thing that shows the importance of context is the fact that when people use the wrong word we sometimes know what word should have been used. When Mrs. Malaprop says, "I would by no means wish a daughter of mine to be a progeny of learning . . . I would have her instructed in geometry, that she might know something of the contagious countries," we understand what she thought she was saying because the context so clearly tells us what words are called for if the sentences are to make sense. A malapropism is a word that is wrongly used in a sentence in place of another word that sounds somewhat like it. And if we couldn't tell from the context what the appropriate word would be, we could never recognize a malapropism.

But of course it would be a mistake to overemphasize contextual influence and say that a word *never* has the same meaning in two different contexts. If this were true, language would be even more difficult to manage than it is now. A person who says, "I believe in the dictionary" and later "I believe in the Bible" is presumably using the word "believe" in the same sense in both contexts. Perhaps sometimes when we say that a word is used twice in the same sense we ignore slight differences that could be important for one purpose or another. It is a good idea to keep in mind that a change in context *may* make a change in the sense, but it doesn't seem that it *must*. In the present paragraph the word "context" has, up to this point, been used three times, in three slightly different (immediate) contexts; but it has about the same meaning each time.

It is only when the context is considerably different that the meaning is likely to change. A person who says, "I believe in the dictionary," and, later, "I don't believe in ghosts," is using the word "believe" in two very different senses. But in each of these contexts it can have only one possible meaning, and when the whole context is taken into account there *may* be no question what that meaning is. "I believe in a federal world government" means about the same as "I believe *there should be* a federal world government." "I believe in extrasensory perception" means about the same as "I believe *there is such a thing* as extrasensory perception." "I believe in woman's intuition" means about the same as "I believe *that some of the things that* women intuit *are true.*"

When a word can have different meanings in different kinds of context, we can say that it has variable meaning. Its meaning *varies,* and it therefore has a variety of senses when it appears in the dictionary. Some words are more variable than others. But the variable meaning of words doesn't ordinarily give us any trouble so long as there is enough contextual control. The trouble arises when the context is not complete enough to rule out all but one possible meaning. If I say, "Henry rents the house," there is no way for you to tell from the sentence itself whether Henry rents the house *from* someone or *to* someone. When a word can have one (but not both) of two (or more) meanings in a certain context, we shall say that the word is ambiguous *in that context.*

The ambiguity of a word is always relative to a context: no word is ambiguous *in itself.* Some words like "freedom," "religion," "democracy," are ambiguous in quite a few contexts, and that is why you have to be careful in interpreting and in using them. Sometimes such words are said to be "meaningless," but the trouble with them is just the opposite; they have so many subtly different meanings that it takes a good deal of skill — more than most writers command — to keep their meanings well under control. And when the writer fails in this task, it's up to the reader. Other words, such as the common nouns are variable in meaning but are hardly ever ambiguous. It takes a good deal of ingenuity to write a medium-sized sentence in which the word "foot" is ambiguous.

A case of ambiguity, as we have defined it, is a case where there is some *doubt* about a way a discourse is to be interpreted, and you have to choose between alternative readings. Unfortunately, this is not the way the word "ambiguity" is always used. When A. E. Housman, in his poem "To an Athlete Dying Young," writes,

> Home they brought him, shoulder high,
> Townsman of a stiller town,

the word "town" has at least two meanings: the young man's village is quieter for the funeral than it was on the day everyone cheered his victory, and also he is now among the noiseless dead. But "town" is not ambiguous here. It has *both* meanings at once, and there is no uncertainty about them at all.

This sort of double meaning, or multiple meaning as it may be called, is also characteristic of one type of pun. There is the old pun, for example, about the two women leaning out of their windows across an alley and shouting at each other angrily: they can never come to an agreement because they are arguing from different premises. Another type of pun is built on *homonyms,* that is, words that have the same sound but different senses ("boy," "buoy"; "recede," "reseed"; "bier," "beer"; "air," "heir"). If you want to call homonyms the same word because they have the same sound you would then have to say that such words have an even more variable meaning than we supposed. On the whole, we may as well call them different words if they are spelt differently, and then we shall not need to say any more about homonyms, except to note that they can give rise to the sort of pun made by Macbeth when he says he will plant circumstantial evidence on the grooms:

> "If he do bleed,
> I'll *gild* the faces of the grooms withal,
> For it must seem their *guilt.*"

This sort of double entendre, whether in pun or poem, is sometimes called "ambiguity," but it is a very different thing from ambiguity in the sense in which we are using the term. The important thing at the moment is to note that there is a difference. The high-pressure context of a poem can squeeze many senses, all at once, out of some of its words; this is the multiple meaning of poetic discourse. But we have ambiguity, in the strict sense, when the context is too loose and flabby to hold the words steadily to *any* definite sense. The poet has managed to say several things at once; the ambiguous writer has not quite succeeded in saying anything.

Vagueness

A statement is either true or false, it can't be half-and-half. (A "half-truth" is false.) And an object is either an airplane or it is not; it can't be more or less an airplane. "True" and "airplane" are *either-or* words, but many other words in our language are not either-or words, but *more-or-less* words. A piece of bread can be more or less stale, an argument more or less convincing, a person more or less rich, tired, or bald. These words refer to qualities that vary in degree or amount. They are terms of comparison, or *comparative terms.* Under this label we shall include all words about which it makes sense to ask: How much? or How many? You can ask, "How rich is the Aga Khan?" or "How stale is the bread?" You can't ask, "How airplane is this object?" and when people ask, as they occasionally do, "How true is this statement?" this seems to be a loose colloquial way of asking, not how *true* it is, but how much *evidence* there is for it — which is quite a different thing.

Most of our common comparative terms are also used to classify things. We speak of bread as being more or less stale; but also, in terms of its degree of staleness, we divide bread into *stale* bread and *fresh* bread. If a person is rich enough we call him "rich," and make a threefold division here between the rich, the poor, and the ones who are neither. If a person loses enough hair, we call him "bald"; if a tire loses enough air, we call it "flat"; and if a driver has enough accidents, we call him "unsafe."

The word "enough" is a key word here, for it leads us to ask questions like this: Exactly *how* dry must bread be in order to be stale? How much money must a man have in order to be rich? How many hairs must a man lose in order to be bald? How many accidents must a driver have, and how serious must they be, if he is to be considered unsafe?

These are all natural questions, and the important point about language that we want to be clear about here is just that *they have no answers*. We have never come to any agreement, tacit or explicit, about these words; there is simply no general rule according to which anyone with less than 196 hairs is bald, or anyone with more than $17,412.35 is rich. How old is middle-aged? Where does red leave off and orange begin? How cold is a cold shoulder? We have never drawn a line at any particular place, and so there is no definite line: this is what we mean when we say that a word is *vague*.

A vague word refers to a certain range of variation in intensity or quantity. Think of a sort of scale, ranging, say, from people with no money to the person who has the most, or from people with no hair to people with bushy tresses, or from bread right out of the oven to bread that has been around for months. In the case of a vague word, there is always a certain part of the scale to which the word definitely, and by universal agreement, applies: anyone who has twenty millions is surely rich, anyone with nothing but a slight fringe of hair is bald, and bread that has begun to mold is definitely stale. Moreover, there is always a certain part of the scale to which the word definitely does *not* apply: a person with only forty-five dollars is *not* rich; a person with hair covering the top of his head is certainly *not* bald; and bread that is only an hour old is *not* stale.

But in between these two parts of the scale there is a *doubtful area* where we have not decided whether to apply the word or not. There will be borderline savings accounts, heads of hair, and loaves of bread that you can describe either way, just as there are people you don't know whether to call "middle-aged" or not. If the word were *precise*, it would be defined so as to draw a sharp line. It is just the nature of a vague word that the line it draws is fuzzy.

As you can see, vagueness is a very different sort of thing from ambiguity. In ambiguity you have a choice between two distinct senses of a word, which may be as unrelated as plane geometry and marital disorders (as in two senses of "triangle"), only there is no way to decide how to choose. In vagueness, you know what the sense is all right, but you don't know *how much* there is of the quality referred to. Thus a word that has several meanings may be vague in some senses but not in others (compare "cold war" and "cold shoulder," "hot jazz" and "hot air"). And even when there is no question about the sense of a word, its doubtful area may shift from context to context. A large child is not the same as a large elephant; in both of these contexts the word is vague, but the doubtful area for children would be in pounds, and for elephants in hundreds of pounds. Compare "hot day," "hot bath," "hot oven" and "hot star," in each of these contexts "hot" means a different degree of temperature, and some of these "hot"s are fuzzier than others: "It's a hot day" is very loosely used, but when the cook book advises a "hot oven" for popovers, this has a pretty definite agreed-upon meaning.

So far, we have defined the word "vague" in such a way that only comparative terms are vague. But it is useful to broaden this a little further. Some words that are not comparative words themselves are defined in terms of other words that *are* comparative words. "Explosion" means "a rapid combustion"; thus, so long as there is no general rule that specifies *how* rapid a combustion must be before it is to be called an explosion, the word "explosion" is vague in *one* respect. Similarly, "democracy," in some of its senses, is vague in some respects. When you want to know whether a given word is vague, then, ask yourself, first, whether there is any question of *degree* involved in applying the word, and second, whether the degree involved is anywhere precisely specified.

It is important to realize that vague words can be very useful. In fact, some of them are useful *because* they are vague: it is handy to be able to report that the room was "crowded," without having to calculate the number of people per square foot; it is equally handy for us to be able to speak of the "context" of a word, without having to specify exactly and for all cases exactly how many words before and after a given word we shall include in its context. As for most other vague words, if we haven't bothered to make them precise it may be simply that we haven't needed to do so. A vague word is useful so long as it marks *some* distinction: that is, as long as we can point out something to which the word surely applies (the New England town meeting is definitely a democracy, in one sense of this word) and something to which the word surely does not apply (the Franco government in Spain is definitely *not* a democracy, in the same sense of this word).

Or take another example. The words "good taste" and "bad taste" are vague: how bad does taste have to be before it is "bad"? When the Senate Judiciary Subcommittee on Juvenile Delinquency was investigating comic books, in the spring of 1954, it was struck by a comic book whose cover showed a man with a bloody axe in one hand, holding up a severed woman's head in the other. The publisher of this comic book, who was testifying, cited it as an example of "good taste." Senator Kefauver, somewhat taken aback, asked the logically correct question to discover whether the publisher really meant anything by this description: how would the cover have to look if it were in *bad* taste? "It would be in bad taste," replied the publisher, "if the head were held a little higher, with the blood dripping out." This showed that he was drawing *some* line, though perhaps a rather odd one, and hence that "good taste" at least meant *something* to him.

Vague words get us into trouble only when we don't notice that they are vague. We expect too much of them, and they let us down. We think there must be a sharp line between "neutrality" and "involvement," when in fact there is just a blurry no man's land. Sheep and goats, chairs and tables, males and females can be separated from each other in a way that will satisfy nearly everyone, for these words have highly determinate meanings. Moreover, nature and human workmanship have provided us with easily distinguishable things instead of borderline cases. But two heads of hair may differ by a single hair, two bank accounts by less than a dollar, and the ages of two people by a few minutes. In such cases, there will be heads of hair, bank accounts, and people's ages that we won't have any generally agreed upon way of describing.

And this is why it is essential for words to be reasonably precise when questions of truth and falsity arise. The main counts of the Government's indictment of Professor Owen Lattimore accused him of "following the Communist line" and being a "promoter of Communist interests." These counts were thrown out by the Court of Appeals on the ground of vagueness, in keeping with the Sixth Amendment, which specifies that a person has a right to know what crime he is accused of before he can be tried. If the words used to describe the crime are not clear, how can he know what he is being tried for, and how can he defend himself? And how can the jury be expected to decide objectively whether he is guilty of it or not?

But of course, no matter how vague a word may be, we can always make it as precise as we wish for particular purposes and in particular contexts. We *can* draw a sharp line when we want to. A herring is a large sardine; that is a vague way of talking. For its convenience, however, the Food and Drug Administration calls a sardine a "herring" only when it is at least nine inches long. That is fairly precise. In common speech, the words "urban" and "rural" are vague. But the United States Census makes a sharper distinction: if a town has a population of 2,500 or more it is "urban," if not, it is "rural." "High-income group" is vague, but Congress,

---

Things were first made, then words.

SIR THOMAS OVERBURY

in a particular act, may arbitrarily draw the line at $25,000. This is a perfectly sensible procedure. Of course, it will always sound odd to say that a person making $25,000 a year is in a "high-income group," whereas a person making $24,999.99 is not. But you have to draw the line *somewhere* if you draw it at all. Where the scale is in terms of pennies, any particular place to draw the line will seem arbitrary.

Sometimes the line drawn may, in fact, be *too* arbitrary for the purpose at hand. If a great deal hinges on the distinction, it may be more than such a slight difference will bear. It doesn't seem fair to pass a student who gets 60 and fail a student who gets 59; we don't feel sure enough about the accuracy of tests and grades to make such an important result depend upon such a minute difference. This is why some educators prefer to use a vaguer scale, such as A, B, C, or Pass, High Pass, Honors, for grading students. Precision is always relative to what we want to do with it. Unnecessary precision is pedantic and fussy, like honing a razor to cut butter. Still, to develop skill in careful thinking, it is sometimes useful to practice a little pedantry. If you know how to make precise distinctions, you are free to decide, in a given case, just how far you ought to go. Each case is different, and only by studying it carefully can you determine what degree of vagueness is probably safe and perhaps desirable.

We would have little trouble in handling vague words, once we understood their habits, if it were not for one ingenious way of misusing them that may impose upon our thinking when we are off guard. It consists in arguing that there is no difference, or no important difference, between two things because the apparent difference is made up of a whole series of small differences. It doesn't matter much whether you smoke ten cigarettes a day or eleven, it doesn't matter much whether you smoke eleven or twelve, and so on. Someone might argue that therefore it doesn't matter whether you smoke ten or forty: there is no difference between heavy smoking and light smoking because any attempt to draw the line, say between thirteen and fourteen, is arbitrary. The amount of freedom you enjoy in one country only differs in degree from the amount of freedom you enjoy in another country; sometimes people argue that since it is only a difference of degree, it is therefore not much of a difference at all: "they are both about the same."

This sort of argument commits the black-or-white fallacy. It is a subtle attempt to paralyze choice by belittling an important difference. It is especially plausible when the distinctions are vague. The prefix "crypto-" has in recent years been used to great advantage in muddling people's thinking about political attitudes. As it is sometimes loosely used, a man can apparently be a disguised, or "crypto-" Communist without knowing it, or, indeed, without doing anything about it. According to this line of thought, a Democrat is a "crypto-liberal," a liberal is a "crypto-socialist," a socialist is a "crypto-communist," and a communist is a traitor; therefore Democrats are traitors, or practically traitors. When put in such a bare form, without any fancy trimmings, this argument doesn't look as though it would fool anyone. But it has been a staple commodity with some rabble rousers, who have done their best to make it appear that there is no important difference between both ends of their equation.

The same method of reasoning sometimes turns up in discussions of the degree of economic difficulty the United States economy may be undergoing at a certain time. There is "inventory correction," "rolling adjustment," "recession," and "depression," and (because the black-or-white fallacy works both ways) there may be an attempt to play down the differences by those who want to show that current troubles are *worse* than they really are (hardly distinguishable from a small depression) and at the same time by those who want to show that current troubles are *not as bad* as they really are (merely a sizeable inventory correction). The only way to get a proper perspective on the situation, and escape both fallacious arguments, is to insist on some definite distinctions between these various ills. For example, let's not call it a depression unless it involves a downward movement on the part of nearly every economic index, and unemployment of at least five million over a period of at least two years. If that seems *too* fine a line, it is easy enough to relax it. But at least we can keep the discussion from bogging down in a mushy terminology like "crypto-depression."

The black-or-white argument is a favorite with extremists, who are blind to the differences between shades of gray because to them the only "real" difference is between black and white. On a scale of cigarette smoking or civil liberty the *big* differences are made up of many *small* differences, but that doesn't make the big difference any less big. There are differences in *kind* and there are differences in *degree,* but some differences in degree are, from a practical point of view, just as crucial as differences in kind. We succeed only in drugging our thinking when we allow these differences to be smudged over by verbal trickery.

FOR DISCUSSION

1. What does "context" mean? Is the context of a particular word always other words, or can the situation itself provide a context?

2. Here are three statements that, standing alone, are ambiguous. The first has at least two possible meanings; the second, three; the third, four. Can you supply verbal or situational contexts, or both, that will compel each of the possible meanings? (*a*) The natives want to have the minister for dinner. (*b*) I shall lose no time in reading it. (*c*) He called up the dumb waiter.

3. How many meanings can you find for the spoken phrase: a pretty little girls school?

4. What is the difference between vagueness and ambiguity?

5. How can the usefulness of certain words depend on their vagueness?

VOCABULARY: qualifications, tax-exempt foundations, papal encyclical, malapropism, extrasensory perception, homonym, tacit, indictment, economic index.

THEME TOPICS: A word is known by the company it keeps. Running through (or down or across or into) some meanings of "run." Vagueness can be a virtue.

Scented Words

H. L. MENCKEN

Oft in the stilly night, ere slumber's chain has bound me, I find myself sweating over a problem both philological and psychological; to wit, why in hell have the used-car dealers of this great republic never devised a better term to designate their profession? What could be more soaring than their idealism — I always think of them, in fact, as one of the great glories of the Rotarian metaphysic — and yet what could be more prosaic and forbidding than the name by which they call themselves? The realtors, if they were of like backwardness, would still be *real-estate agents* and brothers to the ox, and the morticians would still be *undertakers* and brothers to the buzzard. Are the used-car boys, then, too dumb to invent a match for *realtor* and *mortician?* Hardly, for haven't they already got rid of the vulgar and sordid *second-hand* by subisuting the tasty *used,* and do not some of them proceed from *used* to *nearly new* and *experienced?* No, it can't be that. They are smart enough to excogitate something as far beyond *realtor* and *mortician* as either is beyond *mixologist,* for bartender, or *commissionnaire,* for door opener. They have simply fumbled their chance and neglected their duty. They suffer from a form of aphasia, and every lover of beauteous words must hope that it will be as evanescent as it is deplorable.

If my talent for constructive onomatology were as lively as it used to be, I'd throw myself into the breach without further ado and offer them something nifty. There was a time when this gift of mine was so powerful that I tossed off *ecdysiast* for the strip-tease gals and *bootician* for the more recherché bootleggers without blowing a vein, but that, alas, was some years ago, before morticians began to send me Christmas cards. As things

Originally published in *The New Yorker,* April 2, 1949. Copr. © 1949, The New Yorker Magazine, Inc. Reprinted by permission of *The New Yorker* and Alfred A. Knopf, Inc.

stand, the best I can do is lament that all terms based upon the obvious word *service* are barred out, for the keepers of gas stations and roadside feed troughs have already hogged them, including even the verb *to service*, which Robert Louis Stevenson invented in 1893 and then abandoned. It would be hard to imagine any group of Americans more devoted to the dream of Service than the used-car dealers, for even the most earthy of them, when he ropes a prospect, serves him by saving him from the others, but words of the *service* class, as I say, are out, since such forms as *service station, tire service, curb service,* and so on, not only are already hogged but have become banal. For a couple of weeks, I toyed with terms, chiefly from foreign languages, that plausibly adumbrated the used-car dealers' stern and, indeed, almost suicidal ideal of rectitude, but I had to give it up when I found no better sources than the French *probité* and *confidence,* one of which suggests prying grand juries and the other of which has been preempted by the confidence men. That the problem will be solved soon or late, and in a poetic and dashing manner, I am sure; at the time, unhappily, I am unequal to it.

Pondering it, I have been led to cast my eye over some of the more recent bedfellows of *realtor* and *mortician,* and find that several very nobby ones have been invented within the past few years. Perhaps the nobbiest of all is *zymurgeon,* to designate one who serves humanity by working in a brewery. This was thrown to the winds in 1947 by the St. Louis *Star-Times,* which maybe got the idea from a book by the English wordmonger Ivor Brown, who discovered several years ago that the tony word for brewing is *zymurgy. Zymurgy,* at that time, was certainly not new. It had been listed in all the dictionaries, in fact, for nearly a century, but inasmuch as it always appeared near the bottom of the last page, it was overlooked by all previous connoisseurs of verbal delicatessen. It had an analogue, the adjective *zymotic,* which was quite as old, and probably even older. *Zymotic,* however, has nothing to do with the confection of malt liquor. It was used by medical men, in the days before the germ theory of disease, to designate such contagious maladies as smallpox, measles, and typhoid fever, for they were then thought to be produced by a process resembling fermentation. That process, in truth, *did* resemble fermentation more or less, but when Pasteur, Koch, and company began proving that not ferments but bacilli were to blame, *zymotic* disappeared from the medical books, and any doctor who used it today would be dismissed as paleolithic. Both *zymurgy* and *zymotic,* the former suggested by *metallurgy,* were derived originally from a Greek word, *zyme,* meaning a ferment or leaven. The *Star-Times,* starting with *zymurgy,* arrived at *zymurgeon* by thinking of *surgeon,* just as the undertakers arrived at *mortician* by thinking of *physician,* their immemorial pal, and the real-estate boys at *realtor* by thinking of such elegant words as *senator* and *ambassador.* I should add that the *Star-Times* is not indissolubly wedded by *zymurgeon;* it is also flirting with *zymeotechnician,* and may hatch even gaudier ones later on. So far, the brew-workers of St. Louis have not indicated their preference, if, indeed, they have ever heard of the matter at all. My own choice is *zymurgeon*, though I am still willing to hear argument in favor of *zymeotechnician*, and even *zymor*, *zymologist*, *zymiast*, *zymician*, and *zymurgic engineer*. When a brew-master, fearing the return of prohibition, takes a header into one of his vats and is not found until the next morning, he is obviously a *zymocide*. So is a boozer who makes a bet that he can drink thirty kegs of beer in thirty days.

The year 1947 also saw the birth of *sanitor* for janitor, a crown and climax to the process that, some time previously, had worked through *superintendent, custodian, custodian-engineer, custodial engineer*, and, finally, *building engineer*. The new term was born in Louisville and has since made its way to most other cultural centers, though the janitors in the New York public schools are still *custodian-engineers* and those in the warrens of job-holders at Washington are officially *custodian-personnel*. There seems to be a powerful pull, probably inspired by the roaring success of *realtor*, toward the suffix *-or*, and it is thus not surprising that the janitors have come back to it. Many neighborhood butchers and greengrocers are now calling themselves *purveyors*, and virtually all house painters of any tone have become *decorators*. (Meanwhile, not a few interior decorators, disgusted by this invasion from below, have taken to calling themselves *interiorists*.) In many ambitious crafts *-or* is reached by simply turning a traditional *e* into *o*. In 1941, for example, a faction of welders, having seceded in a huff from the American Federation of Labor, changed their name to the more genteel *weldor*, and have since operated a Brotherhood of *Weldors*, Cutters and Helpers of America. The possibilities along this line are manifest. The bartenders, who have scored a failure with *mixologist*, might very well turn to *bartendor*, and the plumbers, who have done almost as badly with *sanitarian* and *sanitary engineer*, might try *plumbor*. Also, there are *truckor, roofor, jewelor, waitor, gardenor*, and *bouncor*. Each of these would borrow some of the fragrance of *realtor*.

The pull of *-or* is so strong that the pedagogues, who began to call themselves *educationists* a decade or so ago, have now gone back to *educator*, which appeared as a rival for the homely *teacher* in Shakespeare's time. I myself once proposed *autor* for dealers in new cars (not used, nearly new, or experienced), but it did not take, maybe because it was too close to *author*, which designates a generally insolvent and contemptible class of men. Nearly all bookkeepers are now *auditors*, and those that are not are *accountants*. *Operator* is used often, as in *rodent operator* or *pest-control operator* (abbreviated to *P.C.O.*), for rat-catcher. The keeper of a necktie shoppe in New York calls himself a *cravateur*, which has a family resemblance to the French *cravatier* and may be only a way stop on the road to *cravator*. In other directions, there is the same steady progress toward euphemism. Some of the sweller jewellers, having muffed *jewellor,* have resorted to *jewellist,* and every rubber in a Turkish bath is now a *physiotherapist.* The regular doctors who specialize in muscle bending formerly used that term, but in 1946 they began to look for something more polished, and now they vacillate between *physiatrist, physiatrician,* and *physicologist,* with the medical journals reporting that *physiatrist* is winning out, though it is hard on the tongue. I add a few more: *home aide,* for servant girl (apparently invented in Canada); *dietician* or *nutritionist,* for cook; *insurance consultant,* for insurance agent (vice *insuror,* which was a flop); and *wedding manager* or *director,* for *shadchen.* The goons who chase small boys playing hooky are no longer *truant officers,* as aforetime, but *attendance officers.* The maids who mop up in hospitals have ceased to be maids and become *nurses' orderlies.* Garbage men are now *sanitary officers,* or, in some towns, *sanitation expediters.* The boys who wrap up packages in stores are *packageers,* builders are *constructioneers,* soda jerks are *fountaineers,* cleaners of cesspools are *septicians,* chimney sweeps (who survive in England) are *fluonomists,* disc jockeys are *transcription directors,* junkmen are *salvagers* or *waste-material dealers,* window dressers are *directors of visual presentation,* washwomen are *clothing refreshers,* and the girls in the ten-cent stores, in certain ultra-progressive communities, have become *counter clerks, sales assistants,* or *service women.*

The hairdressers, as everyone knows, long ago abandoned their ancient designation, traced to 1771, for *beautician, cosmetician, cosmetologist, hair stylist,* and *beauty engineer.* The name *cosmetologist* has been recognized in many states, and also in the District of Columbia, where, in 1938, Congress set up a board to examine practitioners and defined their art as that of doing "arranging, dressing, styling, curling, waving, cleansing, cutting, removing, singeing, bleaching, coloring, or similar work upon the hair of any person by any means, and with hands or mechanical or electrical apparatus or appliances, or by the use of cosmetic preparations, antiseptics, tonics, lotions, or creams, massaging, cleansing, stimulating, exercising, beautifying, or similar work, the scalp, face, neck, arms, bust, or upper part of the body, or manicuring the nails of any person." In their first days of glory, the gals called their dens *parlors, shops, shoppes* (including *beauté shoppés*), and *salons,* but of late they have taken to *center, bar, clinic, laboratory, studio,* and even *villa* and *château.* Like the *chirotonsors,* or barbers, they have pushed their prices so high that they now suffer from a buyers' strike, and have laid in large lines of unguents to be used at home, in the hope of squeezing a few more dollars out of their patrons, who are not customers but *clients* or *patients.*

The morticians also are now using *patient* to designate a customer, though some prefer *case* and a few of the less progressive, at least in their clinical conferences, cling to *body, remains,* and even *stiff* and *meat.* But *corpse,* according to a manual issued by the National Selected Morticians *in* 1941, "is an offensive word." Just why it is offensive is not explained. It dates from the early fourteenth century, was used with no thought of gaucherie by Chaucer, Shakespeare, Milton, Bacon, and Ruskin, and occurs four times in the King James Bible. Some of the ultra- or super-morticians of Hollywood are now toying with *loved one* for the deceased, as readers of Evelyn Waugh's novel of that name well know. The same dreamers call the place where he is on show the *slumber room,* though I gather that the Selected Morticians prefer *reposing room.* So far as I can make out, no one, even in Hollywood, has ever invented a euphemism for *embalmer,* but the atelier in which he works is no longer his *morgue* but his *preparation room, operating room,* or *laboratory.* In circles of any refinement, the term *coffin* has given way to *casket,* though the latter was derided by Nathaniel Hawthorne in 1863 as "a vile modern phrase" (*sic*) that takes all the poetry out of death. *Coffin* came into English from the French centuries ago, but has been under fire since the rise of elegance in Early Victorian days. During the Civil War era, it had a formidable rival in *case,* but *casket* knocked out both afterward, Hawthorne to the contrary not-withstanding. The Selected Morticians say that *coffin* now means only "a special wedge-shaped receptacle," like those still in use both in the British Isles and on the Continent of Europe. But the War Department, perhaps remembering that George Washington is buried in one at Mt. Vernon, sticks to the term.

A man who uses a great many words to express his meaning is like a bad marksman who instead of aiming a single stone at an object takes up a handful and throws at it in hopes he may hit.

SAMUEL JOHNSON

I know an undertaker in Baltimore, of the highest chop, who continues to call his establishment a *funeral parlor,* but most of the others have now substituted *chapel, drawing room,* or *funeral home.* Back in the nineties of the last century, as I am informed by a stenographic report of the Carlyle W. Harris murder trial, there was at least one undertaker in New York who called his place a *store.* The Selected Morticians warn their members that the can or jar in which clean dirt is carried to the loved one's last resting place ("ashes to ashes, dust to dust") is under no circumstances to be called the *sandbox,* even *sotto voce.* In Hollywood, incidentally, burial is going out, at least among Class A movie folk. They are now disposed of by *inhumement, entombment, inurnment, immurement,* or *insarcophagus-ment.* A spot close enough to Valentino to be in his glare of immortality costs something on the order of twenty-five thousand dollars.

Who invented *mortician* is not known, but the records show that it was first used in the *Embalmer's Monthly* early in 1895. It was not, however, until September 17, 1917, that the Selected Morticians launched their very exclusive organization, which is confined to one practitioner in a town and is almost as snobbish as the Porcellian Club, at Harvard. I am told, indeed, by one of its stars that even a former fellow of the Porcellian Club is occasionally backballed, not to mention a member of Phi Beta Kappa or the Union League of Philadelphia. Dr. Louise Pound reported in *Dialect Notes* in 1918 that there were already country undertakers in both central Iowa and western Washington who had grabbed *mortician,* and even debased it to *morticianer,* and since then it has come into such widespread use in all parts of the country that even the *Journal of the American Medical Association,* the bible of the doctors, has formally recognized it. On July 19, 1897, the *Journal* printed a learned article in which morticians and pathologists were jointly given good advice about the use of rubber gloves in their procedures.

In 1940, the cobblers of the United States suddenly decided to call themselves *shoetricians,* apparently in imitation of *mortician* and *physician,* and on February 25th of that year those of Texas and the adjacent states formed the Texas-Southwestern Association of *Shoetricians,* at Forth Worth. But the New York *Times* poked such vicious sport at the new name on March 13th, and so many other newspapers joined in reviling it, that it quickly died the death. The cobblers then went back to *shoe rebuilder,* which had been invented in 1935, and it still survives. Their trade journal is the *Master Shoe Rebuilder,* of Boston, which has a large circulation and has absorbed the archaic *Shoe Repairer.* So far, not many of them have followed the beauticians and morticians in inventing fancy names for their studios, though I have heard of a *shuchâteau* in Denver. The morticians themselves have set up a monthly *Mid-Continent Mortician,* in Minneapolis, but their principal organ is the poetically named *Casket and Sunny Side,* which was founded in 1871 and is still flourishing lushly. Its runner-up, only ten years younger, bears the old-fashioned title of the *American Funeral Director.*

The morticians made one capital mistake at the start of their distinguished career: they neglected to register their new name as a trademark. As a result, it is in the public domain, and anyone who chooses to do so may use it. The realtors were a good deal smarter. *Realtor* is their private property, and whenever any unauthorized person cabbages it, their lawyers clamp down on him hard. Indeed, they even pursue and afflict newspapers and magazines that apply it inadvertently to a heathen and a stranger. This, I suppose, accounts for the fact that Negro real-estate agents have had to invent a name of their own; to wit, *realtist.* But Negro undertakers are free to use *mortician* in a wide and lavish way, and they do so everywhere in the United States.

FOR DISCUSSION

1. How would you describe what this essay is about? Is the title deliberately — and wittily — ambiguous?

2. Is the essay systematically organized? How many subdivisions of the main topic?

3. Is it concerned only with words as words or with the people who use these words? What is Mencken's attitude toward the people? Do you think he is justified?

4. Mencken's style is very much his own. How would you describe it? Is the key to his style a continuous contrast of the ridiculous and the sublime, the informal and the formal, both in what he says and in how he says it? Can you assemble examples of this characteristic, beginning with the opening sentence? How about phrases like "recherché bootleggers" and "used-car dealers' stern and, indeed, almost suicidal ideal of rectitude"?

5. Is Mencken here discussing what Galbraith might call a wordfact? What "facts" are the words trying to give life to?

VOCABULARY: prosaic, aphasia, evanescent, adumbrate, connoisseur, analogue, paleolithic, vacillate, gaucherie, public domain.

THEME TOPICS: Style is the man; or, I know you, Mr. Mencken. Slang can be effective. Tasty words and a tony style. Shock values in language.

The Game of Words

LOUIS B. SALOMON

A word game — that's something we play for fun to take our mind off the capriciousness of the game we play for keeps every time we open our mouth to ask for beer or road directions, every time we write a note to the milkman or a letter to the newspaper. Feeling intuitively how much we have at stake in the *real* language game, we hate to admit to ourselves that it doesn't dance to logical tunes of our own composing, and whenever it misses a step we prefer to pretend that it didn't happen.

Among our many illusions about the way we write or speak, one of the hardest to give up — even when it costs us money — is the assumption that one word stands for one thing or concept, even though the concept may be as atomic as that represented by *a* or *the* or *of*. If, for example, you ever pause to wonder why it costs twice as much to mention, say, a New Zealander in a telegram as it does to mention, say, an Irishman, you will probably shrug off both the expense and the question with, "Oh well, *Irishman* is one word and *New Zealander* is two," and turn right back to building your birdhouse or your chicken house, or whistling your game dog to bring back the game bird so that you can stuff it into your gamebag — provided the gamekeeper hasn't nabbed you as an unlicensed game hunter.

If anyone asks you why *Irishman* is one word and *New Zealander* two, you will probably tell him to go peddle his newspapers, and if driven to it you will spin out some cobwebby sophism to convince yourself that when you say "newspaper" or "wallpaper" you are thinking of a single concept while "wrapping paper" or "carbon paper" represents two concepts. You have, of course, a logical, orderly mind, and you know as surely as you know the reality of a warm bed or a cold martini that language consists of words and words are units of meaning. Otherwise . . . well, hang it all, it otherwise just doesn't make sense.

If any doubt nags you, you can fall back on the dictionaries for support and comfort. Thus the Merriam-Webster *Collegiate* defines *word* as "the smallest unit of speech that has meaning when taken by itself." The *American College Dictionary* calls it "an element which can stand alone as an utterance, not divisible into two or more parts similarly characterized; thus *boy* and *boyish*, but not *-ish* or *boy scout*, the former being less than a word, the latter more."

But doesn't this rather beg the question of why *boy scout* is more than a word, and leave us also wondering why, when a boy scout feels chilly on his campground, he pulls up a camp chair in front of the campfire — or why, if he does his own laundering, he has to support his clothesline with a clothes pole, until he either hangs his duds on a clothes hanger or stows them away in a clothespress? Yet I know people who would lie awake all night figuring out an excuse for believing that *clothes hanger* represents two concepts while *clothesline* only one, rather than admit that the only difference lies in the custom of spacing on the written page that happens to be followed by most of the well-educated writers of English today.

Of course there is always the in-between device of the hyphen. In a sense all standard hyphenated compounds (that is, those that appear in "the dictionary") are weasel words, confessions of vacillation between our sense that they represent a single concept, as nearly as may be, and our filial subservience to the rules of the editor's stylebook. The modern current in English has set in the direction of combination, first via the hyphen, like a timid swimmer hesitantly wetting himself to the knees, and finally the bold plunge, made only in behalf of individual compounds, seldom systematically for all expressions of a type. Your hand-knit sweater is, by definition, handmade; it will keep you warm under the star-spangled (or starlit) sky of a clear autumn night. If, through overexposure in the sun parlor, you should become sun-struck, the doctor will treat you for sunstroke.

Sometimes the in-between stage is lacking, and we have only the fully integrated swimmer and the non-swimmer standing on the dry shore of *apartheid,* with no logical reason why either should not be in the other's place. The finger marks on your highball glass look just like the fingerprints you left on the windowpane (or on the window shade or the window sill). You toss a hand grenade at your enemy, a handball to your friend. Against a head wind you make very little headway.

Trial By Telegraph

The ivy-clad ivory towers may (and do) ring with debate as to whether *boy scout* functions as a single part of speech; whether hyphenated compounds like *well-spent* are single words; whether, in an uninflected language like English, *will go* might not just as well be written *willgo,* thus disposing of the argument over whether English verbs have a future tense. But it occurred to me recently to inquire into the practice of one agency whose approach to the question must be uncompromisingly pragmatic: the Western Union Telegraph Company. When the grammarian sends a birthday wire to his maiden aunt he has to pay by the Company's standard of word-counting, which in turn must have semantic repercussions, since even if you're a grammarian what you have to pay for as a word surely must *be* a word, and a word is a unit of meaning, etc., etc.

The result of my correspondence (by United States mail both ways: one ounce of words for four cents) with a high official of the Company, whose patience must have been sorely tried but whose courtesy never faltered, is as follows: the Company charges hyphenated compounds as single words, and in doubtful cases it accepts the authority of any standard dictionary to which a customer may appeal. Thus if you were sending a wire concerning those slippery rocks which (sometimes) keep your feet out of the creek bed, you could, if money is no object, refer to them as *stepping stones,* or you could go the cheaper way with either *stepping-stones* or *steppingstones,* the three forms being found in as many reputable dictionaries of recent date. (Tennyson characteristically chose the path of moderation when he wrote of those stepping-stones on which men rise from their dead selves to higher things.)

Standard dictionaries of approximately the same vintage, however, seldom vary widely enough to warrant your carrying an armload of reference books each time you visit a branch office of the Telegraph Company. Anyway, even advance planning can't always beat the game. For example, while my learned friends are puzzling why *paving stone* — unlike *hearthstone* or *millstone* — represents two concepts, I note glumly that if I develop a kidney stone it will cost me twice as much to notify them by wire of my affliction as it will if I come down with a gallstone.

If, however, any admirer of this article should send me a brocaded night robe, I'd save money by thanking him telegraphically for a nightdress; whereas if the gift should be a tablecloth I'd pay through the nose for my stuffiness if I called it table linen. If you're about to jump in with "Aha! a tablecloth is a single thing, but table linen includes both tablecloths and napkins," just calm down long enough to remember that a gift of knives, forks, spoons, cups, saucers, etc., could all be acknowledged at the one-word rate as tableware.

Trial By Logic

Probably the notion of the word as the "unit of meaning" is a relic of a far less literate era than ours — of a time when for the majority of people a sentence consisted of a more or less continuous chain of speech-sounds which could be arbitrarily tied off like sausages into units corresponding to concepts. Even then, of course, the locating of the exact phonetic division-points sometimes reflected accident more than logic; the history of words like *adder, apron,* and *nickname* shows that there was a time when the question of whether you were saying *a nadder* or *an adder, an ekename* or *a nekename,* would only have made you squirm with embarrassment. But in an age of almost universal literacy, words of tongue may carry less prestige than words of pen. Granted that in the normal way of life we learn to speak before we learn to read, yet many modern words, like *G.I., O.K., WAC* and *snafu,* could hardly have come into existence without the written language; and we spend the greater part of our life so compulsively manipulating — and being manipulated by — the written language that we have come, whether we admit it to ourselves or not, to regard as a word (hence as a unit of meaning) any meaningful speech-sound or set of speech-sounds which is conventionally represented in writing with a space before and after. This is more or less a linguistic truism; it is only when we try to justify such divisions on logical grounds, or when we subconsciously allow the conventions of writing to shape our thought-processes, that we are likely to find ourselves chasing will-o'-the-wisps in a semantic bog.

The National Institute of Drycleaning, for example, (all *my* dictionaries speak of dry cleaning, not even dry-cleaning) has been campaigning for years in behalf of *drycleaning,* on the ground, as reported in a recent advertisement, that the services its members offer should not be thought of as only cleaning. "They use water and steam as well as solvents, and, for certain fabrics and soil problems, even do wetcleaning." I think these people are waging a real epistemological crusade, not just trying to cut down their telegraph bills.

The basic question is: at what point do two or more closely related concepts merge like mercury drops into a single concept? Does the writing-convention in any case merely reflect our semantic stance, or does the former actually influence our view of the meaning of a verbal symbol?

In the examples given thus far — and many others like them — the original word "parts" are still so clearly recognizable that one often has to consult an up-to-date dictionary to find what practice bears the current seal of approval. But what of words that in another language, or in an earlier form of English, resulted from a mechanical fusing of two or more "separate words," the original forms being known now only to scholars? The Greeks must have been quite conscious of the compound origin of *hippopotamos,* a slightly changed form of which seems to the modern English-speaker as homogeneous as, say, *tiger* or *antelope;* yet our dictionaries list as its synonym *river horse,* which points to the same two separate defining qualities that impressed the Greeks.

People don't worry about a hippopotamus; to most of them it *is* a comically ponderous mammal which they may have seen at the zoo, but a river horse *is* a faintly (so very faintly!) horselike animal that likes to wallow in river mud. If we only wrote it *riverhorse,* we might quit looking for any trace of horsiness or river-addiction, just as precious little horsiness is suggested to the mind of a modern city-dweller by the word *sawhorse.*

You may say, of course, that neither river horses nor sawhorses are "real" horses; that metaphor leads a life outside the laws of logic. Very well, what do we do about real horses? We put one behind the plow or into the paddock and point, as it were, to dual qualities in him as a work horse or a race horse; but as soon as we install him as sultan of an equine harem we merge all his attributes into a "single" concept: studhorse — thus showing, I assume, our trust that he will devote himself single-mindedly to his new duties.

No, you just can't make system out of it, no matter if you try till you have brain fever in your brainpan. If you can't face this you may find solace in a one-word wineglass, or even deaden the pain with fewer refills by pouring the stuff into a two-word water glass. But don't, as you value your sanity, try to rationalize it on any other grounds. That would indeed be to jump out of the frying pan — though not out of the saucepan or the stewpan — into the fire.

And maybe if you just hold on long enough *water glass* (in the sense of *tumbler*) will become *waterglass.* Sometime. Well, anyway, some day.

PART TWO

LANGUAGE IN LITERATURE

The Short Story

The Play

The Poem

THE

SHORT STORY

❦ *Mystery and Surprise* ❦

The Two Bottles of Relish

LORD DUNSANY

Smithers is my name. I'm what you might call a small man, and in a small way of business. I travel for Num-numo, a relish for meats and savories; the world famous relish I ought to say. It's really quite good, no deleterious acids in it, and does not affect the heart; so it is quite easy to push. I wouldn't have got the job if it weren't. But I hope some day to get something that's harder to push, as of course the harder they are to push, the better the pay. At present I can just make my way, with nothing at all over; but then I live in a very expensive flat. It happened like this, and that brings me to my story. And it isn't the story you'd expect from a small man like me, yet there's nobody else to tell it. Those that know anything of it besides me are all for hushing it up.

Well, I was looking for a room to live in in London when first I got my job; it had to be in London, to be central; and I went to a block of buildings, very gloomy they looked, and saw the man that ran them and asked

Reprinted by permission of the author's estate.

206 · The Short Story

him for what I wanted; flats they called them; just a bedroom and a sort of a cupboard. Well, he was showing a man round at the time who was a gent, in fact more than that, so he didn't take much notice of me, the man that ran all those flats didn't, I mean. So I just ran behind for a bit, seeing all sorts of rooms, and waiting till I could be shown my class of thing. We came to a very nice flat, a sitting room, bedroom and bathroom, and a sort of little place that they called a hall. And that's how I came to know Linley. He was the bloke that was being shown round.

"Bit expensive," he said.

And the man that ran the flats turned away to the window and picked his teeth. It's funny how much you can show by a simple thing like that. What he meant to say was that he'd hundreds of flats like that, and thousands of people looking for them, and he didn't care who had them or whether they all went on looking. There was no mistaking him, somehow. And yet he never said a word, only looked away out of the window and picked his teeth. And I ventured to speak to Mr. Linley then; and I said, "How about it, sir, if I paid half, and shared it? I wouldn't be in the way, and I'm out all day, and whatever you said would go, and really I wouldn't be no more in your way than a cat."

You may be surprised at my doing it; and you'll be much more surprised at him accepting it; at least, you would if you knew me, just a small man in a small way of business; and yet I could see at once that he was taking to me more than he was taking to the man at the window.

"But there's only one bedroom," he said.

"I could make up my bed easy in that little room there," I said.

"The Hall," said the man looking round from the window, without taking his toothpick out.

"And I'd have the bed out of the way and hid in the cupboard by any hour you like," I said.

He looked thoughtful, and the other man looked out over London; and in the end, do you know, he accepted.

"Friend of yours?" said the flat man.

"Yes," answered Mr. Linley.

It was really very nice of him.

I'll tell you why I did it. Able to afford it? Of course not. But I heard him tell the flat man that he had just come down from Oxford and wanted to live for a few months in London. It turned out he wanted just to be comfortable and do nothing for a bit while he looked things over and chose a job, or probably just as long as he could afford it. Well, I said to myself, what's the Oxford manner worth in business, especially a business like mine? Why, simply everything you've got. If I picked up only a quarter of it from this Mr. Linley I'd be able to double my sales, and that would soon mean I'd be given something a lot harder to push, with perhaps treble the pay. Worth it every time. And you can make a quarter of an education go twice as far again, if you're careful with it. I mean you don't have to quote the whole of the Inferno to show that you've read Milton; half a line may do it.

An average English word is four letters and a half. By hard, honest labor I've dug all the large words out of my vocabulary and shaved it down till the average is three and a half . . . I never write metropolis *for seven cents, because I can get the same price for* city. *I never write* policeman, *because I can get the same money for* cop.

MARK TWAIN

Well, about that story I have to tell. And you mightn't think that a little man like me could make you shudder. Well, I soon forgot about the Oxford manner when we settled down in our flat. I forgot it in the sheer wonder of the man himself. He had a mind like an acrobat's body, like a bird's body. It didn't want education. You didn't notice whether he was educated or not. Ideas were always leaping up in him, things you'd never have thought of. And not only that, but if any ideas were about, he'd sort of catch them. Time and again I've found him knowing just what I was going to say. Not thought-reading, but what they call intuition. I used to try to learn a bit about chess, just to take my thoughts off Num-numo in the evening, when I'd done with it. But problems I never could do. Yet he'd come along and glance at my problem and say, "You probably move that piece first," and I'd say, "But where?" and he'd say, "Oh, one of those three squares." And I'd say, "But it will be taken on all of them." And the piece a queen all the time, mind you. And he'd say, "Yes, it's doing no good there: you're probably meant to lose it."

And, do you know, he'd be right.

You see he'd been following out what the other man had been thinking. That's what he'd been doing.

Well, one day there was that ghastly murder at Unge. I don't know if you remember it. But Seeger had gone down to live with a girl in a bungalow on the North Downs, and that was the first we had heard of him.

The girl had £200, and he got every penny of it and she utterly disappeared. And Scotland Yard couldn't find her.

Well, I'd happened to read that Seeger had bought two bottles of Num-numo; for the Otherthorpe police had found out everything about him, except what he did with the girl; and that of course attracted my attention or I should have never thought again about the case or said a word of it to Linley. Num-numo was always on my mind, as I always spent every day pushing it, and that kept me from forgetting the other thing. And so one day I said to Linley, "I wonder with all that knack you have for seeing through a chess problem, and thinking of one thing and another, that you don't have a go at that Otherthorpe mystery. It's a problem as much as chess," I said.

"There's not the mystery in ten murders that there is in one game of chess," he answered.

"It's beaten Scotland Yard," I said.

"Has it?" he asked.

"Knocked them end-wise," I said.

"It shouldn't have done that," he said. And almost immediately after he said, "What are the facts?"

We were both sitting at supper and I told him the facts, as I had them straight from the papers. She was a pretty blonde, she was small, she was called Nancy Elth, she had £200, they lived at the bungalow for five days. After that he stayed there for another fortnight, but nobody ever saw her alive again. Seeger said she had gone to South America, but later said he had never said South America, but South Africa. None of her money remained in the bank where she had kept it, and Seeger was shown to have come by at least £150 just at that time. Then Seeger turned out to be a vegetarian, getting all his food from the greengrocer, and that made the constable in the village of Unge suspicious of him, for a vegetarian was something new to the constable. He watched Seeger after that, and it's well he did, for there was nothing that Scotland Yard asked him that he couldn't tell them about him, except of course the one thing. And he told the police at Otherthorpe five or six miles away, and they came and took a hand at it too.

They were able to say, for one thing, that he never went outside the bungalow and its tidy garden ever since she disappeared. You see, the more they watched him the more suspicious they got, as you naturally do if you're watching a man; so that very soon they were watching every move he made, but if it hadn't been for his being a vegetarian they'd never have started to suspect him, and there wouldn't have been enough evidence even for Linley. Not that they found out anything much against him, except that £150 dropping in from nowhere, and it was Scotland Yard that found that, not the police of Otherthorpe.

No, what the constable of Unge found out was about the larch trees, and that beat Scotland Yard utterly, and beat Linley up to the very last, and of course it beat me. There were ten larch trees in the bit of a garden, and he'd made some sort of arrangement with the landlord, Seeger had, before he took the bungalow, by which he could do what he liked with the larch trees. And then from about the time that little Nancy Elth must have died he cut every one of them down. Three times a day he went at it for nearly a week, and when they were all down he cut them up into logs no more than two feet long and laid them all in neat heaps. You never saw such work. And what for? To give an excuse for the axe was one theory. But the excuse was bigger than the axe; it took him a fortnight, hard work every day. And he could have killed a little thing like Nancy Elth without an axe, and cut her up, too. Another theory was that he wanted firewood, to make away with the body. But he never used it. He left it all standing there in those neat stacks. It fairly beat everybody.

Well, those are the facts I told Linley. Oh yes, and he bought a big butcher's knife. Funny thing, they all do. And yet it isn't so funny after all; if you've got to cut a woman up, you've got to cut her up; and you can't do that without a knife. Then, there were some negative facts. He hadn't burned her. Only had a fire in the small stove now and then, and only used it for cooking. They got on to that pretty smartly, the Unge constable did, and the men that were lending him a hand from Otherthorpe. There were some little woody places lying round, shaws they call them in that part of the country, the country people do, and they could climb a tree handy and unobserved and get a sniff at the smoke in almost any direction it might be blowing. They did now and then and there was no smell of flesh burning, just ordinary cooking. Pretty smart of the Otherthorpe police that was, though of course it didn't help to hang Seeger. Then later on the Scotland Yard men went down and got another fact, negative but narrowing things down all the while. And this was the chalk under the bungalow and under the little garden had none of it been disturbed. And he'd never been outside it since Nancy disappeared. Oh yes, and he had a big file besides the knife. But there was no sign of any ground bones found on the file, or any blood on the knife. He'd washed them of course. I told all that to Linley.

Now I ought to warn you before I go any further; I am a small man myself and you probably don't expect anything horrible from me. But I ought to warn you this man was a murderer, or at any rate somebody was; the woman had been made away with, a nice pretty little girl, too, and the man that had done that wasn't necessarily going to stop at things you might think he'd stop at. With the mind to do a thing like that, and with the shadow of the rope to drive him further, you can't say what he'll stop at. Murder tales seem nice things sometimes for a lady to sit and read all by herself by the fire. But murder isn't a nice thing, and when a murderer's desperate and trying to hide his tracks he isn't even as nice as he was before. I'll ask you to bear that in mind. Well, I've warned you.

So I says to Linley, "And what do you make of it?"

"Drains?" said Linley.

"No," I says, "you're wrong there. Scotland Yard has been into that. And the Otherthorpe people before them. They've had a look in the drains, such as they are, a little thing running into a cesspool beyond the garden; and nothing has gone down it, nothing that oughtn't to have, I mean."

He made one or two other suggestions, but Scotland Yard had been before him in every case. That's really the crab of my story, if you'll excuse the expression. You want a man who sets out to be a detective to take his magnifying glass and go down to the spot; to go to the spot before everything; and then to measure the footmarks and pick up the clues and find the knife that the police have overlooked. But Linley never even went near the place, and he hadn't got a magnifying glass, not as I ever saw, and Scotland Yard was before him every time.

In fact they had more clues than anybody could make head or tail of. Every kind of clue to show that he'd murdered the poor little girl; every kind of clue to show that he hadn't disposed of the body; and yet the body wasn't there. It wasn't in South America either, and not much more likely in South Africa. And all the time, mind you, that enormous bunch of chopped larch wood, a clue that was staring everyone in the face and leading nowhere. No, we didn't seem to want any more clues, and Linley never went near the place. The trouble was to deal with the clues we'd got. I was completely mystified; so was Scotland Yard; and Linley seemed to be getting no forwarder; and all the while the mystery was hanging on me. I mean if it were not for the trifle I'd chanced to remember, and if it were not for one chance word I said to Linley, that mystery would have gone the way of all the other mysteries that men have made nothing of, a darkness, a little patch of night in history.

Well, the fact was Linley didn't take much interest in it at first, but I was so absolutely sure that he could do it, that I kept him to the idea. "You can do chess problems," I said.

"That's ten times harder," he said, sticking to his point.

"Then why don't you do this?" I said.

"Then go and take a look at the board for me," said Linley.

That was his way of talking. We'd been a fortnight together, and I knew it by now. He meant to go down to the bungalow at Unge. I know you'll say why didn't he go himself, but the plain truth of it is that if he'd been tearing about the countryside he'd never have been thinking, whereas sitting there in his chair by the fire in our flat there was no limit to the ground he could cover, if you follow my meaning. So down I went by train next day, and got out at Unge station. And there were the North Downs rising up before me.

"It's up there, isn't it?" I said to the porter.

"That's right," he said. "Up there by the lane; and mind to turn to your right when you get to the old yew tree, a very big tree, you can't mistake it, and then . . ." and he told me the way so that I couldn't go wrong. I found them all like that, very nice and helpful. You see it was Unge's day at last; everyone had heard of Unge now; you could have got a letter there any time just then without putting the county or post town; and this was what Unge had to show. I dare say if you tried to find Unge now . . . ; well, anyway, they were making hay while the sun shone.

Well, there the hill was, going up into sunlight, going up like a song.

You don't want to hear about the spring, and all the May colors that came down over everything later on in the day, and all those birds; but I thought, "What a nice place to bring a girl to." And then when I thought that he'd killed her there, well, I'm only a small man, as I said, but when I thought of her on that hill with all the birds singing, I said to myself, "Wouldn't it be odd if it turned out to be me after all that got that man killed, if he did murder her?"

So I soon found my way up to the bungalow and began prying about, looking over the hedge into the garden. And I didn't find much, and I found nothing at all that the police hadn't found already, but there were those heaps of larch logs staring me in the face and looking very queer.

I did a lot of thinking, leaning against the hedge, breathing the smell of the May, and looking over the top of it at the larch logs, and the neat little bungalow the other side of the garden. Lots of theories I thought of; till I came to the best thought of all; and that was that if I left the thinking to Linley, with his Oxford-and-Cambridge education, and only brought him the facts, as he had told me, I should be doing more good in my way than if I tried to do any big thinking. I forgot to say that I had gone to Scotland Yard in the morning. Well, there wasn't really much to tell. What they asked me was, what I wanted. And, not having an answer exactly ready, I didn't find out very much from them.

But it was quite different at Unge; everyone was most obliging; it was their day there, as I said. The constable let me go indoors, so long as I didn't touch anything, and he gave me a look at the garden from the inside. And I saw the stumps of the ten larch trees, and I noticed one thing that Linley said was very observant of me, not that it turned out to be any use, but anyway I was doing my best; I noticed that the stumps

The more a man writes, the more he can write.

WILLIAM HAZLITT

had been all chopped anyhow. And from that I thought that the man that did it didn't know much about chopping. The constable said that was a deduction. So then I said that the axe was blunt when he used it; and that certainly made the constable think, though he didn't actually say I was right this time.

Did I tell you that Seeger never went outdoors, except to the little garden to chop wood, ever since Nancy disappeared? I think I did. Well, it was perfectly true. They'd watched him night and day, one or another of them, and the Unge constable told me that himself. That limited things a good deal. The only thing I didn't like about it was that I felt Linley ought to have found all that out instead of ordinary policemen, and I felt that he could have too. There'd have been romance in a story like that. And they'd never have done it if the news hadn't gone round that the man was a vegetarian and only dealt at the greengrocer's. Likely as not even that was only started out of pique by the butcher. It's queer what little things may trip a man up. Best to keep straight is my motto. But perhaps I'm straying a bit away from my story. I should like to do that forever; forget that it ever was; but I can't.

Well I picked up all sorts of information; clues I suppose I should call it in a story like this; though they none of them seemed to lead anywhere. For instance, I found out everything he ever bought at the village; I could even tell you the kind of salt he bought, quite plain with no phosphates in it, that they sometimes put in to make it tidy. And then he got ice from the fishmonger's, and plenty of vegetables, as I said, from the greengrocer, Mergin and Sons. And I had a bit of talk over it all with the constable. Slugger he said his name was. I wondered why he hadn't come in and searched the place as soon as the girl was missing. "Well, you can't do that," he said. "And besides, we didn't suspect at once, not about the girl, that is. We only suspected there was something wrong about him on account of him being a vegetarian. He stayed a good fortnight after the last that was seen of her. And then we slipped in like a knife. But, you see, no one had been inquiring about her, there was no warrant out."

"And what did you find," I asked Slugger, "when you went in?"

"Just a big file," he said, "and the knife and the axe that he must have got to chop her up with."

"But he got the axe to chop trees with," I said.

"Well, yes," he said, but rather grudgingly.

"And what did he chop them for?" I asked.

"Well, of course my superiors have theories about that," he said, "that they mightn't tell to everybody."

You see, it was those logs that were beating them.

"But did he cut her up at all?" I asked.

"Well, he said that she was going to South America," he answered. Which was really very fair-minded of him.

I don't remember now much else that he told me. Seeger left the plates and dishes all washed up and very neat, he said.

Well, I brought all this back to Linley, going up by the train that started just about sunset. I'd like to tell you about the late spring evening, so calm over that grim bungalow; but you'll want to hear of the murder. Well, I told Linley everything, though much of it didn't seem to me to be worth the telling. The trouble was that the moment I began to leave anything out, he'd know it and make me drag it in. "You can't tell what may be vital," he'd say. "A tin tack swept away by a housemaid might hang a man."

All very well, but be consistent even if you are educated at Eton and

Harrow; and whenever I mentioned Num-numo, which after all was the beginning of the whole story, because he wouldn't have heard of it if it hadn't been for me, and my noticing that Seeger had bought two bottles of it, why then he said that things like that were trivial and we should keep to the main issues. I naturally talked a bit about Num-numo, because only that day I had pushed close on fifty bottles of it in Unge. A murder certainly stimulates people's minds, and Seeger's two bottles gave me an opportunity that only a fool could have failed to make something of. But of course all that was nothing at all to Linley.

You can't see a man's thoughts and you can't look into his mind, so that all the most exciting things in the world can never be told of. But what I think happened all that evening with Linley, while I talked to him before supper, and all through supper, and sitting smoking afterwards in front of our fire, was that his thoughts were stuck at a barrier there was no getting over. And the barrier wasn't the difficulty of finding ways and means by which Seeger might have made away with the body, but the impossibility of finding why he chopped those masses of wood every day for a fortnight and paid, as I'd just found out, £25 to his landlord to be allowed to do it. That's what was beating Linley. As for the ways by which Seeger might have hidden the body, it seemed to me that every way was blocked by the police. If you said he buried it they said the chalk was undisturbed, if you said he carried it away they said he never left the place, if you said he burned it they said no smell of burning was ever noticed when the smoke blew low, and when it didn't they climbed trees after it. I'd taken to Linley wonderfully, and I didn't have to be educated to see there was something big in a mind like his, and I thought that he could have done it. When I saw the police getting in before him like that, and no way that I could see of getting past them, I felt real sorry.

Did anyone come to the house? he asked me once or twice. Did anyone take anything away from it? But we couldn't account for it that way. Then perhaps I made some suggestion that was no good, or perhaps I started talking of Num-numo again, and he interrupted me rather sharply.

"But what would you do, Smithers?" he said. "What would you do yourself?"

"If I'd murdered poor Nancy Elth?" I asked.

"Yes," he said.

"I can't ever imagine doing such a thing," I told him.

He sighed at that, as though it were something against me.

"I suppose I should never be a detective," I said. And he just shook his head.

Then he looked broodingly into the fire for what seemed an hour. And then he shook his head again. We both went to bed after that.

I shall remember the next day all my life. I was till evening, as usual, pushing Num-numo. And we sat down to supper about nine. You couldn't get things cooked at those flats, so of course we had it cold. And Linley began with a salad. I can see it now, every bit of it. Well, I was still a bit full of what I'd done in Unge, pushing Num-numo. Only a fool, I know, would have been unable to push it there; but still, I *had* pushed it; and about fifty bottles, forty-eight to be exact, are something in a small village, whatever the circumstances. So I was talking about it a bit; and then all of a sudden I realized that Num-numo was nothing to Linley, and I pulled myself up with a jerk. It was really very kind of him; do you know what he did? He must have known at once why I stopped talking, and he just stretched out a hand and said: "Would you give me a little of your Num-numo for my salad?"

I was so touched I nearly gave it him. But of course you don't take Num-numo with salad. Only for meats and savories. That's on the bottle.

So I just said to him, "Only for meats and savories." Though I don't know what savories are. Never had any.

I never saw a man's face go like that before.

He seemed still for a whole minute. And nothing speaking about him but that expression. Like a man that's seen a ghost, one is tempted to say. But it wasn't really at all. I'll tell you what he looked like. Like a man that's seen something that no one has ever looked at before, something he thought couldn't be.

And then he said in a voice that was all quite changed, more low and gentle and quiet it seemed, "No good for vegetables, eh?"

"Not a bit," I said.

And at that he gave a kind of sob in his throat. I hadn't thought he could feel things like that. Of course I didn't know what it was all about; but, whatever it was, I thought all that sort of thing would have been knocked out of him at Eton and Harrow, an educated man like that. There were no tears in his eyes but he was feeling something horribly.

And then he began to speak with big spaces between his words, saying, "A man might make a mistake perhaps, and use Num-numo with vegetables."

"Not twice," I said. What else could I say?

And he repeated that after me as though I had told of the end of the world, and adding an awful emphasis to my words, till they seemed all clammy with some frightful significance, and shaking his head as he said it.

Then he was quite silent.

"What is it?" I asked.

"Smithers," he said.

"Yes," I said.

"Smithers," said he.

And I said, "Well?"

"Look here, Smithers," he said, "you must 'phone down to the grocer at Unge and find out from him this."

"Yes?" I said.

"Whether Seeger bought those two bottles, as I expect he did, on the same day, and not a few days apart. He couldn't have done that."

I waited to see if any more was coming, and then I ran out and did what I was told. It took me some time, being after nine o'clock, and only then with the help of the police. About six days apart they said; and so I came back and told old Linley. He looked up at me so hopefully when I came in, but I saw that it was the wrong answer by his eyes.

You can't take things to heart like that without being ill, and when he didn't speak I said, "What you want is a good brandy, and go to bed early."

And he said, "No. I must see someone from Scotland Yard. 'Phone round to them. Say here at once."

But I said, "I can't get an inspector from Scotland Yard to call on us at this hour."

His eyes were all lit up. He was all there all right.

"Then tell them," he said, "they'll never find Nancy Elth. Tell one of them to come here and I'll tell him why." And he added, I think only for me, "They must watch Seeger, till one day they get him over something else."

And, do you know, he came. Inspector Ulton; he came himself.

While we were waiting I tried to talk to Linley. Partly curiosity, I admit. But I didn't want to leave him to those thoughts of his, brooding away by the fire. I tried to ask him what it was all about. But he wouldn't tell me. "Murder is horrible," is all he would say. "And as a man covers his tracks up it only gets worse."

He wouldn't tell me. "There are tales," he said, "that one never wants to hear."

That's true enough, I wish I'd never heard this one. I never did actually. But I guessed it from Linley's last words to Inspector Ulton, the only ones that I overheard. And perhaps this is the point at which to stop reading my story, so that you don't guess it too; even if you think you want murder stories. For don't you rather want a murder story with a bit of romantic twist, and not a story about real foul murder? Well, just as you like.

In came Inspector Ulton, and Linley shook hands in silence and pointed the way to his bedroom; and they went in there and talked in low voices, and I never heard a word.

A fairly hearty-looking man was the inspector when they went into that room.

They walked through our sitting room in silence when they came out, and together they went into the hall, and there I heard the only words they said to each other. It was the Inspector who first broke that silence.

"But why," he said, "did he cut down the trees?"

"Solely," said Linley, "in order to get an appetite."

FOR DISCUSSION

1. A common pattern for the story of mystery and surprise is to pile up many facts, some relevant and some irrelevant, until suddenly the relevant facts leap into such a configuration as to provide an answer to the question. The question of how Seeger disposed of the body is never answered in words in this story. Nonetheless, can you recall at what precise moment you first found the answer for yourself?

2. Had all relevant pieces of information been given to you before you discovered the answer? If so, why did you not see the answer earlier?

3. Look over the story again, or at least the first part of it, and note that the pieces of information now have an obvious significance you did not catch at first. Is the story less interesting or more interesting at second reading? Would you ever want to read it a third or fourth time? Explain your reasons.

4. Are all the pieces of information given about Seeger relevant to a solution of the mystery? Was the file used to sharpen the axe? Is it relevant that this region is a chalk formation? Is it relevant that the salt Seeger bought contained no phosphates?

5. Could the author have given the reader the facts about Seeger without using the sauce-salesman, Smithers, and the thinker, Mr. Linley? What function, if any, does each perform? Could those functions have been performed by one man possessing the traits of both Smithers and Mr. Linley?

6. Sometimes the narrator writes as if he knew the solution of the mystery, and sometimes as if he did not. Find a pair of passages that illustrate this contrast.

7. Does Smithers ever use nonstandard English? Does his language characterize him? Does he ever reveal his lack of knowledge about literature? What does Smithers admire so greatly about Mr. Linley?

8. Did the story shock you as well as surprise you? Do you think it is possible that the body could have been disposed of in the way suggested? If you think it impossible, did that interfere with your enjoyment while you were reading?

The Catbird Seat

JAMES THURBER

Mr. Martin bought the pack of Camels on Monday night in the most crowded cigar store on Broadway. It was theatre time and seven or eight men were buying cigarettes. The clerk didn't even glance at Mr. Martin, who put the pack in his overcoat pocket and went out. If any of the staff at F & S had seen him buy the cigarettes, they would have been astonished, for it was generally known that Mr. Martin did not smoke, and never had. No one saw him.

It was just a week to the day since Mr. Martin had decided to rub out Mrs. Ulgine Barrows. The term "rub out" pleased him because it suggested nothing more than the correction of an error — in this case an error of Mr. Fitweiler. Mr. Martin had spent each night of the past week working out his plan and examining it. As he walked home now he went over it again. For the hundredth time he resented the element of imprecision, the margin of guesswork that entered into the business. The project as he had worked it out was casual and bold, the risks were considerable. Something might go wrong anywhere along the line. And therein lay the cunning of his scheme. No one would ever see in it the cautious, painstaking hand of Edwin Martin, head of the filing department at F & S, of whom Mr. Fitweiler had once said, "Man is fallible but Martin isn't." No one would see his hand, that is, unless it were caught in the act.

Sitting in his apartment, drinking a glass of milk, Mr. Martin reviewed his case against Mrs. Ulgine Barrows, as he had every night for seven nights. He began at the beginning. Her quacking voice and braying laugh had first profaned the halls of F & S on March 7, 1941 (Mr. Martin had a head for dates). Old Roberts, the personnel chief, had introduced her as the newly appointed special adviser to the president of the firm, Mr. Fitweiler. The woman had appalled Mr. Martin instantly, but he hadn't shown it. He had given her his dry hand, a look of studious concentration, and a faint smile. "Well," she had said, looking at the papers on his desk, "are you lifting the oxcart out of the ditch?" As Mr. Martin recalled that moment, over his milk, he squirmed slightly. He must keep his mind on her crimes as a special adviser, not on her peccadillos as a personality.

This he found difficult to do, in spite of entering an objection and sustaining it. The faults of the woman as a woman kept chattering on in his mind like an unruly witness. She had, for almost two years now, baited him. In the halls, in the elevator, even in his own office, into which she romped now and then like a circus horse, she was constantly shouting these silly questions at him. "Are you lifting the oxcart out of the ditch? Are you tearing up the pea patch? Are you hollering down the rain barrel? Are you scraping around the bottom of the pickel barrel? Are you sitting in the catbird seat?"

It was Joey Hart, one of Mr. Martin's two assistants, who had explained what the gibberish meant. "She must be a Dodger fan," he had said. "Red Barber announces the Dodger games over the radio and he uses those expressions — picked 'em up down South." Joey had gone on to explain one or two. "Tearing up the pea patch" meant going on a rampage; "sitting in the catbird seat" mean sitting pretty, like a batter with three balls and no strikes on him. Mr. Martin dismissed all this with an effort. It had been annoying, it had driven him near to distraction, but he was too solid a man to be moved to murder by anything so childish. It was fortunate, he reflected as he passed on to the important charges against Mrs. Barrows, that he had stood up under it so well. He had maintained always an outward appearance of polite tolerance. "Why, I even believe you like the woman," Miss Paird, his other assistant, had once said to him. He had simply smiled.

As it is the mark of great minds to say many things in a few words, so it is that of little minds to use many words to say nothing.

LA ROCHEFOUCAULD

A gavel rapped in Mr. Martin's mind and the case proper was resumed. Mrs. Ulgine Barrows stood charged with willful, blatant, and persistent attempts to destroy the efficiency and system of F & S. It was competent, material, and relevant to review her advent and rise to power. Mr. Martin had got the story from Miss Paird, who seemed always able to find things out. According to her, Mrs. Barrows had met Mr. Fitweiler at a party, where she had rescued him from the embraces of a powerfully built drunken man who had mistaken the president of F & S for a famous retired Middle Western football coach. She had led him to a sofa and somehow worked upon him a monstrous magic. The aging gentleman had jumped to the conclusion there and then that this was a woman of singular attainments, equipped to bring out the best in him and in the firm. A week later he had introduced her into F & S as his special adviser. On that day confusion got its foot in the door. After Miss Tyson, Mr. Brundage, and Mr. Bartlett had been fired and Mr. Munson had taken his hat and stalked out, mailing in his resignation later, old Roberts had been emboldened to speak to Mr. Fitweiler. He mentioned that Mr. Munson's department had been "a little disrupted" and hadn't they perhaps better resume the old system there. Mr. Fitweiler had said certainly not. He had the greatest faith in Mrs. Barrows' ideas. "They require a little seasoning, a little seasoning, is all," he had added. Mr. Roberts had given it up. Mr. Martin reviewed in detail all the changes wrought by Mrs. Barrows. She had begun chipping at the cornices of the firm's edifice and now she was swinging at the foundation stones with a pickaxe.

Mr. Martin came now, in his summing up, to the afternoon of Monday, November 2, 1942 — just one week ago. On that day, at 3 P.M., Mrs. Barrows had bounced into his office. "Boo!" she had yelled. "Are you scraping around the bottom of the pickle barrel?" Mr. Martin had looked at her from under his green eyeshade, saying nothing. She had begun to wander about the office, taking it in with her great, popping eyes. "Do you really need *all* these filing cabinets?" she had demanded suddenly. Mr. Martin's heart had jumped. "Each of these files," he had said, keeping his voice even, "plays an indispensable part in the system of F & S." She had brayed at him, "Well, don't tear up the pea patch!" and gone to the door. From there she had bawled, "But you sure have got a lot of fine scrap in here!" Mr. Martin could no longer doubt that the finger was on his beloved department. Her pickaxe was on the upswing, poised for the first blow. It had not come yet; he had received no blue memo from the enchanted Mr. Fitweiler bearing nonsensical instructions deriving from the obscene woman. But there was no doubt in Mr. Martin's mind that one would be forthcoming. He must act quickly. Already a precious week had gone by. Mr. Martin stood up in his living room, still holding his milk glass. "Gentlemen of the jury," he said to himself, "I demand the death penalty for this horrible person."

The next day Mr. Martin followed his routine, as usual. He polished his glasses more often and once sharpened an already sharp pencil, but not even Miss Paird noticed. Only once did he catch sight of his victim; she swept past him in the hall with a patronizing "Hi!" At five-thirty he walked home, as usual, and had a glass of milk, as usual. He had never drunk anything stronger in his life — unless you could count ginger ale. The late Sam Schlosser, the S of F & S, had praised Mr. Martin at a staff meeting several years before for his temperate habits. "Our most efficient worker neither drinks nor smokes," he had said. "The results speak for themselves." Mr. Fitweiler had sat by, nodding approval.

Mr. Martin was still thinking about that red-letter day as he walked over to the Schraffts on Fifth Avenue near Forty-sixth Street. He got there, as he always did, at eight o'clock. He finished his dinner and the financial page of the *Sun* at a quarter to nine, as he always did. It was his custom after dinner to take a walk. This time he walked down Fifth Avenue at a casual pace. His gloved hands felt moist and warm, his forehead cold. He transferred the Camels from his overcoat to a jacket pocket. He wondered, as he did so, if they did not represent an unnecessary note of strain. Mrs. Barrows smoked only Luckies. It was his idea to puff a few puffs on a Camel (after the rubbing-out) stub it out in the ashtray holding her lipstick-stained Luckies, and thus drag a small red herring across the trail. Perhaps it was not a good idea. It would take time. He might even choke, too loudly.

Mr. Martin had never seen the house on West Twelfth Street where Mrs. Barrows lived, but he had a clear enough picture of it. Fortunately, she had bragged to everybody about her ducky first-floor apartment in the perfectly darling three-story red-brick. There would be no doorman or other attendants; just the tenants of the second and third floors. As he walked along, Mr. Martin realized that he would get there before nine-thirty. He had considered walking north on Fifth Avenue from Schrafft's to a point from which it would take him until ten o'clock to reach the house. At that hour people were less likely to be coming in or going out. But the procedure would have made an awkward loop in the straight thread of his casualness, and he had abandoned it. It was impossible to figure when people would be entering or leaving the house, anyway. There was a great risk at any hour. If he ran into anybody, he would simply have to place the rubbing-out of Ulgine Barrows in the inactive file forever. The same thing would hold true if there were someone in her apartment. In that case he would just say that he had been passing by, recognized her charming house, and thought to drop in.

It was eighteen minutes after nine when Mr. Martin turned into Twelfth Street. A man passed him, and a man and a woman, talking. There was no one within fifty paces when he came to the house, halfway down the block. He was up the steps and in the small vestibule in no time, pressing the bell under the card that said "Mrs. Ulgine Barrows." When the clicking in the lock started, he jumped forward against the door. He got inside fast, closing the door behind him. A bulb in a lantern hung from the hall ceiling on a chain seemed to give a monstrously bright light. There was nobody on the stair, which went up ahead of him along the left wall. A door opened down the hall in the wall on the right. He went toward it swiftly, on tiptoe.

"Well, for God's sake, look who's here!" bawled Mrs. Barrows, and her braying laugh rang out like the report of a shotgun. He rushed past her like a football tackle, bumping her. "Hey, quit shoving!" she said, closing the door behind them. They were in her living room, which seemed to Mr. Martin to be lighted by a hundred lamps. "What's after you?" she said. "You're as jumpy as a goat." He found he was unable to speak. His heart was wheezing in his throat. "I — yes," he finally brought out. She was jabbering and laughing as she started to help him off with his coat. "No, no," he said. "I'll put it here." He took it off and put it on a chair near the door. "Your hat and gloves, too," she said. "You're in a lady's house." He put his hat on top of the coat. Mrs. Barrows seemed larger than he had thought. He kept his gloves on. "I was passing by," he said. "I recognized — is there anyone here?" She laughed louder than ever. "No," she said, "we're all alone. You're as white as a sheet, you funny man. Whatever *has* come over you? I'll mix you a toddy." She started toward a door across the room. "Scotch-and-soda be all right? But say, you don't drink, do you?" She turned and gave him her amused look. Mr. Martin pulled himself together. "Scotch-and-soda will be all right," he heard himself say. He could hear her laughing in the kitchen.

Mr. Martin looked quickly around the living room for the weapon. He had counted on finding one there. There were andirons and a poker and something in a corner that looked like an Indian club. None of them would do. It couldn't be that way. He began to pace around. He came to a desk. On it lay a metal paper knife with an ornate handle. Would it be sharp enough? He reached for it and knocked over a small brass jar. Stamps spilled out of it and it fell to the floor with a clatter. "Hey," Mrs. Barrows yelled from the kitchen, "are you tearing up the pea patch?" Mr. Martin gave a strange laugh. Picking up the knife, he tried its point against his left wrist. It was blunt. It wouldn't do.

When Mrs. Barrows reappeared, carrying two highballs, Mr. Martin, standing there with his gloves on, became acutely conscious of the fantasy he had wrought. Cigarettes in his pocket, a drink prepared for him — it was all too grossly improbable. It was more than that; it was impossible. Somewhere in the back of his mind a vague idea stirred, sprouted. "For heaven's sake, take off those gloves," said Mrs. Barrows. "I always wear them in the house," said Mr. Martin. The idea began to bloom, strange and wonderful. She put the glasses on a coffee table in front of a sofa and sat on the sofa. "Come over here, you odd little man," she said. Mr. Martin went over and sat beside her. It was difficult getting a cigarette out of the pack of Camels, but he managed it. She held a match for him, laughing. "Well," she said, handing him his drink, "this is perfectly marvelous. You with a drink and a cigarette."

Mr. Martin puffed, not too awkwardly, and took a gulp of the highball. "I drink and smoke all the time," he said. He clicked his glass against hers. "Here's nuts to that old windbag, Fitweiler," he said, and gulped again. The stuff tasted awful, but he made no grimace. "Really, Mr. Martin," she said, her voice and posture changing, "you are insulting our employer." Mrs. Barrows was now all special adviser to the president. "I am preparing a bomb," said Mr. Martin, "which will blow the old goat higher than hell." He had only had a little drink, which was not strong. It couldn't be that. "Do you take dope or something?" Mrs. Barrows asked coldly. "Heroin," said Mr. Martin. "I'll be coked to the gills when I bump that old buzzard off." "Mr. Martin!" she shouted, getting to her feet. "That will be all of that. You must go at once." Mr. Martin took another swallow of his drink. He tapped his cigarette out in the ashtray and put the pack of Camels on the coffee table. Then he got up. She stood glaring at him. He walked over and put on his hat and coat. "Not a word about this," he said, and laid an index finger against his lips. All Mrs. Barrows could bring out was "Really!" Mr. Martin put his hand on the doorknob. "I'm sitting in the catbird seat," he said. He stuck his tongue out at her and left. Nobody saw him go.

Mr. Martin got to his apartment, walking, well before eleven. No one saw him go in. He had two glasses of milk after brushing his teeth, and he felt elated. It wasn't tipsiness, because he hadn't been tipsy. Anyway, the walk had worn off all effects of the whiskey. He got in bed and read a magazine for a while. He was asleep before midnight.

Mr. Martin got to the office at eight-thirty the next morning, as usual. At a quarter to nine, Ulgine Barrows, who had never before arrived at work before ten, swept into his office. "I'm reporting to Mr. Fitweiler now!" she shouted. "If he turns you over to the police, it's no more than you deserve!" Mr. Martin gave her a look of shocked surprise. "I beg your pardon?" he said. Mrs. Barrows snorted and bounced out of the room, leaving Miss Paird and Joey Hart staring after her. "What's the matter with that old devil now?" asked Miss Paird. "I have no idea," said Mr. Martin, resuming his work. The other two looked at him and then at each other. Miss Paird got up and went out. She walked slowly past the closed door of Mr. Fitweiler's office. Mrs. Barrows was yelling inside, but she was not braying. Miss Paird could not hear what the woman was saying. She went back to her desk.

Forty-five minutes later, Mrs. Barrows left the president's office and went into her own, shutting the door. It wasn't until half an hour later that Mr. Fitweiler sent for Mr. Martin. The head of the filing department, neat, quiet, attentive, stood in front of the old man's desk. Mr. Fitweiler was pale and nervous. He took his glasses off and twiddled them. He made a small, bruffing sound in his throat. "Martin," he said, "you have been with us more than twenty years." "Twenty-two, sir," said Mr. Martin. "In that time," pursued the president, "your work and your — uh — manner have been exemplary." "I trust so, sir," said Mr. Martin. "I have understood, Martin," said Mr. Fitweiler, "that you have never taken a drink or smoked." "That is correct, sir," said Mr. Martin. "Ah, yes." Mr. Fitweiler polished his glasses. "You may describe what you did after leaving the office yesterday, Martin," he said. Mr. Martin allowed less than a second for his bewildered pause. "Certainly, sir," he said. "I walked home. Then I went to Schrafft's for dinner. Afterward I walked home again. I went to bed

early, sir, and read a magazine for a while. I was asleep before eleven."
"Ah, yes," said Mr. Fitweiler again. He was silent for a moment, searching
for the proper words to say to the head of the filing department. "Mrs.
Barrows," he said finally, "Mrs. Barrows has worked hard, Martin, very
hard. It grieves me to report that she has suffered a severe breakdown. It
has taken the form of a persecution complex accompanied by distressing
hallucinations." "I am very sorry, sir," said Mr. Martin. "Mrs. Barrows is
under the delusion," continued Mr. Fitweiler, "that you visited her last
evening and behaved yourself in an — uh — unseemly manner." He
raised his hand to silence Mr. Martin's little pained outcry. "It is the
nature of these psychological diseases," Mr. Fitweiler said, "to fix upon
the least likely and most innocent party as the — uh — source of
persecution. These matters are not for the lay mind to grasp, Martin.
I've just had my psychiatrist, Doctor Fitch, on the phone. He would not,
of course, commit himself, but he made enough generalizations to sub-
stantiate my suspicions. I suggested to Mrs. Barrows, when she had completed her — uh — story to me this morning, that she visit Doctor Fitch, for
I suspected a condition at once. She flew, I regret to say, into a rage, and
demanded — uh — requested that I call you on the carpet. You may not
know, Martin, but Mrs. Barrows had planned a reorganization of your department — subject to my approval, of course, subject to my approval.
This brought you, rather than anyone else, to her mind — but again that
is a phenomenon for Dr. Fitch and not for us. So, Martin, I am afraid
Mrs. Barrows' usefulness here is at an end." "I am dreadfully sorry, sir,"
said Mr. Martin.

It was at this point that the door to the office blew open with the
suddenness of a gas-main explosion and Mrs. Barrows catapulted through
it. "Is the little rat denying it?" she screamed. "He can't get away with
that!" Mr. Martin got up and moved discreetly to a point beside Mr. Fitweiler's chair. "You drank and smoked at my apartment," she bawled at
Mr. Martin, "and you know it! You called Mr. Fitweiler an old windbag
and said you were going to blow him up when you got coked to the gills
on your heroin!" She stopped yelling to catch her breath and a new glint
came into her popping eyes. "If you weren't such a drab, ordinary little
man," she said, "I'd think you'd planned it all. Sticking your tongue out,
saying you were sitting in the catbird seat, because you thought no one
would believe me when I told it! My God, it's really too perfect!" She
brayed loudly and hysterically, and the fury was on her again. She glared
at Mr. Fitweiler. "Can't you see how he has tricked us, you old fool?
Can't you see his little game?" But Mr. Fitweiler had been surreptitiously
pressing all the buttons under the top of his desk and employees of F & S
began pouring into the room. "Stockton," said Mr. Fitweiler, "you and
Fishbein will take Mrs. Barrows to her home. Mrs. Powell, you will go
with them." Stockton, who had played a little football in high school,

blocked Mrs. Barrows as she made for Mr. Martin. It took him and Fishbein together to force her out of the door into the hall, crowded with stenographers and office boys. She was still screaming imprecations at Mr. Martin, tangled and contradictory imprecations. The hubbub finally died down in the corridor.

"I regret that this has happened," said Mr. Fitweiler. "I shall ask you to dismiss it from your mind, Martin." "Yes, sir," said Mr. Martin, anticipating his chief's "That will be all" by moving to the door. "I will dismiss it." He went out and shut the door, and his step was light and quick in the hall. When he entered his department he had slowed down to his customary gait, and he walked quietly across the room to the W20 file, wearing a look of studious concentration.

FOR DISCUSSION

1. This delightful story falls into four parts, each with its special source of interest. The various parts are, of course, related, each being a new development of the previous one. During the first part some of the humor lies in the incongruity between the violent intentions of Mr. Martin, and the habitual nonviolence of the man. List details that make it seem impossible that such a man could perform such an action.

2. As you read in the early pages about the conflict between Mrs. Ulgine Barrows and the other older employees, were you for her or against her? If you were against her, is there anything humorously incongruous in your sympathizing more with the intended murderer than the intended victim? Is there also an incongruity in requiring her to pay the death penalty for faults no greater than hers? Most people sometimes imagine, only half-seriously, the dreadful things they would like to see happen to someone they dislike. What kind of people carry out these fantasies?

3. The story shifts to its second brief phase when Mr. Martin enters Mrs. Barrows' apartment; it ends when she reappears from the kitchen. Here Mr. Martin's murder-fantasy is confronted by the hard facts of reality. Did the impossibility of such a man performing such an action still seem humorously incongruous at this point? What realistic details helped convince you that his fantastic scheme could not be carried out? Did you want Mr. Martin to fail in his plan?

4. Was it true that the andirons, the poker, the Indian club, and the paper knife were inadequate for his purpose? Mr. Martin had armed himself with a pack of Camels, but not with a weapon. What does this tell you about his true intentions, or his state of mind?

5. The third phase begins with Mrs. Barrows' re-entry from the kitchen; it ends when Mr. Martin leaves the apartment. "A vague idea stirred, sprouted. . . . The idea began to bloom, strange and wonderful." At the time when you read this whole third part of the story did you feel that he had lost his senses, or that he was very much in command of them? When you finished the story did you then revise your first hypothetical interpretation of this scene, or did you not?

6. In the fourth and final phase, Mrs. Barrows is punished, not by death, but by being fired. Thus the initial conflict between her and Mr. Martin ends with him victorious. Note that victory by murder would have been less happy for the reader

— and for Mr. Martin (not to mention Mrs. Barrows) — than is this victory which follows the momentary defeat of his original plan. The humorous incongruity in the fourth phase lies partly in the fact that the woman who tells the truth is not believed, whereas the man who lies is believed. Furthermore she is considered insane for truthfully reporting that he acted insanely. Do you note any further humorous incongruities as you look back over the story?

7. In her last speech, Mrs. Barrows says, "If you weren't such a drab, ordinary little man . . . I'd think you'd planned it all. . . . It's too perfect." Does she give Mr. Martin more credit than is due him, or less? For what reasons was his step light and quick in the hall but quiet again in his office? How much of the David-Goliath theme appears in the story? How prominent is the war between the sexes?

8. Compare the kinds of enjoyment you got from "The Two Bottles of Relish" and "The Catbird Seat." Which story seems more subtle? Which shows you more about human nature?

❦ *Self-Revelation of Character* ❦

I'm a Fool

SHERWOOD ANDERSON

It was a hard jolt for me, one of the most bitterest I ever had to face. And it all came about through my own foolishness, too. Even yet sometimes, when I think of it, I want to cry or swear or kick myself. Perhaps, even now, after all this time, there will be a kind of satisfaction in making myself look cheap by telling of it.

It began at three o'clock one October afternoon as I sat in the grand stand at the fall trotting and pacing meet at Sandusky, Ohio.

To tell the truth, I felt a little foolish that I should be sitting in the grand stand at all. During the summer before I had left my home town with Harry Whitehead and, with a nigger named Burt, had taken a job as swipe with one of the two horses Harry was campaigning through the fall race

From *Horses and Men*, by Sherwood Anderson. Copyright © 1924 by Eleanor Anderson. Reprinted by permission of Harold Ober Associates Incorporated.

meets that year. Mother cried and my sister Mildred, who wanted to get a job as a schoolteacher in our town that fall, stormed and scolded about the house all during the week before I left. They both thought it something disgraceful that one of our family should take a place as a swipe with race horses. I've an idea Mildred thought my taking the place would stand in the way of her getting the job she'd been working so long for.

But after all I had to work, and there was no other work to be got. A big lumbering fellow of nineteen couldn't just hang around the house and I had got too big to mow people's lawns and sell newspapers. Little chaps who could get next to people's sympathies by their sizes were always getting jobs away from me. There was one fellow who kept saying to everyone who wanted a lawn mowed or a cistern cleaned that he was saving money to work his way through college, and I used to lay awake nights thinking up ways to injure him without being found out. I kept thinking of wagons running over him and bricks falling on his head as he walked along the street. But never mind him.

I got the place with Harry and I liked Burt fine. We got along splendid together. He was a big nigger with a lazy sprawling body and soft, kind eyes, and when it came to a fight he could hit like Jack Johnson. He had Bucephalus, a big black pacing stallion that could do 2.09 or 2.10 if he had to, and I had a little gelding named Doctor Fritz that never lost a race all fall when Harry wanted him to win.

We set out from home late in July, in a box car with the two horses and after that, until late November, we kept moving along to the race meets and the fairs. It was a peachy time for me, I'll say that. Sometimes now I think that boys who are raised regular in houses, and never have a fine nigger like Burt for best friend, and go to high schools and college, and never steal anything, or get drunk a little, or learn to swear from fellows who know how, or come walking up in front of a grand stand in their shirt sleeves and with dirty horsy pants on when the races are going on and the grand stand is full of people all dressed up — What's the use of talking about it? Such fellows don't know nothing at all. They've never had no opportunity.

But I did. Burt taught me how to rub down a horse and put the bandages on after a race and steam a horse out and a lot of valuable things for any man to know. He could wrap a bandage on a horse's leg so smooth that if it had been the same color you would think it was his skin, and I guess he'd have been a big driver, too, and got to the top like Murphy and Walter Cox and the others if he hadn't been black.

Gee whiz! it was fun. You got to a county-seat town, maybe say on a Saturday or Sunday, and the fair began the next Tuesday and lasted until Friday afternoon. Doctor Fritz would be, say, in the 2.25 trot on Tuesday afternoon and on Thursday afternoon Bucephalus would knock 'em cold in the "free-for-all" pace. It left you a lot of time to hang around and listen to horse talk, and see Burt knock some yap cold that got too gay, and you'd find out about horses and men and pick up a lot of stuff you could use all the rest of your life, if you had some sense and salted down what you heard and felt and saw.

And then at the end of the week when the race meet was over, and Harry had run home to tend up to his livery-stable business, you and Burt hitched the two horses to carts and drove slow and steady across country, to the place for the next meeting, so as to not overheat the horses, etc., etc., you know.

Gee whizz! Gosh amighty! the nice hickory-nut and beechnut and oaks and other kinds of trees along the roads, all brown and red, and the good smells, and Burt singing a song called "Deep River," and the country girls at the windows of houses and everything. You can stick your colleges up your nose for all me. I guess I know where I got my education.

Why, one of those little burgs of towns you came to on the way, say now on a Saturday afternoon, and Burt says, "Let's lay up here." And you did.

And you took the horses to a livery stable and fed them, and you got your good clothes out of a box and put them on.

And the town was full of farmers gaping, because they could see you were racehorse people, and the kids maybe never see a nigger before and was afraid and run away when the two of us walked down their main street.

And that was before prohibition and all that foolishness, and so you went into a saloon, the two of you, and all the yaps come and stood around, and there was always some one pretended he was horsy and knew things and spoke up and began asking questions, and all you did was to lie and lie all you could about what horses you had, and I said I owned them, and then some fellow said, "Will you have a drink of whisky?" and Burt knocked his eye out the way he could say, offhand like, "Oh, well, all right, I'm agreeable to a little nip. I'll split a quart with you." Gee whizz!

But that isn't what I want to tell my story about. We got home late in November and I promised mother I'd quit the race horses for good. There's a lot of things you've got to promise a mother because she don't know any better.

And so, there not being any work in our town any more than when I left there to go to the races, I went off to Sandusky and got a pretty good place taking care of horses for a man who owned a teaming and delivery and storage and coal and real-estate business there. It was a pretty good place with good eats, and a day off each week, and sleeping on a cot in a big barn, and mostly just shoveling in hay and oats to a lot of big good-enough skates of horses that couldn't have trotted a race with a toad. I wasn't dissatisfied and I could send money home.

And then, as I started to tell you, the fall races come to Sandusky and I got the day off and I went. I left the job at noon and had on my good clothes and my new brown derby hat I'd bought the Saturday before, and a stand-up collar.

First of all I went downtown and walked about with the dudes. I've always thought to myself, "Put up a good front," and so I did it. I had forty dollars in my pocket and so I went into the West House, a big hotel, and walked up to the cigar stand. "Give me three twenty-five-cent cigars," I said. There was a lot of horsemen and strangers and dressed-up people from other towns standing around in the lobby and in the bar, and I mingled amongst them. In the bar there was a fellow with a cane and a Windsor tie on, that it made me sick to look at him. I like a man to be a man and dress up, but not to go put on that kind of airs. So I pushed him aside, kind of rough, and had me a drink of whisky. And then he looked at me, as though he thought maybe he'd get gay, but he changed his mind and didn't say anything. And then I had another drink of whisky, just to show him something, and went out and had a hack out to the races, all to myself, and when I got there I bought myself the best seat I could get up in the grand stand, but didn't go in for any of these boxes. That's putting on too many airs.

Say that which has to be said in such language that you can stand cross-examination on each word.

T. H. HUXLEY

And so there I was, sitting up in the grand stand as gay as you please and looking down on the swipes coming out with their horses, and with their dirty horsy pants on and the horseblankets swung over their shoulders, same as I had been doing all the year before. I liked one thing about the same as the other, sitting up there and feeling grand and being down there and looking up at the yaps and feeling grander and more important, too.

One thing's about as good as another, if you take it just right. I've often said that.

Well, right in front of me, in the grand stand that day, there was a fellow with a couple of girls and they was about my age. The young fellow was a nice guy, all right. He was the kind maybe that goes to college and then comes to be a lawyer or maybe a newspaper editor or something like that, but he wasn't stuck on himself. There are some of that kind are all right and he was one of the ones.

He had his sister with him and another girl and the sister looked around over his shoulder, accidental at first, not intending to start anything — she wasn't that kind — and her eyes and mine happened to meet.

You know how it is. Gee, she was a peach! She had on a soft dress, kind of a blue stuff and it looked carelessly made, but was well sewed and made and everything. I knew that much. I blushed when she looked right at me and so did she. She was the nicest girl I've ever seen in my life. She wasn't stuck on herself and she could talk proper grammar without being like a schoolteacher or something like that. What I mean is, she was O.K. I think maybe her father was well-to-do, but not rich to make her chesty because she was his daughter, as some are. Maybe he owned a drug store or a dry-goods store in their home town, or something like that. She never told me and I never asked.

My own people are all O.K. too, when you come to that. My grandfather was Welsh and over in the old country, in Wales he was — But never mind that.

The first heat of the first race come off and the young fellow setting there with the two girls left them and went down to make a bet. I knew what he was up to, but he didn't talk big and noisy and let everyone around know he was a sport, as some do. He wasn't that kind. Well, he come back and I heard him tell the two girls what horse he'd bet on, and when the heat trotted they all half got to their feet and acted in the excited, sweaty way people do when they've got money down on a race, and the horse they bet on is up there pretty close at the end, and they think maybe he'll come on with a rush, but he never does because he hasn't got the old juice in him, come right down to it.

And then, pretty soon, the horses come out for the 2.18 pace and there was a horse in it I knew. He was a horse Bob French had in his string but Bob didn't own him. He was a horse owned by a Mr. Mathers down at Marietta, Ohio.

This Mr. Mathers had a lot of money and owned some coal mines or something and he had a swell place out in the country, and he was stuck on race horses, but was a Presbyterian or something, and I think more than likely his wife was one, too, maybe a stiffer one than himself. So he never raced his horses hisself, and the story round the Ohio race tracks was that when one of his horses got ready to go to the races he turned them over to Bob French and pretended to his wife he was sold.

So Bob had the horses and he did pretty much as he pleased and you can't blame Bob, at least, I never did. Sometimes he was out to win and sometimes he wasn't. I never cared much about that when I was swiping a horse. What I did want to know was that my horse had the speed and could go out in front, if you wanted him to.

And, as I'm telling you, there was Bob in this race with one of Mr. Mathers' horses, was named "About Ben Ahem" or something like that, and was fast as a streak. He was a gelding and had a mark of 2.21, but could step in .08 or .09.

Because when Burt and I were out, as I've told you, the year before, there was a nigger Burt knew, worked for Mr. Mathers and we went out there one day when we didn't have no race on at the Marietta Fair and our boss Harry was gone home.

And so everyone was gone to the fair but just this one nigger and he took us all through Mr. Mathers' swell house and he and Burt tapped a bottle of wine Mr. Mathers had hid in his bedroom, back in a closet, without his wife knowing, and he showed us this Ahem horse. Burt was always stuck on being a driver but didn't have much chance to get to the top, being a nigger, and he and the other nigger gulped the whole bottle of wine and Burt got a little lit up.

So the nigger let Burt take this About Ben Ahem and step him a mile in a track Mr. Mathers had all to himself, right there on the farm. And Mr. Mathers had one child, a daughter, kinda sick and not very good looking, and she came home and we had to hustle and get About Ben Ahem stuck back in the barn.

I'm only telling you to get everything straight. At Sandusky, that afternoon I was at the fair, this young fellow with the two girls was fussed, being with the girls and losing his bet. You know how a fellow is that way. One of them was his girl and the other his sister. I had figured that out.

"Gee whizz," I says to myself, "I'm going to give him the dope."

He was mighty nice when I touched him on the shoulder. He and the girls were nice to me right from the start and clear to the end. I'm not blaming them.

And so he leaned back and I gave him the dope on About Ben Ahem. "Don't bet a cent on this first heat because he'll go like an oxen hitched to a plow, but when the first heat is over go right down and lay on your pile." That's what I told him.

Well, I never saw a fellow treat any one sweller. There was a fat man sitting beside the little girl, that had looked at me twice by this time, and I at her, and both blushing, and what did he do but have the nerve to turn and ask the fat man to get up and change places with me so I could set with his crowd.

Gee whizz, craps amighty. There I was. What a chump I was to go and get gay up there in the West House bar, and just because that dude was standing there with a cane and that kind of a necktie on, to go and get all balled up and drink that whisky, just to show off.

Of course she would know, me setting right beside her and letting her smell of my breath. I could have kicked myself right down out of that grand stand and all around that race track and made a faster record than most of the skates of horses they had there that year.

Because that girl wasn't any mutt of a girl. What wouldn't I have give right then for a stick of chewing gum to chew, or a lozenger, or some licorice, or most anything. I was glad I had those twenty-five-cent cigars in my pocket and right away I give that fellow one and lit one myself. Then that fat man got up and we changed places and there I was, plunked right down beside her.

They introduced themselves and the fellow's best girl, he had with him, was named Miss Elinor Woodbury, and her father was a manufacturer of barrels from a place called Tiffin, Ohio. And the fellow himself was named Wilbur Wessen and his sister was Miss Lucy Wessen.

I suppose it was their having such swell names that got me off my trolley. A fellow, just because he has been a swipe with a race horse, and works taking care of horses for a man in the teaming, delivery, and storage business isn't any better or worse than any one else. I've often thought that, and said it too.

But you know how a fellow is. There's something in that kind of nice clothes, and the kind of nice eyes she had, and the way she had looked at me, awhile before, over her brother's shoulder, and me looking back at her, and both of us blushing.

I couldn't show her up for a boob, could I?

I made a fool of myself, that's what I did. I said my name was Walter Mathers from Marietta, Ohio, and then I told all three of them the smashingest lie you ever heard. What I said was that my father owned the horse About Ben Ahem and that he had let him out to this Bob French for racing purposes, because our family was proud and had never gone into racing that way, in our own name, I mean. Then I had got started and they were all leaning over and listening, and Miss Lucy Wessen's eyes were shining, and I went the whole hog.

I told about our place down at Marietta, and about the big stables and the grand brick house we had on a hill, up above the Ohio River, but I knew enough not to do it in no bragging way. What I did was to start things and then let them drag the rest out of me. I acted just as reluctant to tell as I could. Our family hasn't got any barrel factory, and since I've known us, we've always been pretty poor, but not asking anything of any one at that, and my grandfather, over in Wales — but never mind that.

We set there talking like we had known each other for years and years, and I went and told them that my father had been expecting maybe this Bob French wasn't on the square, and had sent me up to Sandusky on the sly to find out what I could.

And I bluffed it through I had found out all about the 2.18 pace, in which About Ben Ahem was to start.

I said he would lose the first heat by pacing like a lame cow and then he would come back and skin 'em alive after that. And to back up what I said I took thirty dollars out of my pocket and handed it to Mr. Wilbur Wessen and asked him, would he mind, after the first heat, to go down and place it on About Ben Ahem for whatever odds he could get. What I said was that I didn't want Bob French to see me and none of the swipes.

Sure enough the first heat come off and About Ben Ahem went off his stride, up the back stretch, and looked like a wooden horse or a sick one, and come in to be last. Then this Wilbur Wessen went down to the betting place under the grand stand and there I was with the two girls, and when that Miss Woodbury was looking the other way once, Lucy Wessen kinda, with her shoulder you know, kinda touched me. Not just tucking down, I don't mean. You know how a woman can do. They get close, but not getting gay either. You know what they do. Gee whizz.

And then they give me a jolt. What they had done, when I didn't know, was to get together, and they had decided Wilbur Wessen would bet fifty dollars, and the two girls had gone and put in ten dollars each, of their own money, too. I was sick then, but I was sicker later.

About the gelding, About Ben Ahem, and their winning their money, I wasn't worried a lot about that. It come out O.K. Ahem stepped the next three heats like a bushel of spoiled eggs going to market before they could be found out, and Wilbur Wessen had got nine to two for the money. There was something else eating at me.

Because Wilbur come back, after he had bet the money, and after that he spent most of his time talking to that Miss Woodbury and Lucy Wessen and I was left alone together like on a desert island. Gee, if I'd only been on the square or if there had been any way of getting myself on the square. There ain't any Walter Mathers, like I said to her and them, and there hasn't been one, but if there was, I bet I'd go to Marietta, Ohio, and shoot him tomorrow.

There I was, big boob that I am. Pretty soon the race was over, and Wilbur had gone down and collected our money, and we had a hack downtown, and he stood us a swell supper at the West House, and a bottle of champagne beside.

And I was with that girl and she wasn't saying much, and I wasn't saying much either. One thing I know. She wasn't stuck on me because of the lie about my father being rich and all that. There's a way you know . . . Craps amighty. There's a kind of girl you see just once in your life, and if you don't get busy and make hay, then you're gone for good and all, and might as well go jump off a bridge. They give you a look from inside of them somewhere, and it ain't no vamping, and what it means is — you want that girl to be your wife, and you want nice things around her like flowers and swell clothes, and you want her to have the kids you're going to have, and you want good music played and no ragtime. Gee whizz.

There's a place over near Sandusky, across a kind of bay, and it's called Cedar Point. And after we had supper we went over to it in a launch, all by ourselves. Wilbur and Miss Lucy and that Miss Woodbury had to catch a ten o'clock train back to Tiffin, Ohio, because, when you're out with girls like that you can't get careless and miss any trains and stay out all night, like you can with some kinds of Janes.

And Wilbur blowed himself to the launch and it cost him fifteeen cold plunks, but I wouldn't never have knew if I hadn't listened. He wasn't no tin horn kind of a sport.

Over at the Cedar Point place, we didn't stay around where there was a gang of common kind of cattle at all.

There was big dance halls and dining places for yaps, and there was a beach you could walk along and get where it was dark, and we went there.

She didn't talk hardly at all and neither did I, and I was thinking how glad I was my mother was all right, and always made us kids learn to eat with a fork at table, and not swill soup, and not be noisy and rough like a gang you see around a race track that way.

Then Wilbur and his girl went away up the beach and Lucy and I sat down in a dark place, where there was some roots of old trees the water had washed up, and after that the time, till we had to go back in the launch and they had to catch their trains, wasn't nothing at all. It went like winking your eye.

Here's how it was. The place we were setting in was dark, like I said, and there was the roots from that old stump sticking up like arms, and there was a watery smell, and the night was like — as if you could put your hand out and feel it — so warm and soft and dark and sweet like an orange.

I most cried and I most swore and I most jumped up and danced, I was so mad and happy and sad.

When Wilbur come back from being alone with his girl, and she saw him coming, Lucy she says, "We got to go to the train now," and she was most crying too, but she never knew nothing I knew, and she couldn't be so all busted up. And then, before Wilbur and Miss Woodbury got to where we was, she put her face up and kissed me quick and put her head up against me and she was all quivering and — Gee whizz.

Sometimes I hope I have cancer and die. I guess you know what I mean. We went to the launch across the bay to the train like that, and it was dark, too. She whispered and said it was like she and I could get out of the boat and walk on the water, and it sounded foolish, but I knew what she meant.

And then quick we were right at the depot, and there was a big gang of yaps, the kind that goes to the fairs, and crowded and milling around like cattle, and how could I tell her? "It won't be long because you'll write and I'll write to you." That's all she said.

I got a chance like a hay barn afire. A swell chance I got.

And maybe she would write me, down at Marietta that way, and the letter would come back, and stamped on the front of it by the U.S.A. "there ain't any such guy," or something like that, whatever they stamp on a letter that way.

And me trying to pass myself off for a big-bug and a swell — to her, as decent a little body as God ever made. Craps amighty — a swell chance I got!

And then the train come in, and she got on it, and Wilbur Wessen, he come and shook hands with me, and that Miss Woodbury was nice too and bowed to me, and I at her, and the train went and I busted out and cried like a kid.

Gee, I could have run after that train and made Dan Patch look like a freight train after a wreck but, socks amighty, what was the use? Did you ever see such a fool?

I'll bet you what — if I had an arm broke right now or a train had run over my foot — I wouldn't go to no doctor at all. I'd go set down and let her hurt and hurt — that's what I'd do.

Little do such men know the toil, the pains, the daily, nightly racking of the brains, to range the thoughts, the matter to digest, to cull fit phrases, and reject the rest.

CHARLES CHURCHILL

I'll bet you what — if I hadn't a drunk that booze I'd never been such a boob as to go tell such a lie — that couldn't never be made straight to a lady like her.

I wish I had that fellow here that had on a Windsor tie and carried a cane. I'd smash him for fair. Gosh darn his eyes. He's a big fool — that's what he is.

And if I'm not another you just go find me one and I'll quit working and be a bum and give him my job. I don't care nothing for working, and earning money, and saving it for no such boob as myself.

FOR DISCUSSION

1. On the surface, this is the story of a nineteen-year-old boy who was so anxious to impress an extremely attractive girl that he pretended to a higher socio-economic position than he really possessed. The pretense turned out to be disastrous, for the girl was equally attracted to him and would have been glad to continue the acquaintance, but he felt he dared not let his lie be discovered. Does he think that she liked him only because she supposed his father to live in a fine house and own a stable of racing horses? If he thinks that, then his lie need not be regretted so extremely, for the lie enabled him to step out of character into an evening as delightful as Cinderella's night at the ball.

2. Below the surface this is the story of a big boy at an awkward age in an awkward social position. What do you know about his family's financial position? His mother is "all right" and taught the children better manners than race-track people know, but what about his father? What of his grandfather? Why does the

boy take a job as swipe? To the people in the grandstand how does he cover up the fact that he learned about horses by being a swipe? How does he feel toward people who go to college: the one who takes odd-jobs away from him, for instance; Wilbur Wessen in the grandstand, for instance? How does he feel about people who dress better than he? What did he enjoy about being a swipe? What kind of people enjoy those things?

3. He blames the whisky for his lie. He blames the man with the cane and the Windsor tie for the whisky. Is that an accurate distribution of blame?

4. Summarize the things revealed to the reader which the narrator of the story does not know about himself. Do you understand his self-blame better than he does?

Why I Live at the P.O.

EUDORA WELTY

I was getting along fine with Mama, Papa-Daddy and Uncle Rondo until my sister Stella-Rondo just separated from her husband and came back home again. Mr. Whitaker! Of course I went with Mr. Whitaker first, when he first appeared here in China Grove, taking "Pose Yourself" photos, and Stella-Rondo broke us up. Told him I was one-sided. Bigger on one side than the other, which is a deliberate, calculated falsehood: I'm the same. Stella-Rondo is exactly twelve months to the day younger than I am and for that reason she's spoiled.

She's always had anything in the world she wanted and then she'd throw it away. Papa-Daddy gave her this gorgeous Add-a-Pearl necklace when she was eight years old and she threw it away playing baseball when she was nine, with only two pearls.

So as soon as she got married and moved away from home the first thing she did was separate! From Mr. Whitaker! This photographer with the popeyes she said she trusted. Came home from one of those towns up in Illinois and to our complete surprise brought this child of two.

Mama said she'd like to make her drop dead for a second. "Here you had this marvelous blonde child and never so much as wrote your mother a word about it," says Mama. "I'm thoroughly ashamed of you." But of course she wasn't.

Stella-Rondo just calmly takes off this *hat,* I wish you could see it. She says, "Why, Mama, Shirley-T.'s adopted, I can prove it."

"How?" says Mama, but all I says was, "H'm!" There I was over the hot stove, trying to stretch two chickens over five people and a completely un-expected child into the bargain, without one moment's notice.

"What do you mean — 'H'm!'?" says Stella-Rondo, and Mama says, "I heard that, Sister."

I said that oh, I didn't mean a thing, only that whoever Shirley-T. was, she was the spit-image of Papa-Daddy if he'd cut off his beard, which of course he'd never do in the world. Papa-Daddy's Mama's papa and sulks.

Stella-Rondo got furious! She said, "Sister, I don't need to tell you you got a lot of nerve and always did have and I'll thank you to make no future reference to my adopted child whatsoever!"

"Very well," I said. "Very well, very well. Of course I noticed at once she looks like Mr. Whitaker's side too. That frown. She looks like a cross between Mr. Whitaker and Papa-Daddy."

"Well, all I can say is she isn't."

"She looks exactly like Shirley Temple to me," says Mama, but Shirley-T. just ran away from her.

So the first thing Stella-Rondo did at the table was turn Papa-Daddy against me.

"Papa-Daddy," she says. He was trying to cut up his meat. "Papa-Daddy!" I was taken completely by surprise. Papa-Daddy is about a million years old and's got this long-long beard. "Papa-Daddy, Sister says she fails to understand why you don't cut off your beard."

So Papa-Daddy l-a-y-s down his knife and fork! He's real rich. Mama says he is, he says he isn't. So he says, "Have I heard correctly? You don't understand why I don't cut off my beard?"

"Why," I says, "Papa-Daddy, of course I understand. I did not say any such of a thing, the idea!"

He says, "Hussy!"

I says, "Papa-Daddy, you know I wouldn't any more want you to cut off your beard than the man in the moon. It was the farthest thing from my mind! Stella-Rondo sat there and made that up while she was eating breast of chicken."

But he says, "So the postmistress fails to understand why I don't cut off my beard. Which job I got you through my influence with the government. 'Bird's nest' — is that what you call it?"

Not that it isn't the next to smallest P.O. in the entire state of Mississippi.

I says, "Oh, Papa-Daddy," I says, "I didn't say any such of a thing. I never dreamed it was a bird's nest, I have always been grateful though this is the next to smallest P.O. in the state of Mississippi, and I do not enjoy being referred to as a hussy by my own grandfather."

But Stella-Rondo says, "Yes, you did say it too. Anybody in the world could of heard you, that had ears."

"Stop right there," says Mama, looking at *me.*

So I pulled my napkin straight back through the napkin ring and left the table.

As soon as I was out of the room Mama says, "Call her back, or she'll starve to death," but Papa-Daddy says, "This is the beard I started growing on the Coast when I was fifteen years old." He would of gone on till night-fall if Shirley-T. hadn't lost the Milky Way she ate in Cairo.

So Papa-Daddy says, "I am going out and lie in the hammock, and you can all sit here and remember my words: I'll never cut off my beard as long as I live, even one inch, and I don't appreciate it in you at all." Passed right by me in the hall and went straight out and got in the hammock.

It would be a holiday. It wasn't five minutes before Uncle Rondo suddenly appeared in the hall in one of Stella-Rondo's flesh-colored kimonos, all cut on the bias, like something Mr. Whitaker probably thought was gorgeous.

"Uncle Rondo!" I says. "I didn't know who that was! Where are you going?"

"Sister," he says, "get out of my way, I'm poisoned."

"If you're poisoned stay away from Papa-Daddy," I says. "Keep out of the hammock. Papa-Daddy will certainly beat you on the head if you come within forty miles of him. He thinks I deliberately said he ought to cut off his beard after he got me the P.O., and I've told him and told him and told him, and he acts like he just don't hear me. Papa-Daddy must of gone stone deaf."

"He picked a fine day to do it then," says Uncle Rondo, and before you could say "Jack Robinson" flew out in the yard.

What he'd really done, he'd drunk another bottle of that prescription. He does it every single Fourth of July as sure as shooting, and it's horribly expensive. Then he falls over in the hammock and snores. So he insisted on zigzagging right on out to the hammock, looking like a half-wit.

Papa-Daddy woke up with this horrible yell and right there without moving an inch he tried to turn Uncle Rondo against me. I heard every word he said. Oh, he told Uncle Rondo I didn't learn to read till I was eight years old and he didn't see how in the world I ever got the mail put up at the P.O., much less read it all, and he said if Uncle Rondo could only fathom the lengths he had gone to to get me that job! And he said on the other hand he thought Stella-Rondo had a brilliant mind and deserved credit for getting out of town. All the time he was just lying there swinging as pretty as you please and looping out his beard, and poor Uncle Rondo was *plead-ing* with him to slow down the hammock, it was making him as dizzy as a witch to watch it. But that's what Papa-Daddy likes about a hammock. So Uncle Rondo was too dizzy to get turned against me for the time being.

He's Mama's only brother and is a good case of a one-track mind. Ask anybody. A certified pharmacist.

Just then I heard Stella-Rondo raising the upstairs window. While she was married she got this peculiar idea that it's cooler with the window shut and locked. So she has to raise the window before she can make a soul hear her outdoors.

So she raises the window and says, "*Oh!*" You would have thought she was mortally wounded.

Uncle Rondo and Papa-Daddy didn't even look up, but kept right on with what they were doing. I had to laugh.

I flew up the stairs and threw the door open! I says, "What in the wide world's the matter, Stella-Rondo? You mortally wounded?"

"No," she says, "I am not mortally wounded but I wish you would do me the favor of looking out the window there and telling me what you see."

So I shade my eyes and look out the window.

"I see the front yard," I says.

"Don't you see any human beings?" she says.

"I see Uncle Rondo trying to run Papa-Daddy out of the hammock," I says. "Nothing more. Naturally, it's so suffocating-hot in the house, with all the windows shut and locked, everybody who cares to stay in their right mind will have to go out and get in the hammock before the Fourth of July is over."

"Don't you notice anything different about Uncle Rondo?" asks Stella-Rondo.

"Why, no, except he's got on some terrible-looking flesh-colored contraption I wouldn't be found dead in, is all I can see," I says.

"Never mind, you won't be found dead in it, because it happens to be part of my trousseau, and Mr. Whitaker took several dozen photographs of me in it," says Stella-Rondo. "What on earth could Uncle Rondo *mean* by wearing part of my trousseau out in the broad open daylight without saying so much as 'Kiss my foot,' *knowing* I only got home this morning after my separation and hung my negligee up on the bathroom door, just as nervous as I could be?"

"I'm sure I don't know, and what do you expect me to do about it?" I says. "Jump out the window?"

"No, I expect nothing of the kind. I simply declare that Uncle Rondo looks like a fool in it, that's all," she says. "It makes me sick to my stomach."

"Well, he looks as good as he can," I says. "As good as anybody in reason could." I stood up for Uncle Rondo, please remember. And I said to Stella-Rondo, "I think I would do well not to criticize so freely if I were you and came home with a two-year-old child I had never said a word about, and no explanation whatever about my separation."

"I asked you the instant I entered this house not to refer one more time to my adopted child, and you gave me your word of honor you would not," was all Stella-Rondo would say, and started pulling out every one of her eyebrows with some cheap Kress tweezers.

So I merely slammed the door behind me and went down and made some green-tomato pickle. Somebody had to do it. Of course Mama had turned both the niggers loose; she always said no earthly power could hold one anyway on the Fourth of July, so she wouldn't even try. It turned out that Jaypan fell in the lake and came within a very narrow limit of drowning.

So Mama trots in. Lifts up the lid and says, "H'm! Not very good for your Uncle Rondo in his precarious condition, I must say. Or poor little adopted Shirley-T. Shame on you!"

That made me tired. I says, "Well, Stella-Rondo had better thank her lucky stars it was her instead of me came trotting in with that very peculiar-looking child. Now if it had been me that trotted in from Illinois and brought a peculiar-looking child of two, I shudder to think of the reception I'd of got, much less controlled the diet of an entire family."

"But you must remember, Sister, that you were never married to Mr. Whitaker in the first place and didn't go up to Illinois to live," says Mama, shaking a spoon in my face. "If you had I would of been just as overjoyed to see you and your little adopted girl as I was to see Stella-Rondo, when you wound up with your separation and came on back home."

"You would not," I says.

"Don't contradict me, I would," says Mama.

But I said she couldn't convince me though she talked till she was blue in the face. Then I said, "Besides, you know as well as I do that that child is not adopted."

"She most certainly is adopted," says Mama, stiff as a poker.

I says, "Why, Mama, Stella-Rondo had her just as sure as anything in this world, and just too stuck up to admit it."

"Why, Sister," said Mama. "Here I thought we were going to have a pleasant Fourth of July, and you start right out not believing a word your own baby sister tells you!"

"Just like Cousin Annie Flo. Went to her grave denying the facts of life," I remind Mama.

"I told you if you ever mentioned Auntie Flo's name I'd slap your face," says Mama, and slaps my face.

"All right, you wait and see," I says.

"I," says Mama, "I prefer to take my children's word for anything when it's humanly possible." You ought to see Mama, she weighs two hundred pounds and has real tiny feet.

Just then something perfectly horrible occurred to me.

"Mama," I says, "can that child talk?" I simply had to whisper! "Mama, I wonder if that child can be — you know — in any way? Do you realize," I says, "that she hasn't spoken one single, solitary word to a human being up to the minute? This is the way she looks," I says, and I looked like this.

Well, Mama and I just stood there and stared at each other. It was horrible!

"I remember well that Joe Whitaker frequently drank like a fish," says Mama. "I believed to my soul he drank *chemicals*." And without another word she marches to the foot of the stairs and calls Stella-Rondo.

"Stella-Rondo? O-o-o-o-o! Stella-Rondo!"

"What?" says Stella-Rondo from upstairs. Not even the grace to get up off the bed.

"Can that child of yours talk?" asks Mama.

Stella-Rondo says, "Can she what?"

"Talk! Talk!" says Mama. "Burdyburdyburdyburdy!"

So Stella-Rondo yells back, "Who says she can't talk?"

"Sister says so," says Mama.

"You didn't have to tell me, I know whose word of honor don't mean a thing in this house," says Stella-Rondo.

And in a minute the loudest Yankee voice I ever heard in my life yells out, "OE'm Pop-OE the Sailor-r-r-r Ma-a-n!" and then somebody jumps up and down in the upstairs hall. In another second the house would of fallen down.

"Not only talks, she can tap-dance!" calls Stella-Rondo. "Which is more than some people I won't name can do."

"Why, the little precious darling thing!" Mama says, so surprised. "Just as smart as she can be!" Starts talking baby talk right there. Then she turns on me. "Sister, you ought to be thoroughly ashamed! Run upstairs this instant and apologize to Stella-Rondo and Shirley-T."

"Apologize for what?" I says. "I merely wondered if the child was normal, that's all. Now that she's proved she is, why, I have nothing further to say."

But Mama just turned on her heel and flew out, furious. She ran right upstairs and hugged the baby. She believed it was adopted. Stella-Rondo hadn't done a thing but turn her against me from upstairs while I stood there helpless over the hot stove. So that made Mama, Papa-Daddy and the baby all on Stella-Rondo's side.

Next, Uncle Rondo.

I must say that Uncle Rondo had been marvelous to me at various times in the past and I was completely unprepared to be made to jump out of my skin, the way it turned out. Once Stella-Rondo did something perfectly horrible to him — broke a chain letter from Flanders Field — and he took the radio back he had given her and gave it to me. Stella-Rondo was furious! For six months we all had to call her Stella instead of Stella-Rondo, or she wouldn't answer. I always thought Uncle Rondo had all the brains of the entire family. Another time he sent me to Mammoth Cave, with all expenses paid.

But this would be the day he was drinking that prescription, the Fourth of July.

So at supper Stella-Rondo speaks up and says she thinks Uncle Rondo ought to try to eat a little something. So finally Uncle Rondo said he would try a little cold biscuits and ketchup, but that was all. So *she* brought it to him.

"Do you think it wise to disport with ketchup in Stella-Rondo's flesh-colored kimono?" I says. Trying to be considerate! If Stella-Rondo couldn't watch out for her trousseau, somebody had to.

"Any objections?" asks Uncle Rondo, just about to pour out all the ketchup.

"Don't mind what she says, Uncle Rondo," says Stella-Rondo. "Sister has been devoting this solid afternoon to sneering out my bedroom window at the way you look."

"What's that?" says Uncle Rondo. Uncle Rondo has got the most terrible temper in the world. Anything is liable to make him tear the house down if it comes at the wrong time.

So Stella-Rondo says, "Sister says, 'Uncle Rondo certainly does look like a fool in that pink kimono!'"

Do you remember who it was really said that?

Uncle Rondo spills out all the ketchup and jumps out of his chair and tears off the kimono and throws it down on the dirty floor and puts his foot on it. It had to be sent all the way to Jackson to the cleaners and re-pleated.

"So that's your opinion of your Uncle Rondo, is it?" he says. "I look like a fool, do I? Well, that's the last straw. A whole day in this house with nothing to do, and then to hear you come out with a remark like that behind my back!"

"I didn't say any such of a thing, Uncle Rondo," I says, "and I'm not saying who did, either. Why, I think you look all right. Just try to take care of yourself and not talk and eat at the same time," I says. "I think you better go lie down."

"Lie down my foot," says Uncle Rondo. I ought to of known by that he was fixing to do something perfectly horrible.

So he didn't do anything that night in the precarious state he was in — just played Casino with Mama and Stella-Rondo, and Shirley-T. and gave Shirley-T. a nickel with a head on both sides. It tickled her nearly to death, and she called him "Papa." But at 6:30 a.m. the next morning, he threw a whole five-cent package of some unused one-inch firecrackers from the store as hard as he could into my bedroom and they every one went off. Not one bad one in the string. Anybody else, there'd be one that wouldn't go off.

Well, I'm just terribly susceptible to noise of any kind, the doctor has always told me I was the most sensitive person he had ever seen in his whole life, and I was simply prostrated. I couldn't eat! People tell me they heard it as far as the cemetery, and old Aunt Jep Patterson, that had been holding her own so good, thought it was Judgment Day and she was going to meet her whole family. It's usually so quiet here.

And I'll tell you it didn't take me any longer than a minute to make up my mind what to do. There I was with the whole entire house on Stella-Rondo's side and turned against me. If I have anything at all I have pride.

So I just decided I'd go straight down to the P.O. There's plenty of room there in the back, I says to myself.

Well! I made no bones about letting the family catch on to what I was up to. I didn't try to conceal it.

The first thing they knew, I marched in where they were all playing Old Maid and pulled the electric oscillating fan out by the plug, and everything got real hot. Next I snatched the pillow I'd done the needlepoint on right off the davenport from behind Papa-Daddy. He went "Ugh!" I beat Stella-Rondo up the stairs and finally found my charm bracelet in her bureau drawer under a picture of Nelson Eddy.

"So that's the way the land lies," says Uncle Rondo. There he was, piecing on the ham. "Well, Sister, I'll be glad to donate my army cot if you got any place to set it up, providing you'll leave right this minute and let me get some peace." Uncle Rondo was in France.

"Thank you kindly for the cot and 'peace' is hardly the word I would select if I had to resort to firecrackers at 6:30 A.M. in a young girl's bedroom," I says back to him. "And as to where I intend to go, you seem to forget my position as postmistress of China Grove, Mississippi," I says, "I've always got the P.O."

Well, that made them all sit up and take notice.

I went out front and started digging up some four-o'clocks to plant around the P.O.

"Ah-ah-ah!" says Mama, raising the window. "Those happen to be my four-o'clocks. Everything planted in that star is mine. I've never known you to make anything grow in your life."

"Very well," I says. "But I take the fern. Even you, Mama, can't stand there and deny that I'm the one watered that fern. And I happen to know where I can send in a box top and get a packet of one thousand mixed seeds, no two the same kind, free."

"Oh, where?" Mama wants to know.

But I says, "Too late. You 'tend to your house, and I'll 'tend to mine. You hear things like that all the time if you know how to listen to the radio. Perfectly marvelous offers. Get anything you want free."

So I hope to tell you I marched in and got that radio, and they could of all bit a nail in two, especially Stella-Rondo, that it used to belong to, and she well knew she couldn't get it back, I'd sue for it like a shot. And I very politely took the sewing-machine motor I helped pay the most on to give Mama for Christmas back in 1929, and a good big calendar, with the first-aid remedies on it. The thermometer and the Hawaiian ukulele certainly were rightfully mine, and I stood on the step-ladder and got all my watermelon-rind preserves and every fruit and vegetable I'd put up, every jar. Then I began to pull the tacks out of the bluebird wall vases on the archway to the dining room.

"Who told you you could have those, Miss Priss?" says Mama, fanning as hard as she could.

"I bought 'em and I'll keep track of 'em," I says. "I'll tack 'em up one on each side the post-office window, and you can see 'em when you come to ask me for your mail, if you're so dead to see 'em."

"Not I! I'll never darken the door to that post office again if I live to be a hundred," Mama says. "Ungrateful child! After all the money we spent on you at the Normal."

"Me either," says Stella-Rondo. "You can just let my mail lie there and *rot*, for all I care. I'll never come and relieve you of a single, solitary piece."

"I should worry," I says. "And who you think's going to sit down and write you all those big fat letters and postcards, by the way? Mr. Whitaker? Just because he was the only man ever dropped down in China Grove and you got him — unfairly — is he going to sit down and write you a lengthy correspondence after you come home giving no rhyme nor reason whatsoever for your separation and no explanation for the presence of that child? I may not have your brilliant mind, but I fail to see it."

So Mama says, "Sister, I've told you a thousand times that Stella-Rondo simply got homesick, and this child is far too big to be hers," and she says, "Now, why don't you all just sit down and play Casino?"

Then Shirley-T. sticks out her tongue at me in this perfectly horrible way. She has no more manners than the man in the moon. I told her she was going to cross her eyes like that some day and they'd stick.

"It's too late to stop me now," I says. "You should have tried that yesterday. I'm going to the P.O. and the only way you can possibly see me is to visit me there."

So Papa-Daddy says, "You'll never catch me setting foot in that post office, even if I should take a notion into my head to write a letter some place." He says, "I won't have you reachin' out of that little old window with a pair of shears and cuttin' off any beard of mine. I'm too smart for you!"

"We all are," says Stella-Rondo.

But I said, "If you're so smart, where's Mr. Whitaker?"

So then Uncle Rondo says, "I'll thank you from now on to stop reading all the orders I get on postcards and telling everybody in China Grove what you think is the matter with them," but I says, "I draw my own conclusions and will continue in the future to draw them." I says, "If people want to write their inmost secrets on penny postcards, there's nothing in the wide world you can do about it, Uncle Rondo."

"And if you think we'll ever *write* another postcard you're sadly mistaken," says Mama.

"Cutting off your nose to spite your face then," I says. "But if you're all determined to have no more to do with the U. S. mail, think of this: What will Stella-Rondo do now, if she wants to tell Mr. Whitaker to come after her?"

"Wah!" says Stella-Rondo. I knew she'd cry. She had a conniption fit right there in the kitchen.

"It will be interesting to see how long she holds out," I says. "And now — I am leaving."

"Good-bye," says Uncle Rondo.

"Oh, I declare," says Mama, "to think that a family of mine should quarrel on the Fourth of July, or the day after, over Stella-Rondo leaving old Mr. Whitaker and having the sweetest little adopted child! It looks like we'd all be glad!"

"Wah!" says Stella-Rondo, and has a fresh conniption fit.

"*He* left *her* — you mark my words," I says. "That's Mr. Whitaker. I know Mr. Whitaker. After all, I knew him first. I said from the beginning he'd up and leave her. I foretold every single thing that's happened."

"Where did he go?" asks Mama.

"Probably to the North Pole, if he knows what's good for him," I says.

But Stella-Rondo just bawled and wouldn't say another word. She flew to her room and slammed the door.

"Now look what you've gone and done, Sister," says Mama. "You go apologize."

"I haven't got time, I'm leaving," I says.

"Well, what are you waiting around for?" asks Uncle Rondo.

So I just picked up the kitchen clock and started off, without saying "Kiss my foot" or anything, and never did tell Stella-Rondo good-bye.

There was a nigger girl going along on a little wagon, right in front.

"Nigger girl," I says, "come help me haul these things down the hill. I'm going to live in the post office."

Took her nine trips in her express wagon. Uncle Rondo came out on the porch and threw her a nickel.

And that's the last I've laid eyes on any of my family or my family laid eyes on me for five solid days and nights. Stella-Rondo may be telling the most horrible tales in the world about Mr. Whitaker, but I haven't heard them. As I tell everybody, I draw my own conclusions.

But oh, I like it here. It's ideal, as I've been saying. You see, I've got everything cater-cornered, the way I like it. Hear the radio? All the war news. Radio, sewing machine, book ends, ironing board and that great big piano lamp — peace, that's what I like. Butter-bean vines planted all along the front where the strings are.

Of course, there's not much mail. My family are naturally the main people in China Grove, and if they prefer to vanish from the face of the earth, for all the mail they get or the mail they write, why, I'm not going to open my mouth. Some of the folks here in town are taking up for me and some turned against me. I know which is which. There are always people who will quit buying stamps just to get on the right side of Papa-Daddy.

But here I am, and here I'll stay. I want the world to know I'm happy.

And if Stella-Rondo should come to me this minute, on bended knees, and *attempt* to explain the incidents of her life with Mr. Whitaker, I'd simply put my fingers in both my ears and refuse to listen.

FOR DISCUSSION

1. The narrator apparently believes that it was through the malice of her younger sister that every member of the family was turned against her, so that she had to move out of the house. Does it seem to you that the narrator's defense defends her successfully?

2. Characterize the other members of the family.

3. What would the story lose by being told from the "third person" instead of the "first person" point of view?

4. Whom does the narrator dislike most? Do you think she knows why she dislikes that person? Does she understand herself?

5. Compare "Why I Live at the P.O." with "I'm a Fool."

❧ *Point of View* ❧

Barn Burning

WILLIAM FAULKNER

The store in which the Justice of the Peace's court was sitting smelled of cheese. The boy, crouched on his nail keg at the back of the crowded room, knew he smelled cheese, and more: from where he sat he could see the ranked shelves close-packed with the solid, squat, dynamic shapes of tin cans whose labels his stomach read, not from the lettering which meant nothing to his mind but from the scarlet devils and the silver curve of fish

Copyright 1939 by William Faulkner. Reprinted from *Collected Stories of William Faulkner* by permission of Random House, Inc.

— this, the cheese which he knew he smelled and the hermetic meat which his intestines believed he smelled coming in intermittent gusts momentary and brief between the other constant one, the smell and sense just a little of fear because mostly of despair and grief, the old fierce pull of blood. He could not see the table where the Justice sat and before which his father and his father's enemy (*our enemy* he thought in that despair; *ourn! mine and hisn both! He's my father!*) stood, but he could hear them, the two of them that is, because his father had said no word yet:

"But what proof have you, Mr. Harris?"

"I told you. The hog got into my corn. I caught it up and sent it back to him. He had no fence that would hold it. I told him so, warned him. The next time I put the hog in my pen. When he came to get it I gave him enough wire to patch up his pen. The next time I put the hog up and kept it. I rode down to his house and saw the wire I gave him still rolled on to the spool in his yard. I told him he could have the hog when he paid me a dollar pound fee. That evening a nigger came with the dollar and got the hog. He was a strange nigger. He said, 'He say to tell you wood and hay kin burn.' I said, 'What?' 'That whut he say to tell you,' the nigger said. 'Wood and hay kin burn.' That night my barn burned. I got the stock out but I lost the barn."

"Where is the nigger? Have you got him?"

"He was a strange nigger, I tell you. I don't know what became of him."

"But that's not proof. Don't you see that's not proof?"

"Get that boy up here. He knows." For a moment the boy thought too that the man meant his older brother until Harris said, "Not him. The little one. The boy," and, crouching, small for his age, small and wiry like his father, in patched and faded jeans even too small for him, with straight, uncombed, brown hair and eyes gray and wild as a storm scud, he saw the men between himself and the table part and become a lane of grim faces, at the end of which he saw the Justice, a shabby, collarless, graying man in spectacles, beckoning him. He felt no floor under his bare feet; he seemed to walk beneath the palpable weight of the grim turning faces. His father, stiff in his black Sunday coat donned not for the trial but for the moving, did not even look at him. *He aims for me to lie,* he thought, again with that frantic grief and despair. *And I will have to do hit.*

"What's your name, boy?" the Justice said.

"Colonel Sartoris Snopes," the boy whispered.

"Hey?" the Justice said. "Talk louder. Colonel Sartoris? I reckon anybody named for Colonel Sartoris in this country can't help but tell the truth, can they?" The boy said nothing. *Enemy! Enemy!* he thought; for a moment he could not even see, could not see that the Justice's face was kindly nor discern that his voice was troubled when he spoke to the man named Harris: "Do you want me to question this boy?" But he could hear, and during those subsequent long seconds while there was absolutely no sound in the crowded little room save that of quiet and intent breathing it was as if he had swung outward at the end of a grape vine, over a ravine, and at the top of the swing had been caught in a prolonged instant of mesmerized gravity, weightless in time.

"No!" Harris said violently, explosively. "Damnation! Send him out of here!" Now time, the fluid world, rushed beneath him again, the voices coming to him again through the smell of cheese and sealed meat, the fear and despair and the old grief of blood:

"This case is closed. I can't find against you, Snopes, but I can give you advice. Leave this country and don't come back to it."

His father spoke for the first time, his voice cold and harsh, level, without emphasis: "I aim to. I don't figure to stay in a country among people who . . ." he said something unprintable and vile, addressed to no one.

"That'll do," the Justice said. "Take your wagon and get out of this country before dark. Case dismissed."

His father turned, and he followed the stiff black coat, the wiry figure walking a little stiffly from where a Confederate provost's man's musket ball had taken him in the heel on a stolen horse thirty years ago, followed the two backs now, since his older brother had appeared from somewhere in the crowd, no taller than the father but thicker, chewing tobacco steadily, between the two lines of grim-faced men and out of the store and across the worn gallery and down the sagging steps and among the dogs and half-grown boys in the mild May dust, where as he passed a voice hissed:

"Barn burner!"

Again he could not see, whirling; there was a face in a red haze, moonlike, bigger than the full moon, the owner of it half again his size, he leaping in the red haze toward the face, feeling no blow, feeling no shock when his head struck the earth, scrabbling up and leaping again, feeling no blow this time either and tasting no blood, scrabbling up to see the other boy in full flight and himself already leaping into pursuit as his father's hand jerked him back, the harsh, cold voice speaking above him: "Go get in the wagon."

It stood in a grove of locusts in mulberries across the road. His two hulking sisters in their Sunday dresses and his mother and her sister in calico and sunbonnets were already in it, sitting on and among the sorry residue of the dozen and more movings which even the boy could remember — the battered stove, the broken beds and chairs, the clock inlaid with mother-of-pearl, which would not run, stopped at some fourteen minutes past two o'clock of a dead and forgotten day and time, which had been his

We cannot write well or truly but what we write with gusto.

HENRY DAVID THOREAU

mother's dowry. She was crying, though when she saw him she drew her sleeve across her face and began to descend from the wagon. "Get back," the father said.

"He's hurt. I got to get some water and wash his . . ."

"Get back in the wagon," his father said. He got in too, over the tail-gate. His father mounted to the seat where the older brother already sat and struck the gaunt mules two savage blows with the peeled willow, but without heat. It was not even sadistic; it was exactly that same quality which in later years would cause his descendants to over-run the engine before putting a motor car into motion, striking and reining back in the same movement. The wagon went on, the store with its quiet crowd of grimly watching men dropped behind; a curve in the road hid it. *Forever* he thought. *Maybe he's done satisfied now, now that he has . . .* stopping himself, not to say it aloud even to himself. His mother's hand touched his shoulder.

"Does hit hurt?" she said.

"Naw," he said. "Hit don't hurt. Lemme be."

"Can't you wipe some of the blood off before hit dries?"

"I'll wash to-night," he said. "Lemme be, I tell you."

The wagon went on. He did not know where they were going. None of them ever did or ever asked, because it was always somewhere, always a house of sorts waiting for them a day or two days or even three days away. Likely his father had already arranged to make a crop on another farm before he . . . Again he had to stop himself. He (the father) always did. There was something about his wolflike independence and even courage when the advantage was at least neutral which impressed strangers, as if they got from his latent ravening ferocity not so much a sense of dependability as a feeling that his ferocious conviction in the rightness of his own actions would be of advantage to all whose interest lay with his.

That night they camped, in a grove of oaks and beeches where a spring ran. The nights were still cool and they had a fire against it, of a rail lifted from a nearby fence and cut into lengths — a small fire, neat, niggard almost, a shrewd fire, such fires were his father's habit and custom always, even to freezing weather. Older, the boy might have remarked this and wondered why not a big one; why should not a man who had not only seen the waste and extravagance of war, but who had in his blood an inherent voracious prodigality with material not his own, have burned everything in sight? Then he might have gone a step farther and thought that that was the reason: that niggard blaze was the living fruit of nights passed during those four years in the woods hiding from all men, blue or gray, with his strings of horses (captured horses, he called them). And older still, he might have divined the true reason: that the element of fire spoke to some deep mainspring of his father's being, as the element of steel or of powder spoke to other men, as the one weapon for the preservation of integrity, else breath were not worth the breathing, and hence to be regarded with respect and used with discretion.

But he did not think this now and he had seen those same niggard blazes all his life. He merely ate his supper beside it and was already half asleep over his iron plate when his father called him, and once more he followed the stiff back, the stiff and ruthless limp, up the slope and on to the starlit road where, turning, he could see his father against the stars but without face or depth — a shape black, flat, and bloodless as though cut from tin in the iron folds of the frockcoat which had not been made for him, the voice harsh like tin and without heat like tin:

"You were fixing to tell them. You would have told him." He didn't answer. His father struck him with the flat of his hand on the side of the head, hard but without heat, exactly as he had struck the two mules at the store, exactly as he would strike either of them with any stick in order to kill a horse fly, his voice still without heat or anger. "You're getting to be a man. You got to learn. You got to learn to stick to your own blood or you ain't going to have any blood to stick to you. Do you think either of them, any man there this morning, would? Don't you know all they wanted was a chance to get at me because they knew I had them beat? Eh?" Later, twenty years later, he was to tell himself, "If I had said they wanted only truth, justice, he would have hit me again." But now he said nothing. He was not crying. He just stood there. "Answer me," his father said.

"Yes," he whispered. His father turned.

"Get on to bed. We'll be there to-morrow."

To-morrow they were there. In the early afternoon the wagon stopped before a paintless, two-room house identical almost with the dozen others it had stopped before even in the boy's ten years, and again, as on the other dozen occasions, his mother and aunt got down and began to unload the wagon, although his two sisters and his father and brother had not moved.

"Likely hit ain't fitten for hawgs," one of the sisters said.

"Nevertheless, fit it will and you'll hog it and like it," his father said. "Get out of them chairs and help your Ma unload."

The two sisters got down, big, bovine, in a flutter of cheap ribbons; one of them drew from the jumbled wagon bed a battered lantern, the other a worn broom. His father handed the reins to the older son and began to climb stiffly over the wheel. "When they get unloaded, take the team to the farm and feed them." Then he said, and at first the boy thought he was still speaking to his brother: "Come with me."

"Me?" he said.

"Yes," his father said. "You."

"Abner," his mother said. His father paused and looked back — the harsh level stare beneath the shaggy, graying, irascible brows.

"I reckon I'll have a word with the man that aims to begin to-morrow owning me body and soul for the next eight months."

They went back up the road. A week ago — or before last night, that is — he would have asked where they were going, but not now. His father had struck him before last night but never before had he paused afterward to explain why; it was as if the blow and the following calm, outrageous voice still rang, repercussed, divulging nothing to him save the terrible handicap of being young, the light weight of his few years, just heavy enough to prevent his soaring free of the world as it seemed to be ordered but not heavy enough to keep him footed solid in it, to resist it and try to change the course of its events.

Presently he could see the grove of oaks and cedars and the other flowering trees and shrubs where the house would be, though not the house yet. They walked beside a fence massed with honeysuckle and Cherokee roses and came to a gate swinging open between two brick pillars, and now, beyond a sweep of drive, he saw the house for the first time and at that instant he forgot his father and the terror and despair both, and even when he remembered his father again (who had not stopped) the terror and despair did not return. Because, for all the twelve movings, they had sojourned until now in a poor country, a land of small farms and fields and houses, and he had never seen a house like this before. *Hit's big as a courthouse* he thought quietly, with a surge of peace and joy whose reason he could not have thought into words, being too young for that. *They are safe from him. People whose lives are a part of this peace and dignity are beyond his touch, he no more to them than a buzzing wasp: capable of stinging for a little moment but that's all; the spell of this peace and dignity rendering even the barns and stable and cribs which belong to it impervious to the puny flames he might contrive* . . . this, the peace and joy, ebbing for an instant as he looked again at the stiff black back, the stiff and implacable limp of the figure which was not dwarfed by the house, for the reason that it had never looked big anywhere and which now, against the serene columned backdrop, had more than ever that impervious quality of something cut ruthlessly from tin, depthless, as though, sidewise to the sun, it would cast no shadow. Watching him, the boy remarked the absolutely undeviating course which his father held and saw the stiff foot come squarely down in a pile of fresh droppings where a horse had stood in the drive and which his father could have avoided by a simple change of stride. But it ebbed only for a moment, though he could not have thought this into words either, walking on in the spell of the house, which he could even want but without envy, without sorrow, certainly never with that ravening and jealous rage which unknown to him walked in the ironlike black coat before him: *Maybe he will feel it too. Maybe it will even change him now from what maybe he couldn't help but be.*

They crossed the portico. Now he could hear his father's stiff foot as it came down on the boards with clocklike finality, a sound out of all proportion to the displacement of the body it bore and which was not dwarfed either by the white door before it, as though it had attained to a sort of vicious and ravening minimum not to be dwarfed by anything — the flat, wide, black hat, the formal coat of broadcloth which had once been black but which had now that friction-glazed greenish cast of the bodies of old house flies, the lifted sleeve which was too large, the lifted hand like a curled claw. The door opened so promptly that the boy knew the Negro must have been watching them all the time, an old man with neat grizzled hair, in a linen jacket, who stood barring the door with his body, saying, "Wipe yo foots, white man, fo you come in here. Major ain't home nohow."

"Get out of my way, nigger," his father said, without heat too, flinging the door back and the Negro also and entering, his hat still on his head. And now the boy saw the prints of the stiff foot on the doorjamb and saw them appear on the pale rug behind the machinelike deliberation of the foot which seemed to bear (or transmit) twice the weight which the body compassed. The Negro was shouting "Miss Lula! Miss Lula!" somewhere behind them, then the boy, deluged as though by a warm wave by a suave turn of carpeted stair and a pendant glitter of chandeliers and a mute gleam of gold frames, heard the swift feet and saw her too, a lady — perhaps he had never seen her like before either — in a gray, smooth gown with lace at the throat and an apron tied at the waist and the sleeves turned back, wiping cake or biscuit dough from her hands with a towel as she came up the hall, looking not at his father at all but at the tracks on the blond rug with an expression of incredulous amazement.

"I tried," the Negro cried. "I tole him to . . ."

"Will you please go away?" she said in a shaking voice. "Major de Spain is not at home. Will you please go away?"

His father had not spoken again. He did not speak again. He did not even look at her. He just stood stiff in the center of the rug, in his hat, the shaggy iron-gray brows twitching slightly above the pebble-colored eyes as he appeared to examine the house with brief deliberation. Then with the same deliberation he turned; the boy watched him pivot on the good leg and saw the stiff foot drag round the arc of the turning, leaving a final long and fading smear. His father never looked at it, he never once looked down at the rug. The Negro held the door. It closed behind them, upon the hysteric and indistinguishable woman-wail. His father stopped at the top of the steps and scraped his boot clean on the edge of it. At the gate he stopped again. He stood for a moment, planted stiffly on the stiff foot, looking back at the house. "Pretty and white, ain't it?" he said. "That's sweat. Nigger sweat. Maybe it ain't white enough yet to suit him. Maybe he wants to mix some white sweat with it."

Two hours later the boy was chopping wood behind the house within which his mother and aunt and the two sisters (the mother and aunt, not the two girls, he knew that; even at this distance and muffled by walls the flat loud voices of the two girls emanated an incorrigible idle inertia) were setting up the stove to prepare a meal, when he heard the hooves and saw the linen-clad man on a fine sorrel mare, whom he recognized even before he saw the rolled rug in front of the Negro youth following on a fat bay carriage horse — a suffused, angry face, vanishing, still at full gallop, beyond the corner of the house where his father and brother were sitting in the two tilted chairs; and a moment later, almost before he could have put the axe down, he heard the hooves again and watched the sorrel mare go back out of the yard, already galloping again. Then his father began to shout one of the sisters' names, who presently emerged backward from the kitchen door dragging the rolled rug along the ground by one end while the other sister walked behind it.

"If you ain't going to tote, go on and set up the wash pot," the first said.

"You, Sarty!" the second shouted. "Set up the wash pot!" His father appeared at the door, framed against that shabbiness, as he had been against that other bland perfection, impervious to either, the mother's anxious face at his shoulder.

"Go on," the father said. "Pick it up." The two sisters stooped, broad, lethargic; stooping, they presented an incredible expanse of pale cloth and a flutter of tawdry ribbons.

"If I thought enough of a rug to have to git hit all the way from France I wouldn't keep hit where folks coming in would have to tromp on hit," the first said. They raised the rug.

"Abner," the mother said. "Let me do it."

"You go back and git dinner," his father said. "I'll tend to this."

From the woodpile through the rest of the afternoon the boy watched them, the rug spread flat in the dust beside the bubbling wash-pot, the two sisters stooping over it with that profound and lethargic reluctance, while the father stood over them in turn, implacable and grim, driving them though never raising his voice again. He could smell the harsh homemade lye they were using; he saw his mother come to the door once and look toward them with an expression not anxious now but very like despair; he saw his father turn, and he fell to with the axe and saw from the corner of his eye his father raise from the ground a flattish fragment of field stone and examine it and return to the pot, and this time his mother actually spoke: "Abner. Abner. Please don't. Please, Abner."

Then he was done too. It was dusk; the whippoorwills had already begun. He could smell coffee from the room where they would presently eat the cold food remaining from the mid-afternoon meal, though when he entered the house he realized they were having coffee again probably because there was a fire on the hearth, before which the rug now lay spread over the backs of the two chairs. The tracks of his father's foot were gone. Where they had been were now long, water-cloudy scorifications resembling the sporadic course of a lilliputian mowing machine.

It still hung there while they ate the cold food and then went to bed, scattered without order or claim up and down the two rooms, his mother in one bed, where his father would later lie, the older brother in the other, himself, the aunt, and the two sisters on pallets on the floor. But his father was not in bed yet. The last thing the boy remembered was the depthless, harsh silhouette of the hat and coat bending over the rug and it seemed to him that he had not even closed his eyes when the silhouette was standing over him, the fire almost dead behind it, the stiff foot prodding him awake. "Catch up the mule," his father said.

When he returned with the mule his father was standing in the black door, the rolled rug over his shoulder. "Ain't you going to ride?" he said.

"No. Give me your foot."

He bent his knee into his father's hand, the wiry, surprising power flowed smoothly, rising, he rising with it, on to the mule's bare back (they had owned a saddle once; the boy could remember it though not when or where) and with the same effortlessness his father swung the rug up in front of him. Now in the starlight they retraced the afternoon's path, up the dusty road rife with honeysuckle, through the gate and up the black tunnel of the drive to the lightless house, where he sat on the mule and felt the rough warp of the rug drag across his thighs and vanish.

She was not a woman of many words; for, unlike people in general, she proportioned them to the number of her ideas.

JANE AUSTEN

"Don't you want me to help?" he whispered. His father did not answer and now he heard again that stiff foot striking the hollow portico with that wooden and clocklike deliberation, that outrageous overstatement of the weight it carried. The rug, hunched, not flung (the boy could tell that even in the darkness) from his father's shoulder struck the angle of wall and floor with a sound unbelievably loud, thunderous, then the floor again, unhurried and enormous; a light came on in the house and the boy sat, tense, breathing steadily and quietly and just a little fast, though the foot itself did not increase its beat at all, descending the steps now; now the boy could see him.

"Don't you want to ride now?" he whispered. "We kin both ride now," the light within the house altering now, flaring up and sinking. *He's coming down the stairs now,* he thought. He had already ridden the mule up beside the horse block; presently his father was up behind him and he doubled the reins over and slashed the mule across the neck, but before the animal could begin to trot the hard, thin arm came round him, the hard, knotted hand jerking the mule back to a walk.

In the first red rays of the sun they were in the lot, putting plow gear on the mules. This time the sorrel mare was in the lot before he heard it at all, the rider collarless and even bareheaded, trembling, speaking in a shaking voice as the woman in the house had done, his father merely looking up once before stooping again to the hame he was buckling, so that the man on the mare spoke to his stooping back:

"You must realize you have ruined that rug. Wasn't there anybody here, any of your women . . ." he ceased, shaking,, the boy watching him, the older brother leaning now in the stable door, chewing, blinking slowly and steadily at nothing apparently. "It cost a hundred dollars. But you never had a hundred dollars. You never will. So I'm going to charge you twenty bushels of corn against your crop. I'll add it in your contract and when you come to the commissary you can sign it. That won't keep Mrs. de Spain quiet but maybe it will teach you to wipe your feet off before you enter her home again."

Then he was gone. The boy looked at his father, who still had not spoken or even looked up again, who was now adjusting the logger-head in the hame.

"Pap," he said. His father looked at him — the inscrutable face, the shaggy brows beneath which the gray eyes glinted coldly. Suddenly the boy went toward him, fast, stopping as suddenly. "You done the best you could!" he cried. "If he wanted hit done different why didn't he wait and tell you how? He won't git no twenty bushels! He won't git none! We'll gather hit and hide hit! I kin watch . . ."

"Did you put the cutter back in that straight stock like I told you?"

"No, sir," he said.

"Then go do it."

That was Wednesday. During the rest of that week he worked steadily, at what was within his scope and some which was beyond it, with an industry that did not need to be driven nor even commanded twice; he had this from his mother, with the difference that some at least of what he did he liked to do, such as splitting wood with the half-size axe which his mother and aunt had earned, or saved money somehow, to present him with at Christmas. In company with the two older women (and on one afternoon, even one of the sisters), he built pens for the shoat and the cow which were a part of his father's contract with the landlord, and one afternoon, his father being absent, gone somewhere on one of the mules, he went to the field.

They were running a middle buster now, his brother holding the plow straight while he handled the reins, and walking beside the straining mule, the rich black soil shearing cool and damp against his bare ankles, he thought *Maybe this is the end of it. Maybe even that twenty bushels that seems hard to have to pay for just a rug will be a cheap price for him to stop forever and always from being what he used to be;* thinking, dreaming now, so that his brother had to speak sharply to him to mind the mule: *Maybe he even won't collect the twenty bushels. Maybe it will all add up and balance and vanish — corn, rug, fire, the terror and grief, the being pulled two ways like between two teams of horses — gone, done with for ever and ever.*

Then it was Saturday; he looked up from beneath the mule he was harnessing and saw his father in the black coat and hat. "Not that," his father said. "The wagon gear." And then, two hours later, sitting in the wagon bed behind his father and brother on the seat, the wagon accomplished a final curve, and he saw the weathered paintless store with its tattered tobacco- and patent-medicine posters and the tethered wagons and saddle animals below the gallery. He mounted the gnawed steps behind his father and brother, and there again was the lane of quiet, watching faces for the three of them to walk through. He saw the man in spectacles sitting at the plank table and he did not need to be told this was a Justice of the Peace; he sent one glare of fierce, exultant, partisan defiance at the man in collar and cravat now, whom he had seen but twice before in his life, and that on a galloping horse, who now wore on his face an expression not of rage but of amazed unbelief which the boy could not have known was at the incredible circumstance of being sued by one of his own tenants, and came and stood against his father and cried at the Justice: "He ain't done it! He ain't burnt . . ."

"Go back to the wagon," his father said.

"Burnt?" the Justice said. "Do I understand this rug was burned too?"

"Does anybody here claim it was?" his father said. "Go back to the wagon." But he did not, he merely retreated to the rear of the room, crowded as that other had been, but not to sit down this time, instead, to stand pressing among the motionless bodies, listening to the voices:

"And you claim twenty bushels of corn is too high for the damage you did to the rug?"

"He brought the rug to me and said he wanted the tracks washed out of it. I washed the tracks out and took the rug back to him."

"But you didn't carry the rug back to him in the same condition it was in before you made the tracks on it."

His father did not answer, and now for perhaps half a minute there was no sound at all save that of breathing, the faint, steady suspiration of complete and intent listening.

"You decline to answer that, Mr. Snopes?" Again his father did not answer. "I'm going to find against you, Mr. Snopes. I'm going to find that you were responsible for the injury to Major de Spain's rug and hold you liable for it. But twenty bushels of corn seems a little high for a man in your circumstances to have to pay. Major de Spain claims it cost a hundred dollars. October corn will be worth about fifty cents. I figure that if Major de Spain can stand a ninety-five dollar loss on something he paid cash for, you can stand a five-dollar loss you haven't earned yet. I hold you in damages to Major de Spain to the amount of ten bushels of corn over and above your contract with him, to be paid to him out of your crop at gathering time. Court adjourned."

It had taken no time hardly, the morning was but half begun. He thought they would return home and perhaps back to the field, since they were late, far behind all other farmers. But instead his father passed on behind the wagon, merely indicating with his hand for the older brother to follow with it, and crossed the road toward the blacksmith shop opposite, pressing on after his father, overtaking him, speaking, whispering up at the harsh, calm face beneath the weathered hat: "He won't git no ten bushels, neither. He won't git one. We'll . . ." until his father glanced for an instant down at him, the face absolutely calm, the grizzled eyebrows tangled above the cold eyes, the voice almost pleasant, almost gentle.

"You think so? Well, we'll wait till October anyway."

The matter of the wagon — the setting of a spoke or two and the tightening of the tires — did not take long either, the business of the tires accomplished by driving the wagon into the spring branch behind the shop and letting it stand there, the mules nuzzling into the water from time to time, and the boy on the seat with the idle reins, looking up the slope and through the sooty tunnel of the shed where the slow hammer rang and where his father sat on an upended cypress bolt, easily, either talking or listening, still sitting there when the boy brought the dripping wagon up out of the branch and halted it before the door.

"Take them on to the shade and hitch," his father said. He did so and returned. His father and the smith and a third man squatting on his heels inside the door were talking, about crops and animals; the boy, squatting too in the ammoniac dust and hoof-parings and scales of rust, heard his father tell a long and unhurried story out of the time before the birth of the older brother even when he had been a professional horsetrader. And then his father came up beside him where he stood before a tattered last year's circus poster on the other side of the store, gazing rapt and quiet at the scarlet horses, the incredible poisings and convolutions of tulle and tights and the painted leers of comedians, and said, "It's time to eat."

But not at home. Squatting beside his brother against the front wall, he watched his father emerge from the store and produce from a paper sack a segment of cheese and divide it carefully and deliberately into three with his pocket knife and produce crackers from the same sack. They all three squatted on the gallery and ate, slowly, without talking; then in the store again, they drank from a tin dipper tepid water smelling of the cedar bucket and of living beech trees. And still they did not go home. It was a horse lot this time, a tall rail fence upon and along which men stood and sat and out of which one by one horses were led, to be walked and trotted and then cantered back and forth along the road while the slow swapping and buying went on and the sun began to slant westward, they — the three of them — watching and listening, the older brother with his muddy eyes and his steady, inevitable tobacco, the father commenting now and then on certain of the animals, to no one in particular.

It was after sundown when they reached home. They ate supper by lamplight, then, sitting on the doorstep, the boy watched the night fully accomplish, listening to the whippoorwills and the frogs, when he heard his mother's voice: "Abner! No! No! Oh, God. Oh, God. Abner!" and he rose, whirled, and saw the altered light through the door where a candle stub now burned in a bottleneck on the table and his father, still in the hat and coat, at once formal and burlesque as though dressed carefully for some shabby and ceremonial violence, emptying the reservoir of the lamp back into the five-gallon kerosene can from which it had been filled, while the mother tugged at his arm until he shifted the lamp to the other hand and flung her back, not savagely or viciously, just hard, into the wall, her hands flung out against the wall for balance, her mouth open and in her face the same quality of hopeless despair as had been in her voice. Then his father saw him standing in the door.

"Go to the barn and get that can of oil we were oiling the wagon with," he said. The boy did not move. Then he could speak.

"What . . ." he cried. "What are you . . ."

"Go get that oil," his father said. "Go."

Then he was moving, running, outside the house, toward the stable: this the old habit, the old blood which he had not been permitted to choose for himself, which had been bequeathed him willy nilly and which had run for so long (and who knew where, battening on what of outrage and savagery and lust) before it came to him. *I could keep on*, he thought. *I could run on and on and never look back, never need to see his face again. Only I can't. I can't*, the rusted can in his hand now, the liquid sploshing in it as he ran back to the house and into it, into the sound of his mother's weeping in the next room, and handed the can to his father.

"Ain't you going to even send a nigger?" he cried. "At least you sent a nigger before!"

This time his father didn't strike him. The hand came even faster than the blow had, the same hand which had set the can on the table with almost excruciating care flashing from the can toward him too quick for him to follow it, gripping him by the back of his shirt and on to tiptoe before he had seen it quit the can, the face stooping at him in breathless and frozen ferocity, the cold, dead voice speaking over him to the older brother who leaned against the table, chewing with that steady, curious, sidewise motion of cows.

"Empty the can into the big one and go on. I'll catch up with you."

"Better tie him up to the bedpost," the brother said.

"Do like I told you," the father said. Then the boy was moving, his bunched shirt and the hard, bony hand between his shoulder-blades, his toes touching the floor, across the room and into the other one, past the sisters sitting with spread heavy thighs in the two chairs over the cold hearth, and to where his mother and aunt sat side by side on the bed, the aunt's arms about his mother's shoulders.

"Hold him," the father said. The aunt made a startled movement. "Not you," the father said. "Lennie. Take hold of him. I want to see you do it." His mother took him by the wrist. "You'll hold him better than that. If he gets loose don't you know what he is going to do? He will go up yonder." He jerked his head toward the road. "Maybe I'd better tie him."

"I'll hold him," his mother whispered.

"See you do then." Then his father was gone, the stiff foot heavy and measured upon the boards, ceasing at last.

Then he began to struggle. His mother caught him in both arms, he jerking and wrenching at them. He would be stronger in the end, he knew that. But he had no time to wait for it. "Lemme go!" he cried. "I don't want to have to hit you!"

"Let him go!" the aunt said. "If he don't go, before God, I am going up there myself!"

"Don't you see I can't?" his mother cried. "Sarty! Sarty! No! No! Help me, Lizzie!"

Then he began to struggle. His mother caught him in both arms, he whirled, running, his mother stumbled forward onto her knees behind him, crying to the nearer sister: "Catch him, Net! Catch him!" But that was too late too, the sister (the sisters were twins, born at the same time, yet either of them now gave the impression of being, encompassing as much living meat and volume and weight as any other two of the family) not yet having begun to rise from the chair, her head, face, alone merely turned, presenting to him in the flying instant an astonishing expanse of young female features untroubled by any surprise even, wearing only an expression of bovine interest. Then he was out of the room, out of the house, in the mild dust of the starlit road and the heavy rifeness of honeysuckle, the pale ribbon unspooling with terrific slowness under his running feet, reaching the gate at last and turning in, running, his heart and lungs drumming, on up the drive toward the lighted house, the lighted door. He did not knock, he burst in, sobbing for breath, incapable for the moment of speech; he saw the astonished face of the Negro in the linen jacket without knowing when the Negro had appeared.

"De Spain!" he cried, panted. "Where's . . ." then he saw the white man too emerging from a white door down the hall. "Barn!" he cried. "Barn!"

"What?" the white man said. "Barn?"

"Yes!" the boy cried. "Barn!"

"Catch him!" the white man shouted.

But it was too late this time too. The Negro grasped his shirt, but the entire sleeve, rotten with washing, carried away, and he was out that door too and in the drive again, and had actually never ceased to run even while he was screaming into the white man's face.

Behind him the white man was shouting, "My horse! Fetch my horse!" and he thought for an instant of cutting across the park and climbing the fence into the road, but he did not know the park nor how high the vine-massed fence might be and he dared not risk it. So he ran on down the drive, blood and breath roaring; presently he was in the road again though he could not see it. He could not hear either: the galloping mare was almost upon him before he heard her, and even then he held his course, as if the very urgency of his wild grief and need must in a moment more find him wings, waiting until the ultimate instant to hurl himself aside and into the weed-choked roadside ditch as the horse thundered past and on, for an instant in furious silhouette against the stars, the tranquil early summer night sky which, even before the shape of the horse and rider vanished, stained abruptly and violently upward: a long, swirling roar incredible and soundless, blotting the stars, and he springing up and into the road again, running again, knowing it was too late yet still running even after he heard the shot and, an instant later, two shots, pausing now without knowing he had ceased to run, crying "Pap! Pap!", running again before he knew he had begun to run, stumbling, tripping over something and scrabbling up again without ceasing to run, looking backward over his shoulder at the glare as he got up, running on among the invisible trees, panting, sobbing, "Father! Father!"

All books are divisible into two classes, the books of the hour, and the books of all time. . . . There are good books for the hour, and good ones for all time; bad books for the hour, and bad ones for all time.

JOHN RUSKIN

At midnight he was sitting on the crest of a hill. He did not know it was midnight and he did not know how far he had come. But there was no glare behind him now and he sat now, his back toward what he had called home for four days anyhow, his face toward the dark woods which he would enter when breath was strong again, small, shaking steadily in the chill darkness, hugging himself into the remainder of his thin, rotten shirt, the grief and despair now no longer terror and fear but just grief and despair. *Father. My father,* he thought. "He was brave!" he cried suddenly, aloud but not loud, no more than a whisper: "He was! He was in the war! He was in Colonel Sartoris' cav'ry!" not knowing that his father had gone to that war a private in the fine old European sense, wearing no uniform, admitting the authority of and giving fidelity to no man or army or flag, going to war as Malbrouck himself did: for booty — it meant nothing and less than nothing to him if it were enemy booty or his own.

The slow constellations wheeled on. It would be dawn and then sun-up after a while and he would be hungry. But that would be tomorrow and now he was only cold, and walking would cure that. His breathing was easier now and he decided to get up and go on, and then he found that he had been asleep because he knew it was almost dawn, the night almost over. He could tell that from the whippoorwills. They were everywhere now among the dark trees below him, constant and inflectioned and ceaseless, so that, as the instant for giving over to the day birds drew nearer and nearer, there was no interval at all between them. He got up. He was a little stiff, but walking would cure that too as it would the cold, and soon there would be the sun. He went on down the hill, toward the dark woods within which the liquid silver voices of the birds called unceasing — the rapid and urgent beating of the urgent and quiring heart of the late spring night. He did not look back.

FOR DISCUSSION

1. Here we watch the father, but watch with the eyes of his son. And it is the son's response to him that is the story. The son suffers the keenest compassion for his father, but finally he breaks with his father, turns against him, and does what is necessary to get the father shot. The father's egocentricity and his hatred of others have become so habitual as to be attitudes, not passions. He is described as bloodless, as two-dimensional, as tin rather than iron, lacking in heat. He strikes his mules and his son without anger, and hence without remorse. Do you feel that the trial at the opening of the story was fair to the barn-burner, or unfair? How did the father interpret the trial? In what sense did he "have them beat"?

2. After the first trial the father strikes the boy because he says the boy would have given evidence against him. Would the boy have done so? The boy strikes another boy who calls his father a "barn-burner." Does the boy believe that his father burned the barn?

3. During the second trial the father speaks as if he had carried out instructions for cleaning the rug in all good faith. Do the facts bear him out? Earlier, someone says people shouldn't put a fine rug "where folks coming in would have to tromp on it." Recalling how he dirtied his shoe, how he forced himself into the hallway, and how he swung the dirty shoe as he left, do you agree that he "*had to* tromp on it"?

Review also the events involving the hog that led up to the first barn-burning. Do you find in all these events that Snopes burns barns to retaliate for unprovoked injuries done him, or that he repeatedly provokes what he can call injuries?

4. Do you recall how the devil is said to walk? Why is the father always dressed formally? To whom was the father loyal during the war?

5. The most important question is why the boy turns against his father. Is it because the boy hates being struck? Is it because the boy hates moving in dis-

grace once every year or oftener? Can you find the last point at which the son is not against the father, and the earliest point at which he is against him?

Look back, if necessary, to the initial response of the father and of the son when they first view the fine white house in the country richer than any they have known before. Does the boy's vision of this place as a sort of heaven determine him not to allow it to be destroyed? The boy runs away after the fire but not when he is bringing the oil can. Why does he not run away earlier?

Butcher Bird

WALLACE STEGNER

That summer the boy was alone on the farm except for his parents. His brother was working at Orullian's Grocery in town, and there was no one to run the trap line with or swim with in the dark, weed-smelling reservoir where garter snakes made straight rapid lines in the water and the skaters rowed close to shore. So every excursion was an adventure, even if it was only a trip across the three miles of prairie to Larsen's to get mail or groceries. He was excited at the visit to Garfield's as he was excited by everything unusual. The hot midsummer afternoon was still and breathless, the air harder to breathe than usual. He knew there was a change in weather coming because the gingersnaps in their tall cardboard box were soft and bendable when he snitched two to stick in his pocket. He could tell too by his father's grumpiness accumulated through two weeks of drought, his habit of looking off in the southwest, from which either rain or hot winds might come, that something was brewing. If it was rain everything would be fine, his father would hum under his breath getting breakfast, maybe let him drive the stoneboat or ride the mare down to Larsen's for mail. If it was hot wind they'd have to walk soft and speak softer, and it wouldn't be any fun.

They didn't know the Garfields, who had moved in only the fall before; but people said they had a good big house and a bigger barn and that Mr. Garfield was an Englishman and a little funny talking about scientific farming and making the desert blossom like the rose. The boy's father hadn't wanted to go, but his mother thought it was unneighborly not to call at least once in a whole year when people lived only four miles away.

She was, the boy knew, as anxious for a change, as eager to get out of that atmosphere of waiting to see what the weather would do — that tense and teeth-gritting expectancy — as he was.

He found more than he looked for at Garfield's. Mr. Garfield was tall and bald with a big nose, and talked very softly and politely. The boy's father was determined not to like him right from the start.

When Mr. Garfield said, "Dear, I think we might have a glass of lemonade, don't you?", the boy saw his parents look at each other, saw the beginning of a contemptuous smile on his father's face, saw his mother purse her lips and shake her head ever so little. And when Mrs. Garfield, prim and spectacled, with a habit of tucking her head back and to one side while she listened to anyone talk, brought in the lemonade, the boy saw his father taste his and make a little face behind the glass. He hated any summer drink without ice in it, and had spent two whole weeks digging a dugout icehouse just so that he could have ice water and cold beer when the hot weather came.

But Mr. and Mrs. Garfield were nice people. They sat down in their new parlor and showed the boy's mother the rug and the gramophone. When the boy came up curiously to inspect the little box with the petunia-shaped horn and the little china dog with "His Master's Voice" on it, and the Garfields found that he had never seen or heard a gramophone, they put on a cylinder like a big spool of tightly wound black thread and lowered a needle on it, and out came a man's voice singing in Scotch brogue, and his mother smiled and nodded and said, "My land, Harry Lauder! I heard him once a long time ago. Isn't it wonderful, Sonny?"

It was wonderful all right. He inspected it, reached out his fingers to touch things, wiggled the big horn to see if it was loose or screwed in. His father warned him sharply to keep his hands off, but then Mr. Garfield smiled and said, "Oh, he can't hurt it. Let's play something else," and found a record about the saucy little bird on Nelly's hat that had them all laughing. They let him wind the machine and play the record over again, all by himself, and he was very careful. It was a fine machine. He wished he had one.

About the time he had finished playing his sixth or seventh record, and George M. Cohan was singing "She's a grand old rag, she's a high-flying flag, and forever in peace may she wave," he glanced at his father and discovered that he was grouchy about something. He wasn't taking any part in the conversation but was sitting with his chin in his hand staring out of the window. Mr. Garfield was looking at him a little helplessly. His eyes met the boy's and he motioned him over.

"What do you find to do all summer? Only child, are you?"

"No, sir. My brother's in Whitemud. He's twelve. He's got a job."

"So you come out on the farm to help," said Mr. Garfield. He had his hand on the boy's shoulder and his voice was so kind that the boy lost his shyness and felt no embarrassment at all in being out there in the middle of the parlor with all of them watching.

"I don't help much," he said. "I'm too little to do anything but drive the stoneboat, Pa says. When I'm twelve he's going to get me a gun and then I can go hunting."

"Hunting?" Mr. Garfield said. "What do you hunt?"

"Oh, gophers and weasels. I got a pet weasel. His name's Lucifer."

"Well," said Mr. Garfield. "You seem to be a pretty manly little chap. What do you feed your weasel?"

"Gophers." The boy thought it best not to say that the gophers were live ones he threw into the weasel's cage. He thought probably Mr. Garfield would be a little shocked at that.

Mr. Garfield straightened up and looked round at the grown folks. "Isn't it a shame," he said, "that there are so many predatory animals and pests in this country that we have to spend our time destroying them? I hate killing things."

"I hate weasels," the boy said. "I'm just saving this one till he turns into an ermine, and then I'm going to skin him. Once I speared a weasel with the pitchfork in the chicken coop and he dropped right off the tine and ran up my leg and bit me after he was speared clean through."

He finished breathlessly, and his mother smiled at him, motioning him not to talk so much. But Mr. Garfield was still looking at him kindly. "So you want to make war on the cruel things, the weasels and hawks," he said.

"Yes, sir," the boy said. He looked at his mother and it was all right. He hadn't spoiled anything by telling about the weasels.

"Now that reminds me," Mr. Garfield said, rising. "Maybe I've got something you'd find useful."

He went into another room and came back with a .22 in his hand. "Could you use this?"

"I . . . yes, sir!" the boy said. He had almost, in his excitement, said "I hope to whisk in your piskers," because that was what his father always said when he meant anything real hard.

"If your parents want you to have it," Mr. Garfield said and raised his eyebrows at the boy's mother. He didn't look at the father, but the boy did.

"Can I, Pa?"

"I guess so," his father said. "Sure."

"Thank Mr. Garfield nicely," said his mother.

"Gee," the boy breathed. "Thanks, Mr. Garfield, ever so much."

"There's a promise goes with it," Mr. Garfield said. "I'd like you to promise never to shoot anything with it but the bloodthirsty animals — the cruel ones like weasels and hawks. Never anything like birds or prairie dogs."

"How about butcher birds?"

"Butcher birds?" Mr. Garfield said.

"Shrikes," said the boy's mother. "We've got some over by our place. They kill all sorts of things, snakes and gophers and other birds. They're worse than the hawks because they just kill for the fun of it."

"By all means," said Mr. Garfield. "Shoot all the shrikes you see. A thing that kills for the fun of it . . ." He shook his head and his voice got solemn, almost like the voice of Mr. McGregor, the Sunday School Superintendent in town, when he was asking the benediction. "There's something about the way the war drags on, or maybe just this country," he said, "that makes me hate killing. I just can't bear to shoot anything any more, even a weasel."

The boy's father turned cold eyes away from Mr. Garfield and looked out of the window. One big brown hand, a little dirty from the wheel of the car, rubbed against the day-old bristles on his jaws. Then he stood up and stretched. "Well, we got to be going," he said.

"Oh, stay a little while," Mr. Garfield said. "You just came. I wanted to show you my trees."

The boy's mother stared at him. "Trees?"

He smiled. "Sounds a bit odd out here, doesn't it? But I think trees will grow. I've made some plantings down below."

"I'd love to see them," she said. "Sometimes I'd give almost anything to get into a good deep shady woods. Just to smell it, and feel how cool . . ."

"There's a little story connected with these," Mr. Garfield said. He spoke to the mother alone, warmly. "When we first decided to come out here I said to Martha that if trees wouldn't grow we shouldn't stick it. That's just what I said, 'If trees won't grow we shan't stick it.' Trees are almost the breath of life to me."

The boy's father was shaken by a sudden spell of coughing, and the mother shot a quick look at him and looked back at Mr. Garfield with a light flush on her cheekbones. "I'd love to see them," she said. "I was raised in Minnesota, and I never will get used to a place as barren as this."

"When I think of the beeches back home in England," Mr. Garfield said, and shook his head with a puckering smile round his eyes.

The father lifted himself heavily out of his chair and followed the rest of them out to the coulee edge. Below them willows grew profusely along the almost-dry creek, and farther back from the water there was a grove of perhaps twenty trees about a dozen feet high.

"I'm trying cottonwoods first because they can stand dry weather," Mr. Garfield said.

The mother was looking down with all her longings suddenly plain and naked in her eyes. "It's wonderful," she said. "I'd give almost anything to have some on our place."

"I found the willows close by here," said Mr. Garfield. "Just at the south end of the hills they call Old-Man-on-His-Back, where the stream comes down."

"Stream?" the boy's father said. "You mean that trickle?"

"It's not much of a stream," Mr. Garfield said apologetically. "But . . ."

"Are there any more there?" the mother said.

"Oh, yes. You could get some. Cut them diagonally and push them into any damp ground. They'll grow."

"They'll grow about six feet high," the father said.

"Yes," said Mr. Garfield. "They're not, properly speaking, trees. Still . . ."

"It's getting pretty smothery," the father said rather loudly. "We better be getting on."

This time Mr. Garfield didn't object, and they went back to the car exchanging promises of visits. The father jerked the crank and climbed into the Ford, where the boy was sighting along his gun. "Put that down," his father said. "Don't you know any better than to point a gun around people?"

"It isn't loaded."

"They never are," his father said. "Put it down now."

The Garfields were standing with their arms around each other's waists, waiting to wave good-by. Mr. Garfield reached over and picked something from his wife's dress.

"What was it, Alfred?" she said peering.

"Nothing. Just a bit of fluff."

The boy's father coughed violently and the car started with a jerk. With his head down almost to the wheel still coughing, he waved and the mother and the boy waved as they went down along the badly set cedar posts of the pasture fence. They were almost a quarter of a mile away before the boy, with a last wave of the gun, turned round again and saw that his father was purple with laughter. He rocked the car with his joy, and when his wife said, "Oh, Harry, you big fool," he pointed helplessly to his shoulder. "Would you mind," he said. "Would you mind brushing that bit o' fluff off me showldah?" He roared again, pounding the wheel. "I shawn't stick it," he said. "I bloody well shawn't stick it, you know!"

"It isn't fair to laugh at him," she said. "He can't help being English."

"He can't help being a sanctimonious old mudhen either, braying about his luv-ly luv-ly trees. They'll freeze out the first winter."

"How do you know? Maybe it's like he says — if they get a start they'll grow here as well as anywhere."

"Maybe there's a gold mine in our back yard too, but I'm not gonna dig to see. I couldn't stick it."

"Oh, you're just being stubborn," she said. "Just because you didn't like Mr. Garfield . . ."

He turned on her in heavy amazement. "Well, my God! Did you?"

"I thought he was very nice," she said, and sat straighter in the back seat, speaking loudly above the creak of the springs and cough of the motor. "They're trying to make a home, not just a wheat crop. I liked them."

"Uh, huh." He was not laughing any more now. Sitting beside him, the boy could see that his face had hardened and the cold look had come into his eye again. "So I should start talking like I had a mouthful of bran, and planting trees around the house that'll look like clothesline poles in two months."

"I didn't say that."

"You thought it though." He looked irritably at the sky, misted with the same delusive film of cloud that had fooled him for three days, and spat at the roadside. "You thought it all the time we were there. 'Why aren't you more like Mr. Garfield, he's such a nice man.'" With mincing savagery he swung round and mocked her. "Shall I make it a walnut grove? Or a big maple sugar bush? Or maybe you'd like an orange orchard."

The boy was looking down at his gun, trying not to hear them quarrel, but he knew what his mother's face would be like — hurt and a little flushed, her chin trembling into stubbornness. "I don't suppose you could bear to have a rug on the floor, or a gramophone?" she said.

He smacked the wheel hard. "Of course I could bear it if we could afford it. But I sure as hell would rather do without than be like that old sandhill crane."

"I don't suppose you'd like to take me over to the Old-Man-on-His-Back some day to get some willow slips either."

"What for?"

"To plant down in the coulee, by the dam."

"That dam dries up every August. Your willows wouldn't live till snow flies."

"Well, would it do any harm to try?"

"Oh, shut up!" he said. "Just thinking about that guy and his fluff and his trees gives me the pleefer."

The topless Ford lurched, one wheel at a time, through the deep burnout by their pasture corner, and the boy clambered out with his gun in his hand to slip the loop from the three-strand gate. It was then that he saw the snake, a striped limp ribbon, dangling on the fence, and a moment later the sparrow, neatly butchered and hung by the throat from the barbed wire. He pointed the gun at them. "Lookit!" he said. "Lookit what the butcher bird's been doing."

His father's violent hand waved at him from the seat. "Come on! Get the wire out of the way!"

The boy dragged the gate through the dust, and the Ford went through and up behind the house, perched on the bare edge of the coulee in the midst of its baked yard and framed by the dark fireguard overgrown with Russian thistle. Walking across that yard a few minutes later, the boy felt its hard heat under his sneakers. There was hardly a spear of grass within the fireguard. It was one of his father's prides that the dooryard should be like cement. "Pour your wash water out long enough," he said, "and you'll have a surface so hard it won't even make mud." Religiously he threw his water out three time a day, carrying it sometimes a dozen steps to dump it on a dusty or grassy spot.

The mother had objected at first, asking why they had to live in the middle of an alkali flat, and why they couldn't let grass grow up to the door. But he snorted her down. Everything round the house ought to be bare as a bone. Get a good prairie fire going and it'd jump that guard like nothing, and if they had grass to the door where'd they be? She said why not plow a wider fireguard then, one a fire couldn't jump, but he said he had other things to do besides plowing fifty-foot fireguards.

They were arguing inside when the boy came up on the step to sit down and aim his empty .22 at a fencepost. Apparently his mother had been persistent, and persistence when he was not in a mood for it angered the father worse than anything else. Their talk came vaguely through his concentration, but he shut his ears on it. If that spot on the fencepost was a coyote now, and he held the sight steady, right on it, and pulled the trigger, that old coyote would jump about eighty feet in the air and come down dead as a mackerel, and he could tack his hide on the barn the way Mr. Larsen had one, only the dogs had jumped and torn the tail and hind legs off Mr. Larsen's pelt, and he wouldn't get more than the three-dollar bounty out of it. But then Mr. Larsen had shot his with a shotgun anyway, and the hide wasn't worth much even before the dogs tore it. . . .

"I can't for the life of me see why not," his mother said inside. "We could do it now. We're not doing anything else."

"I tell you they wouldn't grow!" said his father with emphasis on every word. "Why should we run our tongues out doing everything that mealy-mouthed fool does?"

"I don't want anything but the willows. They're easy."

He made his special sound of contempt, half-snort, half-grunt. After a silence she tried again. "They might even have pussies on them in the spring. Mr. Garfield thinks they'd grow, and he used to work in a greenhouse, his wife told me."

"This isn't a greenhouse, for Chrissake."

"Oh, let it go," she said. "I've stood it this long without any green things around. I guess I can stand it some more."

The boy, aiming now toward the gate where the butcher bird, coming back to his prey, would in just a minute fly right into Deadeye's unerring bullet, heard his father stand up suddenly.

"Abused, aren't you?" he said.

The mother's voice rose. "No, I'm not abused! Only I can't see why it would be so awful to get some willows. Just because Mr. Garfield gave me the idea, and you didn't like him . . ."

"You're right I didn't like Mr. Garfield," the father said. "He gave me a pain right under the crupper."

"Because," the mother's voice said bitterly, "he calls his wife 'dear' and puts his arm around her and likes trees. It wouldn't occur to you to put your arm around your wife, would it?"

The boy aimed and held his breath. His mother ought to keep still, because if she didn't she'd get him real mad and then they'd both have to tiptoe around the rest of the day. He heard his father's breath whistle through his teeth, and his voice, mincing, nasty. "Would you like me to kiss you now, *dear?*"

"I wouldn't let you touch me with a ten-foot pole," his mother said. She sounded just as mad as he did, and it wasn't often she let herself get that way. The boy squirmed over when he heard the quick hard steps come up behind him and pause. Then his father's big hand, brown and meaty and felted with fine black hair, reached down over his shoulder and took the .22.

"Let's see this cannon old Scissor-bill gave you," he said.

It was a single-shot, bolt-action Savage, a little rusty on the barrel, the bolt sticky with hardened grease when the father removed it. Sighting up through the barrel, he grunted. "Takes care of a gun like he takes care of his farm. Probably used it to cultivate his luv-ly trees."

He went out into the sleeping porch, and after a minute came back with a rag and a can of machine oil. Hunching the boy over on the step, he sat down and began rubbing the bolt with the oil-soaked rag.

"I just can't bear to shoot anything any more," he said, and laughed suddenly. "I just cawn't stick it, little man." He leered at the boy, who grinned back uncertainly. Squinting through the barrel again, the father breathed through his nose and clamped his lips together, shaking his head.

The sun lay heavy on the baked yard. Out over the corner of the pasture a soaring hawk caught wind and sun at the same time, so that his light breast feathers flashed as he banked and rose. Just wait, the boy thought. Wait till I get my gun working and I'll fix you, you hen-robber. He thought of the three chicks a hawk had struck earlier in the summer, the three balls of yellow with the barred mature plumage just coming through. Two of them dead when he got there and chased the hawk away, the other gasping with its crop slashed wide open and the wheat spilling from it on the ground. His mother had sewed up the crop, and the chicken had lived, but it always looked droopy, like a plant in drought time, and sometimes it would stand and work its bill as if it were choking.

By golly, he thought, I'll shoot every hawk and butcher bird in twenty miles. I'll . . .

"Rustle around and find me a piece of baling wire," his father said. "This barrel looks like a henroost."

Behind the house he found a piece of rusty wire, brought it back and watched his father straighten it, wind a bit of rag round the end, ram it up and down through the barrel, and peer through again. "He's leaded her so you can hardly see the grooves," he said. "But maybe she'll shoot. We'll fill her with vinegar and cork her up to-night."

The mother was behind them, leaning against the jamb and watching. She reached down and rumpled the father's black hair. "The minute you get a gun in your hand you start feeling better," she said. "It's just a shame you weren't born fifty years sooner."

"A gun's a good tool," he said. "It hadn't ought to be misused. Gun like this is enough to make a guy cry."

"Well, you've got to admit it was nice of Mr. Garfield to give it to Sonny," she said. It was the wrong thing to say. The boy had a feeling somehow that she knew it was the wrong thing to say, that she said it just to have one tiny triumph over him. He knew it would make him boiling mad again, even before he heard his father's answer.

"Oh, sure, Mr. Garfield's a fine man. He can preach a better sermon than any homesteader in Saskatchewan. God Almighty! everything he does is better than what I do. All right. All right, *all right!* Why the hell don't you move over there if you like it so well?"

"If you weren't so blind . . . !"

He rose with the .22 in his hand and pushed past her into the house. "I'm not so blind," he said heavily in passing. "You've been throwing that bastard up to me for two hours. It don't take very good eyes to see what that means."

His mother started to say, "All because I want a few little . . ." but the boy cut in on her, anxious to help the situation somehow. "Will it shoot now?" he said.

His father said nothing. His mother looked down at him, shrugged, sighed, smiled bleakly with a tight mouth. She moved aside when the father came back with a box of cartridges in his hand. He ignored his wife, speaking to the boy alone in the particular half-jocular tone he always used with him or the dog when he wasn't mad or exasperated.

"Thought I had these around," he said. "Now we'll see what this smoke-pole will do."

He slipped a cartridge in and locked the bolt, looking round for something to shoot at. Behind him the mother's feet moved on the floor, and her voice came purposefully. "I can't see why you have to act this way," she said. "I'm going over and get some slips myself."

There was a long silence. The angled shade lay sharp as a knife across the baked front yard. The father's cheek was pressed against the stock of the gun, his arms and hands as steady as stone.

"How'll you get there?" he said, whispering down the barrel.

"I'll walk."

"Five miles and back."

"Yes, five miles and back. Or fifty miles and back. If there was any earthly reason why you should mind . . ."

"I don't mind," he said, and his voice was soft as silk. "Go ahead."

Close to his mother's long skirts in the doorway, the boy felt her stiffen as if she had been slapped. He squirmed anxiously, but his desperation could find only the question he had asked before. His voice squeaked on it: "Will it shoot now?"

"See that sparrow out there?" his father said, still whispering. "Right out by that cactus?"

"Harry!" the mother said. "If you shoot that harmless little bird!"

Fascinated, the boy watched his father's dark face against the rifle stock, the locked, immovable left arm, the thick finger crooked inside the trigger guard almost too small to hold it. He saw the sparrow, gray, white-breasted, hopping, obliviously in search of bugs, fifty feet out on the gray earth. "I just . . . can't . . . bear . . . to . . . shoot . . . anything," the father said, his face like dark stone, his lips hardly moving. "I just . . . can't . . . stick it!"

"Harry!" his wife screamed.

The boy's mouth opened, a dark wash of terror shadowed his vision of the baked yard cut by its sharp angle of shade.

"Don't, pa!"

The rocklike figure of his father never moved. The thick finger squeezed slowly down on the trigger, there was a thin, sharp report, and the sparrow jerked and collapsed into a shapeless wad on the ground. It was as if, in the instant of the shot, all its clean outlines vanished. Head, feet, the white breast, the perceptible outlines of the folded wings, disappeared all at once, were crumpled together and lost, and the boy sat beside his father on the step with the echo of the shot still in his ears.

He did not look at either of his parents. He looked only at the crumpled sparrow. Step by step, unable to keep away, he went to it, stooped, and picked it up. Blood stained his fingers, and he held the bird by the tail while he wiped the smeared hand on his overalls. He heard the click as the bolt was shot and the empty cartridge ejected, and he saw his mother come swiftly out of the house past his father, who sat still on the step. Her hands were clenched, and she walked with her head down, as if fighting tears.

"Ma!" the boy said dully. "Ma, what'll I do with it?"

She stopped and turned, and for a moment they faced each other. He saw the dead pallor of her face, the burning eyes, the not-quite-controllable quiver of her lips. But her words, when they came, were flat and level, almost casual.

"Leave it right there," she said. "After a while your father will want to hang it on the barbed wire."

FOR DISCUSSION

1. Little by little, under the stress of the withering heat during the Saskatchewan drought, the world arranges itself into two warring camps. In the middle is the boy from whose point of view the action is seen. Note that the story opens with the boy's aloneness, then it speaks of his parents, but quickly mentions the tension they all feel as they wait for a change in the weather. What is the usual

activity of the boy when his brother is at home? Does the fact that the brother is gone intensify the story as a whole?

2. The conflict between the two warring camps extends into the whole world of the story. List the contrasted opposites in animals or birds, in hobbies, in ways to protect a farmhouse from a prairie fire, in kinds of vegetation, in ways a husband treats his wife, in drinks. What position do the father and the mother take in this conflict? Where are the Garfields in this conflict? When you have completed the list, try to define in general terms what each side stands for.

3. Stegner captures with remarkable success the delicate interaction of the father and mother and son. It is primarily the son's receiving set that we listen in on. Does he change from the mother's side to the father's side at different times, or does he never take sides? How would the story differ if it were told from the father's point of view? from the mother's?

4. In the final crisis, the butcher bird, as contrasted with the sparrow, becomes a symbol of the opposition in the story. What traits does the butcher bird possess? In what sense is the father like that bird? Is anyone in the story like the sparrow?

5. Is the point of the story to prove that it is cruel to shoot sparrows with a .22 even though you are upset by the weather? If that isn't the point, then what is?

✿ *Fantasy* ✿

The Celestial Omnibus

E. M. FORSTER

The boy who resided at Agathox Lodge, 28, Buckingham Park Road, Surbiton, had often been puzzled by the old sign-post that stood almost opposite. He asked his mother about it, and she replied that it was a joke, and not a very nice one, which had been made many years back by some naughty young men, and that the police ought to remove it. For there were two strange things about this sign-post: firstly, it pointed up a blank alley, and, secondly, it had painted on it, in faded characters, the words, "To Heaven."

Reprinted from *The Collected Tales of E. M. Forster*, by permission of Alfred A. Knopf, Inc. Copyright 1947 by Alfred A. Knopf, Inc.

"What kind of young men were they?" he asked.

"I think your father told me that one of them wrote verses, and was expelled from the University and came to grief in other ways. Still, it was a long time ago. You must ask your father about it. He will say the same as I do, that it was put up as a joke."

"So it doesn't mean anything at all?"

She sent him upstairs to put on his best things, for the Bonses were coming to tea, and he was to hand the cakestand.

It struck him, as he wrenched on his tightening trousers, that he might do worse than ask Mr. Bons about the sign-post. His father, though very kind, always laughed at him — shrieked with laughter whenever he or any other child asked a question or spoke. But Mr. Bons was serious as well as kind. He had a beautiful house and lent one books, he was a churchwarden, and a candidate for the County Council; he had donated to the Free Library enormously, he presided over the Literary Society, and had Members of Parliament to stop with him — in short, he was probably the wisest person alive.

Yet even Mr. Bons could only say that the sign-post was a joke — the joke of a person named Shelley.

"Of course!" cried the mother; "I told you so, dear. That was the name."

"Had you never heard of Shelley?" asked Mr. Bons.

"No," said the boy, and hung his head.

"But is there no Shelley in the house?"

"Why, yes!" exclaimed the lady, in much agitation. "Dear Mr. Bons, we aren't such Philistines as that. Two at the least. One a wedding present, and the other, smaller print, in one of the spare rooms."

"I believe we have seven Shelleys," said Mr. Bons, with a slow smile. Then he brushed the cake crumbs off his stomach, and, together with his daughter, rose to go.

The boy, obeying a wink from his mother, saw them all the way to the garden gate, and when they had gone he did not at once return to the house, but gazed for a little up and down Buckingham Park Road.

His parents lived at the right end of it. After No. 39 the quality of the houses dropped very suddenly, and 64 had not even a separate servants' entrance. But at the present moment the whole road looked rather pretty, for the sun had just set in splendour, and the inequalities of rent were drowned in a saffron afterglow. Small birds twittered, and the bread-winners' train shrieked musically down through the cutting — that wonderful cutting which has drawn to itself the whole beauty out of Surbiton, and clad itself, like any Alpine valley, with the glory of the fir and the silver birch and the primrose. It was this cutting that had first stirred desires within the boy — desires for something just a little different, he knew not what, desires that would return whenever things were sunlit, as they were this evening, running up and down inside him, up and down, up and down, till he would feel quite unusual all over, and as likely as not would want to cry. This evening he was even sillier, for he slipped across the road towards the signpost and began to run up the blank alley.

The alley runs between high walls — the walls of the garden of "Ivanhoe" and "Bella Vista," respectively. It smells a little all the way, and is scarcely twenty yards long, including the turn at the end. So not unnaturally the boy soon came to a standstill. "I'd like to kick that Shelley," he exclaimed, and glanced idly at a piece of paper which was pasted on the wall. Rather an odd piece of paper, and he read it carefully before he turned back. This is what he read:

S. AND C.R.C.C.

ALTERATION IN SERVICE

Owing to lack of patronage the Company are regretfully compelled to suspend the hourly service, and to retain only the

Sunrise and Sunset Omnibuses,

which will run as usual. It is to be hoped that the public will patronize an arrangement which is intended for their convenience. As an extra inducement, the Company will, for the first time, now issue

Return Tickets!

(available one day only), which may be obtained of the driver. Passengers are again reminded that *no tickets are issued at the other end,* and that no complaints in this connection will receive consideration from the Company. Nor will the Company be responsible for any negligence or stupidity on the part of Passengers, nor for Hailstorms, Lightning, Loss of Tickets, nor for any Act of God.

          For the Direction.

Now, he had never seen this notice before, nor could he imagine where the omnibus went to. S. of course was for Surbiton, and R.C.C. meant Road Car Company. But what was the meaning of the other C.? Coombe and Malden, perhaps, or possibly "City." Yet it could not hope to compete with the South-Western. The whole thing, the boy reflected, was run on hopelessly unbusinesslike lines. Why no tickets from the other end? And what an hour to start! Then he realized that unless the notice was a hoax, an omnibus must have been starting just as he was wishing the Bonses good-bye. He peered at the ground through the gathering dusk, and there he saw what might or might not be the marks of wheels. Yet nothing had

---

There is no such thing as a dirty theme. There are only dirty writers.

        G. J. NATHAN

come out of the alley. And he had never seen an omnibus at any time in the Buckingham Park Road. No: it must be a hoax, like the sign-post, like the fairy tales, like the dreams upon which he would wake suddenly in the night. And with a sigh he stepped from the alley — right into the arms of his father.

Oh, how his father laughed! "Poor, poor Popsey!" he cried. "Diddums! Diddums! Diddums think he'd walky-palky up to Evvink!" And his mother, also convulsed with laughter, appeared on the steps of Agathox Lodge.

"Don't, Bob!" she gasped. "Don't be so naughty! Oh, you'll kill me! Oh, leave the boy alone!"

But all that evening the joke was kept up. The father implored to be taken too. Was it a very tiring walk? Need one wipe one's shoes on the door-mat? And the boy went to bed feeling faint and sore, and thankful for only one thing — that he had not said a word about the omnibus. It was a hoax, yet through his dreams it grew more and more real, and the streets of Surbiton, through which he saw it driving, seemed instead to become hoaxes and shadows. And very early in the morning he woke with a cry, for he had had a glimpse of its destination.

He struck a match, and its light fell not only on his watch but also on his calendar, so that he knew it to be half-an-hour to sunrise. It was pitch dark, for the fog had come down from London in the night, and all Surbiton was wrapped in its embraces. Yet he sprang out and dressed himself, for he was determined to settle once for all which was real: the omnibus or the streets. "I shall be a fool one way or the other," he thought, "until I know." Soon he was shivering in the road under the gas lamp that guarded the entrance to the alley.

To enter the alley itself required some courage. Not only was it horribly dark, but he now realized it was an impossible terminus for an omnibus. If it had not been for a policeman, whom he heard approaching through the fog, he would never have made the attempt. The next moment he had made the attempt and failed. Nothing. Nothing but a blank alley and a very silly boy gaping at its dirty floor. It *was* a hoax. "I'll tell papa and mamma," he decided. "I deserve it. I deserve that they should know. I am too silly to be alive." And he went back to the gate of Agathox Lodge.

There he remembered that his watch was fast. The sun was not risen; it would not rise for two minutes. "Give the bus every chance," he thought cynically, and returned into the alley.

But the omnibus was there.

II

It had two horses, whose sides were still smoking from their journey, and its two great lamps shone through the fog against the alley's walls, changing their cobwebs and moss into tissues of fairyland. The driver was huddled up in a cape. He faced the blank wall, and how he had managed to drive in so neatly and so silently was one of the many things that the boy never discovered. Nor could he imagine how ever he would drive out.

"Please," his voice quavered through the foul brown air, "please, is that an omnibus?"

"Omnibus est," said the driver, without turning round. There was a moment's silence. The policeman passed, coughing, by the entrance of the alley. The boy crouched in the shadow, for he did not want to be found out. He was pretty sure, too, that it was a Pirate; nothing else, he reasoned, would go from such odd places and at such odd hours.

"About when do you start?" He tried to sound nonchalant.

"At sunrise."

"How far do you go?"

"The whole way."

"And can I have a return ticket which will bring me all the way back?"

"You can."

It is only by writing ill that you can attain to write well.
                                                    SAMUEL JOHNSON

"Do you know, I half think I'll come." The driver made no answer. The sun must have risen, for he unhitched the brake. And scarcely had the boy jumped in before the omnibus was off.

How? Did it turn? There was no room. Did it go forward? There was a blank wall. Yet it was moving — moving at a stately pace through the fog, which had turned from brown to yellow. The thought of warm bed and warmer breakfast made the boy feel faint. He wished he had not come. His parents would not have approved. He would have gone back to them if the weather had not made it impossible. The solitude was terrible; he was the only passenger. And the omnibus, though well-built, was cold and somewhat musty. He drew his coat round him, and in so doing chanced to feel his pocket. It was empty. He had forgotten his purse.

"Stop!" he shouted. "Stop!" And then, being of a polite disposition, he glanced up at the painted notice-board so that he might call the driver by name. "Mr. Browne! stop; oh, do please stop!"

Mr. Browne did not stop, but he opened a little window and looked in at the boy. His face was a surprise, so kind it was and modest.

"Mr. Browne, I've left my purse behind. I've not got a penny. I can't pay for the ticket. Will you take my watch, please? I am in the most awful hole."

"Tickets on this line," said the driver, "whether single or return, can be purchased by coinage from no terrene mint. And a chronometer, though it had solaced the vigils of Charlemagne, or measured the slumbers of Laura, can acquire by no mutation the double-cake that charms the fangless Cerberus of Heaven!" So saying, he handed in the necessary ticket, and, while the boy said "Thank you," continued, "Titular pretensions, I know it well, are vanity. Yet they merit no censure when uttered on a laughing lip, and in an homonymous world are in some sort, useful, since they do serve to distinguish one Jack from his fellow. Remember me, therefore, as Sir Thomas Browne."

"Are you a Sir? Oh, sorry!" He had heard of these gentleman drivers. "It *is* good of you about the ticket. But if you go on at this rate, however does your bus pay?"

"It does not pay. It was not intended to pay. Many are the faults of my equipage; it is compounded too curiously of foreign woods; its cushions tickle erudition rather than promote repose; and my horses are nourished not on the evergreen pastures of the moment, but on the dried bents and clovers of Latinity. But that it pays! — that error at all events was never intended and never attained."

"Sorry again," said the boy rather hopelessly. Sir Thomas looked sad, fearing that, even for a moment, he had been the cause of sadness. He invited the boy to come up and sit beside him on the box, and together they journeyed on through the fog, which was now changing from yellow to white. There were no houses by the road; so it must be either Putney Heath or Wimbledon Common.

"Have you been a driver always?"

"I was a physician once."

"But why did you stop? Weren't you good?"

"As a healer of bodies I had scant success, and several score of my patients preceded me. But as a healer of the spirit I have succeeded beyond my hopes and my deserts. For though my draughts were not better nor subtler than those of other men, yet, by reason of the cunning goblets wherein I offered them, the queasy soul was ofttimes tempted to sip and be refreshed."

"The queasy soul," the boy murmured; "if the sun sets with trees in front of it, and you suddenly come strange all over, is that a queasy soul?"

"Have you felt that?"

"Why, yes."

After a pause he told the boy a little, a very little, about the journey's end. But they did not chatter much, for the boy, when he liked a person, would as soon sit silent in his company as speak, and this, he discovered, was also the mind of Sir Thomas Browne and of many others with whom he was to be acquainted. He heard, however, about the young man Shelley, who was now quite a famous person, with a carriage of his own, and about some of the other drivers who are in the service of the Company. Meanwhile the light grew stronger, though the fog did not disperse. It was now more like mist than fog, and at times would travel quickly across them, as if it was part of a cloud. They had been ascending too, in a most puzzling way; for over two hours the horses had been pulling against the collar, and even if it were Richmond Hill they ought to have been at the top long ago. Perhaps it was Epsom, or even the North Downs; yet the air seemed keener than that which blows on either. And as to the name of their destination, Sir Thomas Browne was silent.

Crash.

"Thunder, by Jove!" said the boy, "and not so far off either. Listen to the echoes! It's more like mountains."

He thought, not very vividly, of his father and mother. He saw them sitting down to sausages and listening to the storm. He saw his own empty place. Then there would be questions, alarms, theories, jokes, consolations. They would expect him back at lunch. To lunch he would not come, nor to tea, but he would be in for dinner, and so his day's truancy would be over. If he had had his purse he would have bought them presents — not that he should have known what to get them.

Crash!

The peal and the lightning came together. The cloud quivered as if it were alive, and torn streamers of mist rushed past. "Are you afraid?" asked Sir Thomas Browne.

"What is there to be afraid of? Is it much farther?"

The horses of the omnibus stopped just as a ball of fire burst up and exploded with a ringing noise that was deafening but clear, like the noise of a blacksmith's forge. All the cloud was shattered.

"Oh, listen, Sir Thomas Browne! No, I mean look; we shall get a view at last. No, I mean listen; that sounds like a rainbow!"

The noise had died into the faintest murmur, beneath which another murmur grew, spreading stealthily, steadily, in a curve that widened but did not vary. And in widening curves a rainbow was spreading from the horses' feet into the dissolving mists.

"But how beautiful! What colours! Where will it stop? It is more like the rainbows you can tread on. More like dreams."

The colour and the sound grew together. The rainbow spanned an enormous gulf. Clouds rushed under it and were pierced by it, and still it grew, reaching forward, conquering the darkness, until it touched something that seemed more solid than a cloud.

The boy stood up. "What is that out there?" he called. "What does it rest on, out at that other end?"

In the morning sunshine a precipice shone forth beyond the gulf. A precipice — or was it a castle? The horses moved. They set their feet upon the rainbow.

"Oh, look!" the boy shouted. "Oh, listen! Those caves — or are they gateways? Oh, look between those cliffs at those ledges. I see people. I see trees!"

"Look also below," whispered Sir Thomas. "Neglect not the diviner Acheron."

The boy looked below, past the flames of the rainbow that licked against their wheels. The gulf also had cleared, and in its depths there flowed an everlasting river. One sunbeam entered and struck a green pool, and as they passed over he saw three maidens rise to the surface of the pool, singing, and playing with something that glistened like a ring.

"You down in the water — " he called.

They answered, "You up on the bridge — " There was a burst of music. "You up on the bridge, good luck to you. Truth in the depth, truth on the height."

"You down in the water, what are you doing?"

Sir Thomas Browne replied: "They sport in the mancipiary possession of their gold"; and the omnibus arrived.

III

The boy was in disgrace. He sat locked up in the nursery of Agathox Lodge, learning poetry for a punishment. His father had said, "My boy! I can pardon anything but untruthfulness," and had caned him, saying at each stroke, "There is *no* omnibus, *no* driver, *no* bridge, *no* mountain; you are a *truant*, a *guttersnipe*, a *liar*." His father could be very stern at times. His mother had begged him to say he was sorry. But he could not say that. It was the greatest day of his life, in spite of the caning and the poetry at the end of it.

He had returned punctually at sunset — driven not by Sir Thomas Browne, but by a maiden lady who was full of quiet fun. They had talked of omnibuses and also of barouche landaus. How far away her gentle voice seemed now! Yet it was scarcely three hours since he had left her up the alley.

His mother called through the door. "Dear, you are to come down and to bring your poetry with you."

He came down, and found that Mr. Bons was in the smoking-room with his father. It had been a dinner party.

"Here is the great traveller!" said his father grimly. "Here is the young gentleman who drives in an omnibus over rainbows, while young ladies sing to him." Pleased with his wit, he laughed.

"After all," said Mr. Bons, smiling, "there is something a little like it in Wagner. It is odd how, in quite illiterate minds, you will find glimmers of Artistic Truth. The case interests me. Let me plead for the culprit. We have all romanced in our time, haven't we?"

"Hear how kind Mr. Bons is," said his mother, while his father said, "Very well. Let him say his Poem, and that will do. He is going away to my sister on Tuesday, and *she* will cure him of this alley-slopering." (Laughter.) "Say your Poem."

The boy began. " 'Standing aloof in giant ignorance.' "

His father laughed again — roared. "One for you, my son! 'Standing aloof in giant ignorance!' I never knew these poets talked sense. Just describes you. Here, Bons, you go in for poetry. Put him through it, will you, while I fetch up the whisky?"

"Yes, give me the Keats," said Mr. Bons. "Let him say his Keats to me."

So for a few moments the wise man and the ignorant boy were left alone in the smoking-room.

" 'Standing aloof in giant ignorance, of thee I dream and of the Cyclades, as one who sits ashore and longs perchance to visit — ' "

"Quite right. To visit what?"

" 'To visit dolphin coral in deep seas,' " said the boy, and burst into tears.

"Come, come! why do you cry?"

"Because — because all these words that only rhymed before, now that I've come back they're me."

Mr. Bons laid the Keats down. The case was more interesting than he had expected. "*You?*" he exclaimed. "This sonnet, *you?*"

"Yes — and look farther on: 'Aye, on the shores of darkness there is light, and precipices show untrodden green.' It *is* so, sir. All these things are true."

"I never doubted it," said Mr. Bons, with closed eyes.

"You — then you believe me? You believe in the omnibus and the driver and the storm and that return ticket I got for nothing and — "

"Tut, tut! No more of your yarns, my boy. I meant that I never doubted the essential truth of Poetry. Some day, when you have read more, you will understand what I mean."

"But, Mr. Bons, it *is* so. There *is* light upon the shores of darkness. I have seen it coming. Light and a wind."

"Nonsense," said Mr. Bons.

"If I had stopped! They tempted me. They told me to give up my ticket — for you cannot come back if you lose your ticket. They called from the river for it, and indeed I was tempted, for I have never been so happy as among those precipices. But I thought of my mother and father, and that I must fetch them. Yet they will not come, though the road starts opposite our house. It has all happened as the people up there warned me, and Mr. Bons has disbelieved me like everyone else. I have been caned. I shall never see that mountain again."

"What's that about me?" said Mr. Bons, sitting up in his chair very suddenly.

"I told them about you, and how clever you were, and how many books you had, and they said, 'Mr. Bons will certainly disbelieve you.' "

"Stuff and nonsense, my young friend. You grow impertinent. I — well — I will settle the matter. Not a word to your father. I will cure you. To-morrow evening I will myself call here to take you for a walk, and at sunset we will go up this alley opposite and hunt for your omnibus, you silly little boy."

His face grew serious, for the boy was not disconcerted, but leapt about the room singing, "Joy! joy! I told them you would believe me. We will drive together over the rainbow. I told them that you would come." After all, could there be anything in the story? Wagner? Keats? Shelley? Sir Thomas Browne? Certainly the case was interesting.

And on the morrow evening, though it was pouring with rain, Mr. Bons did not omit to call at Agathox Lodge.

The boy was ready, bubbling with excitement, and skipping about in a way that rather vexed the President of the Literary Society. They took a turn down Buckingham Park Road, and then — having seen that no one was watching them — slipped up the alley. Naturally enough (for the sun was setting) they ran straight against the omnibus.

"Good heavens!" exclaimed Mr. Bons. "Good gracious heavens!"

It was not the omnibus in which the boy had driven first, nor yet that in which he had returned. There were three horses — black, gray, and white, the gray being the finest. The driver, who turned round at the mention of goodness and of heaven, was a sallow man with terrifying jaws and sunken eyes. Mr. Bons, on seeing him, gave a cry as if of recognition, and began to tremble violently.

The boy jumped in.

"Is it possible?" cried Mr. Bons. "Is the impossible possible?"

"Sir; come in, sir. It is such a fine omnibus. Oh, here is his name — Dan someone."

Mr. Bons sprang in too. A blast of wind immediately slammed the omnibus door, and the shock jerked down all the omnibus blinds, which were very weak on their springs.

"Dan . . . Show me. Good gracious heavens! We're moving."

"Hooray!" said the boy.

Mr. Bons became flustered. He had not intended to be kidnapped. He could not find the door-handle nor push up the blinds. The omnibus was quite dark, and by the time he had struck a match, night had come on outside also. They were moving rapidly.

"A strange, a memorable adventure," he said, surveying the interior of the omnibus, which was large, roomy, and constructed with extreme regularity, every part exactly answering to every other part. Over the door (the handle of which was outside) was written, "Lasciate ogni baldanza voi che

The last thing one settles in writing a book is what one should put in first.

PASCAL

entrate" — at least, that was what was written, but Mr. Bons said that it was Lashy arty something, and that baldanza was a mistake for speranza. His voice sounded as if he was in church. Meanwhile, the boy called to the cadaverous driver for two return tickets. They were handed in without a word. Mr. Bons covered his face with his hand and again trembled. "Do you know who that is!" he whispered, when the little window had shut upon them. "It is the impossible."

"Well, I don't like him as much as Sir Thomas Browne, though I shouldn't be surprised if he had even more in him."

"More in him?" He stamped irritably. "By accident you have made the greatest discovery of the century, and all you can say is that there is more in his man. Do you remember those vellum books in my library, stamped with red lilies? This — sit still, I bring you stupendous news! — *this is the man who wrote them.*"

The boy sat quite still. "I wonder if we shall see Mrs. Gamp?" he asked, after a civil pause.

"Mrs. — ?"

"Mrs. Gamp and Mrs. Harris. I like Mrs. Harris. I came upon them quite suddenly. Mrs. Gamp's bandboxes have moved over the rainbow so badly. All the buttons have fallen out, and two of the pippins off her bedstead tumbled into the stream." ·

"Out there sits the man who wrote my vellum books!" thundered Mr. Bons, "and you talk to me of Dickens and of Mrs. Gamp?"

"I know Mrs. Gamp so well," he apologized. "I could not help being glad to see her. I recognized her voice. She was telling Mrs. Harris about Mrs. Prig."

"Did you spend the whole day in her elevating company?"

"Oh, no. I raced. I met a man who took me out beyond to a race-course. You run, and there are dolphins out at sea."

"Indeed. Do you remember the man's name?"

"Achilles. No; he was later. Tom Jones."

Mr. Bons sighed heavily. "Well, my lad, you have made a miserable mess of it. Think of a cultured person with your opportunities! A cultured person would have known all these characters and known what to have said to each. He would not have wasted his time with a Mrs. Gamp or a Tom Jones. The creations of Homer, of Shakespeare, and of Him who drives us now, would alone have contented him. He would not have raced. He would have asked intelligent questions."

"But, Mr. Bons," said the boy humbly, "you will be a cultured person. I told them so."

"True, true, and I beg you not to disgrace me when we arrive. No gossiping. No running. Keep close to my side, and never speak to these Immortals unless they speak to you. Yes, and give me the return tickets. You will be losing them."

The boy surrendered the tickets, but felt a little sore. After all, he had found the way to this place. It was hard first to be disbelieved and then to be lectured. Meanwhile, the rain had stopped, and moonlight crept into the omnibus through the cracks in the blinds.

"But how is there to be a rainbow?" cried the boy.

"You distract me," snapped Mr. Bons. "I wish to meditate on beauty. I wish to goodness I was with a reverent and sympathetic person."

The lad bit his lip. He made a hundred good resolutions. He would imitate Mr. Bons all the visit. He would not laugh, or run, or sing, or do any of the vulgar things that must have disgusted his new friends last time. He would be very careful to pronounce their names properly, and to remember who knew whom. Achilles did not know Tom Jones — at least, so Mr. Bons said. The Duchess of Malfi was older than Mrs. Gamp — at least, so Mr. Bons said. He would be self-conscious, reticent, and prim. He would never say he liked anyone. Yet, when the blind flew up at a chance touch of his head, all these good resolutions went to the winds, for the omnibus had reached the summit of a moonlit hill, and there was the chasm, and there, across it, stood the old precipices, dreaming, with their feet in the everlasting river. He exclaimed, "The mountain! Listen to the new tune in the water! Look at the camp fires in the ravines," and Mr. Bons, after a hasty glance, retorted, "Water? Camp fires? Ridiculous rubbish. Hold your tongue. There is nothing at all."

Yet, under his eyes, a rainbow formed, compounded not of sunlight and storm, but of moonlight and the spray of the river. The three horses put their feet upon it. He thought it the finest rainbow he had seen, but did not dare to say so, since Mr. Bons said that nothing was there. He leant out — the window had opened — and sang the tune that rose from the sleeping waters.

"The prelude of Rhinegold?" said Mr. Bons suddenly. "Who taught you these *leit motifs*?" He, too, looked out of the window. Then he behaved very oddly. He gave a choking cry and fell back onto the omnibus floor. He writhed and kicked. His face was green.

"Does the bridge make you dizzy?" the boy asked.

"Dizzy!" gasped Mr. Bons. "I want to go back. Tell the driver."

But the driver shook his head.

"We are nearly there," said the boy. "They are asleep. Shall I call? They will be so pleased to see you, for I have prepared them."

Mr. Bons moaned. They moved over the lunar rainbow, which ever and ever broke away behind their wheels. How still the night was! Who would be sentry at the Gate?

"I am coming," he shouted, again forgetting the hundred resolutions. "I am returning — I, the boy."

"The boy is returning," cried a voice to other voices, who repeated, "The boy is returning."

"I am bringing Mr. Bons with me."

Silence.

"I should have said Mr. Bons is bringing me with him."

Profound silence.

"Who stands sentry?"

"Achilles."

And on the rocky causeway, close to the springing of the rainbow bridge, he saw a young man who carried a wonderful shield.

"Mr. Bons, it is Achilles, armed."

"I want to go back," said Mr. Bons.

The last fragment of the rainbow melted, the wheels sang upon the living rock, the door of the omnibus burst open. Out leapt the boy — he could not resist — and sprang to meet the warrior, who, stooping suddenly, caught him on his shield.

"Achilles!" he cried, "let me get down, for I am ignorant and vulgar, and I must wait for Mr. Bons of whom I told you yesterday."

But Achilles raised him aloft. He crouched on the wonderful shield, on heroes and burning cities, on vineyards graven in gold, on every dear passion, every joy, on the entire image of the Mountain that he had discovered, encircled, like it, with an everlasting stream. "No, no," he protested, "I am not worthy. It is Mr. Bons who must be up here."

But Mr. Bons was whimpering, and Achilles trumpeted and cried, "Stand upright upon my shield!"

"Sir, I did not mean to stand! something made me stand. Sir, why do you delay? Here is only the great Achilles, whom you knew."

Mr. Bons screamed, "I see no one. I see nothing. I want to go back." Then he cried to the driver, "Save me! Let me stop in your chariot. I have honoured you. I have quoted you. I have bound you in vellum. Take me back to my world."

The driver replied, "I am the means and not the end. I am the food and not the life. Stand by yourself, as that boy has stood. I cannot save you. For poetry is a spirit; and they that would worship it must worship in spirit and in truth."

Mr. Bons — he could not resist — crawled out of the beautiful omnibus. His face appeared, gaping horribly. His hands followed, one gripping the step, the other beating the air. Now his shoulders emerged, his chest, his stomach. With a shriek of "I see London," he fell — fell against the hard, moonlit rock, fell into it as if it were water, fell through it, vanished, and was seen by the boy no more.

"Where have you fallen to, Mr. Bons? Here is a procession arriving to honour you with music and torches. Here come the men and women whose names you know. The mountain is awake, the river is awake, over the racecourse the sea is awaking those dolphins, and it is all for you. They want you —"

There was the touch of fresh leaves on his forehead. Someone had crowned him.

ΤΕΛΟΣ

From the *Kingston Gazette, Surbiton Times,* and *Raynes Park Observer.* The body of Mr. Septimus Bons has been found in a shockingly mutilated condition in the vicinity of the Bermondsey gas-works. The deceased's pockets contained a sovereign-purse, a silver cigar-case, a bijou pronouncing dictionary, and a couple of omnibus tickets. The unfortunate gentleman had apparently been hurled from a considerable height. Foul play is suspected, and a thorough investigation is pending by the authorities.

FOR DISCUSSION

1. If the "real" world is that part of our experience which other people also share, then the "unreal" world is that part of experience uniquely one's own. Fantasy as a literary form always combines elements of both worlds, and always aims to make the unreal part quite as believable as the real part.

The first paragraph of this story — with the precise information about where the boy lived so you can go there and see for yourself — starts out like a most commonplace paragraph. But the third of the three sentences is, as it says, strange.

That strangeness is asked about, and it turns out to be mainly the strangeness that comes when things of long ago convince us that they once were as much the present as this present of ours now is. Most of the unreal world in this story is of that sort. It is not the unreal world of religious vision, though the place is called Heaven; it is the world of the literary past. Authors and their creations are all vividly alive.

The first paragraph in the story is mostly real, then, with the last sentence unreal. Later, whole pages are unreal. At what places in the story would you say we pass the 50-50 mark moving either from real to unreal or from unreal to real? Did you experience a slight jolt or shock at each such crossing?

2. Does the boy find the first unreal journey and the unreal place quite believable and, in that sense, real? Did you too, as you read? Did you even go so far, after returning from the first journey, as to be in sympathy with the boy and against the unbelieving father?

3. Considerable attention is given to Mr. Bons' literary education, which is indeed superior to that of the boy. And repeatedly he says that the boy behaved wrongly on his first visit. Does the boy take his advice? How suitably does Mr. Bons himself behave once he arrives?

4. If the story suggests that certain human traits are preferable to others, which seem preferred and which not? How does the author make his preference known to the reader?

The Rocking-Horse Winner

D. H. LAWRENCE

There was a woman who was beautiful, who started with all the advantages, yet she had no luck. She married for love, and the love turned to dust. She had bonny children, yet she felt they had been thrust upon her, and she could not love them. They looked at her coldly, as if they were finding fault with her. And hurriedly she felt she must cover up some fault in herself. Yet what it was that she must cover up she never knew. Nevertheless, when her children were present, she always felt the centre of her heart go hard. This troubled her, and in her manner she was all the more gentle and anxious for her children, as if she loved them very much. Only she herself knew that at the centre of her heart was a hard little place that could not feel love, no, not for anybody. Everybody else said of her: "She is such a good mother. She adores her children." Only she herself, and her children themselves, knew it was not so. They read it in each other's eyes.

There were a boy and two little girls. They lived in a pleasant house, with a garden, and they had discreet servants, and felt themselves superior to anyone in the neighbourhood.

Although they lived in style, they felt always an anxiety in the house. There was never enough money. The mother had a small income, and the father had a small income, but not nearly enough for the social position which they had to keep up. The father went into town to some office. But though he had good prospects, these prospects never materialized. There was always the grinding sense of the shortage of money, though the style was always kept up.

At last the mother said: "I will see if I can't make something." But she did not know where to begin. She racked her brains, and tried this thing and the other, but could not find anything successful. The failure made deep lines come into her face. Her children were growing up, they would have to go to school. There must be more money, there must be more money. The father, who was always very handsome and expensive in his tastes, seemed as if he never would be able to do anything worth doing.

And the mother, who had a great belief in herself, did not succeed any better, and her tastes were just as expensive.

And so the house came to be haunted by the unspoken phrase: There must be more money! There must be more money! The children could hear it all the time, though nobody said it aloud. They heard it at Christmas, when the expensive and splendid toys filled the nursery. Behind the shining modern rocking-horse, behind the small doll's house, a voice would start whispering: "There must be more money! There must be more money!" And the children would stop playing, to listen for a moment. They would look into each other's eyes, to see if they had all heard. And each one saw in the eyes of the other two that they too had heard. "There must be more money! There must be more money!"

It came whispering from the springs of the still-swaying rocking-horse, and even the horse, bending his wooden, champing head, heard it. The big doll, sitting so pink and smirking in her new pram, could hear it quite plainly, and seemed to be smirking all the more self-consciously because of it. The foolish puppy, too, that took the place of the teddy-bear, he was looking so extraordinarily foolish for no other reason but that he heard the secret whisper all over the house: "There must be more money!"

Swiftness of mere writing after due energy of preparation, is doubtless the right method; the hot furnace having worked and simmered, let the pure gold flow out at one gush.

THOMAS CARLYLE

Yet nobody ever said it aloud. The whisper was everywhere, and therefore no one spoke it. Just as no one ever says: "We are breathing!" in spite of the fact that breath is coming and going all the time.

"Mother," said the boy Paul one day, "Why don't we keep a car of our own? Why do we always use uncle's, or else a taxi?"

"Because we're the poor members of the family," said the mother.

"But why are we, mother?"

"Well — I suppose," she said slowly and bitterly, "it's because your father has no luck."

The boy was silent for some time.

"Is luck money, mother?" he asked, rather timidly.

"No, Paul. Not quite. It's what causes you to have money."

"Oh!" said Paul vaguely. "I thought when Uncle Oscar said filthy lucker, it meant money."

"Filthy lucre does mean money," said the mother. "But it's lucre, not luck."

"Oh!" said the boy. "Then what is luck, mother?"

"It's what causes you to have money. If you're lucky you have money. That's why it's better to be born lucky than rich. If you're rich, you may lose your money. But if you're lucky, you will always get more money."

"Oh! Will you? And is father not lucky?"

"Very unlucky, I should say," she said bitterly.

The boy watched her with unsure eyes.

"Why?" he asked.

"I don't know. Nobody ever knows why one person is lucky and another unlucky."

"Don't they? Nobody at all? Does nobody know?"

"Perhaps God. But He never tells."

"He ought to, then. And aren't you lucky either, mother?"

"I can't be, if I married an unlucky husband."

"But by yourself, aren't you?"

"I used to think I was, before I married. Now I think I am very unlucky indeed."

"Why?"

"Well — never mind! Perhaps I'm not really," she said.

The child looked at her, to see if she meant it. But he saw, by the lines of her mouth, that she was only trying to hide something from him.

"Well, anyhow," he said stoutly, "I'm a lucky person."

"Why?" said his mother, with a sudden laugh.

He stared at her. He didn't even know why he had said it.

"God told me," he asserted, brazening it out.

"I hope He did, dear!" she said, again with a laugh, but rather bitter.

"He did, mother!"

"Excellent!" said the mother, using one of her husband's exclamations.

The boy saw she did not believe him; or, rather, that she paid no attention to his assertion. This angered him somewhat, and made him want to compel her attention.

He went off by himself, vaguely, in a childish way, seeking for the clue to "luck." Absorbed, taking no heed of other people, he went about with a sort of stealth, seeking inwardly for luck. He wanted luck, he wanted it, he wanted it. When the two girls were playing dolls in the nursery, he would sit on his big rocking-horse, charging madly into space, with a frenzy that made the little girls peer at him uneasily. Wildly the horse careered, the waving dark hair of the boy tossed, his eyes had a strange glare in them. The little girls dared not speak to him.

When he had ridden to the end of his mad little journey, he climbed down and stood in front of his rocking-horse, staring fixedly into its lowered face. Its red mouth was slightly open, its big eye was wide and glassy-bright.

"Now!" he would silently command the snorting steed. "Now, take me to where there is luck! Now take me!"

And he would slash the horse on the neck with the little whip he had asked Uncle Oscar for. He knew the horse could take him to where there was luck, if only he forced it. So he would mount again, and start on his furious ride, hoping at last to get there. He knew he could get there.

"You'll break your horse, Paul!" said the nurse.

"He's always riding like that! I wish he'd leave off!" said his elder sister Joan.

But he only glared down on them in silence. Nurse gave him up. She could make nothing of him. Anyhow he was growing beyond her.

One day his mother and his Uncle Oscar came in when he was on one of his furious rides. He did not speak to them.

"Hallo, you young jockey! Riding a winner?" said his uncle.

"Aren't you growing too big for a rocking-horse? You're not a very little boy any longer, you know," said his mother.

But Paul only gave a blue glare from his big, rather close-set eyes. He would speak to nobody when he was in full tilt. His mother watched him with an anxious expression on her face.

At last he suddenly stopped forcing his horse into the mechanical gallop, and slid down.

"Well, I got there!" he announced fiercely, his blue eyes still flaring, and his sturdy long legs straddling apart.

"Where did you get to?"' asked his mother.

"Where I wanted to go," he flared back at her.

"That's right, son!" said Uncle Oscar. "Don't you stop till you get there. What's the horse's name?"

"He doesn't have a name," said the boy.

"Gets on without all right?" asked the uncle.

"Well, he has different names. He was called Sansovino last week."

"Sansovino, eh? Won the Ascot. How did you know his name?"

"He always talks about horse-races with Bassett," said Joan.

The uncle was delighted to find that his small nephew was posted with all the racing news. Bassett, the young gardener, who had been wounded in the left foot in the war and had got his present job through Oscar Cresswell, whose batman he had been, was a perfect blade of the "turf." He lived in the racing events, and the small boy lived with him.

Oscar Cresswell got it all from Bassett.

"Master Paul comes and asks me, so I can't do more than tell him, sir," said Bassett, his face terribly serious, as if he were speaking of religious matters.

"And does he ever put anything on a horse he fancies?"

"Well — I don't want to give him away — he's a young sport, a fine sport, sir. Would you mind asking him yourself? He sort of takes a pleasure in it, and perhaps he'd feel I was giving him away, sir, if you don't mind."

Bassett was serious as a church.

The uncle went back to his nephew, and took him off for a ride in the car.

"Say, Paul, old man, do you ever put anything on a horse?" the uncle asked.

The boy watched the handsome man closely.

"Why, do you think I oughtn't to?" he parried.

"Not a bit of it! I thought perhaps you might give me a tip for the Lincoln."

The car sped on into the country, going down to Uncle Oscar's place in Hampshire.

"Honour bright?" said the nephew.

"Honour bright, son!" said the uncle.

"Well, then, Daffodil."

"Daffodil! I doubt it, sonny. What about Mirza?"

"I only know the winner," said the boy. "That's Daffodil."

"Daffodil, eh?"

There was a pause. Daffodil was an obscure horse comparatively.

"Uncle!"

"Yes, son?"

"You won't let it go any further, will you? I promised Bassett."

"Bassett be damned, old man! What's he got to do with it?"

"We're partners. We've been partners from the first. Uncle, he lent me my first five shillings, which I lost. I promised him, honour bright, it was only between me and him; only you gave me that ten-shilling note I started winning with, so I thought you were lucky. You won't let it go any further, will you?"

The boy gazed at his uncle from those big, hot, blue eyes, set rather close together. The uncle stirred and laughed uneasily.

"Right you are, son! I'll keep your tip private. Daffodil, eh? How much are you putting on him?"

"All except twenty pounds," said the boy. "I keep that in reserve."

The uncle thought it a good joke.

"You keep twenty pounds in reserve, do you, you young romancer? What are you betting, then?"

"I'm betting three hundred," said the boy gravely. "But it's between you and me, Uncle Oscar! Honour bright?"

The uncle burst into a roar of laughter.

"It's between you and me all right, you young Nat Gould," he said, laughing. "But where's your three hundred?"

"Bassett keeps it for me. We're partners."

"You are, are you! And what is Bassett putting on Daffodil?"

"He won't go quite as high as I do, I expect. Perhaps he'll go a hundred and fifty."

"What, pennies?" laughed the uncle.

"Pounds," said the child, with a surprised look at his uncle. "Bassett keeps a bigger reserve than I do."

Between wonder and amusement Uncle Oscar was silent. He pursued the matter no further, but he determined to take his nephew with him to the Lincoln races.

"Now, son," he said, "I'm putting twenty on Mirza, and I'll put five for you on any horse you fancy. What's your pick?"

"Daffodil, uncle."

"No, not the fiver on Daffodil!"

"I should if it was my own fiver," said the child.

"Good! Good! Right you are! A fiver for me and a fiver for you on Daffodil."

The child had never been to a race-meeting before, and his eyes were blue fire. He pursed his mouth tight, and watched. A Frenchman just in front had put his money on Lancelot. Wild with excitement, he flayed his arms up and down, yelling "Lancelot! Lancelot!" in his French accent.

Daffodil came in first, Lancelot second, Mirza third. The child, flushed and with eyes blazing, was curiously serene. His uncle brought him four five-pound notes, four to one.

"What am I to do with these?" he cried, waving them before the boy's eyes.

"I suppose we'll talk to Bassett," said the boy. "I expect I have fifteen hundred now; and twenty in reserve; and this twenty."

His uncle studied him for some moments.

"Look here, son!" he said. "You're not serious about Bassett and that fifteen hundred, are you?"

"Yes, I am. But it's between you and me, uncle. Honour bright!"

"Honour bright all right, son! But I must talk to Bassett."

"If you'd like to be a partner, uncle, with Bassett and me, we could all be partners. Only, you'd have to promise, honour bright, uncle, not to let it go beyond us three. Bassett and I are lucky, and you must be lucky, because it was your ten shillings I started winning with. . . ."

Uncle Oscar took both Bassett and Paul into Richmond Park for an afternoon, and there they talked.

"It's like this, you see, sir," Bassett said. "Master Paul would get me talking about racing events, spinning yarns, you know, sir. And he was always keen on knowing if I'd made or if I'd lost. It's about a year since, now, that I put five shillings on Blush of Dawn for him — and we lost. Then the luck turned, with that ten shillings he had from you, that we put on Singhalese. And since that time, it's been pretty steady, all things considering. What do you say, Master Paul?"

"We're all right when we're sure," said Paul. "It's when we're not quite sure that we go down."

"Oh, but we're careful then," said Bassett.

"But when are you sure?" smiled Uncle Oscar.

"It's Master Paul, sir," said Bassett, in a secret, religious voice. "It's as if he had it from heaven. Like Daffodil, now, for the Lincoln. That was as sure as eggs."

"Did you put anything on Daffodil?" asked Oscar Cresswell.

"Yes, sir, I made my bet."

"And my nephew?"

Bassett was obstinately silent, looking at Paul.

"I made twelve hundred, didn't I, Bassett? I told uncle I was putting three hundred on Daffodil."

"That's right," said Bassett, nodding.

"But where's the money?" asked the uncle.

"I keep it locked up, sir. Master Paul he can have it any minute he likes to ask for it."

"What, fifteen hundred pounds?"

"And twenty! And forty, that is, with the twenty he made on the course."

"It's amazing!" said the uncle.

"If Master Paul offers you to be partners, sir, I would, if I were you; if you'll excuse me," said Bassett.

Oscar Cresswell thought about it.

"I'll see the money," he said.

Reading maketh a full man; conference a ready man; and writing an exact man.

FRANCIS BACON

They drove home again, and sure enough, Bassett came round to the garden-house with fifteen hundred pounds in notes. The twenty pounds reserve was left with Joe Glee, in the Turf Commission deposit.

"You see, it's all right, uncle, when I'm sure! Then we go strong, for all we're worth. Don't we, Bassett?"

"We do that, Master Paul."

"And when are you sure?" said the uncle, laughing.

"Oh, well, sometimes I'm absolutely sure, like about Daffodil," said the boy; "and sometimes I have an idea; and sometimes I haven't even an idea, have I, Bassett? Then we're careful, because we mostly go down."

"You do, do you! And when you're sure, like about Daffodil, what makes you sure, sonny?"

"Oh, well, I don't know," said the boy uneasily. "I'm sure, you know, uncle; that's all."

"It's as if he had it from heaven, sir," Bassett reiterated.

"I should say so," said the uncle.

But he became a partner. And when the Leger was coming on, Paul was "sure" about Lively Spark, which was a quite inconsiderable horse. The boy insisted on putting a thousand on the horse, Bassett went for five hundred, and Oscar Cresswell two hundred. Lively Spark came in first, and the betting had been ten to one against him. Paul had made ten thousand.

"You see," he said, "I was absolutely sure of him."

Even Oscar Cresswell had cleared two thousand.

"Look here, son," he said, "this sort of thing makes me nervous."

"It needn't, uncle! Perhaps I shan't be sure again for a long time."

"But what are you going to do with your money?" asked the uncle.

"Of course," said the boy, "I started it for mother. She said she had no luck, because father is unlucky, so I thought if I was lucky, it might stop whispering."

"What might stop whispering?"

"Our house. I hate our house for whispering."

"What does it whisper?"

"Why — why" — the boy fidgeted — "why, I don't know. But it's always short of money, you know, uncle."

"I know it, son, I know it."

"You know people send mother writs, don't you, uncle?"

"I'm afraid I do," said the uncle.

"And then the house whispers, like people laughing at you behind your back. It's awful, that is! I thought if I was lucky . . ."

"You might stop it," added the uncle.

The boy watched him with big blue eyes that had an uncanny cold fire in them, and he said never a word.

"Well, then!" said the uncle. "What are we doing?"

"I shouldn't like mother to know I was lucky," said the boy.

"Why not, son?"

"She'd stop me."

"I don't think she would."

"Oh!" — and the boy writhed in an odd way — "I don't want her to know, uncle."

"All right, son! We'll manage it without her knowing."

They managed it very easily. Paul, at the other's suggestion, handed over five thousand pounds to his uncle, who deposited it with the family lawyer, who was then to inform Paul's mother that a relative had put five thousand pounds into his hands, which sum was to be paid out a thousand pounds at a time, on the mother's birthday, for the next five years.

"So she'll have a birthday present of a thousand pounds for five successive years," said Uncle Oscar. "I hope it won't make it all the harder for her later."

Paul's mother had her birthday in November. The house had been "whispering" worse than ever lately, and, even in spite of his luck, Paul could not bear up against it. He was very anxious to see the effect of the birthday letter, telling his mother about the thousand pounds.

When there were no visitors, Paul now took his meals with his parents, as he was beyond the nursery control. His mother went into town nearly every day. She had discovered that she had an odd knack of sketching furs and dress materials, so she worked secretly in the studio of a friend who was the chief "artist" for the leading drapers. She drew the figures of ladies in furs and ladies in silk and sequins for the newspaper advertisements. This young woman artist earned several thousand pounds a year, but Paul's mother only made several hundreds, and she was again dissatisfied. She so wanted to be first in something, and she did not succeed, even in making sketches for drapery advertisements.

She was down to breakfast on the morning of her birthday. Paul watched her face as she read her letters. He knew the lawyer's letter. As his mother read it, her face hardened and became more expressionless. Then a cold, determined look came on her mouth. She hid the letter under the pile of others, and said not a word about it.

"Didn't you have anything nice in the post for your birthday, mother?" said Paul.

"Quite moderately nice," she said, her voice cold and absent.

She went away to town without saying more.

But in the afternoon Uncle Oscar appeared. He said Paul's mother had had a long interview with the lawyer, asking if the whole five thousand could be advanced at once, as she was in debt.

"What do you think, uncle?" said the boy.

"I leave it to you, son."

"Oh, let her have it, then! We can get some more with the other," said the boy.

"A bird in the hand is worth two in the bush, laddie!" said Uncle Oscar.

"But I'm sure to know for the Grand National; or the Lincolnshire; or else the Derby. I'm sure to know for one of them," said Paul.

So Uncle Oscar signed the agreement, and Paul's mother touched the whole five thousand. Then something very curious happened. The voices in the house suddenly went mad, like a chorus of frogs on a spring evening. There were certain new furnishings, and Paul had a tutor. He was really going to Eton, his father's school, in the following autumn. There were flowers in the winter, and a blossoming of the luxury Paul's mother had been used to. And yet the voices in the house, behind the sprays of mimosa and almond blossom, and from under the piles of iridescent cushions, simply trilled and screamed in a sort of ecstasy: "There must be more money! Oh-h-h, there must be more money. Oh, now, now-w! Now-w-w — there must be more money! — more than ever! More than ever!"

It frightened Paul terribly. He studied away at his Latin and Greek with his tutors. But his intense hours were spent with Bassett. The Grand National had gone by: he had not "known," and had lost a hundred pounds. Summer was at hand. He was in agony for the Lincoln. But even for the Lincoln he didn't "know," and he lost fifty pounds. He became wild-eyed and strange, as if something were going to explode in him.

"Let it alone, son! Don't you bother about it!" urged Uncle Oscar. But it was as if the boy couldn't really hear what his uncle was saying.

"I've got to know for the Derby! I've got to know for the Derby!" the child reiterated, his big blue eyes blazing with a sort of madness.

His mother noticed how overwrought he was.

"You'd better go to the seaside. Wouldn't you like to go now to the seaside, instead of waiting? I think you'd better," she said, looking down at him anxiously, her heart curiously heavy because of him.

But the child lifted his uncanny blue eyes.

"I couldn't possibly go before the Derby, mother!" he said. "I couldn't possibly!"

"Why not?" she said, her voice becoming heavy when she was opposed. "Why not? You can still go from the seaside to see the Derby with your Uncle Oscar, if that's what you wish. No need for you to wait here. Besides, I think you care too much about these races. It's a bad sign. My family has been a gambling family, and you won't know till you grow up how much damage it has done. But it has done damage. I shall have to send Bassett away, and ask Uncle Oscar not to talk racing to you, unless you promise to be reasonable about it; go away to the seaside and forget it. You're all nerves!"

"I'll do what you like, mother, so long as you don't send me away till after the Derby," the boy said.

"Send you away from where? Just from this house?"

"Yes," he said, gazing at her.

"Why, you curious child, what makes you care about this house so much, suddenly? I never knew you loved it."

He gazed at her without speaking. He had a secret within a secret, something he had not divulged, even to Bassett or to his Uncle Oscar.

But his mother, after standing undecided and a little bit sullen for some moments, said:

"Very well, then! Don't go to the seaside till after the Derby, if you don't wish it. But promise me you won't let your nerves go to pieces. Promise you won't think so much about horseracing and events, as you call them!"

"Oh, no," said the boy casually. "I won't think much about them, mother. You needn't worry. I wouldn't worry, mother, if I were you."

"If you were me and I were you," said his mother, "I wonder what we should do!"

"But you know you needn't worry, mother, don't you?" the boy repeated.

"I should be awfully glad to know it," she said wearily.

"Oh, well, you can, you know. I mean, you ought to know you needn't worry," he insisted.

"Ought I? Then I'll see about it," she said.

Paul's secret of secrets was his wooden horse, that which had no name. Since he was emancipated from a nurse and a nursery-governess, he had had his rocking-horse removed to his own bedroom at the top of the house.

"Surely, you're too big for a rocking-horse!" his mother had remonstrated.

"Well, you see, mother, till I can have a real horse, I like to have some sort of animal about," had been his quaint answer.

"Do you feel he keeps you company?" she laughed.

"Oh, yes! He's very good, he always keeps me company, when I'm there," said Paul.

So the horse, rather shabby, stood in an arrested prance in the boy's bedroom.

The Derby was drawing near, and the boy grew more and more tense. He hardly heard what was spoken to him, he was very frail, and his eyes were really uncanny. His mother had sudden seizures of uneasiness about him. Sometimes, for half-an-hour, she would feel a sudden anxiety about him that was almost anguish. She wanted to rush to him at once, and know he was safe.

Two nights before the Derby, she was at a big party in town, when one of her rushes of anxiety about her boy, her firstborn, gripped her heart till she could hardly speak. She fought with the feeling, might and main, for she believed in common sense. But it was too strong. She had to leave the dance and go downstairs to telephone to the country. The children's nursery-governess was terribly surprised and startled at being rung up in the night.

"Are the children all right, Miss Wilmot?"

"Oh, yes, they are quite all right."

"Master Paul? Is he all right?"

"He went to bed as right as a trivet. Shall I run up and look at him?"

"No," said Paul's mother reluctantly. "No! Don't trouble. It's all right. Don't sit up. We shall be home fairly soon." She did not want her son's privacy intruded upon.

"Very good," said the governess.

It was about one o'clock when Paul's mother and father drove up to their house. All was still. Paul's mother went to her room and slipped off her white fur coat. She had told her maid not to wait up for her. She heard her husband downstairs, mixing a whisky-and-soda.

And then, because of the strange anxiety at her heart, she stole upstairs to her son's room. Noiselessly she went along the upper corridor. Was there a faint noise? What was it?

She stood, with arrested muscles, outside his door, listening. There was a strange, heavy, and yet not loud noise. Her heart stood still. It was a soundless noise, yet rushing and powerful. Something huge, in violent, hushed motion. What was it? What in God's name was it? She ought to know. She felt that she knew the noise. She knew what it was.

Yet she could not place it. She couldn't say what it was. And on and on it went, like a madness.

Softly, frozen with anxiety and fear, she turned the doorhandle.

The room was dark. Yet in the space near the window, she heard and saw something plunging to and fro. She gazed in fear and amazement.

Then suddenly she switched on the light, and saw her son, in his green pajamas, madly surging on the rocking-horse. The blaze of light suddenly lit him up, as he urged the wooden horse, and lit her up, as she stood, blonde, in her dress of pale green and crystal, in the doorway.

"Paul!" she cried. "Whatever are you doing?"

"It's Malabar!" he screamed, in a powerful, strange voice. "It's Malabar."

His eyes blazed at hers for one strange and senseless second, as he ceased urging his wooden horse. Then he fell with a crash to the ground, and she, all her tormented motherhood flooding upon her, rushed to gather him up.

But he was unconscious, and unconscious he remained, with some brain-fever. He talked and tossed, and his mother sat stonily by his side.

"Malabar! It's Malabar! Bassett, Bassett, I know! It's Malabar!"

So the child cried, trying to get up and urge the rocking-horse that gave him his inspiration.

"What does he mean by Malabar?" asked the heart-frozen mother.

"I don't know," said the father stonily.

"What does he mean by Malabar?" she asked her brother Oscar.

"It's one of the horses running for the Derby," was the answer.

And, in spite of himself, Oscar Cresswell spoke to Bassett, and himself put a thousand on Malabar: at fourteen to one.

The third day of the illness was critical: they were waiting for a change. The boy, with his rather long, curly hair, was tossing ceaselessly on the pillow. He neither slept nor regained consciousness, and his eyes were like blue stones. His mother sat, feeling her heart had gone, turned actually into a stone.

In the evening, Oscar Cresswell did not come, but Bassett sent a message, saying could he come up for one moment, just one moment? Paul's mother was very angry at the intrusion, but on second thought she agreed. The boy was the same. Perhaps Bassett might bring him to consciousness.

The gardener, a shortish fellow with a little brown moustache, and sharp little brown eyes, tiptoed into the room, touched his imaginary cap to Paul's mother, and stole to the bedside, staring with glittering, smallish eyes, at the tossing, dying child.

"Master Paul!" he whispered. "Master Paul! Malabar come in first all right, a clean win. I did as you told me. You've made over seventy thousand pounds, you have; you've got over eighty thousand. Malabar came in all right, Mister Paul."

"Malabar! Malabar! Did I say Malabar, mother? Did I say Malabar? Do you think I'm lucky, mother? I knew Malabar, didn't I? Over eighty thousand pounds! I call that lucky, don't you, mother? Over eighty thousand pounds! I knew, didn't I know I knew? Malabar came in all right. If I ride my horse till I'm sure, then I tell you, Bassett, you can go as high as you like. Did you go for all you were worth, Bassett?"

"I went a thousand on it, Master Paul."

"I never told you, mother, that if I can ride my horse, and get there, then I'm absolutely sure — oh, absolutely! Mother, did I ever tell you? I am lucky."

"No, you never did," said the mother.

But the boy died in the night.

And even as he lay dead, his mother heard her brother's voice saying to her: "My God, Hester, you're eighty-odd thousand to the good and a poor devil of a son to the bad. But, poor devil, poor devil, he's best gone out of a life where he rides his rocking-horse to find a winner."

FOR DISCUSSION

1. In this superb story, riding a rocking horse to find a winner is a symbol. But the symbol is continued so long and developed so richly with meaning that the symbol becomes a fantasy. Its unreality takes on an air of reality. It is treated seriously by two adults. It is deadly serious to the boy himself, being as real and substantial as a bullet, a poison, or a disease.

Laying aside for the present the question of what the riding could symbolize, let us see first its genesis. The boy makes his first ride in order to help whom? How does he learn that help is necessary?

Is it true that children sense their parents' love or lack of love, even penetrating through parental pretenses? Is it true that children sense anxieties in a family as infallibly as they see a Christmas toy? Is it true that children sometimes try to protect their parents, or try to make up in their own lives for deficiencies that the parents felt in theirs?

What other assumptions like these does Lawrence imply in the first three pages? What chain of assumptions leads him to the important conclusion that a woman who can love nobody — neither man nor child — may turn her energies to financial or social success but will still remain empty-hearted?

2. Note the first three paragraphs. Do they carry the tone of particularity which you usually find in fiction, or the tone of generality usually found in science — for instance, in a social welfare case report or a psychological case record?

3. Do you feel that the children would prefer less expensive toys, provided the whispering would stop? Why do the parents spend so much if it increases family anxiety?

4. The language loses some of its tone of abstract generality in the conversation between mother and son, yet some abstraction persists. Point out specific instances.

5. The son sets out to find the luck — the money — which the mother thinks would make her happy. At the time you read of his first riding, did it seem to have any extraordinary and symbolic significance?

Can you recall how you responded to the series of riding and betting episodes? Did they seem fun at any time? Were they frightening at any time?

6. After great exertion and anxiety the son wins a substantial sum of money which he hopes will make his mother happy and stop the whispering. Does it have the desired effect?

Do you think that Eton and Latin are what the boy needs? Or are these like the expensive Christmas toys spoiled by the whispering?

What does the mother now think is needed to make her happy? What does the son think? the uncle? At this point did you think she was capable of being happy? (You may want to check the first part of the story again.)

7. When the child is dead from his feverish and fruitless exertions, the uncle points out that the mother now has what she thought she wanted, and has lost nothing that she prized. Does the author make this point to convince the mother, or to convince the reader?

8. Certainly the author does not expect any reader to believe really that a boy can pick race winners so infallibly in this way. The riding is only a symbol. What kinds of real activity serving approximately the same fruitless purpose could have been used instead in a story that employed realism rather than symbolism and fantasy?

9. If you have read Caldwell's "The Windfall," do you find any similarity between the theme of that realistic story and this symbolic one? Which story do you prefer?

❧ *Symbolism* ❧

The Chrysanthemums

JOHN STEINBECK

The high grey-flannel fog of winter closed off the Salinas Valley from the sky and from all the rest of the world. On every side it sat like a lid on the mountains and made of the great valley a closed pot. On the broad, level land floor the gang plows bit deep and left the black earth shining like metal where the shares had cut. On the foothill ranches across the Salinas River, the yellow stubble fields seemed to be bathed in pale cold sunshine, but there was no sunshine in the valley now in December. The thick willow scrub along the river flamed with sharp and positive yellow leaves.

It was a time of quiet and of waiting. The air was cold and tender. A light wind blew up from the southwest so that the farmers were mildly hopeful of a good rain before long; but fog and rain did not go together.

Across the river, on Henry Allen's foothill ranch there was little work to be done, for the hay was cut and stored and the orchards were plowed up to receive the rain deeply when it should come. The cattle on the higher slopes were becoming shaggy and rough-coated.

Elisa Allen, working in her flower garden, looked down across the yard and saw Henry, her husband, talking to two men in business suits. The three of them stood by the tractor shed, each man with one foot on the side of the little Fordson. They smoked cigarettes and studied the machine as they talked.

Elisa watched them for a moment and then went back to her work. She was thirty-five. Her face was lean and strong and her eyes were as clear as water. Her figure looked blocked and heavy in her gardening costume, a man's black hat pulled low down over her eyes, clod-hopper shoes, a figured print dress almost completely covered by a big corduroy apron with four big pockets to hold the snips, the trowel and scratcher, the seeds and the knife she worked with. She wore heavy leather gloves to protect her hands while she worked.

She was cutting down the old year's chrysanthemum stalks with a pair of short and powerful scissors. She looked down toward the men by the tractor shed now and then. Her face was eager and mature and handsome; even her work with the scissors was over-eager, over-powerful. The chrysanthemum stems seemed too small and easy for her energy.

She brushed a cloud of hair out of her eyes with the back of her glove, and left a smudge of earth on her cheek in doing it. Behind her stood the neat white farm house with red geraniums close-banked around it as high as the windows. It was a hard-swept looking little house, with hard-polished windows, and a clean mud-mat on the front steps.

Elisa cast another glance toward the tractor shed. The strangers were getting into their Ford coupe. She took off a glove and put her strong fingers down into the forest of new green chrysanthemum sprouts that were growing around the old roots. She spread the leaves and looked down among the close-growing stems. No aphids were there, no sowbugs or snails or cutworms. Her terrier fingers destroyed such pests before they could get started.

Elisa started at the sound of her husband's voice. He had come near quietly, and he leaned over the wire fence that protected her flower garden from cattle and dogs and chickens.

"At it again," he said. "You've got a strong new crop coming."

Elisa straightened her back and pulled on the gardening glove again. "Yes. They'll be strong this coming year." In her tone and on her face there was a little smugness.

"You've got a gift with things," Henry observed. "Some of those yellow chrysanthemums you had this year were ten inches across. I wish you'd work out in the orchard and raise some apples that big."

Her eyes sharpened. "Maybe I could do it, too. I've a gift with things, all right. My mother had it. She could stick anything in the ground and make it grow. She said it was having planters' hands that knew how to do it."

"Well, it sure works with flowers," he said.

"Henry, who were those men you were talking to?"

"Why, sure, that's what I came to tell you. They were from the Western Meat Company. I sold those thirty head of three-year-old steers. Got nearly my own price, too."

"Good," she said. "Good for you."

"And I thought," he continued, "I thought how it's Saturday afternoon, and we might go into Salinas for dinner at a restaurant, and then to a picture show — to celebrate, you see."

"Good," she repeated. "Oh, yes. That will be good."

Composition is, for the most part, an effort of slow diligence and steady perseverance, to which the mind is dragged by necessity or resolution.

SAMUEL JOHNSON

Henry put on his joking tone. "There's fights tonight. How'd you like to go to the fights?"

"Oh, no," she said breathlessly. "No, I wouldn't like fights."

"Just fooling, Elisa. We'll go to a movie. Let's see. It's two now. I'm going to take Scotty and bring down those steers from the hill. It'll take us maybe two hours. We'll go in town about five and have dinner at the Cominos Hotel. Like that?"

"Of course I'll like it. It's good to eat away from home."

"All right, then. I'll go get up a couple of horses."

She said, "I'll have plenty of time to transplant some of these sets, I guess."

She heard her husband calling Scotty down by the barn. And a little later she saw the two men ride up the pale yellow hillside in search of the steers.

There was a little square sandy bed kept for rooting the chrysanthemums.

With her trowel she turned the soil over and over, and smoothed it and patted it firm. Then she dug ten parallel trenches to receive the sets. Back at the chrysanthemum bed she pulled out the little crisp shoots, trimmed off the leaves of each one with her scissors and laid it on a small orderly pile.

A squeak of wheels and plod of hoofs came from the road. Elisa looked up. The country road ran along the dense bank of willows and cottonwoods that bordered the river, and up this road came a curious vehicle, curiously drawn. It was an old spring-wagon, with a round canvas top on it like the cover of a prairie schooner. It was driven by an old bay horse and a little grey-and-white burro. A big stubble-bearded man sat between the cover flaps and drove the crawling team. Underneath the wagon, between the hind wheels, a lean and rangy mongrel dog walked sedately. Words were painted on the canvas, in clumsy, crooked letters. "Pots, pans, knives, sisors, lawn mores, Fixed." Two rows of articles, and the triumphantly definitive "Fixed" below. The black paint had run down in little sharp points beneath each letter.

Elisa, squatting on the ground, watched to see the crazy, loose-jointed wagon pass by. But it didn't pass. It turned into the farm road in front of her house, crooked old wheels skirling and squeaking. The rangy dog darted from between the wheels and ran ahead. Instantly the two ranch shepherds flew out at him. Then all three stopped, and with stiff and quivering tails, with taut straight legs, with ambassadorial dignity, they slowly circled, sniffing daintily. The caravan pulled up to Elisa's wire fence and stopped. Now the newcomer dog, feeling outnumbered, lowered his tail and retired under the wagon with raised hackles and bared teeth.

The man on the wagon seat called out, "That's a bad dog in a fight when he gets started."

Elisa laughed. "I see he is. How soon does he generally get started?"

The man caught up her laughter and echoed it heartily. "Sometimes not for weeks and weeks," he said. He climbed stiffly down, over the wheel. The horse and the donkey drooped like unwatered flowers.

Elisa saw that he was a very big man. Although his hair and beard were greying, he did not look old. His worn black suit was wrinkled and spotted with grease. The laughter had disappeared from his face and eyes the moment his laughing voice ceased. His eyes were dark, and they were full of the brooding that gets in the eyes of teamsters and of sailors. The calloused hands he rested on the wire fence were cracked, and every crack was a black line. He took off his battered hat.

"I'm off my general road, ma'am," he said. "Does this dirt road cut over across the river to the Los Angeles highway?"

Elisa stood up and shoved the thick scissors in her apron pocket. "Well, yes, it does, but it winds around and then fords the river. I don't think your team could pull through the sand."

He replied with some asperity, "It might surprise you what them beasts can pull through."

"When they get started?" she asked.

He smiled for a second. "Yes. When they get started."

"Well," said Elisa, "I think you'll have time if you go back to the Salinas road and pick up the highway there."

He drew a big finger down the chicken wire and made it sing. "I ain't in any hurry, ma'am. I go from Seattle to San Diego and back every year. Takes all my time. About six months each way. I aim to follow nice weather."

Elisa took off her gloves and stuffed them in the apron pocket with the scissors. She touched the under edge of her man's hat, searching for fugitive hairs. "That sounds like a nice kind of a way to live," she said.

He leaned confidentially over the fence. "Maybe you noticed the writing on my wagon. I mend pots and sharpen knives and scissors. You got any of them things to do?"

"Oh, no," she said quickly. "Nothing like that." Her eyes hardened with resistance.

"Scissors is the worst thing," he explained. "Most people just ruin scissors trying to sharpen 'em, but I know how. I got a special tool. It's a little bobbit kind of thing, and patented. But it sure does the trick."

"No. My scissors are all sharp."

"All right, then. Take a pot," he continued earnestly, "a bent pot, or a pot with a hole. I can make it like new so you don't have to buy no new ones. That's a saving for you."

"No," she said shortly. "I tell you I have nothing like that for you to do."

His face fell to an exaggerated sadness. His voice took on a whining undertone. "I ain't had a thing to do today. Maybe I won't have no supper tonight. You see I'm off my regular road. I know folks on the highway clear from Seattle to San Diego. They save their things for me to sharpen up because they know I do it so good and save them money."

"I'm sorry," Elisa said irritably. "I haven't anything for you to do."

His eyes left her face and fell to searching the ground. They roamed about until they came to the chrysanthemum bed where she had been working. "What's them plants, ma'am?"

The irritation and resistance melted from Elisa's face. "Oh, those are chrysanthemums, giant whites and yellows. I raise them every year, bigger than anybody around here."

"Kind of a long-stemmed flower? Looks like a quick puff of colored smoke?" he asked.

"That's it. What a nice way to describe them."

"They smell kind of nasty till you get used to them," he said.

"It's a good bitter smell," she retorted, "not nasty at all."

He changed his tone quickly. "I like the smell myself."

"I had ten-inch blooms this year," she said.

The man leaned farther over the fence. "Look. I know a lady down the road a piece, has got the nicest garden you ever seen. Got nearly every kind of flower but no chrysanthemums. Last time I was mending a copper-bottom washtub for her (that's a hard job but I do it good), she said to me, 'If you ever run acrost some nice chrysanthemums I wish you'd try to get me a few seeds.' That's what she told me."

Elisa's eyes grew alert and eager. "She couldn't have known much about chrysanthemums. You can raise them from seed, but it's much easier to root the little sprouts you see there."

"Oh," he said. "I s'pose I can't take none to her, then."

"Why yes you can," Elisa cried. "I can put some in damp sand, and you can carry them right along with you. They'll take root in the pot if you keep them damp. And then she can transplant them."

"She'd sure like to have some, ma'am. You say they're nice ones?"

"Beautiful," she said. "Oh, beautiful." Her eyes shone. She tore off the battered hat and shook out her dark pretty hair. "I'll put them in a flower pot, and you can take them right with you. Come into the yard."

While the man came through the picket fence Elisa ran excitedly along the geranium-bordered path to the back of the house. And she returned carrying a big red flower pot. The gloves were forgotten now. She kneeled on the ground by the starting bed and dug up the sandy soil with her fingers and scooped it into the bright new flower pot. Then she picked up the little pile of shoots she had prepared. With her strong fingers she pressed them into the sand and tamped around them with her knuckles. The man stood over her. "I'll tell you what to do," she said. "You remember so you can tell the lady."

"Yes, I'll try to remember."

"Well, look. These will take root in about a month. Then she must set them out, about a foot apart in good rich earth like this, see?" She lifted a handful of dark soil for him to look at. "They'll grow fast and tall. Now remember this. In July tell her to cut them down, about eight inches from the ground."

"Before they bloom?" he asked.

"Yes, before they bloom." Her face was tight with eagerness. "They'll grow right up again. About the last of September the buds will start."

She stopped and seemed perplexed. "It's the budding that takes the most care," she said hesitantly. "I don't know how to tell you." She looked deep into his eyes, searchingly. Her mouth opened a little, and she seemed to be listening. "I'll try to tell you," she said. "Did you ever hear of planting hands?"

"Can't say I have, ma'am."

"Well, I can only tell you what it feels like. It's when you're picking off the buds you don't want. Everything goes right down into your finger-tips.

You watch your fingers work. They do it themselves. You can feel how it is. They pick and pick the buds. They never make a mistake. They're with the plant. Do you see? Your fingers and the plant. You can feel that, right up your arm. They know. They never make a mistake. You can feel it. When you're like that you can't do anything wrong. Do you see that? Can you understand that?"

She was kneeling on the ground looking up at him. Her breast swelled passionately.

The man's eyes narrowed. He looked away self-consciously. "Maybe I know," he said. "Sometimes in the night in the wagon there ——"

Elisa's voice grew husky. She broke in on him. "I've never lived as you do, but I know what you mean. When the night is dark — why, the stars are sharp-pointed, and there's quiet. Why, you rise up and up! Every pointed star gets driven into your body. It's like that. Hot and sharp and — lovely."

Kneeling there, her hand went out toward his legs in the greasy black trousers. Her hesitant fingers almost touched the cloth. Then her hand dropped to the ground. She crouched low like a fawning dog.

He said, "It's nice, just like you say. Only when you don't have no dinner, it ain't."

She stood up then, very straight, and her face was ashamed. She held the flower pot out to him and placed it gently in his arms. "Here. Put it in your wagon, on the seat, where you can watch it. Maybe I can find something for you to do."

At the back of the house she dug in the can pile and found two old and battered aluminum saucepans. She carried them back and gave them to him. "Here, maybe you can fix these."

His manner changed. He became professional. "Good as new I can fix them." At the back of his wagon he set a little anvil, and out of an oily tool box dug a small machine hammer. Elisa came through the gate to watch him while he pounded out the dents in the kettles. His mouth grew sure and knowing. At a difficult part of the work he sucked his under-lip.

"You sleep right in the wagon?" Elisa asked.

"Right in the wagon, ma'am. Rain or shine I'm dry as a cow in there."

"It must be nice," she said. "It must be very nice. I wish women could do such things."

"It ain't the right kind of a life for a woman."

Her upper lip raised a little, showing her teeth. "How do you know? How can you tell?" she said.

"I don't know, ma'am," he protested. "Of course I don't know. Now here's your kettles, done. You don't have to buy no new ones."

"How much?"

"Oh, fifty cents'll do. I keep my prices down and my work good. That's why I have all them satisfied customers up and down the highway."

Elisa brought him a fifty-cent piece from the house and dropped it in his hand. "You might be surprised to have a rival some time. I can sharpen scissors, too. And I can beat the dents out of little pots. I could show you what a woman might do."

He put his hammer back in the oily box and shoved the little anvil out of sight. "It would be a lonely life for a woman, ma'am, and a scarey life, too, with animals creeping under the wagon all night." He climbed over the singletree, steadying himself with a hand on the burro's white rump. He settled himself in the seat, picked up the lines. "Thank you kindly, ma'am," he said. "I'll do like you told me; I'll go back and catch the Salinas road."

"Mind," she called, "if you're long in getting there, keep the sand damp."

"Sand, ma'am? . . . Sand? Oh, sure. You mean around the chrysanthemums. Sure I will." He clucked his tongue. The beasts leaned luxuriously into their collars. The mongrel dog took his place between the back wheels. The wagon turned and crawled out the entrance road and back the way it had come, along the river.

Elisa stood in front of her wire fence watching the slow progress of the caravan. Her shoulders were straight, her head thrown back, her eyes half-closed, so that the scene came vaguely into them. Her lips moved silently, forming the words "Good-bye — good-bye." Then she whispered, "That's a bright direction. There's a glowing there." The sound of her whisper startled her. She shook herself free and looked about to see whether anyone had been listening. Only the dogs had heard. They lifted their heads toward her from their sleeping in the dust, and then stretched out their chins and settled asleep again. Elisa turned and ran hurriedly into the house.

In the kitchen she reached behind the stove and felt the water tank. It was full of hot water from the noonday cooking. In the bathroom she tore off her soiled clothes and flung them into the corner. And then she scrubbed herself with a little block of pumice, legs and thighs, loins and chest and arms, until her skin was scratched and red. When she had dried herself she stood in front of a mirror in her bedroom and looked at her body. She tightened her stomach and threw out her chest. She turned and looked over her shoulder at her back.

After a while she began to dress, slowly. She put on her newest under-clothing and her nicest stockings and the dress which was the symbol of her prettiness. She worked carefully on her hair, pencilled her eyebrows and rouged her lips.

Before she was finished she heard the little thunder of hoofs and the shouts of Henry and his helper as they drove the red steers into the corral. She heard the gate bang shut and set herself for Henry's arrival.

His step sounded on the porch. He entered the house calling, "Elisa, where are you?"

"In my room, dressing. I'm not ready. There's hot water for your bath. Hurry up. It's getting late."

When she heard him splashing in the tub, Elisa laid his dark suit on the bed, and shirt and socks and tie beside it. She stood his polished shoes on the floor beside the bed. Then she went to the porch and sat primly and stiffly down. She looked toward the river road where the willow-line was still yellow with frosted leaves so that under the high grey fog they seemed a thin band of sunshine. This was the only color in the grey afternoon. She sat unmoving for a long time. Her eyes blinked rarely.

Henry came banging out of the door, shoving his tie inside his vest as he came. Elisa stiffened and her face grew tight. Henry stopped short and looked at her. "Why — why, Elisa. You look so nice!"

"Nice? You think I look nice? What do you mean by 'nice'?"

Henry blundered on. "I don't know. I mean you look different, strong and happy."

"I am strong? Yes, strong. What do you mean 'strong'?"

He looked bewildered. "You're playing some kind of a game," he said helplessly. "It's a kind of a play. You look strong enough to break a calf over your knee, happy enough to eat it like a watermelon."

For a second she lost her rigidity. "Henry! Don't talk like that. You didn't know what you said." She grew complete again. "I'm strong," she boasted. "I never knew before how strong."

Literature and fiction are two entirely different things. Literature is a luxury; fiction is a necessity.

G. K. CHESTERTON

Henry looked down toward the tractor shed, and when he brought his eyes back to her, they were his own again. "I'll get out the car. You can put on your coat while I'm starting."

Elisa went into the house. She heard him drive to the gate and idle down his motor, and then she took a long time to put on her hat. She pulled it here and pressed it there. When Henry turned the motor off she slipped into her coat and went out.

The little roadster bounced along on the dirt road by the river, raising the birds and driving the rabbits into the brush. Two cranes flapped heavily over the willow-line and dropped into the river-bed.

Far ahead on the road Elisa saw a dark speck. She knew.

She tried not to look as they passed it, but her eyes would not obey. She whispered to herself sadly, "He might have thrown them off the road. That wouldn't have been much trouble, not very much. But he kept the pot," she explained. "He had to keep the pot. That's why he couldn't get them off the road."

The roadster turned a bend and she saw the caravan ahead. She swung full around toward her husband so she could not see the little covered wagon and the mismatched team as the car passed them.

In a moment it was over. The thing was done. She did not look back. She said loudly, to be heard above the motor, "It will be good, tonight, a good dinner."

"Now you're changed again," Henry complained. He took one hand from the wheel and patted her knee. "I ought to take you in to dinner oftener. It would be good for both of us. We get so heavy out on the ranch."

"Henry," she asked, "could we have wine at dinner?"

"Sure we could. Say! That will be fine."

She was silent for a while; then she said, "Henry, at those prize fights, do the men hurt each other very much?"

"Sometimes a little, not often. Why?"

"Well, I've read how they break noses, and blood runs down their chests. I've read how the fighting gloves get heavy and soggy with blood."

He looked around at her. "What's the matter, Elisa? I didn't know you read things like that." He brought the car to a stop, then turned to the right over the Salinas River bridge.

"Do any women ever go to the fights?" she asked.

"Oh, sure, some. What's the matter, Elisa? Do you want to go? I don't think you'd like it, but I'll take you if you really want to go."

She relaxed limply in the seat. "Oh, no. No. I don't want to go. I'm sure I don't." Her face was turned away from him. "It will be enough if we can have wine. It will be plenty." She turned up her coat collar so he could not see that she was crying weakly — like an old woman.

FOR DISCUSSION

1. In this story there is a rising, succeeding movement; then a sudden collapse. The collapse comes when the wife sees her chrysanthemums dumped out onto the road. She realizes then that the tinker was not what she had supposed, but was acting up to her so that he could get half a dollar's business out of her. The cause of her collapse is clear and definite, but the cause of the preceding elation is more elusive. Was she elated because (1) she felt she had found someone as interested in flowers as she; (2) she felt she had found someone who experienced life as deeply and keenly as she ("Every pointed star gets driven into your body. . . . Hot and sharp and — lovely."); (3) she fancied she too might find a sense of release traveling? Is her elation caused by all these things, or none of them?

2. At the time you were reading the scene between Elisa and the tinker, did you feel that she was being deceived while you were not? ("He changed his tone quickly. 'I like the smell myself.'" He did not change his tone out of conviction, but out of policy.)

3. Before the tinker comes she says she would not be interested in seeing the fights. Then after her collapse she manifests interest in them, and then a moment later says she is not interested. Thus we have a double reversal of attitude, but what that change signifies is not specified. While she is manifesting interest in the fights she speaks of them as bloody and painful. Do you conclude that momentarily she wants to experience the blood and pain? Do you suppose she would imagine herself giving the blows, or receiving the blows, or neither, or both? Is the husband's remark about her breaking and eating a calf relevant? A second clue to what the fight means to her is that she says having wine will be almost as good as the fights; the fight would be like wine only more so. However, as she settles for wine she cries, weakly and oddly, whereas at her peak of elation she was described as strong.

4. Is any clue given as to what is so desperately lacking in her life?

5. Can the story be satisfactory even if we don't know what everything stands for?

A Hunger Artist

FRANZ KAFKA

During these last decades the interest in professional fasting has markedly diminished. It used to pay very well to stage such great performances under one's own management, but today that is quite impossible. We live in a different world now. At one time the whole town took a lively interest in the hunger artist; from day to day of his fast the excitement mounted; everybody wanted to see him at least once a day; there were people who bought season tickets for the last few days and sat from morning till night

Reprinted from *The Penal Colony*, by Franz Kafka, by permission of Schocken Books Inc., New York; copyright 1948 by Schocken Books Inc.; translated by Willa and Edwin Muir.

in front of his small barred cage; even in the nighttime there were visiting hours, when the whole effect was heightened by torch flares; on fine days the cage was set out in the open air, and then it was the children's special treat to see the hunger artist; for their elders he was often just a joke that happened to be in fashion, but the children stood open-mouthed, holding each other's hands for greater security, marveling at him as he sat there pallid in black tights, with his ribs sticking out so prominently, not even on a seat but down among straw on the ground, sometimes giving a courteous nod, answering questions with a constrained smile, or perhaps stretching an arm through the bars so that one might feel how thin it was, and then again withdrawing deep into himself, paying no attention to anyone or anything, not even to the all-important striking of the clock that was the only piece of furniture in his cage, but merely staring into vacancy with half-shut eyes, now and then taking a sip from a tiny glass of water to moisten his lips.

Besides casual onlookers there were also relays of permanent watchers selected by the public, usually butchers, strangely enough, and it was their task to watch the hunger artist day and night, three of them at a time, in case he should have some secret recourse to nourishment. This was nothing but a formality, instituted to reassure the masses for the initiates knew well enough that during his fast the artist would never in any circumstances, not even under forcible compulsion, swallow the smallest morsel of food; the honor of his profession forbade it. Not every watcher, of course, was capable of understanding this, there were often groups of night watchers who were very lax in carrying out their duties and deliberately huddled together in a retired corner to play cards with great absorption, obviously intending to give the hunger artist the chance of a little refreshment, which they supposed he could draw from some private hoard. Nothing annoyed the artist more than such watchers; they made him miserable; they made his fast seem unendurable; sometimes he mastered his feebleness sufficiently to sing during their watch for as long as he could keep going, to show them how unjust their suspicions were. But that was of little use; they only wondered at his cleverness in being able to fill his mouth even while singing. Much more to his taste were the watchers who sat close up to the bars, who were not content with the dim night lighting of the hall but focused him in the full glare of the electric pocket torch given them by the impresario. The harsh light did not trouble him at all, in any case he could never sleep properly, and he could always drowse a little, whatever the light, at any hour, even when the hall was thronged with noisy onlookers. He was quite happy at the prospect of spending a sleepless night with such watchers; he was ready to exchange jokes with them, to tell them stories out of his nomadic life, anything at all to keep them awake and demonstrate to them again that he had no eatables in his cage and that he was fasting as not one of them could fast. But his happiest moment was when the morning came and an enormous breakfast was brought them, at his expense, on which they flung themselves with the keen appetite of healthy men after a weary night of wakefulness. Of course there were people who argued that this breakfast was an unfair attempt to bribe the watchers, but that was going rather too far, and when they were invited to take on a night's vigil without a breakfast, merely for the sake of the cause, they made themselves scarce, although they stuck stubbornly to their suspicions.

Such suspicions, anyhow, were a necessary accompaniment to the profession of fasting. No one could possibly watch the hunger artist continuously, day and night, and so no one could produce first-hand evidence that the fast had really been rigorous and continuous; only the artist himself could know that, he was therefore bound to be the sole completely satisfied spectator of his own fast. Yet for other reasons he was never satisfied; it was not perhaps mere fasting that had brought him to such skeleton thinness that many people had regretfully to keep away from his exhibitions, because the sight of him was too much for them, perhaps it was dissatisfaction with himself that had worn him down. For he alone knew, what no other initiate knew, how easy it was to fast. It was the easiest thing in the world. He made no secret of this, yet people did not believe him, at the best they set him down as modest, most of them, however, thought he was out for publicity or else was some kind of cheat who found it easy to fast because he had discovered a way of making it easy, and then had the impudence to admit the fact, more or less. He had to put up with all that, and in the course of time had got used to it, but his inner dissatisfaction always rankled, and never yet, after any term of fasting — this must be granted to his credit — had he left the cage of his own free will. The longest period of fasting was fixed by his impresario at forty days, beyond that term he was not allowed to go, not even in great cities, and there was good reason for it, too. Experience had proved that for about forty days the interest of the public could be stimulated by a steadily increasing pressure of advertisement, but after that the town began to lose interest, sympathetic support began notably to fall off; there were of course local variations as between one town and another or one country and another, but as a general rule forty days marked the limit. So on the fortieth day the flower-bedecked cage was opened, enthusiastic spectators filled the hall, a military band played, two doctors entered the cage to measure the results of the fast, which were announced through a megaphone, and finally two young ladies appeared, blissful at having been selected for the honor, to help the hunger artist down the few steps leading to a small table on which was spread a carefully chosen invalid repast. And at this very moment the artist always turned stubborn. True, he would entrust his bony arms to the outstretched helping hands of the ladies bending over him, but stand up he would not.

Why stop fasting at this particular moment, after forty days of it? He had held out for a long time, an illimitably long time; why stop now, when he was in his best fasting form, or rather, not yet quite in his best fasting form? Why should he be cheated of the fame he would get for fasting longer, for being not only the record hunger artist of all time, which presumably he was already, but for beating his own record by a performance beyond human imagination, since he felt that there were no limits to his capacity for fasting? His public pretended to admire him so much, why should it have so little patience with him; if he could endure fasting longer, why shouldn't the public endure it? Besides, he was tired, he was comfortable sitting in the straw, and now he was supposed to lift himself to his full height and go down to a meal the very thought of which gave him a nausea that only the presence of the ladies kept him from betraying, and even that with an effort. And he looked up into the eyes of the ladies who were apparently so friendly and in reality so cruel, and shook his head, which felt too heavy on its strengthless neck. But then there happened yet again what always happened. The impresario came forward, without a word — for the band made speech impossible — lifted his arms in the air above the artist, as if inviting Heaven to look down upon its creature here in the straw, this suffering martyr, which indeed he was, although in quite another sense; grasped him round the emaciated waist, with exaggerated caution, so that the frail condition he was in might be appreciated; and committed him to the care of the blenching ladies, not without secretly giving him a shaking so that his legs and body tottered and swayed. The artist now submitted completely; his head lolled on his breast as if it had landed there by chance; his body was hollowed out; his legs in a spasm of self-preservation clung close to each other at the knees, yet scraped on the ground as if it were not really solid ground, as if they were only trying to find solid ground; and the whole weight of his body, a featherweight after all, relapsed onto one of the ladies, who, looking round for help and panting a little — this post of honor was not at all what she had expected it to be — first stretched her neck as far as she could to keep her face at least free from contact with the artist, then finding this impossible, and her more fortunate companion not coming to her aid but merely holding extended on her own trembling hand the little bunch of knucklebones that was the artist's, to the great delight of the spectators burst into tears and had to be replaced by an attendant who had long been stationed in readiness. Then came the food, a little of which the impresario managed to get between the artist's lips, while he sat in a kind of half-fainting trance, to the accompaniment of

---

If you wish to be a good writer, write.

EPICTETUS

cheerful patter designed to distract the public's attention from the artist's condition; after that, a toast was drunk to the public, supposedly prompted by a whisper from the artist in the impresario's ear; the band confirmed it with a mighty flourish, the spectators melted away, and no one had any cause to be dissatisfied with the proceedings, no one except the hunger artist himself, he only, as always.

So he lived for many years, with small regular intervals of recuperation, in visible glory, honored by the world, yet in spite of that troubled in spirit, and all the more troubled because no one would take his trouble seriously. What comfort could he possibly need? What more could he possibly wish for? And if some good-natured person, feeling sorry for him, tried to console him by pointing out that his melancholy was probably caused by fasting, it could happen, especially when he had been fasting for some time, that he reacted with an outburst of fury and to the general alarm began to shake the bars of his cage like a wild animal. Yet the impresario had a way of punishing these outbreaks which he rather enjoyed putting into operation. He would apologize publicly for the artist's behavior, which was only to be excused, he admitted, because of the irritability caused by fasting; a condition hardly to be understood by well-fed people; then by natural transition he went on to mention the artist's equally incomprehensible boast that he could fast for much longer than he was doing; he praised the high ambition, the good will, the great self-denial undoubtedly implicit in such a statement; and then quite simply countered it by bringing out photographs, which were also on sale to the public, showing the artist on the fortieth day of a fast lying in bed almost dead from exhaustion. This perversion of the truth, familiar to the artist though it was, always unnerved him afresh and proved too much for him. What was a consequence of the premature ending of his fast was here presented as the cause of it! To fight against this lack of understanding, against a whole world of non-understanding, was impossible. Time and again in good faith he stood by the bars listening to the impresario, but as soon as the photographs appeared he always let go and sank with a groan back on to his straw, and the reassured public could once more come close and gaze at him.

A few years later when the witnesses of such scenes called them to mind, they often failed to understand themselves at all. For meanwhile the aforementioned change in public interest had set in; it seemed to happen almost overnight; there may have been profound causes for it, but who was going to bother about that; at any rate the pampered hunger artist suddenly found himself deserted one fine day by the amusement seekers, who went streaming past him to other more favored attractions. For the last time the impresario hurried him over half Europe to discover whether the old interest might still survive here and there; all in vain; everywhere, as if by secret agreement, a positive revulsion from professional fasting was in evidence. Of course it could not really have sprung up so suddenly as all that, and many premonitory symptoms which had not been sufficiently remarked or suppressed during the rush and glitter of success now came retrospectively to mind, but it was now too late to take any countermeasures. Fasting would surely come into fashion again at some future date, yet that was no comfort for those living in the present. What, then, was the hunger artist to do? He had been applauded by thousands in his time and could hardly come down to showing himself in a street booth at village fairs, and as for adopting another profession, he was not only too old for that but too fanatically devoted to fasting. So he took leave of the impresario, his partner in an unparalleled career, and hired himself to a large circus; in order to spare his own feelings he avoided reading the conditions of his contract.

A large circus with its enormous traffic in replacing and recruiting men, animals and apparatus can always find a use for people at any time, even for a hunger artist, provided of course that he does not ask too much, and in this particular case anyhow it was not only the artist who was taken on but his famous and long-known name as well, indeed considering the peculiar nature of his performance, which was not impaired by advancing age, it could not be objected that here was an artist past his prime, no longer at the height of his professional skill, seeking a refuge in some quiet corner of a circus, on the contrary, the hunger artist averred that he could fast as well as ever, which was entirely credible, he even alleged that if he were allowed to fast as he liked, and this was at once promised him without more ado, he could astound the world by establishing a record never yet achieved, a statement which certainly provoked a smile among the other professionals, since it left out of account the change in public opinion, which the hunger artist in his zeal conveniently forgot.

He had not, however, actually lost his sense of the real situation and took it as a matter of course that he and his cage should be stationed, not in the middle of the ring as a main attraction, but outside, near the animal cages, on a site that was after all easily accessible. Large and gaily painted placards made a frame for the cage and announced what was to be seen inside it. When the public came thronging out in the intervals to see the animals, they could hardly avoid passing the hunger artist's cage and stopping there for a moment, perhaps they might even have stayed longer had not those pressing behind them in the narrow gangway, who did not understand why they should be held up on their way towards the excitements of the menagerie, made it impossible for anyone to stand gazing quietly for any length of time. And that was the reason why the hunger artist, who had of course been looking forward to these visiting hours as the main achievement of his life, began instead to shrink from them. At first he could hardly wait for the intervals; it was exhilarating to watch the crowds come streaming his way, until only too soon — not even the most obstinate self-deception, clung to almost consciously, could hold out against the fact — the conviction was borne in upon him that these people, most of them, to judge from their actions, again and again, without exception, were all on their way to the menagerie. And the first sight of them from the distance remained the best. For when they reached his cage he was at once deafened by the storm of shouting and abuse that arose from the two contending factions, which renewed themselves continuously, of those who wanted to stop and stare at him — he soon began to dislike them more than the others — not out of real interest but only out of obstinate self-assertiveness, and those who wanted to go straight on to the animals. When the first great rush was past, the stragglers came along, and these, whom nothing could have prevented from stopping to look at him as long as they had breath, raced past with long strides, hardly even glancing at him, in their haste to get to the menagerie in time. And all too rarely did it happen that he had a stroke of luck, when some father of a family fetched up before him with his children, pointed a finger at the hunger artist and explained at length what the phenomenon meant, telling stories of earlier years when he himself had watched similar but much more thrilling performances, and the children, still rather uncomprehending, since neither inside nor outside school had they been sufficiently prepared for this lesson — what did they care about fasting? — yet showed by the brightness of their intent eyes that new and better times might be coming. Perhaps, said the hunger artist to himself many a time, things would be a little better if his cage were set not quite so near the menagerie. That made it too easy for people to make their choice, to say nothing of what he suffered from the stench of the menagerie, the animals' restlessness by night, the carrying past of raw lumps of flesh for the beasts of prey, the roaring at feeding times, which depressed him continually. But he did not dare to lodge a complaint with the management; after all, he had the animals to thank for the troops of people who passed his cage, among whom there might always be one here and there to take an interest in him, and who could tell where they might seclude him if he called attention to his existence and thereby to the fact that, strictly speaking, he was only an impediment on the way to the menagerie.

A small impediment, to be sure, one that grew steadily less. People grew familiar with the strange idea that they could be expected, in times like these, to take an interest in a hunger artist, and with this familiarity the verdict went out against him. He might fast as much as he could, and he did so; but nothing could save him now, people passed him by. Just try to explain to anyone the art of fasting! Anyone who has no feeling for it cannot be made to understand it. The fine placards grew dirty and illegible, they were torn down; the little notice board telling the number of fast days achieved, which at first was changed carefully every day, had long stayed at the same figure, for after the first few weeks even this small task seemed pointless to the staff; and so the artist simply fasted on and on, as he had once dreamed of doing, and it was no trouble to him, just as he had always foretold, but no one counted the days, no one, not even the artist himself, knew what records he was already breaking, and his heart grew heavy. And when once in a time some leisurely passer-by stopped, made merry over the old figure on the board and spoke of swindling, that was in its way the stupidest lie ever invented by indifference and inborn malice, since it was not the hunger artist who was cheating, he was working honestly, but the world was cheating him of his reward.

Many more days went by, however, and that too came to an end. An overseer's eye fell on the cage one day and he asked the attendants why this perfectly good cage should be left standing there unused with dirty straw inside it; nobody knew, until one man, helped out by the notice board, remembered about the hunger artist. They poked into the straw with sticks and found him in it. "Are you still fasting?" asked the overseer, "when on earth do you mean to stop?" "Forgive me, everybody," whispered the hunger artist; only the overseer, who had his ear to the bars, understood him. "Of course," said the overseer, and tapped his forehead with a finger to let the attendants know what state the man was in, "we forgive you." "I always wanted you to admire my fasting," said the hunger artist. "We do admire it," said the overseer, affably. "But you shouldn't admire it," said the hunger artist. "Well then we don't admire it," said the overseer, "but why shouldn't we admire it?" "Because I have to fast, I can't help it," said the hunger artist. "What a fellow you are," said the overseer, "and why can't you help it?" "Because," said the hunger artist, lifting his head a little and speaking, with his lips pursed, as if for a kiss, right into the overseer's ear, so that no syllable might be lost, "because I couldn't find the food I liked. If I had found it, believe me, I should have made no fuss and stuffed myself like you or anyone else." These were his last words, but in his dimming eyes remained the firm though no longer proud persuasion that he was still continuing to fast.

"Well, clear this out now!" said the overseer, and they buried the hunger artist, straw and all. Into the cage they put a young panther. Even the most insensitive felt it refreshing to see this wild creature leaping around the cage that had so long been dreary. The panther was all right. The food he liked was brought him without hesitation by the attendants; he seemed not even to miss his freedom; his noble body, furnished almost to the bursting point with all that it needed, seemed to carry freedom around with it too; somewhere in his jaws it seemed to lurk; and the joy of life streamed with such ardent passion from his throat that for the onlookers it was not easy to stand the shock of it. But they braced themselves, crowded round the cage, and did not want ever to move away.

FOR DISCUSSION

1. The whole surface story is contained in the first sentence: "During these last decades the interest in professional fasting has markedly diminished." Note how

the following pages do little more than to furnish supporting details, showing vividly the old interest, then the growing indifference until the artist's last superb accomplishment is played to an empty house, without even the artist himself knowing the record he has given his life to set. He is buried along with the straw from his cage. His place is taken by a young panther, the diametrical opposite of the hunger artist. Freedom and the joy of life "streamed with such ardent passion from his throat that for the onlookers it was not easy to stand the shock of it. But they braced themselves, crowded round the cage, and did not want ever to move away." This animal replaced the hunger artist in popularity.

If there is more than a surface meaning to this story, it lies in the suggestion that the change in public taste may not be a change for the good. Would you say that the human condition is closer to that of the hunger artist than to that of the young panther?

2. While the hunger artist is not an appealing figure, he does have a professional ethic, a pride in his art, and a genuine modesty. Search the story for humane values which you think he may have in contrast to the young panther, and which this deeply religious author may prefer.

❦ *The Experience Itself* ❦

The Open Boat

STEPHEN CRANE

A Tale Intended to be after the Fact: Being
the Experience of Four Men from the
Sunk Steamer "Commodore"

I

None of them knew the color of the sky. Their eyes glanced level, and were fastened upon the waves that swept toward them. These waves were of the hue of slate, save for the tops, which were of foaming white, and all of the men knew the colors of the sea. The horizon narrowed and widened, and dipped and rose, and at all times its edge was jagged with waves that seemed thrust up in points like rocks.

Many a man ought to have a bath-tub larger than the boat which here rode upon the sea. These waves were most wrongfully and barbarously

From Stephen Crane, *The Open Boat and Other Tales of Adventure* (New York, 1898).

abrupt and tall, and each froth-top was a problem in small-boat navigation.

The cook squatted in the bottom, and looked with both eyes at the six inches of gunwale which separated him from the ocean. His sleeves were rolled over his fat forearms, and the two flaps of his unbuttoned vest dangled as he bent to bail out the boat. Often he said, "Gawd! that was a narrow clip." As he remarked it he invariably gazed eastward over the broken sea.

The oiler, steering with one of the two oars in the boat, sometimes raised himself suddenly to keep clear of water that swirled in over the stern. It was a thin little oar, and it seemed often ready to snap.

The correspondent, pulling at the other oar, watched the waves and wondered why he was there.

The injured captain, lying in the bow, was at this time buried in that profound dejection and indifference which comes, temporarily at least, to even the bravest and most enduring when, willy-nilly, the firm fails, the army loses, the ship goes down. The mind of the master of a vessel is rooted deep in the timbers of her, though he command for a day or a decade; and this captain had on him the stern impression of a scene in the grays of dawn of seven turned faces, and later a stump of a topmast with a white ball on it, that slashed to and fro at the waves, went low and lower, and down. Thereafter there was something strange in his voice. Although steady, it was deep with mourning, and of a quality beyond oration or tears.

"Keep'er a little more south, Billie," said he.

"A little more south, sir," said the oiler in the stern.

A seat in this boat was not unlike a seat upon a bucking broncho, and, by the same token, a broncho is not much smaller. The craft pranced and reared and plunged like an animal. As each wave came, and she rose for it, she seemed like a horse making at a fence outrageously high. The manner of her scramble over these walls of water is a mystic thing, and, moreover, at the top of them were ordinarily these problems in white water, the foam racing down from the summit of each wave, requiring a new leap, and a leap from the air. Then, after scornfully bumping a crest, she would slide and race and splash down a long incline, and arrive bobbing and nodding in front of the next menace.

A singular disadvantage of the sea lies in the fact that, after successfully surmounting one wave, you discover that there is another behind it, just as important and just as nervously anxious to do something effective in the way of swamping boats. In a ten-foot dinghy one can get an idea of the resources of the sea in the line of waves that is not probable to the average experience, which is never at sea in a dinghy. As each slaty wall of water approached, it shut all else from the view of the men in the boat, and it was not difficult to imagine that this particular wave was the final outburst of the ocean, the last effort of the grim water. There was a terrible grace in the move of the waves, and they came in silence, save for the snarling of the crests.

In the wan light the faces of the men must have been gray. Their eyes must have glinted in strange ways as they gazed steadily astern. Viewed from a balcony, the whole thing would, doubtless, have been weirdly picturesque. But the men in the boat had no time to see it, and if they had had leisure, there were other things to occupy their minds. The sun swung steadily up the sky, and they knew it was broad day because the color of the sea changed from slate to emerald-green streaked with amber lights, and the foam was like tumbling snow. The process of the breaking day was unknown to them. They were aware only of this effect upon the color of the waves that rolled toward them.

In disjointed sentences the cook and the correspondent argued as to the difference between a life-saving station and a house of refuge. The cook had said: "There's a house of refuge just north of the Mosquito Inlet Light, and as soon as they see us they'll come off in their boat and pick us up."

"As soon as who see us?" said the correspondent.

"The crew," said the cook.

"Houses of refuge don't have crews," said the correspondent. "As I understand them, they are only places where clothes and grub are stored for the benefit of shipwrecked people. They don't carry crews."

"Oh, yes, they do," said the cook.

"No, they don't," said the correspondent.

"Well, we're not there yet, anyhow," said the oiler in the stern.

"Well," said the cook, "perhaps it's not a house of refuge that I'm thinking of as being near Mosquito Inlet Light; perhaps it's a life-saving station."

"We're not there yet," said the oiler in the stern.

II

As the boat bounced from the top of each wave the wind tore through the hair of the hatless men, and as the craft plopped her stern down again the spray slashed past them. The crest of each of these waves was a hill, from the top of which the men surveyed for a moment a broad, tumultuous expanse, shining and windriven. It was probably splendid, it was probably glorious, this play of the free sea, wild with lights of emerald and white and amber.

"Bully good thing it's an on-shore wind," said the cook. "If not, where would we be? Wouldn't have a show."

"That's right," said the correspondent.

The busy oiler nodded his assent.

Then the captain, in the bow, chuckled in a way that expressed humor, contempt, tragedy, all in one. "Do you think we've got much of a show now, boys?" said he.

Whereupon the three were silent, save for a trifle of hemming and hawing. To express any particular optimism at this time they felt to be childish and stupid, but they all doubtless possessed this sense of the situation in their minds. A young man thinks doggedly at such times. On the other hand, the ethics of their condition was decidedly against any open suggestion of hopelessness. So they were silent.

"Oh, well," said the captain, soothing his children, "we'll get ashore all right."

But there was that in his tone which made them think; so the oiler quoth, "Yes! if this wind holds."

The cook was bailing. "Yes! if we don't catch hell in the surf."

Canton-flannel gulls flew near and far. Sometimes they sat down on the sea, near patches of brown seaweed that rolled over the waves with a movement like carpets on a line in a gale. The birds sat comfortably in groups, and they were envied by some in the dinghy, for the wrath of the sea was no more to them than it was to a covey of prairie-chickens a thousand miles inland. Often they came very close and stared at the men with black, bead-like eyes. At these times they were uncanny and sinister in their unblinking scrutiny, and the men hooted angrily at them, telling them to be gone. One came, and evidently decided to alight on the top of the captain's head. The bird flew parallel to the boat, and did not circle, but made short sidelong jumps in the air in chicken fashion. His black eyes were wistfully fixed upon the captain's head. "Ugly brute," said the oiler to the bird. "You look as if you were made with a jack-knife." The cook and the correspondent swore darkly at the creature. The captain naturally wished to knock it away with the end of the heavy painter, but he did not dare do it, because anything resembling an emphatic gesture would have cap-sized this freighted boat; and so, with his open hand, the captain gently and carefully waved the gull away. After it had been discouraged from the pursuit the captain breathed easier on account of his hair, and others breathed easier because the bird struck their minds at this time as being somehow gruesome and ominous.

Shakespeare, we may fancy, wrote with rapidity; but not till he had thought with intensity.

THOMAS CARLYLE

In the meantime the oiler and the correspondent rowed; and also they rowed. They sat together in the same seat, and each rowed an oar. Then the oiler took both oars; then the correspondent took both oars, then the oiler; then the correspondent. They rowed and they rowed. The very ticklish part of the business was when the time came for the reclining one in the stern to take his turn at the oars. By the very last star of truth, it is easier to steal eggs from under a hen than it was to change seats in the dinghy.

First the man in the stern slid his hand along the thwart and moved with care, as if he were of Sèvres. Then the man in the rowing-seat slid his hand along the other thwart. It was all done with the most extraordinary care. As the two sidled past each other, the whole party kept watchful eyes on the coming wave, and the captain cried: "Look out, now! Steady, there!"

The brown mats of seaweed that appeared from time to time were like islands, bits of earth. They were traveling, apparently, neither one way nor the other. They were, to all intents, stationary. They informed the men in the boat that it was making progress slowly toward the land.

The captain, rearing cautiously in the bow after the dinghy soared on a great swell, said that he had seen the lighthouse at Mosquito Inlet. Presently the cook remarked that he had seen it. The correspondent was at the oars then, and for some reason he too wished to look at the lighthouse; but his back was toward the far shore, and the waves were important, and for some time he could not seize an opportunity to turn his head. But at last there came a wave more gentle than the others, and when at the crest of it he swiftly scoured the western horizon.

"See it?" said the captain.

"No," said the correspondent, slowly; "I didn't see anything."

"Look again," said the captain. He pointed. "It's exactly in that direction."

At the top of another wave the correspondent did as he was bid, and this time his eyes chanced on a small, still thing on the edge of the swaying horizon. It was precisely like the point of a pin. It took an anxious eye to find a lighthouse so tiny.

"Think we'll make it, Captain?"

"If this wind holds and the boat don't swamp, we can't do much else," said the captain.

The little boat, lifted by each towering sea and splashed viciously by the crests, made progress that in the absence of seaweed was not apparent to those in her. She seemed just a wee thing wallowing, miraculously top up, at the mercy of five oceans. Occasionally a great spread of water, like white flames, swarmed into her.

"Bail her, cook," said the captain, serenely.

"All right, Captain," said the cheerful cook.

III

It would be difficult to describe the subtle brotherhood of men that was here established on the seas. No one said that it was so. No one mentioned it. But it dwelt in the boat, and each man felt it warm him. They were a captain, an oiler, a cook, and a correspondent, and they were friends — friends in a more curiously iron-bound degree than may be common. The hurt captain, lying against the water-jar in the bow, spoke always in a low voice and calmly; but he could never command a more ready and swiftly obedient crew than the motley three of the dinghy. It was more than a mere recognition of what was best for the common safety. There was surely in it a quality that was personal and heartfelt. And after this devotion to the commander of the boat, there was this comradeship, that the correspondent, for instance, who had been taught to be cynical of men, knew even at the time was the best experience of his life. But no one said that it was so. No one mentioned it.

"I wish we had a sail," remarked the captain. "We might try my overcoat on the end of an oar, and give you two boys a chance to rest." So the cook and the correspondent held the mast and spread wide the overcoat; the oiler steered; and the little boat made good way with her new rig. Sometimes the oiler had to scull sharply to keep a sea from breaking into the boat, but otherwise sailing was a success.

Meanwhile the lighthouse had been growing slowly larger. It had now almost assumed color, and appeared like a gray shadow on the sky. The man at the oars could not be prevented from turning his head rather often to try for a glimpse of this little gray shadow.

At last, from the top of each wave, the men in the tossing boat could see land. Even as the lighthouse was an upright shadow on the sky, this land seemed but a long black shadow on the sea. It certainly was thinner than paper. "We must be about opposite New Smyrna," said the cook, who had coasted this shore often in schooners. "Captain, by the way, I believe they abandoned that life-saving station there about a year ago."

"Did they?" said the captain.

The wind slowly died away. The cook and the correspondent were not now obliged to slave in order to hold high the oar; but the waves continued their old impetuous swooping at the dinghy, and the little craft, no longer under way, struggled woundily over them. The oiler or the correspondent took the oars again.

Shipwrecks are *apropos* of nothing. If men could only train for them and have them occur when the men had reached pink condition, there would be less drowning at sea. Of the four in the dinghy none had slept any time worth mentioning for two days and two nights previous to embarking in the dinghy, and in the excitement of clambering about the deck of a foundering ship they had also forgotten to eat heartily.

For these reasons, and for others, neither the oiler nor the correspondent was fond of rowing at this time. The correspondent wondered ingenuously how in the name of all that was sane could there be people who thought it amusing to row a boat. It was not an amusement; it was a diabolical punishment, and even a genius of mental aberrations could never conclude that it was anything but a horror to the muscles and a crime against the back. He mentioned to the boat in general how the amusement of rowing struck him, and the weary-faced oiler smiled in full sympathy. Previously to the foundering, by the way, the oiler had worked double watch in the engine-room of the ship.

"Take her easy now, boys," said the captain. "Don't spend yourselves. If we have to run a surf you'll need all your strength, because we'll sure have to swim for it. Take your time."

Slowly the land arose from the sea. From a black line it became a line of black and a line of white — trees and sand. Finally the captain said that he could make out a house on the shore. "That's the house of refuge, sure," said the cook. "They'll see us before long, and come out after us."

The distant lighthouse reared high. "The keeper ought to be able to make us out now, if he's looking through a glass," said the captain. "He'll notify the life-saving people."

"None of those other boats could have got ashore to give word of the wreck," said the oiler, in a low voice, "else the lifeboat would be out hunting us."

Slowly and beautifully the land loomed out of the sea. The wind came again. It had veered from the northeast to the southeast. Finally a new sound struck the ears of the men in the boat. It was the low thunder of the surf on the shore. "We'll never be able to make the lighthouse now," said the captain. "Swing her head a little more north, Billie."

"A little more north, sir," said the oiler.

You must not suppose, because I am a man of letters, that I never tried to earn an honest living.

BERNARD SHAW

Whereupon the little boat turned her nose once more down the wind, and all but the oarsman watched the shore grow. Under the influence of this expansion doubt and direful apprehension were leaving the minds of the men. The management of the boat was still most absorbing, but it could not prevent a quiet cheerfulness. In an hour, perhaps, they would be ashore.

Their backbones had become thoroughly used to balancing in the boat, and they now rode this wild colt of a dinghy like circus men. The correspondent thought that he had been drenched to the skin, but happening to feel in the top pocket of his coat, he found therein eight cigars. Four of them were soaked with sea-water; four were perfectly scatheless. After a search, somebody produced three dry matches; and thereupon the four waifs rode in their little boat and, with an assurance of an impending rescue shining in their eyes, puffed at the big cigars, and judged well and ill of all men. Everybody took a drink of water.

IV

"Cook," remarked the captain, "there don't seem to be any signs of life about your house of refuge."

"No," replied the cook. "Funny they don't see us!"

A broad stretch of lowly coast lay before the eyes of the men. It was of low dunes topped with dark vegetation. The roar of the surf was plain, and sometimes they could see the white lip of a wave as it spun up the beach. A tiny house was blocked out black upon the sky. Southward, the slim lighthouse lifted its little gray length.

Tide, wind, and waves were swinging the dinghy northward. "Funny they don't see us," said the men.

The surf's roar was here dulled, but its tone was nevertheless thunderous and mighty. As the boat swam over the great rollers the men sat listening to this roar. "We'll swamp sure," said everybody.

It is fair to say here that there was not a life-saving station within twenty miles in either direction; but the men did not know this fact, and in consequence they made dark and opprobrious remarks concerning the eyesight of the nation's life-savers. Four scowling men sat in the dinghy and surpassed records in the invention of epithets.

"Funny they don't see us."

The light-heartedness of a former time had completely faded. To their sharpened minds it was easy to conjure pictures of all kinds of incompetency and blindness and, indeed, cowardice. There was the shore of the populous land, and it was bitter and bitter to them that from it came no sign.

"Well," said the captain, ultimately, "I suppose we'll have to make a try for ourselves. If we stay out here too long, we'll none of us have strength left to swim after the boat swamps."

And so the oiler, who was at the oars, turned the boat straight for the shore. There was a sudden tightening of muscles. There was some thinking.

"If we don't all get ashore," said the captain, — "if we don't all get ashore, I suppose you fellows know where to send news of my finish?"

They then briefly exchanged some addresses and admonitions. As for the reflections of the men, there was a great deal of rage in them. Perchance they might be formulated thus: "If I am going to be drowned — if I am going to be drowned — if I am going to be drowned, why, in the name of the seven mad gods who rule the sea, was I allowed to come thus far and contemplate sand and trees? Was I brought here merely to have my nose dragged away as I was about to nibble the sacred cheese of life? It is preposterous! If this old ninny-woman, Fate, cannot do better than this, she should be deprived of the management of men's fortunes. She is an old hen who knows not her intention. If she has decided to drown me, why did she not do it in the beginning, and save me all this trouble? The whole affair is absurd. . . . But no; she cannot mean to drown me. She dare not drown me. She cannot drown me. Not after all this work!" Afterward the man might have had an impulse to shake his fist at the clouds. "Just you drown me, now, and then hear what I call you!"

The billows that came at this time were more formidable. They seemed always just about to break and roll over the little boat in a turmoil of foam. There was a preparatory and long growl in the speech of them. No mind unused to the sea would have concluded that the dinghy could ascend these sheer heights in time. The shore was still afar. The oiler was a wily surf-man. "Boys," he said swiftly, "she won't live three minutes more, and we're too far out to swim. Shall I take her to sea again, Captain?"

"Yes; go ahead!" said the captain.

This oiler, by a series of quick miracles and fast and steady oarsmanship, turned the boat in the middle of the surf and took her safely to sea again.

There was a considerable silence as the boat bumped over the furrowed sea to deeper water. Then somebody in gloom spoke: "Well, anyhow, they must have seen us from the shore by now."

The gulls went in slanting flight up the wind toward the gray, desolate east. A squall, marked by dingy clouds, and clouds brick-red, like smoke from a burning building, appeared from the southeast.

"What do you think of those life-saving people? Ain't they peaches?"

"Funny they haven't seen us."

"Maybe they think we're out here for sport! Maybe they think we're fishin'. Maybe they think we're damned fools."

It was a long afternoon. A changed tide tried to force them southward, but wind and wave said northward. Far ahead, where coast-line, sea, and sky formed their mighty angle, there were little dots which seemed to indicate a city on the shore.

"St. Augustine?"

The captain shook his head. "Too near Mosquito Inlet."

And the oiler rowed, and then the correspondent rowed; then the oiler rowed. It was a weary business. The human back can become the seat of more aches and pains than are registered in books for the composite anatomy of a regiment. It is a limited area, but it can become the theater of in-numerable muscular conflicts, tangles, wrenches, knots, and other comforts.

"Did you ever like to row, Billie?" asked the correspondent.

"No," said the oiler; "hang it!"

When one exchanged the rowing-seat for a place in the bottom of the boat, he suffered a bodily depression that caused him to be careless of everything save an obligation to wiggle one finger. There was cold sea-water swashing to and fro in the boat, and he lay in it. His head, pillowed on a thwart, was within an inch of the swirl of a wave-crest, and some-times a particularly obstreperous sea came inboard and drenched him once more. But these matters did not annoy him. It is almost certain that if the boat had capsized he would have tumbled comfortably out upon the ocean as if he felt sure that it was a great, soft mattress.

"Look! There's a man on the shore!"

"Where?"

"There! See 'im? See 'im?"

"Yes, sure! He's walking along."

"Now he's stopped. Look! He's facing us!"

"He's waving at us!"

"So he is! By thunder!"

"Ah, now we're all right! Now we're all right! There'll be a boat out here for us in half an hour."

"He's going on. He's running. He's going up to that house there."

The remote beach seemed lower than the sea, and it required a searching glance to discern the little black figure. The captain saw a floating stick, and they rowed to it. A bath towel was by some weird chance in the boat, and tying this on the stick, the captain waved it. The oarsman did not dare turn his head, so he was obliged to ask questions.

"What's he doing now?"

"He's standing still again. He's looking, I think. . . . There he goes again — toward the house. . . . Now he's stopped again."

"Is he waving at us?"

"No, not now; he was, though."

"Look! There comes another man!"

"He's running."

"Look at him go, would you!"

"Why, he's on a bicycle. Now he's met the other man. They're both waving at us. Look!"

"There comes something up the beach."

"What the devil is that thing?"

"Why, it looks like a boat."

"Why, certainly, it's a boat."

"No; it's on wheels."

"Yes, so it is. Well, that must be the life-boat. They drag them along shore on a wagon."

"That's the life-boat, sure."

"No, by ——, it's an omnibus."

"I tell you it's a life-boat."

"It is not! It's an omnibus. I can see it plain. See? One of these big hotel omnibuses."

"By thunder, you're right. It's an omnibus, sure as fate. What do you suppose they are doing with an omnibus? Maybe they are going around collecting the life-crew, hey?"

"That's it, likely. Look! There's a fellow waving a little black flag. He's standing on the steps of the omnibus. There come those other two fellows. Now they're all talking together. Look at the fellow with the flag. Maybe he ain't waving it!"

"That ain't a flag, is it? That's his coat. Why, certainly, that's his coat."

"So it is; it's his coat. He's taken it off and is waving it around his head. But would you look at him swing it!"

"Oh, say, there isn't any life-saving station there. That's just a winter-resort hotel omnibus that has brought over some of the boarders to see us drown."

"What's that idiot with the coat mean? What's he signaling, anyhow?"

"It looks as if he were trying to tell us to go north. There must be a life-saving station up there."

"No; he thinks we're fishing. Just giving us a merry hand. See? Ah, there, Willie!"

"Well, I wish I could make something out of those signals. What do you suppose he means?"

"He don't mean anything; he's just playing."

"Well, if he'd just signal us to try the surf again, or to go to sea and wait, or go north, or go south, or go to hell, there would be some reason in it. But look at him. He just stands there and keeps his coat revolving like a wheel. The ass."

"There come more people."

"Now there's quite a mob. Look. Isn't that a boat?"

"Where? Oh, I see where you mean. No, that's no boat."

"That fellow is still waving his coat."

"He must think we like to see him do that. Why don't he quit it? It don't mean anything."

I would rather risk my future fame upon one lyric than upon ten volumes.

OLIVER WENDELL HOLMES

"I don't know. I think he is trying to make us go north. It must be that there's a life-saving station there somewhere."

"Say, he ain't tired yet. Look at 'im wave!"

"Wonder how long he can keep that up. He's been revolving his coat ever since he caught sight of us. He's an idiot. Why aren't they getting men to bring a boat out? A fishing-boat — one of those big yawls — could come out here all right. Why don't he do something?"

"Oh, it's all right now."

"They'll have a boat out here for us in less than no time, now that they've seen us."

A faint yellow tone came into the sky over the low land. The shadows on the sea slowly deepened. The wind bore coldness with it, and the men began to shiver.

"Holy smoke!" said one, allowing his voice to express his impious mood, "if we keep on monkeying out here! If we've got to flounder out here all night!"

"Oh, we'll never have to stay here all night! Don't you worry. They've seen us now, and it won't be long before they'll come chasing out after us."

The shore grew dusky. The man waving a coat blended gradually into this gloom, and it swallowed in the same manner the omnibus and the group of people. The spray, when it dashed uproariously over the side, made the voyagers shrink and swear like men who were being branded.

"I'd like to catch the chump who waved the coat. I feel like soaking him one, just for luck."

"Why? What did he do?"

"Oh, nothing, but then he seemed so damned cheerful."

In the meantime the oiler rowed, and then the correspondent rowed, and then the oiler rowed. Gray-faced and bowed forward, they mechanically, turn by turn, plied the leaden oars. The form of the lighthouse had vanished from the southern horizon, but finally a pale star appeared, just lifting from the sea. The streaked saffron in the west passed before the all-merging darkness, and the sea to the east was black. The land had vanished, and was expressed only by the low and drear thunder of the surf.

"If I am going to be drowned — if I am going to be drowned — if I am going to be drowned, why in the name of the seven mad gods who rule the sea, was I allowed to come thus far and contemplate sand and trees? Was I brought here merely to have my nose dragged away as I was about to nibble the sacred cheese of life?"

The patient captain, drooped over the water-jar, was sometimes obliged to speak to the oarsman.

"Keep her head up! Keep her head up!"

"Keep her head up, sir." The voices were weary and low.

This was surely a quiet evening. All save the oarsman lay heavily and listlessly in the boat's bottom. As for him, his eyes were just capable of noting the tall black waves that swept forward in a most sinister silence, save for an occasional subdued growl of a crest.

The cook's head was on a thwart, and he looked without interest at the water under his nose. He was deep in other scenes. Finally he spoke. "Billie," he murmured dreamfully, "what kind of pie do you like best?"

V

"Pie!" said the oiler and the correspondent, agitatedly. "Don't talk about those things, blast you!"

"Well," said the cook, "I was just thinking about ham sandwiches, and —"

A night on the sea in an open boat is a long night. As darkness settled finally, the shine of the light, lifting from the sea in the south, changed to full gold. On the northern horizon a new light appeared, a small bluish gleam on the edge of the waters. These two lights were the furniture of the world. Otherwise there was nothing but waves.

Two men huddled in the stern, and distances were so magnificent in the dinghy that the rower was enabled to keep his feet partly warm by thrusting them under his companions. Their legs indeed extended far under the rowing-seat until they touched the feet of the captain forward. Sometimes, despite the efforts of the tired oarsman, a wave came piling into the boat, an icy wave of the night, and the chilling water soaked them anew. They would twist their bodies for a moment and groan, and sleep the dead sleep once more, while the water in the boat gurgled about them as the craft rocked.

The plan of the oiler and the correspondent was for one to row until he lost the ability, and then arouse the other from his sea-water couch in the bottom of the boat.

The oiler plied the oars until his head drooped forward and the overpowering sleep blinded him; and he rowed yet afterward. Then he touched a man in the bottom of the boat, and called his name. "Will you spell me for a little while?" he said meekly.

"Sure, Billie," said the correspondent, awaking and dragging himself to a sitting position. They exchanged places carefully, and the oiler, cuddling down in the sea-water at the cook's side, seemed to go to sleep instantly.

The particular violence of the sea had ceased. The waves came without snarling. The obligation of the man at the oars was to keep the boat headed so that the tilt of the rollers would not capsize her, and to preserve her from filling when the crests rushed past. The black waves were silent and hard to be seen in the darkness. Often one was almost upon the boat before the oarsman was aware.

In a low voice the correspondent addressed the captain. He was not sure that the captain was awake, although this iron man seemed to be always awake. "Captain, shall I keep her making for that light north, sir?"

The same steady voice answered him. "Yes. Keep it about two points off the port bow."

The cook had tied a life-belt around himself in order to get even the warmth which this clumsy cork contrivance could donate, and he seemed almost stove-like when a rower, whose teeth invariably chattered wildly as soon as he ceased his labor, dropped down to sleep.

The correspondent, as he rowed, looked down at the two men sleeping under foot. The cook's arm was around the oiler's shoulders, and, with their fragmentary clothing and haggard faces, they were the babes of the sea — a grotesque rendering of the old babes in the wood.

Later he must have grown stupid at his work, for suddenly there was a growling of water, and a crest came with a roar and a swash into the boat, and it was a wonder that it did not set the cook afloat in his life-belt. The cook continued to sleep, but the oiler sat up, blinking his eyes and shaking with the new cold.

"Oh, I'm awful sorry, Billie," said the correspondent, contritely.

"That's all right, old boy," said the oiler, and lay down again and was asleep.

Presently it seemed that even the captain dozed, and the correspondent thought that he was the one man afloat on all the ocean. The wind had a voice as it came over the waves, and it was sadder than the end.

There was a long, loud swishing astern of the boat, and a gleaming trail of phosphorescence, like blue flame, was furrowed on the black waters. It might have been made by a monstrous knife.

Then there came a stillness, while the correspondent breathed with the open mouth and looked at the sea.

Suddenly there was another swish and another long flash of bluish light, and this time it was alongside the boat, and might almost have been reached with an oar. The correspondent saw an enormous fin speed like a shadow through the water, hurling the crystalline spray and leaving the long glowing trail.

The correspondent looked over his shoulder at the captain. His face was hidden, and he seemed to be asleep. He looked at the babes of the sea. They certainly were asleep. So, being bereft of sympathy, he leaned a little way to one side and swore softly into the sea.

But the thing did not then leave the vicinity of the boat. Ahead or astern, on one side or the other, at intervals long or short, fled the long sparkling streak, and there was to be heard the whiroo of the dark fin. The speed and power of the thing was greatly to be admired. It cut the water like a gigantic and keen projectile.

The presence of this biding thing did not affect the man with the same horror that it would if he had been a picnicker. He simply looked at the sea dully and swore in an undertone.

Nevertheless, it is true that he did not wish to be alone with the thing. He wished one of his companions to awake by chance and keep him company with it. But the captain hung motionless over the water-jar, and the oiler and the cook in the bottom of the boat were plunged in slumber.

VI

"If I am going to be drowned — if I am going to be drowned — if I am going to be drowned, why, in the name of the seven mad gods who rule the sea, was I allowed to come thus far and contemplate sand and trees?"

During this dismal night, it may be remarked that a man would conclude that it was really the intention of the seven mad gods to drown him, despite the abominable injustice of it. For it was certainly an abominable injustice to drown a man who had worked so hard, so hard. The man felt it would be a crime most unnatural. Other people had drowned at sea since galleys swarmed with painted sails, but still —

When it occurs to a man that nature does not regard him as important, and that she feels she would not maim the universe by disposing of him, he at first wishes to throw bricks at the temple, and he hates deeply the fact that there are no bricks and no temples. Any visible expression of nature would surely be pelleted with his jeers.

Then, if there be no tangible thing to hoot, he feels, perhaps, the desire to confront a personification and indulge in pleas, bowed to one knee, and with hands supplicant, saying, "Yes, but I love myself."

A high cold star on a winter's night is the word he feels that she says to him. Thereafter he knows the pathos of his situation.

The men in the dinghy had not discussed these matters, but each had, no doubt, reflected upon them in silence and according to his mind. There was seldom any expression upon their faces save the general one of complete weariness. Speech was devoted to the business of the boat.

To chime the notes of his emotion, a verse mysteriously entered the correspondent's head. He had even forgotten that he had forgotten this verse, but it suddenly was in his mind.

> A soldier of the Legion lay dying in Algiers;
> There was lack of woman's nursing, there was dearth of woman's tears;
> But a comrade stood beside him, and he took that comrade's hand,
> And he said, "I never more shall see my own, my native land."

In his childhood the correspondent had been made acquainted with the fact that a soldier of the Legion lay dying in Algiers, but he had never regarded it as important. Myriads of his school-fellows had informed him of the soldier's plight, but the dinning had naturally ended by making him perfectly indifferent. He had never considered it his affair that a soldier of the Legion lay dying in Algiers, nor had it appeared to him as a matter for sorrow. It was less to him than the breaking of a pencil's point.

Now, however, it quaintly came to him as a human, living thing. It was no longer merely a picture of a few throes in the breast of a poet, meanwhile drinking tea and warming his feet at the grate; it was an actuality — stern, mournful, and fine.

The correspondent plainly saw the soldier. He lay on the sand with his feet out straight and still. While his pale left hand was upon his chest in an attempt to thwart the going of his life, the blood came between his fingers. In the far Algerian distance, a city of low square forms was set against a sky that was faint with the last sunset hues. The correspondent, plying the oars and dreaming of the slow and slower movements of the lips of the soldier, was moved by a profound and perfectly impersonal comprehension. He was sorry for the soldier of the Legion who lay dying in Algiers.

The thing which had followed the boat and waited had evidently grown bored at the delay. There was no longer to be heard the slash of the cutwater, and there was no longer the flame of the long trail. The light in the north still glimmered, but it was apparently no nearer to the boat. Sometimes the boom of the surf rang in the correspondent's ears, and he turned the craft seaward then and rowed harder. Southward, some one had evidently built a watch-fire on the beach. It was too low and too far to be seen, but it made a shimmering, roseate reflection upon the bluff back of it, and this could be discerned from the boat. The wind came stronger, and sometimes a wave suddenly raged out like a mountain-cat, and there was to be seen the sheen and sparkle of a broken crest.

The captain, in the bow, moved on his water-jar and sat erect. "Pretty long night," he observed to the correspondent. He looked at the shore. "Those life-saving people take their time."

"Did you see that shark playing around?"

"Yes, I saw him. He was a big fellow, all right."

"Wish I had known you were awake."

Later the correspondent spoke into the bottom of the boat.

"Billie!" There was a slow and gradual disentanglement. "Billie, will you spell me?"

"Sure," said the oiler.

As soon as the correspondent touched the cold, comfortable sea-water in the bottom of the boat and had huddled close to the cook's life-belt he was deep in sleep, despite the fact that his teeth played all the popular airs. This sleep was so good to him that it was but a moment before he heard a voice call his name in a tone that demonstrated the last stages of exhaustion. "Will you spell me?"

"Sure, Billie."

The light in the north had mysteriously vanished, but the correspondent took his course from the wide-awake captain.

Later in the night they took the boat farther out to sea, and the captain directed the cook to take one oar at the stern and keep the boat facing the seas. He was to call out if he should hear the thunder of the surf. This plan enabled the oiler and the correspondent to get respite together. "We'll give those boys a chance to get into shape again," said the captain. They curled down and, after a few preliminary chatterings and trembles, slept once more the dead sleep. Neither knew they had bequeathed to the cook the company of another shark, or perhaps the same shark.

As the boat caroused on the waves, spray occasionally bumped over the side and gave them a fresh soaking, but this had no power to break their repose. The ominous slash of the wind and the water affected them as it would have affected mummies.

"Boys," said the cook, with the notes of every reluctance in his voice, "she's drifted in pretty close. I guess one of you had better take her to sea again." The correspondent, aroused, heard the crash of the toppled crests.

As he was rowing, the captain gave him some whiskey and water, and this steadied the chills out of him. "If I ever get ashore and anybody shows me even a photograph of an oar — "

At last there was a short conversation.
"Billie! . . . Billie, will you spell me?"
"Sure," said the oiler.

VII

When the correspondent again opened his eyes, the sea and the sky were each of the gray hue of the dawning. Later, carmine and gold was painted upon the waters. The morning appeared finally, in its splendor, with a sky of pure blue, and the sunlight flamed on the tips of the waves.

On the distant dunes were set many little black cottages, and a tall white windmill reared above them. No man, nor dog, nor bicycle appeared on the beach. The cottages might have formed a deserted village.

The voyagers scanned the shore. A conference was held in the boat. "Well," said the captain, "if no help is coming, we might better try a run through the surf right away. If we stay out here much longer we will be too weak to do anything for ourselves at all." The others silently acquiesced in this reasoning. The boat was headed for the beach. The correspondent wondered if none ever ascended the tall wind-tower, and if then they never looked seaward. This tower was a giant, standing with its back to the plight of the ants. It represented in a degree, to the correspondent, the serenity of nature amid the struggles of the individual — nature in the wind, and nature in the vision of men. She did not seem cruel to him then, nor beneficent, nor treacherous, nor wise. But she was indifferent, flatly indifferent. It is, perhaps, plausible that a man in this situation, impressed with the unconcern of the universe, should see the innumerable flaws of his life and have them taste wickedly in his mind and wish for another chance. A distinction between right and wrong seems absurdly clear to him, then, in this new ignorance of the grave-edge, and he understands that if he were given another opportunity he would mend his conduct and his words, and be better and brighter during an introduction or at a tea.

"Now, boys," said the captain, "she is going to swamp sure. All we can do is to work her in as far as possible, and then when she swamps, pile out and scramble for the beach. Keep cool now, and don't jump until she swamps sure."

The oiler took the oars. Over his shoulder he scanned the surf. "Captain," he said, "I think I'd better bring her about, and keep her head-on to the sea, and back her in."

"All right, Billie," said the captain. "Back her in." The oiler swung the boat then, and, seated in the stern, the cook and the correspondent were obliged to look over their shoulders to contemplate the lonely and indifferent shore.

The monstrous inshore rollers heaved the boat high until the men were again enabled to see the white sheets of water scudding up the slanted beach. "We won't get in very close," said the captain. Each time a man could wrest his attention from the rollers, he turned his glance toward the shore, and in the expression of the eyes during this contemplation there was a singular quality. The correspondent, observing the others, knew that they were not afraid, but the full meaning of their glances was shrouded.

As for himself, he was too tired to grapple fundamentally with the fact. He tried to coerce his mind into thinking of it, but the mind was dominated at this time by the muscles, and the muscles said they did not care. It merely occurred to him that if he should drown it would be a shame.

There were no hurried words, no pallor, no plain agitation. The men simply looked at the shore. "Now, remember to get well clear of the boat when you jump," said the captain.

Seaward the crest of a roller suddenly fell with a thunderous crash, and the long white comber came roaring down upon the boat.

"Steady now," said the captain. The men were silent. They turned their eyes from the shore to the comber and waited. The boat slid up the incline, leaped at the furious top, bounced over it, and swung down the long back of the wave. Some water had been shipped, and the cook bailed it out.

But the next crest crashed also. The tumbling, boiling flood of white water caught the boat and whirled it almost perpendicular. Water swarmed in from all sides. The correspondent had his hands on the gunwale at this time, and when the water entered at that place he swiftly withdrew his fingers, as if he objected to wetting them.

The little boat, drunken with this weight of water, reeled and snuggled deeper into the sea.

"Bail her out, cook! Bail her out!" said the captain.

"All right, Captain," said the cook.

"Now, boys, the next one will do for us sure," said the oiler. "Mind to jump clear of the boat."

The third wave moved forward, huge, furious, implacable. It fairly swallowed the dinghy, and almost simultaneously the men tumbled into the sea. A piece of life-belt had lain in the bottom of the boat, and as the correspondent went overboard he held this to his chest with his left hand.

The January water was icy, and he reflected immediately that it was colder than he had expected to find it off the coast of Florida. This appeared to his dazed mind as a fact important enough to be noted at the time. The coldness of the water was sad; it was tragic. This fact was somehow mixed and confused with his opinion of his own situation so that it seemed almost a proper reason for tears. The water was cold.

When he came to the surface he was conscious of little but the noisy water. Afterward he saw his companions in the sea. The oiler was ahead in the race. He was swimming strongly and rapidly. Off to the correspondent's left, the cook's great white and corked back bulged out of the water; and in the rear the captain was hanging with his one good hand to the keel of the overturned dinghy.

There is a certain immovable quality to a shore, and the correspondent wondered at it amid the confusion of the sea.

It seemed also very attractive; but the correspondent knew that it was a long journey, and he paddled leisurely. The piece of life-preserver lay under him, and sometimes he whirled down the incline of a wave as if he were on a hand-sled.

But finally he arrived at a place in the sea where travel was beset with difficulty. He did not pause swimming to inquire what manner of current had caught him, but there his progress ceased. The shore was set before him like a bit of scenery on a stage, and he looked at it, and understood with his eyes each detail of it.

As the cook passed, much farther to the left, the captain was calling to him, "Turn over on your back, cook! Turn over on your back and use the oar."

"All right, sir." The cook turned on his back, and, paddling with an oar, went ahead as if he were a canoe.

Presently the boat also passed to the left of the correspondent, with the captain clinging with one hand to the keel. He would have appeared like a man raising himself to look over a board fence if it were not for the extraordinary gymnastics of the boat. The correspondent marveled that the captain could still hold to it.

They passed on nearer to shore — the oiler, the cook, the captain — and following them went the water-jar, bouncing gaily over the seas.

The correspondent remained in the grip of this strange new enemy, a current. The shore, with its white slope of sand and its green bluff, topped with little silent cottages, was spread like a picture before him. It was very near to him then, but he was impressed as one who, in a gallery, looks at a scene from Brittany or Algiers.

He thought: "I am going to drown? Can it be possible? Can it be possible? Can it be possible?" Perhaps an individual must consider his own death to be the final phenomenon of nature.

But later a wave perhaps whirled him out of this small deadly current, for he found suddenly that he could again make progress toward the shore. Later still he was aware that the captain, clinging with one hand to the keel of the dinghy, had his face turned away from the shore and toward him, and was calling his name. "Come to the boat! Come to the boat!"

In his struggle to reach the captain and the boat, he reflected that when one gets properly wearied drowning must really be a comfortable arrangement — a cessation of hostilities accompanied by a large degree of relief; and he was glad of it, for the main thing in his mind for some moments had been horror of the temporary agony; he did not wish to be hurt.

Presently he saw a man running along the shore. He was undressing with most remarkable speed. Coat, trousers, shirt, everything flew magically off him.

"Come to the boat!" called the captain.

"All right, Captain." As the correspondent paddled, he saw the captain let himself down to bottom and leave the boat. Then the correspondent performed his one little marvel of the voyage. A large wave caught him and flung him with ease and supreme speed completely over the boat and far beyond it. It struck him even then as an event in gymnastics and a true miracle of the sea. An overturned boat in the surf is not a plaything to a swimming man.

The correspondent arrived in water that reached only to his waist, but his condition did not enable him to stand for more than a moment. Each wave knocked him into a heap, and the undertow pulled at him.

Then he saw the man who had been running and undressing, and undressing and running, come bounding into the water. He dragged ashore the cook, and then waded toward the captain; but the captain waved him away and sent him to the correspondent. He was naked — naked as a tree in winter; but a halo was about his head, and he shone like a saint. He gave a strong pull, and a long drag, and a bully heave at the correspondent's hand. The correspondent, schooled in the minor formulae, said, "Thanks, old man." But suddenly the man cried, "What's that?" He pointed a swift finger. The correspondent said, "Go."

In the shallows, face downward, lay the oiler. His forehead touched sand that was periodically, between each wave, clear of the sea.

The correspondent did not know all that transpired afterward. When he achieved safe ground he fell, striking the sand with each particular part of his body. It was as if he had dropped from a roof, but the thud was grateful to him.

It seems that instantly the beach was populated with men with blankets, clothes, and flasks, and women with coffee-pots and all the remedies sacred to their minds. The welcome of the land to the men from the sea was warm and generous; but a still and dripping shape was carried slowly up the beach, and the land's welcome for it could only be the different and sinister hospitality of the grave.

When it came night, the white waves paced to and fro in the moonlight, and the wind brought the sound of the great sea's voice to the men on the shore, and they felt that they could then be interpreters.

FOR DISCUSSION

1. That "The Open Boat" should be called a short story is an indication of the wide variety of writings that fall within that category. Its plot is a simple question: will the men survive or drown? The characters are slightly drawn: they form an eager brotherhood, but each is somewhat individual. Who is most individual from the others, and what are his traits?

2. The central purpose of the author is to show as exactly as possible what the experience was like: the exhaustion of the men, the imminence of each threaten-

ing wave, the nearness yet farness of safety. Part of his method is to refer to certain subjects or themes again and again. List as many as you can of the subjects or themes — like bailing the boat — that are mentioned a half dozen times or more.

3. To avoid monotony the author treats those recurring themes with a slight difference each time. As you looked for sameness in the previous question, now look for difference in his treatment of the same theme each time he mentions it.

4. In part VI the correspondent speaks of nature as being indifferent to his survival. Contrast this attitude with the common religious attitude.

5. At the end of the story, which was the stronger feeling: relief because the correspondent survived or sorrow because the oiler drowned? Does your answer to this question tell you anything about a reader's sympathy in fiction?

❦ *Further Stories for Appreciation* ❦

A Clean, Well-Lighted Place

ERNEST HEMINGWAY

It was late and every one had left the cafe except an old man who sat in the shadow the leaves of the tree made against the electric light. In the day time the street was dusty, but at night the dew settled the dust and the old man liked to sit late because he was deaf and now at night it was quiet and he felt the difference. The two waiters inside the cafe knew that the old man was a little drunk, and while he was a good client they knew that if he became too drunk he would leave without paying, so they kept watch on him.

"Last week he tried to commit suicide," one waiter said.

"Why?"

"He was in despair."

"What about?"

"Nothing."

From *Winner Take Nothing* by Ernest Hemingway. Reprinted by permission of Charles Scribner's Sons.

"How do you know it was nothing?"

"He has plenty of money."

They sat together at a table that was close against the wall near the door of the cafe and looked at the terrace where the tables were all empty except where the old man sat in the shadow of the leaves of the tree that moved slightly in the wind. A girl and a soldier went by in the street. The street light shone on the brass number on his collar. The girl wore no head covering and hurried beside him.

"The guard will pick him up," one waiter said.

"What does it matter if he gets what he's after?"

"He had better get off the street now. The guard will get him. They went by five minutes ago."

The old man sitting in the shadow rapped on his saucer with his glass. The younger waiter went over to him.

"What do you want?"

The old man looked at him. "Another brandy," he said.

"You'll be drunk," the waiter said. The old man looked at him. The waiter went away.

"He'll stay all night," he said to his colleague. "I'm sleepy now. I never get into bed before three o'clock. He should have killed himself last week."

The waiter took the brandy bottle and another saucer from the counter inside the cafe and marched out to the old man's table. He put down the saucer and poured the glass full of brandy.

No man but a blockhead ever wrote, except for money.

SAMUEL JOHNSON

"You should have killed yourself last week," he said to the deaf man. The old man motioned with his finger. "A little more," he said. The waiter poured on into the glass so that the brandy slopped over and ran down the stem into the top saucer of the pile. "Thank you," the old man said. The waiter took the bottle back inside the cafe. He sat down at the table with his colleague again.

"He's drunk now," he said.

"He's drunk every night."

"What did he want to kill himself for?"

"How should I know."

"How did he do it?"

"He hung himself with a rope."

"Who cut him down?"

"His niece."

"Why did they do it?"

"Fear for his soul."

"How much money has he got?"

"He's got plenty."

"He must be eighty years old."

"Anyway I should say he was eighty."

"I wish he would go home. I never get to bed before three o'clock. What kind of hour is that to go to bed?"

"He stays up because he likes it."

"He's lonely. I'm not lonely. I have a wife waiting in bed for me."

"He had a wife once too."

"A wife would be no good to him now."

"You can't tell. He might be better with a wife."

"His niece looks after him."

"I know. You said she cut him down."

"I wouldn't want to be that old. An old man is a nasty thing."

"Not always. This old man is clean. He drinks without spilling. Even now, drunk. Look at him."

"I don't want to look at him. I wish he would go home. He has no regard for those who must work."

The old man looked from his glass across the square, then over at the waiters.

"Another brandy," he said, pointing to his glass. The waiter who was in a hurry came over.

"Finished," he said, speaking with that omission of syntax stupid people employ when talking to drunken people or foreigners. "No more tonight. Close now."

"Another," said the old man.

"No. Finished." The waiter wiped the edge of the table with a towel and shook his head.

The old man stood up, slowly counted the saucers, took a leather coin purse from his pocket and paid for the drinks, leaving half a peseta tip.

The waiter watched him go down the street, a very old man walking unsteadily but with dignity.

"Why didn't you let him stay and drink?" the unhurried waiter asked. They were putting up the shutters. "It is not half past two."

"I want to go home to bed."

"What is an hour?"

"More to me than to him."

"An hour is the same."

"You talk like an old man yourself. He can buy a bottle and drink at home."

"It's not the same."

"No, it is not," agreed the waiter with a wife. He did not wish to be unjust. He was only in a hurry.

"And you? You have no fear of going home before your usual hour?"

"Are you trying to insult me?"

"No, hombre, only to make a joke."

"No," the waiter who was in a hurry said, rising from pulling down the metal shutters. "I have confidence. I am all confidence."

"You have youth, confidence, and a job," the older waiter said. "You have everything."

"And what do you lack?"

"Everything but work."

"You have everything I have."

"No. I have never had confidence and I am not young."

"Come on. Stop talking nonsense and lock up."

"I am of those who like to stay late at the cafe," the older waiter said. "With all those who do not want to go to bed. With all those who need a light for the night."

"I want to go home and into bed."

"We are of two different kinds," the older waiter said. He was now dressed to go home. "It is not only a question of youth and confidence although those things are very beautiful. Each night I am reluctant to close up because there may be some one who needs the cafe."

"Hombre, there are bodegas open all night long."

"You do not understand. This is a clean and pleasant cafe. It is well lighted. The light is very good and also, now, there are shadows of the leaves."

"Good night," said the younger waiter.

"Good night," the other said. Turning off the electric light he continued the conversation with himself. It is the light of course but it is necessary that the place be clean and pleasant. You do not want music. Certainly you do not want music. Nor can you stand before a bar with dignity although that is all that is provided for these hours. What did he fear? It was not fear or dread. It was a nothing that he knew too well. It was all a nothing and a man was nothing too. It was only that and light was all it needed and a certain cleanness and order. Some lived in it and never felt it but he knew it all was nada y pues nada y nada y pues nada. Our nada who art in nada, nada be thy name thy kingdom nada thy will be nada in nada as it is in nada. Give us this nada our daily nada and nada us our nada as we nada our nadas and nada us not into nada but deliver us from nada; pues nada. Hail nothing full of nothing, nothing is with thee. He smiled and stood before a bar with a shining steam pressure coffee machine.

"What's yours?" asked the barman.

"Nada."

"Otro loco mas," said the barman and turned away.

"A little cup," said the waiter.

The barman poured it for him.

"The light is very bright and pleasant but the bar is unpolished," the waiter said.

The barman looked at him but did not answer. It was too late at night for conversation.

"You want another copita?" the barman asked.

"No, thank you," said the waiter and went out. He disliked bars and bodegas. A clean, well-lighted cafe was a very different thing. Now, without thinking further, he would go home to his room. He would lie in the bed and finally, with daylight, he would go to sleep. After all, he said to himself, it is probably only insomnia. Many must have it.

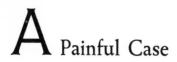

A Painful Case

JAMES JOYCE

Mr. James Duffy lived in Chapelizod because he wished to live as far as possible from the city of which he was a citizen and because he found all the other suburbs of Dublin mean, modern and pretentious. He lived in an old sombre house and from his windows he could look into the disused distillery or upwards along the shallow river on which Dublin is built. The lofty walls of his uncarpeted room were free from pictures. He had himself bought every article of furniture in the room: a black iron bedstead, an iron wash-stand, four cane chairs, a clothes-rack, a coal-scuttle, a fender and irons and a square table on which lay a double desk. A bookcase had beeen made in an alcove by means of shelves of white wood. The bed was clothed with white bedclothes and a black and scarlet rug covered the foot. A little hand-mirror hung above the wash-stand and during the day a white-shaded lamp stood as the sole ornament of the mantelpiece. The books on the white wooden shelves were arranged from below upwards according to bulk. A complete Wordsworth stood at one end of the lowest shelf and a copy of the *Maynooth Catechism*, sewn into the cloth cover of a notebook, stood at one end of the top shelf. Writing materials were always on the desk. In the desk lay a manuscript translation of Hauptmann's *Michael Kramer*, the stage directions of which were writ-

From *Dubliners* by James Joyce. Originally published by B. W. Huebsch, Inc. in 1916. Reprinted by permission of The Viking Press, Inc.

ten in purple ink, and a little sheaf of papers held together by a brass pin. In these sheets a sentence was inscribed from time to time and, in an ironical moment, the headline of an advertisement for *Bile Beans* had been pasted on to the first sheet. On lifting the lid of the desk a faint fragrance escaped — the fragrance of new cedarwood pencils or of a bottle of gum or of an over-ripe apple which might have been left there and forgotten.

Mr. Duffy abhorred anything which betokened physical or mental disorder. A mediaeval doctor would have called him saturnine. His face, which carried the entire tale of his years, was of the brown tint of Dublin streets. On his long and rather large head grew dry black hair and a tawny moustache did not quite cover an unamiable mouth. His cheekbones also gave his face a harsh character; but there was no harshness in the eyes which, looking at the world from under their tawny eyebrows, gave the impression of a man ever alert to greet a redeeming instinct in others but often disappointed. He lived at a little distance from his body, regarding his own acts with doubtful side-glances. He had an odd autobiographical habit which led him to compose in his mind from time to time a short sentence about himself containing a subject in the third person and a predicate in the past tense. He never gave alms to beggars and walked firmly, carrying a stout hazel.

He had been for many years cashier of a private bank in Baggot Street. Every morning he came in from Chapelizod by tram. At midday he went to Dan Burke's and took his lunch — a bottle of lager beer and a small trayful of arrowroot biscuits. At four o'clock he was set free. He dined in an eating-house in George's Street where he felt himself safe from the society of Dublin's gilded youth and where there was a certain plain honesty in the bill of fare. His evenings were spent either before his landlady's piano or roaming about the outskirts of the city. His liking for Mozart's music brought him sometimes to an opera or a concert: these were the only dissipations of his life.

He had neither companions nor friends, church nor creed. He lived his spiritual life without any communion with others, visiting his relatives at Christmas and escorting them to the cemetery when they died. He performed these two social duties for old dignity's sake but conceded nothing further to the conventions which regulate the civic life. He allowed himself to think that in certain circumstances he would rob his bank but, as these circumstances never arose, his life rolled out evenly — an adventureless tale.

One evening he found himself sitting beside two ladies in the Rotunda. The house, thinly peopled and silent, gave distressing prophecy of failure. The lady who sat next to him looked round at the deserted house once or twice and then said:

"What a pity there is such a poor house to-night! It's so hard on people to have to sing to empty benches."

He took the remark as an invitation to talk. He was surprised that she seemed so little awkward. While they talked he tried to fix her permanently in his memory. When he learned that the young girl beside her was her daughter he judged her to be a year or so younger than himself. Her face, which must have been handsome, had remained intelligent. It was an oval face with strongly marked features. The eyes were very dark blue and steady. Their gaze began with a defiant note but was confused by what seemed a deliberate swoon of the pupil into the iris, revealing for an instant a temperament of great sensibility. The pupil reasserted itself quickly, this half-disclosed nature fell again under the reign of prudence, and her astrakhan jacket, moulding a bosom of a certain fullness, struck the note of defiance more definitely.

He met her again a few weeks afterwards at a concert in Earlsfort Terrace and seized the moments when her daughter's attention was diverted to become intimate. She alluded once or twice to her husband but her tone was not such as to make the allusion a warning. Her name was Mrs. Sinico. Her husband's great-great-grandfather had come from Leghorn. Her husband was captain of a mercantile boat plying between Dublin and Holland; and they had one child.

It is better to be able neither to read nor write than to be able to do nothing else.

WILLIAM HAZLITT

Meeting her a third time by accident he found courage to make an appointment. She came. This was the first of many meetings; they met always in the evening and chose the most quiet quarters for their walks together. Mr. Duffy, however, had a distaste for underhand ways and, finding that they were compelled to meet stealthily, he forced her to ask him to her house. Captain Sinico encouraged his visits, thinking that his daughter's hand was in question. He had dismissed his wife so sincerely from his gallery of pleasures that he did not suspect that anyone else would take an interest in her. As the husband was often away and the daughter out giving music lessons Mr. Duffy had many opportunities of enjoying the lady's society. Neither he nor she had had any such adventure before and neither was conscious of any incongruity. Little by little he entangled his thoughts with hers. He lent her books, provided her with ideas, shared his intellectual life with her. She listened to all.

Sometimes in return for his theories she gave out some fact of her own life. With almost maternal solicitude she urged him to let his nature open to the full: she became his confessor. He told her that for some time he had assisted at the meetings of an Irish Socialist Party where he had felt himself a unique figure amidst a score of sober workmen in a garret lit by an inefficient oil-lamp. When the party had divided into three sections, each under its own leader and in its own garret, he had discontinued his attendances. The workmen's discussions, he said, were too timorous; the interest they took in the question of wages was inordinate. He felt that they were hard-featured realists and that they resented an exactitude which was the produce of a leisure not within their reach. No social revolution, he told her, would be likely to strike Dublin for some centuries.

She asked him why did he not write out his thoughts. For what, he asked her, with careful scorn. To compete with phrasemongers, incapable of thinking consecutively for sixty seconds? To submit himself to the criticisms of an obtuse middle class which entrusted its morality to policemen and its fine arts to impresarios?

He went often to her little cottage outside Dublin; often they spent their evenings alone. Little by little, as their thoughts entangled, they spoke of subjects less remote. Her companionship was like a warm soil about an exotic. Many times she allowed the dark to fall upon them, refraining from lighting the lamp. The dark discreet room, their isolation, the music that still vibrated in their ears united them. This union exalted him, wore away the rough edges of his character, emotionalised his mental life. Sometimes he caught himself listening to the sound of his own voice. He thought that in her eyes he would ascend to an angelical stature; and, as he attached the fervent nature of his companion more and more closely to him, he heard the strange impersonal voice which he recognized as his own, insisting on the soul's incurable loneliness. We cannot give ourselves, it said: we are our own. The end of these discourses was that one night during which she had shown every sign of unusual excitement, Mrs. Sinico caught up his hand passionately and pressed it to her cheek.

Mr. Duffy was very much surprised. Her interpretation of his words disillusioned him. He did not visit her for a week; then he wrote to her asking her to meet him. As he did not wish their last interview to be troubled by the influence of their ruined confessional they met in a little cake-shop near the Parkgate. It was cold autumn weather but in spite of the cold they wandered up and down the roads of the Park for nearly three hours. They agreed to break off their intercourse: every bond, he said, is a bond to sorrow. When they came out of the Park they walked in silence towards the tram; but here she began to tremble so violently that, fearing another collapse on her part, he bade her good-bye quickly and left her. A few days later he received a parcel containing his books and music.

Four years passed. Mr. Duffy returned to his even way of life. His room still bore witness of the orderliness of his mind. Some new pieces of music encumbered the music-stand in the lower room and on his shelves stood two volumes by Nietzsche: *Thus Spake Zarathustra* and *The Gay Science*.

He wrote seldom in the sheaf of papers which lay in his desk. One of his sentences, written two months after his last interview with Mrs. Sinico, read: Love between man and man is impossible because there must not be sexual intercourse and friendship between man and woman is impossible because there must be sexual intercourse. He kept away from concerts lest he should meet her. His father died; the junior partner of the bank retired. And still every morning he went into the city by tram and every evening walked home from the city after having dined moderately in George's Street and read the evening paper for dessert.

One evening as he was about to put a morsel of corned beef and cabbage into his mouth his hand stopped. His eyes fixed themselves on a paragraph in the evening paper which he had propped against the water-carafe. He replaced the morsel of food on his plate and read the paragraph attentively. Then he drank a glass of water, pushed his plate to one side, doubled the paper down before him between his elbows and read the paragraph over and over again. The cabbage began to deposit a cold white grease on his plate. The girl came over to him to ask was his dinner not properly cooked. He said it was very good and ate a few mouthfuls of it with difficulty. Then he paid his bill and went out.

He walked along quickly through the November twilight, his stout hazel stick striking the ground regularly, the fringe of the buff *Mail* peeping out of a side-pocket of his tight reefer overcoat. On the lonely road which leads from the Parkgate to Chapelizod he slackened his pace. His stick struck the ground less emphatically and his breath, issuing irregularly, almost with a sighing sound, condensed in the wintry air. When he reached his house he went up at once to his bedroom and, taking the paper from his pocket, read the paragraph again by the failing light of the window. He read it not aloud, but moving his lips as a priest does when he reads the prayers *Secreto*. This was the paragraph:

DEATH OF A LADY AT SYDNEY PARADE

A PAINFUL CASE

To-day at the City of Dublin Hospital the Deputy Coroner (in the absence of Mr. Leverett) held an inquest on the body of Mrs. Emily Sinico, aged forty-three years, who was killed at Sydney Parade Station yesterday evening. The evidence showed that the deceased lady, while attempting to cross the line, was knocked down by the engine of the ten o'clock slow train from Kingstown, thereby sustaining injuries of the head and right side which led to her death.

James Lennon, driver of the engine, stated that he had been in the employment of the railway company for fifteen years. On hearing the guard's whistle he set the train in motion and a second or two afterwards brought it to rest in response to loud cries. The train was going slowly.

P. Dunne, railway porter, stated that as the train was about to start he observed a woman attempting to cross the lines. He ran towards her and shouted, but, before he could reach her, she was caught by the buffer of the engine and fell to the ground.

A Juror. "You saw the lady fall?"

Witness. "Yes."

Police-Sergeant Croly deposed that when he arrived he found the deceased lying on the platform apparently dead. He had the body taken to the waiting-room pending the arrival of the ambulance.

Constable 57 corroborated.

Dr. Halpin, assistant house-surgeon of the City of Dublin Hospital, stated that the deceased had two lower ribs fractured and had sustained severe contusions of the right shoulder. The right side of the head had been injured in the fall. The injuries were not sufficient to have caused death in a normal person. Death, in his opinion, had been probably due to shock and sudden failure of the heart's action.

Mr. H. B. Patterson Finlay, on behalf of the railroad company, expressed his deep regret at the accident. The company had always taken every precaution to prevent people crossing the lines except by the bridges, both by placing notices in every station and by the use of patent spring gates at level crossings. The deceased had been in the habit of crossing the lines late at night from platform to platform and, in view of certain other circumstances of the case, he did not think the railway officials were to blame.

Captain Sinico, of Leoville, Sydney Parade, husband of the deceased, also gave evidence. He stated that the deceased was his wife. He was not in Dublin at the time of the accident as he had arrived only that morning from Rotterdam. They had been married for twenty-two years and had lived happily until about two years ago when his wife began to be rather intemperate in her habits.

Miss Mary Sinico said that of late her mother had been in the habit of going out at night to buy spirits. She, witness, had often tried to reason with her mother and had induced her to join a League. She was not at home until an hour after the accident.

The jury returned a verdict in accordance with the medical evidence and exonerated Lennon from all blame.

The Deputy-Coroner said it was a most painful case, and expressed great sympathy with Captain Sinico and his daughter. He urged on the railway company to take strong measures to prevent the possibility of similar accidents in the future. No blame attached to anyone.

Mr. Duffy raised his eyes from the paper and gazed out of his window on the cheerless evening landscape. The river lay quiet beside the empty distillery and from time to time a light appeared in some house on the Lucan road. What an end! The whole narrative of her death revolted him and it revolted him to think that he had ever spoken to her of what he held sacred. The threadbare phrases, the inane expressions of sympathy, the cautious words of a reporter won over to conceal the details of a commonplace vulgar death attacked his stomach. Not merely had she degraded herself; she had degraded him. He saw the squalid tract of her vice, miserable and malodorous. His soul's companion! He thought of the hobbling wretches whom he had seen carrying cans and bottles to be filled by the barman. Just God, what an end! Evidently she had been unfit to live, without any strength of purpose, an easy prey to habits, one of the wrecks on which civilization has been reared. But that she could have sunk so low! Was it possible he had deceived himself so utterly about her? He remembered her outburst of that night and interpreted it in a harsher sense than he had ever done. He had no difficulty now in approving of the course he had taken.

As the light failed and his memory began to wander he thought her hand touched his. The shock which had first attacked his stomach was now attacking his nerves. He put on his overcoat and hat quickly and went out. The cold air met him on the threshold; it crept into the sleeves of his coat. When he came to the public-house at Chapelizod Bridge he went in and ordered a hot punch.

The proprietor served him obsequiously but did not venture to talk. There were five or six workingmen in the shop discussing the value of a gentleman's estate in County Kildare. They drank at intervals from their huge pint tumblers and smoked, spitting often on the floor and sometimes dragging the sawdust over their spirits with their heavy boots. Mr. Duffy sat on his stool and gazed at them, without seeing or hearing them. After a while they went out and he called for another punch. He sat a long time over it. The shop was very quiet. The proprietor sprawled on the counter reading the *Herald* and yawning. Now and again a tram was heard swishing along the lonely road outside.

As he sat there, living over his life with her and evoking alternately the two images in which he now conceived her, he realized that she was dead, that she had ceased to exist, that she had become a memory. He began to feel ill at ease. He asked himself what else could he have done. He could not have carried on a comedy of deception with her; he could not have lived with her openly. He had done what seemed to him best. How was he to blame? Now that she was gone he understood how lonely her life must have been, sitting night after night alone in that room. His life would be lonely too until he, too, died, ceased to exist, became a memory — if anyone remembered him.

'Tis a vanity common to all writers, to over-value their own productions.   JOHN DRYDEN

It was after nine o'clock when he left the shop. The night was cold and gloomy. He entered the Park by the first gate and walked along under the gaunt trees. He walked through the bleak alleys where they had walked four years before. She seemed to be near him in the darkness. At moments he seemed to feel her voice touch his ear, her hand touch his. He stood still to listen. Why had he withheld life from her? Why had he sentenced her to death? He felt his moral nature falling to pieces.

When he gained the crest of the Magazine Hill he halted and looked along the river towards Dublin, the lights of which burned redly and hospitably in the cold night. He looked down the slope and, at the base, in the shadow of the wall of the Park, he saw some human figures lying. Those venal and furtive lovers filled him with despair. He gnawed the rectitude of his life; he felt that he had been outcast from life's feast. One human being had seemed to love him and he had denied her life and happiness: he had sentenced her to ignominy, a death of shame. He knew that the prostrate creatures down by the wall were watching him and wished him gone. No one wanted him; he was outcast from life's feast. He turned his eyes to the grey gleaming river, winding along towards Dublin. Beyond the river he saw a goods train winding out of Kingsbridge Station, like a worm with a fiery head winding through the darkness, obstinately and laboriously. It passed slowly out of sight; but still he heard in his ears the laborious drone of the engine reiterating the syllables of her name.

He turned back the way he had come, the rhythm of the engine pounding in his ears. He began to doubt the reality of what memory told him. He halted under a tree and allowed the rhythm to die away. He could not feel her near him in the darkness nor her voice touch his ear. He waited for some minutes listening. He could hear nothing: the night was perfectly silent. He listened again: perfectly silent. He felt that he was alone.

Bliss

KATHERINE MANSFIELD

Although Bertha Young was thirty she still had moments like this when she wanted to run instead of walk, to take dancing steps on and off the pavement, to bowl a hoop, to throw something up in the air and catch it again, or to stand still and laugh at — nothing — at nothing, simply.

What can you do if you are thirty and, turning the corner of your own street, you are overcome, suddenly, by a feeling of bliss — absolute bliss! — as though you'd suddenly swallowed a bright piece of that late afternoon sun and it burned in your bosom, sending out a little shower of sparks into every particle, into every finger and toe? . . .

Oh, is there no way you can express it without being "drunk and disorderly"? How idiotic civilization is! Why be given a body if you have to keep it shut up in a case like a rare, rare fiddle?

"No, that about the fiddle is not quite what I mean," she thought, running up the steps and feeling in her bag for the key — she'd forgotten it, as usual — and rattling the letterbox. "It's not what I mean, because — Thank you, Mary" — she went into the hall. "Is nurse back?"

"Yes, M'm."

"And has the fruit come?"

"Yes, M'm. Everything's come."

"Bring the fruit up to the dining-room, will you? I'll arrange it before I go upstairs."

It was dusky in the dining-room and quite chilly. But all the same Bertha threw off her coat; she could not bear the tight clasp of it another moment, and the cold air fell on her arms.

But in her bosom there was still that bright glowing place — that shower of little sparks coming from it. It was almost unbearable. She hardly dared to breathe for fear of fanning it higher, and yet she breathed deeply, deeply. She hardly dared to look into the cold mirror — but she did look, and it gave her back a woman, radiant, with smiling, trembling lips, with big, dark eyes and an air of listening, waiting for something . . . divine to happen . . . that she knew must happen . . . infallibly.

Mary brought in the fruit on a tray and with it a glass bowl, and a blue dish, very lovely, with a strange sheen on it as though it had been dipped in milk.

"Shall I turn on the light, M'm?"

"No, thank you. I can see quite well."

There were tangerines and apples stained with strawberry pink. Some yellow pears, smooth as silk, some white grapes covered with a silver bloom and a big cluster of purple ones. These last she had bought to tone in with the new dining-room carpet. Yes, that did sound rather far-fetched and absurd, but it was really why she had bought them. She had thought in the shop: "I must have some purple ones to bring the carpet up to the table." And it had seemed quite sense at the time.

When she had finished with them and had made two pyramids of these bright round shapes, she stood away from the table to get the effect — and it really was most curious. For the dark table seemed to melt into the dusky light and the glass dish and the blue bowl to float in the air. This, of course in her present mood, was so incredibly beautiful. . . . She began to laugh.

"No, no, I'm getting hysterical." And she seized her bag and coat and ran upstairs to the nursery.

Nurse sat at a low table giving Little B her supper after her bath. The baby had on a white flannel gown and a blue woollen jacket, and her dark, fine hair was brushed up into a funny little peak. She looked up when she saw her mother and began to jump.

"Now, my lovely, eat it up like a good girl," said Nurse, setting her lips in a way that Bertha knew, and that meant she had come into the nursery at another wrong moment.

"Has she been good, Nanny?"

"She's been a little sweet all the afternoon," whispered Nanny. "We went to the park and I sat down on a chair and took her out of the pram and a big dog came along and put its head on my knee and she clutched its ear, tugged it. Oh, you should have seen her."

Bertha wanted to ask if it wasn't rather dangerous to let her clutch at a strange dog's ear. But she did not dare to. She stood watching them, her hands by her side, like the poor little girl in front of the rich little girl with the doll.

The baby looked up at her again, stared, and then smiled so charmingly that Bertha couldn't help crying:

No book is worth anything which is not worth much; nor is it serviceable until it has been read, and reread, and loved, and loved again; and marked, so that you can refer to the passages you want in it as a soldier can seize the weapon he needs in an armory, or a housewife bring the spice she needs from her store.

JOHN RUSKIN

"Oh, Nanny, do let me finish giving her her supper while you put the bath things away."

"Well, M'm, she oughtn't to be changed hands while she's eating," said Nanny, still whispering. "It unsettles her; it's very likely to upset her."

How absurd it was. Why have a baby if it has to be kept — not in a case like a rare, rare fiddle — but in another woman's arms?

"Oh, I must!" said she.

Very offended, Nanny handed her over.

"Now, don't excite her after her supper. You know you do, M'm. And I have such a time with her after!"

Thank heaven! Nanny went out of the room with the bath towels.

"Now I've got you to myself, my little precious," said Bertha, as the baby leaned against her.

She ate delightfully, holding up her lips for the spoon and then waving her hands. Sometimes she wouldn't let the spoon go; and sometimes, just as Bertha had filled it, she waved it away to the four winds.

When the soup was finished Bertha turned round to the fire.

"You're nice — you're very nice!" said she, kissing her warm baby. "I'm fond of you. I like you."

And, indeed, she loved Little B so much — her neck as she bent forward, her exquisite toes as they shone transparent in the firelight — that all her feeling of bliss came back again, and again she didn't know how to express it — what to do with it.

"You're wanted on the telephone," said Nanny, coming back in triumph and seizing *her* Little B.

Down she flew. It was Harry.

"Oh, is that you, Ber? Look here. I'll be late. I'll take a taxi and come along as quickly as I can, but get dinner put back ten minutes — will you? All right?"

"Yes, perfectly. Oh, Harry!"

"Yes?"

What had she to say? She'd nothing to say. She only wanted to get in touch with him for a moment. She couldn't absurdly cry: "Hasn't it been a divine day!"

"What is it?" rapped out the little voice.

"Nothing. *Entendu*," said Bertha, and hung up the receiver, thinking how more than idiotic civilization was.

They had people coming to dinner. The Norman Knights — a very sound couple — he was about to start a theatre, and she was awfully keen on interior decoration, a young man, Eddie Warren, who had just published a little book of poems and whom everybody was asking to dine, and a "find" of Bertha's called Pearl Fulton. What Miss Fulton did, Bertha didn't know. They had met at the club and Bertha had fallen in love with her, as she always did fall in love with beautiful women who had something strange about them.

The provoking thing was that, though they had been about together and met a number of times and really talked, Bertha couldn't yet make her out. Up to a certain point Miss Fulton was rarely, wonderfully frank, but the certain point was there, and beyond that she would not go.

Was there anything beyond it? Harry said, "No." Voted her dullish, and "cold like all blond women, with a touch, perhaps, of anæmia of the brain." But Bertha wouldn't agree with him; not yet, at any rate.

"No, the way she has of sitting with her head a little on one side, and smiling, has something behind it, Harry, and I must find out what that something is."

"Most likely it's a good stomach," answered Harry.

He made a point of catching Bertha's heels with replies of that kind . . . "liver frozen, my dear girl," or "pure flatulence," or "kidney disease," . . . and so on. For some strange reason Bertha liked this, and almost admired it in him very much.

She went into the drawing-room and lighted the fire; then, picking up the cushions, one by one, that Mary had disposed so carefully, she threw them back on to the chairs and the couches. That made all the difference; the room came alive at once. As she was about to throw the last one she surprised herself by suddenly hugging it to her, passionately, passionately. But it did not put out the fire in her bosom. Oh, on the contrary!

The windows of the drawing-room opened on to a balcony overlooking the garden. At the far end, against the wall, there was a tall, slender pear tree in fullest, richest bloom; it stood perfect, as though becalmed against the jade-green sky. Bertha couldn't help feeling, even from this distance, that it had not a single bud or a faded petal. Down below, in the garden beds, the red and yellow tulips, heavy with flowers, seemed to lean upon the dusk. A grey cat, dragging its belly, crept across the lawn, and a black one, its shadow, trailed after. The sight of them, so intent and so quick, gave Bertha a curious shiver.

"What creepy things cats are!" she stammered, and she turned away from the window and began walking up and down. . . .

How strong the jonquils smelled in the warm room. Too strong? Oh, no. And yet, as though overcome, she flung down on a couch and pressed her hands to her eyes.

"I'm too happy — too happy!" she murmured.

And she seemed to see on her eyelids the lovely pear tree with its wide open blossoms as a symbol of her own life.

Really — really — she had everything. She was young. Harry and she were as much in love as ever, and they got on together splendidly and were really good pals. She had an adorable baby. They didn't have to worry about money. They had this absolutely satisfactory house and garden. And friends — modern, thrilling friends, writers and painters and poets or people keen on social questions — just the kind of friends they wanted. And then there were books, and there was music, and she had found a wonderful little dressmaker, and they were going abroad in the summer, and their new cook made the most superb omelettes. . . .

"I'm absurd. Absurd!" She sat up; but she felt quite dizzy, quite drunk. It must have been the spring.

Yes, it was the spring. Now she was so tired she could not drag herself upstairs to dress.

A white dress, a string of jade beads, green shoes and stockings. It wasn't intentional. She had thought of this scheme hours before she stood at the drawing-room window.

Her petals rustled softly into the hall, and she kissed Mrs. Norman

Knight, who was taking off the most amusing orange coat with a procession of black monkeys around the hem and up the fronts.

". . . Why! Why! Why is the middle-class so stodgy — so utterly without a sense of humour! My dear, it's only by a fluke that I am here at all — Norman being the protective fluke. For my darling monkeys so upset the train that it rose to a man and simply ate me with its eyes. Didn't laugh — wasn't amused — that I should have loved. No, just stared — and bored me through and through."

"But the cream of it was," said Norman, pressing a large tortoise-shell-rimmed monocle into his eye, "you don't mind me telling this, Face, do you?" (In their home and among their friends they called each other Face and Mug.) "The cream of it was when she, being full fed, turned to the woman beside her and said: 'Haven't you ever seen a monkey before?'"

"Oh, yes!" Mrs. Norman Knight joined in the laughter. "Wasn't that too absolutely creamy?"

And a funnier thing still was that now her coat was off she did look like a very intelligent monkey — who had even made that yellow silk dress out of scraped banana skins. And her amber ear-rings; they were like little dangling nuts.

"This is a sad, sad fall!" said Mug, pausing in front of Little B's perambulator. "When the perambulator comes into the hall — " and he waved the rest of the quotation away.

The bell rang. It was lean, pale Eddie Warren (as usual) in a state of acute distress.

"It *is* the right house, *isn't* it?" he pleaded.

"Oh, I think so — I hope so," said Bertha brightly.

"I have had such a *dreadful* experience with a taxi-man; he was *most* sinister. I couldn't get him to *stop*. The *more* I knocked and called the *faster* he went. And *in* the moonlight this *bizarre* figure with the *flattened* head *crouching* over the *lit-tle* wheel . . ."

He shuddered, taking off an immense white silk scarf. Bertha noticed that his socks were white, too — most charming.

"But how dreadful!" she cried.

"Yes, it really was," said Eddie, following her into the drawing-room. "I saw myself *driving* through Eternity in a *timeless* taxi."

He knew the Norman Knights. In fact, he was going to write a play for N.K. when the theatre scheme came off.

"Well, Warren, how's the play?" said Norman Knight, dropping his monocle and giving his eye a moment in which to rise to the surface before it was screwed down again.

And Mrs. Norman Knight. "Oh, Mr. Warren, what happy socks!"

"I *am* so glad you like them," said he, staring at his feet. "They seem to have got so *much* whiter since the moon rose." And he turned his lean sorrowful young face to Bertha. "There *is* a moon, you know."

She wanted to cry: "I am sure there is — often — often!"

He really was a most attractive person. But so was Face, crouched before the fire in her banana skins, and so was Mug, smoking a cigarette and saying as he flicked the ash: "Why doth the bridegroom tarry?"

"There he is, now."

Bang went the front door open and shut. Harry shouted: "Hullo, you people. Down in five minutes." And they heard him swarm up the stairs. Bertha couldn't help smiling; she knew how he loved doing things at high pressure. What, after all, did an extra five minutes matter? But he would pretend to himself that they mattered beyond measure. And then he would make a great point of coming into the drawing-room, extravagantly cool and collected.

Harry had such a zest for life. Oh, how she appreciated it in him. And his passion for fighting — for seeking in everything that came up against him another test of his power and of his courage — that, too, she understood. Even when it made him just occasionally, to other people, who didn't know him well, a little ridiculous perhaps. . . . For there were moments when he rushed into battle where no battle was. . . . She talked and laughed and positively forgot until he had come in (just as she had imagined) that Pearl Fulton had not turned up.

"I wonder if Miss Fulton has forgotten?"

"I expect so," said Harry. "Is she on the 'phone?"

"Ah! There's a taxi, now." And Bertha smiled with that little air of proprietorship that she always assumed while her women finds were new and mysterious. "She lives in taxis."

The Master said to Tzu-hsia: "Read to become a gentleman; do not read as the vulgar do."

CONFUCIUS

"She'll run to fat if she does," said Harry coolly, ringing the bell for dinner. "Frightful danger for blond women."

"Harry — don't," warned Bertha, laughing up at him.

Came another tiny moment, while they waited, laughing and talking, just a trifle too much at their ease, a trifle too unaware. And then Miss Fulton, all in silver, with a silver fillet binding her pale blond hair, came in smiling, her head a little on one side.

"Am I late?"

"No, not at all," said Bertha. "Come along." And she took her arm and they moved into the dining-room.

What was there in the touch of that cool arm that could fan — fan —

start blazing — blazing — the fire of bliss that Bertha did not know what to do with?

Miss Fulton did not look at her; but then she seldom did look at people directly. Her heavy eyelids lay upon her eyes and the strange half smile came and went upon her lips as though she lived by listening rather than seeing. But Bertha knew, suddenly, as if the longest, most intimate look had passed between them — as if they had said to each other: "You, too?" — that Pearl Fulton, stirring the beautiful red soup in the grey plate, was feeling just what she was feeling.

And the others? Face and Mug, Eddie and Harry, their spoons rising and falling — dabbing their lips with their napkins, crumbling bread, fiddling with the forks and glasses and talking.

"I met her at the Alpha show — the weirdest little person. She'd not only cut off her hair, but she seemed to have taken a dreadfully good snip off her legs and arms and her neck and her poor little nose as well."

"Isn't she very *liée* with Michael Oat?"

"The man who wrote *Love in False Teeth?*"

"He wants to write a play for me. One act. One man. Decides to commit suicide. Gives all the reasons why he should and why he shouldn't. And just as he has made up his mind either to do it or not to do it — curtain. Not half a bad idea."

"What's he going to call it — 'Stomach Trouble'?"

"I *think* I've come across the *same* idea in a lit-tle French review, *quite* unknown in England."

No, they didn't share it. They were dears — dears — and she loved having them there, at her table, and giving them delicious food and wine. In fact, she longed to tell them how delightful they were, and what a decorative group they made, how they seemed to set one another off and how they reminded her of a play by Tchekof!

Harry was enjoying his dinner. It was part of his — well, not his nature, exactly, and certainly not his pose — his — something or other — to talk about food and to glory in his "shameless passion for the white flesh of the lobster" and "the green of pistachio ices — green and cold like the eyelids of Egyptian dancers."

When he looked up at her and said: "Bertha, this is a very admirable *soufflé!*" she almost could have wept with childlike pleasure.

Oh, why did she feel so tender towards the whole world tonight? Everything was good — was right. All that happened seemed to fill again her brimming cup of bliss.

And still, in the back of her mind, there was the pear tree. It would be silver now, in the light of poor dear Eddie's moon, silver as Miss Fulton, who sat there turning a tangerine in her slender fingers that were so pale a light seemed to come from them.

What she simply couldn't make out — what was miraculous — was how she should have guessed Miss Fulton's mood so exactly and so instantly. For she never doubted for a moment that she was right, and yet what had she to go on? Less than nothing.

"I believe this does happen very, very rarely between women. Never between men," thought Bertha. "But while I am making the coffee in the drawing-room perhaps she will 'give a sign.'"

What she meant by that she did not know, and what would happen after that she could not imagine.

While she thought like this she saw herself talking and laughing. She had to talk because of her desire to laugh.

"I must laugh or die."

But when she noticed Face's funny little habit of tucking something down the front of her bodice — as if she kept a tiny, secret hoard of nuts there, too — Bertha had to dig her nails into her hands — so as not to laugh too much.

It was over at last. And: "Come and see my new coffee machine," said Bertha.

"We only have a new coffee machine once a fortnight," said Harry. Face took her arm this time. Miss Fulton bent her head and followed after.

The fire had died down in the drawing-room to a red, flickering "nest of baby phœnixes," said Face.

"Don't turn up the light for a moment. It is so lovely." And down she crouched by the fire again. She was always cold . . . "without her little red flannel jacket, of course," thought Bertha.

At that moment Miss Fulton "gave the sign."

"Have you a garden?" said the cool, sleepy voice.

This was so exquisite on her part that all Bertha could do was to obey. She crossed the room, pulled the curtains apart, and opened those long windows.

"There!" she breathed.

And the two women stood side by side looking at the slender, flowering tree. Although it was so still it seemed, like the flame of a candle, to stretch up, to point, to quiver in the bright air, to grow taller and taller as they gazed — almost to touch the rim of the round, silver moon.

How long did they stand there? Both, as it were, caught in that circle of unearthly light, understanding each other perfectly, creatures of another world, and wondering what they were to do in this one with all this blissful treasure that burned in their bosoms and dropped, in silver flowers, from their hair and hands?

For ever — for a moment? And did Miss Fulton murmur: "Yes. Just *that*." Or did Bertha dream it?

Then the light was snapped on and Face made the coffee and Harry said: "My dear Mrs. Knight, don't ask me about my baby. I never see her. I shan't feel the slightest interest in her until she has a lover," and Mug took his eye out of the conservatory for a moment and then put it under glass again and Eddie Warren drank his coffee and set down the cup with a face of anguish as though he had drunk and seen the spider.

"What I want to do is to give the young men a show. I believe London is simply teeming with first-chop, unwritten plays. What I want to say to 'em is: 'Here's the theatre. Fire ahead.' "

"You know, my dear, I am going to decorate a room for the Jacob Nathans. Oh, I am so tempted to do a fried-fish scheme, with the backs of the chairs shaped like frying pans and lovely chip potatoes embroidered all over the curtains."

"The trouble with our young writing men is that they are still too romantic. You can't put out to sea without being seasick and wanting a basin. Well, why won't they have the courage of those basins?"

"A *dreadful* poem about a *girl* who was *violated* by a beggar *without* a nose in a lit-tle wood. . . ."

Miss Fulton sank into the lowest, deepest chair and Harry handed round the cigarettes.

A man will write at any time, if he will set himself doggedly to it.
SAMUEL JOHNSON

From the way he stood in front of her shaking the silver box and saying abruptly: "Egyptians? Turkish? Virginian? They're all mixed up." Bertha realized that she not only bored him; he really disliked her. And she decided from the way Miss Fulton said: 'No, thank you, I won't smoke," that she felt it, too, and was hurt.

"Oh, Harry, don't dislike her. You are quite wrong about her. She's wonderful, wonderful. And, besides, how can you feel so differently about someone who means so much to me. I shall try to tell you when we are in bed to-night what has been happening. What she and I have shared."

At those last words something strange and almost terrifying darted into Bertha's mind. And this something blind and smiling whispered to her: "Soon these people will go. The house will be quiet — quiet. The lights will be out. And you and he will be alone together in the dark room — the warm bed. . . ."

She jumped up from her chair and ran over to the piano.

"What a pity someone does not play!" she cried. "What a pity somebody does not play."

For the first time in her life Bertha Young desired her husband.

Oh, she'd loved him — she'd been in love with him, of course, in every other way, but just not in that way. And, equally, of course, she'd understood that he was different. They'd discussed it so often. It had worried her dreadfully at first to find that she was so cold, but after a time it had not seemed to matter. They were so frank with each other — such good pals. That was the best of being modern.

But now — ardently! ardently! The word ached in her ardent body! Was this what that feeling of bliss had been leading up to? But then — then —

"My dear," said Mrs. Norman Knight, "you know our shame. We are the victims of time and train. We live in Hampstead. It's been so nice."

"I'll come with you into the hall," said Bertha. "I loved having you. But you must not miss the last train. That's so awful, isn't it?"

"Have a whiskey, Knight, before you go," called Harry.

"No, thanks, old chap."

Bertha squeezed his hand for that as she shook it.

"Good night, good-bye," she cried from the top step, feeling that this self of hers was taking leave of them for ever.

When she got back into the drawing-room the others were on the move.

". . . Then you can come part of the way in my taxi."

"I shall be *so* thankful *not* to have to face *another* drive *alone* after my *dreadful* experience."

"You can get a taxi at the rank just at the end of the street. You won't have to walk more than a few yards."

"That's a comfort. I'll go and put on my coat."

Miss Fulton moved towards the hall and Bertha was following when Harry almost pushed past.

"Let me help you."

Bertha knew that he was repenting his rudeness — she let him go. What a boy he was in some ways — so impulsive — so — simple.

And Eddie and she were left by the fire.

"I *wonder* if you have seen Bilk's *new* poem called *Table d'Hôte*, said Eddie softly. "It's *so* wonderful. In the last Anthology. Have you got a copy? I'd *so* like to *show* it to you. It begins with an *incredibly* beautiful line: 'Why Must it Always be Tomato Soup?'"

"Yes," said Bertha. And she moved noiselessly to a table opposite the drawing-room door and Eddie glided noiselessly after her. She picked up the little book and gave it to him: they had not made a sound.

While he looked it up she turned her head towards the hall. And she saw . . . Harry with Miss Fulton's coat in his arms and Miss Fulton with her back turned to him and her head bent. He tossed the coat away, put his hands on her shoulders and turned her violently to him. His lips said: "I adore you," and Miss Fulton laid her moonbeam fingers on his cheeks and smiled her sleepy smile. Harry's nostrils quivered: his lips curled back in a hideous grin while he whispered: "Tomorrow," and with her eyelids Miss Fulton said: "Yes."

"Here it is," said Eddie. " 'Why Must it Always be Tomato Soup?' " It's so *deeply* true, don't you feel? Tomato soup is so *dreadfully* eternal."

"If you prefer," said Harry's voice, very loud, from the hall, "I can phone you a cab to come to the door."

"Oh, no. It's not necessary," said Miss Fulton, and she came up to Bertha and gave her the slender fingers to hold.

"Good-bye. Thank you so much."

"Good-bye," said Bertha.

Miss Fulton held her hand a moment longer.

"Your lovely pear tree!" she murmured.

And then she was gone, with Eddie following, like the black cat following the grey cat.

"I'll shut up shop," said Harry, extravagantly cool and collected.

"Your lovely pear tree — pear tree — pear tree!"

Bertha simply ran over to the long windows.

"Oh, what is going to happen now?" she cried.

But the pear tree was as lovely as ever and as full of flower and as still.

The Colonel's Lady

SOMERSET MAUGHAM

All this happened two or three years before the outbreak of the war.

The Peregrines were having breakfast. Though they were alone and the table was long they sat at opposite ends of it. From the walls George Peregrine's ancestors, painted by the fashionable painters of the day, looked down upon them. The butler brought in the morning post. There were several letters for the Colonel, business letters, the *Times* and a small parcel for his wife Evie. He looked at his letters and then, opening the *Times*, began to read it. They finished breakfast and rose from the table. He noticed that his wife hadn't opened the parcel.

"What's that?" he asked.

"Only some books."

"Shall I open it for you?"

"If you like."

He hated to cut string and so with some difficulty untied the knots.

"But they're all the same," he said when he had unwrapped the parcel. "What on earth d'you want six copies of the same book for?" He opened one of them. "Poetry." Then he looked at the title page. *When Pyramids Decay*, he read, by E. K. Hamilton. Eva Katherine Hamilton: that was his wife's maiden name. He looked at her with smiling surprise. "Have you written a book, Evie? You are a slyboots."

"I didn't think it would interest you very much. Would you like a copy?"

"Well, you know poetry isn't much in my line, but — yes, I'd like a copy; I'll read it. I'll take it along to my study. I've got a lot to do this morning."

He gathered up the *Times*, his letters and the book and went out. His study was a large and comfortable room, with a big desk, leather armchairs and what he called "trophies of the chase" on the walls. In the bookshelves were works of reference, books on farming, gardening, fishing and shooting, and books on the last war in which he had won an M.C. and a D.S.O. For before his marriage he had been in the Welsh Guards. At the end of the war he retired and settled down to the life of a country gentleman in the spacious house, some twenty miles from Sheffield, which one of his forebears had built in the reign of George II. George Peregrine had an estate of some fifteen hundred acres which he managed with ability; he was a justice of the peace and performed his duties conscientiously. During the season he rode to hounds two days a week. He was a good shot, a golfer and though now a little over fifty could still play a hard game of tennis. He could describe himself with propriety as an all-round sportsman.

He had been putting on weight lately, but was still a fine figure of a man; tall, with gray curly hair, only just beginning to grow thin on the crown, frank blue eyes, good features and a high colour. He was a public-spirited man, chairman of any number of local organizations and, as became his class and station, a loyal member of the Conservative party. He looked upon it as his duty to see to the welfare of the people on his estate and it was a satisfaction to him to know that Evie could be trusted to tend the sick and succour the poor. He had built a cottage hospital on the outskirts of the village and paid the wages of a nurse out of his own pocket. All he asked of the recipients of his bounty was that at elections, county or general, they should vote for his candidate. He was a friendly man, affable to his inferiors, considerate with his tenants and popular with the neighbouring gentry. He would have been pleased and at the same time slightly embarrassed if someone had told him he was a jolly good fellow. That was what he wanted to be. He desired no higher praise.

It was hard luck that he had no children. He would have been an excellent father, kindly but strict, and would have brought up his sons as a gentleman's sons should be brought up, sent them to Eton, you know, taught them to fish, shoot and ride. As it was, his heir was a nephew, son of his brother killed in a motor accident, not a bad boy, but not a chip off the old block, no, sir, far from it, and would you believe it, his fool of a mother was sending him to a co-educational school. Evie had been a sad disappointment to him. Of course she was a lady, and she had a bit of money of her own; she managed the house uncommonly well and she was a good hostess. The village people adored her. She had been a pretty little thing when he married her, with a creamy skin, light brown hair and a trim figure, healthy too and not a bad tennis player; he couldn't understand why she'd had no children; of course she was faded now, she must be getting on for five and forty; her skin was drab, her hair had lost its sheen and she was as thin as a rail. She was always neat and suitably dressed, but she didn't seem to bother how she looked, she wore no make-up and didn't even use lipstick, sometimes at night when she dolled herself up for a party you could tell that once she'd been quite attractive, but ordinarily she was — well, the sort of woman you simply didn't notice. A nice woman, of course, a good wife, and it wasn't her fault if she was barren, but it was tough on a fellow who wanted an heir of his own loins; she hadn't any vitality, that's what was the matter with her. He supposed he'd been in love with her when he asked her to marry him, at least sufficiently in love for a man who wanted to marry and settle down, but with time he discovered that they had nothing much in common. She didn't care about hunting, and fishing bored her. Naturally they'd drifted apart. He had to do her the justice to admit that she'd never bothered him. There'd been no scenes. They had no quarrels. She seemed to take it for granted that he should go his own way. When he went up to London now and then she never wanted to come with him. He had a girl there, well, she wasn't exactly a girl, she was thirty-five if she was a day, but she was blonde and luscious and he only had to wire ahead of time and they'd dine, do a show and spend the night together. Well, a man, a healthy normal man had to have some fun in his life. The thought crossed his mind that if Evie hadn't been such a good woman she'd have been a better wife; but it was not the sort of thought that he welcomed and he put it away from him.

George Peregrine finished his *Times* and being a considerate fellow rang the bell and told the butler to take the paper to Evie. Then he looked at his watch. It was half-past ten and at eleven he had an appointment with one of his tenants. He had half an hour to spare.

"I'd better have a look at Evie's book," he said to himself.

He took it up with a smile. Evie had a lot of highbrow books in her sitting room, not the sort of books that interested him, but if they amused her he had no objection to her reading them. He noticed that the volume he now held in his hand contained no more than ninety pages. That was all to the good. He shared Edgar Allan Poe's opinion that poems should be short. But as he turned the pages he noticed that several of Evie's had long lines of irregular length and didn't rhyme. He didn't like that. At his first school, when he was a little boy, he remembered learning a poem that began: *The boy stood on the burning deck* and later, at Eton, one that started: *Ruin seize thee, ruthless king,* and then there was Henry V; they'd had to take that one half. He stared at Evie's pages with consternation.

"That's not what I call poetry," he said.

Fortunately it wasn't all like that. Interspersed with the pieces that looked so odd, lines of three or four words and then a line of ten or fifteen, there were little poems, quite short, that rhymed, thank God, with the lines all the same length. Several of the pages were just headed with the word *Sonnet,* and out of curiosity he counted the lines; there were fourteen of them. He read them. They seemed all right, but he didn't quite know what they were all about. He repeated to himself: *Ruin seize thee, ruthless king.*

"Poor Evie," he sighed.

At that moment the farmer he was expecting was ushered into the study, and putting the book down he made him welcome. They embarked on their business.

"I read your book, Evie," he said as they sat down to lunch. "Jolly good. Did it cost you a packet to have it printed?"

"No, I was lucky. I sent it to a publisher and he took it."

"Not much money in poetry, my dear," he said in his good-natured, hearty way.

"No, I don't suppose there is. What did Bannock want to see you about this morning?"

Bannock was the tenant who had interrupted his reading of Evie's poems.

"He's asked me to advance the money for a pedigree bull he wants to buy. He's a good man and I've half a mind to do it."

George Peregrine saw that Evie didn't want to talk about her book and he was not sorry to change the subject. He was glad she had used her maiden name on the title page; he didn't suppose anyone would ever hear about the book, but he was proud of his own unusual name and he wouldn't have liked it if some damned penny-a-liner had made fun of Evie's effort in one of the papers.

During the few weeks that followed he thought it tactful not to ask Evie any questions about her venture into verse and she never referred to it. It might have been a discreditable incident that they had silently agreed not to mention. But then a strange thing happened. He had to go to London on business and he took Daphne out to dinner. That was the name of the girl with whom he was in the habit of passing a few agreeable hours whenever he went to town.

"Oh, George," she said, "is that your wife who's written a book they're all talking about?"

"What on earth d'you mean?"

"Well, there's a fellow I know who's a critic. He took me out to dinner the other night and he had a book with him. 'Got anything for me to read?' I said. 'What's that?' 'Oh, I don't think that's your cup of tea,' he said.

'It's poetry. I've just been reviewing it.' 'No poetry for me,' I said. 'It's about the hottest stuff I ever read,' he said. 'Selling like hot cakes. And it's damned good.'"

"Who's the book by?" asked George.

"A woman called Hamilton. My friend told me that wasn't her real name. He said her real name was Peregrine. 'Funny,' I said, 'I know a fellow called Peregrine.' 'Colonel in the army,' he said. 'Lives near Sheffield.'"

"I'd just as soon you didn't talk about me to your friends," said George with a frown of vexation.

"Keep your shirt on, dearie. Who'd you take me for? I just said, 'It's not the same one.'" Daphne giggled. "My friend said: 'They say he's a regular Colonel Blimp.'"

George had a keen sense of humour.

"You could tell them better than that," he laughed. "If my wife had written a book I'd be the first to know about it, wouldn't I?"

"I suppose you would."

Anyhow the matter didn't interest her and when the Colonel began to talk of other things she forgot about it. He put it out of his mind too. There was nothing to it, he decided, and that silly fool of a critic had just been pulling Daphne's leg. He was amused at the thought of her tackling that book because she had been told it was hot stuff and then finding it just a lot of stuff cut up into unequal lines.

He was a member of several clubs and next day he thought he'd lunch at one in St. James's Street. He was catching a train back to Sheffield early in the afternoon. He was sitting in a comfortable armchair having a glass of sherry before going into the dining-room when an old friend came up to him.

You, for example, clever to a fault, the rough and ready man, who write apace, read somewhat seldomer, think perhaps even less.

ROBERT BROWNING

"Well, old boy, how's life?" he said. "How d'you like being the husband of a celebrity?"

George Peregrine looked at his friend. He thought he saw an amused twinkle in his eyes.

"I don't know what you're talking about," he answered.

"Come off it, George. Everyone knows E. K. Hamilton is your wife. Not often a book of verse has a success like that. Look here, Henry Dashwood is lunching with me. He'd like to meet you."

"Who the devil is Henry Dashwood and why should he want to meet me?"

"Oh, my dear fellow, what do you do with yourself all the time in the country? Henry's about the best critic we've got. He wrote a wonderful review of Evie's book. D'you mean to say she didn't show it you?"

Before George could answer his friend had called a man over. A tall, thin man, with a high forehead, a beard, a long nose and a stoop, just the sort of man whom George was prepared to dislike at first sight. Introductions were effected. Henry Dashwood sat down.

"Is Mrs. Peregrine in London by any chance? I should very much like to meet her," he said.

"No, my wife doesn't like London. She prefers the country," said George stiffly.

"She wrote me a very nice letter about my review. I was pleased. You know, we critics get more kicks than halfpence. I was simply bowled over by her book. It's so fresh and original, very modern without being obscure. She seems to be as much at her ease in free verse as in the classical metres." Then because he was a critic he thought he should criticize. "Some times her ear is a trifle at fault, but you can say the same of Emily Dickinson. There are several of those short lyrics of hers that might have been written by Landor."

All this was gibberish to George Peregrine. The man was nothing but a disgusting highbrow. But the Colonel had good manners and he answered with proper civility. Henry Dashwood went on as though he hadn't spoken.

"But what makes the book so outstanding is the passion that throbs in every line. So many of these young poets are so anaemic, cold, bloodless, dully intellectual, but here you have real naked, earthy passion; of course deep, sincere emotion like that is tragic — ah, my dear Colonel, how right Heine was when he said that the poet makes little songs out of his great sorrows. You know, now and then, as I read and reread those heart-rending pages I thought of Sappho."

This was too much for George Peregrine and he got up.

"Well, it's jolly nice of you to say such nice things about my wife's little book. I'm sure she'll be delighted. But I must bolt. I've got to catch a train and I want to get a bite of lunch."

"Damned fool," he said irritably to himself as he walked upstairs to the dining-room.

He got home in time for dinner and after Evie had gone to bed he went into his study and looked for her book. He thought he'd just glance through it again to see for himself what they were making such a fuss about, but he couldn't find it. Evie must have taken it away.

"Silly," he muttered.

He'd told her he thought it jolly good. What more could a fellow be expected to say? Well, it didn't matter. He lit his pipe and read the *Field* till he felt sleepy. But a week or so later it happened that he had to go into Sheffield for the day. He lunched there at his club. He had nearly finished when the Duke of Haverel came in. This was the great local magnate and of course the Colonel knew him, but only to say how d'you do to; and he was surprised when the Duke stopped at his table.

"We're so sorry your wife couldn't come to us for the week end," he said, with a sort of shy cordiality. "We're expecting rather a nice lot of people."

George was taken aback. He guessed that the Haverels had asked him and Evie over the week end and Evie, without saying a word to him about it, had refused. He had the presence of mind to say he was sorry too.

"Better luck next time," said the Duke pleasantly and moved on.

Colonel Peregrine was very angry and when he got home he said to his wife:

"Look here, what's this about our being asked over to Haverel? Why on earth did you say we couldn't go? We've never been asked before and it's the best shooting in the county."

"I didn't think of that. I thought it would only bore you."

"Damn it all, you might at least have asked me if I wanted to go."

"I'm sorry."

He looked at her closely. There was something in her expression that he didn't quite understand. He frowned.

"I suppose *I* was asked?" he barked.

Evie flushed a little.

"Well, in point of fact you weren't."

"I call it damned rude of them to ask you without asking me."

"I suppose they thought it wasn't your sort of party. The Duchess is rather fond of writers and people like that, you know. She's having Henry Dashwood, the critic, and for some reason he wants to meet me."

"It was damned nice of you to refuse, Evie."

"It's the least I could do," she smiled. She hesitated a moment. "George, my publishers want to give a little dinner party for me one day towards the end of the month and of course they want you to come too."

"Oh, I don't think that's quite my mark. I'll come up to London with you if you like. I'll find someone to dine with."

Daphne.

"I expect it'll be very dull, but they're making rather a point of it. And the day after, the American publisher who's taken my book is giving a cock-tail party at Claridge's. I'd like you to come to that if you wouldn't mind."

"Sounds like a crashing bore, but if you really want me to come I'll come."

"It would be sweet of you."

George Peregrine was dazed by the cocktail party. There were a lot of people. Some of them didn't look so bad, a few of the women were decently turned out, but the men seemed to him pretty awful. He was introduced to everybody as Colonel Peregrine, E. K. Hamilton's husband, you know. The men didn't seem to have anything to say to him, but the women gushed.

"You *must* be proud of your wife. Isn't it *wonderful?* You know. I read it right through at a sitting, I simply couldn't put it down, and when I'd finished I started again at the beginning and read it right through a second time. I was simply *thrilled*."

The English publisher said to him:

"We've not had a success like this with a book of verse for twenty years. I've never seen such reviews."

The American publisher said to him:

"It's swell. It'll be a smash hit in America. You wait and see."

The American publisher had sent Evie a great spray of orchids. Damned ridiculous, thought George. As they came in, people were taken up to Evie and it was evident that they said flattering things to her, which she took with a pleasant smile and a word or two of thanks. She was a trifle flushed with the excitement, but semed quite at her ease. Though he thought the whole thing a lot of stuff and nonsense George noted with approval that his wife was carrying it off in just the right way.

"Well, there's one thing," he said to himself, "you can see she's a lady and that's a damned sight more than you can say of anyone else here."

He drank a good many cocktails. But there was one thing that bothered him. He had a notion that some of the people he was introduced to looked at him in rather a funny sort of way, he couldn't quite make out what it meant, and once when he strolled by two women who were sitting together on a sofa he had the impression that they were talking about him and after he passed he was almost certain they tittered. He was very glad when the party came to an end.

In the taxi on their way back to their hotel Evie said to him:

"You were wonderful, dear. You made quite a hit. The girls simply raved about you; they thought you so handsome."

"Girls," he said bitterly "Old hags."

"Were you bored, dear?"

"Stiff."

She pressed his hand in a gesture of sympathy.

"I hope you won't mind if we wait and go down by the afternoon train. I've got some things to do in the morning."

"No, that's all right. Shopping?"

"I do want to buy one or two things, but I've got to go and be photographed. I hate the idea, but they think I ought to be. For America, you know."

He said nothing. But he thought. He thought it would be a shock to the American public when they saw the portrait of the homely, desiccated little woman who was his wife. He'd always been under the impression that they liked glamour in America.

He went on thinking and next morning when Evie had gone out he went to his club and up to the library. There he looked up recent numbers of the *Times Literary Supplement*, the *New Statesman* and the *Spectator*. Presently he found reviews of Evie's book. He didn't read them very carefully, but enough to see that they were extremely favourable. Then he went to the bookseller's in Piccadilly, where he occasionally bought books. He'd made up his mind that he had to read this damned thing of Evie's properly, but he didn't want to ask her what she'd done with the copy she'd given him. He'd buy one for himself. Before going in he looked in the window and the first thing he saw was a display of *When Pyramids Decay*. Damned silly title! He went in. A young man came forward and asked if he could help him.

"No, I'm just having a look round." It embarrassed him to ask for Evie's book and he thought he'd find it for himself and then take it to the salesman. But he couldn't see it anywhere and at last, finding the young man near him, he said in a carefully casual tone: "By the way, have you got a book called *When Pyramids Decay?*"

"The new edition came in this morning. I'll get a copy."

In a moment the young man returned with it. He was a short, rather stout young man, with a shock of untidy carroty hair and spectacles. George Peregrine, tall, upstanding, very military. towered over him.

"Is this a new edition then?" he asked.

"Yes, sir. The fifth. It might be a novel the way it's selling."

George Peregrine hesitated a moment.

"Why d'you suppose it's such a success? I've always been told no one reads poetry."

"Well, it's good, you know. I've read it meself." The young man, though obviously cultured, had a slight Cockney accent, and George quite instinctively adopted a patronizing attitude. "It's the story they like. Sexy, you know, but tragic."

George frowned a little. He was coming to the conclusion that the young man was rather impertinent. No one had told him anything about there being a story in the damned book and he had not gathered that from reading the reviews. The young man went on.

"Of course it's only a flash in the pan, if you know what I mean. The way I look at it, she was sort of inspired like by a personal experience, like Housman was with *The Shropshire Lad*. She'll never write anything else."

"How much is the book?" said George coldly to stop his chatter. "You needn't wrap it up, I'll just slip it in my pocket."

The November morning was raw and he was wearing a greatcoat.

At the station he bought the evening papers and magazines and he and Evie settled themselves comfortably in opposite corners of a first-class carriage and read. At five o'clock they went along to the restaurant car to have tea and chatted a little. They arrived. They drove home in the car which was waiting for them. They bathed, dressed for dinner, and after dinner Evie, saying she was tired out, went to bed. She kissed him, as was her habit, on the forehead. Then he went into the hall, took Evie's book out of his greatcoat pocket and going into the study began to read it. He didn't read verse very easily and though he read with attention, every word of it, the impression he received was far from clear. Then he began at the beginning again and read it a second time. He read with increasing malaise, but he was not a stupid man and when he had finished he had a distinct understanding of what it was all about. Part of the book was in free verse, part in conventional metres, but the story it related was coherent and plain to the meanest intelligence. It was the story of a passionate love affair between an older woman, married, and a young man. George Peregrine made out the steps of it as easily as if he had been doing a sum in simple addition.

Written in the first person, it began with the tremulous surprise of the woman, past her youth, when it dawned upon her that the young man was in love with her. She hesitated to believe it. She thought she must be deceiving herself. And she was terrified when on a sudden she discovered that she was passionately in love with him. She told herself it was absurd; with the disparity of age between them nothing but unhappiness could come to her if she yielded to her emotion. She tried to prevent him from speaking, but the day came when he told her that he loved her and forced her to tell him that she loved him too. He begged her to run away with him. She couldn't leave her husband, her home; and what life could they look forward to, she an ageing woman, he so young? How could she expect his love to last? She begged him to have mercy on her. But his love was impetuous. He wanted her, he wanted her with all his heart, and at last trembling, afraid, desirous, she yielded to him. Then there was a period of ecstatic happiness. The world, the dull, humdrum world of every day, blazed with glory. Love songs flowed from her pen. The woman worshipped the young, virile body of her lover. George flushed darkly when she praised his broad chest and slim flanks, the beauty of his legs and the flatness of his belly.

Hot stuff, Daphne's friend had said. It was that all right. Disgusting.

There were sad little pieces in which she lamented the emptiness of her life when as must happen he left her, but they ended with a cry that all she had to suffer would be worth it for the bliss that for a while had been hers. She wrote of the long, tremulous nights they passed together and the languor that lulled them to sleep in one another's arms. She wrote of the rapture of brief stolen moments when, braving all danger, their passion overwhelmed them and they surrendered to its call.

She thought it would be an affair of a few weeks, but miraculously it lasted. One of the poems referred to three years having gone by without lessening the love that filled their hearts. It looked as though he continued to press her to go away with him, far away, to a hill town in Italy, a Greek island, a walled city in Tunisia, so that they could be together always, for in another of the poems she besought him to let things be as they were. Their happiness was precarious. Perhaps it was owing to the difficulties they had to encounter and the rarity of their meetings that their love had retained for so long its first enchanting ardour. Then on a sudden the young man died. How, when or where George could not discover. There followed a long, heartbroken cry of bitter grief, grief she could not indulge in, grief that had to be hidden. She had to be cheerful, give dinner parties and go out to dinner, behave as she had always behaved, though the light had gone out of her life and she was bowed down with anguish. The last poem of all was a set of four short stanzas in which the writer, sadly resigned to her loss, thanked the dark powers that rule man's destiny that she had been privileged at least for a while to enjoy the greatest happiness that we poor human beings can ever hope to know.

It was three o'clock in the morning when George Peregrine finally put the book down. It had seemed to him that he heard Evie's voice in every line, over and over again he came upon turns of phrase he had heard her use, there were details that were as familiar to him as to her: there was no doubt about it; it was her own story she had told, and it was as plain as anything could be that she had had a lover and her lover had died. It was not anger so much that he felt, or horror or dismay, though he was dismayed and he was horrified, but amazement. It was as inconceivable that Evie should have had a love affair, and a wildly passionate one at that, as that the trout in a glass case over the chimney piece in his study, the finest he had ever caught, should suddenly wag its tail. He understood now the meaning of the amused look he had seen in the eyes of that man he had spoken with at the club, he understood why Daphne when she was talking about the book had seemed to be enjoying a private joke and why those two women at the cocktail party had tittered when he strolled past them.

He broke out into a sweat. Then on a sudden he was seized with fury and he jumped up to go and awake Evie and ask her sternly for an explanation. But he stopped at the door. After all what proof had he? A book. He remembered that he'd told Evie he thought it jolly good. True, he hadn't read it, but he'd pretended he had. He would look a perfect fool if he had to admit that.

"I must watch my step," he muttered.

He made up his mind to wait for two or three days and think it all over. Then he'd decide what to do. He went to bed, but he couldn't sleep for a long time.

"Evie," he kept on saying to himself. "Evie, of all people."

They met at breakfast next morning as usual. Evie was as she always was, quiet, demure and self-possessed, a middle-aged woman, who made no effort to look younger than she was, a woman who had nothing of what he still called It. He looked at her as he hadn't looked at her for years. She had her usual placid serenity. Her pale blue eyes were untroubled. There was no sign of guilt on her candid brow. She made the same little casual remarks she always made.

"It's nice to get back to the country again after those two hectic days in London. What are you going to do this morning?"

It was incomprehensible.

Three days later he went to see his solicitor. Henry Blane was an old friend of George's as well as his lawyer. He had a place not far from Peregrine's and for years they had shot over one another's preserves. For two days a week he was a country gentleman and for the other five a busy lawyer in Sheffield. He was a tall, robust fellow, with a boisterous manner and a jovial laugh, which suggested that he liked to be looked upon essentially as a sportsman and a good fellow and only incidentally as a lawyer. But he was shrewd and worldly-wise.

"Well, George, what's brought you here today?" he boomed as the Colonel was shown into his office. "Have a good time in London? I'm taking my missus up for a few days next week. How's Evie?"

"It's about Evie I've come to see you," said Peregrine, giving him a suspicious look. "Have you read her book?"

Ready writing makes not good writing; but good writing brings on ready writing.

BEN JONSON

His sensitivity had been sharpened during those last days of troubled thought and he was conscious of a faint change in the lawyer's expression. It was as though he were suddenly on his guard.

"Yes, I've read it. Great success, isn't it? Fancy Evie breaking out into poetry. Wonders will never cease."

George Peregrine was inclined to lose his temper.

"It's made me look a perfect damned fool."

"Oh, what nonsense, George! There's no harm in Evie's writing a book. You ought to be jolly proud of her."

"Don't talk such rot. It's her own story. You know it and everyone else knows it. I suppose I'm the only one who doesn't know who her lover was."

"There is such a thing as imagination, old boy. There's no reason to suppose the whole thing isn't just made up."

"Look here, Henry, we've known one another all our lives. We've had all sorts of good times together. Be honest with me. Can you look me in the face and tell me you believe it's a made-up story?"

Henry Blane moved uneasily in his chair. He was disturbed by the distress in old George's voice.

"You've got no right to ask me a question like that. Ask Evie."

"I daren't," George answered after an anguished pause. "I'm afraid she'd tell me the truth."

There was an uncomfortable silence.

"Who was the chap?"

Henry Blane looked at him straight in the eye.

"I don't know, and if I did I wouldn't tell you."

"You swine. Don't you see what a position I'm in? Do you think it's very pleasant to be made absolutely ridiculous?"

The lawyer lit a cigarette and for some moments silently puffed it.

"I don't see what I can do for you," he said at last.

"You've got private detectives you employ, I suppose. I want you to put them on the job and let them find everything out."

"It's not very pretty to put detectives on one's wife, old boy; and besides, taking for granted for a moment that Evie had an affair, it was a good many years ago and I don't suppose it would be possible to find out a thing. They seem to have covered their tracks pretty carefully."

"I don't care. You put the detectives on. I want to know the truth."

"I won't, George. If you're determined to do that you'd better consult someone else. And look here, even if you got evidence that Evie had been unfaithful to you what would you do with it? You'd look rather silly divorcing your wife because she'd committed adultery ten years ago."

"At all events I could have it out with her."

"You can do that now, but you know just as well as I do, that if you do she'll leave you. D'you want her to do that?"

George gave him an unhappy look.

"I don't know. I always thought she'd been a damned good wife to me. She runs the house perfectly, we never have any servant trouble; she's done wonders with the garden and she's splendid with all the village people. But damn it, I have my self-respect to think of. How can I go on living with her when I know that she was grossly unfaithful to me?"

"Have you always been faithful to her?"

"More or less, you know. After all we've been married for nearly twenty-four years and Evie was never much for bed."

The solicitor slightly raised his eyebrows, but George was too intent on what he was saying to notice.

"I don't deny that I've had a bit of fun now and then. A man wants it. Women are different."

"We only have men's word for that," said Henry Blane, with a faint smile.

"Evie's absolutely the last woman I'd have suspected of kicking over the traces. I mean, she's a very fastidious, reticent woman. What on earth made her write the damned book?"

"I suppose it was a very poignant experience and perhaps it was a relief to her to get it off her chest like that."

"Well, if she had to write it why the devil didn't she write it under an assumed name?"

"She used her maiden name. I suppose she thought that was enough and it would have been if the book hadn't had this amazing boom."

George Peregrine and the lawyer were sitting opposite one another with a desk between them. George, his elbow on the desk, his cheek resting on his hand, frowned at his thought.

"It's so rotten not to know what sort of a chap he was. One can't even tell if he was by way of being a gentleman. I mean, for all I know he may have been a farmhand or a clerk in a lawyer's office."

Henry Blane did not permit himself to smile and when he answered there was in his eyes a kindly, tolerant look.

"Knowing Evie so well I think the probabilities are that he was all right. Anyhow I'm sure he wasn't a clerk in my office."

"It's been such a shock to me," the Colonel sighed. "I thought she was fond of me. She couldn't have written that book unless she hated me."

"Oh, I don't believe that. I don't think she's capable of hatred."

"You're not going to pretend that she loves me."

"No."

"Well, what does she feel for me?"

Henry Blane leaned back in his swivel chair and looked at George reflectively.

"Indifference, I should say."

The Colonel gave a little shudder and reddened.

"After all, you're not in love with her, are you?"

George Peregrine did not answer directly.

"It's been a great blow to me not to have any children, but I've never let her see that I think she's let me down. I've always been kind to her. Within reasonable limits I've tried to do my duty by her."

The lawyer passed a large hand over his mouth to conceal the smile that trembled on his lips.

"It's been such an awful shock to me," Peregrine went on. "Damn it all, even ten years ago Evie was no chicken and God knows, she wasn't much to look at. It's so ugly." He sighed deeply. "What would you do in my place?"

"Nothing."

George Peregrine drew himself bolt upright in his chair and he looked at Henry with the stern set face that he must have worn when he inspected his regiment.

"I can't overlook a thing like this. I've been made a laughing stock. I can never hold up my head again."

"Nonsense," said the lawyer sharply, and then in a pleasant, kindly manner: "Listen, old boy: the man's dead; it all happened a long while back. Forget it. Talk to people about Evie's book, rave about it, tell 'em how proud you are of her. Behave as though you had so much confidence in her, you *knew* she could never have been unfaithful to you. The world moves so quickly and people's memories are so short. They'll forget."

"I shan't forget."

"You're both middle-aged people. She probably does a great deal more for you than you think and you'd be awfully lonely without her. I don't think it matters if you don't forget. It'll be all to the good if you can get it into that thick head of yours that there's a lot more in Evie than you ever had the gumption to see."

"Damn it all, you talk as if *I* was to blame."

"No, I don't think you were to blame, but I'm not so sure that Evie was either. I don't suppose she wanted to fall in love with this boy. D'you remember those verses right at the end? The impression they gave me was that though she was shattered by his death, in a strange sort of way she welcomed it. All through she'd been aware of the fragility of the tie that bound them. He died in the full flush of his first love and had never known that love so seldom endures; he'd only known its bliss and beauty. In her own bitter grief she found solace in the thought that he'd been spared all sorrow."

"All that's a bit over my head, old boy. I see more or less what you mean."

George Peregrine stared unhappily at the inkstand on the desk. He was silent and the lawyer looked at him with curious, yet sympathetic eyes.

"Do you realize what courage she must have had never by a sign to show how dreadfully unhappy she was?" he said gently.

Colonel Peregrine sighed.

"I'm broken. I suppose you're right; it's no good crying over spilt milk and it would only make things worse if I made a fuss."

"Well?"

George Peregrine gave a pitiful little smile.

"I'll take your advice. I'll do nothing. Let them think me a damned fool and to hell with them. The truth is, I don't know what I'd do without Evie. But I'll tell you what, there's one thing I shall never understand till my dying day. What in the name of heaven did the fellow ever see in her?"

The Guest

ALBERT CAMUS

The schoolmaster was watching the two men climb toward him. One was on horseback, the other on foot. They had not yet tackled the abrupt rise leading to the schoolhouse built on the hillside. They were toiling onward, making slow progress in the snow, among the stones, on the vast expanse of the high, deserted plateau. From time to time the horse stumbled. Without hearing anything yet, he could see the breath issuing from the horse's nostrils. One of the men, at least, knew the region. They were following the trail although it had disappeared days ago under a layer of dirty white snow. The schoolmaster calculated that it would take them half an hour to get onto the hill. It was cold; he went back into the school to get a sweater.

He crossed the empty, frigid classroom. On the blackboard the four rivers of France, drawn with four different colored chalks, had been flowing toward their estuaries for the past three days. Snow had suddenly fallen in mid-October after eight months of drought without the transition of rain, and the twenty pupils, more or less, who lived in the villages scattered over the plateau had stopped coming. With fair weather they would return. Daru now heated only the single room that was his lodging, adjoining the classroom and giving also onto the plateau to the east. Like the class windows, his window looked to the south too. On that side the school was a few kilometers from the point where the plateau began to slope toward the south. In clear weather could be seen the purple mass of the mountain range where the gap opened onto the desert.

Somewhat warmed, Daru returned to the window from which he had first seen the two men. They were no longer visible. Hence they must have tackled the rise. The sky was not so dark, for the snow had stopped falling during the night. The morning had opened with a dirty light which had scarcely become brighter as the ceiling of clouds lifted. At two in the afternoon it seemed as if the day were merely beginning. But still this was better than those three days when the thick snow was falling amidst unbroken darkness with little gusts of wind that rattled the double door of the classroom. Then Daru had spent long hours in his room, leaving it only to go to the shed and feed the chickens or get some coal. Fortunately the delivery truck from Tadjid, the nearest village to the north, had brought his supplies two days before the blizzard. It would return in forty-eight hours.

Besides, he had enough to resist a siege, for the little room was cluttered with bags of wheat that the administration left as a stock to distribute to those of his pupils whose families had suffered from the drought. Actually they had all been victims because they were all poor. Every day Daru would distribute a ration to the children. They had missed it, he knew, during these bad days. Possibly one of the fathers or big brothers would come this afternoon and he could supply them with grain. It was just a matter of carrying them over to the next harvest. Now shiploads of wheat were arriving from France and the worst was over. But it would be hard to forget that poverty, that army of ragged ghosts wandering in the sunlight, the plateaus burned to a cinder month after month, the earth shriveled up little by little, literally scorched, every stone bursting into dust under one's foot. The sheep had died then by thousands and even a few men, here and there, sometimes without anyone's knowing.

In contrast with such poverty, he who lived almost like a monk in his remote schoolhouse, nonetheless satisfied with the little he had and with the rough life, had felt like a lord with his whitewashed walls, his narrow couch, his unpainted shelves, his well, and his weekly provision of water and food. And suddenly this snow, without warning, without the foretaste of rain. This is the way the region was, cruel to live in, even without men — who didn't help matters either. But Daru had been born here. Everywhere else, he felt exiled.

He stepped out onto the terrace in front of the schoolhouse. The two men were now halfway up the slope. He recognized the horseman as Balducci, the old gendarme he had known for a long time. Balducci was holding on the end of a rope an Arab who was walking behind him with hands bound and head lowered. The gendarme waved a greeting to which Daru did not reply, lost as he was in contemplation of the Arab dressed in a faded blue jellaba, his feet in sandals but covered with socks of heavy raw wool, his head surmounted by a narrow, short *chèche*. They were approaching. Balducci was holding back his horse in order not to hurt the Arab, and the group was advancing slowly.

Within earshot, Balducci shouted: "One hour to do the three kilometers from El Ameur!" Daru did not answer. Short and square in his thick sweater, he watched them climb. Not once had the Arab raised his head. "Hello," said Daru when they got up onto the terrace. "Come in and warm up." Balducci painfully got down from his horse without letting go the rope. From under his bristling mustache he smiled at the schoolmaster. His little dark eyes, deep-set under a tanned forehead, and his mouth surrounded with wrinkles made him look attentive and studious. Daru took the bridle, led the horse to the shed, and came back to the two men, who were now waiting for him in the school. He led them into his room. "I am going to heat up the classroom," he said. "We'll be more comfortable there." When he entered the room again, Balducci was on the couch. He had undone the rope tying him to the Arab, who had squatted near the stove. His hands still bound, the *chèche* pushed back on his head, he was looking toward the window. At first Daru noticed only his huge lips, fat, smooth, almost Negroid; yet his nose was straight, his eyes were dark and full of fever. The *chèche* revealed an obstinate forehead and, under the weathered skin now rather discolored by the cold, the whole face had a restless and rebellious look that struck Daru when the Arab, turning his face toward him, looked him straight in the eyes. "Go into the other room," said the schoolmaster, "and I'll make you some mint tea." "Thanks," Balducci said. "What a chore! How I long for retirement." And addressing his prisoner in Arabic: "Come on, you." The Arab got up and, slowly, holding his bound wrists in front of him, went into the classroom.

With the tea, Daru brought a chair. But Balducci was already enthroned on the nearest pupil's desk and the Arab had squatted against the teacher's platform facing the stove, which stood between the desk and the window. When he held out the glass of tea to the prisoner, Daru hesitated at the sight of his bound hands. "He might perhaps be untied." "Sure," said Balducci. "That was for the trip." He started to get to his feet. But Daru, setting the glass on the floor, had knelt beside the Arab. Without saying anything, the Arab watched him with his feverish eyes. Once his hands were free, he rubbed his swollen wrists against each other, took the glass of tea, and sucked up the burning liquid in swift little sips.

"Good," said Daru. "And where are you headed?"

Balducci withdrew his mustache from the tea. "Here, son."

"Odd pupils! And you're spending the night?"

"No. I'm going back to El Ameur. And you will deliver this fellow to Tinguit. He is expected at police headquarters."

Balducci was looking at Daru with a friendly little smile.

"What's this story?" asked the schoolmaster. "Are you pulling my leg?"

"No, son. Those are the orders."

"The orders? I'm not . . ." Daru hesitated, not wanting to hurt the old Corsican. "I mean, that's not my job."

"What! What's the meaning of that? In wartime people do all kinds of jobs."

"Then I'll wait for the declaration of war!"

Balducci nodded.

"O.K. But the orders exist and they concern you too. Things are brewing, it appears. There is talk of a forthcoming revolt. We are mobilized, in a way."

Daru still had his obstinate look.

"Listen, son," Balducci said. "I like you and you must understand. There's only a dozen of us at El Ameur to patrol throughout the whole territory of a small department and I must get back in a hurry. I was told to hand this guy over to you and return without delay. He couldn't be kept there. His village was beginning to stir; they wanted to take him back. You must take him to Tinguit tomorrow before the day is over. Twenty kilometers shouldn't faze a husky fellow like you. After that, all will be over. You'll come back to your pupils and your comfortable life."

Behind the wall the horse could be heard snorting and pawing the earth. Daru was looking out the window. Decidedly, the weather was clearing and the light was increasing over the snowy plateau. When all the snow was melted, the sun would take over again and once more would burn the fields of stone. For days, still, the unchanging sky would shed its dry light on the solitary expanse where nothing had any connection with man.

"After all," he said, turning around toward Balducci, "what did he do?" And, before the gendarme had opened his mouth, he asked: "Does he speak French?"

"No, not a word. We had been looking for him for a month, but they were hiding him. He killed his cousin."

"Is he against us?"

"I don't think so. But you can never be sure."

"Why did he kill?"

"A family squabble, I think. One owed the other grain, it seems. It's not at all clear. In short, he killed his cousin with a billhook. You know, like a sheep, *kreezk!*"

Balducci made the gesture of drawing a blade across his throat and the Arab, his attention attracted, watched him with a sort of anxiety. Daru felt a sudden wrath against the man, against all men with their rotten spite, their tireless hates, their blood lust.

But the kettle was singing on the stove. He served Balducci more tea, hesitated, then served the Arab again, who, a second time, drank avidly. His raised arms made the jellaba fall open and the schoolmaster saw his thin, muscular chest.

"Thanks, kid," Balducci said. "And now, I'm off."

He got up and went toward the Arab, taking a small rope from his pocket.

"What are you doing?" Daru asked dryly.

Balducci, disconcerted, showed him the rope.

"Don't bother."

The old gendarme hesitated. "It's up to you. Of course, you are armed?"

"I have my shotgun."

"Where?"

"In the trunk."

"You ought to have it near your bed."

"Why? I have nothing to fear."

"You're crazy, son. If there's an uprising, no one is safe, we're all in the same boat."

"I'll defend myself. I'll have time to see them coming."

Balducci began to laugh, then suddenly the mustache covered the white teeth.

"You'll have time? O.K. That's just what I was saying. You have always been a little cracked. That's why I like you, my son was like that."

At the same time he took out his revolver and put it on the desk.

"Keep it; I don't need two weapons from here to El Ameur."

The revolver shone against the black paint of the table. When the gendarme turned toward him, the schoolmaster caught the smell of leather and horseflesh.

"Listen, Balducci," Daru said suddenly, "every bit of this disgusts me, and first of all your fellow here. But I won't hand him over. Fight, yes, if I have to. But not that."

The old gendarme stood in front of him and looked at him severely.

"You're being a fool," he said slowly. "I don't like it either. You don't get used to putting a rope on a man even after years of it, and you're even ashamed — yes, ashamed. But you can't let them have their way."

"I won't hand him over," Daru said again.

"It's an order, son, and I repeat it."

"That's right. Repeat to them what I've said to you: I won't hand him over."

Balducci made a visible effort to reflect. He looked at the Arab and at Daru. At last he decided.

"No, I won't tell them anything. If you want to drop us, go ahead; I'll not denounce you. I have an order to deliver the prisoner and I'm doing so. And now you'll just sign this paper for me."

"There's no need. I'll not deny that you left him with me."

"Don't be mean with me. I know you'll tell the truth. You're from hereabouts and you are a man. But you must sign, that's the rule."

Daru opened his drawer, took out a little square bottle of purple ink, the red wooden penholder with the "sergeant-major" pen he used for making models of penmanship, and signed. The gendarme carefully folded the paper and put it into his wallet. Then he moved toward the door.

"I'll see you off," Daru said.

"No," said Balducci. "There's no use being polite. You insulted me."

He looked at the Arab, motionless in the same spot, sniffed peevishly, and turned away toward the door. "Good-by, son," he said. The door shut behind him. Balducci appeared suddenly outside the window and then disappeared. His footsteps were muffled by the snow. The horse stirred on the other side of the wall and several chickens fluttered in fright. A moment later Balducci reappeared outside the window leading the horse by the bridle. He walked toward the little rise without turning around and disappeared from sight with the horse following him. A big stone could be heard bouncing down. Daru walked back toward the prisoner, who, without stirring, never took his eyes off him. "Wait," the schoolmaster said in Arabic and went toward the bedroom. As he was going through the door, he had a second thought, went to the desk, took the revolver, and stuck it in his pocket. Then, without looking back, he went into his room.

For some time he lay on his couch watching the sky gradually close over, listening to the silence. It was this silence that had seemed painful to him during the first days here, after the war. He had requested a post in the little town at the base of the foothills separating the upper plateaus from the desert. There, rocky walls, green and black to the north, pink and lavender to the south, marked the frontier of eternal summer. He had been named to a post farther north, on the plateau itself. In the beginning, the solitude and the silence had been hard for him on these wastelands peopled only by stones. Occasionally, furrows suggested cultivation, but they had been dug to uncover a certain kind of stone good for building. The only plowing here was to harvest rocks. Elsewhere a thin layer of soil accumulated in the hollows would be scraped out to enrich paltry village gardens. This is the way it was: bare rock covered three quarters of the region. Towns sprang up, flourished, then disappeared; men came by, loved one another or fought bitterly, then died. No one in this desert, neither he nor his guest, mattered. And yet, outside this desert neither of them, Daru knew, could have really lived.

When he got up, no noise came from the classroom. He was amazed at the unmixed joy he derived from the mere thought that the Arab might have fled and that he would be alone with no decision to make. But the prisoner was there. He had merely stretched out between the stove and the desk. With eyes open, he was staring at the ceiling. In that position, his thick lips were particularly noticeable, giving him a pouting look. "Come," said Daru. The Arab got up and followed him. In the bedroom, the schoolmaster pointed to a chair near the table under the window. The Arab sat down without taking his eyes off Daru.

"Are you hungry?"

"Yes," the prisoner said.

Daru set the table for two. He took flour and oil, shaped a cake in a frying-pan, and lighted the little stove that functioned on bottled gas. While the cake was cooking, he went out to the shed to get cheese, eggs, dates, and condensed milk. When the cake was done he set it on the window sill to cool, heated some condensed milk diluted with water, and beat up the eggs into an omelette. In one of his motions he knocked against the revolver stuck in his right pocket. He set the bowl down, went into the classroom, and put the revolver in his desk drawer. When he came back to the room, night was falling. He put on the light and served the Arab. "Eat," he said. The Arab took a piece of the cake, lifted it eagerly to his mouth, and stopped short.

"And you?" he asked.

"After you. I'll eat too."

The thick lips opened slightly. The Arab hesitated, then bit into the cake determinedly.

The meal over, the Arab looked at the schoolmaster. "Are you the judge?"

"No, I'm simply keeping you until tomorrow."

"Why do you eat with me?"

"I'm hungry."

The Arab fell silent. Daru got up and went out. He brought back a folding bed from the shed, set it up between the table and the stove, perpendicular to his own bed. From a large suitcase which, upright in a corner, served as a shelf for papers, he took two blankets and arranged them on the camp bed. Then he stopped, felt useless, and sat down on his bed. There was nothing more to do or to get ready. He had to look at this man. He looked at him, therefore, trying to imagine his face bursting with rage. He couldn't do so. He could see nothing but the dark yet shining eyes and the animal mouth.

"Why did you kill him?" he asked in a voice whose hostile tone surprised him.

The Arab looked away.

"He ran away. I ran after him."

He raised his eyes to Daru again and they were full of a sort of woeful interrogation. "Now what will they do to me?"

"Are you afraid?"

He stiffened, turning his eyes away.

"Are you sorry?"

The Arab stared at him openmouthed. Obviously he did not understand. Daru's annoyance was growing. At the same time he felt awkward and self-conscious with his big body wedged between the two beds.

"Lie down there," he said impatiently. "That's your bed."

The Arab didn't move. He called to Daru:

"Tell me!"

The schoolmaster looked at him.

"Is the gendarme coming back tomorrow?"

"I don't know."

"Are you coming with us?"

"I don't know. Why?"

The prisoner got up and stretched out on top of the blankets, his feet toward the window. The light from the electric bulb shone straight into his eyes and he closed them at once.

"Why?" Daru repeated, standing beside the bed.

The Arab opened his eyes under the blinding light and looked at him, trying not to blink.

"Come with us," he said.

In the middle of the night, Daru was still not asleep. He had gone to bed after undressing completely; he generally slept naked. But when he suddenly realized that he had nothing on, he hesitated. He felt vulnerable and the temptation came to him to put his clothes back on. Then he shrugged his shoulders; after all, he wasn't a child and, if need be, he could break his adversary in two. From his bed he could observe him, lying on his back, still motionless with his eyes closed under the harsh light. When Daru turned out the light, the darkness seemed to coagulate all of a sudden. Little by little, the night came back to life in the window where the starless sky was stirring gently. The schoolmaster soon made out the body lying at his feet. The Arab still did not move, but his eyes seemed open. A faint wind was prowling around the schoolhouse. Perhaps it would drive away the clouds and the sun would reappear.

During the night the wind increased. The hens fluttered a little and then were silent. The Arab turned over on his side with his back to Daru, who thought he heard him moan. Then he listened for his guest's breathing, become heavier and more regular. He listened to that breath so close to him and mused without being able to go to sleep. In this room where he had been sleeping alone for a year, this presence bothered him. But it bothered him also by imposing on him a sort of brotherhood he knew well but refused to accept in the present circumstances. Men who share the same rooms, soldiers or prisoners, develop a strange alliance as if, having cast off their armor with their clothing, they fraternized every evening, over and above their differences, in the ancient community of dream and fatigue. But Daru shook himself; he didn't like such musings, and it was essential to sleep.

A little later, however, when the Arab stirred slightly, the schoolmaster was still not asleep. When the prisoner made a second move, he stiffened, on the alert. The Arab was lifting himself slowly on his arms with almost the motion of a sleepwalker. Seated upright in bed, he waited motionless without turning his head toward Daru, as if he were listening attentively. Daru did not stir; it had just occurred to him that the revolver was still in the drawer of his desk. It was better to act at once. Yet he continued to observe the prisoner, who, with the same slithery motion, put his feet on the ground, waited again, then began to stand up slowly. Daru was about to call out to him when the Arab began to walk, in a quite natural but extraordinarily silent way. He was heading toward the door at the end of the room that opened into the shed. He lifted the latch with precaution and went out, pushing the door behind him but without shutting it. Daru had not stirred. "He is running away," he merely thought. "Good riddance!" Yet he listened attentively. The hens were not fluttering; the guest must be on the plateau. A faint sound of water reached him, and he didn't know what it was until the Arab again stood framed in the doorway, closed the door carefully, and came back to bed without a sound. Then Daru turned his back on him and fell asleep. Still later he seemed, from the depths of his sleep, to hear furtive steps around the schoolhouse. "I'm dreaming! I'm dreaming!" he repeated to himself. And he went on sleeping.

When he awoke, the sky was clear; the loose window let in a cold, pure air. The Arab was asleep, hunched up under the blankets now, his mouth open, utterly relaxed. But when Daru shook him, he started dreadfully, staring at Daru with wild eyes as if he had never seen him and such a frightened expression that the schoolmaster stepped back. "Don't be afraid. It's me. You must eat." The Arab nodded his head and said yes. Calm had returned to his face, but his expression was vacant and listless.

The coffee was ready. They drank it seated together on the folding bed as they munched their pieces of the cake. Then Daru led the Arab under the shed and showed him the faucet where he washed. He went back into the room, folded the blankets and the bed, made his own bed and put the room in order. Then he went through the classroom and out onto the terrace. The sun was already rising in the blue sky; a soft, bright light was bathing the deserted plateau. On the ridge the snow was melting in spots. The stones were about to reappear. Crouched on the edge of the plateau, the schoolmaster looked at the deserted expanse. He thought of Balducci. He had hurt him, for he had sent him off in a way as if he didn't want to be associated with him. He could still hear the gendarme's farewell and, without knowing why, he felt strangely empty and vulnerable. At that moment, from the other side of the schoolhouse, the prisoner coughed. Daru listened to him almost despite himself and then, furious, threw a pebble that whistled through the air before sinking into the snow. That man's stupid crime revolted him, but to hand him over was contrary to honor. Merely thinking of it made him smart with humiliation. And he cursed at one and the same time his own people who had sent him this Arab and the Arab too who had dared to kill and not managed to get away. Daru got up, walked in a circle on the terrace, waited motionless, and then went back into the schoolhouse.

The Arab, leaning over the cement floor of the shed, was washing his teeth with two fingers. Daru looked at him and said: "Come." He went back into the room ahead of the prisoner. He slipped a hunting-jacket on over his sweater and put on walking-shoes. Standing, he waited until the Arab had put on his *chèche* and sandals. They went into the classroom and the schoolmaster pointed to the exit, saying: "Go ahead." The fellow didn't budge. "I'm coming," said Daru. The Arab went out. Daru went back into the room and made a package of pieces of rusk, dates, and sugar. In the classroom, before going out, he hesitated a second in front of his desk, then crossed the threshold and locked the door. "That's the way," he said. He started toward the east, followed by the prisoner. But, a short distance from the schoolhouse, he thought he heard a slight sound behind them. He retraced his steps and examined the surroundings of the house; there was no one there. The Arab watched him without seeming to understand. "Come on," said Daru.

They walked for an hour and rested beside a sharp peak of limestone. The snow was melting faster and faster and the sun was drinking up the puddles at once, rapidly cleaning the plateau, which gradually dried and vibrated like the air itself. When they resumed walking, the ground rang under their feet. From time to time a bird rent the space in front of them with a joyful cry.

Daru breathed in deeply the fresh morning light. He felt a sort of rapture before the vast familiar expanse, now almost entirely yellow under its dome of blue sky. They walked an hour more, descending toward the south. They reached a level height made up of crumbly rocks. From there on, the plateau sloped down, eastward, toward a low plain where there were a few spindly trees and, to the south, toward outcroppings of rock that gave the landscape a chaotic look.

Daru surveyed the two directions. There was nothing but the sky on the horizon. Not a man could be seen. He turned toward the Arab, who was looking at him blankly. Daru held out the package to him. "Take it," he said. "There are dates, bread, and sugar. You can hold out for two days. Here are a thousand francs too." The Arab took the package and the money but kept his full hands at chest level as if he didn't know what to do with what was being given him. "Now look," the schoolmaster said as he pointed in the direction of the east, "there's the way to Tinguit. You have a two-hour walk. At Tinguit you'll find the administration and the police. They are expecting you." The Arab looked toward the east, still holding the package and the money against his chest. Daru took his elbow and turned him rather roughly toward the south. At the foot of the height on which they stood could be seen a faint path. "That's the trail across the plateau. In a day's walk from here you'll find pasturelands and the first nomads. They'll take you in and shelter you according to their law." The Arab had now turned toward Daru and a sort of panic was visible in his expression. "Listen," he said. Daru shook his head: "No, be quiet. Now I'm leaving you." He turned his back on him, took two long steps in the direction of the school, looked hesitantly at the motionless Arab, and started off again. For a few minutes he heard nothing but his own step resounding on the cold ground and did not turn his head. A moment later, however, he turned around. The Arab was still there on the edge of the hill, his arms hanging now, and he was looking at the schoolmaster. Daru felt something rise in his throat. But he swore with impatience, waved vaguely, and started off again. He had already gone some distance when he again stopped and looked. There was no longer anyone on the hill.

Daru hesitated. The sun was now rather high in the sky and was beginning to beat down on his head. The schoolmaster retraced his steps, at first somewhat uncertainly, then with decision. When he reached the little hill, he was bathed in sweat. He climbed it as fast as he could and stopped, out of breath, at the top. The rock-fields to the south stood out sharply against the blue sky, but on the plain to the east a steamy heat was already rising. And in that slight haze, Daru, with heavy heart, made out the Arab walking slowly on the road to prison.

A little later, standing before the window of the classroom, the schoolmaster was watching the clear light bathing the whole surface of the plateau, but he hardly saw it. Behind him on the blackboard, among the winding

French rivers, sprawled the clumsily chalked-up words he had just read: "You handed over our brother. You will pay for this." Daru looked at the sky, the plateau, and, beyond, the invisible lands stretching all the way to the sea. In this vast landscape he had loved so much, he was alone.

Everything That Rises Must Converge

FLANNERY O'CONNOR

Her doctor had told Julian's mother that she must lose twenty pounds on account of her blood pressure, so on Wednesday nights Julian had to take her downtown on the bus for a reducing class at the Y. The reducing class was designed for working girls over fifty, who weighed from 165 to 200 pounds. His mother was one of the slimmer ones, but she said ladies did not tell their age or weight. She would not ride the buses by herself at night since they had been integrated, and because the reducing class was one of her few pleasures, necessary for her health, and *free*, she said Julian could at least put himself out to take her, considering all she did for him. Julian did not like to consider all she did for him, but every Wednesday night he braced himself and took her.

She was almost ready to go, standing before the hall mirror, putting on her hat, while he, his hands behind him, appeared pinned to the door frame, waiting like Saint Sebastian for the arrows to begin piercing him. The hat was new and had cost her seven dollars and a half. She kept saying, "Maybe I shouldn't have paid that for it. No, I shouldn't have. I'll take it off and return it tomorrow. I shouldn't have bought it."

Julian raised his eyes to heaven. "Yes, you should have bought it," he said. "Put it on and let's go." It was a hideous hat. A purple velvet flap came down on one side of it and stood up on the other; the rest of it was green and looked like a cushion with the stuffing out. He decided it was less comical than jaunty and pathetic. Everything that gave her pleasure was small and depressed him.

She lifted the hat one more time and set it down slowly on top of her head. Two wings of gray hair protruded on either side of her florid face, but her eyes, sky-blue, were as innocent and untouched by experience as they must have been when she was ten. Were it not that she was a widow who had struggled fiercely to feed and clothe and put him through school and who was supporting him still, "until he got on his feet," she might have been a little girl that he had to take to town.

"It's all right, it's all right," he said. "Let's go." He opened the door himself and started down the walk to get her going. The sky was a dying violet and the houses stood out darkly against it, bulbous liver-colored monstrosities of a uniform ugliness though no two were alike. Since this had been a fashionable neighborhood forty years ago, his mother persisted in thinking they did well to have an apartment in it. Each house had a narrow collar of dirt around it in which sat, usually, a grubby child. Julian walked with his hands in his pockets, his head down and thrust forward and his eyes glazed with the determination to make himself completely numb during the time he would be sacrificed to her pleasure.

The door closed and he turned to find the dumpy figure, surmounted by the atrocious hat, coming toward him. "Well," she said, "you only live once and paying a little more for it, I at least won't meet myself coming and going."

"Some day I'll start making money," Julian said gloomily — he knew he never would — "and you can have one of those jokes whenever you take the fit." But first they would move. He visualized a place where the nearest neighbors would be three miles away on either side.

"I think you're doing fine," she said, drawing on her gloves. "You've only been out of school a year. Rome wasn't built in a day."

She was one of the few members of the Y reducing class who arrived in hat and gloves and who had a son who had been to college. "It takes time," she said, "and the world is in such a mess. This hat looked better on me than any of the others, though when she brought it out I said, 'Take that thing back. I wouldn't have it on my head,' and she said, 'Now wait till you see it on,' and when she put it on, I said, 'We-ull,' and she said, 'If you ask me, that hat does something for you and you do something for the hat, and besides,' she said, 'with that hat, you won't meet yourself coming and going.'"

Julian thought he could have stood his lot better if she had been selfish, if she had been an old hag who drank and screamed at him. He walked along, saturated in depression, as if in the midst of his martyrdom he had lost his faith. Catching sight of his long, hopeless, irritated face, she stopped suddenly with a grief-stricken look, and pulled back on his arm. "Wait on me," she said. "I'm going back to the house and take this thing off and tomorrow I'm going to return it. I was out of my head. I can pay the gas bill with that seven-fifty."

He caught her arm in a vicious grip. "You are not going to take it back," he said. "I like it."

"Well," she said, "I don't think I ought..."

"Shut up and enjoy it," he muttered, more depressed than ever.

"With the world in the mess it's in," she said, "it's a wonder we can enjoy anything. I tell you, the bottom rail is on the top."

Julian sighed.

"Of course," she said, "if you know who you are, you can go anywhere." She said this every time he took her to the reducing class. "Most of them in it are not our kind of people," she said, "but I can be gracious to anybody. I know who I am."

"They don't give a damn for your graciousness," Julian said savagely. "Knowing who you are is good for one generation only. You haven't the foggiest idea where you stand now or who you are."

She stopped and allowed her eyes to flash at him. "I most certainly do know who I am," she said, "and if you don't know who you are, I'm ashamed of you."

"Oh hell," Julian said.

"Your great-grandfather was a former governor of this state," she said. "Your grandfather was a prosperous landowner. Your grandmother was a Godhigh."

"Will you look around you," he said tensely, "and see where you are now?" and he swept his arm jerkily out to indicate the neighborhood, which the growing darkness at least made less dingy.

"You remain what you are," she said. "Your great-grandfather had a plantation and two hundred slaves."

"There are no more slaves," he said irritably.

"They were better off when they were," she said. He groaned to see that she was off on that topic. She rolled onto it every few days like a train on an open track. He knew every stop, every junction, every swamp along the way, and knew the exact point at which her conclusion would roll majestically into the station: "It's ridiculous. It's simply not realistic. They should rise, yes, but on their own side of the fence."

"Let's skip it," Julian said.

"The ones I feel sorry for," she said, "are the ones that are half white. They're tragic."

"Will you skip it?"

"Suppose we were half white. We would certainly have mixed feelings."

"I have mixed feelings now," he groaned.

"Well let's talk about something pleasant," she said. "I remember going to Grandpa's when I was a little girl. Then the house had double stairways that went up to what was really the second floor — all the cooking was done on the first. I used to like to stay down in the kitchen on account of the way the walls smelled. I would sit with my nose pressed against the plaster and take deep breaths. Actually the place belonged to the Godhighs but your grandfather Chestny paid the mortgage and saved it for them. They were in reduced circumstances," she said, "but reduced or not, they never forgot who they were."

"Doubtless that decayed mansion reminded them," Julian muttered. He never spoke of it without contempt or thought of it without longing. He had seen it once when he was a child before it had been sold. The double stairways had rotted and been torn down. Negroes were living in it. But it remained in his mind as his mother had known it. It appeared in his dreams regularly. He would stand on the wide porch, listening to the rustle of oak leaves, then wander through the high-ceilinged hall into the parlor that opened onto it and gaze at the worn rugs and faded draperies. It occurred to him that it was he, not she, who could have appreciated it. He preferred its threadbare elegance to anything he could name and it was because of it that all the neighborhoods they had lived in had been a torment to him — whereas she had hardly known the difference. She called her insensitivity "being adjustable."

"And I remember the old darky who was my nurse, Caroline. There was no better person in the world. I've always had a great respect for my colored friends," she said. "I'd do anything in the world for them and they'd . . ."

"Will you for God's sake get off that subject?" Julian said. When he got on a bus by himself, he made it a point to sit down beside a Negro, in reparation as it were for his mother's sins.

"You're mighty touchy tonight," she said. "Do you feel all right?"

"Yes I feel all right," he said. "Now lay off."

She pursed her lips. "Well, you certainly are in a vile humor," she observed. "I just won't speak to you at all."

They had reached the bus stop. There was no bus in sight and Julian, his hands still jammed in his pockets and his head thrust forward, scowled down the empty street. The frustration of having to wait on the bus as well as ride on it began to creep up his neck like a hot hand. The presence of his mother was borne in upon him as she gave a pained sigh. He looked at her bleakly. She was holding herself very erect under the preposterous hat, wearing it like a banner of her imaginary dignity. There was in him an evil urge to break her spirit. He suddenly unloosened his tie and pulled it off and put it in his pocket.

She stiffened. "Why must you look like *that* when you take me to town?" she said. "Why must you deliberately embarrass me?"

"If you'll never learn where you are," he said, "you can at least learn where I am."

"You look like a — thug," she said.

"Then I must be one," he murmured.

"I'll just go home," she said. "I will not bother you. If you can't do a little thing like that for me . . ."

Rolling his eyes upward, he put his tie back on. "Restored to my class," he muttered. He thrust his face toward her and hissed, "True culture is in the mind, the *mind*," he said, and tapped his head, "the mind."

"It's in the heart," she said, "and in how you do things and how you do things is because of who you *are*."

"Nobody in the damn bus cares who you are."

"I care who I am," she said icily.

The lighted bus appeared on top of the next hill and as it approached, they moved out into the street to meet it. He put his hand under her elbow and hoisted her up on the creaking step. She entered with a little smile, as if she were going into a drawing room where everyone had been waiting for her. While he put in the tokens, she sat down on one of the broad front seats for three which faced the aisle. A thin woman with protruding teeth and long yellow hair was sitting on the end of it. His mother moved up beside her and left room for Julian beside herself. He sat down and looked at the floor across the aisle where a pair of thin feet in red and white canvas sandals were planted.

His mother immediately began a general conversation meant to attract anyone who felt like talking. "Can it get any hotter?" she said and removed from her purse a folding fan, black with a Japanese scene on it, which she began to flutter before her.

"I reckon it might could," the woman with the protruding teeth said, "but I know for a fact my apartment couldn't get no hotter."

"It must get the afternoon sun," his mother said. She sat forward and looked up and down the bus. It was half filled. Everybody was white. "I see we have the bus to ourselves," she said. Julian cringed.

"For a change," said the woman across the aisle, the owner of the red and white canvas sandals. "I come on one the other day and they were thick as fleas — up front and all through."

"The world is in a mess everywhere," his mother said. "I don't know how we've let it get in this fix."

"What gets my goat is all those boys from good families stealing automobile tires," the woman with the protruding teeth said. "I told my boy, I said you may not be rich but you been raised right and if I ever catch you in any such mess, they can send you on to the reformatory. Be exactly where you belong."

"Training tells," his mother said. "Is your boy in high school?"

"Ninth grade," the woman said.

"My son just finished college last year. He wants to write but he's selling typewriters until he gets started," his mother said.

The woman leaned forward and peered at Julian. He threw her such a malevolent look that she subsided against the seat. On the floor across the aisle there was an abandoned newspaper. He got up and got it and opened it out in front of him. His mother discreetly continued the conversation in a lower tone but the woman across the aisle said in a loud voice, "Well that's nice. Selling typewriters is close to writing. He can go right from one to the other."

"I tell him," his mother said, "that Rome wasn't built in a day."

Behind the newspaper Julian was withdrawing into the inner compartment of his mind where he spent most of his time. This was a kind of mental bubble in which he established himself when he could not bear to be a part of what was going on around him. From it he could see out and judge but in it he was safe from any kind of penetration from without. It was the only place where he felt free of the general idiocy of his fellows. His mother had never entered it but from it he could see her with absolute clarity.

The old lady was clever enough and he thought that if she had started from any of the right premises, more might have been expected of her. She lived according to the laws of her own fantasy world, outside of which he had never seen her set foot. The law of it was to sacrifice herself for him after she had first created the necessity to do so by making a mess of things. If he had permitted her sacrifices, it was only because her lack of foresight had made them necessary. All of her life had been a struggle to act like a Chestny without the Chestny goods, and to give him everything she thought a Chestny ought to have; but since, said she, it was fun to struggle, why complain? And when you had won, as she had won, what fun to look back on the hard times! He could not forgive her that she had enjoyed the struggle and that she thought *she* had won.

What she meant when she said she had won was that she had brought him up successfully and had sent him to college and that he had turned out so well — good looking (her teeth had gone unfilled so that his could be straightened), intelligent (he realized he was too intelligent to be a success), and with a future ahead of him (there was of course no future ahead of him). She excused his gloominess on the grounds that he was still growing up and his radical ideas on his lack of practical experience. She said he didn't yet know a thing about "life," that he hadn't even entered the real world — when already he was as disenchanted with it as a man of fifty.

The further irony of all this was that in spite of her, he had turned out so well. In spite of going to only a third-rate college, he had, on his own initiative, come out with a first-rate education; in spite of growing up dominated by a small mind, he had ended up with a large one; in spite of all her foolish views, he was free of prejudice and unafraid to face facts. Most miraculous of all, instead of being blinded by love for her as she was for him, he had cut himself emotionally free of her and could see her with complete objectivity. He was not dominated by his mother.

The bus stopped with a sudden jerk and shook him from his meditation. A woman from the back lurched forward with little steps and barely escaped falling in his newspaper as she righted herself. She got off and a large Negro got on. Julian kept his paper lowered to watch. It gave him a certain satisfaction to see injustice in daily operation. It confirmed his view that with a few exceptions there was no one worth knowing within a radius of three hundred miles. The Negro was well dressed and carried a briefcase. He looked around and then sat down on the other end of the seat where the woman with the red and white canvas sandals was sitting. He immediately unfolded a newspaper and obscured himself behind it. Julian's mother's elbow at once prodded insistently into his ribs. "Now you see why I won't ride on these buses by myself," she whispered.

The woman with the red and white canvas sandals had risen at the same time the Negro sat down and had gone further back in the bus and taken the seat of the woman who had got off. His mother leaned forward and cast her an approving look.

Julian rose, crossed the aisle, and sat down in the place of the woman with the canvas sandals. From this position, he looked serenely across at his mother. Her face had turned an angry red. He stared at her, making his eyes the eyes of a stranger. He felt his tension suddenly lift as if he had openly declared war on her.

He would have liked to get in conversation with the Negro and to talk with him about art or politics or any subject that would be above the comprehension of those around them, but the man remained entrenched behind his paper. He was either ignoring the change of seating or had never noticed it. There was no way for Julian to convey his sympathy.

His mother kept her eyes fixed reproachfully on his face. The woman with the protruding teeth was looking at him avidly as if he were a type of monster new to her.

"Do you have a light?" he asked the Negro.

Without looking away from his paper, the man reached in his pocket and handed him a packet of matches.

"Thanks," Julian said. For a moment he held the matches foolishly. A NO SMOKING sign looked down upon him from over the door. This alone would not have deterred him; he had no cigarettes. He had quit smoking some months before because he could not afford it. "Sorry," he muttered and handed back the matches. The Negro lowered the paper and gave him an annoyed look. He took the matches and raised the paper again.

His mother continued to gaze at him but she did not take advantage of his momentary discomfort. Her eyes retained their battered look. Her face seemed to be unnaturally red, as if her blood pressure had risen. Julian allowed no glimmer of sympathy to show on his face. Having got the advantage, he wanted desperately to keep it and carry it through. He would have liked to teach her a lesson that would last her a while, but there seemed no way to continue the point. The Negro refused to come out from behind his paper.

Julian folded his arms and looked stolidly before him, facing her but as if he did not see her, as if he had ceased to recognize her existence. He visualized a scene in which, the bus having reached their stop, he would remain in his seat and when she said, "Aren't you going to get off?" he would look at her as at a stranger who had rashly addressed him. The corner they got off on was usually deserted, but it was well lighted and it would not hurt her to walk by herself the four blocks to the Y. He decided to wait until the time came and then decide whether or not he would let her get off by herself. He would have to be at the Y at ten to bring her back, but he could leave her wondering if he was going to show up. There was no reason for her to think she could always depend on him.

He retired again into the high-ceilinged room sparsely settled with large pieces of antique furniture. His soul expanded momentarily but then he became aware of his mother across from him and the vision shriveled. He studied her coldly. Her feet in little pumps dangled like a child's and did not quite reach the floor. She was training on him an exaggerated look of reproach. He felt completely detached from her. At that moment he could with pleasure have slapped her as he would have slapped a particularly obnoxious child in his charge.

He began to imagine various unlikely ways by which he could teach her a lesson. He might make friends with some distinguished Negro professor or lawyer and bring him home to spend the evening. He would be entirely justified but her blood pressure would rise to 300. He could not push her to the extent of making her have a stroke, and moreover, he had never been successful at making any Negro friends. He had tried to strike up an acquaintance on the bus with some of the better types, with ones that looked like professors or ministers or lawyers. One morning he had sat down next to a distinguished-looking dark brown man who had answered his questions with a sonorous solemnity but who had turned out to be an undertaker. Another day he had sat down beside a cigar-smoking Negro with a diamond ring on his finger, but after a few stilted pleasantries, the Negro had rung the buzzer and risen, slipping two lottery tickets into Julian's hand as he climbed over him to leave.

He imagined his mother lying desperately ill and his being able to secure only a Negro doctor for her. He toyed with that idea for a few minutes and then dropped it for a momentary vision of himself participating as a sympathizer in a sit-in demonstration. This was possible but he did not linger with it. Instead, he approached the ultimate horror. He brought home a beautiful suspiciously Negroid woman. Prepare yourself, he said. There is nothing you can do about it. This is the woman I've chosen. She's intelligent, dignified, even good, and she's suffered and she hasn't thought it *fun*. Now persecute us, go ahead and persecute us. Drive her out of here, but remember, you're driving me too. His eyes were narrowed and through the indignation he had generated, he saw his mother across the aisle, purple-faced, shrunken to the dwarf-like proportions of her moral nature, sitting like a mummy beneath the ridiculous banner of her hat.

He was tilted out of his fantasy again as the bus stopped. The door opened with a sucking hiss and out of the dark a large, gaily dressed, sullen-looking colored woman got on with a little boy. The child, who might have been four, had on a short plaid suit and a Tyrolean hat with a blue feather in it. Julian hoped that he would sit down beside him and that the woman would push in beside his mother. He could think of no better arrangement.

As she waited for her tokens, the woman was surveying the seating possibilities — he hoped with the idea of sitting where she was least wanted. There was something familiar-looking about her but Julian could not place what it was. She was a giant of a woman. Her face was set not only to meet opposition but to seek it out. The downward tilt of her large lower lip was like a warning sign: DON'T TAMPER WITH ME. Her bulging figure was encased in a green crepe dress and her feet overflowed in red shoes. She had on a hideous hat. A purple velvet flap came down on one side of it and stood up on the other; the rest of it was green and looked like a cushion with the stuffing out. She carried a mammoth red pocketbook that bulged throughout as if it were stuffed with rocks.

To Julian's disappointment, the little boy climbed up on the empty seat beside his mother. His mother lumped all children, black and white, into the common category, "cute," and she thought little Negroes were on the whole cuter than little white children. She smiled at the little boy as he climbed on the seat.

Meanwhile the woman was bearing down upon the empty seat beside Julian. To his annoyance, she squeezed herself into it. He saw his mother's face change as the woman settled herself next to him and he realized with satisfaction that this was more objectionable to her than it was to him. Her face seemed almost gray and there was a look of dull recognition in her eyes, as if suddenly she had sickened at some awful confrontation. Julian saw that it was because she and the woman had, in a sense, swapped sons. Though his mother would not realize the symbolic significance of this, she would feel it. His amusement showed plainly on his face.

The woman next to him muttered something unintelligible to herself. He was conscious of a kind of bristling next to him, a muted growling like that of an angry cat. He could not see anything but the red pocketbook upright on the bulging green thighs. He visualized the woman as she had stood waiting for her tokens — the ponderous figure, rising from the red shoes upward over the solid hips, the mammoth bosom, the haughty face, to the green and purple hat.

His eyes widened.

The vision of the two hats, identical, broke upon him with the radiance of a brilliant sunrise. His face was suddenly lit with joy. He could not believe that Fate had thrust upon his mother such a lesson. He gave a loud chuckle so that she would look at him and see that he saw. She turned her eyes on him slowly. The blue in them seemed to have turned a bruised purple. For a moment he had an uncomfortable sense of her innocence, but it lasted only a second before principle rescued him. Justice entitled him to laugh. His grin hardened until it said to her as plainly as if he were saying aloud: Your punishment exactly fits your pettiness. This should teach you a permanent lesson.

Her eyes shifted to the woman. She seemed unable to bear looking at him and to find the woman preferable. He became conscious again of the bristling presence at his side. The woman was rumbling like a volcano about to become active. His mother's mouth began to twitch slightly at one corner. With a sinking heart, he saw incipient signs of recovery on her face and realized that this was going to strike her suddenly as funny and was going to be no lesson at all. She kept her eyes on the woman and an amused smile came over her face as if the woman were a monkey that had stolen her hat. The little Negro was looking up at her with large fascinated eyes. He had been trying to attract her attention for some time.

"Carver!" the woman said suddenly. "Come heah!"

When he saw that the spotlight was on him at last, Carver drew his feet up and turned himself toward Julian's mother and giggled.

"Carver!" the woman said. "You heah me? Come heah!"

Carver slid down from the seat but remained squatting with his back against the base of it, his head turned slyly around toward Julian's mother, who was smiling at him. The woman reached a hand across the aisle and snatched him to her. He righted himself and hung backwards on her knees, grinning at Julian's mother. "Isn't he cute?" Julian's mother said to the woman with the protruding teeth.

"I reckon he is," the woman said without conviction.

The Negress yanked him upright but he eased out of her grip and shot across the aisle and scrambled, giggling wildly, onto the seat beside his love.

"I think he likes me," Julian's mother said, and smiled at the woman. It was the smile she used when she was being particularly gracious to an inferior. Julian saw everything lost. The lesson had rolled off her like rain on a roof.

The woman stood up and yanked the little boy off the seat as if she were snatching him from contagion. Julian could feel the rage in her at having no weapon like his mother's smile. She gave the child a sharp slap across his leg. He howled once and then thrust his head into her stomach and kicked his feet against her shins. "Be-have," she said vehemently.

The bus stopped and the Negro who had been reading the newspaper got off. The woman moved over and set the little boy down with a thump between herself and Julian. She held him firmly by the knee. In a moment he put his hands in front of his face and peeped at Julian's mother through his fingers.

"I see yoooooooo!" she said and put her hand in front of her face and peeped at him.

The woman slapped his hand down. "Quit yo' foolishness," she said, "before I knock the living Jesus out of you!"

Julian was thankful that the next stop was theirs. He reached up and pulled the cord. The woman reached up and pulled it at the same time. Oh my God, he thought. He had the terrible intuition that when they got off the bus together, his mother would open her purse and give the little boy a nickel. The gesture would be as natural to her as breathing. The bus stopped and the woman got up and lunged to the front, dragging the child, who wished to stay on, after her. Julian and his mother got up and followed. As they neared the door, Julian tried to relieve her of her pocketbook.

"No," she murmured, "I want to give the little boy a nickel."

"No!" Julian hissed. "No!"

She smiled down at the child and opened her bag. The bus door opened and the woman picked him up by the arm and descended with him, hanging at her hip. Once in the street she set him down and shook him.

Julian's mother had to close her purse while she got down the bus step but as soon as her feet were on the ground, she opened it again and began to rummage inside. "I can't find but a penny," she whispered, "but it looks like a new one."

"Don't do it!" Julian said fiercely between his teeth. There was a streetlight on the corner and she hurried to get under it so that she could better see into her pocketbook. The woman was heading off rapidly down the street with the child still hanging backward on her hand.

"Oh little boy!" Julian's mother called and took a few quick steps and caught up with them just beyond the lamppost. "Here's a bright new penny for you," and she held out the coin, which shone bronze in the dim light.

The huge woman turned and for a moment stood, her shoulders lifted and her face frozen with frustrated rage, and stared at Julian's mother. Then all at once she seemed to explode like a piece of machinery that had been given one ounce of pressure too much. Julian saw the black fist swing out with the red pocketbook. He shut his eyes and cringed as he heard the woman shout, "He don't take nobody's pennies!" When he opened his eyes, the woman was disappearing down the street with the little boy staring wide-eyed over her shoulder. Julian's mother was sitting on the sidewalk.

"I told you not to do that," Julian said angrily. "I told you not to do that!"

He stood over her for a minute, gritting his teeth. Her legs were stretched out in front of her and her hat was on her lap. He squatted down and looked her in the face. It was totally expressionless. "You got exactly what you deserved," he said. "Now get up."

He picked up her pocketbook and put what had fallen out back in it. He picked the hat up off her lap. The penny caught his eye on the sidewalk and he picked that up and let it drop before her eyes into the purse. Then he stood up and leaned over and held his hands out to pull her up. She remained immobile. He sighed. Rising above them on either side were black apartment buildings, marked with irregular rectangles of light. At the end of the block a man came out of a door and walked off in the opposite direction. "All right," he said, "suppose somebody happens by and wants to know why you're sitting on the sidewalk?"

She took the hand and, breathing hard, pulled heavily up on it and then stood for a moment, swaying slightly as if the spots of light in the darkness were circling around her. Her eyes, shadowed and confused, finally settled on his face. He did not try to conceal his irritation. "I hope this teaches you a lesson," he said. She leaned forward and her eyes raked his face. She seemed trying to determine his identity. Then, as if she found nothing familiar about him, she started off with a headlong movement in the wrong direction.

"Aren't you going to the Y?" he asked.

"Home," she muttered.

"Well, are we walking?"

For answer she kept going. Julian followed along, his hands behind him. He saw no reason to let the lesson she had had go without backing it up with an explanation of its meaning. She might as well be made to understand what had happened to her. "Don't think that was just an uppity Negro woman," he said. "That was the whole colored race which will no longer take your condescending pennies. That was your black double. She can wear the same hat as you, and to be sure," he added gratuitously (because he thought it was funny), "it looked better on her than it did on you. What all this means," he said, "is that the old world is gone. The old manners are obsolete and your graciousness is not worth a damn." He thought bitterly of the house that had been lost for him. "You aren't who you think you are," he said.

She continued to plow ahead, paying no attention to him. Her hair had come undone on one side. She dropped her pocketbook and took no notice. He stooped and picked it up and handed it to her but she did not take it.

"You needn't act as if the world had come to an end," he said, "because it hasn't. From now on you've got to live in a new world and face a few realities for a change. Buck up," he said, "it won't kill you."

She was breathing fast.

"Let's wait on the bus," he said.

"Home," she said thickly.

"I hate to see you behave like this," he said. "Just like a child. I should be able to expect more of you." He decided to stop where he was and make her stop and wait for a bus. "I'm not going any farther," he said, stopping. "We're going on the bus."

She continued to go on as if she had not heard him. He took a few steps and caught her arm and stopped her. He looked into her face and caught his breath. He was looking into a face he had never seen before. "Tell Grandpa to come get me," she said.

He stared, stricken.

"Tell Caroline to come get me," she said.

Stunned, he let her go and she lurched forward again, walking as if one leg were shorter than the other. A tide of darkness seemed to be sweeping her from him. "Mother!" he cried. "Darling, sweetheart, wait!" Crumpling, she fell to the pavement. He dashed forward and fell at her side, crying, "Mamma, Mamma!" He turned her over. Her face was fiercely distorted. One eye, large and staring, moved slightly to the left as if it had become unmoored. The other remained fixed on him, raked his face again, found nothing and closed.

"Wait here, wait here!" he cried and jumped up and began to run for help toward a cluster of lights he saw in the distance ahead of him. "Help, help!" he shouted, but his voice was thin, scarcely a thread of sound. The lights drifted farther away the faster he ran and his feet moved numbly as if they carried him nowhere. The tide of darkness seemed to sweep him back to her, postponing from moment to moment his entry into the world of guilt and sorrow.

THE PLAY

D eath of a Salesman

Certain Private Conversations in Two Acts and a Requiem

ARTHUR   MILLER

ACT ONE

A melody is heard, played upon a flute. It is small and fine, telling of grass and trees and the horizon. The curtain rises.

Before us is the Salesman's house. We are aware of towering, angular shapes behind it, surrounding it on all sides. Only the blue light of the sky falls upon the house and forestage; the surrounding area shows an angry glow of orange. As more light appears, we see a solid vault of apartment houses around the small, fragile-seeming home. An air of the dream clings to the place, a dream rising out of reality. The kitchen at center seems actual enough, for there is a kitchen table with three chairs, and a refrigerator. But no other fixtures are seen. At the back of the kitchen there is a draped entrance, which leads to the living-room.

To the right of the kitchen, on a level raised two feet, is a bedroom furnished only with a brass bedstead and a straight chair. On a shelf over the bed a silver athletic trophy stands. A window opens onto the apartment house at the side.

Behind the kitchen, on a level raised six and a half feet, is the boys' bedroom, at present barely visible. Two beds are dimly seen, and at the back of the room a dormer window. [This bedroom is above the unseen living-room.] At the left a stairway curves up to it from the kitchen.

The entire setting is wholly or, in some places, partially transparent. The roof-line of the house is one-dimensional; under and over it we see the apartment buildings. Before the house lies an apron, curving beyond the forestage into the orchestra. This forward area serves as the back yard as well as the locale of all WILLY's *imaginings and of his city scenes. Whenever the action is in the present the actors observe the imaginary wall-lines, entering the house only through its door at the left. But in the scenes of the past these boundaries are broken, and characters enter or leave a room by stepping "through" a wall onto the forestage.*

From the right, WILLY LOMAN, *the Salesman, enters, carrying two large sample cases. The flute plays on. He hears but is not aware of it. He is past sixty years of age, dressed quietly. Even as he crosses the stage to the doorway of the house, his exhaustion is apparent. He unlocks the door, comes into the kitchen, and thankfully lets his burden down, feeling the soreness of his palms. A word-sigh escapes his lips — it might be "Oh, boy, oh, boy." He closes the door, then carries his cases out into the living-room, through the draped kitchen doorway.*

LINDA, *his wife, has stirred in her bed at the right. She gets out and puts on a robe, listening. Most often jovial, she has developed an iron repression of her exceptions to* WILLY's *behavior — she more than loves him, she admires him, as though his mercurial nature, his temper, his massive dreams and little cruelties, served her only as sharp reminders of the turbulent longings within him, longings which she shares but lacks the temperament to utter and follow to their end.*

LINDA [*hearing* WILLY *outside the bedroom, calls with some trepidation*]: Willy!

WILLY: It's all right. I came back.

LINDA: Why? What happened? [*Slight pause.*] Did something happen, Willy?

WILLY: No, nothing happened.

LINDA: You didn't smash the car, did you?

WILLY [*with casual irritation*]: I said nothing happened. Didn't you hear me?

LINDA: Don't you feel well?

WILLY: I'm tired to the death. [*The flute has faded away. He sits on the bed beside her, a little numb.*] I couldn't make it. I just couldn't make it, Linda.

LINDA [*very carefully, delicately*]: Where were you all day? You look terrible.

WILLY: I got as far as a little above Yonkers. I stopped for a cup of coffee. Maybe it was the coffee.

LINDA: What?

WILLY [*after a pause*]: I suddenly couldn't drive any more. The car kept going off onto the shoulder, y'know?

LINDA [*helpfully*]: Oh. Maybe it was the steering again. I don't think Angelo knows the Studebaker.

WILLY: No, it's me, it's me. Suddenly I realize I'm goin' sixty miles an hour and I don't remember the last five minutes. I'm — I can't seem to — keep my mind to it.

LINDA: Maybe it's your glasses. You never went for your new glasses.

WILLY: No, I see everything. I came back ten miles an hour. It took me nearly four hours from Yonkers.

LINDA [*resigned*]: Well, you'll just have to take a rest, Willy, you can't continue this way.

WILLY: I just got back from Florida.

LINDA: But you didn't rest your mind. Your mind is overactive, and the mind is what counts, dear.

WILLY: I'll start out in the morning. Maybe I'll feel better in the morning. [*She is taking off his shoes.*] These goddam arch supports are killing me.

LINDA: Take an aspirin. Should I get you an aspirin? It'll soothe you.

WILLY [*with wonder*]: I was driving along, you understand? And I was fine. I was even observing the scenery. You can imagine, me looking at scenery, on the road every week of my life. But it's so beautiful up there, Linda, the trees are so thick, and the sun is warm. I opened the windshield and just let the warm air bathe over me. And then all of a sudden I'm goin' off the road! I'm tellin' ya, I absolutely forgot I was driving. If I'd've gone the other way over the white line I might've killed somebody. So I went on again — and five minutes later I'm dreamin' again, and I nearly — [*He presses two fingers against his eyes.*] I have such thoughts, I have such strange thoughts.

LINDA: Willy, dear. Talk to them again. There's no reason why you can't work in New York.

WILLY: They don't need me in New York. I'm the New England man. I'm vital in New England.

LINDA: But you're sixty years old. They can't expect you to keep traveling every week.

WILLY: I'll have to send a wire to Portland. I'm supposed to see Brown

and Morrison tomorrow morning at ten o'clock to show the line. Goddammit, I could sell them!

[*He starts putting on his jacket.*]

LINDA [*taking the jacket from him*]: Why don't you go down to the place
tomorrow and tell Howard you've simply got to work in New York? You're
too accommodating, dear.

WILLY: If old man Wagner was alive I'd a been in charge of New York
now! That man was a prince, he was a masterful man. But that boy of his,
that Howard, he don't appreciate. When I went north the first time, the
Wagner Company didn't know where New England was!

LINDA: Why don't you tell those things to Howard, dear?

WILLY [*encouraged*]: I will, I definitely will. Is there any cheese?

LINDA: I'll make you a sandwich.

WILLY: No, go to sleep. I'll take some milk. I'll be up right away. The
boys in?

LINDA: They're sleeping. Happy took Biff on a date tonight.

WILLY [*interested*]: That so?

LINDA: It was so nice to see them shaving together, one behind the
other, in the bathroom. And going out together. You notice? The whole
house smells of shaving lotion.

WILLY: Figure it out. Work a lifetime to pay off a house. You finally
own it, and there's nobody to live in it.

LINDA: Well, dear, life is a casting off. It's always that way.

WILLY: No, no, some people — some people accomplish something. Did
Biff say anything after I went this morning?

LINDA: You shouldn't have criticized him, Willy, especially after he just
got off the train. You mustn't lose your temper with him.

WILLY: When the hell did I lose my temper? I simply asked him if he
was making any money. Is that a criticism?

LINDA: But, dear, how could he make any money?

WILLY [*worried and angered*]: There's such an undercurrent in him. He
became a moody man. Did he apologize when I left this morning?

LINDA: He was crestfallen, Willy. You know how he admires you. I think
if he finds himself, then you'll both be happier and not fight any more.

WILLY: How can he find himself on a farm? Is that a life? A farmhand?
In the beginning, when he was young, I thought, well, a young man, it's
good for him to tramp around, take a lot of different jobs. But it's more
than ten years now and he has yet to make thirty-five dollars a week!

LINDA: He's finding himself, Willy.

WILLY: Not finding yourself at the age of thirty-four is a disgrace!

LINDA: Shh!

WILLY: The trouble is he's lazy, goddammit!

LINDA: Willy, please!

WILLY: Biff is a lazy bum!

LINDA: They're sleeping. Get something to eat. Go on down.

WILLY: Why did he come home? I would like to know what brought him home.

LINDA: I don't know. I think he's still lost, Willy. I think he's very lost.

WILLY: Biff Loman is lost. In the greatest country in the world a young man with such — personal attractiveness, gets lost. And such a hard worker. There's one thing about Biff — he's not lazy.

LINDA: Never.

WILLY [*with pity and resolve*]: I'll see him in the morning; I'll have a nice talk with him. I'll get him a job selling. He could be big in no time. My God! Remember how they used to follow him around in high school? When he smiled at one of them their faces lit up. When he walked down the street . . .

[*He loses himself in reminiscences.*]

LINDA [*trying to bring him out of it*]: Willy, dear, I got a new kind of American-type cheese today. It's whipped.

WILLY: Why do you get American when I like Swiss?

LINDA: I just thought you'd like a change —

WILLY: I don't want a change! I want Swiss cheese. Why am I always being contradicted?

LINDA [*with a covering laugh*]: I thought it would be a surprise.

WILLY: Why don't you open a window in here, for God's sake?

LINDA [*with infinite patience*]: They're all open, dear.

WILLY: The way they boxed us in here. Bricks and windows, windows and bricks.

LINDA: We should've bought the land next door.

WILLY: The street is lined with cars. There's not a breath of fresh air in the neighborhood. The grass don't grow any more, you can't raise a carrot in the back yard. They should've had a law against apartment houses. Remember those two beautiful elm trees out there? When I and Biff hung the swing between them?

LINDA: Yeah, like being a million miles from the city.

WILLY: They should've arrested the builder for cutting those down. They massacred the neighborhood. [*Lost.*] More and more I think of those days, Linda. This time of year it was lilac and wisteria. And then the peonies would come out, and the daffodils. What fragrance in this room!

LINDA: Well, after all, people have to move somewhere.

WILLY: No, there's more people now.

LINDA: I don't think there's more people. I think —

WILLY: There's more people! That's what's ruining this country! Population is getting out of control. The competition is maddening! Smell the stink from that apartment house! And another one on the other side. . . . How can they whip cheese?

[*On* WILLY's *last line,* BIFF *and* HAPPY *raise themselves up in their beds, listening.*]

LINDA: Go down, try it. And be quiet.

WILLY [*turning to* LINDA, *guiltily*]: You're not worried about me, are you, sweetheart?

BIFF: What's the matter?

HAPPY: Listen!

LINDA: You've got too much on the ball to worry about.

WILLY: You're my foundation and my support, Linda.

LINDA: Just try to relax. You make mountains out of molehills.

WILLY: I won't fight with him any more. If he wants to go back to Texas, let him go.

LINDA: He'll find his way.

WILLY: Sure. Certain men just don't get started till later in life. Like Thomas Edison, I think. Or B. F. Goodrich. One of them was deaf. [*He starts for the bedroom doorway.*] I'll put my money on Biff.

LINDA: And Willy — if it's warm Sunday, we'll drive in the country. And we'll open the windshield, and take lunch.

WILLY: No, the windshields don't open on the new cars.

LINDA: But you opened it today.

WILLY: Me? I didn't. [*He stops.*] Now isn't that peculiar! Isn't that a remarkable ——

[*He breaks off in amazement and fright as the flute is heard distantly.*]

LINDA: What, darling?

WILLY: That is the most remarkable thing.

LINDA: What, dear?

WILLY: I was thinking of the Chevvy. [*Slight pause.*] Nineteen twenty-eight . . . when I had that red Chevvy— [*Breaks off.*] That funny? I coulda sworn I was driving that Chevvy today.

LINDA: Well, that's nothing. Something must've reminded you.

WILLY: Remarkable. Ts. Remember those days? The way Biff used to simonize that car? The dealer refused to believe there was eighty thousand miles on it. [*He shakes his head.*] Heh! [*To* LINDA.] Close your eyes, I'll be right up.

[*He walks out of the bedroom.*]

HAPPY [*to* BIFF]: Jesus, maybe he smashed up the car again!

LINDA [*calling after* WILLY]: Be careful on the stairs, dear! The cheese is on the middle shelf!

[*She turns, goes over to the bed, takes his jacket, and goes out of the bedroom.*]

[*Light has risen on the boys' room. Unseen,* WILLY *is heard talking to himself, "Eighty thousand miles," and a little laugh.* BIFF *gets out of bed, comes downstage a bit, and stands attentively.* BIFF *is two years older than his brother* HAPPY, *well built, but in these days bears a worn air and seems less self-assured. He has succeeded less, and his dreams are stronger and less acceptable than* HAPPY's. HAPPY *is tall, powerfully made. Sexuality is like a visible color on him, or a scent that many women have discovered. He, like his brother, is lost, but in a different way, for he has never allowed himself to turn his face toward defeat and is thus more confused and hard-skinned, although seemingly more content.*]

HAPPY [*getting out of bed*]: He's going to get his license taken away if he keeps that up. I'm getting nervous about him, y'know, Biff?

BIFF: His eyes are going.

HAPPY: No, I've driven with him. He sees all right. He just doesn't keep his mind on it. I drove into the city with him last week. He stops at a green light and then it turns red and he goes.

[*He laughs.*]

BIFF: Maybe he's color-blind.

HAPPY: Pop? Why he's got the finest eye for color in the business. You know that.

BIFF [*sitting down on his bed*]: I'm going to sleep.

HAPPY: You're not still sour on Dad, are you Biff?

BIFF: He's all right, I guess.

WILLY [*underneath them, in the living-room*]: Yes, sir, eighty thousand miles — eighty-two thousand!

BIFF: You smoking?

HAPPY [*holding out a pack of cigarettes*]: Want one?

BIFF [*taking a cigarette*]: I can never sleep when I smell it.

WILLY: What a simonizing job, heh!

HAPPY [*with deep sentiment*]: Funny, Biff, y'know? Us sleeping in here again? The old beds. [*He pats his bed affectionately.*] All the talk that went across those two beds, huh? Our whole lives.

BIFF: Yeah. Lotta dreams and plans.

HAPPY [*with a deep and masculine laugh*]: About five hundred women would like to know what was said in this room.

[*They share a soft laugh.*]

BIFF: Remember that big Betsy something — what the hell was her name — over on Bushwick Avenue?

HAPPY [*combing his hair*]: With the collie dog!

BIFF: That's the one. I got you in there, remember?

HAPPY: Yeah, that was my first time — I think. Boy, there was a pig! [*They laugh, almost crudely.*] You taught me everything I know about women. Don't forget that.

BIFF: I bet you forgot how bashful you used to be. Especially with girls.

HAPPY: Oh, I still am, Biff.

BIFF: Oh, go on.

HAPPY: I just control it, that's all. I think I got less bashful and you got more so. What happened, Biff? Where's the old humor, the old confidence? [*He shakes* BIFF's *knee.* BIFF *gets up and moves restlessly about the room.*] What's the matter?

BIFF: Why does Dad mock me all the time?

HAPPY: He's not mocking you, he ——

BIFF: Everything I say there's a twist of mockery on his face. I can't get near him.

HAPPY: He just wants you to make good, that's all. I wanted to talk to you about Dad for a long time, Biff. Something's — happening to him. He — talks to himself.

BIFF: I noticed that this morning. But he always mumbled.

HAPPY: But not so noticeable. It got so embarrassing I sent him to Florida. And you know something? Most of the time he's talking to you.

BIFF: What's he say about me?

HAPPY: I can't make it out.

BIFF: What's he say about me?

HAPPY: I think the fact that you're not settled, that you're still kind of up in the air . . .

BIFF: There's one or two other things depressing him, Happy.

HAPPY: What do you mean?

BIFF: Never mind. Just don't lay it all to me.

HAPPY: But I think if you just get started — I mean — is there any future for you out there?

BIFF: I tell ya, Hap, I don't know what the future is. I don't know — what I'm supposed to want.

HAPPY: What do you mean?

BIFF: Well, I spent six or seven years after high school trying to work myself up. Shipping clerk, salesman, business of one kind or another. And it's a measly manner of existence. To get on that subway on the hot mornings in summer. To devote your whole life to keeping stock, or making phone calls, or selling or buying. To suffer fifty weeks of the year for the sake of a two-week vacation, when all you really desire is to be outdoors, with your shirt off. And always to have to get ahead of the next fella. And still — that's how you build a future.

HAPPY: Well, you really enjoy it on a farm? Are you content out there?

BIFF [*with rising agitation*]: Hap, I've had twenty or thirty different kinds of jobs since I left home before the war, and it always turns out the same. I just realized it lately. In Nebraska when I herded cattle, and the Dakotas, and Arizona, and now in Texas. It's why I came home now, I guess, because I realized it. This farm I work on, it's spring there now, see? And they've got about fifteen new colts. There's nothing more inspiring or — beautiful than the sight of a mare and a new colt. And it's cool there now, see? Texas is cool now, and it's spring. And whenever spring comes to where I am, I suddenly get the feeling, my God, I'm not gettin' anywhere! What the hell am I doing, playing around with horses, twenty-eight dollars a week! I'm thirty-four years old, I oughta be makin' my future. That's when I come running home. And now, I get here, and I don't know what to do with myself. [*After a pause.*] I've always made a point of not wasting my life, and every time I come back here I know that all I've done is to waste my life.

HAPPY: You're a poet, you know that, Biff? You're a — you're an idealist!

BIFF: No, I'm mixed up very bad. Maybe I oughta get married. Maybe I oughta get stuck into something. Maybe that's my trouble. I'm like a boy. I'm not married, I'm not in business, I just — I'm like a boy. Are you content, Hap? You're a success, aren't you? Are you content?

HAPPY: Hell, no!

BIFF: Why? You're making money, aren't you?

HAPPY [*moving about with energy, expressiveness*]: All I can do now is wait for the merchandise manager to die. And suppose I get to be merchandise manager? He's a good friend of mine, and he just built a terrific estate on Long Island. And he lived there about two months and sold it, and now he's building another one. He can't enjoy it once it's finished. And I know that's just what I would do. I don't know what the hell I'm workin' for. Sometimes I sit in my apartment — all alone. And I think of the rent I'm paying. And it's crazy. But then, it's what I always wanted. My own apartment, a car, and plenty of women. And still, goddammit, I'm lonely.

BIFF [*with enthusiasm*]: Listen, why don't you come out West with me?

HAPPY: You and I, heh?

BIFF: Sure, maybe we could buy a ranch. Raise cattle, use our muscles. Men built like we are should be working out in the open.

HAPPY [*avidly*]: The Loman Brothers, heh?

BIFF [*with vast affection*]: Sure, we'd be known all over the counties!

HAPPY [*enthralled*]: That's what I dream about, Biff. Sometimes I want to just rip my clothes off in the middle of the store and outbox that goddam merchandise manager. I mean I can outbox, outrun, and outlift anybody in that store, and I have to take orders from those common, petty sons-of-bitches till I can't stand it any more.

BIFF: I'm tellin' you kid, if you were with me I'd be happy out there.

HAPPY [*enthused*]: See, Biff, everybody around me is so false that I'm constantly lowering my ideals . . .

BIFF: Baby, together we'd stand up for one another, we'd have someone to trust.

HAPPY: If I were around you ——

BIFF: Hap, the trouble is we weren't brought up to grub for money. I don't know how to do it.

HAPPY: Neither can I!

BIFF: Then let's go!

HAPPY: The only thing is — what can you make out there?

BIFF: But look at your friend. Builds an estate and then hasn't the peace of mind to live in it.

HAPPY: Yeah, but when he walks into the store the waves part in front of him. That's fifty-two thousand dollars a year coming through the revolving door, and I got more in my pinky finger that he's got in his head.

BIFF: Yeah, but you just said ——

HAPPY: I gotta show some of those pompous, self-important executives over there that Hap Loman can make the grade. I want to walk into the store the way he walks in. Then I'll go with you, Biff. We'll be together yet, I swear. But take those two we had tonight. Now weren't they gorgeous creatures?

BIFF: Yeah, yeah, most gorgeous I've had in years.

HAPPY: I get that any time I want, Biff. Whenever I feel disgusted. The only trouble is, it gets like bowling or something. I just keep knockin' them over and it doesn't mean anything. You still run around a lot?

BIFF: Naa. I'd like to find a girl — steady, somebody with substance.

HAPPY: That's what I long for.

BIFF: Go on! You'd never come home.

HAPPY: I would! Somebody with character, with resistance! Like Mom, y'know? You're gonna call me a bastard when I tell you this. That girl Charlotte I was with tonight is engaged to be married in five weeks.

[*He tries on his new hat.*]

BIFF: No kiddin'!

HAPPY: Sure, the guy's in line for the vice-presidency of the store. I don't know what gets into me, maybe I just have an overdeveloped sense of competition or something, but I went and ruined her, and furthermore I can't get rid of her. And he's the third executive I've done that to. Isn't that a crummy characteristic? And to top it all, I go to their weddings [*Indignantly, but laughing.*] Like I'm not supposed to take bribes. Manufacturers offer me a hundred-dollar bill now and then to throw an order their way. You know how honest I am, but it's like this girl, see. I hate myself for it. Because I don't want the girl, and, still, I take it and — I love it!

BIFF: Let's go to sleep.

HAPPY: I guess we didn't settle anything, heh?

BIFF: I just got one idea that I think I'm going to try.

HAPPY: What's that?

BIFF: Remember Bill Oliver?

HAPPY: Sure, Oliver is very big now. You want to work for him again?

BIFF: No, but when I quit he said something to me. He put his arm on my shoulder, and he said, "Biff, if you ever need anything, come to me."

HAPPY: I remember that. That sounds good.

BIFF: I think I'll go to see him. If I could get ten thousand or even seven or eight thousand dollars I could buy a beautiful ranch.

HAPPY: I bet he'd back you. 'Cause he thought highly of you, Biff. I mean, they all do. You're well liked, Biff. That's why I say to come back here, and we both have the apartment. And I'm tellin' you, Biff, any babe you want . . .

BIFF: No, with a ranch I could do the work I like and still be something. I just wonder though. I wonder if Oliver still thinks I stole that carton of basketballs.

HAPPY: Oh, he probably forgot that long ago. It's almost ten years. You're too sensitive. Anyway, he didn't really fire you.

BIFF: Well, I think he was going to. I think that's why I quit. I was never sure whether he knew or not. I know he thought the world of me, though. I was the only one he'd let lock up the place.

WILLY [*below*]: You gonna wash the engine, Biff?

HAPPY: Shh!

[BIFF *looks at* HAPPY, *who is gazing down, listening.* WILLY *is mumbling in the parlor.*]

HAPPY: You hear that?

[*They listen.* WILLY *laughs warmly.*]

BIFF [*growing angry*]: Doesn't he know Mom can hear that?

WILLY: Don't get your sweater dirty, Biff!

[*A look of pain crosses* BIFF's *face.*]

HAPPY: Isn't that terrible? Don't leave again, will you? You'll find a job here. You gotta stick around. I don't know what to do about him, it's getting embarrassing.

WILLY: What a simonizing job!

BIFF: Mom's hearing that!

WILLY: No kiddin', Biff, you got a date? Wonderful!

HAPPY: Go on to sleep. But talk to him in the morning, will you?

BIFF [*reluctantly getting into bed*]: With her in the house. Brother!

HAPPY [*getting into bed*]: I wish you'd have a good talk with him.

[*The light on their room begins to fade.*]

BIFF: [*to himself in bed*]: That selfish, stupid . . .

HAPPY: Sh . . . Sleep, Biff.

[*Their light is out. Well before they have finished speaking,* WILLY's *form is dimly seen below in the darkened kitchen. He opens the refrigerator, searches in there, and takes out a bottle of milk. The apartment houses are fading out, and the entire house and surroundings become covered with leaves. Music insinuates itself as the leaves appear.*]

WILLY: Just wanna be careful with those girls, Biff, that's all. Don't make any promises. No promises of any kind. Because a girl, y'know, they always believe what you tell 'em, and you're very young, Biff, you're too young to be talking seriously to girls.

[*Light rises on the kitchen.* WILLY, *talking, shuts the refrigerator door and comes downstage to the kitchen table. He pours milk into a glass. He is totally immersed in himself, smiling faintly.*]

WILLY: Too young entirely, Biff. You want to watch your schooling first. Then when you're all set, there'll be plenty of girls for a boy like you. [*He smiles broadly at a kitchen chair.*] That so? The girls pay for you? [*He laughs.*] Boy, you must really be makin' a hit.

[WILLY *is gradually addressing — physically — a point offstage, speaking through the wall of the kitchen, and his voice has been rising in volume to that of a normal conversation.*]

WILLY: I been wondering why you polish the car so careful. Ha! Don't leave the hubcaps, boys. Get the chamois to the hubcaps. Happy, use newspapers on the windows, it's the easiest thing. Show him how to do it, Biff! You see, Happy? Pad it up, use it like a pad. That's it, that's it, good work. You're doin' all right, Hap. [*He pauses, then nods in approbation for a few seconds, then looks upward.*] Biff, first thing we gotta do when we get time is clip that big branch over the house. Afraid it's gonna fall in a storm and hit the roof. Tell you what. We get a rope and sling her around, and then we climb up there with a couple of saws and take her down. Soon as you finish the car, boys, I wanna see ya. I got a surprise for you, boys.

BIFF [*offstage*]: Whatta ya got, Dad?

WILLY: No, you finish first. Never leave a job till you're finished — remember that. [*Looking toward the "big trees."*] Biff, up in Albany I saw a beautiful hammock. I think I'll buy it next trip, and we'll hang it right between those two elms. Wouldn't that be something? Just swingin' there under those branches. Boy, that would be . . .

[YOUNG BIFF *and* YOUNG HAPPY *appear from the direction* WILLY *was addressing.* HAPPY *carries rags and a pail of water.* BIFF, *wearing a sweater with a block "S," carries a football.*]

BIFF [*pointing in the direction of the car offstage*]: How's that, Pop, professional?

WILLY: Terrific. Terrific job, boys. Good work, Biff.

HAPPY: Where's the surprise, Pop?

WILLY: In the back seat of the car.

HAPPY: Boy!

[*He runs off.*]

BIFF: What is it, Dad? Tell me, what'd you buy?

WILLY [*laughing, cuffs him*]: Never mind, something I want you to have.

BIFF [*turns and starts off*]: What is it, Hap?

HAPPY [*offstage*]: It's a punching bag!

BIFF: Oh, Pop!

WILLY: It's got Gene Tunney's signature on it!

[HAPPY *runs offstage with a punching bag.*]

BIFF: Gee, how'd you know we wanted a punching bag?

WILLY: Well, it's the finest thing for the timing.

HAPPY [*lies down on his back and pedals with his feet*]: I'm losing weight, you notice, Pop?

WILLY [*to* HAPPY]: Jumping rope is good too.

BIFF: Did you see the new football I got?

WILLY [*examining the ball*]: Where'd you get a new ball?

BIFF: The coach told me to practice my passing.

WILLY: That so? And he gave you the ball, heh?

BIFF: Well, I borrowed it from the locker room.

[*He laughs confidently.*]

WILLY [*laughing with him at the theft*]: I want you to return that.

HAPPY: I told you he wouldn't like it!

BIFF [*angrily*]: Well, I'm bringing it back!

WILLY [*stopping the incipient argument, to* HAPPY]: Sure, he's gotta practice with a regulation ball, doesn't he? [*To* BIFF.] Coach'll probably congratulate you on your initiative!

BIFF: Oh, he keeps congratulating my initiative all the time, Pop.

WILLY: That's because he likes you. If somebody else took that ball there'd be an uproar. So what's the report, boys, what's the report?

BIFF: Where'd you go this time, Dad? Gee we were lonesome for you.

WILLY [*pleased, puts an arm around each boy and they come down to the apron*]: Lonesome, heh?

BIFF: Missed you every minute.

WILLY: Don't say? Tell you a secret, boys. Don't breathe it to a soul. Someday I'll have my own business, and I'll never have to leave home any more.

HAPPY: Like Uncle Charley, heh?

WILLY: Bigger than Uncle Charley! Because Charley is not — liked. He's liked, but he's not — well liked.

BIFF: Where'd you go this time, Dad?

WILLY: Well, I got on the road, and I went north to Providence. Met the Mayor.

BIFF: The Mayor of Providence!

WILLY: He was sitting in the hotel lobby.

BIFF: What'd he say?

WILLY: He said, "Morning!" And I said, "You got a fine city here, Mayor." And then he had coffee with me. And then I went to Waterbury. Waterbury is a fine city. Big clock city, the famous Waterbury clock. Sold a nice bill there. And then Boston — Boston is the cradle of the Revolution. A fine city. And a couple of other towns in Mass., and on to Portland and Bangor and straight home!

BIFF: Gee, I'd love to go with you sometime, Dad.

WILLY: Soon as summer comes.

HAPPY: Promise?

WILLY: You and Hap and I, and I'll show you all the towns. America is full of beautiful towns and fine, upstanding people. And they know me, boys, they know me up and down New England. The finest people. And when I bring you fellas up, there'll be open sesame for all of us, 'cause one thing, boys: I have friends. I can park my car in any street in New England, and the cops protect it like their own. This summer, heh?

BIFF AND HAPPY [*together*]: Yeah! You bet!

WILLY: We'll take our bathing suits.

HAPPY: We'll carry your bags, Pop!

WILLY: Oh, won't that be something! Me comin' into the Boston stores with you boys carryin' my bags. What a sensation!

[BIFF *is prancing around, practicing passing the ball.*]

WILLY: You nervous, Biff, about the game?

BIFF: Not if you're gonna be there.

WILLY: What do they say about you in school, now that they made you captain?

HAPPY: There's a crowd of girls behind him every time the classes change.

BIFF [*taking* WILLY's *hand*]: This Saturday, Pop, this Saturday — just for you, I'm going to break through for a touchdown.

HAPPY: You're supposed to pass.

BIFF: I'm takin' one play for Pop. You watch me, Pop, and when I take off my helmet, that means I'm breakin' out. Then you watch me crash through that line!

WILLY [*kisses* BIFF]: Oh, wait'll I tell this in Boston!

[BERNARD *enters in knickers. He is younger than* BIFF, *earnest and loyal, a worried boy.*]

BERNARD: Biff, where are you? You're supposed to study with me today.

WILLY: Hey, looka Bernard. What're you lookin' so anemic about, Bernard?

BERNARD: He's gotta study, Uncle Willy. He's got Regents next week.

HAPPY [*taunting, spinning* BERNARD *around*]: Let's box, Bernard!

BERNARD: Biff! [*He gets away from* HAPPY.] Listen, Biff, I heard Mr. Birnbaum say that if you don't start studyin' math he's gonna flunk you, and you won't graduate. I heard him!

WILLY: You better study with him, Biff. Go ahead now.

BERNARD: I heard him!

BIFF: Oh, Pop, you didn't see my sneakers!

[*He holds up a foot for* WILLY *to look at.*]

WILLY: Hey, that's a beautiful job of printing!

BERNARD [*wiping his glasses*]: Just because he printed University of Virginia on his sneakers doesn't mean they've got to graduate him, Uncle Willy!

WILLY [*angrily*]: What're you talking about? With scholarships to three universities they're gonna flunk him?

BERNARD: But I heard Mr. Birnbaum say ——

WILLY: Don't be a pest, Bernard! [*To his boys*]: What an anemic!

BERNARD: Okay, I'm waiting for you in my house, Biff.

[BERNARD *goes off. The* LOMANS *laugh.*]

WILLY: Bernard is not well liked, is he?

BIFF: He's liked, but he's not well liked.

HAPPY: That's right, Pop.

WILLY: That's just what I mean. Bernard can get the best marks in school, y'understand, but when he gets out in the business world, y'understand, you are going to be five times ahead of him. That's why I thank Almighty God you're both built like Adonises. Because the man who makes an appearance in the business world, the man who creates personal interest, is the man who gets ahead. Be liked and you will never want. You take me, for instance. I never have to wait in line to see a buyer. "Willy Loman is here!" That's all they have to know, and I go right through.

BIFF: Did you knock them dead, Pop?

WILLY: Knocked 'em cold in Providence, slaughtered 'em in Boston.

HAPPY [*on his back, pedaling again*]: I'm losing weight, you notice, Pop?

[LINDA *enters, as of old, a ribbon in her hair, carrying a basket of washing.*]

LINDA [*with youthful energy*]: Hello, dear!

WILLY: Sweetheart!

LINDA: How'd the Chevvy run?

WILLY: Chevrolet, Linda, is the greatest car ever built. [*To the boys.*] Since when do you let your mother carry wash up the stairs?

BIFF: Grab hold there, boy!

HAPPY: Where to, Mom?

LINDA: Hang them up on the line. And you better go down to your friends, Biff. The cellar is full of boys. They don't know what to do with themselves.

BIFF: Ah, when Pop comes home they can wait!

WILLY [*laughs appreciatively*]: You better go down and tell them what to do, Biff.

BIFF: I think I'll have them sweep out the furnace room.

WILLY: Good work, Biff.

BIFF⁻ [*goes through wall-line of kitchen to doorway at back and calls down*]: Fellas! Everybody sweep out the furnace room! I'll be right down!

VOICES: All right! Okay, Biff.

BIFF: George and Sam and Frank, come out back! We're hangin' up the wash! Come on, Hap, on the double!

[*He and* HAPPY *carry out the basket.*]

LINDA: The way they obey him!

WILLY: Well, that's training, the training. I'm tellin' you, I was sellin' thousands and thousands, but I had to come home.

LINDA: Oh, the whole block'll be at that game. Did you sell anything?

WILLY: I did five hundred gross in Providence and seven hundred gross in Boston.

LINDA: No! Wait a minute, I've got a pencil. [*She pulls pencil and paper out of her apron pocket.*] That makes your commission . . . Two hundred — my God! Two hundred and twelve dollars!

WILLY: Well, I didn't figure it yet, but . . .

LINDA: How much did you do?

WILLY: Well, I — I did — about a hundred and eighty gross in Providence. Well, no — it came to — roughly two hundred gross on the whole trip.

LINDA [*without hesitation*]: Two hundred gross. That . . .

[*She figures.*]

WILLY: The trouble was that three of the stores were half closed for inventory in Boston. Otherwise I woulda broke records.

LINDA: Well, it makes seventy dollars and some pennies. That's very good.

WILLY: What do we owe?

LINDA: Well, on the first there's sixteen dollars on the refrigerator ——

WILLY: Why sixteen?

LINDA: Well, the fan belt broke, so it was a dollar eighty.

WILLY: But it's brand new.

LINDA: Well, the man said that's the way it is. Till they work themselves in, y'know.

[*They move through the wall-line into the kitchen.*]

WILLY: I hope we didn't get stuck on that machine.

LINDA: They got the biggest ads of any of them!

WILLY: I know, it's a fine machine. What else?

LINDA: Well, there's nine-sixty for the washing machine. And for the vacuum cleaner there's three and a half due on the fifteenth. Then the roof, you got twenty-one dollars remaining.

WILLY: It don't leak, does it?

LINDA: No, they did a wonderful job. Then you owe Frank for the carburetor.

WILLY: I'm not going to pay that man! That goddam Chevrolet, they ought to prohibit the manufacture of that car!

LINDA: Well, you owe him three and a half. And odds and ends, comes to around a hundred and twenty dollars by the fifteenth.

WILLY: A hundred and twenty dollars! My God, if business don't pick up I don't know what I'm gonna do!

LINDA: Well, next week you'll do better.

WILLY: Oh, I'll knock 'em dead next week. I'll go to Hartford. I'm very well liked in Hartford. You know, the trouble is, Linda, people don't seem to take to me.

[*They move onto the forestage.*]

LINDA: Oh, don't be foolish.

WILLY: I know it when I walk in. They seem to laugh at me.

LINDA: Why? Why would they laugh at you? Don't talk that way, Willy. [WILLY *moves to the edge of the stage.* LINDA *goes into the kitchen and starts to darn stockings.*]

WILLY: I don't know the reason for it, but they just pass me by. I'm not noticed.

LINDA: But you're doing wonderful, dear. You're making seventy to a hundred dollars a week.

WILLY: But I gotta be at it ten, twelve hours a day. Other men — I don't know — they do it easier. I don't know why — I can't stop myself — I talk too much. A man oughta come in with a few words. One thing about Charley. He's a man of few words, and they respect him.

LINDA: You don't talk too much, you're just lively.

WILLY [*smiling*]: Well, I figure, what the hell, life is short, a couple of jokes. [*To himself*]: I joke too much! [*The smile goes.*]

LINDA: Why? You're ——

WILLY: I'm fat. I'm very — foolish to look at, Linda. I didn't tell you, but Christmas time I happened to be calling on F. H. Stewarts, and a salesman I know, as I was going in to see the buyer I heard him say something about — walrus. And I — I cracked him right across the face. I won't take that. I simply will not take that. But they do laugh at me. I know that.

LINDA: Darling . . .

WILLY: I gotta overcome it. I know I gotta overcome it. I'm not dressing to advantage, maybe.

LINDA: Willy, darling, you're the handsomest man in the world ——

WILLY: Oh, no, Linda.

LINDA: To me you are. [*Slight pause.*] The handsomest. [*From the darkness is heard the laughter of a woman.* WILLY *doesn't turn to it, but it continues through* LINDA's *lines.*]

LINDA: And the boys, Willy. Few men are idolized by their children the way you are. [*Music is heard as behind a scrim, to the left of the house.* THE WOMAN, *dimly seen, is dressing.*]

WILLY [*with great feeling*]: You're the best there is, Linda, you're a pal, you know that? On the road — on the road I want to grab you sometimes and just kiss the life outa you. [*The laughter is loud now, and he moves into a brightening area at the left, where* THE WOMAN *has come from behind the scrim and is standing, putting on her hat, looking into a "mirror" and laughing.*]

WILLY: 'Cause I get so lonely — especially when business is bad and there's nobody to talk to. I get the feeling that I'll never sell anything again, that I won't make a living for you, or a business, a business for the boys. [*He talks through* THE WOMAN's *subsiding laughter;* THE WOMAN *primps at the "mirror."*] There's so much I want to make for ——

THE WOMAN: Me? You didn't make me, Willy. I picked you.

WILLY [*pleased*]: You picked me?

THE WOMAN [*who is quite proper-looking,* WILLY's *age*]: I did. I've been sitting at that desk watching all the salesmen go by, day in, day out. But you've got such a sense of humor, and we do have such a good time together, don't we?

WILLY: Sure, sure. [*He takes her in his arms.*] Why do you have to go now?

THE WOMAN: It's two o'clock . . .

WILLY: No, come on in!

[*He pulls her.*]

THE WOMAN: . . . my sister'll be scandalized. When'll you be back?

WILLY: Oh, two weeks about. Will you come up again?

THE WOMAN: Sure thing. You do make me laugh. It's good for me. [*She squeezes his arm, kisses him.*] And I think you're a wonderful man.

WILLY: You picked me, heh?

THE WOMAN: Sure. Because you're so sweet. And such a kidder.

WILLY: Well, I'll see you next time I'm in Boston.

THE WOMAN: I'll put you right through to the buyers.

WILLY [*slapping her bottom*]: Right. Well, bottoms up!

THE WOMAN [*slaps him gently and laughs*]: You just kill me, Willy. [*He suddenly grabs her and kisses her roughly.*] You kill me. And thanks for the stockings. I love a lot of stockings. Well, good night.

WILLY: Good night. And keep your pores open!

THE WOMAN: Oh, Willy!

[THE WOMAN *bursts out laughing, and* LINDA's *laughter blends in.* THE WOMAN *disappears into the dark. Now the area at the kitchen table brightens.* LINDA *is sitting where she was at the kitchen table, but now is mending a pair of her silk stockings.*]

LINDA: You are, Willy. The handsomest man. You've got no reason to feel that ——

WILLY [*coming out of* THE WOMAN's *dimming area and going over to* LINDA]: I'll make it all up to you, Linda, I'll ——

LINDA: There's nothing to make up, dear. You're doing fine, better than ——

WILLY [*noticing her mending*]: What's that?

LINDA: Just mending my stockings. They're so expensive ——

WILLY [*angrily, taking them from her*]: I won't have you mending stockings in this house! Now throw them out!

[LINDA *puts the stockings in her pocket.*]

BERNARD [*entering on the run*]: Where is he? If he doesn't study!

WILLY [*moving to the forestage, with great agitation*]: You'll give him the answers!

BERNARD: I do, but I can't on a Regents! That's a state exam! They're liable to arrest me!

WILLY: Where is he? I'll whip him, I'll whip him!

LINDA: And he'd better give back that football, Willy, it's not nice.

WILLY: Biff! Where is he? Why is he taking everything?

LINDA: He's too rough with the girls, Willy. All the mothers are afraid of him!

WILLY: I'll whip him!

BERNARD: He's driving the car without a license!

[THE WOMAN'S *laugh is heard.*]

WILLY: Shut up!

LINDA: All the mothers ——

WILLY: Shut up!

BERNARD [*backing quietly away and out*]: Mr. Birnbaum says he's stuck up.

WILLY: Get outa here!

BERNARD: If he doesn't buckle down he'll flunk math!

[*He goes off.*]

LINDA: He's right, Willy, you've gotta ——

WILLY [*exploding at her*]: There's nothing the matter with him! You want him to be a worm like Bernard? He's got spirit, personality . . .

[*As he speaks,* LINDA, *almost in tears, exits into the living-room.* WILLY *is alone in the kitchen, wilting and staring. The leaves are gone. It is night again, and the apartment houses look down from behind.*]

WILLY: Loaded with it. Loaded! What is he stealing? He's giving it back, isn't he? Why is he stealing? What did I tell him? I never in my life told him anything but decent things.

[HAPPY *in pajamas has come down the stairs;* WILLY *suddenly becomes aware of* HAPPY'S *presence.*]

HAPPY: Let's go now, come on.

WILLY [*sitting down at the kitchen table*]: Huh! Why did she have to wax the floors herself? Every time she waxes the floors she keels over. She knows that!

HAPPY: Shh! Take it easy. What brought you back tonight?

WILLY: I got an awful scare. Nearly hit a kid in Yonkers. God! Why didn't I go to Alaska with my brother Ben that time! Ben! That man was a genius, that man was success incarnate! What a mistake! He begged me to go.

HAPPY: Well, there's no use in ——

WILLY: You guys! There was a man started with the clothes on his back and ended up with diamond mines!

HAPPY: Boy, someday I'd like to know how he did it.

WILLY: What's the mystery? The man knew what he wanted and went out and got it! Walked into a jungle, and comes out, the age of twenty-one, and he's rich! The world is an oyster, but you don't crack it open on a mattress!

HAPPY: Pop, I told you I'm gonna retire you for life.

WILLY: You'll retire me for life on seventy goddam dollars a week? And your women and your car and your apartment, and you'll retire me for life! Christ's sake, I couldn't get past Yonkers today! Where are you guys, where are you? The woods are burning! I can't drive a car!

[CHARLEY *has appeared in the doorway. He is a large man, slow of speech, laconic, immovable. In all he says, despite what he says, there is pity, and, now, trepidation. He has a robe over pajamas, slippers on his feet. He enters the kitchen.*]

CHARLEY: Everything all right?

HAPPY: Yeah, Charley, everything's . . .

WILLY: What's the matter?

CHARLEY: I heard some noise. I thought something happened. Can't we do something about the walls? You sneeze in here, and in my house hats blow off.

HAPPY: Let's go to bed, Dad. Come on.

[CHARLEY *signals to* HAPPY *to go.*]

WILLY: You go ahead, I'm not tired at the moment.

HAPPY [*to* WILLY]: Take it easy, huh?

[*He exits.*]

WILLY: What're you doin' up?

CHARLEY [*sitting down at the kitchen table opposite* WILLY]: Couldn't sleep good. I had a heartburn.

WILLY: Well, you don't know how to eat.

CHARLEY: I eat with my mouth.

WILLY: No, you're ignorant. You gotta know about vitamins and things like that.

CHARLEY: Come on, let's shoot. Tire you out a little.

WILLY [*hesitantly*]: All right. You got cards?

CHARLEY [*taking a deck from his pocket*]: Yeah, I got them. Someplace. What is it with those vitamins?

WILLY [*dealing*]: They build up your bones. Chemistry.

CHARLEY: Yeah, but there's no bones in a heartburn.

WILLY: What are you talkin' about? Do you know the first thing about it?

CHARLEY: Don't get insulted.

WILLY: Don't talk about something you don't know anything about.

[*They are playing. Pause.*]

CHARLEY: What're you doin' home?

WILLY: A little trouble with the car.

CHARLEY: Oh. [*Pause.*] I'd like to take a trip to California.

WILLY: Don't say.

CHARLEY: You want a job?

WILLY: I got a job, I told you that. [*After a slight pause.*] What the hell are you offering me a job for?

CHARLEY: Don't get insulted.

WILLY: Don't insult me.

CHARLEY: I don't see no sense in it. You don't have to go on this way.

WILLY: I got a good job. [*Slight pause.*] What do you keep comin' in here for?

CHARLEY: You want me to go?

WILLY [*after a pause, witheringly*]: I can't understand it. He's going back to Texas again. What the hell is that?

CHARLEY: Let him go.

WILLY: I got nothin' to give him, Charley, I'm clean, I'm clean.

CHARLEY: He won't starve. None a them starve. Forget about him.

WILLY: Then what have I got to remember?

CHARLEY: You take it too hard. To hell with it. When a deposit bottle is broken you don't get your nickel back.

WILLY: That's easy enough for you to say.

CHARLEY: That ain't easy for me to say.

WILLY: Did you see the ceiling I put up in the living-room?

CHARLEY: Yeah, that's a piece of work. To put up a ceiling is a mystery to me. How do you do it?

WILLY: What's the difference?

CHARLEY: Well, talk about it.

WILLY: You gonna put up a ceiling?

CHARLEY: How could I put up a ceiling?

WILLY: Then what the hell are you bothering me for?

CHARLEY: You're insulted again.

WILLY: A man who can't handle tools is not a man. You're disgusting.

CHARLEY: Don't call me disgusting, Willy.

[UNCLE BEN, *carrying a valise and an umbrella, enters the forestage from around the right corner of the house. He is a stolid man, in his sixties, with a mustache and an authoritative air. He is utterly certain of his destiny, and there is an aura of far places about him. He enters exactly as* WILLY *speaks.*]

WILLY: I'm getting awfully tired, Ben.

[BEN's *music is heard.* BEN *looks around at everything.*]

CHARLEY: Good, keep playing; you'll sleep better. Did you call me Ben?

[BEN *looks at his watch.*]

WILLY: That's funny. For a second there you reminded me of my brother Ben.

BEN: I only have a few minutes.

[*He strolls, inspecting the place.* WILLY *and* CHARLEY *continue playing.*]

CHARLEY: You never heard from him again, heh? Since that time?

WILLY: Didn't Linda tell you? Couple of weeks ago we got a letter from his wife in Africa. He died.

CHARLEY: That so.

BEN [*chuckling*]: So this is Brooklyn, eh?

CHARLEY: Maybe you're in for some of his money.

WILLY: Naa, he had seven sons. There's just one opportunity I had with that man . . .

BEN: I must make a train, William. There are several properties I'm looking at in Alaska.

WILLY: Sure, sure! If I'd gone with him to Alaska that time, everything would've been totally different.

CHARLEY: Go on, you'd froze to death up there.

WILLY: What're you talking about?

BEN: Opportunity is tremendous in Alaska, William. Surprised you're not up there.

WILLY: Sure, tremendous.

CHARLEY: Heh?

WILLY: There was the only man I ever met who knew the answers.

CHARLEY: Who?

BEN: How are you all?

WILLY [*taking a pot, smiling*]: Fine, fine.

CHARLEY: Pretty sharp tonight.

BEN: Is Mother living with you?

WILLY: No, she died a long time ago.

CHARLEY: Who?

BEN: That's too bad. Fine specimen of a lady, Mother.

WILLY [*to* CHARLEY]: Heh?

BEN: I'd hoped to see the old girl.

CHARLEY: Who died?

BEN: Heard anything from Father, have you?

WILLY [*unnerved*]: What do you mean, who died?

CHARLEY [*taking a pot*]: What're you talkin' about?

BEN [*looking at his watch*]: William, it's half-past eight!

WILLY [*as though to dispel his confusion he angrily stops* CHARLEY'S *hand*]: That's my build!

CHARLEY: I put the ace ——

WILLY: If you don't know how to play the game I'm not gonna throw my money away on you!

CHARLEY [*rising*]: It was my ace, for God's sake!

WILLY: I'm through, I'm through!

BEN: When did Mother die?

WILLY: Long ago. Since the beginning you never knew how to play cards.

CHARLEY [*picks up the cards and goes to the door*]: All right! Next time I'll bring a deck with five aces.

WILLY: I don't play that kind of game!

CHARLEY [*turning to him*]: You ought to be ashamed of yourself.

WILLY: Yeah?

CHARLEY: Yeah!

[*He goes out.*]

WILLY [*slamming the door after him*]: Ignoramus!

BEN [*as* WILLY *comes toward him through the wall-line of the kitchen*]: So you're William.

WILLY [*shaking* BEN's *hand*]: Ben! I've been waiting for you so long! What's the answer? How did you do it?

BEN: Oh, there's a story in that.

[LINDA *enters the forestage, as of old, carrying the wash basket.*]

LINDA: Is this Ben?

BEN [*gallantly*]: How do you do, my dear.

LINDA: Where've you been all these years? Willy's always wondered why you ——

WILLY [*pulling* BEN *away from her impatiently*]: Where is Dad? Didn't you follow him? How did you get started?

BEN: Well, I don't know how much you remember.

WILLY: Well, I was just a baby, of course, only three or four year old ——

BEN: Three years and eleven months.

WILLY: What a memory, Ben!

BEN: I have many enterprises, William, and I have never kept books.

WILLY: I remember I was sitting under the wagon in — was it Nebraska?

BEN: It was South Dakota, and I gave you a bunch of wild flowers.

WILLY: I remember you walking away down some open road.

BEN [*laughing*]: I was going to find Father in Alaska.

WILLY: Where is he?

BEN: At that age I had a very faulty view of geography, William. I discovered after a few days that I was heading due south, so instead of Alaska, I ended up in Africa.

LINDA: Africa!

WILLY: The Gold Coast!

BEN: Principally diamond mines.

LINDA: Diamond mines!

BEN: Yes, my dear. But I've only a few minutes ——

WILLY: No! Boys! Boys! [YOUNG BIFF *and* HAPPY *appear.*] Listen to this. This is your Uncle Ben, a great man! Tell my boys, Ben!

BEN: Why, boys, when I was seventeen I walked into the jungle, and when I was twenty-one I walked out. [*He laughs.*] And by God I was rich.

WILLY [*to the boys*]: You see what I been talking about? The greatest things can happen!

BEN [*glancing at his watch*]: I have an appointment in Ketchikan Tuesday week.

WILLY: No, Ben! Please tell about Dad. I want my boys to hear. I want them to know the kind of stock they spring from. All I remember is a man with a big beard, and I was in Mamma's lap, sitting around a fire, and some kind of high music.

BEN: His flute. He played the flute.

WILLY: Sure, the flute, that's right!

[*New music is heard, a high, rollicking tune.*]

BEN: Father was a very great and a very wild-hearted man. We would start in Boston, and he'd toss the whole family into the wagon, and then he'd drive the team right across the country; through Ohio, and Indiana, Michigan, Illinois, and all the Western states. And we'd stop in the towns and sell the flutes that he'd made on the way. Great inventor, Father. With one gadget he made more in a week than a man like you could make in a lifetime.

WILLY: That's just the way I'm bringing them up, Ben — rugged, well liked, all-around.

BEN: Yeah? [*To* BIFF.] Hit that, boy — hard as you can.

[*He pounds his stomach.*]

BIFF: Oh, no, sir!

BEN [*taking boxing stance*]: Come on, get to me!

[*He laughs.*]

WILLY: Go to it, Biff! Go ahead, show him!

BIFF. Okay!

[*He cocks his fists and starts in.*]

LINDA [*to* WILLY]: Why must he fight, dear?

BEN [*sparring with* BIFF]: Good boy! Good boy!

WILLY: How's that, Ben, heh?

HAPPY: Give him the left, Biff!

LINDA: Why are you fighting?

BEN: Good boy!

[*Suddenly comes in, trips* BIFF, *and stands over him, the point of his umbrella poised over* BIFF's *eye.*]

LINDA: Look out, Biff!

BIFF: Gee!

BEN [*patting* BIFF's *knee*]: Never fight fair with a stranger, boy. You'll never get out of the jungle that way. [*Taking* LINDA's *hand and bowing.*] It was an honor and a pleasure to meet you, Linda.

LINDA [*withdrawing her hand coldly, frightened*]: Have a nice — trip.

BEN [*to* WILLY]: And good luck with your — what do you do?

WILLY: Selling.

BEN: Yes. Well . . .

[*He raises his hand in farewell to all.*]

WILLY: No, Ben, I don't want you to think . . . [*He takes* BEN's *arm to show him.*] It's Brooklyn, I know, but we hunt too.

BEN: Really, now.

WILLY: Oh, sure, there's snakes and rabbits and — that's why I moved out here. Why, Biff can fell any one of these trees in no time! Boys! Go right over to where they're building the apartment house and get some sand. We're gonna rebuild the entire front stoop right now! Watch this, Ben!

BIFF: Yes, sir! On the double, Hap!

HAPPY [*as he and* BIFF *run off*]: I lost weight, Pop, you notice?

[CHARLEY *enters in knickers, even before the boys are gone.*]

CHARLEY: Listen, if they steal any more from that building the watchman'll put the cops on them!

LINDA [*to* WILLY]: Don't let Biff . . .

[BEN *laughs lustily.*]

WILLY: You shoulda seen the lumber they brought home last week. At least a dozen six-by-tens worth all kinds a money.

CHARLEY: Listen, if that watchman ——

WILLY: I gave them hell, understand. But I got a couple of fearless characters there.

CHARLEY: Willy, the jails are full of fearless characters.

BEN [*clapping* WILLY *on the back, with a laugh at* CHARLEY]: And the stock exchange, friend!

WILLY [*joining in* BEN's *laughter*]: Where are the rest of your pants?

CHARLEY: My wife bought them.

WILLY: Now all you need is a golf club and you can go upstairs and go to sleep. [*To* BEN.] Great athlete! Between him and his son Bernard they can't hammer a nail!

BERNARD [*rushing in*]: The watchman's chasing Biff!

WILLY [*angrily*]: Shut up! He's not stealing anything!

LINDA [*alarmed, hurrying off left*]: Where is he? Biff, dear!

[*She exits.*]

WILLY [*moving toward the left, away from* BEN]: There's nothing wrong. What's the matter with you?

BEN: Nervy boy. Good!

WILLY [*laughing*]: Oh, nerves of iron, that Biff!

CHARLEY: Don't know what it is. My New England man comes back and he's bleedin', they murdered him up there.

WILLY: It's contacts, Charley, I got important contacts!

CHARLEY [*sarcastically*]: Glad to hear it, Willy. Come in later, we'll shoot a little casino. I'll take some of your Portland money.

[*He laughs at* WILLY *and exits.*]

WILLY [*turning to* BEN]: Business is bad, it's murderous. But not for me, of course.

BEN: I'll stop by on my way back to Africa.

WILLY [*longingly*]: Can't you stay a few days? You're just what I need, Ben, because I — I have a fine position here, but I — well, Dad left when I was such a baby, and I never had a chance to talk to him and I still feel — kind of temporary about myself.

BEN: I'll be late for my train.

[*They are at opposite ends of the stage.*]

WILLY: Ben, my boys — can't we talk? They'd go into the jaws of hell for me, see, but I ——

BEN: William, you're being first-rate with your boys. Outstanding, manly chaps!

WILLY [*hanging on to his words*]: Oh, Ben, that's good to hear! Because sometimes I'm afraid that I'm not teaching them the right kind of — Ben, how should I teach them?

BEN [*giving great weight to each word, and with a certain vicious audacity*]: William, when I walked into the jungle, I was seventeen. When I walked out I was twenty-one. And, by God, I was rich!

[*He goes off into darkness around the right corner of the house.*]

WILLY: . . . was rich! That's just the spirit I want to imbue them with! To walk into a jungle! I was right! I was right! I was right!

[BEN *is gone, but* WILLY *is still speaking to him as* LINDA, *in nightgown and robe, enters the kitchen, glances around for* WILLY, *then goes to the door of the house, looks out and sees him. Comes down to his left. He looks at her.*]

LINDA: Willy, dear? Willy?

WILLY: I was right!

LINDA: Did you have some cheese? [*He can't answer.*] It's very late, darling. Come to bed, heh?

WILLY [*looking straight up*]: Gotta break your neck to see a star in this yard.

LINDA: You coming in?

WILLY: Whatever happened to that diamond watch fob? Remember? When Ben came from Africa that time? Didn't he give me a watch fob with a diamond in it?

LINDA: You pawned it, dear. Twelve, thirteen years ago. For Biff's radio correspondence course.

WILLY: Gee, that was a beautiful thing. I'll take a walk.

LINDA: But you're in your slippers.

WILLY [*starting to go around the house at the left*]: I was right! I was! [*Half to* LINDA, *as he goes, shaking his head.*] What a man! There was a man worth talking to. I was right!

LINDA [*calling after* WILLY]: But in your slippers, Willy!

[WILLY *is almost gone when* BIFF, *in his pajamas, comes down the stairs and enters the kitchen.*]

BIFF: What is he doing out there?

LINDA: Sh!

BIFF: God Almighty, Mom, how long has he been doing this?

LINDA: Don't, he'll hear you.

BIFF: What the hell is the matter with him?

LINDA: It'll pass by morning.

BIFF: Shouldn't we do anything?

LINDA: Oh, my dear, you should do a lot of things, but there's nothing to do, so go to sleep.

[HAPPY *comes down the stairs and sits on the steps.*]

HAPPY: I never heard him so loud, Mom.

LINDA: Well, come around more often; you'll hear him.

[*She sits down at the table and mends the lining of* WILLY's *jacket.*]

BIFF: Why didn't you ever write me about this, Mom?

LINDA: How would I write to you? For over three months you had no address.

BIFF: I was on the move. But you know I thought of you all the time. You know that, don't you, pal?

LINDA: I know, dear, I know. But he likes to have a letter. Just to know that there's still a possibility for better things.

BIFF: He's not like this all the time, is he?

LINDA: It's when you come home he's always the worst.

BIFF: When I come home?

LINDA: When you write you're coming, he's all smiles, and talks about the future, and — he's just wonderful. And then the closer you seem to come, the more shaky he gets, and then, by the time you get here, he's arguing, and he seems angry at you. I think it's just that maybe he can't bring himself to — to open up to you. Why are you so hateful to each other? Why is that?

BIFF [*evasively*]: I'm not hateful, Mom.

LINDA: But you no sooner come in the door than you're fighting!

BIFF: I don't know why. I mean to change. I'm tryin', Mom, you understand?

LINDA: Are you home to stay now?

BIFF: I don't know. I want to look around, see what's doin'.

LINDA: Biff, you can't look around all your life, can you?

BIFF: I just can't take hold, Mom. I can't take hold of some kind of a life.

LINDA: Biff, a man is not a bird, to come and go with the springtime.

BIFF: Your hair . . . [*He touches her hair.*] Your hair got so gray.

LINDA: Oh, it's been gray since you were in high school. I just stopped dyeing it, that's all.

BIFF: Dye it again, will ya? I don't want my pal looking old.

[*He smiles.*]

LINDA: You're such a boy! You think you can go away for a year and . . . You've got to get it into your head now that one day you'll knock on this door and there'll be strange people here ——

BIFF: What are you talking about? You're not even sixty, Mom.

LINDA: But what about your father?

BIFF [*lamely*]: Well, I meant him too.

HAPPY: He admires Pop.

LINDA: Biff, dear, if you don't have any feeling for him, then you can't have any feeling for me.

BIFF: Sure I can, Mom.

LINDA: No. You can't just come to see me, because I love him. [*With a threat, but only a threat, of tears.*] He's the dearest man in the world to me, and I won't have anyone making him feel unwanted and low and blue. You've got to make up your mind now, darling, there's no leeway any more. Either he's your father and you pay him that respect, or else you're not to come here. I know he's not easy to get along with — nobody knows that better than me — but . . .

WILLY [*from the left, with a laugh*]: Hey, hey, Biffo!

BIFF [*starting to go out after* WILLY]: What the hell is the matter with him?

[HAPPY *stops him.*]

LINDA: Don't — don't go near him!

BIFF: Stop making excuses for him! He always, always wiped the floor with you. Never had an ounce of respect for you.

HAPPY: He's always had respect for ——

BIFF: What the hell do you know about it?

HAPPY [*surlily*]: Just don't call him crazy!

BIFF: He's got no character — Charley wouldn't do this. Not in his own house — spewing out that vomit from his mind.

HAPPY: Charley never had to cope with what he's got to.

BIFF: People are worse off than Willy Loman. Believe me, I've seen them!

LINDA: Then make Charley your father, Biff. You can't do that, can you? I don't say he's a great man. Willy Loman never made a lot of money. His name was never in the paper. He's not the finest character that ever lived. But he's a human being, and a terrible thing is happening to him. So attention must be paid. He's not to be allowed to fall into his grave like an old dog. Attention, attention must be finally paid to such a person. You called him crazy ——

BIFF: I don't mean ——

LINDA: No, a lot of people think he's lost his — balance. But you don't have to be very smart to know what his trouble is. The man is exhausted.

HAPPY: Sure!

LINDA: A small man can be just as exhausted as a great man. He works for a company thirty-six years this March, opens up unheard-of territories to their trademark, and now in his old age they take his salary away.

HAPPY [*indignantly*]: I didn't know that, Mom.

LINDA: You never asked, my dear! Now that you get your spending money someplace else you don't trouble your mind with him.

HAPPY: But I gave you money last ——

LINDA: Christmas time, fifty dollars! To fix the hot water it cost ninety-seven fifty! For five weeks he's been on straight commission, like a beginner, an unknown!

BIFF: Those ungrateful bastards!

LINDA: Are they any worse than his sons? When he brought them business, when he was young, they were glad to see him. But now his old friends, the old buyers that loved him so and always found some order to hand him in a pinch — they're all dead, retired. He used to be able to make six, seven calls a day in Boston. Now he takes his valises out of the car and puts them back and takes them out again and he's exhausted. Instead of walking he talks now. He drives seven hundred miles, and when he gets there no one knows him any more, no one welcomes him. And what goes through a man's mind, driving seven hundred miles home without having earned a cent? Why shouldn't he talk to himself? Why? When he has to go to Charley and borrow fifty dollars a week and pretend to me that it's his pay? How long can that go on? How long? You see what I'm sitting here and waiting for? And you tell me he has no character? The man who never worked a day but for your benefit? When does he get the medal for that? Is this his reward — to turn around at the age of sixty-three and find his sons, who he loved better than his life, one a philandering bum ——

HAPPY: Mom!

LINDA: That's all you are, my baby! [*To* BIFF.] And you! What's happened to the love you had for him? You were such pals! How you used to talk to him on the phone every night! How lonely he was till he could come home to you!

BIFF: All right, Mom. I'll live here in my room, and I'll get a job. I'll keep away from him, that's all.

LINDA: No, Biff. You can't stay here and fight all the time.

BIFF: He threw me out of this house, remember that.

LINDA: Why did he do that? I never knew why.

BIFF: Because I know he's a fake and he doesn't like anybody around who knows!

LINDA: Why a fake? In what way? What do you mean?

BIFF: Just don't lay it all at my feet. It's between me and him — that's all I have to say. I'll chip in from now on. He'll settle for half my pay check. He'll be all right. I'm going to bed.

[*He starts for the stairs.*]

LINDA: He won't be all right.

BIFF [*turning on the stairs, furiously*]: I hate this city and I'll stay here. Now what do you want?

LINDA: He's dying, Biff.

[HAPPY *turns quickly to her, shocked.*]

BIFF [*after a pause*]: Why is he dying?

LINDA: He's been trying to kill himself.

BIFF [*with great horror*]: How?

LINDA: I live from day to day.

BIFF: What're you talking about?

LINDA: Remember I wrote you that he smashed up the car again? In February?

BIFF: Well?

LINDA: The insurance inspector came. He said that they have evidence. That all these accidents in the last year — weren't — weren't — accidents.

HAPPY: How can they tell that? That's a lie.

LINDA: It seems there's a woman . . . [*She takes a breath as*]

⎰BIFF [*sharply but contained*]: What woman?

⎱LINDA [*simultaneously*]: . . . and this woman . . .

LINDA: What?

BIFF: Nothing. Go ahead.

LINDA: What did you say?

BIFF: Nothing. I just said what woman?

HAPPY: What about her?

LINDA: Well, it seems she was walking down the road and saw his car. She says that he wasn't driving fast at all, and that he didn't skid. She says he came to that little bridge, and then deliberately smashed into the railing, and it was only the shallowness of the water that saved him.

BIFF: Oh, no, he probably just fell asleep again.

LINDA: I don't think he fell asleep.

BIFF: Why not?

LINDA: Last month . . . [*With great difficulty.*] Oh, boys, it's so hard to say a thing like this! He's just a big stupid man to you, but I tell you there's more good in him than in many other people. [*She chokes, wipes her eyes.*] I was looking for a fuse. The lights blew out, and I went down the cellar. And behind the fuse box — it happened to fall out — was a length of rubber pipe — just short.

HAPPY: No kidding?

LINDA: There's a little attachment on the end of it. I knew right away. And sure enough, on the bottom of the water heater there's a new little nipple on the gas pipe.

HAPPY [*angrily*]: That — jerk.

BIFF: Did you have it taken off?

LINDA: I'm — I'm ashamed to. How can I mention it to him? Every day I go down and take away that little rubber pipe. But, when he comes home, I put it back where it was. How can I insult him that way? I don't know what to do. I live from day to day, boys. I tell you, I know every thought in his mind. It sounds so old-fashioned and silly, but I tell you he put his whole life into you and you've turned your backs on him. [*She is bent over in the chair, weeping, her face in her hands.*] Biff, I swear to God! Biff, his life is in your hands!

HAPPY [*to* BIFF]: How do you like that damned fool!

BIFF [*kissing her*]: All right, pal, all right. It's all settled now. I've been remiss. I know that, Mom. But now I'll stay, and I swear to you, I'll apply myself. [*Kneeling in front of her, in a fever of self-reproach.*] It's just — you see, Mom, I don't fit in business. Not that I won't try. I'll try, and I'll make good.

HAPPY: Sure you will. The trouble with you in business was you never tried to please people.

BIFF: I know. I——

HAPPY: Like when you worked for Harrison's. Bob Harrison said you were tops, and then you go and do some damn fool thing like whistling whole songs in the elevator like a comedian.

BIFF [*against* HAPPY]: So what? I like to whistle sometimes.

HAPPY: You don't raise a guy to a responsible job who whistles in the elevator!

LINDA: Well, don't argue about it now.

HAPPY: Like when you'd go off and swim in the middle of the day instead of taking the line around.

BIFF [*his resentment rising*]: Well, don't you run off? You take off sometimes, don't you? On a nice summer day?

HAPPY: Yeah, but I cover myself!

LINDA: Boys!

HAPPY: If I'm going to take a fade the boss can call any number where I'm supposed to be and they'll swear to him that I just left. I'll tell you something that I hate to say, Biff, but in the business world some of them think you're crazy.

BIFF [*angered*]: Screw the business world!

HAPPY: All right, screw it! Great, but cover yourself!

LINDA: Hap, Hap!

BIFF: I don't care what they think! They've laughed at Dad for years, and you know why? Because we don't belong in this nuthouse of a city! We should be mixing cement on some open plain, or — or carpenters. A carpenter is allowed to whistle!

[WILLY *walks in from the entrance of the house, at left.*]

WILLY: Even your grandfather was better than a carpenter. [*Pause. They watch him.*] You never grew up. Bernard does not whistle in the elevator, I assure you.

BIFF [*as though to laugh* WILLY *out of it*]: Yeah, but you do, Pop.

WILLY: I never in my life whistled in an elevator! And who in the business world thinks I'm crazy?

BIFF: I didn't mean it like that, Pop. Now don't make a whole thing out of it, will ya?

WILLY: Go back to the West! Be a carpenter, a cowboy, enjoy yourself!

LINDA: Willy, he was just saying ——

WILLY: I heard what he said!

HAPPY [*trying to quiet* WILLY]: Hey, Pop, come on now . . .

WILLY [*continuing over* HAPPY's *line*]: They laugh at me, heh? Go to Filene's, go to the Hug, go to Slattery's, Boston. Call out the name Willy Loman and see what happens! Big Shot!

BIFF: All right, Pop.

WILLY: Big!

BIFF: All right!

WILLY: Why do you always insult me?

BIFF: I didn't say a word. [*To* LINDA.] Did I say a word?

LINDA: He didn't say anything, Willy.

WILLY [*going to the doorway of the living-room*]: All right, good night, good night.

LINDA: Willy, dear, he just decided . . .

WILLY [*to* BIFF]: If you get tired hanging around tomorrow, paint the ceiling I put up in the living-room.

BIFF: I'm leaving early tomorrow.

HAPPY: He's going to see Bill Oliver, Pop.

WILLY [*interestedly*]: Oliver? For what?

BIFF [*with reserve, but trying, trying*]: He always said he'd stake me. I'd like to go into business, so maybe I can take him up on it.

LINDA: Isn't that wonderful?

WILLY: Don't interrupt. What's wonderful about it? There's fifty men in the City of New York who'd stake him. [*To* BIFF.] Sporting goods?

BIFF: I guess so. I know something about it and ——

WILLY: He knows something about it! You know sporting goods better than Spalding, for God's sake! How much is he giving you?

BIFF: I don't know, I didn't even see him yet, but ——

WILLY: Then what're you talkin' about?

BIFF [*getting angry*]: Well, all I said was I'm gonna see him, that's all!

WILLY [*turning away*]: Ah, you're counting your chickens again.

BIFF [*starting left for the stairs*]: Oh, Jesus, I'm going to sleep!

WILLY [*calling after him*]: Don't curse in this house!

BIFF [*turning*]: Since when did you get so clean?

HAPPY [*trying to stop them*]: Wait a . . .

WILLY: Don't use that language to me! I won't have it!

HAPPY [*grabbing* BIFF, *shouts*]: Wait a minute! I got an idea. I got a feasible idea. Come here, Biff, let's talk this over now, let's talk some sense here. When I was down in Florida last time, I thought of a great idea to sell sporting goods. It just came back to me. You and I, Biff — we have a line, the Loman Line. We train a couple of weeks, and put on a couple of exhibitions, see?

WILLY: That's an idea!

HAPPY: Wait! We form two basketball teams, see? Two waterpolo teams. We play each other. It's a million dollars' worth of publicity. Two brothers, see? The Loman Brothers. Displays in the Royal Palms — all the hotels. And banners over the ring and basketball court: "Loman Brothers." Baby, we could sell sporting goods!

WILLY: That is a one-million dollar idea!

LINDA: Marvelous!

BIFF: I'm in great shape as far as that's concerned.

HAPPY: And the beauty of it is, Biff, it wouldn't be like a business. We'd be out playin' ball again . . .

BIFF [*enthused*]: Yeah, that's . . .

WILLY: Million-dollar . . .

HAPPY: And you wouldn't get fed up with it, Biff. It'd be the family again. There'd be the old honor, and comradeship, and if you wanted to go off for a swim or somethin' — well, you'd do it! Without some smart cooky gettin' up ahead of you!

WILLY: Lick the world. You guys together could absolutely lick the civilized world.

BIFF: I'll see Oliver tomorrow. Hap, if we could work that out . . .

LINDA: Maybe things are beginning to ——

WILLY [*wildly enthused, to* LINDA]: Stop interrupting! [*To* BIFF.] But don't wear sport jacket and slacks when you see Oliver.

BIFF: No, I'll ——

WILLY: A business suit, and talk as little as possible, and don't crack any jokes.

BIFF: He did like me. Always liked me.

LINDA: He loved you!

WILLY [*to* LINDA]: Will you stop? [*To* BIFF.] Walk in very serious. You are not applying for a boy's job. Money is to pass. Be quiet, fine, and serious. Everybody likes a kidder, but nobody lends him money.

HAPPY: I'll try to get some myself, Biff. I'm sure I can.

WILLY: I see great things for you kids, I think your troubles are over. But remember, start big and you'll end big. Ask for fifteen. How much you gonna ask for?

BIFF: Gee, I don't know ——

WILLY: And don't say "Gee." "Gee" is a boy's word. A man walking in for fifteen thousand dollars does not say "Gee!"

BIFF: Ten, I think, would be top though.

WILLY: Don't be so modest. You always started too low. Walk in with a big laugh. Don't look worried. Start off with a couple of your good stories to lighten things up. It's not what you say, it's how you say it — because personality always wins the day.

LINDA: Oliver always thought the highest of him ——

WILLY: Will you let me talk?

BIFF: Don't yell at her, Pop, will ya?

WILLY [*angrily*]: I was talking, wasn't I?

BIFF: I don't like you yelling at her all the time, and I'm tellin' you, that's all.

WILLY: What're you, takin' over this house?

LINDA: Willy ——

WILLY [*turning to her*]: Don't take his side all the time, goddammit!

BIFF [*furiously*]: Stop yelling at her!

WILLY [*suddenly pulling on his cheek, beaten down, guilt ridden*]: Give my best to Bill Oliver — he may remember me.

[*He exits through the living-room doorway.*]

LINDA [*her voice subdued*]: What'd you have to start that for? [BIFF *turns away.*] You see how sweet he was as soon as you talked hopefully? [*She goes over to* BIFF.] Come up and say good night to him. Don't let him go to bed that way.

HAPPY: Come on, Biff, let's back him up.

LINDA: Please, dear. Just say good night. It takes so little to make him happy. Come. [*She goes through the living-room doorway, calling upstairs from within the living-room.*] Your pajamas are hanging in the bathroom, Willy!

HAPPY [*looking toward where* LINDA *went out*]: What a woman! They broke the mold when they made her. You know that, Biff?

BIFF: He's off salary. My God, working on commission!

HAPPY: Well, let's face it: he's no hot-shot selling man. Except that sometimes, you have to admit, he's a sweet personality.

BIFF [*deciding*]: Lend me ten bucks, will ya? I want to buy some new ties.

HAPPY: I'll take you to a place I know. Beautiful stuff. Wear one of my striped shirts tomorrow.

BIFF: She got gray. Mom got awful old. Gee, I'm gonna go in to Oliver tomorrow and knock him for a ——

HAPPY: Come on up. Tell that to Dad. Let's give him a whirl. Come on.

BIFF [*steamed up*]: You know, with ten thousand bucks, boy!

HAPPY [*as they go into the living-room*]: That's the talk, Biff, that's the first time I've heard the old confidence out of you! [*From within the living-room, fading off.*] You're gonna live with me, kid, and any babe you want just say the word . . .

[*The last lines are hardly heard. They are mounting the stairs to their parents' bedroom.*]

LINDA [*entering her bedroom and addressing* WILLY, *who is in the bath-*

room. She is straightening the bed for him]: Can you do anything about the shower? It drips.

WILLY [*from the bathroom*]: All of a sudden everything falls to pieces! Goddam plumbing, oughta be sued, those people. I hardly finished putting it in and the thing . . .

[*His words rumble off.*]

LINDA: I'm just wondering if Oliver will remember him. You think he might?

WILLY [*coming out of the bathroom in his pajamas*]: Remember him? What's the matter with you, you crazy? If he'd've stayed with Oliver he'd be on top by now! Wait'll Oliver gets a look at him. You don't know the average caliber any more. The average young man today—[*he is getting into bed*]—is got a caliber of zero. Greatest thing in the world for him was to bum around.

[BIFF *and* HAPPY *enter the bedroom. Slight pause.*]

WILLY [*stops short, looking at* BIFF]: Glad to hear it, boy.

HAPPY: He wanted to say good night to you, sport.

WILLY [*to* BIFF]: Yeah. Knock him dead, boy. What'd you want to tell me?

BIFF: Just take it easy, Pop. Good night.

[*He turns to go.*]

WILLY [*unable to resist*]: And if anything falls off the desk while you're talking to him—like a package or something—don't pick it up. They have office boys for that.

LINDA: I'll make a big breakfast—

WILLY: Will you let me finish? [*To* BIFF.] Tell him you were in the business in the West. Not farm work.

BIFF: All right, Dad.

LINDA: I think everything—

WILLY [*going right through her speech*]: And don't undersell yourself. No less than fifteen thousand dollars.

BIFF [*unable to bear him*]: Okay. Good night, Mom.

[*He starts moving.*]

WILLY: Because you got a greatness in you, Biff, remember that. You got all kinds of greatness . . .

[*He lies back, exhausted.* BIFF *walks out.*]

LINDA [*calling after* BIFF]: Sleep well, darling!

HAPPY: I'm gonna get married, Mom. I wanted to tell you.

LINDA: Go to sleep, dear.

HAPPY [*going*] : I just wanted to tell you.

WILLY: Keep up the good work. [HAPPY *exits.*] God . . . remember that Ebbets Field game? The championship of the city?

LINDA: Just rest. Should I sing to you?

WILLY: Yeah. Sing to me. [LINDA *hums a soft lullaby.*] When that team came out—he was the tallest, remember?

LINDA: Oh, yes. And in gold.

[BIFF *enters the darkened kitchen, takes a cigarette, and leaves the house. He comes downstage into a golden pool of light. He smokes, staring at the night.*]

WILLY: Like a young god. Hercules—something like that. And the sun, the sun all around him. Remember how he waved to me? Right up from the field, with the representatives of three colleges standing by? And the buyers I brought, and the cheers when he came out—Loman, Loman, Loman! God Almighty, he'll be great yet. A star like that, magnificent, can never really fade away!

[*The light on* WILLY *is fading. The gas heater begins to glow through the kitchen wall, near the stairs, a blue flame beneath red coils.*]

LINDA [*timidly*]: Willy dear, what has he got against you?

WILLY: I'm so tired. Don't talk any more.

[BIFF *slowly returns to the kitchen. He stops, stares toward the heater.*]

LINDA: Will you ask Howard to let you work in New York?

WILLY: First thing in the morning. Everything'll be all right.

[BIFF *reaches behind the heater and draws out a length of rubber tubing. He is horrified and turns his head toward* WILLY'S *room, still dimly lit, from which the strains of* LINDA'S *desperate but monotonous humming rise.*]

WILLY [*staring through the window into the moonlight*]: Gee, look at the moon moving between the buildings!

[BIFF *wraps the tubing around his hand and quickly goes up the stairs.*]

CURTAIN

ACT TWO

Music is heard, gay and bright. The curtain rises as the music fades away.
   WILLY, *in shirt sleeves, is sitting at the kitchen table, sipping coffee, his hat in his lap.* LINDA *is filling his cup when she can.*

WILLY: Wonderful coffee. Meal in itself.

LINDA: Can I make you some eggs?

WILLY: No. Take a breath.

LINDA: You look so rested, dear.

WILLY: I slept like a dead one. First time in months. Imagine, sleeping till ten on a Tuesday morning. Boys left nice and early, heh?

LINDA: They were out of here by eight o'clock.

WILLY: Good work!

LINDA: It was so thrilling to see them leaving together. I can't get over the shaving lotion in this house!

WILLY [*smiling*]: Mmm ——

LINDA: Biff was very changed this morning. His whole attitude seemed to be hopeful. He couldn't wait to get downtown to see Oliver.

WILLY: He's heading for a change. There's no question, there simply are certain men that take longer to get—solidified. How did he dress?

LINDA: His blue suit. He's so handsome in that suit. He could be a— anything in that suit!

[WILLY *gets up from the table.* LINDA *holds his jacket for him.*]

WILLY: There's no question, no question at all. Gee, on the way home tonight I'd like to buy some seeds.

LINDA [*laughing*]: That'd be wonderful. But not enough sun gets back there. Nothing'll grow any more.

WILLY: You wait, kid, before it's all over we're gonna get a little place out in the country, and I'll raise some vegetables, a couple of chickens . . .

LINDA: You'll do it yet, dear.

[WILLY *walks out of his jacket.* LINDA *follows him.*]

WILLY: And they'll get married, and come for a weekend. I'd build a little guest house. 'Cause I got so many fine tools, all I'd need would be a little lumber and some peace of mind.

LINDA [*joyfully*]: I sewed the lining . . .

WILLY: I could build two guest houses, so they'd both come. Did he decide how much he's going to ask Oliver for?

LINDA [*getting him into the jacket*]: He didn't mention it, but I imagine ten or fifteen thousand. You going to talk to Howard today?

WILLY: Yeah. I'll put it to him straight and simple. He'll just have to take me off the road.

LINDA: And Willy, don't forget to ask for a little advance, because we've got the insurance premium. It's the grace period now.

WILLY: That's a hundred . . . ?

LINDA: A hundred and eight, sixty-eight. Because we're a little short again.

WILLY: Why are we short?

LINDA: Well, you had the motor job on the car . . .

WILLY: That goddamn Studebaker!

LINDA: And you got one more payment on the refrigerator . . .

WILLY: But it just broke again!

LINDA: Well, it's old, dear.

WILLY: I told you we should've bought a well-advertised machine. Charley bought a General Electric and it's twenty years old and it's still good, that son-of-a-bitch.

LINDA: But, Willy ——

WILLY: Whoever heard of a Hastings refrigerator? Once in my life I would like to own something outright before it's broken! I'm always in a race with the junkyard! I just finished paying for the car and it's on its last legs. The refrigerator consumes belts like a goddam maniac. They time those things. They time them so when you finally paid for them, they're used up.

LINDA [*buttoning up his jacket as he unbuttons it*]: All told, about two hundred dollars would carry us, dear. But that includes the last payment on the mortgage. After this payment, Willy, the house belongs to us.

WILLY: It's twenty-five years!

LINDA: Biff was nine years old when we bought it.

WILLY: Well, that's a great thing. To weather a twenty-five year mortgage is ——

LINDA: It's an accomplishment.

WILLY: All the cement, the lumber, the reconstruction I put in this house! There ain't a crack to be found in it any more.

LINDA: Well, it served its purpose.

WILLY: What purpose? Some stranger'll come along, move in, and that's that. If only Biff would take this house, and raise a family . . . [*He starts to go.*] Goodbye, I'm late.

LINDA [*suddenly remembering*]: Oh, I forgot! You're supposed to meet them for dinner.

WILLY: Me?

LINDA: At Frank's Chop House on Forty-eighth near Sixth Avenue.

WILLY: Is that so! How about you?

LINDA: No, just the three of you. They're gonna blow you to a big meal!

WILLY: Don't say! Who thought of that?

LINDA: Biff came to me this morning, Willy, and he said, "Tell Dad, we want to blow him to a big meal." Be there six o'clock. You and your two boys are going to have dinner.

WILLY: Gee whiz! That's really somethin'. I'm gonna knock Howard for a loop, kid. I'll get an advance, and I'll come home with a New York job. Goddammit, now I'm gonna do it!

LINDA: Oh, that's the spirit, Willy!

WILLY: I will never get behind a wheel the rest of my life!

LINDA: It's changing, Willy, I can feel it changing!

WILLY: Beyond a question. G'by, I'm late.

[*He starts to go again.*]

LINDA [*calling after him as she runs to the kitchen table for a handkerchief*]: You got your glasses?

WILLY [*feels for them, then comes back in*]. Yeah, yeah, got my glasses.

LINDA [*giving him the handkerchief*]: And a handkerchief.

WILLY: Yeah, handerchief.

LINDA: And your saccharine?

WILLY: Yeah, my saccharine.

LINDA: Be careful on the subway stairs.

[*She kisses him, and a silk stocking is seen hanging from her hand.* WILLY *notices it.*]

WILLY: Will you stop mending stockings? At least while I'm in the house. It gets me nervous. I can't tell you. Please.

[LINDA *hides the stocking in her hand as she follows* WILLY *across the forestage in front of the house.*]

LINDA: Remember, Frank's Chop House.

WILLY [*passing the apron*]: Maybe beets would grow out there.

LINDA [*laughing*]: But you tried so many times.

WILLY: Yeah. Well, don't work hard today.

[*He disappears around the right corner of the house.*]

LINDA: Be careful!

[*As* WILLY *vanishes,* LINDA *waves to him. Suddenly the phone rings. She runs across the stage and into the kitchen and lifts it.*]

LINDA: Hello? Oh, Biff! I'm so glad you called, I just . . . Yes, sure, I just told him. Yes, he'll be there for dinner at six o'clock, I didn't forget. Listen, I was just dying to tell you. You know that little rubber pipe I told you about? That he connected to the gas heater? I finally decided to go down the cellar this morning and take it away and destroy it. But it's gone! Imagine? He took it away himself, it isn't there! [*She listens.*] When? Oh, then you took it. Oh — nothing, it's just that I'd hoped he'd taken it away himself. Oh, I'm not worried, darling, because this morning he left in such high spirits, it was like the old days! I'm not afraid any more. Did Mr. Oliver see you? . . . Well, you wait there then. And make a nice impression on him, darling. Just don't perspire too much before you see him. And have a nice time with Dad. He may have big news too! . . . That's right, a New York job. And be sweet to him tonight, dear. Be loving to him. Because he's only a little boat looking for a harbor. [*She is trembling with sorrow and joy.*] Oh, that's wonderful, Biff, you'll save his life. Thanks, darling. Just put your arm around him when he comes into the restaurant. Give him a smile. That's the boy . . . Goodbye, dear. . . . You got your comb? . . . That's fine. Goodbye, Biff dear.

[*In the middle of her speech,* HOWARD WAGNER, *thirty-six, wheels on a small typewriter table on which is a wire-recording machine and proceeds to plug it in. This is on the left forestage. Light slowly fades on* LINDA *as it rises on* HOWARD. *Howard is intent on threading the machine and only glances over his shoulder as* WILLY *appears.*]

WILLY: Pst! Pst!

HOWARD: Hello, Willy, come in.

WILLY: Like to have a little talk with you, Howard.

HOWARD: Sorry to keep you waiting. I'll be with you in a minute.

WILLY: What's that, Howard?

HOWARD: Didn't you ever see one of these? Wire recorder.

WILLY: Oh. Can we talk a minute?

HOWARD: Records things. Just got delivery yesterday. Been driving me crazy, the most terrific machine I ever saw in my life. I was up all night with it.

WILLY: What do you do with it?

HOWARD: I bought it for dictation, but you can do anything with it. Listen to this. I had it home last night. Listen to what I picked up. The first one is my daughter. Get this. [*He flicks the switch and "Roll out the Barrel" is heard being whistled.*] Listen to that kid whistle.

WILLY: That is lifelike, isn't it?

HOWARD: Seven years old. Get that tone.

WILLY: Ts, ts. Like to ask a little favor if you . . .

[*The whistling breaks off, and the voice of* HOWARD's *daughter is heard.*]

HIS DAUGHTER: "Now you, Daddy."

HOWARD: She's crazy for me! [*Again the same song is whistled.*] That's me! Ha!

[*He winks.*]

WILLY: You're very good!

[*The whistling breaks off again. The machine runs silent for a moment.*]

HOWARD: Sh! Get this now, this is my son.

HIS SON: "The capital of Alabama is Montgomery; the capital of Arizona is Phoenix; the capital of Arkansas is Little Rock; the capital of California is Sacramento . . ." *and on, and on.*

HOWARD [*holding up five fingers*]: Five years old, Willy!

WILLY: He'll make an announcer some day!

HIS SON [*continuing*]: "The capital . . ."

HOWARD: Get that — alphabetical order! [*The machine breaks off suddenly.*] Wait a minute. The maid kicked the plug out.

WILLY: It certainly is a ——

HOWARD: Sh, for God's sake!

HIS SON: "It's nine o'clock, Bulova watch time. So I have to go to sleep."

WILLY: That really is ——

HOWARD: Wait a minute! The next is my wife.

[*They wait.*]

HOWARD'S VOICE: "Go on, say something." [*Pause.*] "Well, you gonna talk?"

HIS WIFE: "I can't think of anything."

HOWARD'S VOICE: "Well, talk — it's turning."

HIS WIFE [*shyly, beaten*]: "Hello." [*Silence.*] "Oh, Howard, I can't talk into this . . ."

HOWARD [*snapping the machine off*]: That was my wife.

WILLY: That is a wonderful machine. Can we ——

HOWARD: I tell you, Willy, I'm gonna take my camera, and my bandsaw, and all my hobbies, and out they go. This is the most fascinating relaxation I ever found.

WILLY: I think I'll get one myself.

HOWARD: Sure, they're only a hundred and a half. You can't do without it. Supposing you wanna hear Jack Benny, see? But you can't be at home at that hour. So you tell the maid to turn the radio on when Jack Benny comes on, and this automatically goes on with the radio . . .

WILLY: And when you come home you . . .

HOWARD: You can come home twelve o'clock, one o'clock, any time you like, and you get yourself a Coke and sit yourself down, throw the switch, and there's Jack Benny's program in the middle of the night!

WILLY: I'm definitely going to get one. Because lots of time I'm on the road, and I think to myself, what I must be missing on the radio!

HOWARD: Don't you have a radio in the car?

WILLY: Well, yeah, but who ever thinks of turning it on?

HOWARD: Say, aren't you supposed to be in Boston?

WILLY: That's what I want to talk to you about, Howard. You got a minute?

[*He draws a chair in from the wing.*]

HOWARD: What happened? What're you doing here?

WILLY: Well . . .

HOWARD: You didn't crack up again, did you?

WILLY: Oh, no. No . . .

HOWARD: Geez, you had me worried there for a minute. What's the trouble?

WILLY: Well, tell you the truth, Howard. I've come to the decision that I'd rather not travel any more.

HOWARD: Not travel! Well, what'll you do?

WILLY: Remember, Christmas time, when you had the party here? You said you'd try to think of some spot for me here in town.

HOWARD: With us?

WILLY: Well, sure.

HOWARD: Oh, yeah, yeah. I remember. Well, I couldn't think of anything for you, Willy.

WILLY: I tell ya, Howard. The kids are all grown up, y'know. I don't need much any more. If I could take home — well, sixty-five dollars a week, I could swing it.

HOWARD: Yeah, but Willy, see I ——

WILLY: I tell ya why, Howard. Speaking frankly and between the two of us, y'know — I'm just a little tired.

HOWARD: Oh, I could understand that, Willy. But you're a road man, Willy, and we do a road business. We've only got a half-dozen salesmen on the floor here.

WILLY: God knows, Howard, I never asked a favor of any man. But I was with the firm when your father used to carry you in here in his arms.

HOWARD: I know that, Willy, but ——

WILLY: Your father came to me the day you were born and asked me what I thought of the name of Howard, may he rest in peace.

HOWARD: I appreciate that, Willy, but there just is no spot here for you. If I had a spot I'd slam you right in, but I just don't have a single solitary spot.

[*He looks for his lighter.* WILLY *has picked it up and gives it to him. Pause.*]

WILLY [*with increasing anger*]: Howard, all I need to set my table is fifty dollars a week.

HOWARD: But where am I going to put you, kid?

WILLY: Look, it isn't a question of whether I can sell merchandise, is it?

HOWARD: No, but it's a business, kid, and everybody's gotta pull his own weight.

WILLY [*desperately*]: Just let me tell you a story, Howard——

HOWARD: 'Cause you gotta admit, business is business.

WILLY [*angrily*]: Business is definitely business, but just listen for a minute. You don't understand this. When I was a boy — eighteen, nineteen — I was already on the road. And there was a question in my mind as to whether selling had a future for me. Because in those days I had a yearning to go to Alaska. See, there were three gold strikes in one month in Alaska, and I felt like going out. Just for the ride, you might say.

HOWARD [*barely interested*]: Don't say.

WILLY: Oh, yeah, my father lived many years in Alaska. He was an adventurous man. We've got quite a little streak of self-reliance in our family. I thought I'd go out with my older brother and try to locate him, and maybe settle in the North with the old man. And I was almost decided to go, when I met a salesman in the Parker House. His name was Dave Singleman. And he was eighty-four years old, and he'd drummed merchandise in thirty-one states. And old Dave, he'd go up to his room, y'understand, put on his green velvet slippers — I'll never forget — and pick up his phone and call the buyers, and without ever leaving his room, at the age of eighty-four, he made his living. And when I saw that, I realized that selling was the greatest career a man could want. 'Cause what could be more satisfying than to be able to go, at the age of eighty-four, into twenty or thirty different cities, and pick up a phone, and be remembered and loved and helped by so many different people? Do you know? when he died — and by the way he died the death of a salesman, in his green velvet slippers in the smoker of the New York, New Haven and Hartford, going into Boston — when he died, hundreds of salesmen and buyers were at his funeral. Things were sad on a lotta trains for months after that. [*He stands up.* HOWARD *has not looked at him.*] In those days there was personality in it, Howard. There was respect, and comradeship, and gratitude in it. Today, it's all cut and dried, and there's no chance for bringing friendship to bear — or personality. You see what I mean? They don't know me any more.

HOWARD [*moving away to the right*]: That's just the thing, Willy.

WILLY: If I had forty dollars a week — that's all I'd need. Forty dollars, Howard.

HOWARD: Kid, I can't take blood from a stone. I ——

WILLY [*desperation is on him now*]. Howard, the year Al Smith was nominated, your father came to me and ——

HOWARD [*starting to go off*]: I've got to see some people, kid.

WILLY [*stopping him*]: I'm talking about your father! There were promises made across this desk! You mustn't tell me you've got people to see — I put thirty-four years into this firm, Howard, and now I can't pay my insurance! You can't eat the orange and throw the peel away — a man is not a piece of fruit! [*After a pause.*] Now pay attention. Your father — in 1928 I had a big year. I averaged a hundred and seventy dollars a week in commissions.

HOWARD [*impatiently*]: Now, Willy, you never averaged ——

WILLY [*banging his hand on the desk*]: I averaged a hundred and seventy dollars a week in the year of 1928! And your father came to me — or rather, I was in the office here — it was right over this desk — and he put his hand on my shoulder ——

HOWARD [*getting up*]: You'll have to excuse me, Willy, I gotta see some people. Pull yourself together. [*Going out.*] I'll be back in a little while.

[*On* HOWARD's *exit, the light on his chair grows very bright and strange.*]

WILLY: Pull myself together! What the hell did I say to him? My God, I was yelling at him! How could I! [WILLY *breaks off, staring at the light, which occupies the chair, animating it. He approaches this chair, standing across the desk from it.*] Frank, Frank, don't you remember what you told me that time? How you put your hand on my shoulder, and Frank . . .

[*He leans on the desk and as he speaks the dead man's name he accidentally switches on the recorder, and instantly*]

HOWARD's SON: ". . . of New York is Albany. The capital of Ohio is Cincinnati, the capital of Rhode Island is . . ."

[*The recitation continues.*]

WILLY [*leaping away with fright, shouting*]: Ha! Howard! Howard! Howard!

HOWARD [*rushing in*]: What happened?

WILLY [*pointing at the machine, which continues nasally, childishly, with the capital cities*]: Shut it off! Shut it off!

HOWARD [*pulling the plug out*]: Look, Willy . . .

WILLY [*pressing his hand to his eyes*]: I gotta get myself some coffee. I'll get some coffee . . .

[WILLY *starts to walk out.* HOWARD *stops him.*]

HOWARD [*rolling up the cord*]: Willy, look . . .

WILLY: I'll go to Boston.

HOWARD: Willy, you can't go to Boston for us.

WILLY: Why can't I go?

HOWARD: I don't want you to represent us. I've been meaning to tell you for a long time now.

WILLY: Howard, are you firing me?

HOWARD: I think you need a good long rest, Willy.

WILLY: Howard ——

HOWARD: And when you feel better, come back, and we'll see if we can work something out.

WILLY: But I gotta earn money, Howard. I'm in no position to ——

HOWARD: Where are your sons? Why don't your sons give you a hand?

WILLY: They're working on a very big deal.

HOWARD: This is no time for false pride, Willy. You go to your sons and you tell them that you're tired. You've got two great boys, haven't you?

WILLY: Oh, no question, no question, but in the meantime . . .

HOWARD: Then that's that, heh?

WILLY: All right, I'll go to Boston tomorrow.

HOWARD: No, no.

WILLY: I can't throw myself on my sons. I'm not a cripple!

HOWARD: Look, kid, I'm busy this morning.

WILLY [*grasping* HOWARD's *arm*]: Howard, you've got to let me go to Boston!

HOWARD [*hard, keeping himself under control*]: I've got a line of people to see this morning. Sit down, take five minutes, and pull yourself together, and then go home, will ya? I need the office, Willy. [*He starts to go, turns, remembering the recorder, starts to push off the table holding the recorder.*] Oh, yeah. Whenever you can this week, stop by and drop off the samples. You'll feel better, Willy, and then come back and we'll talk. Pull yourself together, kid, there's people outside.

[HOWARD *exits, pushing the table off left.* WILLY *stares into space, exhausted. Now the music is heard —* BEN's *music — first distantly, then closer, closer. As* WILLY *speaks,* BEN *enters from the right. He carries valise and umbrella.*]

WILLY: Oh, Ben, how did you do it? What is the answer? Did you wind up the Alaska deal already?

BEN: Doesn't take much time if you know what you're doing. Just a short business trip. Boarding ship in an hour. Wanted to say goodbye.

WILLY: Ben, I've got to talk to you.

BEN [*glancing at his watch*]: Haven't time, William.

WILLY [*crossing the apron to* BEN]: Ben, nothing's working out. I don't know what to do.

BEN: Now, look here, William. I've bought timberland in Alaska and I need a man to look after things for me.

WILLY: God, timberland! Me and my boys in those grand outdoors!

BEN: You've a new continent at your doorstep, William. Get out of these cities, they're full of talk and time payments and courts of law. Screw on your fists and you can fight for a fortune up there.

WILLY: Yes, yes! Linda! Linda!

[LINDA *enters as of old, with the wash.*]

LINDA: Oh, you're back?

BEN: I haven't much time.

WILLY: No, wait! Linda, he's got a proposition for me in Alaska.

LINDA: But you've got —— [*To* BEN.] He's got a beautiful job here.

WILLY: But in Alaska, kid, I could ——

LINDA: You're doing well enough, Willy!

BEN [*to* LINDA]: Enough for what, my dear?

LINDA [*frightened of* BEN *and angry at him*]: Don't say those things to him! Enough to be happy right here, right now. [*To* WILLY, *while* BEN *laughs.*] Why must everybody conquer the world? You're well liked, and the boys love you, and someday —— [*To* BEN.] — why, old man Wagner told him just the other day that if he keeps it up he'll be a member of the firm, didn't he, Willy?

WILLY: Sure, sure. I am building something with this firm, Ben, and if a man is building something he must be on the right track, mustn't he?

BEN: What are you building? Lay your hand on it. Where is it?

WILLY [*hesitantly*]: That's true, Linda, there's nothing.

LINDA: Why? [*To* BEN.] There's a man eighty-four years old ——

WILLY: That's right, Ben, that's right. When I look at that man I say, what is there to worry about?

BEN: Bah!

WILLY: It's true, Ben. All he has to do is go into any city, pick up the phone, and he's making his living and you know why?

BEN [*picking up his valise*]: I've got to go.

WILLY [*holding* BEN *back*]: Look at this boy!

[BIFF, *in his high school sweater, enters carrying suitcase.* HAPPY *carries* BIFF's *shoulder guards, gold helmet, and football pants.*]

WILLY: Without a penny to his name, three great universities are begging for him, and from there the sky's the limit, because it's not what you do, Ben. It's who you know and the smile on your face! It's contacts, Ben, contacts! The whole wealth of Alaska passes over the lunch table at the Commodore Hotel, and that's the wonder, the wonder of this country, that a man can end with diamonds here on the basis of being liked. [*He turns to* BIFF.] And that's why when you get out on that field today it's important. Because thousands of people will be rooting for you and loving you. [*To* BEN, *who has again begun to leave.*] And Ben! when he walks into a business office his name will sound out like a bell and all the doors will open to him! I've seen it, Ben, I've seen it a thousand times! You can't feel it with your hand like timber, but it's there!

BEN: Goodbye, William.

WILLY: Ben, am I right? Don't you think I'm right? I value your advice.

BEN: There's a new continent at your doorstep, William. You could walk out rich. Rich!

[*He is gone.*]

WILLY: We'll do it here, Ben! You hear me? We're gonna do it here!

[YOUNG BERNARD *rushes in. The gay music of the* BOYS *is heard.*]

BERNARD: Oh, gee, I was afraid you left already!

WILLY: Why? What time is it?

BERNARD: It's half-past one!

WILLY: Well, come on, everybody! Ebbets Field next stop! Where's the pennants?

[*He rushes through the wall-line of the kitchen and out into the living-room.*]

LINDA [*to* BIFF]: Did you pack your fresh underwear?

BIFF [*who has been limbering up*]: I want to go!

BERNARD: Biff, I'm carrying your helmet, ain't I?

HAPPY: No, I'm carrying the helmet.

BERNARD: Oh, Biff, you promised me.

HAPPY: I'm carrying the helmet.

BERNARD: How am I going to get in the locker room?

LINDA: Let him carry the shoulder guards.

[*She puts her coat and hat on in the kitchen.*]

BERNARD: Can I, Biff? 'Cause I told everybody I'm going to be in the locker room.

HAPPY: In Ebbets Field it's the clubhouse.

BERNARD: I meant the clubhouse. Biff!

HAPPY: Biff!

BIFF [*grandly, after a slight pause*]: Let him carry the shoulder guards.

HAPPY [*as he gives* BERNARD *the shoulder guards*]: Stay close to us now.

[WILLY *rushes in with the pennants.*]

WILLY [*handing them out*]: Everybody wave them when Biff comes out on the field. [HAPPY *and* BERNARD *run off.*] You set now, boy?

[*The music has died away.*]

BIFF: Ready to go, Pop. Every muscle is ready.

WILLY [*at the edge of the apron*]: You realize what this means?

BIFF: That's right, Pop.

WILLY [*feeling* BIFF'S *muscles*]: You're comin' home this afternoon captain of the All-Scholastic Championship Team of the City of New York.

BIFF: I got it, Pop. And remember, pal, when I take off my helmet, that touchdown is for you.

WILLY: Let's go! [*He is starting out, with his arm around* BIFF, *when* CHARLEY *enters, as of old, in knickers.*] I got no room for you, Charley.

CHARLEY: Room? For what?

WILLY: In the car.

CHARLEY: You goin' for a ride? I wanted to shoot some casino.

WILLY [*furiously*]: Casino! [*Incredulously.*] Don't you realize what today is?

LINDA: Oh, he knows, Willy. He's just kidding you.

WILLY: That's nothing to kid about!

CHARLEY: No, Linda, what's goin' on?

LINDA: He's playing in Ebbets Field.

CHARLEY: Baseball in this weather?

WILLY: Don't talk to him. Come on, come on!

[*He is pushing them out.*]

CHARLEY: Wait a minute, didn't you hear the news?

WILLY: What?

CHARLEY: Don't you listen to the radio? Ebbets Field just blew up.

WILLY: You go to hell! [CHARLEY *laughs. Pushing them out.*] Come on, come on! We're late.

CHARLEY [*as they go*]: Knock a homer, Biff, knock a homer!

WILLY [*the last to leave, turning to* CHARLEY]: I don't think that was funny, Charley. This is the greatest day of his life.

CHARLEY: Willy, when are you going to grow up?

WILLY: Yeah, heh? When this game is over, Charley, you'll be laughing out of the other side of your face. They'll be calling him another Red Grange. Twenty-five thousand a year.

CHARLEY [*kidding*]: Is that so?

WILLY: Yeah, that's so.

CHARLEY: Well, then, I'm sorry, Willy. But tell me something.

WILLY: What?

CHARLEY: Who is Red Grange?

WILLY: Put up your hands. Goddam you, put up your hands!

[CHARLEY, *chuckling, shakes his head and walks away, around the left corner of the stage.* WILLY *follows him. The music rises to a mocking frenzy.*]

WILLY: Who the hell do you think you are, better than everybody else? You don't know everything, you big, ignorant, stupid . . . Put up your hands!

[*Light rises, on the right side of the forestage, on a small table in the reception room of* CHARLEY's *office. Traffic sounds are heard.* BERNARD, *now mature, sits whistling to himself. A pair of tennis rackets and an overnight bag are on the floor beside him.*]

WILLY [*offstage*]: What are you walking away for? Don't walk away! If you're going to say something say it to my face! I know you laugh at me behind my back. You'll laugh out of the other side of your goddam face after this game. Touchdown! Touchdown! Eighty thousand people! Touchdown! Right between the goal posts.

[BERNARD *is a quiet, earnest, but self-assured young man.* WILLY's *voice is coming from right upstage now.* BERNARD *lowers his feet off the table and listens.* JENNY, *his father's secretary, enters.*]

JENNY [*distressed*]: Say, Bernard, will you go out in the hall?

BERNARD: What is that noise? Who is it?

JENNY: Mr. Loman. He just got off the elevator.

BERNARD [*getting up*]: Who's he arguing with?

JENNY: Nobody. There's nobody with him. I can't deal with him any more, and your father gets all upset everytime he comes. I've got a lot of typing to do, and your father's waiting to sign it. Will you see him?

WILLY [*entering*]: Touchdown! Touch — [*He sees* JENNY.] Jenny, Jenny, good to see you. How're ya? Workin'? Or still honest?

JENNY: Fine. How've you been feeling?

WILLY: Not much any more, Jenny. Ha, ha!

[*He is surprised to see the rackets.*]

BERNARD: Hello, Uncle Willy.

WILLY [*almost shocked*]: Bernard! Well, look who's here!

[*He comes quickly, guiltily, to* BERNARD *and warmly shakes his hand.*]

BERNARD: How are you? Good to see you.

WILLY: What are you doing here?

BERNARD: Oh, just stopped by to see Pop. Get off my feet till my train leaves. I'm going to Washington in a few minutes.

WILLY: Is he in?

BERNARD: Yes, he's in his office with the accountant. Sit down.

WILLY [*sitting down*]: What're you going to do in Washington?

BERNARD: Oh, just a case I've got there, Willy.

WILLY: That so? [*Indicating the rackets.*] You going to play tennis there?

BERNARD: I'm staying with a friend who's got a court.

WILLY: Don't say. His own tennis court. Must be fine people, I bet.

BERNARD: They are, very nice. Dad tells me Biff's in town.

WILLY [*with a big smile*]: Yeah, Biff's in. Working on a very big deal, Bernard.

BERNARD: What's Biff doing?

WILLY: Well, he's been doing very big things in the West. But he decided to establish himself here. Very big. We're having dinner. Did I hear your wife had a boy?

BERNARD: That's right. Our second.

WILLY: Two boys! What do you know!

BERNARD: What kind of a deal has Biff got?

WILLY: Well, Bill Oliver — very big sporting-goods man — he wants Biff very badly. Called him in from the West. Long distance, carte blanche, special deliveries. Your friends have their own private tennis courts?

BERNARD: You still with the old firm, Willy?

WILLY [*after a pause*]: I'm — I'm overjoyed to see how you made the grade, Bernard, overjoyed. It's an encouraging thing to see a young man really — really — Looks very good for Biff — very — [*He breaks off, then.*] Bernard ——

[*He is so full of emotion, he breaks off again.*]

BERNARD: What is it, Willy?

WILLY [*small and alone*]: What — what's the secret?

BERNARD: What secret?

WILLY: How — how did you? Why didn't he ever catch on?

BERNARD: I wouldn't know that, Willy.

WILLY [*confidently, desperately*]: You were his friend, his boyhood friend. There's something I don't understand about it. His life ended after that Ebbets Field game. From the age of seventeen nothing good ever happened to him.

BERNARD: He never trained himself for anything.

WILLY: But he did, he did. After high school he took so many correspondence courses. Radio mechanics, television; God knows what, and never made the slightest mark.

BERNARD [*taking off his glasses*]: Willy, do you want to talk candidly?

WILLY [*rising, facing* BERNARD]: I regard you as a very brilliant man, Bernard. I value your advice.

BERNARD: Oh, the hell with the advice, Willy. I couldn't advise you. There's just one thing I've always wanted to ask you. When he was supposed to graduate. and the math teacher flunked him ——

WILLY: Oh, that son-of-a-bitch ruined his life.

BERNARD: Yeah, but, Willy, all he had to do was go to summer school and make up that subject.

WILLY: That's right, that's right.

BERNARD: Did you tell him not to go to summer school?

WILLY: Me? I begged him to go. I ordered him to go!

BERNARD: Then why wouldn't he go?

WILLY: Why? Why! Bernard, that question has been trailing me like a ghost for the last fifteen years. He flunked the subject, and laid down and died like a hammer hit him!

BERNARD: Take it easy, kid.

WILLY: Let me talk to you — I got nobody to talk to. Bernard, Bernard, was it my fault? Y'see? It keeps going around in my mind, maybe I did something to him. I got nothing to give him.

BERNARD: Don't take it so hard.

WILLY: Why did he lay down? What is the story there? You were his friend!

BERNARD: Willy, I remember, it was June, and our grades came out. And he'd flunked math.

WILLY: That son-of-a-bitch!

BERNARD: No, it wasn't right then. Biff just got very angry, I remember, and he was ready to enroll in summer school.

WILLY [*surprised*]: He was?

BERNARD: He wasn't beaten by it at all. But then, Willy, he disappeared from the block for almost a month. And I got the idea that he'd gone up to New England to see you. Did he have a talk with you then?

[WILLY *stares in silence.*]

BERNARD: Willy?

WILLY [*with a strong edge of resentment in his voice*]: Yeah, he came to Boston. What about it?

BERNARD: Well, just that when he came back — I'll never forget this, it always mystifies me. Because I'd thought so well of Biff, even though he'd always taken advantage of me. I loved him, Willy, y'know? And he came back after that month and took his sneakers — remember those sneakers with "University of Virginia" printed on them? He was so proud of those, wore them every day. And he took them down in the cellar, and burned them up in the furnace. We had a fist fight. It lasted at least half an hour. Just the two of us, punching each other down the cellar, and crying right through it. I've often thought of how strange it was that I knew he'd given up his life. What happened in Boston, Willie?

[WILLY *looks at him as at an intruder.*]

BERNARD: I just bring it up because you asked me.

WILLY [*angrily*]: Nothing. What do you mean, "What happened?" What's that got to do with anything?

BERNARD: Well, don't get sore.

WILLY: What are you trying to do, blame it on me? If a boy lays down is that my fault?

BERNARD: Now, Willy, don't get ——

WILLY: Well, don't — don't talk to me that way! What does that mean, "What happened?"

[CHARLEY *enters. He is in his vest, and he carries a bottle of bourbon.*]

CHARLEY: Hey, you're going to miss that train.

[*He waves the bottle.*]

BERNARD: Yeah, I'm going. [*He takes the bottle.*] Thanks, Pop. [*He picks up his rackets and bag.*] Goodbye, Willy, and don't worry about it. You know, "If at first you don't succeed . . ."

WILLY: Yes, I believe in that.

BERNARD: But sometimes, Willy, it's better for a man just to walk away.

WILLY: Walk away?

BERNARD: That's right.

WILLY: But if you can't walk away?

BERNARD [*after a slight pause*]: I guess that's when it's tough. [*Extending his hand.*] Goodbye, Willy.

WILLY [*shaking* BERNARD's *hand*]: Goodbye, boy.

CHARLEY [*an arm on* BERNARD's *shoulder*]: How do you like this kid? Gonna argue a case in front of the Supreme Court.

BERNARD [*protesting*]: Pop!

WILLY [*genuinely shocked, pained, and happy*]: No! The Supreme Court!

BERNARD: I gotta run. 'Bye, Dad!

CHARLEY: Knock 'em dead, Bernard!

[BERNARD *goes off.*]

WILLY [*as* CHARLEY *takes out his wallet*]: The Supreme Court! And he didn't even mention it!

CHARLEY [*counting out money on the desk*]: He don't have to — he's gonna do it.

WILLY: And you never told him what to do, did you? You never took any interest in him.

CHARLEY: My salvation is that I never took any interest in anything. There's some money — fifty dollars. I got an accountant inside.

WILLY: Charley, look . . . [*With difficulty.*] I got my insurance to pay. If you can manage it — I need a hundred and ten dollars.

[CHARLEY *doesn't reply for a moment; merely stops moving.*]

WILLY: I'd draw it from my bank but Linda would know, and I . . .

CHARLEY: Sit down, Willy.

WILLY [*moving toward the chair*]: I'm keeping an account of everything, remember. I'll pay every penny back.

[*He sits.*]

CHARLEY: Now listen to me, Willy.

WILLY: I want you to know I appreciate . . .

CHARLEY [*sitting down on the table*]: Willy, what're you doin'? What the hell is goin' on in your head?

WILLY: Why? I'm simply . . .

CHARLEY: I offered you a job. You can make fifty dollars a week. And I won't send you on the road.

WILLY: I've got a job.

CHARLEY: Without pay? What kind of a job is a job without pay? [*He rises.*] Now, look, kid, enough is enough. I'm no genius but I know when I'm being insulted.

WILLY: Insulted!

CHARLEY: Why don't you want to work for me?

WILLY: What's the matter with you? I've got a job.

CHARLEY: Then what're you walkin' in here every week for?

WILLY [*getting up*]: Well, if you don't want me to walk in here ——

CHARLEY: I am offering you a job.

WILLY: I don't want your goddam job!

CHARLEY: When the hell are you gonna grow up?

WILLY [*furiously*]: You big ignoramus, if you say that to me again I'll rap you one! I don't care how big you are!

[*He's ready to fight.*]

[*Pause.*]

CHARLEY [*kindly, going to him*]: How much do you need, Willy?

WILLY: Charley, I'm strapped, I'm strapped. I don't know what to do I was just fired.

CHARLEY: Howard fired you?

WILLY: That snotnose. Imagine that? I named him. I named him Howard.

CHARLEY: Willy, when're you gonna realize that them things don't mean anything? You named him Howard, but you can't sell that. The only thing you got in this world is what you can sell. And the funny thing is that you're a salesman, and you don't know that.

WILLY: I've always tried to think otherwise, I guess. I always felt that if a man was impressive, and well liked, that nothing ——

CHARLEY: Why must everybody like you? Who liked J. P. Morgan? Was he impressive? In a Turkish bath he'd look like a butcher. But with his pockets on he was very well liked. Now listen, Willy, I know you don't like me, and nobody can say I'm in love with you, but I'll give you a job because — just for the hell of it, put it that way. Now what do you say?

WILLY: I — I just can't work for you, Charley.

CHARLEY: What're you, jealous of me?

WILLY: I can't work for you, that's all, don't ask me why.

CHARLEY [*angered, takes out more bills*]: You been jealous of me all your life, you damned fool! Here, pay your insurance.

[*He puts the money in* WILLY's *hand.*]

WILLY: I'm keeping strict accounts.

CHARLEY: I've got some work to do. Take care of yourself. And pay your insurance.

WILLY [*moving to the right*]: Funny, y'know? After all the highways, and the trains, and the appointments, and the years, you end up worth more dead than alive.

CHARLEY: Willy, nobody's worth nothin' dead. [*After a slight pause.*] Did you hear what I said?

[WILLY *stands still, dreaming.*]

CHARLEY: Willy!

WILLY: Apologize to Bernard for me when you see him. I didn't mean to argue with him. He's a fine boy. They're all fine boys, and they'll end up big — all of them. Someday they'll all play tennis together. Wish me luck, Charley. He saw Bill Oliver today.

CHARLEY: Good luck.

WILLY [*on the verge of tears*]: Charley, you're the only friend I got. Isn't that a remarkable thing?

[*He goes out.*]

CHARLEY: Jesus!

[CHARLEY *stares after him a moment and follows. All light blacks out. Suddenly raucous noise is heard, and a red glow rises behind the screen at right.* STANLEY, *a young waiter, appears, carrying a table, followed by* HAPPY, *who is carrying two chairs.*]

STANLEY [*putting the table down*]: That's all right, Mr. Loman, I can handle it myself.

[*He turns and takes the chairs from* HAPPY *and places them at the table.*]

HAPPY [*glancing around*]: Oh, this is better.

STANLEY: Sure, in the front there you're in the middle of all kinds a noise. Whenever you got a party, Mr. Loman, you just tell me and I'll put you back here. Y'know, there's a lotta people they don't like it private, because when they go out they like to see a lotta action around them because they're sick and tired to stay in the house by theirself. But I know you, you ain't from Hackensack. You know what I mean?

HAPPY [*sitting down*]: So how's it coming, Stanley?

STANLEY: Ah, it's a dog's life. I only wish during the war they'd a took me in the Army. I coulda been dead by now.

HAPPY: My brother's back, Stanley.

STANLEY: Oh, he come back, heh? From the Far West.

HAPPY: Yeah, big cattle man, my brother, so treat him right. And my father's coming too.

STANLEY: Oh, your father too!

HAPPY: You got a couple of nice lobsters?

STANLEY: Hundred per cent big.

HAPPY: I want them with the claws.

STANLEY: Don't worry, I don't give you no mice. [HAPPY *laughs.*] How about some wine? It'll put a head on the meal.

HAPPY: No. You remember, Stanley, that recipe I brought you from overseas? With the champagne in it?

STANLEY: Oh, yeah, sure. I still got it tacked up yet in the kitchen. But that'll have to cost a buck apiece anyways.

HAPPY: That's all right.

STANLEY: What'd you do, hit a number or somethin'?

HAPPY: No, it's a little celebration. My brother is — I think he pulled off a big deal today. I think we're going into business together.

STANLEY: Great! That's the best for you. Because a family business, you know what I mean? — that's the best.

HAPPY: That's what I think.

STANLEY: 'Cause what's the difference? Somebody steals? It's in the family. Know what I mean? [*Sotto voce.*] Like this bartender here. The boss is goin' crazy what kinda leak he's got in the cash register. You put it in but it don't come out.

HAPPY [*raising his hand*]: Sh!

STANLEY: What?

HAPPY: You notice I wasn't lookin' right or left, was I?

STANLEY: No.

HAPPY: And my eyes are closed.

STANLEY: So what's the —— ?

HAPPY: Strudel's comin'.

STANLEY [*catching on, looks around*]: Oh, no, there's no ——
[*He breaks off as a furred, lavishly dressed girl enters and sits at the next table. Both follow her with their eyes.*]

STANLEY: Geez, how'd ya know?

HAPPY: I got radar or something. [*Staring directly at her profile.*] Ooooooooo . . . Stanley.

STANLEY: I think that's for you, Mr. Loman.

HAPPY: Look at that mouth. Oh, God. And the binoculars.

STANLEY: Geez, you got a life, Mr. Loman.

HAPPY: Wait on her.

STANLEY [*going to the girl's table*]: Would you like a menu, ma'am?

GIRL: I'm expecting someone, but I'd like a ——

HAPPY: Why don't you bring her — excuse me, miss, do you mind? I sell champagne, and I'd like you to try my brand. Bring her a champagne, Stanley.

GIRL: That's awfully nice of you.

HAPPY: Don't mention it. It's all company money.
[*He laughs.*]

GIRL: That's a charming product to be selling, isn't it?

HAPPY: Oh, gets to be like everything else. Selling is selling, y'know.

GIRL: I suppose.

HAPPY: You don't happen to sell, do you?

GIRL: No, I don't sell.

HAPPY: Would you object to a compliment from a stranger? You ought to be on a magazine cover.

GIRL [*looking at him a little archly*]: I have been.
[STANLEY *comes in with a glass of champagne.*]

HAPPY: What'd I say before, Stanley? You see? She's a cover girl.

STANLEY: Oh, I could see, I could see.

HAPPY [*to the* GIRL]: What magazine?

GIRL: Oh, a lot of them. [*She takes the drink.*] Thank you.

HAPPY: You know what they say in France, don't you? "Champagne is the drink of the complexion" — H'ya Biff!

[BIFF *has entered and sits with* HAPPY.]

BIFF: Hello, kid. Sorry I'm late.

HAPPY: I just got here. Uh, Miss —— ?

GIRL: Forsythe.

HAPPY: Miss Forsythe, this is my brother.

BIFF: Is Dad here?

HAPPY: His name is Biff. You might've heard of him. Great football player.

GIRL: Really? What team?

HAPPY: Are you familiar with football?

GIRL: No, I'm afraid I'm not.

HAPPY: Biff is a quarterback with the New York Giants.

GIRL: Well, that is nice, isn't it?

[*She drinks.*]

HAPPY: Good health.

GIRL: I'm happy to meet you.

HAPPY: That's my name. Hap. It's really Harold, but at West Point they called me Happy.

GIRL [*now really impressed*]: Oh, I see. How do you do?

[*She turns her profile.*]

BIFF: Isn't Dad coming?

HAPPY: You want her?

BIFF: Oh, I could never make that.

HAPPY: I remember the time that idea would never come into your head. Where's the old confidence, Biff?

BIFF: I just saw Oliver ——

HAPPY: Wait a minute. I've got to see that old confidence again. Do you want her? She's on call.

BIFF: Oh, no.

[*He turns to look at the* GIRL.]

HAPPY: I'm telling you. Watch this. [*Turning to the* GIRL.] Honey? [*She turns to him.*] Are you busy?

GIRL: Well, I am . . . but I could make a phone call.

HAPPY: Do that, will you, honey? And see if you can get a friend. We'll be here for a while. Biff is one of the greatest football players in the country.

GIRL [*standing up*]: Well, I'm certainly happy to meet you.

HAPPY: Come back soon.

GIRL: I'll try.

HAPPY: Don't try, honey, try hard.

[*The* GIRL *exits.* STANLEY *follows, shaking his head in bewildered admiration.*]

HAPPY: Isn't that a shame now? A beautiful girl like that? That's why I can't get married. There's not a good woman in a thousand. New York is loaded with them, kid!

BIFF: Hap, look ——

HAPPY: I told you she was on call!

BIFF [*strangely unnerved*]: Cut it out, will ya. I want to say something to you.

HAPPY: Did you see Oliver?

BIFF: I saw him all right. Now look, I want to tell Dad a couple of things and I want you to help me.

HAPPY: What? Is he going to back you?

BIFF: Are you crazy? You're out of your goddam head, you know that?

HAPPY: Why? What happened?

BIFF [*breathlessly*]: I did a terrible thing today, Hap. It's been the strangest day I ever went through. I'm all numb, I swear.

HAPPY: You mean he wouldn't see you?

BIFF: Well, I waited six hours for him, see? All day. Kept sending my name in. Even tried to date his secretary so she'd get me to him, but no soap.

HAPPY: Because you're not showin' the old confidence, Biff. He remembered you, didn't he?

BIFF [*stopping* HAPPY *with a gesture*]: Finally, about five o'clock, he comes out. Didn't remember who I was or anything. I felt like such an idiot, Hap.

HAPPY: Did you tell him my Florida idea?

BIFF: He walked away. I saw him for one minute. I got so mad I could've torn the walls down! How the hell did I ever get the idea I was a salesman there? I even believed myself that I'd been a salesman for him! And then he gave me one look and — I realized what a ridiculous lie my whole life has been. We've been talking in a dream for fifteen years. I was a shipping clerk.

HAPPY: What'd you do?

BIFF [*with great tension and wonder*]: Well, he left, see. And the secretary went out. I was all alone in the waiting room. I don't know what came over me, Hap. The next thing I know I'm in his office — paneled walls, everything. I can't explain it. I — Hap, I took his fountain pen.

HAPPY: Geez, did he catch you?

BIFF: I ran out. I ran down all eleven flights. I ran and ran and ran.

HAPPY: That was an awful dumb — what'd you do that for?

BIFF [*agonized*]: I don't know, I just — wanted to take something, I don't know. You gotta help me, Hap, I'm gonna tell Pop.

HAPPY: You crazy? What for?

BIFF: Hap, he's got to understand that I'm not the man somebody lends that kind of money to. He thinks I've been spiting him all these years and it's eating him up.

HAPPY: That's just it. You tell him something nice.

BIFF: I can't.

HAPPY: Say you got a lunch date with Oliver tomorrow.

BIFF: So what do I do tomorrow?

HAPPY: You leave the house tomorrow and come back at night and say Oliver is thinking it over. And he thinks it over for a couple of weeks, and gradually it fades away and nobody's the worse.

BIFF: But it'll go on forever!

HAPPY: Dad is never so happy as when he's looking forward to something!

[WILLY *enters.*]

HAPPY: Hello, scout!

WILLY: Gee, I haven't been here in years!

[STANLEY *has followed* WILLY *in and sets a chair for him.* STANLEY *starts off but* HAPPY *stops him.*]

HAPPY: Stanley!

[STANLEY *stands by, waiting for an order.*]

BIFF [*going to* WILLY *with guilt, as to an invalid*]: Sit down, Pop. You want a drink?

WILLY: Sure, I don't mind.

BIFF: Let's get a load on.

WILLY: You look worried.

BIFF: N-no. [*To* STANLEY.] Scotch all around. Make it doubles.

STANLEY: Doubles, right.

[*He goes*]

WILLY: You had a couple already, didn't you?

BIFF: Just a couple, yeah.

WILLY: Well, what happened, boy? [*Nodding affirmatively, with a smile.*] Everything go all right?

BIFF [*takes a breath, then reaches out and grasps* WILLY's *hand*]: Pal . . . [*He is smiling bravely, and* WILLY *is smiling too.*] I had an experience today.

HAPPY: Terrific, Pop.

WILLY: That so? What happened?

BIFF [*high, slightly alcoholic, above the earth*]: I'm going to tell you everything from first to last. It's been a strange day. [*Silence. He looks around, composes himself as best he can, but his breath keeps breaking the rhythm of his voice.*] I had to wait quite a while for him, and ——

WILLY: Oliver?

BIFF: Yeah, Oliver. All day, as a matter of cold fact. And a lot of — instances — facts, Pop, facts about my life came back to me. Who was it, Pop? Who ever said I was a salesman with Oliver?

WILLY: Well, you were.

BIFF: No, Dad, I was a shipping clerk.

WILLY: But you were practically ——

BIFF [*with determination*]: Dad, I don't know who said it first, but I was never a salesman for Bill Oliver.

WILLY: What're you talking about?

BIFF: Let's hold on to the facts tonight, Pop. We're not going to get anywhere bullin' around. I was a shipping clerk.

WILLY [*angrily*]: All right, now listen to me ——

BIFF: Why don't you let me finish?

WILLY: I'm not interested in stories about the past or any crap of that kind because the woods are burning, boys, you understand? There's a big blaze going on all around. I was fired today.

BIFF [*shocked*]: How could you be?

WILLY: I was fired, and I'm looking for a little good news to tell your mother, because the woman has waited and the woman has suffered. The gist of it is that I haven't got a story left in my head, Biff. So don't give me a lecture about facts and aspects. I am not interested. Now what've you got to say to me?

[STANLEY *enters with three drinks. They wait until he leaves.*]

WILLY: Did you see Oliver?

BIFF: Jesus, Dad!

WILLY: You mean you didn't go up there?

HAPPY: Sure he went up there.

BIFF: I did. I — saw him. How could they fire you?

WILLY [*on the edge of his chair*]: What kind of a welcome did he give you?

BIFF: He won't even let you work on commission?

WILLY: I'm out! [*Driving.*] So tell me, he gave you a warm welcome!

HAPPY: Sure, Pop, sure!

BIFF [*driven*]: Well, it was kind of ——

WILLY: I was wondering if he'd remember you. [*To* HAPPY.] Imagine, man doesn't see him for ten, twelve years and gives him that kind of a welcome!

HAPPY: Damn right!

BIFF [*trying to return to the offensive*]: Pop, look ——

WILLY: You know why he remembered you, don't you? Because you impressed him in those days.

BIFF: Let's talk quietly and get this down to the facts, huh?

WILLY [*as though* BIFF *had been interrupting*]: Well, what happened? It's great news, Biff. Did he take you into his office or'd you talk in the waiting-room?

BIFF: Well, he came in, see, and ——

WILLY [*with a big smile*]: What'd he say? Betcha he threw his arm around you.

BIFF: Well, he kinda ——

WILLY: He's a fine man. [*To* HAPPY.] Very hard man to see, y'know.

HAPPY [*agreeing*]: Oh, I know.

WILLY [*to* BIFF]: Is that where you had the drinks?

BIFF: Yeah, he gave me a couple of — no, no!

HAPPY [*cutting in*]: He told him my Florida idea.

WILLY: Don't interrupt. [*To* BIFF.] How'd he react to the Florida idea?

BIFF: Dad, will you give me a minute to explain?

WILLY: I've been waiting for you to explain since I sat down here! What happened? He took you into his office and what?

BIFF: Well — I talked. And — and he listened, see.

WILLY: Famous for the way he listens, y'know. What was his answer?

BIFF: His answer was — [*He breaks off, suddenly angry.*] Dad, you're not letting me tell you what I want to tell you!

WILLY [*accusing, angered*]: You didn't see him, did you?

BIFF: I did see him!

WILLY: What'd you insult him or something? You insulted him, didn't you?

BIFF: Listen, will you let me out of it, will you just let me out of it!

HAPPY: What the hell!

WILLY: Tell me what happened!

BIFF [*to* HAPPY]: I can't talk to him!

[*A single trumpet note jars the ear. The light of green leaves stains the house, which holds the air of night and a dream. Young* BERNARD *enters and knocks on the door of the house.*]

YOUNG BERNARD [*frantically*]: Mrs. Loman, Mrs. Loman!

HAPPY: Tell him what happened!

BIFF [*to* HAPPY]: Shut up and leave me alone!

WILLY: No, no! You had to go and flunk math!

BIFF: What math? What're you talking about?

YOUNG BERNARD: Mrs. Loman, Mrs. Loman!

[LINDA *appears in the house, as of old.*]

WILLY [*wildly*]: Math, math, math!

BIFF: Take it easy, Pop!

YOUNG BERNARD: Mrs. Loman!

WILLY [*furiously*]: If you hadn't flunked you'd've been set by now!

BIFF: Now, look, I'm gonna tell you what happened and you're going to listen to me.

YOUNG BERNARD: Mrs. Loman!

BIFF: I waited six hours ——

HAPPY: What the hell are you saying?

BIFF: I kept sending in my name but he wouldn't see me. So finally he . . .

[*He continues unheard as light fades low on the restaurant.*]

YOUNG BERNARD: Biff flunked math!

LINDA: No!

YOUNG BERNARD: Birnbaum flunked him! They won't graduate him!

LINDA: But they have to. He's gotta go to the university. Where is he? Biff! Biff!

YOUNG BERNARD: No, he left. He went to Grand Central.

LINDA: Grand — You mean he went to Boston!

YOUNG BERNARD: Is Uncle Willy in Boston?

LINDA: Oh, maybe Willy can talk to the teacher. Oh, the poor, poor boy!

[*Light on house area snaps out.*]

BIFF [*at the table, now audible, holding up a gold fountain pen*]: . . . so I'm washed up with Oliver, you understand? Are you listening to me?

WILLY [*at a loss*]: Yeah, sure. If you hadn't flunked ——

BIFF: Flunked what? What're you talking about?

WILLY: Don't blame everything on me! I didn't flunk math — you did! What pen?

HAPPY: That was awful dumb, Biff, a pen like that is worth ——

WILLY [*seeing the pen for the first time*]: You took Oliver's pen?

BIFF [*weakening*]: Dad, I just explained it to you.

WILLY: You stole Bill Oliver's fountain pen!

BIFF: I didn't exactly steal it! That's just what I've been explaining to you!

HAPPY: He had it in his hand and just then Oliver walked in, so he got nervous and stuck it in his pocket!

WILLY: My God, Biff!

BIFF: I never intended to do it, Dad!

OPERATOR'S VOICE: Standish Arms, good evening!

WILLY [*shouting*]: I'm not in my room!

BIFF [*frightened*]: Dad, what's the matter?

[*He and* HAPPY *stand up.*]

OPERATOR: Ringing Mr. Loman for you!

WILLIE: I'm not there, stop it!

BIFF [*horrified, gets down on one knee before* WILLY]: Dad, I'll make good, I'll make good. [WILLY *tries to get to his feet.* BIFF *holds him down.*] Sit down now.

WILLY: No, you're no good, you're no good for anything.

BIFF: I am, Dad, I'll find something else, you understand? Now don't worry about anything. [*He holds up* WILLY'S *face.*] Talk to me, Dad.

OPERATOR: Mr. Loman does not answer. Shall I page him?

WILLY [*attempting to stand, as though to rush and silence the* OPERATOR]: No, no, no!

HAPPY: He'll strike something, Pop.

WILLY: No, no . . .

BIFF [*desperately, standing over* WILLY]: Pop, listen! Listen to me! I'm telling you something good. Oliver talked to his partner about the Florida idea. You listening? He — he talked to his partner, and he came to me . . . I'm going to be all right, you hear? Dad, listen to me, he said it was just a question of the amount!

WILLY: Then you . . . got it?

HAPPY: He's gonna be terrific, Pop!

WILLY [*trying to stand*]: Then you got it, haven't you? You got it! You got it!

BIFF [*agonized, holds* WILLY *down*]: No, no. Look, Pop. I'm supposed to have lunch with them tomorrow. I'm just telling you this so you'll know that I can still make an impression, Pop. And I'll make good somewhere, but I can't go tomorrow, see?

WILLY: Why not? You simply ——

BIFF: But the pen, Pop!

WILLY: You give it to him and tell him it was an oversight!

HAPPY: Sure, have lunch tomorrow!

BIFF: I can't say that ——

WILLY: You were doing a crossword puzzle and accidentally used his pen!

BIFF: Listen, kid, I took those balls years ago, now I walk in with his fountain pen? That clinches it, don't you see? I can't face him like that! I'll try elsewhere.

PAGE'S VOICE: Paging Mr. Loman!

WILLY: Don't you want to be anything?

BIFF: Pop, how can I go back?

WILLY: You don't want to be anything, is that what's behind it?

BIFF [*now angry at* WILLY *for not crediting his sympathy*]: Don't take it that way! You think it was easy walking into the office after what I'd done to him? A team of horses couldn't have dragged me back to Bill Oliver!

WILLY: Then why'd you go?

BIFF: Why did I go? Why did I go? Look at you! Look at what's become of you!

[*Off left,* THE WOMAN *laughs.*]

WILLY: Biff, you're going to go to that lunch tomorrow, or ——

BIFF: I can't go. I've got no appointment!

HAPPY: Biff, for . . . !

WILLY: Are you spiting me?

BIFF: Don't take it that way! Goddammit!

WILLY [*strikes* BIFF *and falters away from the table*]: You rotten little louse! Are you spiting me?

THE WOMAN: Someone's at the door, Willy!

BIFF: I'm no good, can't you see what I am?

HAPPY [*separating them*]: Hey, you're in a restaurant! Now cut it out, both of you! [THE GIRLS *enter.*] Hello, girls, sit down.

[*The* WOMAN *laughs, off left.*]

MISS FORSYTHE: I guess we might as well. This is Letta.

THE WOMAN: Willy, are you going to wake up?

BIFF [*ignoring* WILLY]: How're ya, miss, sit down. What do you drink?

MISS FORSYTHE: Letta might not be able to stay long.

LETTA: I gotta get up very early tomorrow. I got jury duty. I'm so excited! Were you fellows ever on a jury?

BIFF: No, but I been in front of them! [THE GIRLS *laugh*.] This is my father.

LETTA: Isn't he cute? Sit down with us, Pop.

HAPPY: Sit him down, Biff!

BIFF [*going to him*]: Come on, slugger, drink us under the table. To hell with it! Come on, sit down, pal.

[*On* BIFF's *insistence*, WILLY *is about to sit.*]

THE WOMAN [*now urgently*]: Willy, are you going to answer the door!

[THE WOMAN's *call pulls* WILLY *back. He starts right, befuddled.*]

BIFF: Hey, where are you going?

WILLY: Open the door.

BIFF: The door?

WILLY: The washroom . . . the door . . . where's the door?

BIFF [*leading* WILLY *to the left*]: Just go straight down.

[WILLY *moves left.*]

THE WOMAN: Willy, Willy, are you going to get up, get up, get up, get up?

[WILLY *exits left.*]

LETTA: I think it's sweet you bring your daddy along.

MISS FORSYTHE: Oh, he isn't really your father!

BIFF [*at left, turning to her resentfully*]: Miss Forsythe, you've just seen a prince walk by. A fine, troubled prince. A hard-working, unappreciated prince. A pal, you understand? A good companion. Always for his boys.

LETTA: That's so sweet.

HAPPY: Well, girls, what's the program? We're wasting time. Come on, Biff. Gather round. Where would you like to go?

BIFF: Why don't you do something for him?

HAPPY: Me!

BIFF: Don't you give a damn for him, Hap?

HAPPY: What're you talking about? I'm the one who ——

BIFF: I sense it, you don't give a good goddam about him. [*He takes the rolled-up hose from his pocket and puts it on the table in front of* HAPPY.] Look what I found in the cellar, for Christ's sake. How can you bear to let it go on?

HAPPY: Me? Who goes away? Who runs off and ——

BIFF: Yeah, but he doesn't mean anything to you. You could help him — I can't! Don't you understand what I'm talking about? He's going to kill himself, don't you know that?

HAPPY: Don't I know it! Me!

BIFF: Help, help him! Jesus . . . help him . . . Help me, help me, I can't bear to look at his face!

[*Ready to weep, he hurries out, up right.*]

HAPPY [*starting after him*]: Where are you going?

MISS FORSYTHE: What's he so mad about?

HAPPY: Come on, girls, we'll catch up with him.

MISS FORSYTHE [*as* HAPPY *pushes her out*]: I don't like that temper of his!

HAPPY: He's just a little overstrung, he'll be all right!

WILLY [*off left, as* THE WOMAN *laughs*]: Don't answer! Don't answer!

LETTA: Don't you want to tell your father ——

HAPPY: No, that's not my father. He's just a guy. Come on, we'll catch Biff, and honey, we're going to paint this town! Stanley, where's the check! Hey, Stanley!

[*They exit.* STANLEY *looks toward left.*]

STANLEY [*calling to* HAPPY *indignantly*]: Mr. Loman! Mr. Loman!

[STANLEY *picks up a chair and follows them off. Knocking is heard off left.* THE WOMAN *enters, laughing.* WILLY *follows her. She is in a black slip; he is buttoning his shirt. Raw, sensuous music accompanies their speech.*]

WILLY: Will you stop laughing? Will you stop?

THE WOMAN: Aren't you going to answer the door? He'll wake the whole hotel.

WILLY: I'm not expecting anybody.

THE WOMAN: Whyn't you have another drink, honey, and stop being so damn self-centered?

WILLY: I'm so lonely.

THE WOMAN: You know you ruined me, Willy? From now on, whenever you come to the office, I'll see that you go right through to the buyers. No waiting at my desk any more, Willy. You ruined me.

WILLY: That's nice of you to say that.

THE WOMAN: Gee, you are self-centered! Why so sad? You are the saddest, self-centeredest soul I ever did see-saw. [*She laughs. He kisses her.*] Come on inside, drummer boy. It's silly to be dressing in the middle of the night. [*As the knocking is heard.*] Aren't you going to answer the door?

WILLY: They're knocking on the wrong door.

THE WOMAN: But I felt the knocking. And he heard us talking in here. Maybe the hotel's on fire!

WILLY [*his terror rising*]: It's a mistake.

THE WOMAN: Then tell him to go away!

WILLY: There's nobody there.

THE WOMAN: It's getting on my nerves, Willy. There's somebody standing out there and it's getting on my nerves!

WILLY [*pushing her away from him*]: All right, stay in the bathroom here, and don't come out. I think there's a law in Massachusetts about it, so don't come out. It may be that new room clerk. He looked very mean. So don't come out. It's a mistake, there's no fire.

[*The knocking is heard again. He takes a few steps away from her, and she vanishes into the wing. The light follows him, and now he is facing* YOUNG BIFF, *who carries a suitcase.* BIFF *steps toward him. The music is gone.*]

BIFF: Why didn't you answer?

WILLY: Biff! What are you doing in Boston?

BIFF: Why didn't you answer? I've been knocking for five minutes, I called you on the phone ——

WILLY: I just heard you. I was in the bathroom and had the door shut. Did anything happen home?

BIFF: Dad — I let you down.

WILLY: What do you mean?

BIFF: Dad . . .

WILLY: Biffo, what's this about? [*Putting his arm around* BIFF.] Come on, let's go downstairs and get you a malted.

BIFF: Dad, I flunked math.

WILLY: Not for the term?

BIFF: The term. I haven't got enough credits to graduate.

WILLY: You mean to say Bernard wouldn't give you the answers?

BIFF: He did, he tried, but I only got a sixty-one.

WILLY: And they wouldn't give you your points?

BIFF: Birnbaum refused absolutely I begged him, Pop, but he won't give me those points. You gotta talk to him before they close the school. Because if he saw the kind of man you are, and you just talked to him in your way, I'm sure he'd come through for me. The class came right before practice, see, and I didn't go enough. Would you talk to him? He'd like you, Pop. You know the way you could talk.

WILLY: You're on. We'll drive right back.

BIFF: Oh, Dad, good work! I'm sure he'll change it for you!

WILLY: Go downstairs and tell the clerk I'm checkin' out. Go right down.

BIFF: Yes, Sir! See, the reason he hates me, Pop — one day he was late for class so I got up at the blackboard and imitated him. I crossed my eyes and talked with a lithp.

WILLY [*laughing*]: You did? The kids like it?

BIFF: They nearly died laughing!

WILLY: Yeah? What'd you do?

BIFF: The thquare root of thixthy twee is . . . [WILLY *bursts out laughing;* BIFF *joins him.*] And in the middle of it he walked in!

[WILLY *laughs and* THE WOMAN *joins in offstage.*]

WILLY [*without hesitation*]: Hurry downstairs and ——

BIFF: Somebody in there?

WILLY: No, that was next door.

[THE WOMAN *laughs offstage.*]

BIFF: Somebody got in your bathroom!

WILLY: No, it's the next room, there's a party ——

THE WOMAN [*enters, laughing. She lisps this*]: Can I come in? There's something in the bathtub, Willy, and it's moving!

[WILLY *looks at* BIFF, *who is staring open-mouthed and horrified at* THE WOMAN.]

WILLY: Ah — you better go back to your room. They must be finished painting by now. They're painting her room so I let her take a shower here. Go back, go back . . .

[*He pushes her.*]

THE WOMAN [*resisting*]: But I've got to get dressed, Willy, I can't ——

WILLY: Get out of here! Go back, go back . . . [*Suddenly striving for the ordinary.*] This is Miss Francis, Biff, she's a buyer. They're painting her room. Go back, Miss Francis, go back . . .

THE WOMAN: But my clothes, I can't go out naked in the hall!

WILLY [*pushing her offstage*]: Get outa here! Go back, go back!

[BIFF *slowly sits down on his suitcase as the argument continues offstage.*]

THE WOMAN: Where's my stockings? You promised me stockings, Willy!

WILLY: I have no stockings here!

THE WOMAN: You had two boxes of size nine sheers for me, and I want them!

WILLY: Here, for God's sake, will you get outa here!

THE WOMAN [*enters holding a box of stockings*]: I just hope there's nobody in the hall. That's all I hope. [*To* BIFF.] Are you football or baseball?

BIFF: Football.

THE WOMAN [*angry, humiliated*]: That's me too. G'night.

[*She snatches her clothes from* WILLY, *and walks out.*]

WILLY [*after a pause*]: Well, better get going. I want to get to the school first thing in the morning. Get my suits out of the closet. I'll get my valise. [BIFF *doesn't move.*] What's the matter? [BIFF *remains motionless, tears falling.*] She's a buyer. Buys for J. H. Simmons. She lives down the hall — they're painting. You don't imagine — [*He breaks off. After a pause.*] Now listen, pal, she's just a buyer. She sees merchandise in her room and they have to keep it looking just so . . . [*Pause. Assuming command.*] All right, get my suits. [BIFF *doesn't move.*] Now stop crying and do as I say. I gave you an order. Biff, I gave you an order! Is that what you do when I give you an order? How dare you cry! [*Putting his arm around* BIFF.] Now look, Biff, when you grow up you'll understand about these things. You mustn't — you mustn't overemphasize a thing like this. I'll see Birnbaum first thing in the morning.

BIFF: Never mind.

WILLY [*getting down beside* BIFF]: Never mind! He's going to give you those points. I'll see to it.

BIFF: He wouldn't listen to you.

WILLY: He certainly will listen to me. You need those points for the U. of Virginia.

BIFF: I'm not going there.

WILLY: Heh? If I can't get him to change that mark you'll make it up in summer school. You've got all summer to ——

BIFF [*his weeping breaking from him*]: Dad . . .

WILLY [*infected by it*]: Oh, my boy . . .

BIFF: Dad . . .

WILLY: She's nothing to me, Biff. I was lonely, I was terribly lonely.

BIFF: You — you gave her Mama's stockings!

[*His tears break through and he rises to go.*]

WILLY [*grabbing for* BIFF]: I gave you an order!

BIFF: Don't touch me, you — liar!

WILLY: Apologize for that!

BIFF: You fake! You phony little fake! You fake!

[*Overcome, he turns quickly and weeping fully goes out with his suitcase.* WILLY *is left on the floor on his knees.*]

WILLY: I gave you an order! Biff, come back here or I'll beat you! Come back here! I'll whip you!

[STANLEY *comes quickly in from the right and stands in front of* WILLY.]

WILLY [*shouts at* STANLEY]: I gave you an order . . .

STANLEY: Hey, let's pick it up, pick it up, Mr. Loman. [*He helps* WILLY *to his feet.*] Your boys left with the chippies. They said they'll see you home.

[*A second waiter watches some distance away.*]

WILLY: But we were supposed to have dinner together.

[*Music is heard,* WILLY'*s theme.*]

STANLEY: Can you make it?

WILLY: I'll — sure, I can make it. [*Suddenly concerned about his clothes.*] Do I — I look all right?

STANLEY: Sure, you look all right.

[*He flicks a speck off* WILLY'*s lapel.*]

WILLY: Here — here's a dollar.

STANLEY: Oh, your son paid me. It's all right.

WILLY [*putting it in* STANLEY'*s hand*]: No, take it. You're a good boy.

STANLEY: Oh, no, you don't have to . . .

WILLY: Here — here's some more, I don't need it any more. [*After a slight pause.*] Tell me — is there a seed store in the neighborhood?

STANLEY: Seeds? You mean like to plant?

[*As* WILLY *turns,* STANLEY *slips the money back into his jacket pocket.*]

WILLY: Yes. Carrots, peas . . .

STANLEY: Well, there's hardware stores on Sixth Avenue, but it may be too late now.

WILLY [*anxiously*]: Oh, I better hurry. I've got to get some seeds. [*He starts off to the right.*] I've got to get some seeds, right away. Nothing's planted. I don't have a thing in the ground.

[WILLY *hurries out as the light goes down.* STANLEY *moves over to the right after him, watches him off. The other waiter has been staring at* WILLY.]

STANLEY [*to the waiter*]: Well, whatta you looking at?

[*The waiter picks up the chairs and moves off right.* STANLEY *takes the table and follows him. The light fades on this area. There is a long pause, the sound of the flute coming over. The light gradually rises on the kitchen, which is empty.* HAPPY *appears at the door of the house, followed by* BIFF. HAPPY *is carrying a large bunch of long-stemmed roses. He enters the kitchen, looks around for* LINDA. *Not seeing her, he turns to* BIFF, *who is just outside the house door, and makes a gesture with his hands, indicating "Not here, I guess." He looks into the living-room and freezes. Inside,* LINDA, *unseen, is seated,* WILLY's *coat on her lap. She rises ominously and quietly moves toward* HAPPY, *who backs up into the kitchen, afraid.*]

HAPPY: Hey, what're you doing up? [LINDA *says nothing but moves toward him implacably.*] Where's Pop? [*He keeps backing to the right, and now* LINDA *is in full view in the doorway to the living-room.*] Is he sleeping?

LINDA: Where were you?

HAPPY [*trying to laugh it off*]: We met two girls, Mom, very fine types. Here, we brought you some flowers. [*Offering them to her.*] Put them in your room, Ma.

[*She knocks them to the floor at* BIFF's *feet. He has now come inside and closed the door behind him. She stares at* BIFF, *silent.*]

HAPPY: Now what'd you do that for? Mom, I want you to have some flowers ——

LINDA [*cutting* HAPPY *off, violently to* BIFF]: Don't you care whether he lives or dies?

HAPPY [*going to the stairs*]: Come upstairs, Biff.

BIFF [*with a flare of disgust, to* HAPPY]: Go away from me! [*To* LINDA.] What do you mean, lives or dies? Nobody's dying around here, pal.

LINDA: Get out of my sight! Get out of here!

BIFF: I wanna see the boss.

LINDA: You're not going near him!

BIFF: Where is he?

[*He moves into the living-room and* LINDA *follows.*]

LINDA [*shouting after* BIFF]: You invite him for dinner. He looks forward to it all day — [BIFF *appears in his parents' bedroom, looks around, and exits*] — and then you desert him there. There's no stranger you'd do that to!

HAPPY: Why? He had a swell time with us. Listen, when I — [LINDA *comes back into the kitchen*] — desert him I hope I don't outlive the day!

LINDA: Get out of here.

HAPPY: Now look, Mom . . .

LINDA: Did you have to go to women tonight? You and your lousy rotten whores!

[BIFF *re-enters the kitchen.*]

HAPPY: Mom, all we did was follow Biff around trying to cheer him up! [*To* BIFF.] Boy, what a night you gave me!

LINDA: Get out of here, both of you, and don't come back! I don't want you tormenting him any more. Go on now, get your things together! [*To* BIFF.] You can sleep in his apartment. [*She starts to pick up the flowers and stops herself.*] Pick up this stuff; I'm not your maid any more. Pick it up, you bum, you!

[HAPPY *turns his back to her in refusal.* BIFF *slowly moves over and gets down on his knees, picking up the flowers.*]

LINDA: You're a pair of animals! Not one, not another living soul would have had the cruelty to walk out on that man in a restaurant!

BIFF [*not looking at her*]: Is that what he said?

LINDA: He didn't have to say anything. He was so humiliated he nearly limped when he came in.

HAPPY: But, Mom, he had a great time with us ——

BIFF [*cutting him off violently*]: Shut up!

[*Without another word,* HAPPY *goes upstairs.*]

LINDA: You! You didn't even go in to see if he was all right!

BIFF [*still on the floor in front of* LINDA, *the flowers in his hand; with self-loathing*]: No. Didn't. Didn't do a damned thing. How do you like that, heh? Left him babbling in a toilet.

LINDA: You louse. You . . .

BIFF: Now you hit it on the nose! [*He gets up, throws the flowers in the wastebasket.*] The scum of the earth, and you're looking at him!

LINDA: Get out of here!

BIFF: I gotta talk to the boss, Mom. Where is he?

LINDA: You're not going near him. Get out of this house!

BIFF [*with absolute assurance, determination*]: No. We're gonna have an abrupt conversation, him and me.

LINDA: You're not talking to him!

[*Hammering is heard from outside the house, off right.* BIFF *turns toward the noise.*]

LINDA [*suddenly pleading*]: Will you please leave him alone?

BIFF: What's he doing out there?

LINDA: He's planting the garden!

BIFF [*quietly*]: Now? Oh, my God!

[BIFF *moves outside,* LINDA *following. The light dies down on them and comes up on the center of the apron as* WILLY *walks into it. He is carrying a flashlight, a hoe, and a handful of seed packets. He raps the top of the hoe sharply to fix it firmly, and then moves to the left, measuring off the distance with his foot. He holds the flashlight to look at the seed packets, reading off the instructions. He is in the blue of night.*]

WILLY: Carrots . . . quarter-inch apart. Rows . . . one-foot rows. [*He measures it off.*] One foot. [*He puts down a package and measures off.*] Beets. [*He puts down another package and measures again.*] Lettuce. [*He reads the package, puts it down.*] One foot — [*He breaks off as* BEN *appears at the right and moves slowly down to him.*] What a proposition, ts, ts. Terrific, terrific. 'Cause she's suffered, Ben, the woman has suffered. You understand me? A man can't go out the way he came in, Ben, a man has got to add up to something. You can't, you can't — [BEN *moves toward him as though to interrupt.*] You gotta consider, now. Don't answer so quick. Remember, it's a guaranteed twenty-thousand-dollar proposition. Now look, Ben, I want you to go through the ins and outs of this thing with me. I've got nobody to talk to, Ben, and the woman has suffered, you hear me?

BEN [*standing still, considering*]: What's the proposition?

WILLY: It's twenty thousand dollars on the barrelhead. Guaranteed, gilt-edged, you understand?

BEN: You don't want to make a fool of yourself. They might not honor the policy.

WILLY: How can they dare refuse? Didn't I work like a coolie to meet every premium on the nose? And now they don't pay off? Impossible!

BEN: It's called a cowardly thing, William.

WILLY: Why? Does it take more guts to stand here the rest of my life ringing up a zero?

BEN [*yielding*]: That's a point, William. [*He moves, thinking, turns.*] And twenty thousand — that *is* something one can feel with the hand, it is there.

WILLY [*now assured, with rising power*]: Oh, Ben, that's the whole beauty of it! I see it like a diamond, shining in the dark, hard and rough, that I can pick up and touch in my hand. Not like — an appointment! This would not be another damned-fool appointment, Ben, and it changes all the aspects. Because he thinks I'm nothing, see, and so he spites me. But the funeral — [*Straightening up.*] Ben, that funeral will be massive! They'll come from Maine, Massachusetts, Vermont, New Hampshire! All the old-timers with the strange license plates — that boy will be thunder-struck, Ben, because he never realized — I am known! Rhode Island, New York, New Jersey — I am known, Ben, and he'll see it with his eyes once and for all. He'll see what I am, Ben! He's in for a shock, that boy!

BEN [*coming down to the edge of the garden*]: He'll call you a coward.

WILLY [*suddenly fearful*]: No, that would be terrible.

BEN: Yes. And a damned fool.

WILLY: No, no, he mustn't, I won't have that!

[*He is broken and desperate.*]

BEN: He'll hate you, William.

[*The gay music of the* BOYS *is heard.*]

WILLY: Oh, Ben, how do we get back to all the great times? Used to be so full of light, and comradeship, the sleigh-riding in winter, and the ruddiness on his cheeks. And always some kind of good news coming up, always something nice coming up ahead. And never even let me carry the valises in the house, and simonizing, simonizing that little red car! Why, why can't I give him something and not have him hate me?

BEN: Let me think about it. [*He glances at his watch.*] I still have a little time. Remarkable proposition, but you've got to be sure you're not making a fool of yourself.

[BEN *drifts off upstage and goes out of sight.* BIFF *comes down from the left.*]

WILLY [*suddenly conscious of* BIFF, *turns and looks up at him, then begins picking up the packages of seeds in confusion*]: Where the hell is that seed? [*Indignantly.*] You can't see nothing out here! They boxed in the whole goddam neighborhood!

BIFF: There are people all around here. Don't you realize that?

WILLY: I'm busy. Don't bother me.

BIFF [*taking the hoe from* WILLY]: I'm saying good-bye to you, Pop. [WILLY *looks at him, silent, unable to move.*] I'm not coming back any more.

WILLY: You're not going to see Oliver tomorrow?

BIFF: I've got no appointment, Dad.

WILLY: He put his arm around you, and you've got no appointment?

BIFF: Pop, get this now, will you? Everytime I've left it's been a fight that sent me out of here. Today I realized something about myself and I tried to explain it to you and I — I think I'm just not smart enough to make any sense out of it for you. To hell with whose fault it is or anything like that. [*He takes* WILLY's *arm.*] Let's just wrap it up, heh? Come on in, we'll tell Mom.

[*He gently tries to pull* WILLY *to left.*]

WILLY [*frozen, immobile, with guilt in his voice*]: No, I don't want to see her.

BIFF: Come on!

[*He pulls again, and* WILLY *tries to pull away.*]

WILLY [*highly nervous*]: No, no, I don't want to see her.

BIFF [*tries to look into* WILLY's *face, as if to find the answer there*]: Why don't you want to see her?

WILLY [*more harshly now*]: Don't bother me, will you?

BIFF: What do you mean, you don't want to see her? You don't want them calling you yellow, do you? This isn't your fault; it's me, I'm a bum. Now come inside! [WILLY *strains to get away.*] Did you hear what I said to you?

[WILLY *pulls away and quickly goes by himself into the house.* BIFF *follows.*]

LINDA [*to* WILLY]: Did you plant, dear?

BIFF [*at the door, to* LINDA]: All right, we had it out. I'm going and I'm not writing any more.

LINDA [*going to* WILLY *in the kitchen*]: I think that's the best way, dear. 'Cause there's no use drawing it out, you'll just never get along.

[WILLY *doesn't respond.*]

BIFF: People ask where I am and what I'm doing, you don't know, and you don't care. That way it'll be off your mind and you can start brightening up again. All right? That clears it, doesn't it? [WILLY *is silent, and* BIFF *goes to him.*] You gonna wish me luck, scout? [*He extends his hand.*] What do you say?

LINDA: Shake his hand, Willy.

WILLY [*turning to her, seething with hurt*]: There's no necessity to mention the pen at all, y'know.

BIFF [*gently*]: I've got no appointment, Dad.

WILLY [*erupting fiercely*]: He put his arm around . . . ?

BIFF: Dad, you're never going to see what I am, so what's the use of arguing? If I strike oil I'll send you a check. Meantime forget I'm alive.

WILLY [*to* LINDA]: Spite, see?

BIFF: Shake hands, Dad.

WILLY: Not my hand.

BIFF: I was hoping not to go this way.

WILLY: Well, this is the way you're going. Goodbye.

[BIFF *looks at him a moment, then turns sharply and goes to the stairs.*]

WILLY [*stops him with*]: May you rot in hell if you leave this house!

BIFF [*turning*]: Exactly what is it that you want from me?

WILLY: I want you to know, on the train, in the mountains, in the valleys, wherever you go, that you cut down your life for spite!

BIFF: No, no.

WILLY: Spite, spite, is the word of your undoing! And when you're down and out, remember what did it. When you're rotting somewhere beside the railroad tracks, remember, and don't you dare blame it on me!

BIFF: I'm not blaming it on you!

WILLY: I won't take the rap for this, you hear?

[HAPPY *comes down the stairs and stands on the bottom step, watching.*]

BIFF: That's just what I'm telling you!

WILLY [*sinking into a chair at the table, with full accusation*]: You're trying to put a knife in me — don't think I don't know what you're doing!

BIFF: All right, phony! Then let's lay it on the line.

[*He whips the rubber tube out of his pocket and puts it on the table.*]

HAPPY: You crazy ——

LINDA: Biff!

[*She moves to grab the hose, but* BIFF *holds it down with his hand.*]

BIFF: Leave it there. Don't move it!

WILLY [*not looking at it*]: What is that?

BIFF: *You* know goddam well what that is.

WILLY [*caged, wanting to escape*]: I never saw that.

BIFF: You saw it. The mice didn't bring it into the cellar! What is this supposed to do, make a hero out of you? This supposed to make me sorry for you?

WILLY: Never heard of it.

BIFF: There'll be no pity for you, you hear it? No pity!

WILLY [*to* LINDA]: You hear the spite!

BIFF: No, you're going to hear the truth — what you are and what I am!

LINDA: Stop it!

WILLY: Spite!

HAPPY [*coming down toward* BIFF]: You cut it now!

BIFF [*to* HAPPY]: The man don't know who we are! The man is gonna know! [*To* WILLY.] We never told the truth for ten minutes in this house!

HAPPY: We always told the truth!

BIFF [*turning on him*]: You big blow, are you the assistant buyer? You're one of the two assistants to the assistant, aren't you?

HAPPY: Well, I'm practically ——

BIFF: You're practically full of it! We all are! And I'm through with it. [*To* WILLY.] Now hear this, Willy, this is me.

WILLY: I know you!

BIFF: You know why I had no address for three months? I stole a suit in Kansas City and I was in jail. [*To* LINDA, *who is sobbing.*] Stop crying. I'm through with it.

[LINDA *turns away from them, her hands covering her face.*]

WILLY: I suppose that's my fault!

BIFF: I stole myself out of every good job since high school!

WILLY: And whose fault is that?

BIFF: And I never got anywhere because you blew me so full of hot air I could never stand taking orders from anybody! That's whose fault it is!

WILLY: I hear that!

LINDA: Don't, Biff!

BIFF: It's goddam time you heard that! I had to be boss big shot in two weeks, and I'm through with it!

WILLY: Then hang yourself! For spite, hang yourself!

BIFF: No! Nobody's hanging himself, Willy! I ran down eleven flights with a pen in my hand today. And suddenly I stopped, you hear me? And in the middle of that office building, do you hear this? I stopped in the middle of that building and I saw — the sky. I saw the things that I love in this world. The work and the food and time to sit and smoke. And I looked at the pen and said to myself, what the hell am I grabbing this for? Why am I trying to become what I don't want to be? What am I doing in an office, making a contemptuous, begging fool of myself, when all I want is out there, waiting for me the minute I say I know who I am! Why can't I say that, Willy?

[*He tries to make* WILLY *face him, but* WILLY *pulls away and moves to the left.*]

WILLY [*with hatred, threateningly*]: The door of your life is wide open!

BIFF: Pop! I'm a dime a dozen, and so are you!

WILLY [*turning on him now in an uncontrolled outburst*]: I am not a dime a dozen! I am Willy Loman, and you are Biff Loman!

[BIFF *starts for* WILLY, *but is blocked by* HAPPY. *In his fury,* BIFF *seems on the verge of attacking his father.*]

BIFF: I am not a leader of men, Willy, and neither are you. You were never anything but a hard-working drummer who landed in the ash can like all of the rest of them! I'm one dollar an hour, Willy! I tried seven states and couldn't raise it. A buck an hour! Do you gather my meaning? I'm not bringing home any prizes any more, and you're going to stop waiting for me to bring them home!

WILLY [*directly to* BIFF]: You vengeful, spiteful mut!

[BIFF *breaks from* HAPPY. WILLY, *in fright, starts up the stairs.* BIFF *grabs him.*]

BIFF [*at the peak of his fury*]: Pop, I'm nothing! I'm nothing, Pop. Can't you understand that? There's no spite in it any more. I'm just what I am, that's all.

[BIFF's *fury has spent itself, and he breaks down, sobbing, holding on to* WILLY, *who dumbly fumbles for* BIFF's *face.*]

WILLY [*astonished*]: What're you doing? What're you doing? [*To* LINDA.] Why is he crying?

BIFF [*crying, broken*]: Will you let me go, for Christ's sake? Will you take that phony dream and burn it before something happens? [*Struggling to contain himself, he pulls away and moves to the stairs.*] I'll go in the morning. Put him — put him to bed.

[*Exhausted,* BIFF *moves up the stairs to his room.*]

WILLY [*after a long pause, astonished, elevated*]: Isn't that — isn't that remarkable? Biff — he likes me!

LINDA: He loves you, Willy!

HAPPY [*deeply moved*]: Always did, Pop.

WILLY: Oh, Biff! [*Staring wildly.*] He cried! Cried to me. [*He is choking with his love, and now cries out his promise.*] That boy — that boy is going to be magnificent!

[BEN *appears in the light just outside the kitchen.*]

BEN: Yes, outstanding, with twenty thousand behind him.

LINDA [*sensing the racing of his mind, fearfully, carefully*]: Now come to bed, Willy. It's all settled now.

WILLY [*finding it difficult not to rush out of the house*]: Yes, we'll sleep. Come on. Go to sleep, Hap.

BEN: And it does take a great kind of a man to crack the jungle.

[*In accents of dread,* BEN's *idyllic music starts up.*]

HAPPY [*his arm around* LINDA]: I'm getting married, Pop, don't forget it. I'm changing everything. I'm gonna run that department before the year is up. You'll see, Mom.

[*He kisses her.*]

BEN: The jungle is dark but full of diamonds, Willy.

[WILLY *turns, moves, listening to* BEN.]

LINDA: Be good. You're both good boys, just act that way, that's all.

HAPPY: 'Night, Pop.

[*He goes upstairs.*]

LINDA [*to* WILLY]: Come dear.

BEN [*with greater force*]: One must go in to fetch a diamond out.

WILLY [*to* LINDA, *as he moves slowly along the edge of the kitchen, toward the door*]: I just want to get settled down, Linda. Let me sit alone for a little.

LINDA [*almost uttering her fear*]: I want you upstairs.

WILLY [*taking her in his arms*]: In a few minutes, Linda. I couldn't sleep right now. Go on, you look awful tired.

[*He kisses her.*]

BEN: Not like an appointment at all. A diamond is rough and hard to the touch.

WILLY: Go on now. I'll be right up.

LINDA: I think this is the only way, Willy.

WILLY: Sure, it's the best thing.

BEN: Best thing!

WILLY: The only way. Everything is gonna be — go on, kid, get to bed. You look so tired.

LINDA: Come right up.

WILLY: Two minutes.

[LINDA *goes into the living-room, then reappears in her bedroom.* WILLY *moves just outside the kitchen door.*]

WILLY: Loves me. [*Wonderingly.*] Always loved me. Isn't that a remarkable thing? Ben, he'll worship me for it!

BEN [*with promise*]: It's dark there, but full of diamonds.

WILLY: Can you imagine that magnificence with twenty thousand dollars in his pocket?

LINDA [*calling from her room*]: Willy! Come up!

WILLY [*calling into the kitchen*]: Yes! Yes! Coming! It's very smart, you realize that, don't you, sweetheart? Even Ben sees it. I gotta go, baby. 'By! By! [*Going over to* BEN, *almost dancing.*] Imagine? When the mail comes he'll be ahead of Bernard again!

BEN: A perfect proposition all around.

WILLY: Did you see how he cried to me? Oh, if I could kiss him, Ben!

BEN: Time, William, time!

WILLY: Oh, Ben, I always knew one way or another we were gonna make it, Biff and I!

BEN [*looking at his watch*]: The boat. We'll be late.

[*He moves slowly off into the darkness.*]

WILLY [*elegiacally, turning to the house*]: Now when you kick off, boy, I want a seventy-yard boot, and get right down the field under the ball, and when you hit, hit low and hit hard, because it's important, boy. [*He swings around and faces the audience.*] There's all kinds of important people in the stands, and the first thing you know . . . [*Suddenly realizing he is alone.*] Ben! Ben, where do I . . . ? [*He makes a sudden movement of search.*] Ben, how do I . . . ?

LINDA [*calling*]: Willy, you coming up?

WILLY [*uttering a gasp of fear, whirling about as if to quiet her*]: Sh! [*He turns around as if to find his way; sounds, faces, voices, seem to be swarming in upon him and he flicks at them, crying.*] Sh! Sh! [*Suddenly music, faint and high, stops him. It rises in intensity, almost to an unbearable scream. He goes up and down on his toes, and rushes off around the house.*] Shhh!

LINDA: Willy?

[*There is no answer.* LINDA *waits.* BIFF *gets up off his bed. He is still in his clothes.* HAPPY *sits up.* BIFF *stands listening.*]

LINDA [*with real fear*]: Willy, answer me! Willy!

[*There is the sound of a car starting and moving away at full speed.*]

LINDA: No!

BIFF [*rushing down the stairs*]: Pop!

[*As the car speeds off, the music crashes down in a frenzy of sound, which becomes the soft pulsation of a single cello string.* BIFF *slowly returns to his bedroom. He and* HAPPY *gravely don their jackets.* LINDA *slowly walks out of her room. The music has developed into a dead march. The leaves of day are appearing over everything.* CHARLEY *and* BERNARD, *somberly dressed, appear and knock on the kitchen door.* BIFF *and* HAPPY *slowly descend the stairs to the kitchen as* CHARLEY *and* BERNARD *enter. All stop a moment when* LINDA, *in clothes of mourning, bearing a little bunch of roses, comes through the draped doorway into the kitchen. She goes to* CHARLEY *and takes his arm. Now all move toward the audience, through the wall-line of the kitchen. At the limit of the apron,* LINDA *lays down the flowers, kneels, and sits back on her heels. All stare down at the grave.*]

REQUIEM

CHARLEY: It's getting dark, Linda.

[LINDA *doesn't react. She stares at the grave.*]

BIFF: How about it, Mom? Better get some rest, heh? They'll be closing the gate soon.

[LINDA *makes no move. Pause.*]

HAPPY [*deeply angered*]: He had no right to do that. There was no necessity for it. We would've helped him.

CHARLEY [*grunting*]: Hmmm.

BIFF: Come along, Mom.

LINDA: Why didn't anybody come?

CHARLEY: It was a very nice funeral.

LINDA: But where are all the people he knew? Maybe they blame him.

CHARLEY: Naa. It's a rough world, Linda. They wouldn't blame him.

LINDA: I can't understand it. At this time especially. First time in thirty-five years we were just about free and clear. He only needed a little salary. He was even finished with the dentist.

CHARLEY: No man only needs a little salary.

LINDA: I can't understand it.

BIFF: There were a lot of nice days. When he'd come home from a trip; or on Sundays, making the stoop; finishing the cellar; putting on the new porch; when he built the extra bathroom; and put up the garage. You know something, Charley, there's more of him in that front stoop than in all the sales he ever made.

CHARLEY: Yeah. He was a happy man with a batch of cement.

LINDA: He was so wonderful with his hands.

BIFF: He had the wrong dreams. All, all, wrong.

HAPPY [*almost ready to fight* BIFF]: Don't say that!

BIFF: He never knew who he was.

CHARLEY [*stopping* HAPPY's *movement and reply. To* BIFF]: Nobody dast blame this man. You don't understand: Willy was a salesman. And for a salesman, there is no rock bottom to the life. He don't put a bolt to a nut, he don't tell you the law or give you medicine. He's a man way out there in the blue, riding on a smile and a shoeshine. And when they start not smiling back — that's an earthquake. And then you get yourself a couple of spots on your hat, and you're finished. Nobody dast blame this man. A salesman is got to dream, boy. It comes with the territory.

BIFF: Charley, the man didn't know who he was.

HAPPY [*infuriated*]: Don't say that!

BIFF: Why don't you come with me, Happy?

HAPPY: I'm not licked that easily. I'm staying right in this city, and I'm gonna beat this racket! [*He looks at* BIFF, *his chin set.*] The Loman Brothers!

BIFF: I know who I am, kid.

HAPPY: All right, boy. I'm gonna show you and everybody else that Willy Loman did not die in vain. He had a good dream. It's the only dream you can have — to come out number-one man. He fought it out here, and this is where I'm gonna win it for him.

BIFF [*with a hopeless glance at* HAPPY, *bends toward his mother*]: Let's go, Mom.

LINDA: I'll be with you in a minute. Go on, Charley. [*He hesitates.*] I want to, just for a minute. I never had a chance to say goodbye.

[CHARLEY *moves away, followed by* HAPPY. BIFF *remains a slight distance up and left of* LINDA. *She sits there, summoning herself. The flute begins, not far away, playing behind her speech.*]

LINDA: Forgive me, dear. I can't cry. I don't know what it is, but I can't cry. I don't understand it. Why did you ever do that? Help me, Willy, I can't cry. It seems to me that you're just on another trip. I keep expecting you. Willy, dear, I can't cry. Why did you do it? I search and search and I search, and I can't understand it, Willy. I made the last payment on the house today. Today, dear. And there'll be nobody home. [*A sob rises in her throat.*] We're free and clear. [*Sobbing more fully, released.*] We're free. [BIFF *comes slowly toward her.*] We're free . . . We're free . . .

[BIFF *lifts her to her feet and moves out up right with her in his arms.* LINDA *sobs quietly.* BERNARD *and* CHARLEY *come together and follow them, followed by* HAPPY. *Only the music of the flute is left on the darkening stage as over the house the hard towers of the apartment buildings rise into sharp focus.*]

THE CURTAIN FALLS

FOR DISCUSSION

"Death of a Salesman" has received innumerable prizes and awards, among them the Theatre Club Award, the New York Drama Critics Circle Award, the American Theatre Wing Award, *Billboard's* Donaldson Award, and the Pulitzer Prize. The Book-of-the-Month Club, choosing a printed play for the first time in its history, made this work the choice for its readers.

After reading both the play and its author's essay "Tragedy and the Common Man" (page 644) study the following questions, checking back into the play to refresh your memory where necessary. The questions may serve for discussion in class or as topics for critical papers. Since in a work of art everything relates to everything else, you will find that these questions overlap.

1. In Willy's last scene when the sound of the car is heard the audience suddenly understands that he is going to commit suicide. Check back through the play to see what references are made to his suicide plans.

2. What happens in the course of the play to convince Willy finally that he must kill himself? Assuming that people can act from mixed motives, review the evidence that he kills himself to provide Biff with the insurance money. Review the evidence that he kills himself because he can no longer face his own predicament. Would this latter motive reflect a strength or a weakness? Consider that question in the light of the author's comment (page 645) that "the tragic feeling is evoked in us when we are in the presence of a character who is ready to lay down his life, if need be, to secure one thing — his sense of personal dignity."

3. In one sense the play spans twenty-four hours. In another sense it spans Willy's whole life, beginning when his own father left home. Try to define why each flashback scene is introduced where it is: perhaps because it is the scene Willy wants to remember; perhaps because it explains what the audience needs to know; or perhaps for some other reason. Do the flashback scenes with the high school boys show life as you think it really was? or do you think that those scenes are dressed up by what Willy wishes had happened?

4. Speaking of the theme of the play, the author once said: "It is the tragedy of a man who did believe that he alone was not meeting the qualifications laid down for mankind by those clean-shaven frontiersmen who inhabit the peaks of broadcasting and advertising offices." Is Ben a real person like the other people in the flashback scenes, or is he a fiction in Willy's mind — a personification of the individualistic frontier dream of American life?

5. The play can be said to unfold both forward and backward in time. At the end of the first act the audience looks forward almost hopefully to Willy's meeting with Howard and to Biff's meeting with Bill Oliver. The audience then sees what happens the day of the second act. But also the second act unfolds backward, for we learn many things about the past which help explain the present of Willy and Biff. Show that as each new event unfolds in the present, an event in the past unfolds to explain it.

6. The relation between Willy and Charley is complex and revealing. Try to explain why each behaves as he does to the other, keeping your conjectures close to the hints given in the play.

7. Apparently the traumatic experience of Biff when he found a woman in his father's hotel room is an important factor in his own collapse. Try to explain why this experience would have such an enduring effect on him.

8. Is the audience expected to regard Willy's relations with The Woman as being so seriously sinful as to justify all the misery which descends on the family? What would Linda's attitude have been if she had learned about The Woman?

9. Why does Biff steal? Does Ben condone some dishonesty?

10. Speaking of the theme of the play, the author once remarked: "It is the growth of illusion until it destroys the individual and leaves the children to whom he transmitted it incapable of dealing with reality. Every man has an image of himself which fails in one way or another to correspond with reality. The closer a man gets to knowing himself, the less likely he is to trip up on his illusions."

What is Willy's illusion about himself? Is it of recent origin? How does it trip him up? Is it transmitted equally to both his sons?

11. Is Willy's illusion, as you defined it in question 10, the same thing as the misleading advice issued to mankind by Ben and those "clean-shaven frontiersmen" mentioned in question 4?

Does old Dave Singleman, whose funeral was attended by hundreds of sales-men and buyers, have any part in Willy's illusion? Did Dave Singleman ever really exist, or is he just part of American folklore? If he did exist and succeed, then why didn't Willy Loman succeed too? Have times changed too much? or did Willy lack the personal qualities possessed by Dave?

12. In his essay the author says (page 646): "The tragic right is a condition of life, a condition in which the human personality is able to flower and realize itself. The wrong is the condition which suppresses man, perverts the flowing out of his love and creative instinct." Where in the play do you find references to the flowing out of love and creative instinct — who experienced it when? What in the play thwarts love and creativity?

13. At least three ways of life are formulated in the play:

"It's not what you do, Ben. It's who you know and the smile on your face! It's contacts, Ben, contacts!"

"When I was seventeen I walked into the jungle, and when I was twenty-one I walked out. And by God I was rich."

"The only thing you got in the world is what you can sell."

Are these formulas all common in American life? In this play do they seem to be wise formulas?

Acting Version of Sophocles' *King Oedipus*

WILLIAM BUTLER YEATS

OEDIPUS. Children, descendants of old Cadmus, why do you come before me, why do you carry the branches of suppliants, while the city smokes with incense and murmurs with prayer and lamentation? I would not learn from any mouth but yours, old man, therefore I question you myself. Do you know of anything that I can do and have not done? How can I, being the man I am, being King Oedipus, do other than all I know? I were indeed hard of heart did I not pity such suppliants.

PRIEST. Oedipus, King of my country, you can see our ages who are before your door; some it may be too young for such a journey, and some too old, Priests of Zeus such as I, and these chosen young men; while the rest of the people crowd the marketplaces with their suppliant branches, for the city stumbles towards death, hardly able to raise up its head. A blight has fallen upon the fruitful blossoms of the land, a blight upon flock and field and upon the bed of marriage — plague ravages the city. Oedipus, King, not god but foremost of living men, seeing that when you first came to this town of Thebes you freed us from that harsh singer, the riddling sphinx, we beseech you, all we suppliants, to find some help. Whether you find it by your power as a man, or because, being near the gods, a god has whispered you. Uplift our State; think upon your fame; your coming brought us luck, be lucky to us still, remember that it is better to rule over men than over a waste place, since neither walled town nor ship is anything if it be empty and no man within it.

OEDIPUS. My unhappy children! I know well what need has brought you, what suffering you endure, yet sufferers though you be, there is not a single one whose suffering is as mine — each mourns himself, but my soul mourns the city, myself, and you. It is not therefore as if you came to arouse a sleeping man. No! Be certain that I have wept many tears and searched hither and thither for some remedy. I have already done the only thing that came in to my head for all my search. I have sent the son of Menoeceus, Creon, my own wife's brother, to the Pythian House of Phoebus, to hear if deed or word of mine may yet deliver this town. I am troubled, for he is a long time away — a longer time than should be — but when he comes I shall not be an honest man unless I do whatever the god commands.

PRIEST. You have spoken at the right time. They have just signalled to us that Creon has arrived.

OEDIPUS. O King Apollo, may he bring brighter fortune, for his face is shining.

PRIEST. He brings good news, for he is crowned with bay.

OEDIPUS. We shall know soon. Brother-in-law, Menoeceus' son, what news from the god?

CREON. Good news; for pain turns to pleasure when we have set the crooked straight.

OEDIPUS. But what is the oracle? — so far the news is neither good nor bad.

CREON. If you would hear it with all these about you, I am ready to speak. Or do we go within?

OEDIPUS. Speak before all. The sorrow I endure is less for my own life than these.

CREON. Then, with your leave, I speak. Our lord Phoebus bids us drive out a defiling thing that has been cherished in this land.

OEDIPUS. By what purification?

CREON. King Laius was our king before you came to pilot us.

OEDIPUS. I know — but not of my own knowledge, for I never saw him.

CREON. He was killed; and the god now bids us revenge it on his murderers, whoever they be.

OEDIPUS. Where shall we come upon their track after all these years? Did he meet his death in house or field, at home or in some foreign land?

CREON. In a foreign land: he was journeying to Delphi.

OEDIPUS. Did no fellow-traveller see the deed? Was there none there who could be questioned?

CREON. All perished but one man who fled in terror and could tell for certain but one thing of all he had seen.

OEDIPUS. One thing might be a clue to many things.

CREON. He said that they were fallen upon by a great troop of robbers.

OEDIPUS. What robbers would be so daring unless bribed from here?

CREON. Such things were indeed guessed at, but Laius once dead no avenger arose. We were amid our troubles.

OEDIPUS. But when royalty had fallen what troubles could have hindered search?

CREON. The riddling sphinx put those dark things out of our thoughts — we thought of what had come to our own doors.

OEDIPUS. But I will start afresh and make the dark things plain. In doing right by Laius I protect myself, for whoever slew Laius might turn a hand against me. Come, my children, rise up from the altar steps; lift up these suppliant boughs and let all the children of Cadmus be called hither that I may search out everything and find for all happiness or misery as god wills.

PRIEST. May Phoebus, sender of the oracle, come with it and be our saviour and deliverer.

(The CHORUS *enter.)*

CHORUS. What message comes to famous Thebes from the Golden House?
What message of disaster from that sweet-throated Zeus?
What foul things that our fathers saw, do the seasons bring?
Or what that no man ever saw, what new monstrous thing?
Trembling in every limb I raise my loud importunate cry,
And in a sacred terror wait the Delian god's reply.

Apollo chase the god of death that leads no shouting men,
Bears no rattling shield and yet consumes this form with pain,
Famine takes what the plague spares, and all the crops are lost;
No new life fills the empty place — ghost flits after ghost.
To that god-trodden western shore, as flit benighted birds.
Sorrow speaks to sorrow and finds no comfort in words.

Hurry him from the land of Thebes with a fair wind behind
Out on to that formless deep where not a man can find
Hold for an anchor fluke, for all is world-enfolding sea;
Master of the thundercloud, set the lightning free,
And add the thunder-stone to that and fling them on his head
For death is all the fashion now, till even death be dead.

We call against the pallid face of this god-hated god
The springing heel of Artemis in the hunting sandal shod,
The towsel-headed Maenads, blown torch and drunken sound,
The stately Lysian king himself with golden fillet crowned,
And in his hands the golden bow and the stretched golden string,
And Bacchus' wine-ensanguined face that all the Maenads sing.

OEDIPUS. You are praying, and it may be that your prayer will be answered; that if you hear my words and do my bidding you may find help out of all your trouble. This is my proclamation, children of Cadmus. Whoever among you knows by what man Laius, son of Labdicus, was killed, must tell all he knows. If he fear for himself and being guilty denounce himself, he shall be in the less danger, suffering no worse thing than banishment. If on the other hand there be one that knows that a foreigner did the deed, let him speak, and I shall give him a reward and my thanks: but if any man keep silent from fear or to screen a friend, hear all what I will do to that man. No one in this land shall speak to him, nor offer sacrifice beside him; but he shall be driven from their homes as if he himself had done the deed. And in this I am the ally of the Pythian God and of the murdered man, and I pray that the murderer's life may, should he be so hidden and screened, drop from him and perish away, whoever he may be, whether he did the deed with others or by himself alone: and on you I lay it to make — so far as man may — these words good, for my sake, and for the god's sake, and for the sake of this land. And even if the god had not spurred us to it, it were a wrong to leave the guilt unpurged, when one so noble, and he your king, had perished; and all have sinned that could have searched it out and did not: and now since it is I who hold the power which he held once, and have his wife for wife — she who would have borne him heirs had he but lived — I take up this cause even as I would were it that of my own father. And if there be any who do not obey me in it, I pray that the gods send them neither harvest of the earth nor fruit of the womb; but let them be wasted by this plague, or by one more dreadful still. But may all be blessed for ever who hear my words and do my will.

CHORUS. We do not know the murderer, and it were indeed more fitting that Phoebus, who laid the task upon us, should name the man.

OEDIPUS. No man can make the gods speak against their will.

CHORUS. Then I will say what seems the next best thing.

OEDIPUS. If there is a third course, show it.

CHORUS. I know that our lord, Tiresias, is the seer most like to our lord Phoebus, and through him we may unravel all.

OEDIPUS. So I was advised by Creon, and twice already have I sent to bring him.

CHORUS. If we lack his help we have nothing but vague and ancient rumours.

OEDIPUS. What rumours are they? I would examine every story.

CHORUS. Certain wayfarers were said to have killed the king.

OEDIPUS. I know. I know. But who was there that saw it?

CHORUS. If there is such a man, and terror can move him, he will not keep silence when they have told him of your curses.

OEDIPUS. He that such a deed did not terrify will not be terrified because of a word.

CHORUS. But there is one who shall convict him. For the blind prophet comes at last — in whom alone of all men the truth lives.

(*Enter* TIRESIAS, *led by a boy.*)

OEDIPUS. Tiresias, master of all knowledge, whatever may be spoken, whatever is unspeakable, whatever omens of earth and sky reveal, the plague is among us, and from that plague, Great Prophet, protect us and save us. Phoebus in answer to our question says that it will not leave us till we have found the murderers of Laius, and driven them into exile or put them to death. Do you therefore neglect neither the voice of birds, nor any other sort of wisdom, but rescue yourself, rescue the State, rescue me, rescue all that are defiled by the deed. For we are in your hands, and what greater task falls to a man than to help other men with all he knows and has.

TIRESIAS. Aye, and what worse task than to be wise and suffer for it. I know this well; it slipped out of mind, or I would never have come.

OEDIPUS. What now?

TIRESIAS. Let me go home. You will bear your burden to the end more easily, and I bear mine — if you but give me leave for that.

OEDIPUS. Your words are strange and unkind to the State that bred you.

TIRESIAS. I see that you, on your part, keep your lips tight shut, and therefore I have shut mine that I may come to no misfortune.

OEDIPUS. For god's love do not turn away — if you have knowledge. We suppliants implore you on our knees.

TIRESIAS. You are fools — I will bring misfortune neither upon you nor upon myself.

OEDIPUS. What is this? You know all and will say nothing? You are minded to betray me and Thebes?

TIRESIAS. Why do you ask these things? You will not learn them from me.

OEDIPUS. What! Basest of the base! You would enrage the very stones. Will you never speak out? Cannot anything touch you?

TIRESIAS. The future will come of itself though I keep silent.

OEDIPUS. Then seeing that come it must, you had best speak out.

TIRESIAS. I will speak no further. Rage if you have a mind to; bring out all the fierceness that is in your heart.

OEDIPUS. That will I. I will not spare to speak my thoughts. Listen to what I have to say. It seems to me that you have helped to plot the deed; and, short of doing it with your own hands, have done the deed yourself. Had you eyesight I would declare that you alone had done it.

TIRESIAS. So that is what you say? I charge you to obey the decree that you yourself have made, and from this day out to speak neither to these nor to me. You are the defiler of this land.

OEDIPUS. So brazen in your impudence? How do you hope to escape punishment?

TIRESIAS. I have escaped; my strength is in my truth.

OEDIPUS. Who taught you this? You never got it by your art.

TIRESIAS. You, because you have spurred me to speech against my will.

OEDIPUS. What speech? Speak it again that I may learn it better.

TIRESIAS. You are but tempting me — you understood me well enough.

OEDIPUS. No; not so that I can say I know it; speak it again.

TIRESIAS. I say that you are yourself the murderer that you seek.

OEDIPUS. You shall rue it for having spoken twice such outrageous words.

TIRESIAS. Would you that I say more that you may be still angrier?

OEDIPUS. Say what you will. I will not let it move me.

TIRESIAS. I say that you are living with your next of kin in unimagined shame.

OEDIPUS. Do you think you can say such things and never smart for it?

TIRESIAS. Yes, if there be strength in truth.

OEDIPUS. There is; yes — for everyone but you. But not for you that are maimed in ear and in eye and in wit.

TIRESIAS. You are but a poor wretch flinging taunts that in a little while everyone shall fling at you.

OEDIPUS. Night — endless night has covered you up so that you can neither hurt me nor any man that looks upon the sun.

TIRESIAS. Your doom is not to fall by me. Apollo is enough: it is his business to work out your doom.

OEDIPUS. Was it Creon that planned this or you yourself?

TIRESIAS. Creon is not your enemy; you are your own enemy.

OEDIPUS. Power, ability, position, you bear all burdens, and yet what envy you create! Great must that envy be if envy of my power in this town — a power put into my hands unsought — has made trusty Creon, my old friend Creon, secretly long to take that power from me; if he has suborned this scheming juggler, this quack and trickster, this man with eyes for his gains and blindness in his art. Come, come, where did you prove yourself a seer? Why did you say nothing to set the townsmen free when the riddling sphinx was here? Yet that riddle was not for the first-comer to read; it needed the skill of a seer. And none such had you! Neither found by help of birds, nor straight from any god. No, I came; I silenced her, I the ignorant Oedipus, it was I that found the answer in my mother wit, untaught by any birds. And it is I that you would pluck out of my place, thinking to stand close to Creon's throne. But you and the plotter of all this shall mourn despite your zeal to purge the land. Were you not an old man, you had already learnt how bold you are and learnt it to your cost.

CHORUS. Both this man's words and yours, Oedipus, have been said in anger. Such words cannot help us here, nor any but those that teach us to obey the oracle.

TIRESIAS. King though you are, the right to answer when attacked belongs to both alike. I am not subject to you, but to Loxias; and therefore I shall never be Creon's subject. And I tell you, since you have taunted me with blindness, that though you have your sight, you cannot see in what misery you stand, nor where you are living, nor with whom, unknowing what you do — for you do not know the stock you come of — you have been your own kin's enemy be they living or be they dead. And one day a mother's curse and father's curse alike shall drive you from this land in dreadful haste with darkness upon those eyes. Therefore, heap your scorn on Creon and on my message if you have a mind to; for no one of living men shall be crushed as you shall be crushed.

OEDIPUS. Begone this instant! Away, away! Get thee from these doors!

TIRESIAS. I had never come but that you sent for me.

OEDIPUS. I did not know you were mad.

TIRESIAS. I may seem mad to you, but your parents thought me sane.

OEDIPUS. My parents! Stop! Who was my father?

TIRESIAS. This day shall you know your birth; and it will ruin you.

OEDIPUS. What dark words you always speak!

TIRESIAS. But are you not most skilful in the unravelling of dark words?

OEDIPUS. You mock me for that which made me great?

TIRESIAS. It was that fortune that undid you.

OEDIPUS. What do I care? For I delivered all this town.

TIRESIAS. Then I will go: boy, lead me out of this.

OEDIPUS. Yes, let him lead you. You take vexation with you.

TIRESIAS. I will go: but first I will do my errand. For frown though you may you cannot destroy me. The man for whom you look, the man you have been threatening in all the proclamation about the death of Laius, that man is here. He seems, so far as looks go, an alien; yet he shall be found a native Theban and shall nowise be glad of that fortune. A blind man, though now he has his sight; a beggar, though now he is most rich; he shall go forth feeling the ground before him with his stick; so you go in and think on that, and if you find I am in fault say that I have no skill in prophecy.

(TIRESIAS *is led out by the boy.*)
(OEDIPUS *enters the palace.*)

CHORUS. The Delphian rock has spoken out, now must a wicked mind
Planner of things I dare not speak and of this bloody wrack,
Pray for feet that run as fast as the four hoofs of the wind:
Cloudy Parnassus and the Fates thunder at his back.

That sacred crossing place of lines upon Parnassus' head,
Lines drawn through North and South, and drawn through West and East,
That navel of the world bids all men search the mountain wood,
The solitary cavern, till they have found that infamous beast.

(CREON *enters from the house.*)

CREON. Fellow-citizens, having heard that King Oedipus accuses me of dreadful things, I come in my indignation. Does he think that he has suffered wrong from me in these present troubles, or anything that could lead to wrong, whether in word or deed? How can I live under blame like that? What life would be worth having if by you here, and by my nearest friends, called a traitor through the town?

CHORUS. He said it in anger, and not from his heart out.

CREON. He said it was I put up the seer to speak those falsehoods.

CHORUS. Such things were said.

CREON. And had he his right mind saying it?

CHORUS. I do not know — I do not know what my masters do.

(OEDIPUS *enters.*)

OEDIPUS. What brought you here? Have you a face so brazen that you come to my house — you the proved assassin of its master — the certain robber of my crown. Come, tell me in the face of the gods what cowardice, or folly, did you discover in me that you plotted this? Did you think that I would not see what you were at till you had crept upon me, or seeing it would not ward it off? What madness to seek a throne, having neither friends nor followers.

CREON. Now, listen, hear my answer, and then you may with knowledge judge between us.

OEDIPUS. You are plausible, but waste words now that I know you.

CREON. Hear what I have to say. I can explain it all.

OEDIPUS. One thing you will not explain away — that you are my enemy.

CREON. You are a fool to imagine that senseless stubbornness sits well upon you.

OEDIPUS. And you to imagine that you can wrong a kinsman and escape the penalty.

CREON. That is justly said I grant you; but what is this wrong that you complain of?

OEDIPUS. Did you advise, or not, that I should send for that notorious prophet?

CREON. And I am of the same mind still.

OEDIPUS. How long is it then since Laius —

CREON. What, what about him?

OEDIPUS. Since Laius was killed by an unknown hand?

CREON. That was many years ago.

OEDIPUS. Was this prophet at his trade in those days?

CREON. Yes; skilled as now and in equal honour.

OEDIPUS. Did he speak of me at any time?

CREON. Never certainly when I was within earshot.

OEDIPUS. And did you make inquiry into the murder?

CREON. We made inquiry but learnt nothing.

OEDIPUS. And why did he not tell out his story then?

CREON. I do not know. Where I lack light I am silent.

OEDIPUS. This much at least you know and can say out.

CREON. What is that? If I know it I will say it.

OEDIPUS. That if he had not consulted you he would never have said that it was I who killed Laius.

CREON. You know best what he said; but now, question for question.

OEDIPUS. Question your fill — I cannot be proved guilty of that blood.

CREON. Answer me then. Are you not married to my sister?

OEDIPUS. That cannot be denied.

CREON. And do you not rule as she does? And with a like power?

OEDIPUS. I give her all she asks for.

CREON. And am not I the equal of you both?

OEDIPUS. Yes: and that is why you are so false a friend.

CREON. Not so; reason this out as I reason it, and first weigh this: who would prefer to lie awake amid terrors rather than to sleep in peace, granting that his power is equal in both cases. Neither I nor any sober-minded man. You give me what I ask and let me do what I want, but were I king I would have to do things I did not want to do. Is not influence and no trouble with it better than any throne, am I such a fool as to hunger after unprofitable honours? Now all are glad to see me, everyone wishes me well, all that want a favour from you ask speech of me — finding in that their hope. Why should I give up these things and take those? No wise mind is treacherous. I am no contriver of plots, and if another took to them he would not come to me for help. And in proof of this go to the Pythian Oracle, and ask if I have truly told what the gods said: and after that, if you have found that I have plotted with the Soothsayer, take me and kill me; not by the sentence of one mouth only — but of two mouths, yours and my own. But do not condemn me in a corner, upon some fancy and without proof. What right have you to declare a good man bad or a bad good? It is as bad a thing to cast off a true friend, as it is for a man to cast away his own life — but you will learn these things with certainty when the time comes; for time alone shows a just man; though a day can show a knave.

CHORUS. King! He has spoken well, he gives himself time to think; a headlong talker does not know what he is saying.

OEDIPUS. The plotter is at his work, and I must counterplot headlong, or he will get his ends and I miss mine.

CREON. What will you do then? Drive me from the land?

OEDIPUS. Not so; I do not desire your banishment — but your death.

CREON. You are not sane.

OEDIPUS. I am sane at least in my own interest.

CREON. You should be in mine also.

OEDIPUS. No, for you are false.

CREON. But if you understand nothing?

OEDIPUS. Yet I must rule.

CREON. Not if you rule badly.

OEDIPUS. Hear him, O Thebes!

CREON. Thebes is for me also, not for you alone.

CHORUS. Cease, princes: I see Jocasta coming out of the house; she comes just in time to quench the quarrel.

(JOCASTA *enters.*)

JOCASTA. Unhappy men! Why have you made this crazy uproar? Are you not ashamed to quarrel about your own affairs when the whole country is in trouble? Go back into the palace, Oedipus, and you, Creon, to your own house. Stop making all this noise about some petty thing.

CREON. Your husband is about to kill me — or to drive me from the land of my fathers.

OEDIPUS. Yes: for I have convicted him of treachery against me.

CREON. Now may I perish accursed if I have done such a thing.

JOCASTA. For god's love believe it, Oedipus. First, for the sake of his oath, and then for my sake, and for the sake of these people here.

CHORUS (*all*). King, do what she asks.

OEDIPUS. What would you have me do?

CHORUS. Not to make a dishonourable charge, with no more evidence than rumour, against a friend who has bound himself with an oath.

OEDIPUS. Do you desire my exile or my death?

CHORUS. No, by Helios, by the first of all the gods, may I die abandoned by Heaven and earth if I have that thought. What breaks my heart is that our public griefs should be increased by your quarrels.

OEDIPUS. Then let him go, though I am doomed thereby to death or to be thrust dishonoured from the land; it is your lips, not his, that move me to compassion; wherever he goes my hatred follows him.

CREON. You are as sullen in yielding as you were vehement in anger, but such natures are their own heaviest burden.

OEDIPUS. Why will you not leave me in peace and begone?

CREON. I will go away; what is your hatred to me; in the eyes of all here I am a just man.

(*He goes.*)

CHORUS. Lady, why do you not take your man in to the house?

JOCASTA. I will do so when I have learned what has happened.

CHORUS. The half of it was blind suspicion bred of talk; the rest the wounds left by injustice.

JOCASTA. It was on both sides?

CHORUS. Yes.

JOCASTA. What was it?

CHORUS. Our land is vexed enough. Let the thing alone now that it is over.

(*Exit leader of chorus.*)

JOCASTA. In the name of the gods, king, what put you in this anger?

OEDIPUS. I will tell you; for I honour you more than these men do. The cause is Creon and his plots against me.

JOCASTA. Speak on, if you can tell clearly how this quarrel arose.

OEDIPUS. He says that I am guilty of the blood of Laius.

JOCASTA. On his own knowledge, or on hearsay?

OEDIPUS. He has made a rascal of a seer his mouthpiece.

JOCASTA. Do not fear that there is truth in what he says. Listen to me, and learn to your comfort that nothing born of woman can know what is to come. I will give you proof of that. An oracle came to Laius once, I will not say from Phoebus, but from his ministers, that he was doomed to die by the hand of his own child sprung from him and me. When his child was but three days old Laius bound its feet together and had it thrown by sure hands upon a trackless mountain; and when Laius was murdered at the place where three highways meet, it was, or so at least the rumour says, by foreign robbers. So Apollo did not bring it about that the child should kill its father, nor did Laius die in the dreadful way he feared by his child's hand. Yet that was how the message of the seers mapped out the future. Pay no attention to such things. What the god would show he will need no help to show it, but bring it to light himself.

OEDIPUS. What restlessness of soul, lady, has come upon me since I heard you speak, what a tumult of the mind!

JOCASTA. What is this new anxiety? What has startled you?

OEDIPUS. You said that Laius was killed where three highways meet.

JOCASTA. Yes: that was the story.

OEDIPUS. And where is the place?

JOCASTA. In Phocis where the road divides branching off to Delphi and to Daulia.

OEDIPUS. And when did it happen? How many years ago?

JOCASTA. News was published in this town just before you came into power.

OEDIPUS. O Zeus! What have you planned to do unto me?

JOCASTA. He was tall; the silver had just come into his hair; and in shape not greatly unlike to you.

OEDIPUS. Unhappy that I am! It seems that I have laid a dreadful curse upon myself, and did not know it.

JOCASTA. What do you say? I tremble when I look on you, my king.

OEDIPUS. And I have a misgiving that the seer can see indeed. But I will know it all more clearly, if you tell me one thing more.

JOCASTA. Indeed, though I tremble I will answer whatever you ask.

OEDIPUS. Had he but a small troop with him; or did he travel like a great man with many followers?

JOCASTA. There were but five in all — one of them a herald; and there was one carriage with Laius in it.

OEDIPUS. Alas! It is now clear indeed. Who was it brought the news, lady?

JOCASTA. A servant — the one survivor.

OEDIPUS. Is he by chance in the house now?

JOCASTA. No; for when he found you reigning instead of Laius he besought me, his hand clasped in mine, to send him to the fields among the cattle that he might be far from the sight of this town; and I sent him. He was a worthy man for a slave and might have asked a bigger thing.

OEDIPUS. I would have him return to us without delay.

JOCASTA. Oedipus, it is easy. But why do you ask this?

OEDIPUS. I fear that I have said too much, and therefore I would question him.

JOCASTA. He shall come, but I too have a right to know what lies so heavy upon your heart, my king.

OEDIPUS. Yes: and it shall not be kept from you; now that my fear has grown so heavy. Nobody is more to me than you, nobody has the same right to learn my good or evil luck. My father was Polybius of Corinth — my mother the Dorian Merope, and I was held the foremost man in all that town until a thing happened — a thing to startle a man, though not to make him angry as it made me. We were sitting at the table, and a man who had drunk too much cried out that I was not my father's son — and I, though angry, restrained my anger for that day; but the next day went to my father and my mother and questioned them. They were indignant at the taunt and that comforted me — and yet the man's words rankled, for they had spread a rumour through the town. Without consulting my father or my mother I went to Delphi, but Phoebus told me nothing of the thing for which I came, but much of other things — things of sorrow and of terror: that I should live in incest with my mother, and beget a brood that men would shudder to look upon; that I should be my father's murderer. Hearing those words I fled out of Corinth, and from that day have but known where it lies when I have found its direction by the stars. I sought where I might escape those infamous things — the doom that was laid upon me. I came in my flight to that very spot where you tell me this king perished. Now, lady, I will tell you the truth. When I had come close up to those three roads, I came upon a herald, and a man like him you have described seated in a carriage. The man who held the reins and the old man himself would not give me room, but thought to force me from the path, and I struck the driver in my anger. The old man, seeing what I had done, waited till I was passing him and then struck me upon the head. I paid him back in full, for I knocked him out of the carriage with a blow of my stick. He rolled on his back, and after that I killed them all. If this stranger were indeed Laius, is there a more miserable man in the world than the man before you? Is there a man more hated of Heaven? No stranger, no citizen, may receive him into his house, not a soul may speak to him, and no mouth but my own mouth has laid this curse upon me. Am I not wretched? May I be swept from this world before I have endured this doom!

CHORUS. These things, O King, fill us with terror; yet hope till you speak with him that saw the deed, and have learnt all.

OEDIPUS. Till I have learnt all, I may hope. I await the man that is coming from the pastures.

JOCASTA. What is it that you hope to learn?

OEDIPUS. I will tell you. If this tale agrees with yours, then I am clear.

JOCASTA. What tale of mine?

OEDIPUS. He told you that Laius met his death from robbers; if he keeps to that tale now and speaks of several slayers I am not the slayer. But if he says one lonely wayfarer, then beyond a doubt the scale dips to me.

JOCASTA. Be certain of this much at least, his first tale was of robbers. He cannot revoke that tale — the city heard it and not I alone. Yet, if he should somewhat change his story, king, at least he cannot make the murder of Laius square with prophecy; for Loxius plainly said of Laius that he would die by the hand of my child. That poor innocent did not kill him, for it died before him. Therefore from this out I would not for all divination can do so much as look to my right hand or to my left hand, or fear at all.

OEDIPUS. You have judged well; and yet for all that, send and bring this peasant to me.

JOCASTA. I will send without delay. I will do all that you would have of me — but let us come in to the house.

(*They go in to the house.*)

CHORUS. For this one thing above all I would be praised as a man,
That in my words and my deeds I have kept those laws in mind
Olympian Zeus, and that high clear Empyrean,
Fashioned, and not some man or people of mankind,
Even those sacred laws nor age nor sleep can blind.

A man becomes a tyrant out of insolence,
He climbs and climbs, until all people call him great,
He seems upon the summit, and God flings him thence;
Yet an ambitious man may lift up a whole State,
And in his death be blessed, in his life fortunate.

And all men honour such; but should a man forget
The holy images, the Delphian Sybil's trance
And the world's navel stone, and not be punished for it
And seem most fortunate, or even blessed perchance,
Why should we honour the gods, or join the sacred dance?

(JOCASTA *enters from the palace.*)

JOCASTA. It has come into my head, citizens of Thebes, to visit every altar of the gods, a wreath in my hand and a dish of incense. For all manner of alarms trouble the soul of Oedipus, who instead of weighing new oracles by old, like a man of sense, is at the mercy of every mouth that speaks terror. Seeing that my words are nothing to him, I cry to you, Lysian Apollo, whose altar is the first I meet: I come, a suppliant, bearing symbols of prayer; O make us clean, for now we are all afraid, seeing him afraid, even as they who see the helmsman afraid.

(*Enter* MESSENGER.)

MESSENGER. May I learn from you, strangers, where is the home of King Oedipus? Or better still, tell me where he himself is, if you know.

CHORUS. This is his house, and he himself, stranger, is within it, and this lady is the mother of his children.

MESSENGER. Then I call a blessing upon her, seeing what man she has married.

JOCASTA. May God reward those words with a like blessing, stranger. But what have you come to seek or to tell?

MESSENGER. Good news for your house, lady, and for your husband.

JOCASTA. What news? From whence have you come?

MESSENGER. From Corinth, and you will rejoice at the message I am about to give you; yet, maybe, it will grieve you.

JOCASTA. What is it? How can it have this double power?

MESSENGER. The people of Corinth, they say, will take him for king.

JOCASTA. How then? Is old Polybius no longer on the throne?

MESSENGER. No. He is in his tomb.

JOCASTA. What do you say? Is Polybius dead, old man?

MESSENGER. May I drop dead if it is not the truth.

JOCASTA. Away! Hurry to your master with this news. O oracle of the gods, where are you now? This is the man whom Oedipus feared and shunned lest he should murder him, and now this man has died a natural death, and not by Oedipus.

(*Enter* OEDIPUS.)

OEDIPUS. Jocasta, dearest wife, why have you called me from the house?

JOCASTA. Listen to this man, and judge to what the oracles of the gods have come.

OEDIPUS. And he — who may he be? And what news has he?

JOCASTA. He has come from Corinth to tell you that your father, Polybius, is dead.

OEDIPUS. How, stranger? Let me have it from your own mouth.

MESSENGER. If I am to tell the story, the first thing is that he is dead and gone.

OEDIPUS. By some sickness or by treachery?

MESSENGER. A little thing can bring the aged to their rest.

OEDIPUS. Ah! He died, it seems, from sickness?

MESSENGER. Yes; and of old age.

OEDIPUS. Alas! Alas! Why, indeed, my wife, should one look to the Pythian seer, or to the birds that scream above our heads? For they would have it that I was doomed to kill my father. And now he is dead — hid already beneath the earth. And here am I — who had no part in it, unless indeed he died from longing for me. If that were so, I may have caused his death; but Polybius has carried the oracles with him into Hades — the oracles as men have understood them — and they are worth nothing.

JOCASTA. Did I not tell you so, long since?

OEDIPUS. You did, but fear misled me.

JOCASTA. Put this trouble from you.

OEDIPUS. Those bold words would sound better, were not my mother living. But as it is — I have some grounds for fear; yet you have said well.

JOCASTA. Yet your father's death is a sign that all is well.

OEDIPUS. I know that: but I fear because of her who lives.

MESSENGER. Who is this woman who makes you afraid?

OEDIPUS. Merope, old man, the wife of Polybius.

MESSENGER. What is there in her to make you afraid?

OEDIPUS. A dreadful oracle sent from Heaven, stranger.

MESSENGER. Is it a secret, or can you speak it out?

OEDIPUS. Loxius said that I was doomed to marry my own mother, and to shed my father's blood. For that reason I fled from my house in Corinth; and I did right though there is great comfort in familiar faces.

MESSENGER. Was it indeed for that reason that you went into exile?

OEDIPUS. I did not wish, old man, to shed my father's blood.

MESSENGER. King, have I not freed you from that fear?

OEDIPUS. You shall be fittingly rewarded.

MESSENGER. Indeed, to tell the truth, it was for that I came; to bring you home and be the better for it ——

OEDIPUS. No! I will never go to my parents' home.

MESSENGER. Ah, my son, it is plain enough, you do not know what you do.

OEDIPUS. How, old man? For the gods' love, tell me.

MESSENGER. If for these reasons you shrink from going home.

OEDIPUS. I am afraid lest Phoebus has spoken true.

MESSENGER. You are afraid of being made guilty through Merope?

OEDIPUS. That is my constant fear.

MESSENGER. A vain fear.

OEDIPUS. How so, if I was born of that father and mother?

MESSENGER. Because they were nothing to you in blood.

OEDIPUS. What do you say? Was Polybius not my father?

MESSENGER. No more nor less than myself.

OEDIPUS. How can my father be no more to me than you who are nothing to me?

MESSENGER. He did not beget you any more than I.

OEDIPUS. No? Then why did he call me his son?

MESSENGER. He took you as a gift from these hands of mine.

OEDIPUS. How could he love so dearly what came from another's hands?

MESSENGER. He had been childless.

OEDIPUS. If I am not your son, where did you get me?

MESSENGER. In a wooded valley of Cythaeron.

OEDIPUS. What brought you wandering there?

MESSENGER. I was in charge of mountain sheep.

OEDIPUS. A shepherd — a wandering, hired man.

MESSENGER. A hired man who came just in time.

OEDIPUS. Just in time — had it come to that?

MESSENGER. Have not the cords left their marks upon your ankles?

OEDIPUS. Yes, that is an old trouble.

MESSENGER. I took your feet out of the spancel.

OEDIPUS. I have had those marks from the cradle.

MESSENGER. They have given you the name you bear.

OEDIPUS. Tell me, for the gods' sake, was that deed my mother's or my father's?

MESSENGER. I do not know — he who gave you to me knows more of that than I.

OEDIPUS. What? You had me from another? You did not chance on me yourself?

MESSENGER. No. Another shepherd gave you to me.

OEDIPUS. Who was he? Can you tell me who he was?

MESSENGER. I think that he was said to be of Laius' household.

OEDIPUS. The king who ruled this country long ago?

MESSENGER. The same — the man was herdsman in his service.

OEDIPUS. Is he alive, that I might speak with him?

MESSENGER. You people of this country should know that.

OEDIPUS. Is there anyone here present who knows the herd he speaks of? Anyone who has seen him in the town pastures? The hour has come when all must be made clear.

CHORUS. I think he is the very herd you sent for but now. Jocasta can tell you better than I.

JOCASTA. Why ask about that man? Why think about him? Why waste a thought on what this man has said? What he has said is of no account.

OEDIPUS. What, with a clue like that in my hands and fail to find out my birth?

JOCASTA. For God's sake, if you set any value upon your life, give up this search — my misery is enough.

OEDIPUS. Though I be proved the son of a slave, yes, even of three generations of slaves, you cannot be made base born.

JOCASTA. Yet, hear me, I implore you. Give up this search.

OEDIPUS. I will not hear of anything but searching the whole thing out.

JOCASTA. I am only thinking of your good — I have advised you for the best.

OEDIPUS. Your advice makes me impatient.

JOCASTA. May you never come to know who you are, unhappy man!

OEDIPUS. Go, someone, bring the herdsman here — and let that woman glory in her noble blood.

JOCASTA. Alas, alas, miserable man! Miserable! That is all that I can call you now or forever.

(She goes out.)

CHORUS. Why has the lady gone, Oedipus, in such a transport of despair? Out of this silence will burst a storm of sorrows.

OEDIPUS. Let come what will. However lowly my origin I will discover it. That woman, with all a woman's pride, grows red with shame at my base birth. I think myself the child of Good Luck, and that the years are my foster-brothers. Sometimes they have set me up, and sometimes thrown me down, but he that has Good Luck for mother can suffer no dishonour. That is my origin, nothing can change it, so why should I renounce this search into my birth?

CHORUS. Oedipus' nurse, mountain of many a hidden glen,
Be honoured among men;
A famous man, deep thoughted, and his body strong;
Be honoured in dance and song.

Who met in the hidden glen? Who let his fancy run
Upon nymph of Helicon?
Lord Pan or Lord Apollo or the mountain Lord,
By the Bacchantes adored?

OEDIPUS. If I, who have never met the man, may venture to say so, I think that the herdsman we await approaches; his venerable age matches with this stranger's, and I recognise as servants of mine those who bring him. But you, if you have seen the man before, will know the man better than I.

CHORUS. Yes, I know the man who is coming; he was indeed in Laius' service, and is still the most trusted of the herdsmen.

OEDIPUS. I ask you first, Corinthian stranger, is this the man you mean?

MESSENGER. He is the very man.

OEDIPUS. Look at me, old man! Answer my questions. Were you once in Laius' service?

HERDSMAN. I was: not a bought slave, but reared up in the house.

OEDIPUS. What was your work — your manner of life?

HERDSMAN. For the best part of my life I have tended flocks.

OEDIPUS. Where, mainly?

HERDSMAN. Cythaeron or its neighbourhood.

OEDIPUS. Do you remember meeting with this man there?

HERDSMAN. What man do you mean?

OEDIPUS. This man. Did you ever meet him?

HERDSMAN. I cannot recall him to mind.

MESSENGER. No wonder in that, master; but I will bring back his memory. He and I lived side by side upon Cythaeron. I had but one flock and he had two. Three full half-years we lived there, from spring to autumn, and every winter I drove my flock to my own fold, while he drove his to the fold of Laius. Is that right? Was it not so?

HERDSMAN. True enough; though it was long ago.

MESSENGER. Come, tell me now — do you remember giving me a boy to rear as my own foster-son?

HERDSMAN. What are you saying? Why do you ask me that?

MESSENGER. Look at that man, my friend, he is the child you gave me.

HERDSMAN. A plague upon you! Cannot you hold your tongue?

OEDIPUS. Do not blame him, old man; your own words are more blameable.

HERDSMAN. And how have I offended, master?

OEDIPUS. In not telling of that boy he asks of.

HERDSMAN. He speaks from ignorance, and does not know what he is saying.

OEDIPUS. If you will not speak with a good grace you shall be made to speak.

HERDSMAN. Do not hurt me for the love of God, I am an old man.

OEDIPUS. Someone there, tie his hands behind his back.

HERDSMAN Alas! Wherefore? What more would you learn?

OEDIPUS. Did you give this man the child he speaks of?

HERDSMAN. I did: would I had died that day!

OEDIPUS. Well, you may come to that unless you speak the truth.

HERDSMAN. Much more am I lost if I speak it.

OEDIPUS. What! Would the fellow make more delay?

HERDSMAN. No, no. I said before that I gave it to him.

OEDIPUS. Where did you come by it? Your own child, or another?

HERDSMAN. It was not my own child — I had it from another.

OEDIPUS. From any of those here? From what house?

HERDSMAN. Do not ask any more, master; for the love of God do not ask.

OEDIPUS. You are lost if I have to question you again.

HERDSMAN. It was a child from the house of Laius.

OEDIPUS. A slave? Or one of his own race?

HERDSMAN. Alas! I am on the edge of dreadful words.

OEDIPUS. And I of hearing: yet hear I must.

HERDSMAN. It was said to have been his own child. But your lady within can tell you of these things best.

OEDIPUS. How? It was she who gave it to you?

HERDSMAN. Yes, king.

OEDIPUS. To what end?

HERDSMAN. That I should make away with it.

OEDIPUS. Her own child?

HERDSMAN. Yes: from fear of evil prophecies.

OEDIPUS. What prophecies?

HERDSMAN. That he should kill his father.

OEDIPUS. Why, then, did you give him up to this old man?

HERDSMAN. Through pity, master, believing that he would carry him to whatever land he had himself come from — but he saved him for dreadful misery; for if you are what this man says, you are the most miserable of all men.

OEDIPUS. O! O! All brought to pass! All truth! Now O Light, may I look my last upon you, having been found accursed in bloodshed, accursed in marriage, and in my coming into the world accursed!

(He rushes into the palace.)

CHORUS. What can the shadow-like generations of man attain
But build up a dazzling mockery of delight that under their touch dissolves again?
Oedipus seemed blessed, but there is no man blessed amongst men.

Oedipus overcame the woman-breasted Fate;
He seemed like a strong tower against Death and first among the fortunate;
He sat upon the ancient throne of Thebes and all men called him great.
But, looking for a marriage bed, he found the bed of his birth,
Tilled the field his father had tilled, cast seed into the same abounding earth;
Entered through the door that had sent him wailing forth.

Begetter and begot as one! How could that be hid?
What darkness cover up that marriage bed? Time watches, he is eagle-eyed,
And all the works of man are known and every soul is tried.

Would you had never come to Thebes, nor to this house,
Nor riddled with the woman-breasted Fate, beaten off death and succoured us,
That I had never raised this song, heartbroken Oedipus.

SECOND MESSENGER *(coming from the house)*. Friends and kinsmen of this house! What deeds must you look upon, what burden of sorrow bear, if true to race you still love the House of Labdicus. For not Istar nor Phasis could wash this house clean, so many misfortunes have been brought upon it, so many has it brought upon itself, and those misfortunes are always the worst that a man brings upon himself.

CHORUS. Great already are the misfortunes of this house, and you bring us a new tale.

SECOND MESSENGER. A short tale in the telling; Jocasta, our queen, is dead.

CHORUS. Alas, miserable woman, how did she die?

SECOND MESSENGER. By her own hand. It cannot be as terrible to you as to one that saw it with his eyes, yet so far as words can serve, you shall see it. When she had come into the vestibule, she ran half crazed towards her marriage bed, clutching at her hair with the fingers of both hands, and once within the chamber dashed the doors together behind her. Then called upon the name of Laius, long since dead, remembering that son who killed the father and upon the mother begot an accursed race. And wailed because of that marriage wherein she had borne a twofold race — husband by husband, children by her child. Then Oedipus with a shriek burst in and rushing here and there asked for a sword, asked where he would find the wife that was no wife but a mother who had borne his children and himself. Nobody answered him, we all stood dumb; but supernatural power helped him for, with a dreadful shriek, as though beckoned, he sprang at the double doors, drove them in, burst the bolts out of their sockets, and rushed into the room. There we saw the woman hanging in a swinging halter, and with a terrible cry he loosened the halter from her neck. When that unhappiest woman lay stretched upon the ground, we saw another dreadful sight. He dragged the golden brooches from her dress and lifting them struck them upon his eyeballs, crying out, 'You have looked enough upon those you ought never to have looked upon, failed long enough to know those that you should have known; henceforth you shall be dark.' He struck his eyes, not once, but many times, lifting his hands and speaking such or like words. The blood poured down and not with a few slow drops, but all at once over his beard in a dark shower as it were hail.

(The chorus *wails and he steps further on to the stage.)*

Such evils have come forth from the deeds of those two and fallen not on one alone but upon husband and wife. They inherited much happiness, much good fortune; but to-day, ruin, shame, death, and loud crying, all evils that can be counted up, all, all are theirs.

chorus. Is he any quieter?

second messenger. He cries for someone to unbar the gates and to show to all the men of Thebes his father's murderer, his mother's — the unholy word must not be spoken. It is his purpose to cast himself out of the land that he may not bring all this house under his curse. But he has not the strength to do it. He must be supported and led away. The curtain is parting; you are going to look upon a sight which even those who shudder must pity.

(Enter oedipus.*)*

oedipus. Woe, woe is me! Miserable, miserable that I am! Where am I? Where am I going? Where am I cast away? Who hears my words?

chorus. Cast away indeed, dreadful to the sight of the eye, dreadful to the ear.

oedipus. Ah, friend, the only friend left to me, friend still faithful to the blind man! I know that you are there blind though I am, I recognise your voice.

chorus. Where did you get the courage to put out your eyes? What unearthly power drove you to that?

OEDIPUS. Apollo, friends, Apollo, but it was my own hand alone, wretched that I am, that quenched these eyes.

CHORUS. You were better dead than blind.

OEDIPUS. No, it is better to be blind. What sight is there that could give me joy? How could I have looked into the face of my father when I came among the dead, aye, or on my miserable mother, since against them both I sinned such things that no halter can punish. And what to me this spectacle, town, statue, wall, and what to me this people, since I, thrice wretched, I noblest of Theban men, have doomed myself to banishment, doomed myself when I commanded all to thrust out the unclean thing.

CHORUS. It had indeed been better if that herdsman had never taken your feet out of the bonds or brought you back to life.

OEDIPUS. O three roads, O secret glen; O coppice and narrow way where three roads met; you that drank up the blood I spilt, the blood that was my own, my father's blood; remember what deeds I wrought for you to look upon, and then, when I had come hither, the new deeds that I wrought. O marriage bed that gave me birth and after that gave children to your child, creating an incestuous kindred of fathers, brothers, sons, wives, and mothers. Yes, all the shame and the uncleanness that I have wrought among men.

CHORUS. For all my pity I shudder and turn away.

OEDIPUS. Come near, condescend to lay your hands upon a wretched man; listen, do not fear. My plague can touch no man but me. Hide me somewhere out of this land for God's sake, or kill me, or throw me into the sea where you shall never look upon me more.

(*Enter* CREON *and attendants.*)

CHORUS. Here Creon comes at a fit moment, you can ask of him what you, will, help or counsel, for he is now in your place. He is king.

OEDIPUS. What can I say to him? What can I claim, having been altogether unjust to him?

CREON. I have not come in mockery, Oedipus, nor to reproach you. Lead him in to the house as quickly as you can. Do not let him display his misery before strangers.

OEDIPUS. I must obey, but first, since you have come in so noble a spirit, you will hear me.

CREON. Say what you will.

OEDIPUS. I know that you will give her that lies within such a tomb as befits your own blood, but there is something more, Creon. My sons are men and can take care of themselves, but my daughters, my two unhappy daughters, that have ever eaten at my own table and shared my food, watch over my daughters, Creon. If it is lawful, let me touch them with my hands. Grant it, prince, grant it, noble heart. I would believe could I touch them that I still saw them.

(ISMENE *and* ANTIGONE *are led in by attendants.*)

But do I hear them sobbing? Has Creon pitied me and sent my children, my darlings? Has he done this?

CREON. Yes, I ordered it, for I know how greatly you have always loved them.

OEDIPUS. Then may you be blessed, and may Heaven be kinder to you than it has been to me. My children, where are you? Come hither — hither — come to the hands of him whose mother was your mother; the hands that put out your father's eyes, eyes once as bright as your own; his, who understanding nothing, seeing nothing, became your father by her that bore him. I weep when I think of the bitter life that men will make you live, and the days that are to come. Into what company dare you go, to what festival, but that you shall return home from it not sharing in the joys, but bathed in tears. When you are old enough to be married, what man dare face the reproach that must cling to you and to your children? What misery is there lacking? Your father killed his father, he begat you at the spring of his own being, offspring of her that bore him. That is the taunt that would be cast upon you and on the man that you should marry. That man is not alive; my children, you must wither away in barrenness. Ah, son of Menoeceus, listen. Seeing that you are the only father now left to them, for we their parents are lost, both of us lost, do not let them wander in beggary — are they not your own kindred? — do not let them sink down into my misery. No, pity them, seeing them utterly wretched in helpless childhood if you do not protect them. Show me that you promise, generous man, by touching me with your hand. (CREON *touches him.*) My children, there is much advice that I would give you were you but old enough to understand, but all I can do now is bid you pray that you may live wherever you are let live, and that your life be happier than your father's.

CREON. Enough of tears. Pass into the house.

OEDIPUS. I will obey, though upon conditions.

CREON. Conditions?

OEDIPUS. Banish me from this country. I know that nothing can destroy me, for I wait some incredible fate; yet cast me upon Cythaeron, chosen by my father and my mother for my tomb.

CREON. Only the gods can say yes or no to that.

OEDIPUS. No, for I am hateful to the gods.

CREON. If that be so you will get your wish the quicker. They will banish that which they hate.

OEDIPUS. Are you certain of that?

CREON. I would not say it if I did not mean it.

OEDIPUS. Then it is time to lead me within.

CREON. Come, but let your children go.

OEDIPUS. No, do not take them from me.

CREON. Do not seek to be master; you won the mastery but could not keep it to the end.

(*He leads* OEDIPUS *into the palace, followed by* ISMENE, ANTIGONE, *and attendants.*)

CHORUS. Make way for Oedipus. All people said
'That is a fortunate man';
And now what storms are beating on his head?
Call no man fortunate that is not dead.
The dead are free from pain.

FOR DISCUSSION

1. One thinks of *Oedipus* as a tragedy — never as a murder mystery. That fact is significant, for the mystery element is very prominent, and we shall be interested at various points in seeing why *Oedipus* is not just a mystery.

The initial question is "Who killed Laius?" Motivation to find the answer to that question is very strong: the oracle says the whole city will continue to be plagued until the answer is found.

At the end of the play the mystery is solved: everyone knows the answer. However, for everyone to know the answer is not simply a problem in finding an eyewitness to identify the murderer. Who were the two surviving eyewitnesses? At the time the play begins, exactly what does each know, and what does each not know about the murder? What does the play suggest as the reason for the Theban shepherd to keep silent so many years. As a matter of fact, does the Theban shepherd ever tell who killed Laius?

2. In the course of the play a second and still more excruciatingly painful question is raised: has Oedipus fulfilled the prophecies against him to (a) murder his father and (b) marry his mother?

It is convenient to divide the play into parts according to who supplies pertinent information to Oedipus. The chief persons are, in order, (1) Creon, (2) Tiresias, (3) Jocasta, (4) the Corinthian messenger, (5) the Theban shepherd.

The play opens with the Chorus, representing the citizens of Thebes, informing Oedipus of the plague. What reasons do they give why he would (a) want to help them, and (b) possess special capabilities for helping them? He replies that he has already taken a step which may lead to a solution: he has sent Creon to the oracle to find out what to do.

Creon returns and gives the god's formula for relief: find the killer of Laius and drive him from the city.

3. Oedipus asks whether any witness survives and what information he may have given. What answer does he get? In view of what we learn later in the play, is that information accurate? Can you see any reason why the witness should have given out false testimony at the time?

4. Oedipus now voices a new motive why he will discover the murderer. What clue does that give to Oedipus' character?

After the Chorus has responded, Oedipus proclaims that everyone must reveal whatever he knows about the crime. What punishment does Oedipus proclaim against anyone who shall "keep silent from fear"?

5. In response to the proclamation the Chorus suggests that Tiresias the blind prophet be sent for and also mentions again the surviving eyewitness. Tiresias enters and Oedipus solicits him to use his occult powers.

Tiresias' response is negative: he asks to be excused. Put yourself in Tiresias' place, knowing what he knows, and determine why he behaves as he does. Put yourself in Oedipus' place and determine why he responds to Tiresias' first non-compliance as he does.

6. Tiresias challenges Oedipus to rage against him, and Oedipus accepts the challenge by accusing Tiresias of having been an accomplice to the deed. Tiresias retaliates by saying Oedipus performed the deed. Later in the play we discover this to be true: in fact, the murder mystery is solved at this point in the play. But do you see any evidence that anyone believes the truth here revealed by the prophet? Explain why it is not now believed. Does Tiresias seem to care that he is not understood and believed? Would Sophocles' audience have known who killed Laius? If so, then what interest would they have in the play? Does the reader ordinarily lose interest in a mere mystery when the mystery is solved?

7. Tiresias gives Oedipus a second piece of truth about the past and later elaborates upon the details. What is that second piece of truth? Is it believed, and if not, why not?

8. Oedipus now taunts the prophet by referring to (a) his professional competence, and (b) his physical infirmity. Count the number of times that light and dark, blindness and sight are mentioned by the two antagonists.

9. When Oedipus calls Tiresias mad, Tiresias drops a third piece of information. What is it?

10. Finally Tiresias departs, prophesying in dark words. In what respects does the full prophecy come true by the end of the play? Is the prophecy understood at this point by anyone? Who is present? Could Tiresias have spoken in clear words? Had he done so, how would the play have been changed? Is his use of dark words rather than clear words adequately motivated?

11. Now Creon enters. What factors have inspired Oedipus' theory that Creon is responsible for Tiresias' words? Is Oedipus rash in his accusation of Creon, knowing only what he knows? Is Oedipus rash in his pardon, knowing only what he knows?

12. Jocasta tries to find out what caused the quarrel between her brother and her husband. Soon she tells the story about the prophecy concerning the son of Laius. What purpose does she express for telling it?

13. What information does her story give Oedipus that he had not had before? What conclusion does he now draw tentatively? Is there good reason for not being completely convinced? What does he not yet even suspect?

14. In telling the story of his life in Corinth Oedipus gives the audience — and perhaps Jocasta and the Chorus — information not given before. What is the significance of that information at this point? Does it cause the audience to fear more than Oedipus fears, more than Jocasta fears?

15. Jocasta argues that even if Oedipus is the slayer of Laius, and hence subject to banishment, he may yet be consoled that he has not fulfilled the prophecies. In what sense would there be any consolation in that? Does she, at this point, fear something beyond his banishment? Does he? What reason do they have to fear more? What reasons do they have yet for hope against that fear?

16. While everyone waits for the Theban shepherd to arrive, a Corinthian messenger appears. Does he think he bears good news? Explain Jocasta's response to the news. Is Oedipus relieved by the news? What motivates the messenger to tell how Oedipus came to Corinth? What does the messenger not know about Oedipus?

Why does Oedipus exclaim when he learns that someone gave the infant to the Corinthian?

17. Shortly before this, Jocasta willingly sent for the Theban shepherd. Now she indicates reluctance to have him come; indeed she implores Oedipus to give up the search. What does she know that Oedipus does not know? Is there anything she does not know? Recount the various occasions on which she got her information.

18. Oedipus misinterprets her reluctance; how does he explain it? Is he being rash to continue the search? Is he thinking of his situation in its entirety?

19. When first asked whether he gave a child to the Corinthian shepherd, the Theban evades the answer, and a moment later deplores what the messenger says. How much does this Theban know? How long has he known it? Explain why this knowledge has not been revealed previously.

20. The Theban provides the second half of the story about Oedipus' origin. Recall what information he was originally sent for to provide; is that information ever given?

21. Oedipus now realizes his dreadful situation and rushes into the palace. Later we learn that he called first for a sword. What would he have done with it? Would the play be a better tragedy if he had found a sword at this time?

22. Contrast the next scene between Oedipus and Creon and the previous scene between them. What purpose, if any, does this scene serve?

23. What purpose is served by the scene between Oedipus and his two daughters?

THE POEM

P opular Ballads

Sir Patrick Spens

The king sits in Dunfermline toune,
    Drinking the blude-red wine:
"O whar will I get guid sailor,
    To sail this schip of mine?"

Up and spak an eldern knicht,
    Sat at the kings richt kne:
"Sir Patrick Spens is the best sailor
    That sails upon the se."

The king has written a braid letter,[1]
    And signed it wi his hand,
And sent it to Sir Patrick Spens,
    Was walking on the sand.

The first line that Sir Patrick red,
    A loud lauch[2] lauched he;
The next line that Sir Patrick red,
    The teir blinded his ee[3]

[1] letter written on a broad sheet.
[2] laugh.
[3] eye.

"O wha is this has don this deid,
   This ill deid don to me,
To send me out this time o' the yeir,
   To sail upon the se!

"Mak hast, mak haste, my mirry men all,
   Our guid schip sails the morne":
"O say na sae, my master deir,
   For I feir a deadlie storme.

"Late late yestreen I saw the new moone,
   Wi the auld moone in hir arme,[4]
And I feir, I feir, my deir master,
   That we will cum to harme."

O our Scots nobles wer richt laith[5]
   To weet their cork-heild schoone;[6]
Bot lang owre[7] a' the play wer playd,
   Thair hats they swam aboone.[8]

O lang, lang may their ladies sit,
   Wi thair fans into their hand,
Or eir they se Sir Patrick Spens
   Cum sailing to the land.

O lang, lang may the ladies stand,
   Wi thair gold kems[9] in their hair,
Waiting for thair ain deir lords,
   For they'll see thame na mair.

Haf owre,[10] haf owre to Aberdour,
   It's fiftie fadom deip,
And thair lies guid Sir Patrick Spens,
   Wi the Scots lords at his feit.

---

[4] The bright crescent is the new moon; the old moon in her arm is the barely visible remainder of the disc. It was thought to be a bad omen when the new moon rose late at night.

[5] loath.

[6] cork-heeled shoes.

[7] before.

[8] Their hats swam above their bodies.

[9] combs.

[10] half way.

The Three Ravens

There were three ravens sat on a tree,
   Downe a downe, hay down, hay downe.
There were three ravens sat on a tree,
   With a downe
There were three ravens sat on a tree,
They were as blacke as they might be.
   With a downe derrie, derrie, derrie, downe, downe.

The one of them said to his mate,
"Where shall we our breakefast take?"

"Downe in yonder greene field,
There lies a knight slain under his shield.

"His hounds they lie downe at his feete,
So well they can their master keepe.

"His haukes they flie so eagerly,
There's no fowle dare him come nie."

Downe there comes a fallow doe,
As great with yong as she might goe.

She lift up his bloudy hed,
And kist his wounds that were so red.

She got him up upon her backe,
And carried him to earthen lake.[1]

She buried him before the prime,
She was dead herself ere even-song time.

God send every gentleman
Such haukes, such hounds, and such a leman.[2]

[1] pit.
[2] sweetheart.

Poetry must be as new as foam and as old as the rock.

                                RALPH WALDO EMERSON

The Twa Corbies

As I was walking all alane,
I heard twa corbies[1] making a mane;[2]
The tane[3] unto the t'other say,
"Where sall we gang and dine to-day?"

"In behint yon auld fail dyke,[4]
I wot there lies a new slain knight;
And naebody kens[5] that he lies there,
But his hawk, his hound, and lady fair.

"His hound is to the hunting gane,
His hawk to fetch the wild-fowl hame,
His lady's ta'en another mate,
So we may mak our dinner sweet.

"Ye'll sit on his white hause-bane,[6]
And I'll pike out his bonny blue een;[7]
Wi' ae lock o' his gowden hair
We'll theek[8] our nest when it grows bare.

"Mony a one for him makes mane,
But nane sall ken where he is gane;
O'er his white banes, when they are bare,
The wind sall blaw for evermair."

[1] carrion crows.
[2] literally, a moan; more freely, any talk.
[3] the one.
[4] turf wall.
[5] knows.
[6] neck-bone.
[7] eyes.
[8] thatch.

FOR DISCUSSION

THE POPULAR BALLADS During the Middle Ages, ballads such as these were passed along orally from generation to generation. Especially talented individuals may have composed the first versions and may have contributed to later alterations, but these ballads survived in their present forms only because of their significance to the masses of ordinary people. Illiterate and semi-literate people love stories, are deeply moved by them, and have tenacious memories. But in countless retellings, details drop out and only the stark outlines remain. Short lines, simple stanza forms, and often a refrain suggest that ballads were often chanted or sung.

"Sir Patrick Spens" The narratives of the ballads are boldly told: they give the main external events, leaving the audience to fill in the intervening material and the emotional significance. Thus, in one stanza Spens deplores the orders to make the voyage, but in the next stanza he is ordering his men to make haste. Again, the Scottish nobles hated even to get their imported shoes wet, but before the play was played out their hats swam above their heads.

Note the significant details: What was the king doing when he decided to commission the voyage? What was Spens doing when he received the letter? What was his first response to the letter? His second? What picture do you get of the noble ladies?

"The Three Ravens" and "The Twa Corbies" These two companion pieces had a special significance to the medieval audience, for all medieval society was built on the ideal of personal loyalty to one's immediate superior. With respect to that ideal, what is the significance of each of the two contrasting pieces? Was the "leman" in "The Three Ravens" a doe, or a woman, or a woman like a doe?

Is "The Twa Corbies" a portrait of a bad knight or just an unfortunate knight? Why do you suppose both poems have survived? What effect is enhanced by putting the stories in the mouths of scavenging birds?

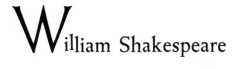

William Shakespeare

Sonnet 18

Shall I compare thee to a summer's day?
Thou art more lovely and more temperate:
Rough winds do shake the darling buds of May,
And summer's lease hath all too short a date:[1]
Sometimes too hot the eye of heaven shines,
And often is his gold complexion dimmed;
And every fair from fair sometime declines,[2]
By chance, or nature's changing course untrimmed;[3]
But thy eternal summer shall not fade,
Nor lose possession of that fair thou owest[4]
Nor shall Death brag thou wander'st in his shade,
When in eternal lines to time thou growest:
   So long as men can breathe or eyes can see,
   So long lives this,[5] and this gives life to thee.

[1] does not last long enough.
[2] Every beautiful thing sometimes falls short of beauty.
[3] thrown off balance; a ship is trimmed by arranging its ballast.
[4] ownest.
[5] this sonnet.

Sonnet 29

When, in disgrace with fortune and men's eyes,
I all alone beweep my outcast state,
And trouble deaf heaven with my bootless cries,
And look upon myself, and curse my fate,
Wishing me like to one more rich in hope,
Featured like him, like him with friends possessed,
Desiring this man's art and that man's scope,
With what I most enjoy contented least;
Yet in these thoughts myself almost despising,
Haply I think on thee — and then my state,
Like to the lark at break of day arising
From sullen earth, sings hymns at heaven's gate;
   For thy sweet love remembered such wealth brings
   That then I scorn to change my state with kings.

Sonnet 73

That time of year thou mayst in me behold
When yellow leaves, or none, or few, do hang
Upon those boughs which shake against the cold,
Bare ruined choirs, where late the sweet birds sang.
In me thou see'st the twilight of such day
As after sunset fadeth in the west,
Which by and by black night doth take away,
Death's second self, that seals up all in rest.
In me thou see'st the glowing of such fire
That on the ashes of his youth doth lie,
As the death-bed whereon it must expire,
Consumed with that which it was nourished by.
   This thou perceivest, which makes thy love more strong,
   To love that well which thou must leave ere long.

FOR DISCUSSION

WILLIAM SHAKESPEARE (1564-1616)   Poetry is harder to read than prose, partly because the word order of poetry often is radically different from the word order of prose, and partly also because things which are explained at length in prose are often only implied in poetry. But poetry also has a musicality absent from prose — rhythm, repetition of sounds, and often rhyme. Shakespeare's sonnets are difficult because of the compression of language, but they nevertheless communicate an immediate pleasure because they are melodious in sound and rhythm as well as rich in imagery.

Sonnet 18 The loved one is said to be more lovely and more temperate than a summer's day. In what respects is summer less lovely and temperate? At what point does the poet cease to describe summer?

Sonnet 29 The poet says that when he is dissatisfied with his accomplishments, and dissatisfied with his dissatisfaction, he then thinks joyously of his love and is content. How does his list of complaints differ from those that would probably be listed by a man of the twentieth century?

Sonnet 73 "Choirs" are the places for the singers, not the singers themselves. To check your understanding of the language, answer these questions: What other words in the poem refer to the same thing as do "bare ruined choirs"? What is the antecedent of "which" in the seventh line? What words mean the same as "Death's second self"? What words mean the same as "the death-bed"? What is "it" in the eleventh line? What is consumed? In the last line is it life or the poet that must be left ere long?

Note the similarity in the beginnings of the first three sentences, and the "such . . . as" or "such . . . that" constructions in the second and third sentences What makes this poem difficult? Are the words strange?

John Donne

Song

Go and catch a falling star,
    Get with child a mandrake[1] root,
Tell me where all past years are,
    Or who cleft the Devil's foot;
Teach me to hear mermaids singing,
Or to keep off envy's stinging,
            And find
            What wind
Serves to advance an honest mind.

If thou be'st born to strange sights,
    Things invisible to see,
Ride ten thousand days and nights
    Till age snow white hairs on thee;
Thou, when thou return'st wilt tell me
All strange wonders that befell thee,
            And swear
            No where
Lives a woman true and fair.

---

[1] an herb with a forked rib, supposed to resemble a human being and, if eaten, to promote conception.

If thou find'st one let me know,
 Such a pilgrimage were sweet;
Yet do not, I would not go,
 Though at next door we might meet;
Though she were true when you met her,
And last till you write your letter,
 Yet she
 Will be
False, ere I come, to two or three.

FOR DISCUSSION

JOHN DONNE (1572-1631) The first stanza tells the reader to do some seven things. What do all seven tasks have in common? What does this list of tasks suggest about the mood of the writer?

The poem, like a joke, depends for its effect on the final punch line. How does the verse form facilitate the surprise of the last line? Where does each stanza move quickly, and where slowly?

Sir John Suckling

Why So Pale and Wan?

Why so pale and wan, fond lover?
 Prithee, why so pale?
Will, when looking well can't move her,
 Looking ill prevail?
 Prithee, why so pale?

Why so dull and mute, young sinner?
 Prithee, why so mute?
Will, when speaking well can't win her,
 Saying nothing do't?
 Prithee, why so mute?

Quit, quit for shame! This will not move
 This cannot take her.
If of herself she will not love,
 Nothing can make her:
 The devil take her!

Sir John Suckling (1609-1642)   The conventional lover of the Renaissance was supposed to sigh, grow pale, and languish for an extended period before daring to declare his love. Here the poet makes light of such a lover.

Like the preceding poem by Donne, this too has a punch line. Compare the level of diction in the punch line and in the previous lines. Compare also the speed of movement of the last line and the previous lines. Do you find any early preparation for this kind of sudden last line?

Robert Herrick

To the Virgins, to Make Much of Time

Gather ye rosebuds while ye may,
    Old Time is still a-flying;
And this same flower that smiles to-day,
    To-morrow will be dying.

The glorious lamp of heaven, the sun,
    The higher he's a-getting,
The sooner will his race be run,
    And nearer he's to setting.

That age is best which is the first,
    When youth and blood are warmer;
But being spent, the worse, and worst
    Times, still succeed the former.

Then be not coy, but use your time,
    And while ye may, go marry;
For, having lost but once your prime,
    You may forever tarry.

Robert Herrick (1591-1674)   Picking up a theme from the Latin poets, the seventeenth-century lyricists repeatedly urged the reader to seize today since tomorrow we die. Here that theme is expressed with unequaled lightness, delicacy, and charm.

Who seems to be speaking to the virgins, urging them to marry while they can?

Andrew Marvell

To His Coy Mistress

Had we but world enough, and time,
This coyness, Lady, were no crime.
We would sit down, and think which way
To walk, and pass our long love's day.
Thou by the Indian Ganges' side
Shouldst rubies find; I by the tide
Of Humber would complain. I would
Love you ten years before the Flood,
And you should, if you please, refuse
Till the conversion of the Jews.
My vegetable love should grow
Vaster than empires and more slow;
An hundred years should go to praise
Thine eyes, and on thy forehead gaze;
Two hundred to adore each breast,
But thirty thousand to the rest;
An age at least to every part,
And the last age should show your heart.
For, Lady, you deserve this state,
Nor would I love at lower rate.

But at my back I always hear
Time's wingèd chariot hurrying near;
And yonder all before us lie
Deserts of vast eternity.
Thy beauty shall no more be found,
Nor, in thy marble vault, shall sound
My echoing song; then worms shall try
That long-preserved virginity,
And your quaint honor turn to dust,
And into ashes all my lust:
The grave's a fine and private place,
But none, I think, do there embrace.

Now therefore, while the youthful hue
Sits on thy skin like morning dew,
And while thy willing soul transpires
At every pore with instant fires,
Now let us sport us while we may,
And now, like amorous birds of prey,

Rather at once our time devour
Than languish in his slow-chapped power.
Let us roll all our strength and all
Our sweetness up into one ball,
And tear our pleasures with rough strife
Thorough the iron gates of life;
Thus, though we cannot make our sun
Stand still, yet we will make him run.

FOR DISCUSSION

ANDREW MARVELL (1621-1678)   In sharp contrast to the previous poem, by
Herrick, Marvell here expresses the *carpe diem* ("seize the day") theme with
terrible power and a cosmic scope.

Compare the progression of ideas in Herrick's poem and this one.   Who is the
speaker in this poem?

Note the exaggerated richness and leisure suggested in the first twenty lines.
Why does the poet call his love "vegetable"?   What is the meaning of "would" in
the twentieth line ("Nor would I love at lower rate.")?

In what respect does the second verse paragraph contrast with the first?   What
figure in Greek mythology is suggested by "Time's wingèd chariot"?   Why is the
chariot behind instead of above the speaker?   Why is eternity called a "desert"?

Note that the tomb is treated as a shocking alternative to the lover's bower.

In the last lines, why does the poet suggest that the lovers be like birds of
prey rather than, for instance, song birds?   What is meant by "slow-chapped"?
Who is slow-chapped?

William Blake

London

I wander through each chartered street,
Near where the chartered Thames does flow,
And mark in every face I meet
Marks of weakness, marks of woe.

In every cry of every man,
In every infant's cry of fear,
In every voice, in every ban,
The mind-forged manacles I hear:

How the chimney-sweeper's cry
Every blackening church appalls,
And the hapless soldier's sigh
Runs in blood down palace walls.

But most, through midnight streets I hear
How the youthful harlot's curse
Blasts the new-born infant's tear,
And blights with plagues the marriage hearse.

The Clod and the Pebble

"Love seeketh not itself to please,
    Nor for itself hath any care,
But for another gives its ease,
    And builds a Heaven in Hell's despair."

So sang a little Clod of Clay,
    Trodden with the cattle's feet,
But a Pebble of the brook
    Warbled out these metres meet:

"Love seeketh only Self to please,
    To bind another to Its delight,
Joys in another's loss of ease,
    And builds a Hell in Heaven's despite."

Finally, most of us (imagist poets) believe that concentration is the very essence of poetry.   AMY LOWELL

The Little Black Boy

My mother bore me in the southern wild,
    And I am black, but O my soul is white!
White as an angel is the English child,
    But I am black, as if bereaved of light.

My mother taught me underneath a tree,
    And, sitting down before the heat of day,
She took me on her lap and kissèd me,
    And, pointing to the east, began to say:

"Look on the rising sun; — there God does live,
   And gives his light, and gives his heat away;
And flowers and trees and beasts and men receive
   Comfort in morning, joy in the noon-day.

"And we are put on earth a little space,
   That we may learn to bear the beams of love;
And these black bodies and this sunburnt face
   Is but a cloud, and like a shady grove.

"For when our souls have learned the heat to bear,
   The cloud will vanish, we shall hear his voice,
Saying: 'Come out from the grove, my love and care,
   And round my golden tent like lambs rejoice.' "

Thus did my mother say, and kissèd me;
   And thus I say to little English boy,
When I from black, and he from white cloud free,
   And round the tent of God like lambs we joy,

I'll shade him from the heat, till he can bear
   To lean in joy upon our father's knee;
And then I'll stand and stroke his silver hair,
   And be like him, and he will then love me.

FOR DISCUSSION

WILLIAM BLAKE (1757-1827) "London" Note the use of "mark" as verb and as noun in lines 3 and 4; does the meaning of the noun affect the meaning of the verb? Note more repetition in the second stanza. What would "mind-forged manacles" be? In the third stanza, does "appall" carry any hidden color reference? Are soldiers represented as defending the good of all classes? What line of reasoning would place the youthful harlot as the enemy of the new-born infant? What is unusual about the last two words in the poem?

What does Blake seem to hold responsible for the plight of these Londoners?

"The Clod and the Pebble" Make a point by point contrast between the first and last stanzas. Is one opinion more appropriate than the other to each speaker?

"The Little Black Boy" Here Blake treats with fascinating insight the psychological complexity of the black boy's attitude toward himself as a member of a white-dominated society.

In the first stanza the black boy acquiesces in the view that blackness is inferior to whiteness; at least he calls the English boy an angel by virtue of his whiteness, and acknowledges that his own blackness signifies his deprivation from the light. Even while he acquiesces, however, he protects his own self-esteem against too deep an injury: he avers that his blackness is only skin-deep; his soul is white.

512 · *The Poem*

The middle of the poem constitutes the theological promise his mother has told him. In heaven things are different. There it is better protection to have a black body than a white one.

Carried away with this happy vision, the black boy resolves that, when in heaven he and the English boy joy together around the tent of God, "I'll shade him from the heat," before "our" father's knee, and for this generous protection I'll "be like him, and he will then love me."

Robert Burns

A Red, Red Rose

O, my luve is like a red, red rose,
    That's newly sprung in June.
O, my luve is like the melodie,
    That's sweetly played in tune.

As fair art thou, my bonnie lass,
    So deep in luve am I,
And I will luve thee still, my dear,
    Till a' the seas gang dry.

Till a' the seas gang dry, my dear,
    And the rocks melt wi' the sun!
And I will luve thee still, my dear,
    While the sands o' life shall run.

And fare thee weel, my only luve,
    And fare thee weel a while!
And I will come again, my luve,
    Tho' it were ten thousand mile!

FOR DISCUSSION

ROBERT BURNS (1759-1796) This is one of the most greatly admired love lyrics in the language. Can you account for its popularity? Consider such matters as ease or difficulty of understanding, sound, imagery, rhyme, and stanza form. Why do you think so many of Burns's poems have been set to music?

William Wordsworth

Lines Written in Early Spring

I heard a thousand blended notes
While in a grove I sate reclined,
In that sweet mood when pleasant thoughts
Bring sad thoughts to the mind.

To her fair works did Nature link
The human soul that through me ran;
And much it grieved my heart to think
What Man has made of Man.

Through primrose tufts, in that sweet bower,
The periwinkle trailed its wreaths;
And 'tis my faith that every flower
Enjoys the air it breathes.

The birds around me hopped and played,
Their thoughts I cannot measure, —
But the least motion which they made,
It seemed a thrill of pleasure.

The budding twigs spread out their fan
To catch the breezy air;
And I must think, do all I can,
That there was pleasure there.

If this belief from heaven be sent,
If such be Nature's holy plan,
Have I not reason to lament
What Man has made of Man?

A prize poem is like a prize sheep . . . Prize sheep are good for nothing but to make tallow candles, and prize poems are good for nothing but to light them.

T. B. MACAULAY

514 · *The Poem*

My Heart Leaps Up

My heart leaps up when I behold
   A rainbow in the sky:
So was it when my life began,
So is it now I am a man,
So be it when I shall grow old,
   Or let me die!
The Child is father of the Man:
And I could wish my days to be
Bound each to each by natural piety.

The World Is Too Much with Us

The world is too much with us; late and soon,
Getting and spending, we lay waste our powers:
Little we see in Nature that is ours;
We have given our hearts away, a sordid boon!
The Sea that bares her bosom to the moon;
The winds that will be howling at all hours
And are up-gathered now like sleeping flowers;
For this, for everything, we are out of tune;
It moves us not. — Great God! I'd rather be
A Pagan suckled in a creed outworn;
So might I, standing on this pleasant lea,
Have glimpses that would make me less forlorn;
Have sight of Proteus rising from the sea;
Or hear old Triton blow his wreathèd horn.

FOR DISCUSSION

WILLIAM WORDSWORTH (1770-1850) "Lines Written in Early Spring" As the poet describes the flowers, the birds, and the budding twigs, what do they have in common with each other? with him? What is it that man has made of man, and how does it fit in with Wordsworth's idea of nature?

"My Heart Leaps Up" In what sense is the child father of the man? What could the poet mean by "natural piety"?

"The World Is Too Much with Us" The opening words are explained in the first four lines. Would you say that "the world" in the first line means the world of Nature? To what does "a sordid boon" refer?

What words in the first four lines are explained by the second four lines? What virtues does the poet find in a pagan creed? Can the poet embrace paganism? Why?

Looking at the poem as a whole, tell what way of life is contrasted with what other way.

Do you find evidence of "natural piety" in this poem?

John Keats

La Belle Dame Sans Merci

"Ah, what can ail thee, Knight-at-arms,
    Alone and palely loitering?
The sedge has withered from the lake,
    And no birds sing.

"Ah, what can ail thee, Knight-at-arms,
    So haggard and so woe-begone?
The squirrel's granary is full,
    And the harvest's done.

"I see a lily on thy brow
    With anguish moist and fever-dew,
And on thy cheeks a fading rose
    Fast withereth too."

"I met a lady in the meads,
    Full beautiful — a faery's child;
Her hair was long, her foot was light,
    And her eyes were wild.

"I made a garland for her head,
    And bracelets too, and fragrant zone;
She looked at me as she did love,
    And made sweet moan.

"I set her on my pacing steed,
    And nothing else saw all day long;
For sidelong would she bend, and sing
    A faery's song.

"She found me roots of relish sweet,
   And honey wild and manna-dew;
And sure in language strange she said,
   'I love thee true.'

"She took me to her elfin grot,
   And there she gazed and sighed full sore,
And there I shut her wild, wild eyes —
   With kisses four.

"And there she lullèd me asleep,
   And there I dreamed — ah! woe betide! —
The latest dream I ever dreamed
   On the cold hill's side.

"I saw pale kings, and princes too,
   Pale warriors, death-pale were they all:
They cried — 'La belle Dame sans Merci
   Hath thee in thrall!'

"I saw their starved lips in the gloam
   With horrid warning gapèd wide,
And I awoke, and found me here
   On the cold hill side.

"And this is why I sojourn here
   Alone and palely loitering,
Though the sedge is withered from the lake,
   And no birds sing."

FOR DISCUSSION

JOHN KEATS (1795-1821) An ancient theme in folklore and popular ballads concerns the supernatural (often fairy) damsel who casts a spell upon the young man, and later deserts him. A knight thus deserted is the subject of this delicate and musical ballad. At the time Keats wrote "La Belle Dame Sans Merci" (The beautiful lady without pity), he was deeply in love with a girl who lacked his depth and intensity. How does knowing the above facts affect your reading of the poem?

Rearrange the words in lines 9 and 10 so that they follow the word order usual to prose.

Later when Keats revised the poem he made several changes, of which the most striking occurred in lines 31 and 32:

      And there I shut her wild sad eyes
      So kiss'd to sleep.

Is the revision an improvement?

Percy Bysshe Shelley

Ode to the West Wind

1

O wild West Wind, thou breath of Autumn's being,
Thou, from whose unseen presence the leaves dead
Are driven, like ghosts from an enchanter fleeing,

Yellow, and black, and pale, and hectic red,
Pestilence-stricken multitudes! O thou
Who chariotest to their dark wintry bed

The wingèd seeds, where they lie cold and low,
Each like a corpse within its grave, until
Thine azure sister of the Spring shall blow

Her clarion o'er the dreaming earth, and fill
(Driving sweet buds like flocks to feed in air)
With living hues and odors plain and hill:

Wild Spirit, which art moving everywhere;
Destroyer and Preserver; hear, oh hear!

2

Thou on whose stream, 'mid the steep sky's commotion,
Loose clouds like earth's decaying leaves are shed,
Shook from the tangled boughs of heaven and ocean,

Angels of rain and lightning! there are spread
On the blue surface of thine airy surge,
Like the bright hair uplifted from the head

Of some fierce Mænad[1] even from the dim verge
Of the horizon to the zenith's height,
The locks of the approaching storm. Thou dirge

Of the dying year, to which this closing night
Will be the dome of a vast sepulchre,
Vaulted with all thy congregated might

[1] a priestess or female worshipper of Bacchus, god of wine.

Of vapors, from whose solid atmosphere
Black rain, and fire, and hail, will burst: Oh hear!

3

Thou who didst waken from his summer-dreams
The blue Mediterranean, where he lay,
Lulled by the coil of his crystalline streams,

Beside a pumice isle in Baiae's[2] bay,
And saw in sleep old palaces and towers
Quivering within the wave's intenser day,

All overgrown with azure moss, and flowers
So sweet, the sense faints picturing them! Thou
For whose path the Atlantic's level powers

Cleave themselves into chasms, while far below
The sea-blooms and the oozy woods which wear
The sapless foliage of the ocean know

Thy voice, and suddenly grow gray with fear
And tremble and despoil themselves: Oh hear!

4

If I were a dead leaf thou mightest bear;
If I were a swift cloud to fly with thee;
A wave to pant beneath thy power, and share

The impulse of thy strength, only less free
Than Thou, O uncontrollable! If even
I were as in my boyhood, and could be

The comrade of thy wanderings over heaven,
As then, when to outstrip thy skyey speed
Scarce seemed a vision; I would ne'er have striven

As thus with thee in prayer in my sore need.
Oh! lift me as a wave, a leaf, a cloud!
I fall upon the thorns of life! I bleed!

A heavy weight of hours has chained and bowed
One too like thee — tameless, and swift, and proud.

[2] a seaport near Naples.

5

Make me thy lyre, ev'n as the forest is:
What if my leaves are falling like its own!
The tumult of thy mighty harmonies

Will take from both a deep, autumnal tone,
Sweet though in sadness. Be thou, Spirit fierce,
My spirit! Be thou me, impetuous one!

Drive my dead thoughts over the universe,
Like withered leaves, to quicken a new birth!
And, by the incantation of this verse,

Scatter, as from an unextinguished hearth
Ashes and sparks, my words among mankind!
Be through my lips to unawakened earth

The trumpet of a prophecy! O wind,
If Winter comes, can Spring be far behind?

Song to the Men of England

Men of England, wherefore plough
For the lords who lay ye low?
Wherefore weave with toil and care
The rich robes your tyrants wear?

Wherefore feed, and clothe, and save,
From the cradle to the grave,
Those ungrateful drones who would
Drain your sweat — nay, drink your blood?

Wherefore, bees of England, forge
Many a weapon, chain, and scourge,
That these stingless drones may spoil
The forced produce of your toil?

Have ye leisure, comfort, calm,
Shelter, food, love's gentle balm?
Or what is it ye buy so dear
With your pain and with your fear?

The seed ye sow, another reaps;
The wealth ye find, another keeps;
The robes ye weave, another wears;
The arms ye forge, another bears.

Sow seed — but let no tyrant reap;
Find wealth — let no impostor heap;
Weave robes — let not the idle wear;
Forge arms — in your defense to bear.

Shrink to your cellars, holes, and cells;
In halls ye deck another dwells.
Why shake the chains ye wrought? Ye see
The steel ye tempered glance on ye.

With plough and spade, and hoe and loom,
Trace your grave, and build your tomb,
And weave your winding-sheet, till fair
England be your sepulchre.

FOR DISCUSSION

PERCY BYSSHE SHELLEY (1792-1822) "Ode to the West Wind" This poem is sometimes described as an incantation (literally, the chanting of a magic spell). What is the poet asking of the West Wind?

This superbly melodious lyric falls into two main parts. The earlier stanzas describe the progress of the wind across the world; the later stanzas establish a relation between the poet and the wind. Where does the division come between the two main parts? What different subjects are treated in the earlier stanzas?

In the later stanzas, what various relationships are established between the wind and the poet? What lines seem to express the theme of the poem? Describe the rhyme scheme.

"Song to the Men of England" Though Shelley is most widely known for his lyrics, he also was deeply concerned about social issues, as in this poem. He was strongly influenced by the reformer, William Godwin, whose writings were studied by later anarchists.

At Manchester on August 16, 1819, a crowd assembled intending to petition Parliament for a redress of grievances regarding taxation and representation. The crowd was fired upon by soldiers. The event became known as the Manchester Massacre, and was the occasion for this poem.

Note the relation of the laboring class to the governing class as it appears in the poem. Has this doctrine been accepted in any modern government?

Alfred, Lord Tennyson

Ulysses

It little profits that an idle king,
By this still hearth, among these barren crags,
Matched with an aged wife, I mete and dole
Unequal laws unto a savage race,
That hoard, and sleep, and feed, and know not me.
I cannot rest from travel. I will drink
Life to the lees. All times I have enjoyed
Greatly, have suffered greatly, both with those
That loved me, and alone; on shore, and when
Through scudding drifts the rainy Hyades
Vexed the dim sea. I am become a name;
For always roaming with a hungry heart
Much have I seen and known; cities of men,
And manners, climates, councils, governments,
Myself not least, but honored of them all;
And drunk delight of battle with my peers,
Far on the ringing plains of windy Troy.
I am a part of all that I have met.
Yet all experience is an arch wherethrough
Gleams that untraveled world, whose margin fades
Forever and forever when I move.
How dull it is to pause, to make an end,
To rust unburnished, not to shine in use!
As though to breathe were life. Life piled on life
Were all too little, and of one to me
Little remains. But every hour is saved
From that eternal silence, something more,
A bringer of new things; and vile it were
For some three suns to store and hoard myself,
And this gray spirit yearning in desire
To follow knowledge like a sinking star,
Beyond the utmost bound of human thought.
    This is my son, mine own Telemachus,
To whom I leave the scepter and the isle —
Well-loved of me, discerning to fulfill
This labor, by slow prudence to make mild
A rugged people, and through soft degrees

Subdue them to the useful and the good.
Most blameless is he, centered in the sphere
Of common duties, decent not to fail
In offices of tenderness, and pay
Meet adoration to my household gods,
When I am gone. He works his work, I mine.
   There lies the port; the vessel puffs her sail;
There gloom the dark broad seas. My mariners,
Souls that have toiled, and wrought, and thought with me —
That ever with a frolic welcome took
The thunder and the sunshine, and opposed
Free hearts, free foreheads — you and I are old;
Old age hath yet his honor and his toil;
Death closes all. But something ere the end,
Some work of noble note, may yet be done,
Not unbecoming men that strove with gods.
The lights begin to twinkle from the rocks;
The long day wanes; the slow moon climbs; the deep
Moans round with many voices. Come, my friends,
'Tis not too late to seek a newer world.
Push off, and sitting well in order smite
The sounding furrows; for my purpose holds
To sail beyond the sunset, and the baths
Of all the western stars, until I die.
It may be that the gulfs will wash us down
It may be we shall touch the Happy Isles,
And see the great Achilles, whom we knew.
Though much is taken, much abides; and though
We are not now that strength which in old days
Moved earth and heaven, that which we are, we are;
One equal temper of heroic hearts,
Made weak by time and fate, but strong in will
To strive, to seek, to find, and not to yield.

FOR DISCUSSION

ALFRED, LORD TENNYSON (1809-1892) Homer's *Odyssey* ends with the return of the hero to his native land, which he repossesses. However, in Canto 26 of the *Inferno*, Dante has the hero leave home again to sail past the Strait of Gibraltar, which the ancients regarded as the end of the world. Following the hint from Dante, Tennyson supposes that after high adventures in the Trojan war and years of voyaging afterward, Ulysses could never be content to settle down with his long-suffering wife Penelope, his ignorant tribesmen, and his blameless but unexciting son Telemachus.

Does Ulysses seem to patronize his wife, his son, and his people as if he were trying to justify deserting them? What arguments can you suggest for his *not* leaving home? Is Ulysses' quest anything more than adventurousness?

R obert Browning

My Last Duchess

That's my last Duchess painted on the wall,
Looking as if she were alive. I call
That piece a wonder, now: Frà Pandolf's hand
Worked busily a day, and there she stands.
Will't please you sit and look at her? I said
"Frà Pandolf" by design, for never read
Strangers like you that pictured countenance,
The depth and passion of its earnest glance,
But to myself they turned (since none puts by
The curtain I have drawn for you, but I)
And seemed as they would ask me, if they durst,
How such a glance came there; so, not the first
Are you to turn and ask thus. Sir, 'twas not
Her husband's presence only, called that spot
Of joy into the Duchess' cheek: perhaps
Frà Pandolf chanced to say, "Her mantle laps
Over my lady's wrist too much," or "Paint
Must never hope to reproduce the faint
Half-flush that dies along her throat:" such stuff
Was courtesy, she thought, and cause enough
For calling up that spot of joy. She had
A heart — how shall I say? — too soon made glad,
Too easily impressed: she liked whate'er
She looked on, and her looks went everywhere.
Sir, 'twas all one! My favor at her breast,
The dropping of the daylight in the West,
The bough of cherries some officious fool
Broke in the orchard for her, the white mule
She rode with round the terrace — all and each
Would draw from her alike the approving speech,
Or blush, at least. She thanked men, — good! but thanked
Somehow — I know not how — as if she ranked
My gift of a nine-hundred-years-old name
With anybody's gift. Who'd stoop to blame
This sort of trifling? Even had you skill
In speech — (which I have not) — to make your will

Quite clear to such an one, and say, "Just this
Or that in you disgusts me; here you miss,
Or there exceed the mark" — and if she let
Herself be lessoned so, nor plainly set
Her wits to yours, forsooth, and made excuse,
— E'en then would be some stooping, and I choose
Never to stoop. Oh sir, she smiled, no doubt,
Whene'er I passed her; but who passed without
Much the same smile? This grew; I gave commands;
Then all smiles stopped together. There she stands
As if alive. Will't please you rise? We'll meet
The company below, then. I repeat,
The Count your master's known munificence
Is ample warrant that no just pretence
Of mine for dowry will be disallowed;
Though his fair daughter's self, as I avowed
At starting, is my object. Nay, we'll go
Together down, sir. Notice Neptune, though,
Taming a sea-horse, thought a rarity,
Which Claus of Innsbruck cast in bronze for me!

FOR DISCUSSION

ROBERT BROWNING (1812-1889)   The speaker, the Duke of Ferrara, is negotiating with some emissary for the hand of a Count's daughter. He reveals himself
as he talks about "my last duchess." Concerning line 26, the author explained
"the commands were that she should be put to death, or he might have had her
shut up in a convent."

If you have studied the short stories illustrating self-revelation of character
(pages 225-245) you are aware that a person trying to give one impression often
reveals himself quite unintentionally. Here is a man negotiating for a second
wife, but unintentionally telling us — and perhaps his listener — all too much
about his treatment of his first wife. As you hear him, what picture do you form
of his first wife? What do you find he loves most? If you were the emissary, what
would you tell the Count?

Matthew Arnold

Dover Beach

The sea is calm tonight,
The tide is full, the moon lies fair
Upon the straits; on the French coast the light
Gleams and is gone; the cliffs of England stand,

Glimmering and vast, out in the tranquil bay.
Come to the window, sweet is the night air!
Only, from the long line of spray
Where the sea meets the moon-blanched sand,
Listen! you hear the grating roar
Of pebbles which the waves draw back, and fling,
At their return, up the high strand,
Begin, and cease; and then again begin,
With tremulous cadence slow; and bring
The eternal note of sadness in.

Sophocles, long ago,
Heard it on the Aegean, and it brought
Into his mind the turbid ebb and flow
Of human misery; we
Find also in the sound a thought,
Hearing it by this distant northern sea.

The Sea of Faith
Was once, too, at the full, and round earth's shore
Lay like the folds of a bright girdle furled;
But now I only hear
Its melancholy, long, withdrawing roar,
Retreating, to the breath
Of the night-wind, down the vast edges drear
And naked shingles of the world.

Ah, love, let us be true
To one another! for the world, which seems
To lie before us like a land of dreams,
So various, so beautiful, so new,
Hath really neither joy, nor love, nor light,
Nor certitude, nor peace, nor help for pain;
And we are here as on a darkling plain,
Swept with confused alarms of struggle and flight,
Where ignorant armies clash by night.

FOR DISCUSSION

MATTHEW ARNOLD (1822-1888) Standing at Dover, where England is closest to France, the poet hears in the sound of the sea, "the eternal note of sadness." He recalls that Sophocles, the great tragedian of classic Greece, also perceived the sadness. Once the world was encompassed with Faith, but now it is retreating. The poet ends with a dismayed view of his modern world, and a plea to his love, "Let us be true to one another."

How adequate would such love be as a bulwark against the world described in the last stanza?

Thomas Hardy

In Time of "The Breaking of Nations"

I

Only a man harrowing clods
    In a slow silent walk
With an old horse that stumbles and nods
    Half asleep as they stalk.

II

Only thin smoke without flame
    From the heaps of couch-grass;
Yet this will go onward the same
    Though Dynasties pass.

III

Yonder a maid and her wight
    Come whispering by:
War's annals will cloud into night
    Ere their story die.

At the Draper's

"I stood at the back of the shop, my dear,
But you did not perceive me.
Well, when they deliver what you were shown
I shall know nothing of it, believe me!"
And he coughed and coughed as she paled and said,
"Oh, I didn't see you come in there —
Why couldn't you speak?" — "Well, I didn't. I left
That you should not notice I'd been there.

"You were viewing some lovely things.
'*Soon required for a widow of latest fashion*';
And I knew 'twould upset you to meet the man
Who had to be cold and ashen,

And screwed in a box before they could dress you
'*In the last new note in mourning,*'
As they defined it. So, not to distress you,
I left you to your adorning."

The Man He Killed

"Had he and I but met
By some old ancient inn,
We should have sat us down to wet
Right many a nipperkin!

"But ranged as infantry,
And staring face to face,
I shot at him as he at me,
And killed him in his place.

"I shot him dead because —
Because he was my foe,
Just so: my foe of course he was;
That's clear enough; although

"He thought he'd 'list, perhaps,
Off-hand like — just as I —
Was out of work — had sold his traps —
No other reason why.

"Yes; quaint and curious war is!
You shoot a fellow down
You'd treat if met where any bar is,
Or help to half-a-crown."

FOR DISCUSSION

THOMAS HARDY (1840-1928) "In Time of 'The Breaking of Nations'" When the nations have broken each other, what is it that will remain on the enduring earth?

Does the plainness of the style suit the theme?

"At the Draper's" What kind of husband is he — with his cough — that would confront his wife with what he had heard? Is it a plausible reason he suggests for not making his presence known? Is the poem an indictment of the husband, the wife, both, neither?

Is the conversation any different from the language of casual talk?

"The Man He Killed" How did the two soldiers happen to be in the army? What similarity in theme do you find between this poem and the first of the Hardy poems printed here?

A. E. Housman

Is My Team Ploughing

"Is my team ploughing,
　　That I was used to drive
And hear the harness jingle
　　When I was man alive?"

Aye, the horses trample,
　　The harness jingles now;
No change though you lie under
　　The land you used to plough.

"Is football playing
　　Along the river shore,
With lads to chase the leather,
　　Now I stand up no more?"

Aye, the ball is flying,
　　The lads play heart and soul;
The goal stands up, the keeper
　　Stands up to keep the goal.

"Is my girl happy,
　　That I thought hard to leave,
And has she tired of weeping
　　As she lies down at eve?"

Aye, she lies down lightly,
　　She lies not down to weep:
Your girl is well contented.
　　Be still, my lad, and sleep.

"Is my friend hearty,
　　Now I am thin and pine;
And has he found to sleep in
　　A better bed than mine?"

Aye, lad, I lie easy,
 I lie as lads would choose;
I cheer a dead man's sweetheart.
 Never ask me whose.

Could Man Be Drunk For Ever

Could man be drunk for ever
 With liquor, love, or fights,
Lief should I rouse at morning
 And lief lie down of nights.

But men at whiles are sober
 And think by fits and starts,
And if they think, they fasten
 Their hands upon their hearts.

When I Was One-and-Twenty

When I was one-and-twenty
 I heard a wise man say,
"Give crowns and pounds and guineas
 But not your heart away;
Give pearls away and rubies
 But keep your fancy free."
But I was one-and-twenty,
 No use to talk to me.

When I was one-and-twenty
 I heard him say again,
"The heart out of the bosom
 Was never given in vain;
'Tis paid with sighs a-plenty
 And sold for endless rue."
And I am two-and-twenty,
 And oh, 'tis true, 'tis true.

Oh, When I Was in Love with You

Oh, when I was in love with you,
 Then I was clean and brave,
And miles around the wonder grew
 How well did I behave.

And now the fancy passes by,
 And nothing will remain,
And miles around they'll say that I
 Am quite myself again.

Loveliest of Trees

Loveliest of trees, the cherry now
Is hung with bloom along the bough,
And stands about the woodland ride
Wearing white for Eastertide.

Now, of my threescore years and ten,
Twenty will not come again,
And take from seventy springs a score,
It only leaves me fifty more.

And since to look at things in bloom
Fifty springs are little room,
About the woodlands I will go
To see the cherry hung with snow.

FOR DISCUSSION

A. E. HOUSMAN (1859-1936) "Is My Team Ploughing" The dead man asks about the four things he loves best. Why are the four not arranged in a different order? Who replies to the dead man's questions? At what point in the story did you discover who was answering the questions? Was your first interpretation of the sixth stanza changed when you finished reading the eighth?

"Could Man Be Drunk For Ever" What is the double meaning of drunkenness and sobriety in this poem?

"When I Was One-and-Twenty" For whom is this a humorous poem, and for whom is it poignant?

"Oh, When I Was in Love with You" Compare and contrast this poem with the previous one.

"Loveliest of Trees" This lyric too has its humorous aspect: what is it? Isn't it verbose to spend one third of a poem saying that somebody is twenty years old?

Edwin Arlington Robinson

Miniver Cheevy

Miniver Cheevy, child of scorn,
    Grew lean while he assailed the seasons;
He wept that he was ever born,
    And he had reasons.

Miniver loved the days of old
    When swords were bright and steeds were prancing;
The vision of a warrior bold
    Would set him dancing.

Miniver sighed for what was not,
    And dreamed, and rested from his labors;
He dreamed of Thebes and Camelot,
    And Priam's neighbors.

Miniver mourned the ripe renown
    That made so many a name so fragrant;
He mourned Romance, now on the town,
    And Art, a vagrant.

Miniver loved the Medici,
    Albeit he had never seen one;
He would have sinned incessantly
    Could he have been one.

Miniver cursed the commonplace
    And eyed a khaki suit with loathing;
He missed the medieval grace
    Of iron clothing.

Miniver scorned the gold he sought,
    But sore annoyed was he without it;
Miniver thought, and thought, and thought,
    And thought about it.

Miniver Cheevy, born too late,
  Scratched his head and kept on thinking;
Miniver coughed, and called it fate,
  And kept on drinking.

Good poetry could not have been otherwise written than it is.

RALPH WALDO EMERSON

Richard Cory

Whenever Richard Cory went down town,
  We people on the pavement looked at him:
He was a gentleman from sole to crown,
  Clean favored, and imperially slim.

And he was always quietly arrayed,
  And he was always human when he talked;
But still he fluttered pulses when he said,
  "Good-morning," and he glittered when he walked.

And he was rich — yes, richer than a king —
  And admirably schooled in every grace:
In fine, we thought that he was everything
  To make us wish that we were in his place.

So on we worked, and waited for the light,
  And went without the meat, and cursed the bread;
And Richard Cory, one calm summer night,
  Went home and put a bullet through his head.

FOR DISCUSSION

E. A. ROBINSON (1869-1935) "Miniver Cheevy" Try to account for the rollicking enjoyment most readers find in this poem. Do you respect Miniver's scholarship? Do you admire his romanticism? Does his love of the past cause him to escape by drinking? Or does his desire to escape cause both his love of the past and his drinking? Describe the verse movement. Is anything unusual about the rhymes?

"Richard Cory" There is more to this poem than the shock ending. What are some of the things the poem suggests about such men and such towns?

From *The Children of the Night* by Edwin Arlington Robinson, published by Charles Scribner's Sons.

Robert Frost

The Death of the Hired Man

Mary sat musing on the lamp-flame at the table
Waiting for Warren. When she heard his step,
She ran on tip-toe down the darkened passage
To meet him in the doorway with the news
And put him on his guard. "Silas is back."
She pushed him outward with her through the door
And shut it after her. "Be kind," she said.
She took the market things from Warren's arms
And set them on the porch, then drew him down
To sit beside her on the wooden steps.

"When was I ever anything but kind to him?
But I'll not have the fellow back," he said.
"I told him so last haying, didn't I?
'If he left then,' I said, 'that ended it.'
What good is he? Who else will harbor him
At his age for the little he can do?
What help he is there's no depending on.
Off he goes always when I need him most.
'He thinks he ought to earn a little pay,
Enough at least to buy tobacco with,
So he won't have to beg and be beholden.'
'All right,' I say, 'I can't afford to pay
Any fixed wages, though I wish I could.'
'Someone else can.' 'Then someone else will have to.'
I shouldn't mind his bettering himself
If that was what it was. You can be certain,
When he begins like that, there's someone at him
Trying to coax him off with pocket-money, —
In haying time, when any help is scarce.
In winter he comes back to us. I'm done."

"Sh! not so loud: he'll hear you," Mary said.

"I want him to: he'll have to soon or late."

"He's worn out. He's asleep beside the stove.
When I came up from Rowe's I found him here,
Huddled against the barn-door fast asleep,
A miserable sight, and frightening, too —
You needn't smile — I didn't recognize him —
I wasn't looking for him — and he's changed.
Wait till you see."

           "Where did you say he'd been?"

"He didn't say. I dragged him to the house,
And gave him tea and tried to make him smoke.
I tried to make him talk about his travels.
Nothing would do: he just kept nodding off."

"What did he say? Did he say anything?"

"But little."

         "Anything? Mary, confess

He said he'd come to ditch the meadow for me."

"Warren!"

         "But did he? I just want to know."

"Of course he did. What would you have him say?
Surely you wouldn't grudge the poor old man
Some humble way to save his self-respect.
He added, if you really care to know,
He meant to clear the upper pasture, too.
That sounds like something you have heard before?
Warren, I wish you could have heard the way
He jumbled everything. I stopped to look
Two or three times — he made me feel so queer —
To see if he was talking in his sleep.
He ran on Harold Wilson — you remember —
The boy you had in haying four years since.
He's finished school, and teaching in his college.
Silas declares you'll have to get him back.
He says they two will make a team for work.
Between them they will lay this farm as smooth!
The way he mixed that in with other things.
He thinks young Wilson a likely lad, though daft

On education — you know how they fought
All through July under the blazing sun,
Silas up on the cart to build the load,
Harold along beside to pitch it on."

"Yes, I took care to keep well out of earshot."

"Well, those days trouble Silas like a dream.
You wouldn't think they would. How some things linger!
Harold's young college boy's assurance piqued him.
After so many years he still keeps finding
Good arguments he sees he might have used.
I sympathize. I know just how it feels
To think of the right thing to say too late.
Harold's associated in his mind with Latin.
He asked me what I thought of Harold's saying
He studied Latin like the violin
Because he liked it — that an argument!
He said he couldn't make the boy believe
He could find water with a hazel prong —
Which showed how much good school had ever done him.
He wanted to go over that. But most of all
He thinks if he could have another chance
To teach him how to build a load of hay — "

"I know, that's Silas' one accomplishment.
He bundles every forkful in its place,
And tags and numbers it for future reference,
So he can find and easily dislodge it
In the unloading. Silas does that well!
He takes it out in bunches like big birds' nests.
You never see him standing on the hay
He's trying to lift, straining to lift himself."

"He thinks if he could teach him that, he'd be
Some good perhaps to someone in the world.
He hates to see a boy the fool of books.
Poor Silas, so concerned for other folk,
And nothing to look backward to with pride,
And nothing to look forward to with hope,
So now and never any different."

Part of a moon was falling down the west,
Dragging the whole sky with it to the hills.
Its light poured softly in her lap. She saw
And spread her apron to it. She put out her hand
Among the harp-like morning-glory strings,

Taut with the dew from garden bed to eaves,
As if she played unheard the tenderness
That wrought on him beside her in the night.
"Warren," she said, "he has come home to die:
You needn't be afraid he'll leave you this time."

"Home," he mocked gently.

                      "Yes, what else but home?
It all depends on what you mean by home.
Of course he's nothing to us, anymore
Than was the hound that came a stranger to us
Out of the woods, worn out upon the trail."

"Home is the place where, when you have to go there,
They have to take you in."

                        "I should have called it
Something you somehow haven't to deserve."
Warren leaned out and took a step or two,
Picked up a little stick, and brought it back
And broke it in his hand and tossed it by.
"Silas has better claims on us, you think,
Than on his brother? Thirteen little miles
As the road winds would bring him to his door.
Silas has walked that far no doubt today.
Why didn't he go there? His brother's rich,
A somebody — director in the bank."

"He never told us that."

                      "We know it though."

"I think his brother ought to help, of course.
I'll see to that if there is need. He ought of right
To take him in, and might be willing to —
He may be better than appearances.
But have some pity on Silas. Do you think
If he'd had any pride in claiming kin
Or anything he looked for from his brother,
He'd keep so still about him all this time?"

"I wonder what's between them."

                        "I can tell you.
Silas is what he is — we wouldn't mind him —
But just the kind that kinsfolk can't abide.
He never did a thing so very bad.

He don't know why he isn't quite as good
As anyone. He won't be made ashamed
To please his brother, worthless though he is."

"I can't think Si ever hurt anyone."

"No, but he hurt my heart the way he lay
And rolled his old head on that sharp-edged chair-back.
He wouldn't let me put him on the lounge.
You must go in and see what you can do.
I made the bed up for him there tonight.
You'll be surprised at him — how much he's broken.
His working days are done; I'm sure of it."

"I'd not be in a hurry to say that."

"I haven't been. Go, look, see for yourself.
But, Warren, please remember how it is:
He's come to help you ditch the meadow.
He has a plan. You mustn't laugh at him.
He may not speak of it, and then he may.
I'll sit and see if that small sailing cloud
Will hit or miss the moon."

                    It hit the moon.
Then there were three there, making a dim row,
The moon, the little silver cloud, and she.

Warren returned — too soon, it seemed to her,
Slipped to her side, caught up her hand and waited.

"Warren," she questioned.

                  "Dead," was all he answered.

FOR DISCUSSION

ROBERT FROST (born 1875) The dramatic tension of this poem is a remarkable accomplishment, for no action occurs in it except what the title tells us will occur: the hired man dies. Yet somehow the poem demands breathless attentiveness. Such attentiveness is called forth partly by the poet's subtle use of language as language, and partly by what is often called the "universality" of the theme. As for the language, look at these early lines.

                   "Silas is back."
She pushed him outward with her through the door
And shut it after her. "Be kind," she said.
She took the market things from Warren's arms
And set them on the porch, then drew him down
To sit beside her on the wooden steps.

Is the vocabulary plain or fancy? Does every word count? Would you call "market things" poetic? Do you suppose she actually spoke just these words reported? Why has the poet reported these words?

Note how the characterization of the wife and the husband, and the interrelation of the two, is unfolded phrase by phrase in these sentences: "She pushed him outward (she seems aggressive) with her (she seems not aggressive but engaged in an important mission) through the door And shut it after her (she must talk with him about something important, and for some reason someone inside the house mustn't hear). She took the market things from Warren's arms (she helps him unload, but also she is detaining him: the things ought to go in the kitchen) And set them on the porch, then drew him down To sit beside her on the wooden steps." (They share their lives, respecting each other. Later on we discover that he runs the farm but she understands people.) Why tell the reader what material the steps are made of? Where do the accents fall in the last line quoted? Do they fall where they would fall in prose? Is the word order in this passage the same as it would be in prose?

As to the "universality" of theme, note the two definitions of home. Those are "quotable quotes" as perfect as the familiar quotations from Shakespeare. Note too the universalized womanliness of Mary, the maleness of Warren. More central, note the motivation of the old man, a most common man, proud of the one thing he does well, offended (and a little defensive) at the college boy who finds the liberal arts fun but is skeptical of the folk method for locating water. Why do you suppose the college boy stuck in his mind for so many years?

Note the ego-protection which the old man uses when he comes to ask for shelter. Why does Mary insist that Warren must not shatter this ego-protection? Why do you suppose the old man chose this house to come to?

What else have Mary and Warren taken in because it needed to be taken in? Mary and Warren both give a definition of home; is each definition characteristic of the speaker, or might one have given the other's definition?

What would you change if you were re-writing this as a short story in prose?

Carl Sandburg

Chicago

Hog Butcher for the World,
Tool Maker, Stacker of Wheat,
Player with Railroads and the Nation's Freight Handler;
Stormy, husky, brawling,
City of the Big Shoulders:

From *Chicago Poems* by Carl Sandburg. Copyright 1916 by Holt, Rinehart and Winston, Inc. Copyright 1944 by Carl Sandburg. Reprinted by permission of Holt, Rinehart and Winston, Inc.

They tell me you are wicked and I believe them, for I have seen your painted
    women under the gas lamps luring the farm boys.
And they tell me you are crooked and I answer: Yes, it is true I have seen
    the gunman kill and go free to kill again.
And they tell me you are brutal and my reply is: On the faces of women and
    children I have seen the marks of wanton hunger.
And having answered so I turn once more to those who sneer at this my city,
    and I give them back the sneer and say to them:
Come and show me another city with lifted head singing so proud to be alive
    and coarse and strong and cunning.
Flinging magnetic curses amid the toil of piling job on job, here is a tall bold
    slugger set vivid against the little soft cities;
Fierce as a dog with tongue lapping for action, cunning as a savage pitted
    against the wilderness,
                    Bareheaded,
                    Shoveling,
                    Wrecking,
                    Planning,
                    Building, breaking, rebuilding,
Under the smoke, dust all over his mouth, laughing with white teeth,
Under the terrible burden of destiny laughing as a young man laughs,
Laughing even as an ignorant fighter laughs who has never lost a battle,
Bragging and laughing that under his wrist is the pulse, and under his ribs
    the heart of the people,
                    Laughing!
Laughing the stormy, husky, brawling laughter of Youth, half-naked, sweat-
    ing, proud to be Hog Butcher, Tool Maker, Stacker of Wheat, Player
    with Railroads and Freight Handler to the Nation.

FOR DISCUSSION

CARL SANDBURG (born 1878)   That "Chicago" is different from earlier poems is
obvious. Try to define the differences, mentioning rhyme scheme, rhythm, and
the "beauty" of the words. In what ways does the language fit the subject? What
would have been lost if the first lines had read as follows?

    He Butchers Hogs for the World,
    Makes Tools, Stacks Wheat,
    Plays with Railroads and Handles the Nation's Freight. . . .

    What seems to be Sandburg's implied attitude toward the wickedness, the
crookedness, and the brutality of the city?

---

*Poetry is a comforting piece of fiction set to more or less lascivious
music.*

                              H. L. MENCKEN

William Butler Yeats

Sailing to Byzantium

That is no country for old men. The young
In one another's arms, birds in the trees
(Those dying generations) at their song,
The salmon-falls, the mackerel-crowded seas,
Fish, flesh, or fowl, commend all summer long
Whatever is begotten, born, and dies.
Caught in that sensual music, all neglect
Monuments of unaging intellect.

An aged man is but a paltry thing,
A tattered coat upon a stick, unless
Soul clap its hands and sing, and louder sing
For every tatter in its mortal dress;
Nor is there singing school but studying
Monuments of its own magnificence;
And therefore I have sailed the seas and come
To the holy city of Byzantium.

O sages, standing in God's holy fire
As in the gold mosaic of a wall,
Come from the holy fire, perne in a gyre
And be the singing-masters of my soul.
Consume my heart away — sick with desire
And fastened to a dying animal
It knows not what it is — and gather me
Into the artifice of eternity.

Once out of nature I shall never take
My bodily form from any natural thing,
But such a form as Grecian goldsmiths make
Of hammered gold and gold enamelling
To keep a drowsy emperor awake;
Or set upon a golden bough to sing
To lords and ladies of Byzantium
Of what is past, or passing, or to come.

FOR DISCUSSION

WILLIAM BUTLER YEATS (1865-1939)   Here, as so often in literature, a change in life is spoken of as a journey. So the aged poet journeys from "this country," described in first stanza, to Byzantium, described in the last two stanzas. Yeats once wrote that in ancient Byzantium (now Istanbul) "religious, aesthetic, and practical life were one." The journey here described suggests also a change from the interests of (1) the young, and (2) the perishable senses, to an interest in the "unaging intellect."

Notice the fecundity symbols in the first stanza: for what reason do salmon leap up falls? In the first stanza does the poet emphasize birth or death or both?

The second and transitional stanza contrasts the singing soul and the tattered coat. What is the more common term for what is here the coat? Why is the coat tattered? How does the soul learn to sing? What is the antecedent of "its" in the sixth line of the stanza?

In the third stanza the old man begs the aid of the sages in continuing the process described in the second stanza. They are to be the singing masters of his soul; they are to burn away the sensual desire emitted from the dying animal in which his soul is housed.

Once he is dead (out of nature) what form will he choose to take? He may have been thinking of a "tree made of gold and silver with artificial birds that sang" supposed to have stood in the Emperor's palace in Byzantium.

Even if you were not given a clue by the theme of the poem, would you consider this imagery and language sensual or intellectual? What poems you have read could be called sensual?

Gerard Manley Hopkins

God's Grandeur

The world is charged with the grandeur of God.
    It will flame out, like shining from shook foil;
    It gathers to a greatness, like the ooze of oil
Crushed. Why do men then now not reck his rod?
Generations have trod, have trod, have trod;
    And all is seared with trade; bleared, smeared with toil;
    And wears man's smudge and shares man's smell: the soil
Is bare now, nor can foot feel, being shod.

The selections from Hopkins are from *Poems of Gerard Manley Hopkins;* third edition edited by W. H. Gardner; copyright 1948 by Oxford University Press, Inc.; reprinted by permission.

And for all this, nature is never spent;
    There lives the dearest freshness deep down things;
And though the last lights of the black West went
    Oh, morning, at the brown brink eastward, springs —
Because the Holy Ghost over the bent
    World broods with warm breast and with ah! bright wings.

The Windhover

TO CHRIST OUR LORD

I caught this morning morning's minion, king-
    dom of daylight's dauphin, dapple-dawn-drawn Falcon, in his riding
    Of the rolling level underneath him steady air, and striding
High there, how he rung upon the rein of a wimpling wing
In his ecstasy! then off, off forth on swing,
    As a skate's heel sweeps smooth on a bow-bend: the hurl and gliding
    Rebuffed the big wind. My heart in hiding
Stirred for a bird, — the achieve of, the mastery of the thing!

Brute beauty and valor and act, oh, air, pride, plume, here
    Buckle! And the fire that breaks from thee then, a billion
Times told lovelier, more dangerous, O my chevalier!

    No wonder of it: sheer plod makes plough down sillion
Shine, and blue-bleak embers, ah, my dear,
    Fall, gall themselves, and gash gold-vermilion.

Spring

    Nothing is so beautiful as spring —
      When weeds, in wheels, shoot long and lovely and lush;
      Thrush's eggs look little low heavens, and thrush
    Through the echoing timber does so rinse and wring
    The ear, it strikes like lightnings to hear him sing;
      The glassy peartree leaves and blooms, they brush
      The descending blue; that blue is all in a rush
    With richness; the racing lambs too have fair their fling.

    What is all this juice and all this joy?
      A strain of the earth's sweet being in the beginning
    In Eden garden. — Have, get, before it cloy,
      Before it cloud, Christ, Lord, and sour with sinning,
    Innocent mind and Mayday in girl and boy.
      Most, O maid's child, thy choice and worthy the winning.

FOR DISCUSSION

GERARD MANLY HOPKINS (1844-1889)   Having vowed, as a Jesuit, to devote his life to the service of God, Hopkins made no effort to publish his poems. Not until thirty years after his death did they appear. Then they were received with great acclaim, though also with bafflement.

His poetry was bolder than anything else being written at that time. His purpose in omitting so many function words was "to crowd out every grammatical or toneless element," and to weight his lines with heavy accents. One critic has spoken of his "passionate emotion which seems to utter all its words in one." An admirer explains, "what obscurity we may find is due, not to a clouded imagination or an unsettled intellect, but to his lightning dashes from image to image, so quick that we are unable at first to perceive the points of contact."

"God's Grandeur"   The thesis of this poem calls to mind Wordsworth's sonnet "The World Is Too Much with Us" (page 514), for this poem too deplores man's materialism which obscures the grandeur of nature. However, this poem, written by a Jesuit priest, represents the grandeur of nature as emanating from the Christian God. Compare that viewpoint with the one expressed in Wordsworth's sonnet.

Does "charged" in the first line refer to indebtedness, or to being filled with energy like an electrical battery? "Foil" in the second line is probably gold, since art objects in gold foil were treasured by primitive peoples long before gold was prized for its rarity. "Oil crushed" in the third and fourth lines is probably that pressed from olives. What is the meaning of "reck his rod"?

Does any passage in Wordsworth correspond to "nor can foot feel, being shod"? Does any passage in Hopkins's poem "The Windhover" speak of the dearest freshness which is deep down in things? In the third line from the last, what is it that springs? In what sense or senses is the world "bent"?

Where would conjunctions and prepositions be placed if this were prose? Find a passage where Hopkins uses a series of slow, heavy accents without unaccented syllables between.

Notice his repetition of similar sounds: the *r*'s and *g*'s in the first line; the *f*'s and *sh*'s in the second; the *seared . . . bleared, smeared* in the sixth line.

"The Windhover"   The theme of the poem is that the grandeur of God breaks out suddenly through earthly beauty. That breaking forth is demonstrated while we watch the windhover (a variety of falcon) flying, and while we watch a new furrow being ploughed. The earthly beauty of the flying and of the ploughing is first described. Then in both examples a deeper fire shines forth. On the level of the physical image, the fire can be pictured as a reflection of the rising sun, both gold and red. But of course the breaking forth of the fire is also meant to indicate a religious revelation.

The poem can be paraphrased in these terms:

This morning I caught sight of the favorite of the morning, the prince of the kingdom of daylight, the Falcon, drawn against the dappled dawn, as he rode the steady air rolling but level beneath him. Striding high there, how, in his ecstasy, he spiraled as if reined (held to the center) by his rippled wing! Then off he went forth on a swinging curve as the heel of a skate sweeps in a smooth bent-bow curve: his hurled gliding beat back the big wind. My hidden heart stirred like the bird — oh, the achievement, the mastery of the thing! Then brute beauty and valor and action and — oh! — air, and plumed pride all give way here (they buckle and are broken by the heat coming in the next line). And the fire reflected from thee (the falcon as the sun reflects from his breast) is a counted billion times lovelier and more dangerous (than the brute beauty, etc., that buckled), O my knight.

And no wonder (this process occurs) for the sheer plod (of a work-horse) makes the plough down a furrow shine and the blue-bleak embers (of soil) — ah my dear — fall and break themselves open, and reveal gold vermillion (in the rising sunlight.)

"Spring" The first stanza is a consummately fine lyric on spring. The second stanza first compares our beautiful, joyous world in the spring to the sweet, new, and innocent world before the Fall in Eden. In the last sentence the poet admonishes Christ, our Lord, to seize ("have, get") the likewise innocent minds of children while they are still in their Mayday — before their lives cloy, cloud, and turn sour with sinning. This must be done since children were chosen by Christ (the maid's child) and were declared most worth winning.

Stephen Vincent Benét

President Lincoln

Lincoln, six feet one in his stocking feet,
The lank man, knotty and tough as a hickory rail,
Whose hands were always too big for white-kid gloves,
Whose wit was a coonskin sack of dry, tall tales,
Whose weathered face was homely as a plowed field —
Abraham Lincoln, who padded up and down
The sacred White House in nightshirt and carpet-slippers,
And yet could strike young hero-worshipping Hay
As dignified past any neat, balanced, fine
Plutarchan sentences carved in a Latin bronze;
The low clown out of the prairies, the ape-buffoon,
The small-town lawyer, the crude small-time politician,
State-character but comparative failure at forty
In spite of ambition enough for twenty Caesars,
Honesty rare as a man without self-pity,
Kindness as large and plain as a prairie wind,
And a self-confidence like an iron bar:
This Lincoln, President now by the grace of luck,
Disunion, politics, Douglas and a few speeches

Which make the monumental booming of Webster
Sound empty as the belly of a burst drum,
Lincoln shambled in to the Cabinet meeting
And sat, ungainly and awkward. Seated so
He did not seem so tall nor quite so strange
Though he was strange enough. His new broadcloth suit
Felt tight and formal across his big shoulders still
And his new shiny top-hat was not yet battered
To the bulging shape of the old familiar hat
He'd worn at Springfield, stuffed with its hoard of papers.
He was pretty tired. All week the office-seekers
Had plagued him as the flies in fly-time plague
A gaunt-headed, patient horse. The children weren't well
And Mollie was worried about them so sharp with her tongue.
But he knew Mollie and tried to let it go by.
Men tracked dirt in the house and women liked carpets.
Each had a piece of the right, that was all most people could stand.

Look at his Cabinet here. There were Seward and Chase,
Both of them good men, couldn't afford to lose them,
But Chase hates Seward like poison and Seward hates Chase
And both of 'em think they ought to be President
Instead of me. When Seward wrote me that letter
The other day, he practically told me so.
I suppose a man who was touchy about his pride
Would send them both to the dickens when he found out,
But I can't do that as long as they do their work.
The Union's too big a horse to keep changing the saddle
Each time it pinches you. As long as you're sure
The saddle fits, you're bound to put up with the pinches
And not keep fussing the horse.

                                    When I was a boy
I remember figuring out when I went to town
That if I had just one pumpkin to bump in a sack
It was hard to carry, but once you could get two pumpkins,
One in each end of the sack, it balanced things up.
Seward and Chase'll do for my pair of pumpkins.
And as for me — if anyone else comes by
Who shows me that he can manage this job of mine
Better than I can — well, he can have the job.
It's harder sweating than driving six cross mules,
But I haven't run into that other fellow yet
And till or supposing I meet him, the job's my job
And nobody else's.
                    Seward and Chase don't know that.

They'll learn it, in time.
                    Wonder how Jefferson Davis
Feels, down there in Montgomery, about Sumter.
He must be thinking pretty hard and fast,
For he's an able man, no doubt of that.
We were born less than forty miles apart,
Less than a year apart — he got the start
Of me in age, and raising too, I guess,
In fact, from all you hear about the man,
If you set out to pick one of us two
For President, by birth and folks and schooling,
General raising, training up in office,
I guess you'd pick him, nine times out of ten
And yet, somehow, I've got to last him out.

These thoughts passed through the mind in a moment's flash,
Then that mind turned to business.
                              It was the calling
Of seventy-five thousand volunteers.

FOR DISCUSSION

STEPHEN VINCENT BENÉT (1898-1943) Introducing a person in a long narrative poem — such as *John Brown's Body,* from which these lines are taken — allows the use of more varied methods than the prose writer would use. Note the repeated use of frontier figures of speech in describing the frontiersman: "like a hickory rail," "a coonskin sack," "a plowed field." Notice also the dry, witty folk-sayings: "honesty rare as a man without self-pity," "each had a bit of the right. . . ." Note then how the point of view moves inside the man's mind, showing his patient tolerance of his wife, and then finally his thoughts about himself as he broods over the problems of his cabinet and the nation. Notice the dramatic effect of the last sentence as the deep revery is broken into by war preparations.

My words are little jars
For you to take and put upon a shelf.
Their shapes are quaint and beautiful,
And they have many pleasant colours and lustres
To recommend them.

AMY LOWELL

T. ♦ S. Eliot

The Love Song of J. Alfred Prufrock

S'io credesse che mia risposta fosse
A persona che mai tornasse al mondo,
Questa fiamma staria senza piu scosse.
Ma perciocche giammai di questo fondo
Non torno vivi alcun, s'i'odo il vero,
Senza tema d'infamia ti rispondo.[1]

Let us go then, you and I,
When the evening is spread out against the sky
Like a patient etherised upon a table;
Let us go, through certain half-deserted streets,
The muttering retreats
Of restless nights in one-night cheap hotels
And sawdust restaurants with oyster-shells:
Streets that follow like a tedious argument
Of insidious intent
To lead you to an overwhelming question . . .
Oh, do not ask, "What is it?"
Let us go and make our visit.

In the room the women come and go
Talking of Michelangelo.

The yellow fog that rubs its back upon the window-panes,
The yellow smoke that rubs its muzzle on the window-panes
Licked its tongue into the corners of the evening,
Lingered upon the pools that stand in drains,
Let fall upon its back the soot that falls from chimneys,
Slipped by the terrace, made a sudden leap,
And seeing that it was a soft October night,
Curled once about the house, and fell asleep.

[1] "If I thought my answer were to one who ever could return to the world, this flame should shake no more; but since, if what I hear be true, none ever did return alive from this depth, without fear of infamy I answer thee." — Dante, *Inferno*, xxvii, 61-66.

And indeed there will be time
For the yellow smoke that slides along the street,
Rubbing its back upon the window-panes;
There will be time, there will be time
To prepare a face to meet the faces that you meet;
There will be time to murder and create,
And time for all the works and days of hands
That lift and drop a question on your plate;
Time for you and time for me,
And time yet for a hundred indecisions,
And for a hundred visions and revisions,
Before the taking of a toast and tea.

In the room the women come and go
Talking of Michelangelo.

And indeed there will be time
To wonder, "Do I dare?" and, "Do I dare?"
Time to turn back and descend the stair,
With a bald spot in the middle of my hair —
(They will say: "How his hair is growing thin!")
My morning coat, my collar mounting firmly to the chin,
My necktie rich and modest, but asserted by a simple pin —
(They will say: "But how his arms and legs are thin!")
Do I dare
Disturb the universe?
In a minute there is time
For decisions and revisions which a minute will reverse.

For I have known them all already, known them all:
Have known the evenings, mornings, afternoons,
I have measured out my life with coffee spoons;
I know the voices dying with a dying fall
Beneath the music from a farther room.
    So how should I presume?

And I have known the eyes already, known them all —
The eyes that fix you in a formulated phrase,
And when I am formulated, sprawling on a pin,
When I am pinned and wriggling on the wall,
Then how should I begin
To spit out all the butt-ends of my days and ways?
    And how should I presume?

And I have known the arms already, known them all —-
Arms that are braceleted and white and bare
(But in the lamplight, downed with light brown hair!)
Is it perfume from a dress
That makes me so digress?
Arms that lie along a table, or wrap about a shawl.
    And should I then presume?
    And how should I begin?

       ❖   ❖   ❖   ❖   ❖

Shall I say, I have gone at dusk through narrow streets
And watched the smoke that rises from the pipes
Of lonely men in shirt-sleeves, leaning out of windows? . . .

I should have been a pair of ragged claws
Scuttling across the floors of silent seas.

       ❖   ❖   ❖   ❖   ❖

And the afternoon, the evening, sleeps so peacefully!
Smoothed by long fingers,
Asleep . . . tired . . . or it malingers,
Stretched on the floor, here beside you and me.
Should I, after tea and cakes and ices,
Have the strength to force the moment to its crisis?
But though I have wept and fasted, wept and prayed,
Though I have seen my head (grown slightly bald) brought in upon a platter,
I am no prophet — and here's no great matter;
I have seen the moment of my greatness flicker
And I have seen the eternal Footman hold my coat, and snicker,
And in short, I was afraid.

And would it have been worth it, after all,
After the cups, the marmalade, the tea,
Among the porcelain, among some talk of you and me,
Would it have been worth while,
To have bitten off the matter with a smile,
To have squeezed the universe into a ball
To roll it toward some overwhelming question,
To say: "I am Lazarus, come from the dead,

Come back to tell you all, I shall tell you all" —
If one, settling a pillow by her head,
    Should say: "That is not what I meant at all;
    That is not it, at all."

And would it have been worth it, after all,
Would it have been worth while,
After the sunsets and the dooryards and the sprinkled streets,
After the novels, after the teacups, after the skirts that trail along the floor —
And this, and so much more? —
It is impossible to say just what I mean!
But as if a magic lantern threw the nerves in patterns on a screen:
Would it have been worth while
If one, settling a pillow or throwing off a shawl,
And turning toward the window, should say:
    "That is not it at all,
    That is not what I meant, at all."

    ❋   ❋   ❋   ❋   ❋

No! I am not Prince Hamlet, nor was meant to be;
Am an attendant lord, one that will do
To swell a progress, start a scene or two,
Advise the prince; no doubt, an easy tool,
Deferential, glad to be of use,
Politic, cautious, and meticulous;
Full of high sentence, but a bit obtuse;
At times, indeed, almost ridiculous —
Almost, at times, the Fool.

I grow old . . . I grow old . . .
I shall wear the bottoms of my trousers rolled.

Shall I part my hair behind? Do I dare to eat a peach?
I shall wear white flannel trousers, and walk upon the beach.
I have heard the mermaids singing, each to each.

I do not think that they will sing to me.

I have seen them riding seaward on the waves
Combing the white hair of the waves blown back
When the wind blows the water white and black.

We have lingered in the chambers of the sea
By sea-girls wreathed with seaweed red and brown
Till human voices wake us, and we drown.

FOR DISCUSSION

T. S. Eliot (1888-1965) Often the dramatic monologue reveals only as much of the speaker's character as is pertinent to the important action pending. In "My Last Duchess" (page 523) the important action pending is the Duke's second marriage; pertinent to it is his animosity toward his lovely first wife — perhaps his murder of her. In "Ulysses" (page 521) the hero's adventurous past is pertinent to his important voyage pending.

This poem tells us much about the speaker's character; but no important action is pending — unless it be a walk through the evening streets to take another toast and tea. So to put this poem into the form of a dramatic monologue is ironic.

To call it a love song is also ironic, for Prufrock is incapable of love — unless it can be said that he loves himself.

Prufrock is a modern neurotic — cultivated, but helpless, purposeless, and indecisive. Any impulse toward action has become so habitually inhibited that now all his psychic energy is diverted into circular introspection. He is neither alive nor dead: he is etherized. His congenial time of day is evening, neither night nor day. His food and drink is toast and tea. He is neither young nor old. His atmosphere is a yellow fog.

The opposite to Prufrock is whole-hearted vigor: that of Michelangelo, of Lazarus risen from the dead, of John the Baptist later beheaded. The opposite to Prufrock is any seer of visions. Prufrock is capable only of revisions and indecisions. Vigor for good is as impossible for Prufrock as vigor for evil: he can no more murder than he can create. The cat leaps, but then falls asleep.

Though Prufrock's impotence is general, it affects also his love relationships: he is fearful to commit himself. Disembodied arms he can face, but the sight of light brown hair upon them in the lamplight distresses him.

Much of the elusiveness of the poem comes from the fact that it conveys the form of Prufrock's neurosis, but not its content. We know that great questions trouble him, but neither he nor we ever learn what those great questions are.

The poem contains numerous allusions. What religious ceremony contrasts with "the taking of a toast and tea"? Prufrock describes himself as an insect formulated by a phrase. Does the word formulated sound like the name of the substance used to preserve biological specimens? To squeeze the universe into a ball suggests Andrew Marvell's great figure of speech (page 509). Is Prufrock like or unlike Marvell's lover? It was Chaucer's Oxford scholar whose speech was full of "high sentence," but which character in *Hamlet* is most sententious, "almost, at times, the fool"? What words does the name Prufrock suggest to you?

Poetry should surprise by a fine excess, and not by singularity.

JOHN KEATS

Archibald MacLeish

Ars Poetica

A poem should be palpable and mute
As a globed fruit

Dumb
As old medallions to the thumb

Silent as the sleeve-worn stone
Of casement ledges where the moss has grown —

A poem should be wordless
As the flight of birds

   •   •   •   •   •

A poem should be motionless in time
As the moon climbs

Leaving, as the moon releases
Twig by twig the night-entangled trees,

Leaving, as the moon behind the winter leaves,
Memory by memory the mind —

A poem should be motionless in time
As the moon climbs

   ❋   ❋   ❋   ❋   ❋   ❋

A poem should be equal to:
Not true

For all the history of grief
An empty doorway and a maple leaf

For love
The leaning grasses and two lights above the sea —

A poem should not mean
But be

From *Collected Poems, 1917-1952*, by Archibald MacLeish; by permission of Houghton Mifflin Company.

You, Andrew Marvell

And here face down beneath the sun
And here upon earth's noonward height
To feel the always coming on
The always rising of the night

To feel creep up the curving east
The earthy chill of dusk and slow
Upon those under lands the vast
And ever climbing shadow grow

And strange at Ecbatan the trees
Take leaf by leaf the evening strange
The flooding dark about their knees
The mountains over Persia change

And now at Kermanshah the gate
Dark empty and the withered grass
And through the twilight now the late
Few travelers in the westward pass

And Baghdad darken and the bridge
Across the silent river gone
And through Arabia the edge
Of evening widen and steal on

And deepen on Palmyra's street
The wheel rut in the ruined stone
And Lebanon fade out and Crete
High through the clouds and overblown

And over Sicily the air
Still flashing with the landward gulls
And loom and slowly disappear
The sails above the shadowy hulls

And Spain go under and the shore
Of Africa the gilded sand
And evening vanish and no more
That low pale light across that land

Nor now the long light on the sea

And here face downward in the sun
To feel how swift how secretly
The shadow of the night comes on . . .

FOR DISCUSSION

ARCHIBALD MACLEISH (born 1892) "Ars Poetica" Though this poem is entitled the "Art of Poetry," the reader discovers within a few words that it contains nothing like the kind of definitions of poetry written even by such accomplished poets as Wordsworth and Coleridge. It does not describe the poem as something on a page, but as an experience inside the reader.

If the images are not to be meaningless, they must be puzzled over, pictured one way and then another. For instance, referring to the second section, have you ever seen the climbing moon leave twig by twig the trees? Where is the moon with respect to the twigs of the pictured trees? In what sense does the moon "leave" the twigs? Why "twig by twig"? Is a tree "night-entangled" before the moon gets to it, while the moon is behind it, or after the moon has left it?

Is it the moon or a poem that "leaves, memory by memory the mind"? What is the similarity between "twigs" and "memories," between "night-entangled trees" and "the mind"?

Note the background music of *m*'s and *p*'s and *l*'s in "A poem should be palpable and mute As a globed fruit." Note more *m*'s and *l*'s in the third and fourth lines along with the *d*'s: "Dumb As old medallions to the thumb." Note next the frequent *s*'s "Silent as the sleeve-worn stone Of casement ledges where the moss has grown." Do you note other intentional repetitions of consonants?

Note the positions of the rhymes in the first section. Does a word in a one-word line move as quickly as if it were in a five-word line? Note, for instance, the single word in the third line. Note too that this is a rhyme-word and that rhyme-words are usually the last words in each line. If "Dumb" is to be regarded as the last word in the line, what words can be supposed to precede it? Now test the modulation in rhythm by reading aloud.

Note also in the first section that the sensations of taste and touch and sight and perhaps smell are all reported in terms of sound — or, more properly, soundlessness: "mute," "dumb," "silent," "wordless."

Note that each of the three sections of the poem begins and also ends with "A poem should be. . . ." After the poet has established the reader's expectation by five exact repetitions of this phrase, note the dramatic alteration made upon the phrase at the end of the poem. See what happens to that previously inconspicuous linking verb.

"You, Andrew Marvell" Alluding to Andrew Marvell's famous metaphor, "But at my back I always hear Time's wingèd chariot hurrying near" (page 508), MacLeish celebrates the swift passage of twilight as it sweeps round the world from the Far East bringing darkness with it.

Where is the "here" of the poem? What time is it "here"? Is it significant that the cities mentioned are all capitals of ancient and formerly advanced cultures?

What does time annihilate in Marvell's poem (page 508)? What does it annihilate in this poem? Is any defense mentioned against such annihilation?

Kenneth Fearing

Portrait

The clear brown eyes, kindly and alert, with 12-20 vision, give confident regard to the passing world through R. K. Lampert & Company lenses
framed in gold;
His soul, however, is all his own;
Arndt Brothers necktie and hat (with feather) supply a touch of youth.

With his soul his own, he drives, drives, chats and drives,
The first and second bicuspids, lower right, replaced by bridgework, while
two incisors have porcelain crowns;

(Render unto Federal, state, and city Caesar, but not unto time;
Render nothing unto time until Amalgamated Death serves final notice, in
proper form;

The vault is ready;
The will has been drawn by Clagget, Clagget, Clagget & Brown;
The policies are adequate, Confidential's best, reimbursing for disability,
partial or complete, with double indemnity should the end be a pure
and simple accident)

Nothing unto time,
Nothing unto change, nothing unto fate,
Nothing unto you, and nothing unto me, or to any other known or unknown
party or parties, living or deceased;

But Mercury shoes, with special arch supports, take much of the wear and
tear;
On the course, a custombuilt driver corrects a tendency to slice;
Love's ravages have been repaired (it was a textbook case) by Drs. Schultz,
Lightner, Mannheim, and Goode,
While all of it is enclosed in excellent tweed, with Mr. Baumer's personal
attention to the shoulders and the waist;

And all of it now roving, chatting amiably through space in a Plymouth 6,
With his soul (his own) at peace, soothed by Walter Lippman, and sustained by Haig & Haig.

Travelogue in a Shooting-Gallery

There is a jungle, there is a jungle, there is a vast, vivid, wild, wild, marvelous, marvelous, marvelous jungle,
Open to the public during business hours,
A jungle not very far from an Automat, between a hat store there, and a
radio shop.

There, there, whether it rains, or it snows, or it shines,
Under the hot, blazing, cloudless, tropical neon skies that the management
always arranges there,
Rows and rows of marching ducks, dozens and dozens and dozens of ducks,
move steadily along on smoothly-oiled ballbearing feet,
Ducks as big as telephone books, slow and fearless, and out of this world,
While lines and lines of lions, lions, rabbits, panthers, elephants, crocodiles,
zebras, apes,
Filled with jungle hunger and jungle rage and jungle love,
Stalk their prey on endless, endless rotary belts through never-ending forests,
and burning deserts, and limitless veldts,
To the sound of tom-toms, equipped with silencers, beaten by thousands of
savages there.

And there it is that all the big game hunters go, there the traders and the
explorers come,
Leanfaced men with windswept eyes who arrive by streetcar, auto or sub-
way, taxi or on foot, streetcar or bus,
And they nod, and they say, and they need no more:
"There . . . there . . .
There they come, and there they go."

And weighing machines, in this civilized jungle, will read your soul like an
open book, for a penny at a time, and tell you all,
There, there, where smoking is permitted,
In a jungle that lies, like a rainbow's end, at the very end of every trail,
There, in the only jungle in the whole wide world where ducks are waiting
for streetcars,
And hunters can be psychoanalyzed, while they smoke and wait for ducks.

American Rhapsody (4)

First you bite your fingernails. And then you comb your hair again. And
then you wait. And wait.
(They say, you know, that first you lie. And then you steal, they say. And
then, they say, you kill.)

Then the doorbell rings. Then Peg drops in. And Bill. And Jane. And Doc.
And first you talk, and smoke, and hear the news and have a drink. Then you
walk down the stairs.
And you dine, then, and go to a show after that, perhaps, and after that a
night spot, and after that come home again, and climb the stairs again,
and again go to bed.

But first Peg argues, and Doc replies. First you dance the same dance and
you drink the same drink you always drank before.
And the piano builds a roof of notes above the world.
And the trumpet weaves a dome of music through space. And the drum
makes a ceiling over space and time and night.
And then the table-wit. And then the check. Then home again to bed.
But first, the stairs.

And do you now, baby, as you climb the stairs, do you still feel as you felt
back there?
Do you feel again as you felt this morning? And the night before? And then
the night before that?

(They say, you know, that first you hear voices. And then you have visions,
they say. Then, they say, you kick and scream and rave.)
Or do you feel: What is one more night in a lifetime of nights?
What is one more death, or friendship, or divorce out of two, or three? Or
four? Or five?
One more face among so many, many faces, one more life among so many
million lives?

But first, baby, as you climb and count the stairs (and they total the same)
did you, sometime or somewhere, have a different idea?
Is this, baby, what you were born to feel, and do, and be?

FOR DISCUSSION

KENNETH FEARING (born 1902) "Portrait" In a unique way this poem shows what man has made of man. What various men have made this man? What part of him is said to remain his own? Does that part seem of much value? What agencies affect even that part?

What allusion lies in the words "Render unto . . . Caesar"? What effect is achieved by the jagged alternation of such a passage with a passage connoting commercial transactions? What is the connotation of the passage beginning "Nothing unto time . . ." and ending "living or deceased"?

As you re-read the poem, what various meanings does the word "drive" take on in the second stanza?

"Travelogue in a Shooting Gallery" On the surface this is an enthusiastic description of the wonders of a shooting gallery, yet no reader can escape the sense that the enthusiasm is ironic. What elements in the poem convince you that the apparent admiration is not sincere?

Surely the poem implies more than that the poet has no taste for shooting galleries; what does it imply?

"American Rhapsody (4)" The title does for this poem what the enthusiasm did for the previous poem: it establishes a high standard of expectation, so that actuality is bitterly disappointing.

By what method does the poet emphasize the flatness and drabness of the evening?

How would you phrase the theme of the poem, either satirically or seriously?

W. H. Auden

Musée des Beaux Arts

About suffering they were never wrong,
The Old Masters: how well they understood
Its human position; how it takes place
While someone else is eating or opening a window or just walking dully
    along;
How, when the aged are reverently, passionately waiting
For the miraculous birth, there always must be
Children who did not specially want it to happen, skating
On a pond at the edge of the wood:
They never forgot

That even the dreadful martyrdom must run its course
Anyhow in a corner, some untidy spot
Where the dogs go on with their doggy life and the torturer's horse
Scratches its innocent behind on a tree.
In Breughel's *Icarus*, for instance: how everything turns away
Quite leisurely from the disaster; the ploughman may
Have heard the splash, the forsaken cry,
But for him it was not an important failure; the sun shone
As it had to on the white legs disappearing into the green
Water; and the expensive delicate ship that must have seen
Something amazing, a boy falling out of the sky,
Had somewhere to get to and sailed calmly on.

In Memory of W. B. Yeats

1

He disappeared in the dead of winter:
The brooks were frozen, the air-ports almost deserted,
And snow disfigured the public statues;
The mercury sank in the mouth of the dying day.
O all the instruments agree
The day of his death was a dark cold day.

Far from his illness
The wolves ran on through the evergreen forests,
The peasant river was untempted by the fashionable quays;
By mourning tongues
The death of the poet was kept from his poems.

But for him it was his last afternoon as himself,
An afternoon of nurses and rumors;
The provinces of his body revolted,
The current of his feeling failed: he became his admirers.

Now he is scattered among a hundred cities
And wholly given over to unfamiliar affections;
To find his happiness in another kind of wood
And be punished under a foreign code of conscience.
The words of a dead man
Are modified in the guts of the living.

But in the importance and noise of to-morrow
When the brokers are roaring like beasts on the floor of the Bourse,
And the poor have the sufferings to which they are fairly accustomed

And each in the cell of himself is almost convinced of his freedom;
A few thousand will think of this day
As one thinks of a day when one did something slightly unusual.

O all the instruments agree
The day of his death was a dark cold day.

2

You were silly like us: your gift survived it all;
The parish of rich women, physical decay,
Yourself; mad Ireland hurt you into poetry.
Now Ireland has her madness and her weather still,
For poetry makes nothing happen: it survives
In the valley of its saying where executives
Would never want to tamper; it flows south
From ranches of isolation and the busy griefs,
Raw towns that we believe and die in; it survives,
A way of happening, a mouth.

3

Earth, receive an honored guest;
William Yeats is laid to rest:
Let the Irish vessel lie
Emptied of its poetry.

Time that is intolerant
Of the brave and innocent,
And indifferent in a week
To a beautiful physique,

Worships language and forgives
Everyone by whom it lives;
Pardons cowardice, conceit,
Lays its honors at their feet.

Time that with this strange excuse
Pardoned Kipling and his views,
And will pardon Paul Claudel,
Pardons him for writing well.

In the nightmare of the dark
All the dogs of Europe bark,
And the living nations wait,
Each sequestered in its hate;

Intellectual disgrace
Stares from every human face,
And the seas of pity lie
Locked and frozen in each eye.

Follow, poet, follow right
To the bottom of the night,
With your unconstraining voice
Still persuade us to rejoice;

With the farming of a verse
Make a vineyard of the curse,
Sing of human unsuccess
In a rapture of distress;

In the deserts of the heart
Let the healing fountain start,
In the prison of his days
Teach the free man how to praise.

FOR DISCUSSION

W. H. Auden (born 1907) "Musee des Beaux Arts" The thesis of the poem appears in the first line and a half. The remainder of the first stanza explains the thesis. The second stanza exemplifies it again by referring to a specific painting by an Old Master. The title of the poem is the name of the museum that owns the painting.

How does the passage about the aged and the children in the first stanza exemplify the thesis? Who is "they" in line 9?

"In Memory of W. B. Yeats" Using the death of Yeats as a point of departure, this poem comments on the relation of the modern poet to his audience. The poet had an audience, but it was small — a few thousand.

The third section is written with a dogged regularity that has been associated for centuries with funeral verse.

Notice the wit of the fourth line of the poem. What double comment is made by "the mercury sank in the mouth of the dying day"? What is implied by the assertion that "all the instruments agree. . . ."?

What effect is achieved by the reference to the wolves and the peasant rivers in lines 8 and 9?

What relation between a poet and his poems is implied in the words "the death of the poet was kept from his poems"?

Compare the view of the contemporary world given in the fifth and sixth stanzas of part 3 with that given toward the end of "Dover Beach" (page 525).

Stephen Spender

The Landscape Near an Aerodrome

More beautiful and soft than any moth
With burring furred antennae feeling its huge path
Through dusk, the air-liner with shut-off engines
Glides over suburbs and the sleeves set trailing tall
To point the wind. Gently, broadly, she falls,
Scarcely disturbing charted currents of air.

Lulled by descent, the travelers across sea
And across feminine land indulging its easy limbs
In miles of softness, now let their eyes trained by watching
Penetrate through dusk the outskirts of this town
Here where industry shows a fraying edge.
Here they may see what is being done.

Beyond the winking masthead light
And the landing-ground, they observe the outposts
Of work: chimneys like lank black fingers
Or figures frightening and mad: and squat buildings
With their strange air behind trees, like women's faces
Shattered by grief. Here where few houses
Moan with faint light behind their blinds
They remark the unhomely sense of complaint, like a dog
Shut out and shivering at the foreign moon.

In the last sweep of love, they pass over fields
Behind the aerodrome, where boys play all day
Hacking dead grass: whose cries, like wild birds,
Settle upon the nearest roofs
But soon are hid under the loud city.

Then, as they land, they hear the tolling bell
Reaching across the landscape of hysteria
To where, larger than all the charcoaled batteries
And imaged towers against that dying sky,
Religion stands, the church blocking the sun.

The Funeral

Death is another milestone on their way.
With laughter on their lips and with winds blowing round them
They record simply
How this one excelled all others in making driving-belts.

This is festivity, it is the time of statistics
When they record what one unit contributed:
They are glad as they lay him back in the earth
And thank him for what he gave them.

They walk home remembering the straining red flags,
And with pennons of song still fluttering through their blood
They speak of the world-state
With its towns like brain-centers and its pulsing arteries.

They think how one life hums, revolves and toils,
One cog in a golden and singing hive:
Like spark from fire, its task happily achieved,
It falls away quietly.

No more are they haunted by the individual grief
Nor the crocodile tears of European genius,
The decline of a culture
Mourned by scholars who dream of the ghosts of Greek boys.

FOR DISCUSSION

STEPHEN SPENDER (born 1909) "The Landscape Near an Aerodrome" The lyric poet of the twentieth century has available to him new subjects. Here an airliner coming in for a landing is compared to the flight of a giant moth. The approach of the plane occasions a survey of the modern industrial city. In the final line the poet indicts the church as an obstacle to enlightenment.

"The Funeral" Is this satire or praise for the absorption of the individual into the socialist state? Is the last stanza the poet's indictment of European classic culture? or is it instead an ironic statement of that indictment as phrased by modern socialism?

Dylan Thomas

In My Craft or Sullen Art

In my craft or sullen art
Exercised in the still night
When only the moon rages
And the lovers lie abed
With all their griefs in their arms,
I labour by singing light
Not for ambition or bread
Or the strut and trade of charms
On the ivory stages
But for the common wages
Of their most secret heart.
Not for the proud man apart
From the raging moon I write
On these spindrift pages
Not for the towering dead
With their nightingales and psalms
But for the lovers, their arms
Round the griefs of the ages,
Who pay no praise or wages
Nor heed my craft or art.

The Force That Through the Green Fuse Drives the Flower

The force that through the green fuse drives the flower
Drives my green age; that blasts the roots of trees
Is my destroyer.
And I am dumb to tell the crooked rose
My youth is bent by the same wintry fever.

The force that drives the water through the rocks
Drives my red blood; that dries the mouthing streams
Turns mine to wax.
And I am dumb to mouth unto my veins
How at the mountain spring the same mouth sucks.

The hand that whirls the water in the pool
Stirs the quicksand; that ropes the blowing wind
Hauls my shroud sail.
And I am dumb to tell the hanging man
How of my clay is made the hangman's lime.

The lips of time leech to the fountain head;
Love drips and gathers, but the fallen blood
Shall calm her sores.
And I am dumb to tell a weather's wind
How time has ticked a heaven round the stars.

And I am dumb to tell the lover's tomb
How at my sheet goes the same crooked worm.

Fern Hill

Now as I was young and easy under the apple boughs
About the lilting house and happy as the grass was green,
   The night above the dingle starry,
    Time let me hail and climb
  Golden in the heydays of his eyes,
And honoured among wagons I was prince of the apple towns
And once below a time I lordly had the trees and leaves
    Trail with daisies and barley
  Down the rivers of the windfall light.

And as I was green and carefree, famous among the barns
About the happy yard and singing as the farm was home,
   In the sun that is young once only,
    Time let me play and be
  Golden in the mercy of his means,
And green and golden I was huntsman and herdsman, the calves
Sang to my horn, the foxes on the hills barked clear and cold,
    And the sabbath rang slowly
  In the pebbles of the holy streams.

All the sun long it was running, it was lovely, the hay-
Fields high as the house, the tunes from the chimneys, it was air
   And playing, lovely and watery
    And fire green as grass.
   And nightly under the simple stars
As I rode to sleep the owls were bearing the farm away,
All the moon long I heard, blessed among stables, the night-jars
   Flying with the ricks, and the horses
    Flashing into the dark.

And then to awake, and the farm, like a wanderer white
With the dew, come back, the cock on his shoulder: it was all
   Shining, it was Adam and maiden,
     The sky gathered again
   And the sun grew round that very day.
So it must have been after the birth of the simple light
In the first, spinning place, the spellbound horses walking warm
   Out of the whinnying green stable
   On to the fields of praise.

And honoured among foxes and pheasants by the gay house
Under the new made clouds and happy as the heart was long,
   In the sun born over and over,
     I ran my heedless ways,
   My wishes raced through the house-high hay
And nothing I cared, at my sky blue trades, that time allows
In all his tuneful turning so few and such morning songs
   Before the children green and golden
     Follow him out of grace,

Nothing I cared, in the lamb white days, that time would take me
Up to the swallow thronged loft by the shadow of my hand,
   In the moon that is always rising,
     Nor that riding to sleep
   I should hear him fly with the high fields
And wake to the farm forever fled from the childless land.
Oh as I was young and easy in the mercy of his means,
     Time held me green and dying
   Though I sang in my chains like the sea.

FOR DISCUSSION

DYLAN THOMAS (1914-1953) Dylan Thomas once remarked that he wanted to be *read*, not *read into*. Nonetheless he is most difficult to read. He altered some of his poems as many as two hundred times, each time increasing their concentration and allusiveness. Though his poetic output is small, it is of high quality.

"In My Craft or Sullen Art" Poetry is a craft; could "craft" also suggest the adjective "crafty" to go with "sullen" as an attribute of the recalcitrance and difficulty of the poet's medium?

When "lovers lie abed with all their griefs in their arms," those griefs being "the griefs of the ages," are we to understand that love is full of grief, or that the lovers have no real griefs (*all* meaning *only*)?

Traditionally poets have labored by lamp-light. What would Thomas's "singing light" be?

Both Homer and Virgil speak of two gates for dreams: through the horn gates true dreams pass; through the ivory gates false dreams pass. Might this allusion be relevant to "the strut and trade of charms on the ivory stages"?

Keats wrote as his epitaph, "Here lies one whose name was writ in water." Might this be relevant to Thomas's "spindrift pages"?

In what sense can poetry be for the lovers if they never heed that poetry?

Do you find any rhyme scheme?

"The Force . . ." The tone of Thomas's poetry is usually celebrative; his subjects are the three elemental ones: birth, reproduction, and death. His images are extremely compressed, sometimes to the point of incomprehensibility. Nonetheless, his exuberant lyric power is inescapable.

The theme of this poem is the acceptance of life in its entirety, for death is inseparable from birth and love, and human life is inseparable from the other natural phenomena. The first three lines of each stanza repeat a four-element statement of identity: (1) fulfillment in the non-human world equals (2) fulfillment in me, equals (3) destruction in the non-human world, equals (4) destruction in me. Then follow in each stanza two lines introduced by "And I am dumb to tell. . . ."

"Fern Hill" is both a celebration and a lament. The first stanzas recount the joyous innocence and confidence of childhood. In the last stanza, after earlier premonitions, this joyousness is displaced by haunting disillusion and the prospect of death. The fourth stanza provides the further implication that this change from innocence to knowledge is the universal change, first prefigured in the Fall of Man and his dire expulsion from Eden by the avenging angel.

For two and a half stanzas the boy's experience is daytime; then he falls asleep, the farm is carried away, and as he wakes the farm returns still fresh and dewy. But as children follow time (Pied Piper-like) "out of grace," the night becomes haunted, and when they wake the farm is "forever fled from the childless land."

Thomas uses multiple images: the words used sound like other words unused. "Once below a time," meaning once before the time of disillusionment, suggests "once upon a time." "All the sun long," suggests "all the day long."

The stanzas repeat certain intricate patterns like parallel structures. Note, for instance, the unusual but similar figures of speech that form the second half of the second lines of the first, second, and fifth stanzas: "happy as the grass was green," "singing as the farm was home," "happy as the heart was long." These and other expressions are greatly compressed: "lamb white days" is a compression of "days innocent and young and fresh as a white lamb" (the religious significance of the lamb is clearly relevant).

In the first and second stanzas, time, like the avenging angel, "in the mercy of his means" is lenient, and mentioned only in the second half of each stanza. But in the second half of the fifth stanza and the first of the sixth, time leads the youth away "by the shadow of my hand" (not time's hand) up into the dread "swallow-thronged loft." Then the poet realizes that even while he had been "young and easy" he had also been dying, "though I sang in my chains like the sea."

PART THREE

❧

LANGUAGE ABOUT LITERATURE

What Literature Is

How Writers Mean

WHAT

LITERATURE IS

What Literature Is For

S. I. HAYAKAWA

Our first and most obvious conclusion is that since the expression of individual feelings is central to literature, affective elements are of the utmost importance in all literary writing. In the evaluation of a novel, poem, play, or short story, as well as in the evaluation of sermons, moral exhortations, political speeches, and directive utterances generally, the usefulness of the given piece of writing as a "map" of actual "territories" is often secondary — sometimes quite irrelevant. If this were not the case, *Gulliver's Travels, Alice in Wonderland, The Scarlet Letter,* or Emerson's *Essays* would have no excuse for existence.

Secondly, when we say that a given piece of affective writing is true, we do not mean "scientifically true." It may mean merely that we agree with the sentiment; it may also mean that we believe that an attitude has been accurately expressed; again, it may mean that the attitudes it evokes are believed to be such as will lead us to better social or personal conduct. There is no end to the meanings "true" may have. People who feel that science and literature or science and religion are in necessary conflict do so because they habitually think in opposites of black and white, true and false, good and evil. To such people, if science is "true," then literature or religion is nonsense; if literature or religion is "true," science is merely "pretentious ignorance." What should be understood when people tell us that certain statements are "scientifically true" is that they are useful and verifiable formulations, suitable for the purposes of organized co-operative workmanship. What should be understood when people tell us that the plays of Shakespeare or the poems of Milton or Dante are "eternally true" is that they produce in us attitudes toward our fellow men, an understanding of ourselves, or feelings of deep moral obligation that are valuable to humanity under any conceivable circumstances.

Thirdly, let us consider an important shortcoming of the language of reports and of science writing. John Smith in love with Mary is not William Brown in love with Jane; William Brown in love with Jane is not Henry Jones in love with Anne; Henry Jones in love with Anne is not Robert Browning in love with Elizabeth Barrett. Each of these situations is unique; no two loves are exactly alike — in fact, no love even between the same people is *exactly* the same from day to day. Science, seeking as always laws of the widest possible applicability and the greatest possible generality, would abstract from these situations *only what they have in common.* But each of these lovers is conscious only of the *uniqueness* of his own feelings; each feels, as we all know, that he is the first one in the world ever to have so loved.

How is that sense of difference conveyed? It is here that affective uses of language play their most important part. The infinity of differences in our feelings towards all the many experiences that we undergo are too subtle to be reported; they must be expressed. And we express them by the complicated manipulation of tones of voice, of rhythms, of connotations, of affective facts, of metaphors, of allusions, of every affective device of language at our command.

Frequently the feelings to be expressed are so subtle or complex that a few lines of prose or verse are not enough to convey them. It is sometimes necessary, therefore, for authors to write entire books, carrying their readers through numbers of scenes, situations, and adventures, pushing their sympathies now this way and now that, arousing in turn their fighting spirit, their tenderness, their sense of tragedy, their laughter, their superstitiousness, their cupidity, their sensuousness, their piety. Only in such ways, sometimes, can the *exact* feelings an author wants to express be re-created in his readers. This, then, is the reason that novels, poems, dramas, stories, allegories, and parables exist: to convey such propositions as "Life is tragic" or "Susanna is beautiful," not by telling us so, but by putting us through a whole series of experiences that make us feel toward life or toward Susanna as the author did. *Literature is the most exact expression of feelings, while science is the most exact kind of reporting.* Poetry, which condenses all the affective resources of language into patterns of infinite rhythmical subtlety, may be said to be *the language of expression at its highest degree of efficiency.*

In a very real sense, then, people who have read good literature have lived more than people who cannot or will not read. To have read *Gulliver's Travels* is to have had the experience, with Jonathan Swift, of turning sick at the stomach at the conduct of the human race; to read *Huckleberry Finn* is to feel what it is like to drift down the Mississippi River on a raft; to have read Byron is to have suffered with him his rebellions and neuroses and to have enjoyed with him his nose-thumbing at society; to have read *Native Son* is to know how it feels to be frustrated in the particular way in which Negroes in Chicago are frustrated. This is the great task that affective communication performs: it enables us to feel how others felt about life, even if they lived thousands of miles away and centuries ago. It is not true that we have only one life to live; if we can read, we can live as many more lives and as many kinds of lives as we wish.

Here, the reader may object by asking, are we not twisting language somewhat to talk about "living" other lives than one's own? In one sense, the objection is correct; two different meanings of the word "live" are involved in the expressions "living one's own life" and "living other people's lives in books." Human life, however, is "lived" at more than one level; we inhabit both the extensional world and the world of words (and other symbols). "Living other people's lives in books" means, as we shall use the expression here, *symbolic experience* — sometimes called "vicarious experience."

In the enjoyment and contemplation of a work of literary or dramatic art — a novel, a play, a moving picture — *we find our deepest enjoyment when the leading characters in the story to some degree symbolize ourselves.* Jessie Jenkins at the movie, watching Ann Sheridan being kissed by a handsome man, sighs as contentedly as if she herself were being kissed — and *symbolically,* she is. In other words, she identifies herself with Ann Sheridan and Ann Sheridan's role in the story. Humphrey Bogart fighting a crowd of villains is watched by thousands of men who clench their hands as if *they* were doing the fighting — which they are, *symbolically.* As we identify ourselves with the people in the story, the dramatist or the novelist puts us through *organized sequences of symbolic experiences.*

The differences between actual and symbolic experiences are great — one is not scarred by watching a moving-picture battle, nor is one nourished by watching people in a play having dinner. Furthermore, actual experiences come to us in highly disorganized fashion: meals, arguments with the landlady, visits to the doctor about one's fallen arches, and so on, inter-rupt the splendid course of romance. The novelist, however, *abstracts* only the events relevant to his story and then *organizes* them into a meaningful sequence. This business of abstracting (selecting) events and organizing them so that they bear some meaningful relationship to each other and to the central "theme" of a novel or play constitutes the "story-teller's art." Plot construction, development of character, narrative structure, climax, denouement, and all the other things one talks about in technical literary criticism have reference to this organizing of symbolic experiences so that the whole complex of symbolic experiences (i.e., the finished story or play) will have the desired impact on the reader.

All literary and dramatic enjoyment, whether of nursery tales in childhood or of moving pictures later on or of "great literature," appears to involve to some degree the reader's imaginative identification of himself with the roles portrayed and his projection of himself into the situations described in the story.[1] Whether a reader is able to identify himself with the characters of a story depends both on the maturity of the story and the maturity of the reader. If a mature reader finds difficulty identifying himself with the hero of a cowboy story, it is because he finds the hero too simple-minded a character to serve as an acceptable symbol for himself, and the villains and the events too improbable to serve as symbols for his own enemies and his own problems. On the other hand, an immature reader, reading the same story, may have a deep need to imagine himself a courageous cowboy, and may also be too inexperienced or uneducated to know what kinds of people or events are probable or improbable — in which case he may enjoy the story enormously. Again, the immature reader, confronted with a story in which the central character is someone far removed from him in outlook and background (say, for example, an eighteenth-century French cardinal, involved in problems and events the reader has never heard of or thought about before) will find it impossible to find in the "hero" any kind of symbol for himself — and will therefore lay the book aside as "too dry."

One of the reasons for calling some people immature is that they are in-capable of confronting defeat, tragedy, or unpleasantness of any kind. Such persons usually cannot endure an "unhappy ending" *even in a set of sym-bolic experiences.* Hence the widespread passion for happy endings in popular literature, so that even stories about unhappy events have to be made, in the end, to "come out all right." The immature constantly need to be reassured that everything will always come out all right.

Readers who mature as they grow older, however, steadily increase the

---

[1] At what age does the capacity for imaginative identification of oneself with the roles portrayed in a story begin? The writer would suggest, on the basis of very limited observation, that it begins around the age of two or earlier. An interesting test case is to read the story of the Three Bears to a very small child to see when he begins to iden-tify himself with Baby Bear.

depth and range and subtlety of their symbolic experiences. Under the guidance of skilled writers who have accurately observed the world and were able to organize their observations in significant ways, the mature reader may symbolically experience what it feels like to be a Chinese peasant woman, a Roman emperor, an early nineteenth-century poet, a Greek philosopher, an irresolute Prince of Denmark, or a dispossessed Mexican sharecropper. He may symbolically experience murder, guilt, religious exaltation, bankruptcy, the loss of friends, the discovery of gold mines or new philosophical principles, or the sense of desolation following a locust invasion in North Dakota. Each new symbolic experience means the enrichment of his insight into people and events.

The immature reader, satisfied with the narrow range of characters that popular literature offers for the reader to identify himself with (almost invariably handsome young men or beautiful young women of acceptable social status, income level, and skin color), and satisfied with the narrow range of symbolic experiences offered (love, love, and more love), may read abundantly the offerings of the drugstore newsstand and the gift-shop lending library all his life without appreciably increasing his knowledge or his sympathies.

Poetry is the journal of a sea animal living on land, wanting to fly in the air. Poetry is a search for syllables to shoot at the barriers of the unknown and the unknowable. Poetry is a phantom script telling how rainbows are made and why they go away.

CARL SANDBURG

If, on the other hand, we are mature readers, we progress in our reading, each new extension and exercise of our imaginations making possible still further extensions. Gradually, the "maps" which we have inside our heads become fuller, more accurate, pictures of the actual "territories" of human character and behavior under many different conditions and in many different times. Gradually, too, our increased insight gives us sympathy with our fellow human beings everywhere. The Kings of Egypt, the Tibetan priest behind his ceremonial mask, the Roman political exile, and the embittered Harlem youth are presented to us by the novelist, the poet, and the playwright, at levels of vivid and intimate description, so that we learn how they lived, what they worried about, and how they felt. When the lives of other people, of whatever time and place, are examined in this way, we discover to our amazement that they are all people. This discovery is the basis of all civilized human relationships. If we remain uncivilized — whether in community, industrial, national, or international relationships —

it is largely because most of us have not yet made this discovery. Literature is one of the important instruments to that end.

By means of scientific communication, then, with its international systems of weights and measures, international systems of botanical and zoological nomenclature, international mathematical symbols, we are enabled to exchange information with each other, pool our observations, and acquire collective control over our environment. By means of affective communication — by conversation and gesture when we can see each other, but by literature and other arts when we cannot — we come to understand each other, to cease being brutishly suspicious of each other, and gradually to realize the profound community that exists between us and our fellow men. Science, in short, makes us able to co-operate; the arts enlarge our sympathies so that we become willing to co-operate.

We are today equipped technologically to be able to get practically anything we want. But our wants are crude. There seems to be only one motivation strong enough to impel us to employ our technological capacities to the full, and that is the desire for "military security." The most expensive concerted national effort in every major nation goes into preparations for a war that nobody wants to start. The immediate task of the future, then, is not only to extend the use of scientific method into fields such as economics and politics where superstition now reigns and makes calamity inevitable. It is also to bring, through the affective power of the arts and of literature, civilizing influences to bear upon our savage wills. We must not only be *able* to work together; we must actively *want* to work together.

FOR DISCUSSION

1. What are three differences between writing as a report of actual experience and writing as literature?

2. Is it reasonable to say that people who have read good literature have lived more than people who have not read?

3. What are some differences between actual and symbolic experiences?

4. Why does a mature reader find it difficult to identify himself with the hero of a cowboy story?

5. Are people who always want happy endings immature?

6. In what way does literature contribute to civilization?

VOCABULARY: affective, verifiable, uniqueness, connotation, cupidity, extensional world, denouement, nomenclature, concerted.

THEME TOPICS: A story that gave me symbolic experience. A story that added to my knowledge of life. A story that deepened my sympathies with other human beings. The superficiality of the last cowboy movie I saw. A story does not have to be realistic to be true.

The Act of Language

JOHN CIARDI

At the beginning of *The Divine Comedy*, Dante finds himself in a Dark Wood, lost from the light of God. It was no single, specific evil act that led Dante into that darkness but, rather, the sin of omission. Its name is Acedia, the fourth of the Seven Deadly Sins, and by us generally translated "Sloth."

In American-English, however, Sloth may seem to imply mere physical laziness and untidiness. The torpor of Acedia, it must be understood, is spiritual rather than physical. It is to know the good, but to be lax in its pursuit.

Whether one thinks of it as a sin or as a behavioral failure, Acedia is also the one fault for which no artist can be forgiven. Time, as W. H. Auden wrote in his poem titled *In Memory of W. B. Yeats*:

> *Worships language and forgives*
> *Everyone by whom it lives;*
> *Pardons cowardice, conceit,*
> *Lays its honors at their feet.*

In place of cowardice and conceit, Auden might have cited any catalogue of pride, envy, wrath, avarice, gluttony or carnality, and he could still have said that time forgives. The poet may cheat anything else and still win honor from time, but he may not cheat the poem and live.

For a man is finally defined by what he does with his attention. It was Simone Weil who said, "Absolute attention is absolute prayer." I do not, of course, know what an absolute attention is, except as an absolutely unattainable goal. But certainly to seek that increasing purity and concentration of one's attention that will lead to more and more meaningful perception, is not only possible but is the basic human exercise of any art. In must be added, however, that *in art it does not matter what one pays attention to; the quality of the attention is what counts.*

I have just made a dangerous statement; one that will probably breed protest, that will be difficult to explain, and that will turn out in the end to be only partly true. It is still necessary to make the statement first, and then to go the long way round to explaining why it is necessary, and in what way it is true.

From *The Saturday Evening Post*, March 19, 1960. Reprinted by permission of the author.

The need to go the long way round brings matters back to another parable of poetry that one may read in Dante's opening situation. The language of parables is always likely to be apt to the discussion of poetry.

As soon as Dante realizes that he is in darkness, he looks up and sees the first light of the dawn shawling the shoulders of a little hill. (In Dante, the Sun is always a symbol of God as Divine Illumination.) The allegory should be clear enough: The very realization that one is lost is the beginning of finding oneself.

What happens next is the heart of the matter. His goal in sight, Dante tries to race straight up the hill — to reach the light, as it were, by direct assault. Note that common sense would certainly be on Dante's side. There is the light and there is the hill: go to it. Nothing could be simpler. Nor, as Dante discovers, could anything be more false. Almost immediately his way is blocked by three beasts. These beasts — a Leopard, a Lion and a She-wolf — represent all the sins of the world. They represent, therefore, the world's total becloudment of any man's best attention, for all that has ever lured any man away from his own good is contained within them.

The three beasts drive Dante back into the darkness. There Dante comes on the soul of Virgil, who symbolizes Human Reason. In that role Virgil explains that a man may reach the light only by going the long way round. Dante must risk the dangerous descent into Hell — to the recognition of sin. And he must make the arduous ascent of Purgatory — to the renunciation of sin. Only then may he enter, bit by bit, the final presence of the light, which is to say, Heaven.

The point of the parable is that in art as in theology — as in all things that concern a man in his profoundest being — the long way round is the only way home. Short cuts are useful only in mechanics. The man who seeks mortal understanding must go the long, encompassing way of his deepest involvement.

Americans, susceptible as they are to the legend of mechanical know-how and get-it-done, may especially need to be told that there is no easy digest of understanding and no gift package of insight. May they learn, too, that "common sense," useful as it can be in its own sphere, cannot lead a man as deeply into himself as he must be led if he is to enter a meaningful experience of art or of life. Every man who looks long enough at the stars must come to feel their other-reality engulfing his mortal state, and nothing from the world's efficiencies and practicalities is specific to that awareness in him.

Poetry is written of that man under the stars in trouble and in joy, and the truth of poetry cannot be spoken meaningfully in simple common-sense assertions. In poetry, as in all our deepest emotions, many feelings and many thoughts and half-thoughts happen at once. Often these feelings and thoughts are in conflict:

We love and hate the same thing, desire it and dread it, need it and are destroyed by it. Always, too, there are more thoughts and feelings in a profound experience than we can put a finger on. What has common sense to say to such states of man? Common sense tends always to the easier assumption that only one thing is "really" happening in a man at one time, and that a simple, straightforward course of action will take care of it.

Such an assumption can only blind one to poetry. To read a poem with no thought in mind but to paraphrase it into a single, simple, and usually high-minded, prose statement is the destruction of poetry. Nor does it make much difference that one can quote poetry, and good poetry, in defense of such destruction. At the end of *Ode on a Grecian Urn,* John Keats wrote:

> *"Beauty is truth, truth beauty," — that is all*
> *Ye know on earth, and all ye need to know.*

Heaven knows how many enthusiasts have used these lines as evidence that poetry is somehow an act of inspiration not to be measured by any criteria but an undefined devotion to "beauty," "truth" and "inspiring message."

But if beauty and truth are all that Grecian urns and men need know on earth, Keats makes evident by his own practice that a poet also needs to know a great deal about his trade, and that he must be passionately concerned for its basic elements.

Those basic elements are not beauty and truth but *rhythm, diction, image* and *form.* Certainly Keats cared about beauty and truth. Any sensitive man must care. No matter that one must forever fumble at the definition of such ideas; they are still matters of ultimate concern. But so was Dante's yearning for the light, and he discovered at once that it can be reached only by the long way round.

The poet's way round is by way of rhythm, diction, image and form. It is the right, the duty and the joy of his trade to be passionate about these things. To be passionate about them in the minutest and even the most frivolous detail. To be passionate about them, if need be, to the exclusion of what is generally understood by "sincerity" and "meaning." To be more passionate about them than he is about the cold war, the Gunpowder Plot, the next election, abolition, the H-bomb, the Inquisition, juvenile delinquency, the Spanish Armada, or his own survival.

The good poets have not generally sneered at the world of affairs. Some have, but many others have functioned well within that world. Yet the need and the right of all poets to detach themselves from the things of the world in order to pursue the things of the poetic trade have always been inseparable from their success as poets.

The poet must be passionate about the four elements of his trade for the most fundamental of reasons. He must be so because those passions are both a joy and an addiction within him. Because they are the life of the poem, without which nothing of value can happen either in the poem or to the reader. Because writing a poem is a more sentient way of living than not writing it, because no poem can be written well except as these passions inform it, and because only when the poem is so written can the beauty and truth of that more sentient way of living be brought to mortal consequence.

The act of poetry may seem to have very simple surfaces, but it is always compounded of many things at once. As Robert Frost wrote in *Two Tramps in Mud Time:*

> *Only where love and need are one,*
> *And the work is play for mortal stakes,*
> *Is the deed ever really done*
> *For Heaven and the future's sakes.*

The voice of common sense rises immediately in protest. "Mystification!" it cries. "A poem still has to *mean* something. What does it *mean?*" And the poet must answer, "Never what you think. Not when you ask the question in that way."

But how shall the question be asked? Let the questioner listen first to a kind of statement he has probably passed over without enough attention. He can find one such in Walter Pater's essay on Winckelman. "Let us understand by poetry," wrote Pater, "all literary production which attains the power of giving pleasure by its form as distinct from its matter."

He can find another in a book titled *The Fire and the Fountain* by the English poet and critic John Press. "The essence of the poet," wrote Press, "is to be found less in his opinion than in his idiom." He may even find one in a textbook titled *Reading Poems*, in which Prof. Wright Thomas says, "The *subject* is a very poor indication of what the *poem* is" — to which I should add only that it is no indication whatever.

But if the meaning is not in the subject, what then does a poem mean? It means always and above all else the poet's deep involvement in the four basic elements of his trade. It means not the subject but the way the poetic involvement transfigures the subject. It means, that is to say, the very act of language by which it comes into existence. The poem may purport to be about anything from pussy willows to battleships, but the meaning of any poem is its act of language.

Because it is an act of language, a good poem is deeply connected with everything men are and do. For language is certainly one of the most fundamental activities in which human beings engage. Take away a man's language, and you take most of his ability to think and to experience. Enrich his language, and you cannot fail to enrich his experience. Any man who has let great language into his head is the richer for it.

He is not made richer by what is being said. It is the language itself that brings his enrichment. Could poetry be meaningful aside from its act of language, it would have no reason for being, and the whole history of poetry could be reduced to a series of simple paraphrases.

Consider as simple a passage as the beginning of Herrick's *Upon Julia's Clothes:*

> *Whenas in silks my Julia goes,*
> *Then, then, methinks, how sweetly flows*
> *The liquefaction of her clothes.*

Who can read those lines without a thrill of pleasure? But now consider the paraphrase: "I like the rustle of Julia's silks when she walks." The poetry and the paraphrase are certainly about equal in subject matter. The difference is that the poetry is a full and rich act of language, whereas the paraphrase, though faultless, lacks, among other things, measure, pause, stress, rhyme and the pleasure of lingering over the word "liquefaction."

"But what is Julia doing there?" cries that voice of common sense. "She must have something to do with the poem or she wouldn't be in it!"

The owner of that voice would do well to ponder the relation between a good portrait and its subject. The subject is there, to be sure — at least in most cases. But the instant the painter puts one brush stroke on the canvas and then another, the two brush strokes take on a relation to each other and to the space around them. The two then take on a relation to the third, and it to them. And so forth. The painting immediately begins to exert its own demands upon the painter, its own way of going. Immediately the subject begins to disappear.

All too soon, for that matter, the subject will have changed with age or will have died. After a while no living person will have any recollection of what the subject looked like. All that will remain then is a portrait head which must be either self-validating or worthless. Because the subject cannot validate the painting, he or she will have become irrelevant. All that can finally validate the portrait is the way in which the painter engaged the act of painting.

And one more thing — the good artist always thinks in long terms. He knows, even at the moment of the painting, that both he and the subject will disappear. Any good painter will be painting for the painting — for the time when the subject will have blown away into time.

So with poetry. The one final and enduring meaning of any poem lies not in what it seems to have set out to say, but in its act of language.

> *An artist (in literature) appeals to that part of our being which is not dependable on wisdom; to that in us which is a gift and not an acquisition — and, therefore, more permanently enduring. He speaks to our capacity for delight and wonder, to the sense of mystery surrounding our lives; to our sense of pity, and beauty, and pain.*
>
> JOSEPH CONRAD

The only test of that act of language is the memory of the race. Bad poetry is by nature forgettable; it is, therefore, soon forgotten. But good poetry, like any good act of language, hooks onto human memory and stays there. Write well, and there will always be someone somewhere who carries in his mind what you have written. It will stay in memory because man is the language animal, and because his need of language is from the roots of his consciousness. That need in him is not a need for meaning. Rather, good language in him takes possession of meaning; it fills him with a resonance that the best of men understand only dimly, but without which no man is entirely alive. Poetry is that presence and the resonance. As Archibald MacLeish put it in his much-discussed *Ars Poetica:*

> *A poem should not mean*
> *But be.*

If the reader truly wishes to engage poetry, let him forget meaning. Let him think rather: "I shall summon great language to mind. I shall summon language so fully, so resonantly and so precisely used that it will bring all my meanings to me." Then let him turn to poetry, and let him listen to the passions of the poet's trade.

Listen to great rhythms. Here is the opening stanza of John Donne's *The Anniversarie:*

> *All Kings, and all their favorites,*
> *All glory of honours, beauties, wits,*
> *The Sun it selfe, which makes times as they passe,*
> *Is elder by a yeare, now, than it was*
> *When thou and I first one another saw:*
> *All other things, to their destruction draw,*
> *   Only our love hath no decay,*
> *This, no to morrow hath, nor yesterday.*
> *Running, it never runs from us away,*
> *But truly keeps his first, last, everlasting day.*

Worldly things pass away, but true love is constant, says the subject matter. All true enough and tried enough. But listen to the rhythm enforce itself upon the saying, especially in the last four lines. For present purposes, let the voice ignore the lesser accents. Let it stress only those syllables printed in capital letters below, while observing the pauses as indicated by the slash marks. And forget the meaning. Read for the voice emphasis and the voice pauses:

> *Only OUR LOVE hath no deCAY//*
> *THIS//no to MOrrow hath//nor YESterday//*
> *RUNning//it never runs from us aWAY//*
> *But truly keeps his FIRST//LAST//EVerlasting DAY.*

Not all rhythms are so percussive, so measured out by pauses, and so metrically irregular. Listen to this smoother rhythm from Poe's *Israfel:*

If I could dwell
Where Israfel
  Hath dwelt, and he where I,
He might not sing so wildly well
  A mortal melody,
While a bolder note than his might swell
  From my lyre within the sky.

Or the rhythm may be percussive, but without substantial pauses, as in the last line of this passage from the end of Gerard Manley Hopkins' *Felix Randal,* an elegy for a blacksmith:

How far from then forethought of, all thy more boisterous years,
When thou at the random grim forge, powerful amidst peers,
Didst fettle for the great gray drayhorse his bright and battering sandal.

Listen to the hammerfall of that last line: "Didst FEttle for the GREAT GRAY DRAYhorse his BRIGHT and BAttering SANdal."

Or listen to the spacing of the "ah" sounds as a rhythmic emphasis in the last line of this final passage from Meredith's *Lucifer in Starlight:*

Around the ancient track marched, rank on rank,
The ARmy of unALterable LAW.

Percussive, smooth, flowing or studded with pauses — there is no end to the variety and delight of great language rhythms. For the poet, his rhythms are forever more than a matter of making a "meaningful" statement; they are a joy in their own right. No poet hates meaning. But the poet's passion is for the triumph of language. No reader can come to real contact with a poem until he comes to it through the joy of that rhythmic act of language.

As for rhythm, so for diction. The poet goes to language — or it comes to him and he receives it — for his joy in the precision of great word choices. Give him such a line as Whitman's "I witness the corpse with the dabbled hair," and he will register the corpse, to be sure, but it will be "dabbled" he seizes upon with the joy of a botanist coming on a rare specimen. So when Keats speaks of Ruth amid "the alien corn" or when Theodore Roethke speaks of sheep "strewn" on a field, the good reader will certainly care about the dramatic situation of the poem, but he cannot fail to answer with a special joy to "alien" and to "strewn."

What, after all, is the subject as compared to his joy in such rich precision? Thousands of English poems have described the passing of winter and the coming of spring. Certainly there is little in that subject as a subject to attract him. But listen to the pure flutefall of the word choices I have italicized in the following passage from Stanley Kunitz's *Deciduous Bough,* and note how the self-delight in language makes everything immediate and new again:

> Winter that *coils* in the thicket now
> Will *glide* from the field, the *swinging* rain
> Be *knotted* with flowers, on every bough
> A bird will *meditate* again.

"Poetry," said Coleridge, "is the best words in the best order." How can anyone reading the Kunitz passage escape a sense that the language is being ultimately and unimprovably selected? The delight one feels in coming on such language is not only in the experience of perfection but also in the fact that perfection has been made to seem not only effortless but inevitable.

And let this much more be added to the idea of poetic meaning: Nothing in a good poem happens by accident; every word, every comma, every variant spelling must enter as an act of the poet's choice. A poem is a machine for making choices. The mark of the good poet is his refusal to make easy or cheap choices. The better the poet, the greater the demands he makes upon himself, and the higher he sets his level of choice. Thus, a good poem is not only an act of mind but an act of devotion to mind. The poet who chooses cheaply or lazily is guilty of aesthetic acedia, and he is lost thereby. The poet who spares himself nothing in his search for the most demanding choices is shaping a human attention that offers itself as a high and joyful example to all men of mind and devotion. Every act of great language, whatever its subject matter, illustrates an idea of order and a resonance of human possibility without which no man's mind can sense its own fullest dimensions.

As for rhythm and diction, so for imagery. To be sure, every word is at root an image, and poetic images must be made of words. Yet certainly there is in a well-constructed image an effect that cannot be said to rise from any one word choice, but from the total phrasing.

So for the sensory shiver of Keats' "The silver snarling trumpets 'gan to chide." So for the wonderfully woozy effect of John Frederick Nims' "The drunk clambering on his undulant floor." So for the grand hyperbole of Howard Nemerov saying that the way a young girl looks at him "sets his knees to splashing like two waves."

We learn both imagination and precision from the poet's eye. And we learn correspondences. Consider the following image from *Aereopagus* by Louis MacNeice, a poem as playful as it is serious, in which MacNeice describes Athens as a cradle of the western mind. Cradles, he makes clear, generally contain children, and all those boy-gods and girl-goddesses had their childish side:

> . . . *you still may glimpse*
> *The child-eyed Fury tossing her shock of snakes,*
> *Careering over the Parthenon's ruined playpen.*

It is a bit shocking to have the Parthenon spoken of as a playpen, but once the shock has passed, what a triumph there is in the figure: everything corresponds! Think how much would have been lost had the Parthenon a surviving roof, or had its general proportions or the placement of the pillars — slats — resisted the comparison. The joy of it is that, despite the first shock, nothing resists the comparison; and we find that the surprise turns out to be a true correspondence.

One of the poet's happiest — and most mortal — games is in seeking such correspondences. But what flows from them is more than a game. Every discovery of a true correspondence is an act of reason and an instruction to the mind. For intelligence does not consist of masses of factual detail. It consists of seeing essential likenesses and essential differences and of relating them, allowing for differences within the likenesses and for likenesses within the differences. Mentality is born of analogy.

Note, too, that the image-idea of "ruined playpen" does not simply happen, but is prepared for in "child-eyed." And note, further, the nice double meaning of "careering" as both "a wild rush" and "to make a career of."

A good extended image, that is to say, is made of various elements and is marked by both sequence and structure. Thus we have already touched upon the essence of the fourth element of the poet's trade: form.

There are many kinds of poetic form, but since all are based on pattern and sequence, let a tightly patterned poem illustrate. Here is Emily Dickinson's *The Soul Selects:*

> *The soul selects her own society,*
> *Then shuts the door;*
> *On her divine majority*
> *Obtrude no more.*
>
> *Unmoved, she notes the chariot's pausing*
> *At her low gate;*
> *Unmoved, an emperor is kneeling*
> *Upon her mat.*
>
> *I've known her from an ample nation*
> *Choose one;*
> *Then close the valves of her attention*
> *Like stone.*

Whatever the hunters of beauty and truth find for their pleasure in such a poem, the poet's joy will be in its form and management. He responds to the passion of the language for its own sparseness, to the pattern of rhyme and half-rhyme, to the flavor of the images (connotation), and to the way those flavors relate to one another. He responds to the interplay of the four-foot feminine lines (feminine lines end on an unaccented syllable) and the two-foot masculine lines (which end on an accented syllable).

And he responds, above all, to the way those two-foot lines develop in the last stanza into two boldly stroked syllables apiece (monosyllabic feet) so that the emotion held down throughout the poem by the sparseness of the language is hammered into sensation by the beat of those last two words: "Like stone" — thud! thud!

Beauty and truth are no irrelevancies, but they are abstractions that must remain meaningless to poetry until they are brought to being in the management of a specific form. It is that management the poet must love: the joy of sensing the poem fall into inescapable form, and therefore into inescapable experience. For the poet's trade is not to talk about experience, but to make it happen. His act of making is all he knows of beauty and truth. It is, in fact, his way of knowing them. His only way of knowing them.

As I. A. Richards, poet and scholar of the language, put it in a recent poem titled *The Ruins:*

> *Sometimes a word is wiser much than men:*
> *"Faithful" e.g., "responsible" and "true."*
> *And words it is, not poets, make up poems.*
> *Our words, we say, but we are theirs, too,*
> *For words made men and may unmake again.*

And now, at last, it is time to repeat the statement from which this long way round began. "In art," I said, "it does not matter what one pays attention to; the quality of the attention is what counts." It is time to amend that necessary false statement.

For it does matter where the poet fixes his attention. Attention must be to *something*. That something, however, is so casually connected with the subject of the poem that any reader will do well to dismiss the subject as no more than a point of departure. Any impassioning point of departure will do. The poet, being a man, must believe something, but what that something is does not matter so long as he believes it strongly enough to be passionate about it. What he believes, moreover, may be touched off by an image, a rhythm, or the quality of a word *in pursuit of which the subject is invented.*

The poem, in any case, is not in its point of departure, but in its journey to itself. That journey, the act of the poem, is its act of language. That act is the true final subject and meaning of any poem. It is to that act of language the poet shapes his most devoted attention — to the fullness of rhythm, diction, image and form. Only in that devotion can he seize the world and make it evident.

Acknowledgements: Archibald MacLeish, from *Collected Poems*, published by Houghton Mifflin; Gerard Manley Hopkins, from *Poems of Gerard Manley Hopkins*, published by Oxford University Press; I. A. Richards, from *Poets and the Past*, published by Andre Emmerich Gallery; Robert Frost, from *The Complete Poems of Robert Frost*, published by Henry Holt; Stanley Kunitz, from *Deciduous Bough;* W. H. Auden, from *In Memory of W. B. Yeats*, published by Random House; Louis MacNeice, from *Ten Burnt Offerings*, published by Oxford University Press.

1. Hayakawa in "What Literature Is For" (pages 571-576) discusses literature as chiefly the "organizing of symbolic experiences." Ciardi, on the other hand, minimizes subject-matter in favor of "the act of language." Are the two points of view really in conflict? How do they supplement one another?

2. What is Ciardi's thesis? Does he state it explicitly?

3. What does he mean when he says that in poetry "many feelings and many thoughts and half-thoughts happen at once"? Could the presence or absence of such complexity be used to help evaluate the greatness of a poem? Of a story or movie?

4. What are the basic elements of a poet's trade?

5. What does Ciardi mean when he says that "the meaning of any good poem is its act of language"?

6. Explain Ciardi's comparison of the subject of a poem with the subject of a portrait. How does the comparison help explain the continuing importance of, say, a play by Shakespeare?

VOCABULARY: behavioral, assumption, paraphrase, criteria, sentient, self-validating.

THEME TOPICS: An analysis of a short poem for rhythm, diction, image, and form. No good poem can be paraphrased. Subject doesn't matter in poetry any more than it does in music. A good poem makes many things happen at once.

Settling the Colonel's Hash

MARY McCARTHY

Seven years ago, when I taught in a progressive college, I had a pretty girl student in one of my classes who wanted to be a short-story writer. She was not studying writing with me, but she knew that I sometimes wrote short stories, and one day, breathless and glowing, she came up to me in the hall, to tell me that she had just written a story that her writing teacher, a Mr. Converse, was terribly excited about. "He thinks it's wonderful," she said, "and he's going to help me fix it up for publication."

I asked what the story was about; the girl was a rather simple being who loved clothes and dates. Her answer had a deprecating tone. It was just about a girl (herself) and some sailors she had met on the train. But then her face, which had looked perturbed for a moment, gladdened.

"Mr. Converse is going over it with me and we're going to put in the symbols."

Another girl in the same college, when asked by us in her sophomore orals why she read novels (one of the pseudo-profound questions that ought never to be put) answered in a defensive flurry: "Well, *of course* I don't read them to find out what happens to the hero."

At the time, I thought these notions were peculiar to progressive education: it was old-fashioned or regressive to read a novel to find out what happens to the hero or to have a mere experience empty of symbolic pointers. But I now discover that this attitude is quite general, and that readers and students all over the country are in a state of apprehension, lest they read a book or story literally and miss the presence of a symbol. And like everything in America, this search for meanings has become a socially competitive enterprise; the best reader is the one who detects the most symbols in a given stretch of prose. And the benighted reader who fails to find any symbols humbly assents when they are pointed out to him; he accepts his mortification.

I had no idea how far this process had gone until last spring, when I began to get responses to a story I had published in *Harper's*. I say "story" because that was what it was called by *Harper's*. I myself would not know quite what to call it; it was a piece of reporting or a fragment of autobiography — an account of my meeting with an anti-Semitic army colonel. It began in the club car of a train going to St. Louis; I was wearing an apple-green shirtwaist and a dark-green skirt and pink earrings; we got into an argument about the Jews. The colonel was a rather dapper, flashy kind of Irish-American with a worldly blue eye; he took me, he said, for a sculptress, which made me feel, to my horror, that I looked Bohemian and therefore rather suspect. He was full of the usual profound clichés that anti-Semites air, like original epigrams, about the Jews: that he could tell a Jew, that they were different from other people, that you couldn't trust them in business, that some of his best friends were Jews, that he distinguished between a Jew and a kike, and finally that, of course, he didn't agree with Hitler: Hitler went too far; the Jews were human beings.

All the time we talked, and I defended the Jews, he was trying to get my angle, as he called it; he thought it was abnormal for anybody who wasn't Jewish not to feel as he did. As a matter of fact, I have a Jewish grandmother, but I decided to keep this news to myself: I did not want the colonel to think that I had any interested reason for speaking on behalf of the Jews, that is, that I was prejudiced. In the end, though, I got my comeuppance. Just as we were parting, the colonel asked me my married name, which is Broadwater, and the whole mystery was cleared up for him, instantly; he supposed I was married to a Jew and that the name was spelled B-r-o-d-w-a-t-e-r. I did not try to enlighten him; I let him think what he wanted; in a certain sense, he was right; he had unearthed my Jewish grandmother or her equivalent.

There were a few details that I must mention to make the next part clear: in my car, there were two nuns, whom I talked to as a distraction from the colonel and the moral problems he raised. He and I finally had lunch together in the St. Louis railroad station, where we continued the discussion. It was a very hot day. I had a sandwich; he had roast-beef hash. We both had an old-fashioned.

The whole point of this "story" was that it really happened; it is written in the first person; I speak of myself in my own name, McCarthy; at the end, I mention my husband's name, Broadwater. When I was thinking about writing the story, I decided not to treat it fictionally; the chief interest, I felt, lay in the fact that it happened, in real life, last summer, to the writer herself, who was a good deal at fault in the incident. I wanted to embarrass myself and, if possible, the reader too.

Yet, strangely enough, many of my readers preferred to think of this account as fiction. I still meet people who ask me, confidentially, "That story of yours about the colonel — was it really true?" It seemed to them perfectly natural that I would write a fabrication, in which I figured under my own name, and sign it, though in my eyes this would be like perjuring yourself in court or forging checks. Shortly after the "story" was published, I got a kindly letter from a man in Mexico, in which he criticized the menu from an artistic point of view: he thought salads would be better for hot weather and it would be more in character for the narrator-heroine to have a martini. I did not answer the letter, though I was moved to, because I had the sense that he would not understand the distinction between what *ought* to have happened and what *did* happen.

Then in April I got another letter, from an English teacher in a small college in the Middle West, that reduced me to despair. I am going to cite it at length.

"My students in freshman English chose to analyze your story, 'Artists in Uniform,' from the March issue of *Harper's*. For a week I heard oral discussions on it and then the students wrote critical analyses. In so far as it is possible, I stayed out of their discussions, encourging them to read the story closely with your intentions as a guide to their understanding. Although some of them insisted that the story has no other level than the realistic one, most of them decided it has symbolic overtones.

"The question is: how closely do you want the symbols labeled? They wrestled with the nuns, the author's two shades of green with pink accents, with the 'materialistic godlessness' of the colonel. . . . A surprising number wanted exact symbols; for example, they searched for the significance of the colonel's eating hash and the author eating a sandwich. . . . From my standpoint, the story was an entirely satisfactory springboard for understanding the various shades of prejudice, for seeing how much of the artist goes into his painting. If it is any satisfaction to you, our campus was alive with discussions about 'Artists in Uniform.' We liked the story and we thought it amazing that an author could succeed in making readers dislike the author — for a purpose, of course!"

I probably should have answered this letter, but I did not. The gulf seemed to me too wide. I could not applaud the backward students who insisted that the story has no other level than the realistic one without giving offense to their teacher, who was evidently a well-meaning person. But I shall try now to address a reply, not to this teacher and her unfortunate class, but to a whole school of misunderstanding. There were no symbols in this story; there was no deeper level. The nuns were in the story because they were on the train; the contrasting greens were the dress I happened to be wearing; the colonel had hash because he had hash; materialistic godlessness meant just what it means when a priest thunders it from the pulpit — the phrase, for the first time, had meaning for me as I watched and listened to the colonel.

But to clarify the misunderstanding, one must go a little further and try to see what a literary symbol is. Now in one sense, the colonel's hash and my sandwich can be regarded as symbols; that is, they typify the colonel's food tastes and mine. (The man in Mexico had different food tastes which he wished to interpose into our reality.) The hash and the sandwich might even be said to show something very obvious about our characters and bringing-up, or about our sexes; I was a woman, he was a man. And though on another day I might have ordered hash myself, that day I did not, because the colonel and I, in our disagreement, were polarizing each other.

The hash and the sandwich, then, could be regarded as symbols of our disagreement, almost conscious symbols. And underneath our discussion of the Jews, there was a thin sexual current running, as there always is in such random encounters or pickups (for they have a strong suggestion of the illicit.) The fact that I ordered something conventionally feminine and he ordered something conventionally masculine represented, no doubt, our awareness of a sexual possibility; even though I was not attracted to the colonel, nor he to me, the circumstances of our meeting made us define ourselves as a woman and a man.

The sandwich and the hash were our provisional, *ad hoc* symbols of ourselves. But in this sense all human actions are symbolic because they represent the person who does them. If the colonel had ordered a fruit salad with whipped cream, this too would have represented him in some way; given his other traits, it would have pointed to a complexity in his character that the hash did not suggest.

In the same way, the contrasting greens of my dress were a symbol of my taste in clothes and hence representative of me — all too representative. I suddenly saw, in the club car, when I got an "artistic" image of myself flashed back at me from the men's eyes. I had no wish to stylize myself as an artist, that is, to parade about as a symbol of flamboyant unconventionality, but apparently I had done so unwittingly when I picked those colors off a rack, under the impression that they suited me or "expressed my personality" as salesladies say.

My dress, then, was a symbol of the perplexity I found myself in with the colonel; I did not want to be categorized as a member of a peculiar minority — an artist or a Jew; but brute fate and the colonel kept resolutely cramming me into both those uncomfortable pigeonholes. I wished to be regarded as ordinary or rather as universal, to be anybody and therefore everybody (that is, in one sense, I wanted to be on the colonel's side, majestically above minorities); but every time the colonel looked at my dress and me in it with my pink earrings I shrank to minority status, and felt the dress in the heat shriveling me, like the shirt of Nessus, the centaur, that consumed Hercules.

But this is not what the students meant when they wanted the symbols "labeled." They were searching for a more recondite significance than that afforded by the trite symbolism of ordinary life, in which a dress is a social badge. They supposed that I was engaging in literary or artificial symbolism, which would lead the reader out of the confines of reality into the vast fairy tale of myth, in which the color green would have an emblematic meaning (or did the two greens signify for them what the teacher calls "shades" of prejudice), and the colonel's hash, I imagine, would be some sort of Eucharistic mincemeat.

Apparently, the presence of the nuns assured them there were overtones of theology; it did not occur to them (a) that the nuns were there because pairs of nuns are a standardized feature of summer Pullman travel, like crying babies, and perspiring businessmen in the club car, and (b) that if I thought the nuns worth mentioning, it was also because of something very simple and directly relevant: the nuns and the colonel and I all had something in common — we had all at one time been Catholics — and I was seeking common ground with the colonel, from which to turn and attack his position.

In any account of reality, even a televised one, which comes closest to being a literal transcript or replay, some details are left out as irrelevant (though nothing is really irrelevant). The details that are not eliminated have to stand as symbols of the whole, like stenographic signs, and of course there is an art of selection, even in a newspaper account: the writer, if he has any ability, is looking for the revealing detail that will sum up the picture for the reader in a flash of recognition.

But the art of abridgment and condensation, which is familiar to anybody who tries to relate an anecdote, or give a direction — the art of natural symbolism, which is at the basis of speech and all representation — has at bottom a centripetal intention. It hovers over an object, and event, or series of events and tries to declare what it is. Analogy (that is, comparison to other objects) is inevitably one of its methods. "The weather was soupy," i.e., like soup. "He wedged his way in," i.e., he had to enter, thin edge first, as a wedge enters, and so on. All this is obvious. But these metaphorical aids to communication are a far cry from literary symbolism, as taught in the schools and practiced by certain fashionable writers. Literary symbolism is centrifugal and flees from the object, the event, into the incorporeal distance, where concepts are taken for substance and floating ideas and archetypes assume a hieratic authority.

In this dream-forest, symbols become arbitrary; all counters are interchangeable; anything can stand for anything else. The colonel's hash can be a Eucharist or a cannibal feast or the banquet of Atreus, or all three, so long as the actual dish set before the actual man is disparaged. What is depressing about this insistent symbolization is the fact that while it claims to lead to the infinite, it quickly reaches very finite limits — there are only so many myths on record, and once you have got through Bulfinch, the Scandinavian, and the Indian, there is not much left. And if all stories reduce themselves to myth and symbol, qualitative differences vanish, and there is only a single, monotonous story.

American fiction of the symbolist school demonstrates this mournful truth, without precisely intending to. A few years ago, when the mode was at its height, chic novels and stories fell into three classes: those which had a Greek myth for their framework, which the reader was supposed to detect, like finding the faces in the clouds in old newspaper puzzle contests; those which had symbolic modern figures, dwarfs, hermaphrodites, and cripples, illustrating maiming and loneliness; and those which contained symbolic animals, cougars, wild cats, and monkeys. One young novelist, a product of the Princeton school of symbolism, had all three elements going at once, like the ringmaster of a three-ring circus, with the freaks, the animals, and the statues.

The quest for symbolic referents had as its object, of course, the deepening of the writer's subject and the reader's awareness. But the result was paradoxical. At the very moment when American writing was penetrated by the symbolic urge, it ceased to be able to create symbols of its own. Babbitt, I suppose, was the last important symbol to be created by an American writer; he gave his name to a type that henceforth would be recognizable to everybody. He passed into the language. The same thing could be said, perhaps, though to a lesser degree, of Caldwell's Tobacco Road, Eliot's Prufrock, and possibly of Faulkner's Snopeses. The discovery of new symbols is not the only function of a writer, but the writer who cares about this must be fascinated by reality itself, as a butterfly collector is fascinated by the glimpse of a new specimen. Such a specimen was Mme. Bovary or M. Homais or M. de Charlus or Jupien; these specimens were precious to their discoverers, not because they repeated an age-old pattern but because their markings were new. Once the specimen has been described, the public instantly spots other examples of the kind, and the world seems suddenly full of Babbitts and Charlus, where none had been noted before.

A different matter was Joyce's Mr. Bloom. Mr. Bloom can be called a symbol of eternal recurrence — the wandering Jew, Ulysses the voyager — but he is a symbol thickly incarnate, fleshed out in a Dublin advertising canvasser. He is not *like* Ulysses or vaguely suggestive of Ulysses; he is Ulysses, circa 1905. Joyce evidently believed in a cyclical theory of history, in which everything repeated itself; he also subscribed in youth to the doctrine that declares that the Host, a piece of bread, is also God's body and blood. How it can be both things at the same time, transubstantially, is a mystery, and Mr. Bloom is just such a mystery: Ulysses in the visible appearance of a Dublin advertising canvasser.

Mr. Bloom is not a symbol of Ulysses, but Ulysses-Bloom together, one and indivisible, symbolize or rather demonstrate eternal recurrence. I hope I make myself clear. The point is transubstantiation: Bloom and Ulysses are transfused into each other and neither reality is diminished. Both realities are locked together, like the protons and neutrons of an atom. *Finnegans Wake* is a still more ambitious attempt to create a fusion, this time a myriad fusion, and to exemplify the mystery of how a thing can be itself and at the same time be something else. The world is many and it is also one.

But the clarity and tension of Joyce's thought brought him closer in a way to the strictness of allegory than to the diffuse practices of latter-day symbolists. In Joyce, the equivalences and analogies are very sharp and distinct, as in a pun, and the real world is almost querulously audible, like the voices of the washerwoman on the Liffey that come into Earwicker's dream. But this is not true of Joyce's imitators or of the imitators of his imitators, for whom reality is only a shadowy pretext for the introduction of a whole *corps de ballet* of dancing symbols in mythic draperies and animal skins.

Let me make a distinction. There are some great writers, like Joyce or Melville, who have consciously introduced symbolic elements into their work; and there are great writers who have written fables or allegories. In both cases, the writer makes it quite clear to the reader how he is to be read; only an idiot would take *Pilgrim's Progress* for a realistic story, and even a young boy, reading *Moby Dick*, realizes that there is something more than whale-fishing here, though he may not be able to name what it is. But the great body of fiction contains only what I have called natural symbolism, in which selected events represent or typify a problem, a kind of society or psychology, a philosophical theory, in the same way that they do in real life. What happens to the hero becomes of the highest importance. This symbolism needs no abstruse interpretation, and abstruse interpretation will only lead the reader away from the reality that the writer is trying to press on his attention.

I shall give an example or two of what I mean by natural symbolism and I shall begin with a rather florid one: Henry James' *The Golden Bowl*. This is the story of a rich American girl who collects European objects. One of these objects is a husband, Prince Amerigo, who proves to be unfaithful. Early in the story, there is a visit to an antique shop in which the Prince picks out a gold bowl for his fiancée and finds, to his annoyance, that it is cracked. It is not hard to see that the cracked bowl is a symbol, both of the Prince himself, who is a valuable antique but a little flawed, morally, and also of the marriage, which represents an act of acquisition or purchase on the part of the heroine and her father. If the reader should fail to notice the analogy, James calls his attention to it in the title.

I myself would not regard this symbol as necessary to this particular history; it seems to me, rather, an ornament of the kind that was fashionable in the architecture and interior decoration of the period, like stylized sheaves of corn or palms on the façade of a house. Nevertheless, it is handsome and has an obvious appropriateness to the theme. It introduces the reader into the Gilded Age attitudes of the novel. I think there is also a scriptural echo in the title that conveys the idea of punishment. But having seen and felt the weight of meaning that James put into this symbol, one must not be tempted to press further and look at the bowl as a female sex symbol, a chalice, a Holy Grail, and so on; a book is not a pious excuse for reciting a litany of associations.

My second example is from Tolstoy's *Anna Karenina*. Toward the beginning of the novel, Anna meets the man who will be her lover, Vronsky, on the Moscow-St. Petersburg express; as they meet, there has been an accident; a workman has been killed by the train. This is the beginning of Anna's doom, which is completed when she throws herself under a train and is killed; and the last we see of Vronsky is in a train, with a toothache; he is off to the wars. The train is necessary to the plot of the novel, and I believe it is also symbolic, both of the iron forces of material progress that Tolstoy hated so and that played a part in Anna's moral destruction, and also of those iron laws of necessity and consequence that govern human action when it remains on the sensual level.

One can read the whole novel, however, without being conscious that the train is a symbol; we do not have to "interpret" to feel the import of doom and loneliness in the train's whistle — the same import we ourselves can feel when we hear a train whistle blow in the country, even today. Tolstoy was a deeper artist than James, and we cannot be sure that the train was a conscious device with him. The appropriateness to Anna's history may have been only a *felt* appropriateness; everything in Tolstoy has such a supreme naturalness that one shrinks from attributing contrivance to him, as if it were a sort of fraud. Yet he worked very hard on his novels — I forget how many times Countess Tolstoy copied out *War and Peace* by hand.

The impression one gets from his diaries is that he wrote by ear; he speaks repeatedly, even as an old man, of having to start a story over again because he has the wrong tone, and I suspect that he did not think of the train as a symbol but that it sounded "right" to him, because it was, in that day, an almost fearsome emblem of ruthless and impersonal force, not only to a writer of genius but to the poorest peasant in the fields. And in Tolstoy's case I think it would be impossible, even for the most fanciful critic, to extricate the train from the novel and try to make it say something that the novel itself does not say directly. Every detail in Tolstoy has an almost cruel and viselike mean-ingfulness and truth to itself that makes it tautological to talk of symbolism; he was a moralist and to him the tiniest action, even the curiosities of physi-cal appearance, Vronsky's bald spot, the small white hands of Prince Andrei, told a moral tale.

It is now considered very old-fashioned and tasteless to speak of an author's "philosophy of life" as something that can be harvested from his work. Actually, most of the great authors did have a "philosophy of life" which they were eager to communicate to the public; this was one of their motives for writing. And to disentangle a moral philosophy from a work that evidently contains one is far less damaging to the author's purpose and the integrity of his art than to violate his imagery by symbol-hunting, as though reading a novel were a sort of paper-chase.

The images of a novel or a story belong, as it were, to a family, very closely knit and inseparable from each other; the parent "idea" of a story or a novel generates events and images all bearing a strong family resemblance. And to understand a story or a novel, you must look for the parent "idea," which is usually in plain view, if you read quite carefully and literally what the author says.

I will go back, for a moment, to my own story, to show how this can be done. Clearly, it is about the Jewish question, for that is what the people are talking about. It also seems to be about artists, since the title is "Artists in Uniform." Then there must be some relation between artists and Jews. What is it? They are both minorities that other people claim to be able to recognize by their appearance. But artists and Jews do not care for this categorization; they want to be universal, that is, like everybody else. They do not want to wear their destiny as a badge, as the soldier wears his uniform. But this aim is really hopeless, for life has formed them as Jews or artists, in a way that immediately betrays them to the majority they are trying to melt into. In my conversation with the colonel, I was endeavoring to play a double game. I was trying to force him into a minority by treating anti-Semitism as an aberration, which, in fact, I believe it is. On his side, the colonel resisted this attempt and tried to show that anti-Semitism was normal, and he was normal, while I was the queer one. He declined to be categorized as anti-Semite; he regarded himself as an independent thinker, who by a happy chance thought the same as everybody else.

I imagined I had a card up my sleeve; I had guessed that the colonel was Irish (i.e., that he belonged to a minority) and presumed that he was a Catholic. I did not see how he could possibly guess that I, with my Irish name and Irish appearance, had a Jewish grandmother in the background. Therefore when I found I had not convinced him by reasoning, I played my last card; I told him that the Church, his Church, forbade anti-Semitism. I went even further; I implied that God forbade it, though I had no right to do this, since I did not believe in God, but was only using Him as a whip to crack over the colonel, to make him feel humble and inferior, a raw Irish Catholic lad under discipline. But the colonel, it turned out, did not believe in God, either, and I lost. And since, in a sense, I had been cheating all along in this game we were playing, I had to concede the colonel a sort of moral victory in the end; I let him think that my husband was Jewish and that that "explained" everything satisfactorily.

Now there are a number or morals or meanings in this little tale, starting with the simple one: don't talk to strangers on a train. The chief moral or meaning (what I learned, in other words, from this experience) was this: you cannot be a universal unless you accept the fact that you are a singular, that is, a Jew or an artist or what-have-you. What the colonel and I were discussing, and at the same time illustrating and enacting, was the definition of a human being. I was trying to be something better than a human being; I was trying to be the voice of pure reason; and pride went before a fall. The colonel, without trying, was being something worse than a human being, and somehow we found ourselves on the same plane — facing each other, like mutually repellent twins. Or, put in another way: it is dangerous to be drawn into discussions of the Jews with anti-Semites: you delude yourself that you are spreading light, but you are really sinking into muck; if you endeavor to be dispassionate, you are really claiming for yourself a privileged position, a little mountain top, from which you look down, impartially, on both the Jews and the colonel.

Anti-Semitism is a horrible disease from which nobody is immune, and it has a kind of evil fascination that makes an enlightened person draw near the source of infection, supposedly in a scientific spirit, but really to sniff the vapors and dally with the possibility. The enlightened person who lunches with the colonel in order, as she tells herself, to improve him, is cheating herself, having her cake and eating it. This attempted cheat, on my part, was related to the question of the artist and the green dress; I wanted to be an artist but not to pay the price of looking like one, just as I was willing to have Jewish blood but not willing to show it, where it would cost me something — the loss of superiority in an argument.

These meanings are all there, quite patent, to anyone who consents to look *into* the story. They were *in* the experience itself, waiting to be found and considered. I did not perceive them all at the time the experience was happening; otherwise, it would not have taken place, in all probability — I should have given the colonel a wide berth. But when I went back over the experience, in order to write it, I came upon these meanings, protruding at me, as it were, from the details of the occasion. I put in the green dress and my mortification over it because they were part of the truth, just as it had occurred, but I did not see how they were related to the general question of anti-Semitism and my grandmother until they *showed* me their relation in the course of writing.

Every short story, at least for me, is a little act of discovery. A cluster of details presents itself to my scrutiny, like a mystery that I will understand in the course of writing or sometimes not fully until afterward, when, if I have been honest and listened to these details carefully, I will find that they are connected and that there is a coherent pattern. The pattern is *in* experience itself; you do not impose it from the outside and if you try to, you will find that the story is taking the wrong tack, dribbling away from you into artificiality or inconsequence. A story that you do not learn something from while you are writing it, that does not illuminate something for you, is dead, finished before you started it. The "idea" of a story is implicit in it, on the one hand; on the other hand, it is always ahead of the writer, like a form dimly discerned in the distance; he is working *toward* the "idea."

It can sometimes happen that you begin a story thinking that you know the "idea" of it and find, when you are finished, that you have said something quite different and utterly unexpected to you. Most writers have been haunted all their lives by the "idea" of a story or a novel that they think they want to write and see very clearly: Tolstoy always wanted to write a novel about the Decembrists and instead, almost against his will, wrote *War and Peace;* Henry James thought he wanted to write a novel about Napoleon. Probably these ideas for novels were too set in their creators' minds to inspire creative discovery.

In any work that is truly creative, I believe, the writer cannot be omniscient in advance about the effects that he proposes to produce. The suspense in a novel is not only in the reader, but in the novelist himself, who is intensely curious too about what will happen to the hero. Jane Austen may know in a general way that Emma will marry Mr. Knightley in the end (the reader knows this too, as a matter of fact); the suspense for the author lies in the how, in the twists and turns of circumstance, waiting but as yet unknown, that will bring the consummation about. Hence, I would say to the student of writing that outlines, patterns, arrangements of symbols may have a certain usefulness at the outset for some kinds of minds, but in the end they will have to be scrapped. If the story does not contradict the outline, overrun the pattern, break the symbols, like an insurrection against authority, it is surely a stillbirth. The natural symbolism of reality has more messages to communicate than the dry Morse code of the disengaged mind.

The tree of life, said Hegel, is greener than the tree of thought; I have quoted this before but I cannot forbear from citing it again in this context. This is not an incitement to mindlessness or an endorsement of realism in the short story (there are several kinds of reality, including interior reality); it means only that the writer must be, first of all, a listener and observer, who can pay attention to reality, like an obedient pupil, and who is willing, always, to be surprised by the messages reality is sending through to him. And if he gets the messages correctly he will not have to go back and put in the symbols; he will find that the symbols are there, staring at him significantly from the commonplace.

FOR DISCUSSION

1. How would you categorize McCarthy's beginning?

2. Does McCarthy consider it benighted to read novels just to find out what happens to the hero?

3. What chief effect on the reader did McCarthy expect to achieve in writing the story about the Colonel?

4. What in the letter from a freshman English teacher reduced McCarthy to despair?

5. In one sense the choice of food and of dress was symbolic. In another sense the choice was not. Explain.

6. What kind of symbolism leads away from the work of art, and what kind leads into it?

7. What moral does McCarthy find in her own story? Was the moral clear to the author before she wrote? Is there an "idea" in every story?

Vocabulary: deprecate, comeuppance, recondite, Eucharistic, transubstantially, querulously, florid, litany, aberration.

Theme Topics: Natural symbolism in a story or poem. The "idea" in a story or poem.

The Making of a Poem

STEPHEN SPENDER

Apology

It would be inexcusable to discuss my own way of writing poetry unless I were able to relate this to a wider view of the problems which poets attempt to solve when they sit down at a desk or table to write, or walk around composing their poems in their heads. There is a danger of my appearing to put across my own experiences as the general rule, when every poet's way of going about his work and his experience of being a poet are different, and when my own poetry may not be good enough to lend my example any authority.

Yet the writing of poetry is an activity which makes certain demands of attention on the poet and which requires that he should have certain qualifications of ear, vision, imagination, memory and so on. He should be able to think in images, he should have as great a mastery of language as a painter has over his palette, even if the range of his language be very limited. All this means that, in ordinary society, a poet has to adapt himself, more or less consciously, to the demands of his vocation, and hence the peculiarities of poets and the condition of inspiration which many people have said is near to madness. One poet's example is only his adaptation of his personality to the demands of poetry, but if it is clearly stated it may help us to understand other poets, and even something of poetry.

Today we lack very much a whole view of poetry, and have instead many one-sided views of certain aspects of poetry which have been advertised as the only aims which poets should attempt. Movements such as free verse, imagism, surrealism, expressionism, personalism and so on, tend to make people think that poetry is simply a matter of not writing in metre of rhyme, or of free association, or of thinking in images, or of a kind of drawing room madness (surrealism) which corresponds to drawing room communism. Here is a string of ideas: Night, dark, stars, immensity, blue, voluptuous, clinging, columns, clouds, moon, sickle, harvest, vast camp fire, hell. Is this poetry? A lot of strings of words almost as simple as this are set down on the backs of envelopes and posted off to editors or to poets by the vast army of amateurs who think that to be illogical is to be poetic, with that fond question. Thus

I hope that this discussion of how poets work will imply a wider and completer view of poets.

Concentration

The problem of creative writing is essentially one of concentration, and the supposed eccentricities of poets are usually due to mechanical habits or rituals developed in order to concentrate. Concentration, of course, for the purposes of writing poetry, is different from the kind of concentration required for working out a sum. It is a focussing of the attention in a special way, so that the poet is aware of all the implications and possible developments of his idea, just as one might say that a plant was not concentrating on developing mechanically in one direction, but in many directions, towards the warmth and light with its leaves, and towards the water with its roots, all at the same time.

Schiller liked to have a smell of rotten apples, concealed beneath the lid of his desk, under his nose when he was composing poetry. Walter de la Mare has told me that he must smoke when writing. Auden drinks endless cups of tea. Coffee is my own addiction, besides smoking a great deal, which I hardly ever do except when I am writing. I notice also that as I attain a greater concentration, this tends to make me forget the taste of the cigarette in my mouth, and then I have a desire to smoke two or even three cigarettes at a time, in order that the sensation from the outside may penetrate through the wall of concentration which I have built round myself.

For goodness sake, though, do not think that rotten apples or cigarettes or tea have anything to do with the quality of the work of a Schiller, a de la Mare, or an Auden. They are a part of a concentration which has already been attained rather than the causes of concentration. De la Mare once said to me that he thought the desire to smoke when writing poetry arose from a need, not of a stimulus, but to canalize a distracting leak of his attention away from his writing towards the distraction which is always present in one's environment. Concentration may be disturbed by someone whistling in the street or the ticking of a clock. There is always a slight tendency of the body to sabotage the attention of the mind by providing some distraction. If this need for distraction can be directed into one channel — such as the odor of rotten apples or the taste of tobacco or tea — then other distractions outside oneself are put out of competition.

Another possible explanation is that the concentrated effort of writing poetry is a spiritual activity which makes one completely forget, for the time being, that one has a body. It is a disturbance of the balance of body and mind and for this reason one needs a kind of anchor of sensation with the physical world. Hence the craving for a scent or taste or even, sometimes, for sexual activity. Poets speak of the necessity of writing poetry rather than of a liking for doing it. It is spiritual compulsion, a straining of the mind to attain heights surrounded by abysses and it cannot be entirely happy, for in the most important sense, the only reward worth having is absolutely denied: for, however confident a poet may be, he is never quite sure that all his energy is not misdirected nor that what he is writing is great poetry. At the moment when art attains its highest attainment it reaches beyond its medium of words or paints or music, and the artist finds himself realizing that these instruments are inadequate to the spirit of what he is trying to say.

Different poets concentrate in different ways. In my own mind I make a sharp distinction between two types of concentration: one is immediate and complete, the other is plodding and only completed by stages. Some poets write immediately works which, when they are written, scarcely need revision. Others write their poems by stages, feeling their way from rough draft to rough draft, until finally, after many revisions, they have produced a result which may seem to have very little connection with their early sketches.

These two opposite processes are vividly illustrated in two examples drawn from music: Mozart and Beethoven. Mozart thought out symphonies, quartets, even scenes from operas, entirely in his head — often on a journey or perhaps while dealing with pressing problems — and then he transcribed them, in their completeness, onto paper. Beethoven wrote fragments of themes in note books which he kept beside him, working on and developing them for years. Often his first ideas were of a clumsiness which makes scholars marvel how he could, at the end, have developed from them such miraculous results.

Thus genius works in different ways to achieve its ends. But although the Mozartian type of genius is the more brilliant and dazzling, genius, unlike virtuosity, is judged by greatness of results, not by brilliance of performance. The result must be the fullest development in a created æsthetic form of an original moment of insight, and it does not matter whether genius devotes a lifetime to producing a small result if that result be immortal. The difference between two types of genius is that one type (the Mozartian) is able to plumb the greatest depths of his own experience by the tremendous effort of a moment, the other (the Beethovenian) must dig deeper and deeper into his consciousness, layer by layer. What counts in either case is the vision which sees and pursues and attains the end; the logic of the artistic purpose.

A poet may be divinely gifted with a lucid and intense and purposive intellect; he may be clumsy and slow; that does not matter, what matters is integrity of purpose and the ability to maintain the purpose without losing oneself. Myself, I am scarcely capable of immediate concentration in poetry. My mind is not clear, my will is weak, I suffer from an excess of ideas and a weak sense of form. For every poem that I begin to write, I think of at least ten which I do not write down at all. For every poem which I do write down, there are seven or eight which I never complete.

The method which I adopt therefore is to write down as many ideas as possible, in however rough a form, in note books (I have at least twenty of these, on a shelf beside my desk, going back over fifteen years). I then make use of some of the sketches and discard others.

The best way of explaining how I develop the rough ideas which I use, is to take an example. Here is a Notebook begun in 1944. About a hundred pages of it are covered with writing, and from this have emerged about six poems. Each idea, when it first occurs is given a number. Sometimes the ideas do not get beyond one line. For example No. 3 (never developed) is the one line: —

A language of flesh and roses.

I shall return to this line in a few pages, which I speak of inspiration. For the moment, I turn to No. 13, because here is an idea which has been developed to its conclusion. The first sketch begins thus: —

a) There are some days when the sea lies like a harp
Stretched flat beneath the cliffs. The waves
Like wires burn with the sun's copper glow
[*all the murmuring blue
every silent*]

Between whose spaces every image
Of sky [*field and*] hedge and field and boat
Dwells like the huge face of the afternoon.
[*Lies*]

When the heat grows tired, the afternoon
Out of the land may breathe a sigh
[*Across these wires like a hand. They vibrate
With*]
Which moves across those wires like a soft hand
[*Then the vibration*]
Between whose spaces the vibration holds
Every bird-cry, dog's bark, man-shout
And creak of rollock from the land and sky
With all the music of the afternoon.

Obviously these lines are attempts to sketch out an idea which exists clearly enough on some level of the mind where it yet eludes the attempt to state it. At this stage, a poem is like a face which one seems to be able to visualize clearly in the eye of memory, but when one examines it mentally or tries to think it out, feature by feature, it seems to fade.

The idea of this poem is a vision of the sea. The faith of the poet is that if this vision is clearly stated it will be significant. The vision is of the sea stretched under a cliff. On top of the cliff there are fields, hedges, houses. Horses draw carts along lanes, dogs bark far inland, bells ring in the distance.

The shore seems laden with hedges, roses, horses and men, all high above the sea, on a very fine summer day when the ocean seems to reflect and absorb the shore. Then the small strung-out glittering waves of the sea lying under the shore are like the strings of a harp which catch the sunlight. Between these strings lies the reflection of the shore. Butterflies are wafted out over the waves, which they mistake for the fields of the chalky landscape, searching them for flowers. On a day such as this, the land, reflected in the sea, appears to enter into the sea, as though it lies under it, like Atlantis. The wires of the harp are like a seen music fusing seascape and landscape.

Looking at this vision in another way, it obviously has symbolic value. The sea represents death and eternity, the land represents the brief life of the summer and of one human generation which passes into the sea of eternity. But let me here say at once that although the poet may be conscious of this aspect of his vision, it is exactly what he wants to avoid stating, or even being too concerned with. His job is to recreate his vision, and let it speak its moral for itself. The poet must distinguish clearly in his own mind between that which most definitely must be said and that which must not be said. The unsaid inner meaning is revealed in the music and the tonality of the poem, and the poet is conscious of it in his knowledge that a certain tone of voice, a certain rhythm, are necessary.

In the next twenty versions of the poem I felt my way towards the clarification of the seen picture, the music and the inner feeling. In the first version quoted above there is the phrase in the second and third lines

> The waves
> Like wires burn with the sun's copper glow.

This phrase fuses the image of the sea with the idea of music, and it is therefore a key-phrase, because the theme of the poem is the fusion of the land with the sea. Here, then are several versions of these one and a quarter lines, in the order in which they were written: —

b)   The waves are wires
    Burning as with the secret song of fires

c)   The day burns in the trembling wires
    With a vast music golden in the eyes

d)   The day glows on its trembling wires
    Singing a golden music in the eyes

e)   The day glows on its burning wires
    Like waves of music golden to the eyes.

f) Afternoon burns upon its wires
    Lines of music dazzling the eyes

g) Afternoon gilds its tingling wires
    To a visual silent music of the eyes

In the final version, these two lines appear as in the following stanza: —

h) There are some days the happy ocean lies
    Like an unfingered harp, below the land.

    Afternoon gilds all the silent wires
    Into a burning music of the eyes.

    On mirroring paths between those fine-strung fires
    The shore, laden with roses, horses, spires,
    Wanders in water, imaged above ribbed sand.

Inspiration

The hard work evinced in these examples, which are only a fraction of the work put into the whole poem, may cause the reader to wonder whether there is no such thing as inspiration, or whether it is merely Stephen Spender who is uninspired. The answer is that everything in poetry is work except inspiration, whether this work is achieved at one swift stroke, as Mozart wrote his music, or whether it is a slow process of evolution from stage to stage. Here again, I have to qualify the word "work," as I qualified the word "concentration": the work on a line of poetry may take the form of putting a version aside for a few days, weeks or years, and then taking it up again, when it may be found that the line has, in the interval of time, almost rewritten itself.

Inspiration is the beginning of a poem and it is also its final goal. It is the first idea which drops into the poet's mind and it is the final idea which he at last achieves in words. In between this start and this winning post there is the hard race, the sweat and toil.

Paul Valéry speaks of the *"une ligne donnée"* of a poem. One line is given to the poet by God or by nature, the rest he has to discover for himself.

My own experience of inspiration is certainly that of a line or a phrase or a word or sometimes something still vague, a dim cloud of an idea which I feel must be condensed into a shower of words. The peculiarity of the key word or line is that it does not merely attract, as, say, the word "braggadocio" attracts. It occurs in what seems to be an active, male, germinal form as though it were the centre of a statement requiring a beginning and an end, and as though it had an impulse in a certain direction. Here are examples: —

A language of flesh and roses

This phrase (not very satisfactory in itself) brings to my mind a whole series of experiences and the idea of a poem which I shall perhaps write some years hence. I was standing in the corridor of a train passing through the Black Country. I saw a landscape of pits and pitheads, artificial mountains, jagged yellow wounds in the earth, everything transformed as though by the toil of an enormous animal or giant tearing up the earth in search of prey or treasure. Oddly enough, a stranger next to me in the corridor echoed my inmost thought. He said: "Everything there is man-made." At this moment the line flashed into my head

A language of flesh and roses.

The sequence of my thought was as follows: the industrial landscape which seems by now a routine and act of God which enslaves both employers and workers who serve and profit by it, is actually the expression of man's will. Men willed it to be so, and the pitheads, slag-heaps and the ghastly disregard of anything but the pursuit of wealth, are a symbol of modern man's mind. In other words, the world which we create — the world of slums and telegrams and newspapers — is a kind of language of our inner wishes and thoughts. Although this is so, it is obviously a language which has got outside our control. It is a confused language, an irresponsible senile gibberish. This thought greatly distressed me, and I started thinking that if the phenomena created by humanity are really like words in a language, what kind of language do we really aspire to? All this sequence of thought flashed into my mind with the answer which came before the question: *A language of flesh and roses.*

I hope this example will give the reader some idea of what I mean by inspiration. Now the line, which I shall not repeat again, is a way of thinking imaginatively. If the line embodies some of the ideas which I have related above, these ideas must be further made clear in other lines. That is the terrifying challenge of poetry. Can I think out the logic of images? How easy it is to explain here the poem that I would have liked to write! How difficult it would be to write it. For writing it would imply living my way through the imaged experience of all these ideas, which here are mere abstractions, and such an effort of imaginative experience requires a lifetime of patience and watching.

Here is an example of a cloudy form of thought germinated by the word *cross,* which is the key word of the poem which exists formlessly in my mind. Recently my wife had a son. On the first day that I visited her after the boy's birth, I went by bus to the hospital. Passing through the streets on the top of the bus, they all seemed very clean, and the thought occurred to me that everything was prepared for our child. Past generations have toiled so that any child born today inherits, with his generation, cities, streets, organization, the most elaborate machinery for living. Everything has been provided for him by people dead long before he was born. Then, naturally enough, sadder thoughts colored this picture for me, and I reflected how he also inherited vast maladjustments, vast human wrongs. Then I thought of the child as like a pin-point of present existence, the moment incarnate, in whom the whole of the past, and all possible futures *cross*. This word *cross* somehow suggested the whole situation to me of a child born into the world and also of the form of a poem about his situation. When the word *cross* appeared in the poem, the idea of the past should give place to the idea of the future and it should be apparent that the *cross* in which present and future meet is the secret of an individual human existence. And here again, the unspoken secret which lies beyond the poem, the moral significance of other meanings of the word "cross" begins to glow with its virtue that should never be said and yet should shine through every image in the poem.

This account of inspiration is probably weak beside the accounts that other poets might give. I am writing of my own experience, and my own inspiration seems to me like the faintest flash of insight into the nature of reality beside that of other poets whom I can think of. However, it is possible that I describe here a kind of experience which, however slight it may be, is far truer to the real poetic experience than Aldous Huxley's account of how a young poet writes poetry in his novel *Time Must Have a Stop*. It is hard to imagine anything more self-conscious and unpoetic than Mr. Huxley's account.

Memory

If the art of concentrating in a particular way is the discipline necessary for poetry to reveal itself, memory exercised in a particular way is the natural gift of poetic genius. The poet, above all else, is a person who never forgets certain sense-impressions which he has experienced and which he can re-live again and again as though with all their original freshness.

All poets have this highly developed sensitive apparatus of memory, and they are usually aware of experiences which happened to them at the earliest age and which retain their pristine significance throughout life. The meeting of Dante and Beatrice when the poet was only nine years of age is the experience which became a symbol in Dante's mind around which the *Divine Comedy* crystallized. The experience of nature which forms the subject of Wordsworth's poetry was an extension of a childhood vision of "natural presences" which surrounded the boy Wordsworth. And his decision in later life to live in the Lake District was a decision to return to the scene of these childhood memories which were the most important experiences in his poetry. There is evidence for the importance of this kind of memory in all the creative arts, and the argument certainly applies to prose which is creative. Sir Osbert Sitwell has told me that his book *Before the Bombardment*, which contains an extremely civilized and satiric account of the social life of Scarborough before and during the last war, was based on his observations of life in that resort before he had reached the age of twelve.

It therefore is not surprising that although I have no memory for telephone numbers, addresses, faces and where I have put this morning's correspondence, I have a perfect memory for the sensation of certain experiences which are crystallized for me around certain associations. I could demonstrate this from my own life by the overwhelming nature of associations which, suddenly aroused, have carried me back so completely into the past, particularly into my childhood, that I have lost all sense of the present time and place. But the best proofs of this power of memory are found in the odd lines of poems written in note books fifteen years ago. A few fragments of unfinished poems enable me to enter immediately into the experiences from which they were derived, the circumstances in which they were written, and the unwritten feelings in the poem that were projected but never put into words.

> . . . Knowledge of a full sun
> That runs up his big sky, above
> The hill, then in those trees and throws
> His smiling on the turf.

That is an incomplete idea of fifteen years ago, and I remember exactly a balcony of a house facing a road, and, on the other side of the road, pine trees, beyond which lay the sea. Every morning the sun sprang up, first of all above the horizon of the sea, then it climbed to the tops of the trees and shone on my window. And this memory connects with the sun that shines through my window in London now in spring and early summer. So that the memory is not exactly a memory. It is more like one prong upon which a whole calendar of similar experiences happening throughout years collect. A memory once clearly stated ceases to be a memory, it becomes perpetually present, because every time we experience something which recalls it, the clear and lucid original experience imposes its formal beauty on the new experiences. It is thus no longer a memory but an experience lived through again and again.

Turning over these old note books, my eye catches some lines, in a projected long poem, which immediately re-shape themselves into the following short portrait of a woman's face: —

> Her eyes are gleaming fish
> Caught in her nervous face, as if in a net.
> Her hair is wild and fair, haloing her cheeks
> Like a fantastic flare of Southern sun.
> There is madness in her cherishing her children.
> Sometimes, perhaps a single time in years,
> Her wandering fingers stoop to arrange some flowers —
> Then in her hands her whole life stops and weeps.

It is perhaps true to say that memory is the faculty of poetry, because the imagination itself is an exercise of memory. There is nothing we imagine which we do not already know. And our ability to imagine is our ability to remember that we have already once experienced and to apply it to some different situation. Thus the greatest poets are those with memories so great that they extend beyond their strongest experiences to their minutest observations of people and things far outside their own self-centredness (the weakness of memory is its self-centredness: hence the narcissistic nature of most poetry).

Here I can detect my own greatest weakness. My memory is defective and self-centred. I lack the confidence in using it to create situations outside myself, although I believe that, in theory, there are very few situations in life which a poet should not be able to imagine, because it is a fact that most poets have experienced almost every situation in life. I do not mean by this that a poet who writes about a Polar Expedition has actually been to the North Pole. I mean, though, that he has been cold, hungry, etc., so that it is possible for him by remembering imaginatively his own felt experiences to know what it is like to explore the North Pole. That is where I fail. I cannot write about going to the North Pole.

Faith

It is evident that a faith in their vocation, mystical in intensity, sustains poets. There are many illustrations from the lives of poets to show this, and Shakespeare's sonnets are full of expressions of his faith in the immortality of his lines.

From my experience I can clarify the nature of this faith. When I was nine, we went to the Lake District, and there my parents read me some of the poems of Wordsworth. My sense of the sacredness of the task of poetry began then, and I have always felt that a poet's was a sacred vocation, like a saint's. Since I was nine, I have wanted to be various things, for example, Prime Minister (when I was twelve). Like some other poets I am attracted by the life of power and the life of action, but I am still more repelled by them. Power involves forcing oneself upon the attention of historians by doing things and occupying offices which are, in themselves, important, so that what is truly powerful is not the soul of a so-called powerful and prominent man but the position which he fills and the things which he does. Similarly, the life of "action" which seems so very positive is, in fact, a selective, even a negative kind of life. A man of action does one thing or several things because he does not do something else. Usually men who do very spectacular things fail completely to do the ordinary things which fill the lives of most normal people, and which would be far more heroic and spectacular perhaps, if they did not happen to be done by many people. Thus in practice the life of action has always seemed to me an act of cutting oneself off from life.

Although it is true that poets are vain and ambitious, their vanity and ambition is of the purest kind attainable in this world, for the saint renounces ambition. They are ambitious to be accepted for what they ultimately are as revealed by their inmost experiences, their finest perceptions, their deepest feelings, their uttermost sense of truth, in their poetry. They cannot cheat about these things, because the quality of their own being is revealed not in the noble sentiments which their poetry expresses, but in sensibility, control of language, rhythm and music, things which cannot be attained by a vote of confidence from an electorate, or by the office of Poet Laureate. Of course, work is tremendously important, but, in poetry, even the greatest labor can only serve to reveal the intrinsic qualities of soul of the poet as he really is.

Since there can be no cheating, the poet, like the saint, stands in all his works before the bar of a perpetual day of judgment. His vanity of course is pleased by success, though even success may contribute to his understanding that popularity does not confer on him the favorable judgment of all the ages which he seeks. For what does it mean to be praised by one's own age, which is soaked in crimes and stupidity, except perhaps that future ages, wise where we are foolish, will see him as a typical expression of this age's crimes and stupidity? Nor is lack of success a guarantee of great poetry, though there are some who pretend that it is. Nor can the critics, at any rate beyond a certain limited point of technical judgment, be trusted.

The poet's faith is therefore, firstly, a mystique of vocation, secondly, a faith in his own truth, combined with his own devotion to a task. There can really be no greater faith than the confidence that one is doing one's utmost to fulfill one's high vocation, and it is this that has inspired all the greatest poets. At the same time this faith is coupled with a deep humility because one knows that, ultimately, judgment does not rest with oneself. All one can do is to achieve nakedness, to be what one is with all one's faculties and perceptions, strengthened by all the skill which one can acquire, and then to stand before the judgment of time.

In my note books, I find the following Prose Poem, which expresses these thoughts:

> Bring me peace bring me power bring me assurance. Let me reach the bright day, the high chair, the plain desk, where my hand at last controls the words, where anxiety no longer undermines me. If I don't reach these I'm thrown to the wolves, I'm a restless animal wandering from place to place, from experience to experience.
>
> Give me the humility and the judgment to live alone with the deep and rich satisfaction of my own creating: not to be thrown into doubt by a word of spite or disapproval.
>
> In the last analysis don't mind whether your work is good or bad so long as it has the completeness, the enormity of the whole world which you love.

Song

Inspiration and song are the irreducible final qualities of a poet which make his vocation different from all others. Inspiration is an experience in which a line or an idea is given to one, and perhaps also a state of mind in which one writes one's best poetry. Song is far more difficult to define. It is the music which a poem as yet unthought of will assume, the empty womb of poetry for ever in the poet's consciousness, waiting for the fertilizing seed.

Sometimes, when I lie in a state of half-waking, half-sleeping, I am conscious of a stream of words which seem to pass through my mind, without their having a meaning, but they have a sound, a sound of passion, or a sound recalling poetry that I know. Again sometimes when I am writing, the music of the words I am trying to shape takes me far beyond the words, I am aware of a rhythm, a dance, a fury, which is as yet empty of words.

In these observations, I have said little about headaches, midnight oil, pints of beer or of claret, love affairs, and so on, which are supposed to be stations on the journey of poets through life. There is no doubt that writing poetry, when a poem appears to succeed, results in an intense physical excitement, a sense of release and ecstasy. On the other hand, I dread writing poetry, for, I suppose, the following reasons: a poem is a terrible journey, a painful effort of concentrating the imagination; words are an extremely difficult medium to use, and sometimes when one has spent days trying to say a thing clearly one finds that one has only said it dully; above all, the writing of a poem brings one face to face with one's own personality with all its familiar and clumsy limitations. In every other phase of existence, one can exercise the orthodoxy of a conventional routine: one can be polite to one's friends, one can get through the day at the office, one can pose, one can draw attention to one's position in society, one is — in a word — dealing with men. In poetry, one is wrestling with a god.

Usually, when I have completed a poem, I think "this is my best poem," and I wish to publish it at once. This is partly because I only write when I have something new to say, which seems more worth while than what I have said before, partly because optimism about my present and future makes me despise my past. A few days after I have finished a poem, I relegate it to the past of all my other wasted efforts, all the books I do not wish to open.

Perhaps the greatest pleasure I have got from poems that I have written is when I have heard some lines quoted which I have not at once recognized. And I have thought "how good and how interesting," before I have realized that they are my own.

In common with other creative writers I pretend that I am not, and I am, exceedingly affected by unsympathetic criticism, whilst praise usually makes me suspect that the reviewer does not know what he is talking about. Why are writers so sensitive to criticism? Partly, because it is their business to be sensitive, and they are sensitive about this as about other things. Partly, because every serious creative writer is really in his heart concerned with reputation and not with success (the most successful writer I have known, Sir Hugh Walpole, was far and away the most unhappy about his reputation, because the "highbrows" did not like him). Again, I suspect that every writer is secretly writing for *someone*, probably for a parent or teacher who did not believe in him in childhood. The critic who refuses to "understand" immediately becomes identified with this person, and the understanding of many admirers only adds to the writer's secret bitterness if this one refusal persists.

Gradually one realizes that there is always this someone who will not like one's work. Then, perhaps, literature becomes a humble exercise of faith in being all that one can be in one's art, of being more than oneself, expecting little, but with a faith in the mystery of poetry which gradually expands into a faith in the mysterious service of truth.

Yet what failures there are! And how much mud sticks to one; mud not thrown by other people but acquired in the course of earning one's living, answering or not answering the letters which one receives, supporting or not supporting public causes. All one can hope is that this mud is composed of little grains of sand which will produce pearls.

FOR DISCUSSION

1. Does Spender begin his discussion by following the convention that one should state his purpose in the first paragraph?

2. According to Spender, what natural endowments are required of a poet?

3. How does Spender explain the eccentricities commonly attributed to poets?

4. What meaning did the word "cross" have when Spender put it into a poem?

5. Judging from the time and effort that goes into the writing of a poem, would you expect a poem to be understandable at a first reading?

6. Does Spender expect a poet to be indifferent to favorable and unfavorable criticism?

VOCABULARY: virtuosity, rollock, germinal, pithead, senile, gibberish, incarnate, pristine, mystique.

THEME TOPICS: The child's experience and the poet's report. Spender's and Ciardi's accounts of poetry. Spender's and McCarthy's accounts of symbolism.

Theory of Modes

Fictional Modes: Introduction

In the second paragraph of the *Poetics* Aristotle speaks of the differences in works of fiction which are caused by the different elevations of the characters in them. In some fictions, he says, the characters are better than we are, in others worse, in still others on the same level. This passage has not received much attention from modern critics, as the importance Aristotle assigns to goodness and badness seems to indicate a somewhat narrowly moralistic view of literature. Aristotle's words for good and bad, however, are *spoudaios* and *phaulos*, which have a figurative sense of weighty and light. In literary fictions the plot consists of somebody doing something. The somebody, if an individual, is the hero, and the something he does or fails to do is what he can do, or could have done, on the level of the postulates made about him by the author and the consequent expectations of the audience. Fictions, therefore, may be classified, not morally, but by the hero's power of action, which may be greater than ours, less, or roughly the same. Thus:

1. If superior in *kind* both to other men and to the environment of other men, the hero is a divine being, and the story about him will be a *myth* in the common sense of a story about a god. Such stories have an important place in literature, but are as a rule found outside the normal literary categories.

2. If superior in *degree* to other men and to his environment, the hero is the typical hero of *romance*, whose actions are marvelous but who is himself identified as a human being. The hero of romance moves in a world in which the ordinary laws of nature are slightly suspended: prodigies of courage and endurance, unnatural to us, are natural to him, and enchanted weapons, talking animals, terrifying ogres and witches, and talismans of miraculous power violate no rule of probability once the postulates of romance have been established. Here we have moved from myth, properly so called, into legend, folk tale, *märchen*, and their literary affiliates and derivatives.

3. If superior in degree to other men but not to his natural environment, the hero is a leader. He has authority, passions, and powers of expression far greater than ours, but what he does is subject both to social criticism and

to the order of nature. This is the hero of the *high mimetic* mode, of most epic and tragedy, and is primarily the kind of hero that Aristotle had in mind.

4. If superior neither to other men nor to his environment, the hero is one of us: we respond to a sense of his common humanity, and demand from the poet the same canons of probability that we find in our own experience. This gives us the hero of the *low mimetic* mode, of most comedy and of realistic fiction. "High" and "low" have no connotations of comparative value, but are purely diagrammatic, as they are when they refer to Biblical critics or Anglicans. On this level the difficulty in retaining the word "hero," which has a more limited meaning among the preceding modes, occasionally strikes an author. Thackeray thus feels obliged to call *Vanity Fair* a novel without a hero.

5. If inferior in power or intelligence to ourselves, so that we have the sense of looking down on a scene of bondage, frustration, or absurdity, the hero belongs to the *ironic* mode. This is still true when the reader feels that he is or might be in the same situation, as the situation is being judged by the norms of a greater freedom.

Looking over this table, we can see that European fiction, during the last fifteen centuries, has steadily moved its center of gravity down the list. In the pre-medieval period literature is closely attached to Christian, late Classical, Celtic, or Teutonic myths. If Christianity had not been both an imported myth and a devourer of rival ones, this phase of Western literature would be easier to isolate. In the form in which we possess it, most of it has already moved into the category of romance. Romance divides into two main forms: a secular form dealing with chivalry and knight-errantry, and a religious form devoted to legends of saints. Both lean heavily on miraculous violations of natural law for their interest as stories. Fictions of romance dominate literature until the cult of the prince and the courtier in the Renaissance brings the high mimetic mode into the foreground. The characteristics of this mode are most clearly seen in the genres of drama, particularly tragedy, and national epic. Then a new kind of middle-class culture introduces the low mimetic, which predominates in English literature from Defoe's time to the end of the nineteenth century. In French literature it begins and ends about fifty years earlier. During the last hundred years, most serious fiction has tended increasingly to be ironic in mode.

Something of the same progression may be traced in Classical literature too, in a greatly foreshortened form. Where a religion is mythological and polytheistic, where there are promiscuous incarnations, deified heroes and kings of divine descent, where the same adjective "godlike" can be applied either to Zeus or to Achilles, it is hardly possible to separate the mythical, romantic, and high mimetic strands completely. Where the religion is theological, and insists on a sharp division between divine and human natures, romance becomes more clearly isolated, as it does in the legends of Christian chivalry and sanctity, in the Arabian Nights of Mohammedanism, in the stories of the judges and thaumaturgic prophets of Israel. Similarly, the inability of the Classical world to shake off the divine leader in its later period has much to do with the abortive development of low mimetic and ironic modes that got barely started with Roman satire. At the same time the establishing of the high mimetic mode, the developing of a literary tradition with a consistent sense of an order of nature in it, is one of the great feats of Greek civilization. Oriental fiction does not, so far as I know, get very far away from mythical and romantic formulas.

We shall here deal chiefly with the five epochs of Western literature, as given above, using Classical parallels only incidentally. In each mode a distinction will be useful between naive and sophisticated literature. The word naive I take from Schiller's essay on naive and sentimental poetry: I mean by it, however, primitive or popular, whereas in Schiller it means something more like Classical. The word sentimental also means something else in English, but we do not have enough genuine critical terms to dispense with it. In quotation marks, therefore, "sentimental" refers to a later recreation of an earlier mode. Thus Romanticism is a "sentimental" form of romance, and the fairy tale, for the most part, a "sentimental" form of folk tale. Also there is a general distinction between fictions in which the hero becomes isolated from his society, and fictions in which he is incorporated into it. This distinction is expressed by the words "tragic" and "comic" when they refer to aspects of plot in general and not simply to forms of drama.

Tragic Fictional Modes

Tragic stories, when they apply to divine beings, may be called Dionysiac. These are stories of dying gods, like Hercules with his poisoned shirt and his pyre, Orpheus torn to pieces by the Bacchantes, Balder murdered by the treachery of Loki, Christ dying on the cross and marking with the words "Why hast thou forsaken me?" a sense of his exclusion, as a divine being, from the society of the Trinity.

The association of a god's death with autumn or sunset does not, in literature, necessarily mean that he is a god "of" vegetation or the sun, but only that he is a god capable of dying, whatever his department. But as a god is superior to nature as well as to other men, the death of a god appropriately involves what Shakespeare, in *Venus and Adonis,* calls the "solemn sympathy" of nature, the word solemn having here some of its etymological connections with ritual. Ruskin's pathetic fallacy can hardly be a fallacy when a god is the hero of the action, as when the poet of *The Dream of the Rood* tells us that all creation wept at the death of Christ. Of course there is never any real fallacy in making a purely imaginative alignment between man and nature, but the use of "solemn sympathy" in a piece of more realistic fiction indicates that the author is trying to give his hero some of the overtones of the mythical mode. Ruskin's example of a pathetic fallacy is "the cruel, crawling foam" from Kingsley's ballad about a girl drowned in the tide. But the fact that the foam is so described gives to Kingsley's Mary a faint coloring of the myth of Andromeda.

The same associations with sunset and the fall of the leaf linger in romance, where the hero is still half a god. In romance the suspension of natural law and the individualizing of the hero's exploits reduce nature largely to the animal and vegetable world. Much of the hero's life is spent with animals, or at any rate the animals that are incurable romantics, such as horses, dogs, and falcons, and the typical setting of romance is the forest. The hero's death or isolation thus has the effect of a spirit passing out of nature, and evokes a mood best described as elegiac. The elegiac presents a heroism unspoiled by irony. The inevitability in the death of Beowulf, the treachery in the death of Roland, the malignancy that compasses the death of the martyred saint, are of much greater emotional importance than any ironic complications of hybris and hamartia that may be involved. Hence the elegiac is often accompanied by a diffused, resigned, melancholy sense of the passing of time, of the old order changing and yielding to a new one: one thinks of Beowulf looking, while he is dying, at the great stone monuments of the eras of history that vanished before him. In a very late "sentimental" form the same mood is well caught in Tennyson's *Passing of Arthur*.

Tragedy in the central or high mimetic sense, the fiction of the fall of a leader (he has to fall because that is the only way in which a leader can be isolated from his society), mingles the heroic with the ironic. In elegiac romance the hero's mortality is primarily a natural fact, the sign of his humanity; in high mimetic tragedy it is also a social and moral fact. The tragic hero has to be of a properly heroic size, but his fall is involved both with a sense of his relation to society and with a sense of the supremacy of natural law, both of which are ironic in reference. Tragedy belongs chiefly to the two indigenous developments of tragic drama in fifth-century Athens and seventeenth-century Europe from Shakespeare to Racine. Both belong to a period of social history in which an aristocracy is fast losing its effective power but still retains a good deal of ideological prestige.

The central position of high mimetic tragedy in the five tragic modes, balanced midway between godlike heroism and all-too-human irony, is expressed in the traditional concept of catharsis. The words pity and fear may be taken as referring to the two general directions in which emotion moves, whether towards an object or away from it. Naive romance, being closer to the wish-fulfilment dream, tends to absorb emotion and communicate it internally to the reader. Romance, therefore, is characterized by the acceptance of pity and fear, which in ordinary life relate to pain, as forms of pleasure. It turns fear at a distance, or terror, into the adventurous; fear at contact, or horror, into the marvellous, and fear without an object, or dread (*Angst*) into a pensive melancholy. It turns pity at a distance, or concern, into the theme of chivalrous rescue; pity at contact, or tenderness, into a languid and relaxed charm, and pity without an object (which has no name but is a kind of animism, or treating everything in nature as though it had human feelings) into creative fantasy. In sophisticated romance the characteristics peculiar to the form are less obvious, especially in tragic romance, where the theme of inevitable death works against the marvellous, and often forces it into the background. In *Romeo and Juliet*, for instance, the marvellous survives only in Mercutio's speech on Queen Mab. But this play is marked as closer to romance than the later tragedies by the softening influences that work in the opposite direction from catharsis, draining off the irony, so to speak, from the main characters.

In high mimetic tragedy pity and fear become, respectively, favorable and adverse moral judgement, which are relevant to tragedy but not central to it. We pity Desdemona and fear Iago, but the central tragic figure is Othello, and our feelings about him are mixed. The particular thing called tragedy that happens to the tragic hero does not depend on his moral status. If it is causally related to something he has done, as it generally is, the tragedy is in the inevitability of the consequences of the act, not in its moral significance as an act. Hence the paradox that in tragedy pity and fear are raised and cast out. Aristotle's hamartia or "flaw," therefore, is not necessarily wrongdoing, much less moral weakness: it may be simply a matter of being a strong character in an exposed position, like Cordelia. The exposed position is usually the place of leadership, in which a character is exceptional and isolated at the same time, giving us that curious blend of the inevitable and the incongruous which is peculiar to tragedy. The principle of the hamartia of leadership can be more clearly seen in naive high mimetic tragedy, as we get it in *The Mirror for Magistrates* and similar collections of tales based on the theme of the wheel of fortune.

In low mimetic tragedy, pity and fear are neither purged nor absorbed into pleasures, but are communicated externally, as sensations. In fact the word "sensational" could have a more useful meaning in criticism if it were not merely an adverse value-judgement. The best word for low mimetic or domestic tragedy is, perhaps, pathos, and pathos has a close relation to the sensational reflex of tears. Pathos presents its hero as isolated by a weakness which appeals to our sympathy because it is on our own level of experience. I speak of a hero, but the central figure of pathos is often a woman or a child (or both, as in the death-scenes of Little Eva and Little Nell), and we have a whole procession of pathetic female sacrifices in English low mimetic fiction from Clarissa Harlowe to Hardy's Tess and James's Daisy Miller. We notice that while tragedy may massacre a whole cast, pathos is usually concentrated on a single character, partly because low mimetic society is more strongly individualized.

Again, in contrast to high mimetic tragedy, pathos is increased by the inarticulateness of the victim. The death of an animal is usually pathetic, and so is the catastrophe of defective intelligence that is frequent in modern American literature. Wordsworth, who as a low mimetic artist was one of our great masters of pathos, makes his sailor's mother speak in a flat, dumpy, absurdly inadequate style about her efforts to salvage her son's clothes and "other property" — or did before bad criticism made him spoil his poem. Pathos is a queer ghoulish emotion, and some failure of expression, real or simulated, seems to be peculiar to it. It will always leave a fluently plangent funeral elegy to go and batten on something like Swift's memoir of Stella. Highly articulate pathos is apt to become a factitious appeal to self-pity, or tear-jerking. The exploiting of fear in the low mimetic is also sensational, and is a kind of pathos in reverse. The terrible figure in this tradition, exemplified by Heathcliff, Simon Legree, and the villains of Dickens, is normally a ruthless figure strongly contrasted with some kind of delicate virtue, generally a helpless victim in his power.

The root idea of pathos is the exclusion of an individual on our own level from a social group to which he is trying to belong. Hence the central tradition of sophisticated pathos is the study of the isolated mind, the story of how someone recognizably like ourselves is broken by a conflict between the inner and outer world, between imaginative reality and the sort of reality which is established by a social consensus. Such tragedy may be concerned, as it often is in Balzac, with a mania or obsession about rising in the world, this being the central low mimetic counterpart of the fiction of the fall of the leader. Or it may deal with the conflict of inner and outer life, as in *Madame Bovary* and *Lord Jim*, or with the impact of inflexible morality on experience, as in Melville's *Pierre* and Ibsen's *Brand*. The type of character involved here we may call by the Greek word *alazon*, which means impostor, someone who pretends or tries to be something more than he is. The most popular types of *alazon* are the *miles gloriosus* and the learned crank or obsessed philosopher.

We are most familiar with such characters in comedy, where they are looked at from the outside, so that we see only the social mask. But the *alazon* may be one aspect of the tragic hero as well: the touch of *miles gloriosus* in Tamburlaine, even in Othello, is unmistakable, as is the touch of the obsessed philosopher in Faustus and Hamlet. It is very difficult to study a case of obsession, or even hypocrisy, from the inside, in a dramatic medium: even Tartuffe, as far as his dramatic function is concerned, is a study of parasitism rather than hypocrisy. The analysis of obsession belongs more naturally to prose fiction or to a semi-dramatic medium like the Browning monologue. For all the differences in technique and attitude, Conrad's Lord Jim is a lineal descendant of the *miles gloriosus*, of the same family as Shaw's Sergius or Synge's playboy, who are parallel types in a dramatic and comic setting. It is, of course, quite possible to take the *alazon* at his own valuation: this is done for instance by the creators of the inscrutable gloomy heroes in Gothic thrillers, with their wild or piercing eyes and their dark hints of interesting sins. The result as a rule is not tragedy so much as the kind of melodrama which may be defined as comedy without humor. When it rises out of this, we have a study of obsession presented in terms of fear instead of pity: that is, the obsession takes the form of an unconditioned will that drives its victim beyond the normal limits of humanity. One of the clearest examples is Heathcliff, who plunges through death itself into vampirism; but there are many others, ranging from Conrad's Kurtz to the mad scientists of popular fiction.

The conception of irony meets us in Aristotle's *Ethics,* where the *eiron* is the man who deprecates himself, as opposed to the *alazon.* Such a man makes himself invulnerable, and, though Aristotle disapproves of him, there is no question that he is a predestined artist, just as the *alazon* is one of his predestined victims. The term irony, then, indicates a technique of appearing to be less than one is, which in literature becomes most commonly a technique of saying as little and meaning as much as possible, or, in a more general way, a pattern of words that turns away from direct statement or its own obvious meaning. (I am not using the word ironic itself in any unfamiliar sense, though I am exploring some of its implications.)

The ironic fiction-writer, then, deprecates himself and, like Socrates, pretends to know nothing, even that he is ironic. Complete objectivity and suppression of all explicit moral judgements are essential to his method. Thus pity and fear are not raised in ironic art: they are reflected to the reader from the art. When we try to isolate the ironic as such, we find that it seems to be simply the attitude of the poet as such, a dispassionate construction of a literary form, with all assertive elements, implied or expressed, eliminated. Irony, as a mode, is born from the low mimetic; it takes life exactly as it finds it. But the ironist fables without moralizing, and has no object but his subject. Irony is naturally a sophisticated mode, and the chief difference between sophisticated and naive irony is that the naive ironist calls attention to the fact that he is being ironic, whereas sophisticated irony merely states, and lets the reader add the ironic tone himself. Coleridge, noting an ironic comment in Defoe, points out how Defoe's subtlety could be made crude and obvious simply by over-punctuating the same words with italics, dashes, exclamation points, and other signs of being oneself aware of irony.

Tragic irony, then, becomes simply the study of tragic isolation as such, and it thereby drops out the element of the special case, which in some degree is in all the other modes. Its hero does not necessarily have any tragic hamartia or pathetic obsession: he is only somebody who gets isolated from his society. Thus the central principle of tragic irony is that whatever exceptional happens to the hero should be causally out of line with his character. Tragedy is intelligible, not in the sense of having any pat moral to go with it, but in the sense that Aristotle had in mind when he spoke of discovery or recognition as essential to the tragic plot. Tragedy is intelligible because its catastrophe is plausibly related to its situation. Irony isolates from the tragic situation the sense of arbitrariness, of the victim's having been unlucky, selected at random or by lot, and no more deserving of what happens to him than anyone else would be. If there is a reason for choosing him for catastrophe, it is an inadequate reason, and raises more objections than it answers.

Thus the figure of a typical or random victim begins to crystallize in domestic tragedy as it deepens in ironic tone. We may call this typical victim the *pharmakos* or scapegoat. We meet a *pharmakos* figure in Hawthorne's Hester Prynne, in Melville's Billy Budd, in Hardy's Tess, in the Septimus of *Mrs. Dalloway*, in stories of persecuted Jews and Negroes, in stories of artists whose genius makes them Ishmaels of a bourgeois society. The *pharmakos* is neither innocent nor guilty. He is innocent in the sense that what happens to him is far greater than anything he has done provokes, like the mountaineer whose shout brings down an avalanche. He is guilty in the sense that he is a member of a guilty society, or living in a world where such injustices are an inescapable part of existence. The two facts do not come together; they remain ironically apart. The *pharmakos*, in short, is in the situation of Job. Job can defend himself against the charge of having done something that makes his catastrophe morally intelligible; but the success of his defense makes it morally unintelligible.

Thus the incongruous and the inevitable, which are combined in tragedy, separate into opposite poles of irony. At one pole is the inevitable irony of human life. What happens to, say, the hero of Kafka's *Trial* is not the result of what he has done, but the end of what he is, which is an "all too human" being. The archetype of the inevitably ironic is Adam, human nature under sentence of death. At the other pole is the incongruous irony of human life, in which all attempts to transfer guilt to a victim give that victim something of the dignity of innocence. The archetype of the incongruously ironic is Christ, the perfectly innocent victim excluded from human society. Halfway between is the central figure of tragedy, who is human and yet of a heroic size which often has in it the suggestion of divinity. His archetype is Prometheus, the immortal titan rejected by the gods for befriending men. The Book of Job is not a tragedy of the Promethean type, but a tragic irony in which the dialectic of the divine and the human nature works itself out. By justifying himself as a victim of God, Job tries to make himself into a tragic Promethean figure, but he does not succeed.

These references may help to explain something that might otherwise be a puzzling fact about modern literature. Irony descends from the low mimetic: it begins in realism and dispassionate observation. But as it does so, it moves steadily towards myth, and dim outlines of sacrificial rituals and dying gods begin to reappear in it. Our five modes evidently go around in a circle. This reappearance of myth in the ironic is particularly clear in Kafka and in Joyce. In Kafka, whose work, from one point of view, may be said to form a series of commentaries on the Book of Job, the common contemporary types of tragic irony, the Jew, the artist, Everyman, and a kind of sombre Chaplin clown, are all found, and most of these elements are combined, in a comic form, in Joyce's Shem. However, ironic myth is frequent enough elsewhere, and many features of ironic literature are unintelligible without it. Henry James learned his trade mainly from the realists and naturalists of the nineteenth century, but if we were to judge, for example, the story called *The Altar of the Dead* purely by low mimetic standards, we should have to call it a tissue of improbable coincidence, inadequate motivation, and inconclusive resolution. When we look at it as ironic myth, a story of how the god of one person is the *pharmakos* of another, its structure becomes simple and logical.

Comic Fictional Modes

The theme of the comic is the integration of society, which usually takes the form of incorporating a central character into it. The mythical comedy corresponding to the death of the Dionysiac god is Apollonian, the story of how a hero is accepted by a society of gods. In Classical literature the theme of acceptance forms part of the stories of Hercules, Mercury, and other deities who had a probation to go through, and in Christian literature it is the theme of salvation, or, in a more concentrated form, of assumption: the comedy that stands just at the end of Dante's *Commedia*. The mode of romantic comedy corresponding to the elegiac is best described as idyllic, and its chief vehicle is the pastoral. Because of the social interest of comedy, the idyllic cannot equal the introversion of the elegiac, but it preserves the theme of escape from society to the extent of idealizing a simplified life in the country or on the frontier (the pastoral of popular modern literature is the Western story). The close association with animal and vegetable nature that we noted in the elegiac recurs in the sheep and pleasant pastures (or the cattle and ranches) of the idyllic, and the same easy connection with myth recurs in the fact that such imagery is often used, as it is in the Bible, for the theme of salvation.

The clearest example of high mimetic comedy is the Old Comedy of Aristophanes. The New Comedy of Menander is closer to the low mimetic, and through Plautus and Terence its formulas were handed down to the Renaissance, so that there has always been a strongly low mimetic bias to social comedy. In Aristophanes there is usually a central figure who constructs his (or her) own society in the teeth of strong opposition, driving off one after another all the people who come to prevent or exploit him, and eventually achieving a heroic triumph, complete with mistresses, in which he is sometimes assigned the honors of a reborn god. We notice that just as there is a catharsis of pity and fear in tragedy, so there is a catharsis of the corresponding comic emotions, which are sympathy and ridicule, in Old Comedy. The comic hero will get his triumph whether what he has done is sensible or silly, honest or rascally. Thus Old Comedy, like the tragedy contemporary with it, is a blend of the heroic and the ironic. In some plays this fact is partly concealed by Aristophanes' strong desire to get his own opinion of what

the hero is doing into the record, but his greatest comedy, *The Birds*, preserves an exquisite balance between comic heroism and comic irony.

New Comedy normally presents an erotic intrigue between a young man
and a young woman which is blocked by some kind of opposition, usually
paternal, and resolved by a twist in the plot which is the comic form of
Aristotle's "discovery," and is more manipulated than its tragic counterpart.
At the beginning of the play the forces thwarting the hero are in control of
the play's society, but after a discovery in which the hero becomes wealthy
or the heroine respectable, a new society crystallizes on the stage around the
hero and his bride. The action of the comedy thus moves towards the
incorporation of the hero into the society that he naturally fits. The hero himself is seldom a very interesting person: in conformity with low mimetic
decorum, he is ordinary in his virtues, but socially attractive. In Shakespeare
and in the kind of romantic comedy that most closely resembles his there is a
development of these formulas in a more distinctively high mimetic direction.
In the figure of Prospero we have one of the few approaches to the Aristo-
phanic technique of having the whole comic action projected by a central
character. Usually Shakespeare achieves his high mimetic pattern by making
the struggle of the repressive and the desirable societies a struggle between
two levels of existence, the former like our own world or worse, the latter
enchanted and idyllic. This point will be dealt with more fully later.

For the reasons given above the domestic comedy of later fiction carries
on with much the same conventions as were used in the Renaissance. Domestic comedy is usually based on the Cinderella archetype, the kind of thing
that happens when Pamela's virtue is rewarded, the incorporation of an individual very like the reader into the society aspired to by both, a society
ushered in with a happy rustle of bridal gowns and banknotes. Here again,
Shakespearean comedy may marry off eight or ten people of approximately
equal dramatic interest, just as a high mimetic tragedy may kill the same
number, but in domestic comedy such diffusion of sexual energy is more rare.
The chief difference between high and low mimetic comedy, however, is that
the resolution of the latter more frequently involves a social promotion. More
sophisticated writers of low mimetic comedy often present the same success-
story formula with the moral ambiguities that we have found in Aristophanes.
In Balzac or Stendhal a clever and ruthless scoundrel may achieve the same
kind of success as the virtuous heroes of Samuel Smiles and Horatio Alger.
Thus the comic counterpart of the *alazon* seems to be the clever, likeable, un-
principled *picaro* of the picaresque novel.

In studying ironic comedy we must start with the theme of driving out the
pharmakos from the point of view of society. This appeals to the kind of
relief we are expected to feel when we see Jonson's Volpone condemned to
the galleys, Shylock stripped of his wealth, or Tartuffe taken off to prison.
Such a theme, unless touched very lightly, is difficult to make convincing, for
the reasons suggested in connection with ironic tragedy. Insisting on the

theme of social revenge on an individual, however great a rascal he may be, tends to make him look less involved in guilt and the society more so. This is particularly true of characters who have been trying to amuse either the actual or the internal audience, and who are the comic counterparts of the tragic hero as artist. The rejection of the entertainer, whether fool, clown, buffoon, or simpleton, can be one of the most terrible ironies known to art, as the rejection of Falstaff shows, and certain scenes in Chaplin.

In some religious poetry, for example at the end of *Paradiso,* we can see that literature has an upper limit, a point at which an imaginative vision of an eternal world becomes an experience of it. In ironic comedy we begin to see that art has also a lower limit in actual life. This is the condition of savagery, the world in which comedy consists of inflicting pain on a helpless victim, and tragedy in enduring it. Ironic comedy brings us to the figure of the scapegoat ritual and the nightmare dream, the human symbol that concentrates our fears and hates. We pass the boundary of art when this symbol becomes existential, as it does in the black man of a lynching, the Jew of a pogrom, the old woman of a witch hunt, or anyone picked up at random by a mob, like Cinna the poet in *Julius Caesar.* In Aristophanes the irony sometimes edges very close to mob violence because the attacks are personal: one thinks of all the easy laughs he gets, in play after play, at the pederasty of Cleisthenes or the cowardice of Cleonymus. In Aristophanes the word *pharmakos* means simply scoundrel, with no nonsense about it. At the conclusion of *The Clouds,* where the poet seems almost to be summoning a lynching party to go and burn down Socrates' house, we reach the comic counterpart of one of the greatest masterpieces of tragic irony in literature, Plato's *Apology.*

But the element of *play* is the barrier that separates art from savagery, and playing at human sacrifice seems to be an important theme of ironic comedy. Even in laughter itself some kind of deliverance from the unpleasant, even the horrible, seems to be very important. We notice this particularly in all forms of art in which a large number of auditors are simultaneously present, as in drama, and, still more obviously, in games. We notice too that playing at sacrifice has nothing to do with any historical descent from sacrificial ritual, such as has been suggested for Old Comedy. All the features of such ritual, the king's son, the mimic death, the executioner, the substituted victim, are far more explicit in Gilbert and Sullivan's *Mikado* than they are in Aristophanes. There is certainly no evidence that baseball has descended from a ritual of human sacrifice, but the umpire is quite as much of a *pharmakos* as if it had: he is an abandoned scoundrel, a greater robber than Barabbas; he has the evil eye; the supporters of the losing team scream for his death. At play, mob emotions are boiled in an open pot, so to speak; in the lynching mob they are in a sealed furnace of what Blake would call moral virtue. The gladiatorial combat, in which the audience has the actual power of life and death over the people who are entertaining them, is perhaps the most concentrated of all the savage or demonic parodies of drama.

The fact that we are now in an ironic phase of literature largely accounts for the popularity of the detective story, the formula of how a man-hunter locates a *pharmakos* and gets rid of him. The detective story begins in the Sherlock Holmes period as an intensification of low mimetic, in the sharpening of attention to details that makes the dullest and most neglected trivia of daily living leap into mysterious and fateful significance. But as we move further away from this we move toward a ritual drama around a corpse in which a wavering finger of social condemnation passes over a group of "suspects" and finally settles on one. The sense of a victim chosen by lot is very strong, for the case against him is only plausibly manipulated. If it were really inevitable, we should have tragic irony, as in *Crime and Punishment,* where Raskolnikoff's crime is so interwoven with his character that there can be no question of any "whodunit" mystery. In the growing brutality of the crime story (a brutality protected by the convention of the form, as it is conventionally impossible that the man-hunter can be mistaken in believing that one of his suspects is a murderer), detection begins to merge with the thriller as one of the forms of melodrama. In melodrama two themes are important: the triumph of moral virtue over villainy, and the consequent idealizing of the moral views assumed to be held by the audience. In the melodrama of the brutal thriller we come as close as it is normally possible for art to come to the pure self-righteousness of the lynching mob.

We should have to say, then, that all forms of melodrama, the detective story in particular, were advance propaganda for the police state, in so far as that represents the regularizing of mob violence, if it were possible to take them seriously. But it seems not to be possible. The protecting wall of play is still there. Serious melodrama soon gets entangled with its own pity and fear: the more serious it is, the more likely it is to be looked at ironically by the reader, its pity and fear seen as sentimental drivel and owlish solemnity, respectively. One pole of ironic comedy is the recognition of the absurdity of naive melodrama, or, at least, of the absurdity of its attempt to define the enemy of society as a person outside that society. From there it develops toward the opposite pole, which is true comic irony or satire, and which defines the enemy of society as a spirit within that society. Let us arrange the forms of ironic comedy from this point of view.

Cultivated people go to a melodrama to hiss the villain with an air of condescension: they are making a point of the fact that they cannot take his villainy seriously. We have here a type of irony which exactly corresponds to that of two other major arts of the ironic age, advertising and propaganda. These arts pretend to address themselves seriously to a subliminal audience of cretins, an audience that may not even exist, but which is assumed to be simple-minded enough to accept at their face value the statements made about the purity of a soap or a government's motives. The rest of us, realizing that irony never says precisely what it means, take these arts ironically, or, at least, regard them as a kind of ironic game. Similarly, we read murder stories with a strong sense of the unreality of the villainy involved. Murder is doubtless a serious crime, but if private murder really were a major threat to our civilization it would not be relaxing to read about it. We may compare the abuse showered on the pimp in Roman comedy, which was similarly based on the indisputable ground that brothels are immoral.

The next step is an ironic comedy addressed to the people who can realize that murderous violence is less an attack on a virtuous society by a malignant individual than a symptom of that society's own viciousness. Such a comedy would be the kind of intellectualized parody of melodramatic formulas represented by, for instance, the novels of Graham Greene. Next comes the ironic comedy directed at the melodramatic spirit itself, an astonishingly persistent tradition in all comedy in which there is a large ironic admixture. One notes a recurring tendency on the part of ironic comedy to ridicule and scold an audience assumed to be hankering after sentiment, solemnity, and the triumph of fidelity and approved moral standards. The arrogance of Jonson and Congreve, the mocking of bourgeois sentiment in Goldsmith, the parody of melodramatic situations in Wilde and Shaw, belong to a consistent tradition. Molière had to please his king, but was not temperamentally an exception. To comic drama one may add the ridicule of melodramatic romance in the novelists, from Fielding to Joyce.

Finally comes the comedy of manners, the portrayal of a chattering-monkey society devoted to snobbery and slander. In this kind of irony the characters who are opposed to or excluded from the fictional society have the sympathy of the audience. Here we are close to a parody of tragic irony, as we can see in the appalling fate of the relatively harmless hero of Evelyn Waugh's *A Handful of Dust*. Or we may have a character who, with the sympathy of the author or audience, repudiates such a society to the point of deliberately walking out of it, becoming thereby a kind of *pharmakos* in reverse. This happens for instance at the conclusion of Aldous Huxley's *Those Barren Leaves*. It is more usual, however, for the artist to present an ironic deadlock in which the hero is regarded as a fool or worse by the fictional society, and yet impresses the real audience as having something more valuable than his society has. The obvious example, and certainly one of the greatest, is Dostoievsky's *The Idiot*, but there are many others. *The Good Soldier Schweik, Heaven's My Destination* and *The Horse's Mouth* are instances that will give some idea of the range of the theme.

What we have said about the return of irony to myth in tragic modes thus holds equally well for comic ones. Even popular literature appears to be slowly shifting its center of gravity from murder stories to science fiction — or at any rate a rapid growth of science fiction is certainly a fact about contemporary popular literature. Science fiction frequently tries to imagine what life would be like on a plane as far above us as we are above savagery; its setting is often of a kind that appears to us as technologically miraculous. It is thus a mode of romance with a strong inherent tendency to myth.

The conception of a sequence of fictional modes should do something, let us hope, to give a more flexible meaning to some of our literary terms. The words "romantic" and "realistic," for instance, as ordinarily used, are relative or comparative terms: they illustrate tendencies in fiction, and cannot be used as simply descriptive adjectives with any sort of exactness. If we take the sequence *De Raptu Proserpinae, The Man of Law's Tale, Much Ado About Nothing, Pride and Prejudice, An American Tragedy,* it is clear that each work is "romantic" compared to its successors and "realistic" compared to its predecessors. On the other hand, the term "naturalism" shows up in its proper perspective as a phase of fiction which, rather like the detective story, though in a very different way, begins as an intensification of low mimetic, an attempt to describe life exactly as it is, and ends, by the very logic of that attempt, in pure irony. Thus Zola's obsession with ironic formulas gave him a reputation as a detached recorder of the human scene.

The difference between the ironic *tone* that we may find in low mimetic or earlier modes and the ironic *structure* of the ironic mode itself is not hard to sense in practice. When Dickens, for instance, uses irony the reader is invited to share in the irony, because certain standards of normality common to author and reader are assumed. Such assumptions are a mark of a relatively popular mode: as the example of Dickens indicates, the gap between serious and popular fiction is narrower in low mimetic than in ironic writing. The literary acceptance of relatively stable social norms is closely connected with the *reticence* of low mimetic as compared to ironic fiction. In low mimetic modes characters are usually presented as they appear to others, fully dressed and with a large section of both their physical lives and their inner monologue carefully excised. Such an approach is entirely consistent with the other conventions involved.

If we were to make this distinction the basis of a comparative value-judgement, which would, of course, be a moral value-judgement disguised as a critical one, we should be compelled either to attack low mimetic conventions for being prudish and hypocritical and leaving too much of life out, or to attack ironic conventions for not being wholesome, healthy, popular, reassuring, and sound, like the conventions of Dickens. As long as we are concerned simply to distinguish between the conventions, we need only remark that the low mimetic is one step more heroic than the ironic, and that low mimetic reticence has the effect of making its characters, on the average, more heroic, or at least more dignified, than the characters in ironic fiction.

We may also apply our scheme to the principles of selection on which a writer of fiction operates. Let us take, as a random example, the use of ghosts in fiction. In a true myth there can obviously be no consistent distinction between ghosts and living beings. In romance we have real human beings, and consequently ghosts are in a separate category, but in a romance a ghost as a rule is merely one more character: he causes little surprise because his appearance is no more marvellous than many other events. In high mimetic, where we are within the order of nature, a ghost is relatively easy to introduce because the plane of experience is above our own, but when he appears he is an awful and mysterious being from what is perceptibly another world. In low mimetic, ghosts have been, ever since Defoe, almost entirely confined to a separate category of "ghost stories." In ordinary low mimetic fiction they are inadmissible, "in complaisance to the scepticism of a reader," as Fielding puts it, a skepticism which extends only to low mimetic conventions. The few exceptions, such as *Wuthering Heights,* go a long way to prove the rule — that is, we recognize a strong influence of romance in *Wuthering Heights.* In some forms of ironic fiction, such as the later works of Henry James, the ghost begins to come back as a fragment of a disintegrating personality.

Once we have learned to distinguish the modes, however, we must then learn to recombine them. For while one mode constitutes the underlying tonality of a work of fiction, any or all of the other four may be simultaneously present. Much of our sense of the subtlety of great literature comes from this modal counterpoint. Chaucer is a medieval poet specializing mainly in romance, whether sacred or secular. Of his pilgrims, the knight and the parson clearly present the norms of the society in which he functions as a poet, and, as we have them, the *Canterbury Tales* are contained by these two figures, who open and close the series. But to overlook Chaucer's mastery of low mimetic and ironic techniques would be as wrong as to think of him as a modern novelist who got into the Middle Ages by mistake. The tonality of *Antony and Cleopatra* is high mimetic, the story of the fall of a great leader. But it is easy to look at Mark Antony ironically, as a man enslaved by passion; it is easy to recognize his common humanity with ourselves; it is easy to see in him a romantic adventurer of prodigious courage and endurance betrayed by a witch; there are even hints of a superhuman being whose legs bestrid the ocean and whose downfall is a conspiracy of fate, explicable only to a soothsayer. To leave out any of these would oversimplify and belittle the play. Through such an analysis we may come to realize that the two essential facts about a work of art, that it is contemporary with its own time and that it is contemporary with ours, are not opposed but complementary facts.

Our survey of fictional modes has also shown us that the mimetic tendency itself, the tendency to verisimilitude and accuracy of description, is one of two poles of literature. At the other pole is something that seems to be connected both with Aristotle's word *mythos* and with the usual meaning of myth. That is, it is a tendency to tell a story which is in origin a story about characters who can do anything, and only gradually becomes attracted toward a tendency to tell a plausible or credible story. Myths of gods merge into legends of heroes; legends of heroes merge into plots of tragedies and comedies; plots of tragedies and comedies merge into plots of more or less realistic fiction. But these are change of social context rather than of literary form, and the constructive principles of story-telling remain constant through them, though of course they adapt to them. Tom Jones and Oliver Twist are typical enough as low mimetic characters, but the birth-mystery plots in which they are involved are plausible adaptations of fictional formulas that go back to Menander, and from Menander to Euripides' *Ion,* and from Euripides to legends like those of Perseus and Moses. We note in passing that imitation of nature in fiction produces, not truth or reality, but plausibility, and plausibility varies in weight from a mere perfunctory concession in a myth or folk tale to a kind of censor principle in a naturalistic novel. Reading forward in history, therefore, we may think of our romantic, high mimetic and low mimetic modes as a series of *displaced* myths, *mythoi* or plot-formulas progressively moving over towards the opposite pole of verisimilitude, and then, with irony, beginning to move back.

FOR DISCUSSION

1. In this volume there are no pure "myths" in Frye's sense of the term, but there are "high mimetic," "low mimetic," and "ironic" works. Classify into those categories the chief characters of the following works: "Why I Live at the P.O."; "The Open Boat"; "Oedipus"; "The Colonel's Lady"; "Ulysses"; "Miniver Cheevy"; "American Rhapsody"; "A Clean, Well-Lighted Place."

2. "The Celestial Omnibus" establishes the postulates of romance. This having been done, what improbabilities are accepted by the reader?

3. From the short stories in this volume list several in which the hero becomes isolated from his society and several in which he becomes incorporated into it.

4. Which of Frye's statements about pity and fear in high mimetic tragedy apply to "Oedipus," and which of them about pity and fear in low mimetic tragedy apply to "Death of a Salesman"?

5. Describe the emotions aroused by Frost's "The Death of the Hired Man."

6. Is the father in "Barn Burning" a terrible figure, and does he have any helpless victim in his power?

7. What mania or obsession appears in "The Rocking Horse Winner"? Is the story presented in terms of fear or of pity?

8. In which stories do you find an *alazon* in the sense of someone who *pretends* or *tries* to be something more than he is?

9. Camus's "The Guest" is an example of sophisticated, rather than naive, irony. What ironic events are presented by the author without having the irony pointed out? Is Daru's final isolation "causally out of line with his character"?

10. Is Oedipus a *pharmakos*? Is Willy Loman? Is the hunger artist?

11. "The Hunger Artist," whatever else it may be, is a story of an obsession, and is low mimetic. Does it also have some qualities of myth?

12. What elegiac elements are found in TV Westerns?

13. In "The Catbird Seat," what constitutes the "twist in the plot" that corresponds to "discovery" in tragedy? Into what society is the hero now re-incorporated? Is there a moral ambiguity in his extreme success? Does Mr. Martin turn out to have been a *picaro*? Is Mrs. Barrows something of a *pharmakos*? Do you also

feel that she is over-punished, and that society is somewhat guilty at the end? Do Martin, Fitweiler, Stockton, Fishbein and Mrs. Powell became a mob, with Doctor Fitch presiding as high priest over the sacrificial ritual?

14. In "The Two Bottles of Relish," what "dullest and most neglected trivia of daily living leap into mysterious and fateful significance"? Not all readers feel this story to be repulsive and revolting as they first experience it, yet all readers would declare actual cannibalism to be intolerable. Does Frye give any explanation of why such a melodramatic story fails to be intolerably offensive to a reader? Is cannibalism a real problem in our society?

15. Is "The Catbird Seat" an ironic parody of the melodramatic spirit?

Speech on Receiving the Nobel Prize

WILLIAM FAULKNER

I feel that this award was not made to me as a man but to my work — a life's work in the agony and sweat of the human spirit; not for glory and least of all for profit, but to create out of the materials of the human spirit something which did not exist before. So this award is only mine in trust. It will not be difficult to find a dedication for the money part of it commensurate with the purpose and significance of its origin. But I would like to do the same with the acclaim too, by using this moment as a pinnacle from which I might be listened to by the young men and women already dedicated to the same anguish and travail, among whom is already that one who will someday stand here where I am standing.

Our tragedy today is a general and universal physical fear so long sustained by now that we can even bear it. There are no longer problems of the spirit. There is only the question: When will I be blown up? Because of this, the young man or woman writing today has forgotten the problems of the human heart in conflict with itself which alone can make good writing because only that is worth writing about, worth the agony and the sweat.

He must learn them again. He must teach himself that the basest of all things is to be afraid; and teaching himself that, forget it forever, leaving no room in his workshop for anything but the old verities and truths of the heart, the old universal truths lacking which any story is ephemeral and

Speech delivered at Stockholm, December 10, 1950. Reprinted from *The Faulkner Reader* (Random House, 1954).

doomed — love and honor and pity and pride and compassion and sacrifice. Until he does so he labors under a curse. He writes not of love but of lust, of defeats in which nobody loses anything of value, of victories without hope and worst of all without pity or compassion. His griefs grieve on no universal bones, leaving no scars. He writes not of the heart but of the glands.

The greater part of a writer's time is spent in reading, in order to write; a man will turn over half a library to make one book.

SAMUEL JOHNSON

Until he relearns these things he will write as though he stood among and watched the end of man. I decline to accept the end of man. It is easy enough to say that man is immortal simply because he will endure; that when the last ding-dong of doom has clanged and faded from the last worthless rock hanging tideless in the last red and dying evening, that even then there will still be one more sound: that of his puny inexhaustible voice, still talking. I refuse to accept this. I believe that man will not merely endure: he will prevail. He is immortal, not because he alone among creatures has an inexhaustible voice, but because he has a soul, a spirit capable of compassion and sacrifice and endurance. The poet's, the writer's, duty is to write about these things. It is his privilege to help man endure by lifting his heart, by reminding him of the courage and honor and hope and pride and compassion and pity and sacrifice which have been the glory of his past. The poet's voice need not merely be the record of man, it can be one of the props, the pillars to help him endure and prevail.

FOR DISCUSSION

1. What is Faulkner's key idea?

2. Do you agree that "our tragedy today is a general and universal physical fear"?

3. If you have read anything by Faulkner, do you believe it represents the kind of writing he here recommends?

4. This speech was made on a great and significant occasion. Does the dignity of its language reflect that situation? What stylistic elements help convey the dignity?

5. Can you find examples of vivid phrasing? Of figures of speech?

VOCABULARY: commensurate, travail, verities, ephemeral.

THEME TOPICS: The writer's duty. Compassion, sacrifice, endurance in a Faulkner story. Our general tragedy.

HOW

WRITERS MEAN

Hemingway in Cuba

ROBERT MANNING

On the shore of Havana's back harbor a stubborn hulk rests in drydock and erodes with time. Its engine and expensive fishing tackle are gone. The fading letters of its name, *Pilar,* are still visible on the stern. "No one else should sail the *Pilar,*" says Mary Hemingway. She had hoped to have it towed to sea and sunk off the port of Cojimar, deep into the fishing hole where a strike came at last to the old man "who fished alone in the Gulf Stream and he had gone eighty-four days now without taking a fish." The Cuban government's red tape prevented that, so the *Pilar* now decays in the Caribbean sun.

Ten miles from Havana, in the village of San Francisco de Paula, is Hemingway's longtime home away from home. The plantation he called Finca Vigia (Lookout Farm), with its big limestone villa and thirteen acres of banana trees, tropical shrubs, and casual gardens, stands much as he and his wife left it in 1960 when he came home to the States for the last time. It is

From *The Atlantic,* August 1965. Reprinted by permission of the author.

now a Cuban government museum. Some Cubans who ran the place for "Papa" still live and work there, caring for the grounds and the sprawling villa and pointing out to visitors the pool where "Papa" swam, the big bedroom where he wrote, and the tall white tower where he would sit to work or to stare from his heights toward the spread of Havana.

Who in my generation was not moved by Hemingway the writer and fascinated by Hemingway the maker of his own legend? "Veteran out of the wars before he was twenty," as Archibald MacLeish described him. "Famous at twenty-five; thirty a master." Wine-stained moods in the sidewalk cafés and roistering nights in Left Bank *boîtes*. Walking home alone in the rain. Talk of death, and scenes of it, in the Spanish sun. Treks and trophies in Tanganyika's green hills. Duck-shooting in the Venetian marshes. Fighting in, and writing about, two world wars. Loving and drinking and fishing out of Key West and Havana. Swaggering into Toots Shor's or posturing in *Life* magazine or talking a verbless sort of Choctaw for the notebooks of Lillian Ross and the pages of the *New Yorker*.

By the time I got the opportunity to meet him, he was savoring the highest moment of his fame — he had just won the Nobel Prize for Literature — but he was moving into the twilight of his life. He was fifty-five but looked older, and was trying to mend a ruptured kidney, a cracked skull, two compressed and one cracked vertebra, and bad burns suffered in the crash of his airplane in the Uganda bush the previous winter. Those injuries, added to half a dozen head wounds, more than 200 shrapnel scars, a shot-off kneecap, wounds in the feet, hands, and groin, had slowed him down. The casually comfortable Cuban villa had become more home than any place he'd had, and days aboard the *Pilar* were his substitute for high adventure abroad.

In a telephone conversation between San Francisco de Paula and New York, Hemingway had agreed to be interviewed on the occasion of his Nobel award, but he resisted at first because one of the magazines I worked with had recently published a penetrating article on William Faulkner. "You guys cut him to pieces, to pieces," Hemingway said. "No, it was a good piece," I said, "and it would have been even better if Faulkner had seen the writer."

"Give me a better excuse," Hemingway said, and then thought of one himself. He saw the arrival of a visitor as an opportunity to fish on the *Pilar* after many weeks of enforced idleness. "Bring a heavy sweater, and we'll go out on the boat," he said. "I'll explain to Mary that you're coming down to cut me up and feed me to William Faulkner."

A handsome young Cuban named René, who had grown up on Hemingway's place as his all-round handyman, chauffeur, and butler, was at Havana Airport to meet me and hustle my luggage, which included a batch of new phonograph records and, as a last-minute addition, a gift from Marlene Dietrich. On hearing that someone was going to Cuba to see her old friend, she sent along a newly released recording called "Shake, Rattle, and Roll," which now may be vaguely remembered as the Java man artifact in the evolution of popular rock 'n' roll. "Just like the Kraut," said Hemingway. He found the sentiment more appealing than the music.

A big man. Even after allowing for all the descriptions and photographs, the first impression of Hemingway in the flesh was size. He was barefoot and barelegged, wearing only floppy khaki shorts and a checked sport shirt, its tail tumbling outside. He squinted slightly through round silver-framed glasses, and a tentative smile, the sort that could instantly turn into a sneer or snarl, showed through his clipped white beard. Idleness had turned him to paunch, and he must have weighed then about 225 pounds, but there was no other suggestion of softness in the burly, broad-shouldered frame, and he had the biceps and calves of an N.F.L. linebacker.

"Drink?" Hemingway asked. The alacrity of the reply pleased him, and the smile broadened into a laugh. He asked René to mix martinis and said, "Thank God you're a drinking man. I've been worried ever since I told you to come down. There was a photographer here for three days a while ago who didn't drink. He was the cruelest man I've ever met. Cruelest man in the world. Made us stand in the sun for hours at a time. And he didn't drink." With stiff caution, he sank into a large overstuffed chair which had been lined back, sides, and bottom with big art and picture books to brace his injured back.

Hemingway sipped and said, "Now, if you find me talking in monosyllables or without any verbs, you tell me, because I never really talk that way. She [he meant Lillian Ross] told me she wanted to write a piece of homage to Hemingway. That's what she told me when I agreed to see her up in New York." He laughed. "I knew her for a long time. Helped her with her first big piece, on Sidney Franklin."

"I don't mind talking tonight," Hemingway said, "because I never work at night. There's a lot of difference between night thinking and day thinking. Night thoughts are usually nothing. The work you do at night you always will have to do over again in the daytime anyhow. So let's talk. When I talk, incidentally, it's just talk. But when I write I mean it for good."

The living room was nearly fifty feet long and high-ceilinged, with gleaming white walls that set off the Hemingways' small but choice collection of paintings (including a Miró, two by Jean Gris, a Klee, a Braque — since stolen from the villa — and five André Massons), a few trophy heads from the African safaris. In another room, near the entrance to a large tile-floored dining room, was an oil portrait of Hemingway in his thirties, wearing a flowing, open-collar white shirt. "It's an old-days picture of me as Kid Balzac by Waldo Pierce," said Hemingway. "Mary has it around because she likes it."

He rubbed the tight-curled white beard and explained that he wore it because when clean-shaven his skin was afflicted with sore spots if he spent much time in the sun. "I'll clip the damned thing off for Christmas, so as not to run against Santa Claus," he said, "and if I rest the hide a couple of weeks at a time, I may be able to keep it off. Hope so anyway."

In one large corner of the living room stood a six-foot-high rack filled with dozens of magazines and newspapers from the States, London, and Paris. In casual piles, books littered windowsills and tables and spilled a trail into two large rooms adjacent. One was a thirty-by-twenty-foot library whose floor-to-ceiling shelves sagged with books. The other was Hemingway's large but crowded bedroom study — littered with correspondence in varied stages of attention or neglect. There were neat piles of opened letters together with stamped and addressed replies; cardboard boxes overflowing with the shards of correspondence that had been opened, presumably read, and one day might be filed; a couple of filing cabinets, whose mysteries probably were best known to a part-time stenographer the Hemingways brought in from Havana a day or two at a time when needed. There was also a large lion skin, in the gaping mouth of which lay half a dozen letters and pair of manila envelopes. "That's the Urgent in-box," Hemingway explained.

The villa seemed awash with books — nearly 400, including two dozen cookbooks, in Mary Hemingway's bedroom; more than 500, mostly fiction, history, and music, in the big sitting room; another 300, mostly French works of history and fiction, in an elegantly tiled room called the Venetian Room; nearly 2000 in the high-shelved library, these carefully divided into history, military books, biography, geography, natural history, some fiction, and a large collection of maps; 900 volumes, mostly military manuals and textbooks, history and geography in Spanish, and sports volumes, in Hemingway's bedroom. In the tall tower he kept another 400 volumes, including foreign editions of his own works, and some 700 overflowed into shelves and tabletops in the finca's small guesthouse. All the books, including Hemingway's collection of autographed works by many of his contemporaries, were impounded at the villa by the Castro regime, though Mrs. Hemingway was able to take away some of the paintings and personal belongings.

From the kitchen came sounds and smells of dinner in preparation. René emerged with two bottles of a good Bordeaux from a cellar that was steadily replenished from France and Italy. Evening sounds grew strident in the soft tropical outdoors. Distant dogs yelped. Near the house, a hoot owl broke into short, sharp cries. "That's the Bitchy Owl," Hemingway said. "He'll go on like that all night. He's lived here longer than we have.

"I respect writing very much," he said abruptly, "the writer not at all, except as the instrument to do the writing. When a writer retires deliberately from life or is forced out of it by some defect, his writing has a tendency to atrophy, just like a man's limb when it's not used.

"I'm not advocating the strenuous life for everyone or trying to say it's the choice form of life. Anyone who's had the luck or misfortune to be an athlete has to keep his body in shape. The body and mind are closely coordinated. Fattening of the body can lead to fattening of the mind. I would be tempted to say that it can lead to fattening of the soul, but I don't know anything about the soul." He halted, broodingly, as if reflecting on his own aches and pains, his too ample paunch, a blood pressure that was too high, and a set of muscles that were suffering too many weeks of disuse. "However, in everyone the process of fattening or wasting away will set in, and I guess one is as bad as the other."

He had been reading about medical discoveries which suggested to him that a diet or regimen or treatment that may work for one man does not necessarily work for another. "This was known years ago, really, by people who make proverbs. But now doctors have discovered that certain men need more exercise than others; that certain men are affected by alcohol more than others; that certain people can assimilate more punishment in many ways than others.

"Take Primo Carnera, for instance. Now he was a real nice guy, but he was so big and clumsy it was pitiful. Or take Tom Wolfe, who just never could discipline his mind to his tongue. Or Scott Fitzgerald, who just couldn't drink." He pointed to a couch across the room. "If Scott had been drinking with us and Mary called us to dinner, Scott'd make it to his feet all right, but then he'd probably fall down. Alcohol was just poison to him. Because all these guys had these weaknesses, it won them sympathy and favor, more sometimes than a guy without those defects would get."

For a good part of his adult life Hemingway was, of course, a ten-goal drinker, and he could hold it well. He was far more disciplined in this regard, though, than the legend may suggest. Frequently when he was working hard, he would drink nothing, except perhaps a glass or two of wine with meals. By rising at about daybreak or half an hour thereafter, he had put in a full writing day by ten or eleven in the morning and was ready for relaxation when others were little more than under way.

As in his early days, Hemingway in the late years worked with painful slowness. He wrote mostly in longhand, frequently while standing at a bookcase in his bedroom; occasionally he would typewrite ("when trying to keep up with dialogue"). For years he carefully logged each day's work. Except for occasional spurts when he was engaged in relatively unimportant efforts, his output ran between 400 and 700 words a day. Mary Hemingway remembers very few occasions when it topped 1000 words.

He did not find writing to be quick or easy. "I always hurt some," he remarked.

Hemingway was capable of great interest in and generosity toward younger writers and some older writers, but as he shows in *A Moveable Feast* (written in 1957-1959 and finished in the spring of 1961), he had a curious and unbecoming compulsion to poke and peck at the reputations of many of his literary contemporaries. Gertrude Stein, Sherwood Anderson, T. S. Eliot, not to mention Fitzgerald, Wolfe, Ford Madox Ford, James Gould Cozzens, and others, were invariably good for a jab or two if their names came up. As for the critics — "I often feel," he said, "that there is now a rivalry between writing and criticism, rather than the feeling that one should help the other." Writers today could not learn much from the critics. "Critics should deal more with dead writers. A living writer can learn a lot from dead writers."

Fiction-writing, Hemingway felt, was to invent out of knowledge. "To invent out of knowledge means to produce inventions that are true. Every man should have a built-in automatic drivel detector operating inside him. It also should have a manual drill and a crank handle in case the machine breaks down. If you're going to write, you have to find out what's bad for you. Part of that you learn fast, and then you learn what's good for you.

"But back to inventing. In *The Old Man and the Sea* I knew two or three things about the situation, but I didn't know the story." He hesitated, filling the intervals with a vague movement of his hands. "I didn't even know if that big fish was going to bite for the old man when it started smelling around the bait. I had to write on, inventing out of knowledge. You reject everything that is not or can't be completely true. I didn't know what was going to happen for sure in *For Whom the Bell Tolls* or *Farewell to Arms*. I was inventing."

Philip Young's *Ernest Hemingway*, published in 1953, had attributed much of Hemingway's inspiration or "invention" to his violent experiences as a boy and in World War I.

"If you haven't read it, don't bother," Hemingway volunteered. "How would you like it if someone said that everything you've done in your life was done because of some trauma. Young had a theory that was like — you know, the Procrustean bed, and he had to cut me to fit into it."

During dinner, the talk continued on writing styles and techniques. Hemingway thought too many contemporary writers defeated themselves through addiction to symbols. "No good book has ever been written that has in it symbols arrived at beforehand and stuck in." He waved a chunk of French bread. "That kind of symbol sticks out like — like raisins in raisin bread. Raisin bread is all right, but plain bread is better."

He mentioned Santiago, his old fisherman, in roughly these terms: Santiago was never alone because he had his friend and enemy, the sea, and the things that lived in the sea, some of which he loved and others he hated. He loved the sea, but the sea is a great whore, as the book made clear. He had tried to make everything in the story real — the boy, the sea, and the marlin and the sharks, the hope being that each would then mean many things. In that way, the parts of a story become symbols, but they are not first designed or planted as symbols.

The Bitchy Owl hooted the household to sleep. I was awakened by tropical birds at the dawn of a bright and promising day. This was to be Hemingway's first fishing trip on *Pilar* since long before his African crash. By six thirty he was dressed in yesterday's floppy shorts and sport shirt, barefooted, and hunched over his New York *Times,* one of the six papers he and Mary read every day. From the record player came a mixture of Scarlatti, Beethoven, Oscar Peterson, and a remake of some 1928 Louis Armstrong.

At brief intervals Hemingway popped a pill into his mouth. "Since the crash I have to take so many of them they have to fight among themselves unless I space them out," he said.

While we were breakfasting, a grizzled Canary Islander named Gregorio, who served as the *Pilar's* first mate, chef, caretaker, and bartender, was preparing the boat for a day at sea. By nine o'clock, with a young nephew to help him, he had fueled the boat, stocked it with beer, whiskey, wine, and a bottle of tequila, a batch of fresh limes, and food for a large seafood lunch afloat. As we made out of Havana Harbor, Gregorio at the wheel and the young boy readying the deep-sea rods, reels, and fresh bait-fish, Hemingway pointed out landmarks and waved jovially to passing skippers. They invariably waved back, occasionally shouting greetings to "Papa." He sniffed the sharp sea air with delight and peered ahead for the dark line made by the Gulf Stream. "Watch the birds," he said. "They show us when the fish are up."

Mary Hemingway had matters to handle at the finca and in the city, so she could not come along, but out of concern for Hemingway's health she exacted a promise. In return for the long-missed fun of a fishing expedition, he agreed to take it easy and to return early, in time for a nap before an art exhibit to which he and Mary had promised their support. He was in a hurry, therefore, to reach good fishing water. Gregorio pushed the boat hard to a stretch of the Gulf Stream off Cojimar. Hemingway relaxed into one of the two cushioned bunks in the boat's open-ended cabin.

"It's wonderful to get out on the water. I need it." He gestured toward the ocean. "It's the last free place there is, the sea. Even Africa's about gone; it's at war, and that's going to go on for a very long time."

The *Pilar* fished two rods from its high antenna-like outriggers and two from seats at the stern, and at Hemingway's instruction, Gregorio and the boy baited two with live fish carefully wired to the hooks, and two with artificial lures. A man-o'-war bird gliding lazily off the coast pointed to the first school of the day, and within an hour the *Pilar* had its first fish, a pair of bonito sounding at the end of the outrigger lines. Before it was over, the day was to be one of the best fishing days in many months, with frequent good runs of bonito and dolphin and pleasant interludes of quiet in which to sip drinks, to soak up the Caribbean sun, and to talk.

Sometimes moody, sometimes erupting with boyish glee at the strike of a tuna or the golden blue explosion of a hooked dolphin, and sometimes — as if to defy or outwit his wounds — pulling himself by his arms to the flying bridge to steer the *Pilar* for a spell, Hemingway talked little of the present, not at all of the future, and a great deal of the past.

He recalled when Scribner's sent him first galley proofs of *For Whom the Bell Tolls*. "I remember, I spent ninety hours on the proofs of that book without once leaving the hotel room. When I finished, I thought the type was so small nobody would ever buy the book. I'd shot my eyes, you see. I had corrected the manuscript several times but still was not satisfied. I told Max Perkins about the type, and he said if I really thought it was too small, he'd have the whole book reprinted. That's a real expensive thing, you know. He was a sweet guy. But Max was right, the type was all right."

"Do you ever read any of your stuff over again?"

"Sometimes I do," he said. "When I'm feeling low. It makes you feel good to look back and see you can write."

"Is there anything you've written that you would do differently if you could do it over?"

"Not yet."

New York. "It's a very unnatural place to live. I could never live there. And there's not much fun going to the city now. Max is dead. Granny Rice is dead. He was a wonderful guy. We always used to go to the Bronx Zoo and look at the animals."

The Key West days, in the early thirties, were a good time. "There was a fighter there — he'd had one eye ruined, but he was still pretty good, and he decided to start fighting again. He wanted to be his own promoter. He asked me if I would referee his bout each week. I told him, 'Nothing doing,' he shouldn't go in the ring anymore. Any fighter who knew about his bad eye would just poke his thumb in the other one and then beat his head off.

"The fighter said, 'The guys come from somewhere else won't know 'bout my eye, and no one around here in the Keys gonna dare poke my eye.'

"So I finally agreed to referee for him. This was the Negro section, you know, and they really introduced me: 'And the referee for tonight, the world-famous millionaire, sportsman, and playboy, Mister Ernest Hemingway!'" Hemingway chuckled. "Playboy was the greatest title they thought they could give a man." Chuckle again. "How can the Nobel Prize move a man who has heard plaudits like that?"

Frequently a sharp cry from Gregorio on the flying bridge interrupted the talk. "Feesh! Papa, feesh!" Line would snap from one of the outriggers, and a reel begin to snarl. "You take him," Hemingway would say, or if two fish struck at once, as frequently happened, he would leap to one rod and I to the other.

For all the hundreds of times it had happened to him, he still thrilled with delight at the quivering run of a bonito or the slash of a dolphin against the sky. "Ah, beautiful! A beautiful fish. Take him softly now. Easy. Easy. Work him with style. That's it. Rod up slowly. Now reel in fast. *Suave!*

Suave! Don't break his mouth. If you jerk, you'll break his mouth, and the hook will go."

When action lulled, he would scan the seascape for clues to better spots. Once a wooden box floated in the near distance, and he ordered Gregorio toward it. "We'll fish that box," he said, explaining that small shrimp seek shelter from the sun beneath flotsam or floating patches of seaweed and these repositories of food attract dolphin. At the instant the lures of the stern rods passed the box, a dolphin struck and was hooked, to be pumped and reeled in with the heavy-duty glass rod whose butt rested in a leather rod holder strapped around the hips.

He talked about the act of playing a fish as if it were an English sentence. "The way to do it, the style, is not just an idle concept. It is simply the way to get done what is supposed to be done; in this case it brings in the fish. The fact that the right way looks pretty or beautiful when it's done is just incidental."

Hemingway had written only one play, *The Fifth Column*. Why no others?

"If you write a play, you have to stick around and fix it up," he said. "They always want to fool around with them to make them commercially successful, and you don't like to stick around that long. After I've written, I want to go home and take a shower."

Almost absently he plucked James Joyce out of the air. "Once Joyce said to me he was afraid his writing was too suburban and that maybe he should get around a bit and see the world, the way I was doing. He was under great discipline, you know — his wife, his work, his bad eyes. And his wife said, yes, it *was* too suburban. 'Jim could do with a spot of that lion-hunting.' How do you like that? A *spot* of lion-hunting!

"We'd go out, and Joyce would fall into an argument or a fight. He couldn't even see the man, so he'd say, 'Deal with him, Hemingway! Deal with him!' " Hemingway paused. "In the big league it is not the way it says in the books."

Hemingway was not warm toward T. S. Eliot. He preferred to praise Ezra Pound, who at that time was still confined in St. Elizabeth's mental hospital in Washington. "Ezra Pound is a great poet, and whatever he did, he has been punished greatly, and I believe should be freed to go and write poems in Italy, where he is loved and understood. He was the master of Eliot. I was a member of an organization which Pound founded with Natalia Barney in order to get Eliot out of his job in a bank so he could be free to write poetry. It was called Bel Esprit. Eliot, I believe, was able to get out of his job and edit a review and write poetry freely due to the backing of other people than this organization. But the organization was typical of Pound's generosity and interest in all forms of the arts regardless of any benefits to himself or of the possibilities that the people he encouraged would be his rivals.

"Eliot is a winner of the Nobel Prize. I believe it might well have gone to Pound, as a poet. Pound certainly deserved punishment, but I believe this would be a good year to release poets and allow them to continue to write poetry. . . . Ezra Pound, no matter what he may think, is not as great a poet as Dante, but he is a very great poet for all his errors."

Dusk was coming when the *Pilar* turned toward Havana Harbor, its skipper steering grandly from the flying bridge. What remained of the bottle of tequila and a half of lime rested in a holder cut into the mahogany rail near the wheel. "To ward off sea serpents," Hemingway explained, passing the bottle for a ceremonial homecoming swig.

At the docks, René reported that the gallery opening had been postponed. Hemingway was overjoyed. "Now we can relax for a while and then get some sleep. We went out and had a good day and got pooped. Now we can sleep."

Hemingway's good spirits on his return helped to diminish his wife's concern about his over-extending himself. She served up a hot oyster stew, and later, clutching an early nightcap, Hemingway sprawled with pleased fatigue in his big armchair and talked of books he had recently read. He had started Saul Bellow's *The Adventures of Augie March,* but didn't like it. "But when I'm working," he said, "and read to get away from it, I'm inclined to make bad judgments about other people's writing." He thought Bellow's very early book, *Dangling Man,* much better.

One of the post-war writers who had impressed him most was John Horne Burns, who wrote *The Gallery* and two other novels and then, in 1953, died in circumstances that suggested suicide. "There was a fellow who wrote a fine book and then a stinking book about a prep school, and then he just blew himself up," Hemingway mused, adding a gesture that seemed to ask, How do you explain such a thing? He stared at nothing, seeming tired and sad.

"You know," he said, "my father shot himself."

There was silence. It had frequently been said that Hemingway never cared to talk about his father's suicide.

"Do you think it took courage?" I asked.

Hemingway pursed his lips and shook his head. "No. It's everybody's right, but there's a certain amount of egotism in it and a certain disregard of others." He turned off that conversation by picking up a handful of books. "Here are a few things you might like to look at before you turn off the light." He held out *The Retreat,* by P. H. Newby, Max Perkins' selected letters, *The Jungle Is Neutral,* by Frederick S. Chapman, and Malcolm Cowley's *The Literary Situation.*

By seven the next morning a rabble of dogs yipped and yelped in the yard near the finca's small guesthouse. René had been to town and returned with the mail and newspapers. Hemingway, in a tattered robe and old slippers, was already half through the *Times.*

"Did you finish the Cowley book last night?" he asked. "Very good, I think. I never realized what a tough time writers have economically, if they have it as tough as Malcolm says they do."

He was reminded of his early days in Paris. "It never seemed like hardship to me. It was hard work, but it was fun. I was working, and I had a wife and kid to support. I remember, first I used to go to the market every morning and get the stuff for Bumby's [his first son, John] bottle. His mother had to have her sleep." Lest this should be taken as a criticism, he added, "That's characteristic, you know, of the very finest women. They need their sleep, and when they get it, they're wonderful."

Another part of the routine in the Paris days, to pick up eating money, was Hemingway's daily trip to a gymnasium to work as a sparring partner for fighters. The pay was two dollars an hour. "That was very good money then, and I didn't get marked up very much. I had one rule: never provoke a fighter. I tried not to get hit. They had plenty of guys they could knock around."

He reached for the mail, slit open one from a pile of fifteen letters. It was from a high school English teacher in Miami, Florida, who complained that her students rarely read good literature and relied for "knowledge" on the movies, television, and radio. To arouse their interest, she wrote, she told them about Hemingway's adventures and pressed them to read his writings. "Therefore in a sense," she concluded, "you are the teacher in my tenth grade classroom. I thought you'd like to know it." Hemingway found the letter depressing: "Pretty bad if kids are spending all that time away from books."

The next fishing expedition was even better than the first — fewer fish, but two of them were small marlin, one about eighty pounds, the other eighty-five, that struck simultaneously and were boated, Hemingway's with dispatch, the second at a cost of amateurish sweat and agony that was the subject of as much merriment as congratulations. It was a more sprightly occasion, too, because Mary Hemingway was able to come along. A bright, generous, and energetic woman, Hemingway's fourth wife cared for him well, anticipated his moods and his desires, enjoyed and played bountiful hostess to his friends, diplomatically turned aside some of the most taxing demands on his time and generosity. More than that, she shared his love and the broad mixture of interests — books, good talk, traveling, fishing, shooting — that were central to Hemingway's life. His marriage to her was plainly the central and guiding personal relationship of his last fifteen years.

Hemingway gazed happily at the pair of marlin. "We're back in business," he said, and gave Mary a hug. "This calls for celebration," said Mary.

"Off to the Floridita," said Hemingway.

The Floridita was once one of those comfortably shoddy Havana saloons where the food was cheap and good and the drinking serious. By then, enjoying a prosperity that was due in no small part to its reputation as the place you could see and maybe even drink with Papa Hemingway, it had taken on a red-plush grandeur and even had a velvet cord to block off the dining room entrance. "It looks crummy now," Hemingway said, "but the drinking's as good as ever."

The Floridita played a special role in Hemingway's life. "My not living in the United States," he explained, "does not mean any separation from the tongue or even the country. Any time I come to the Floridita I see Americans from all over. It can even be closer to America in many ways than being in New York. You go there for a drink or two, and see everybody from everyplace. I live in Cuba because I love Cuba — that does not mean a dislike for anyplace else. And because here I get privacy when I write. If I want to see anyone, I just go into town, or the Air Force guys come out to the place, naval characters and all — guys I knew in the war. I used to have privacy in Key West, but then I had less and less when I was trying to work, and there were too many people around, so I'd come over here and work in the Ambos Mundos Hotel."

The Floridita's bar was crowded, but several customers obligingly slid away from one section that had been designated long before by the proprietor as "Papa's Corner." Smiles. "Hello, Papa." Handshakes all around. "Three *Papa Dobles*," said Hemingway, and the barkeep hastened to manufacture three immense daiquiris according to a Floridita recipe that relies more on grapefruit juice than on lemon or lime juice. The *Papa Doble* was a heavy seller in those days at $1.25, and a bargain at that.

Two sailors off a U.S. aircraft carrier worked up nerve to approach the author and ask for an autograph. "I read all your books," said one of them.

"What about you?" Hemingway said to the other.

"I don't read much," the young sailor said.

"Get started," Hemingway said.

The Floridita's owner appeared, with embraces for the Hemingways and the news that he was installing a modern men's room. Hemingway noted sadly that all the good things were passing. "A wonderful old john back there," he said. "Makes you want to shout: Water closets of the world unite; you have nothing to lose but your chains."

There were some other chances in later years to talk with Hemingway, in Cuba and New York, and there were a few letters in between — from Finca Vigia or Spain or France, or from Peru, where he went to fish with the Hollywood crew that made the film of *The Old Man and the Sea*. "Here's the chiropractor who fixed up my back," said the inscription on a postcard-size photograph from Peru showing him and an immense marlin he landed off Puerto Blanco.

Trips to New York grew less frequent and did not seem to amuse or entertain him. Unlike the old days and nights at Shor's or Twenty-one, he later usually preferred to see a few friends and dine in his hotel suite. Top health never really seemed to come back to him. He was having trouble with his weight, blood pressure, and diet. He was still working, though, as the stylishly written pages of *A Moveable Feast* show. (How much else he was producing then is not clear. Mrs. Hemingway, together with Scribner's and Hemingway's authorized biographer, Carlos Baker, and his old friend Malcolm

Cowley, is sifting a trunkload of manuscripts that include some short stories, several poems, some fragments of novels, and at least one long completed novel about the sea — written to be part of a trilogy about land, sea, and air.)

His curiosity about the world, about people, about the old haunts (that word probably ought to be taken both ways) remained zestful, and so did his willingness to talk books and authors.

Once NBC did an hour-long radio documentary featuring recollections by many people who knew Hemingway, including some who were no longer friends. Sidney Franklin's comments annoyed him. "I never traveled with Franklin's bullfighting 'troup,'" Hemingway said. "That is all ballroom bananas. I did pay for one of his operations, though, and tried to get him fights in Madrid when no promoter would have him, and staked him to cash so he wouldn't have to pawn his fighting suits." Max Eastman had retold on the broadcast his version of the memorable fight between him and Hemingway at Scribner's over Eastman's reflections on whether Hemingway really had any hair on his chest. "He was sort of comic," said Hemingway. "There used to be a character had a monologue something like Listen to What I Done to Philadelphia Jack O'Brien. Eastman is weakening though. In the original version he stood me on my head in a corner, and I screamed in a high-pitched voice."

Hemingway added: "None of this is of the slightest importance, and I never blow the whistle on anyone, nor dial N for Narcotics if I find a friend or enemy nursing the pipe."

On a later occasion, a dean of theology wrote in the *New Republic* an article entitled "The Mystique of Merde" about those he considered to be "dirty" writers, and put Hemingway near the top of his list. A newsmagazine reprinted part of the article, and when he read it, Hemingway, then in Spain, addressed as a rebuttal to the dean a hilarious short lecture on the true meaning of the word *merde* and its use as a word of honor among the military and theatrical people. It is, Hemingway explained, what all French officers say to one another when going on an especially dangerous mission or to their deaths, instead of *au revoir*, good-bye, good luck old-boy, or any similar wet phrases. "I use old and bad words when they are necessary, but that does not make me a dirty writer," he said. For the dean, he had a dirty word. But he did not send the note to him; the writing of it turned his irritation into a shrug.

The Hemingways left Cuba in July of 1960 and went to Key West. From there, with luggage that filled a train compartment, they went to New York to live for a while in a small apartment. Later they moved to the new place Hemingway had bought in Ketchum, Idaho, close to the kind of shooting, fishing, walking that had beguiled him as a young boy in upper Michigan. He went to Spain for six weeks that summer to follow his friend Ordoñez and his rival, Dominguin, in their *mano a mano* tour of bullfights and to write

The Dangerous Summer, bullfight pieces commissioned by *Life* magazine. I have the impression that he didn't think very much of them, but he didn't say. His spirits seemed low after that and ostensibly stayed that way, though he apparently kept at work out in Ketchum almost until the day his gun went off.

The rereading of the notes and letters from which these glimpses of Hemingway are drawn — for glimpses are all they are — induces a curious thought: It is possible that to have known him, at least to have known him superficially and late in his life, makes it more rather than less difficult to understand him.

He made himself easy to parody, but he was impossible to imitate. He sometimes did or said things that seemed almost perversely calculated to obscure his many gallantries and generosities and the many enjoyments and enthusiasms he made possible for others. He could be fierce in his sensitivity to criticism and competitive in his craft to the point of vindictiveness, but he could laugh at himself ("I'm Ernie Hemorrhoid, the poor man's Pyle," he announced when he put on his war correspondent's uniform) and could enjoy the pure pride of believing that he had accomplished much of what he set out to do forty-five years before in a Parisian loft.

The private Hemingway was an artist. The public Hemingway was an experience, one from which small, sharp remembrances linger as persistently as the gusty moments:

A quiet dinner in New York when he remarked out of a rueful silence, and with a hint of surprise, "You know — all the beautiful women I know are growing old."

A misty afternoon in Cuba when he said, "If I could be something else, I'd like to be a painter."

A letter from the clinic in Rochester, Minnesota, where doctors were working him over: he reported "everything working o.k." — the blood pressure down from 250/125 to 130/80, and the weight down to 175 pounds, low for that big frame. He was two months behind, he said, on a book that was supposed to come out that fall — the fall of 1961.

And last of all, a Christmas card with the extra message in his climbing script: "We had fun, didn't we?"

FOR DISCUSSION

1. The article opens with a description of a fishing boat, but the passage implies more than it says. What does it imply?

2. In the fourth paragraph why does the author put together the fact that Hemingway had just won the Nobel Prize and that he had suffered many injuries?

3. What does Hemingway say about the effectiveness of symbols in a work of art?

4. Does Hemingway indicate that he planned his novels from beginning to end? Did he write quickly or slowly? What did he mean when he said "I always hurt some"?

5. How much of the "Hemingway legend" is alluded to in the course of the article?

VOCABULARY: boîtes, strident, atrophy, regimen, a ten-goal drinker, trauma, Procrustean, grizzled, outriggers, flotsam, rabble, ostensibly, vindictiveness.

THEME TOPICS: Manning's character sketch. Playing a fish.

Tragedy and the Common Man

ARTHUR MILLER

In this age few tragedies are written. It has often been held that the lack is due to a paucity of heroes among us, or else that the modern man has had the blood drawn out of his organs of belief by the skepticism of science, and the heroic attack on life cannot feed on an attitude of reserve and circumspection. For one reason or another, we are often held to be below tragedy — or tragedy above us. The inevitable conclusion is, of course, that the tragic mode is archaic, fit only for the very highly placed, the kings or the kingly, and where this admission is not made in so many words it is most often implied.

I believe that the common man is as apt a subject for tragedy in its highest sense as kings were. On the face of it this ought to be obvious in the light of modern psychiatry, which bases its analysis upon classic formulations, such as the Oedipus and Orestes complexes, for instance, which were enacted by royal beings, but which apply to everyone in similar emotional situations.

More simply, when the question of tragedy in art is not at issue, we never hesitate to attribute to the well-placed and the exalted the very same mental processes as the lowly. And finally, if the exaltation of tragic action were truly a property of the high-bred character alone, it is inconceivable that the mass of mankind should cherish tragedy above all other forms, let alone be capable of understanding it.

As a general rule, to which there may be exceptions unknown to me, I think the tragic feeling is evoked in us when we are in the presence of a character who is ready to lay down his life, if need be, to secure one thing — his sense of personal dignity.

From Orestes to Hamlet, Medea to Macbeth, the underlying struggle is that of the individual attempting to gain his "rightful" position in his society. Sometimes he is one who has been displaced from it, sometimes one who seeks to attain it for the first time, but the fateful wound from which the inevitable events spiral is the wound of indignity, and its dominant force is indignation. Tragedy, then, is a consequence of a man's total compulsion to evaluate himself justly.

In the sense of having been initiated by the hero himself, the tale always reveals what has been called his "tragic flaw," a failing that is not peculiar to grand or elevated characters. Nor is it necessarily a weakness. The flaw, or crack in the character, is really nothing — and need be nothing, but his inherent unwillingness to remain passive in the face of what he conceives to be a challenge to his dignity, his image of his rightful status. Only the passive, only those who accept their lot without active retaliation, are "flawless." Most of us are in that category.

But there are among us today, as there always have been, those who act against the scheme of things that degrades them, and in the process of action everything we have accepted out of fear or insensitivity or ignorance is shaken before us and examined, and from this total onslaught by an individual against the seemingly stable cosmos surrounding us — from this total examination of the "unchangeable" environment — comes the terror and the fear that is classically associated with tragedy.

More important, from this total questioning of what has previously been unquestioned, we learn. And such a process is not beyond the common

---

But I became a writer all the same, and shall remain one until the end of the chapter, just as a cow goes on giving milk all her life, even though what appears to be her self-interest urges her to give gin.

H. L. MENCKEN

man. In revolutions around the world, these past thirty years, he has demonstrated again and again this inner dynamic of all tragedy.

Insistence upon the rank of the tragic hero, or the so-called nobility of his character, is really but a clinging to the outward forms of tragedy. If rank or nobility of character was indispensable, then it would follow that the problems of those with rank were the particular problems of tragedy. But surely the right of one monarch to capture the domain from another no longer raises our passions, nor are our concepts of justice what they were to the mind of an Elizabethan king.

The quality in such plays that does shake us, however, derives from the underlying fear of being displaced, the disaster inherent in being torn away from our chosen image of what and who we are in this world. Among us today this fear is as strong, and perhaps stronger, than it ever was. In fact, it is the common man who knows this fear best.

Now, if it is true that tragedy is the consequence of a man's total compulsion to evaluate himself justly, his destruction in the attempt posits a wrong or an evil in his environment. And this is precisely the morality of tragedy and its lesson. The discovery of the moral law, which is what the enlightenment of tragedy consists of, is not the discovery of some abstract or metaphysical quality.

The tragic right is a condition of life, a condition in which the human personality is able to flower and realize itself. The wrong is the condition which suppresses man, perverts the flowing out of his love and creative instinct. Tragedy enlightens — and it must, in that it points the heroic finger at the enemy of man's freedom. The thrust for freedom is the quality in tragedy which exalts. The revolutionary questioning of the stable environment is what terrifies. In no way is the common man debarred from such thoughts or such actions.

Seen in this light, our lack of tragedy may be partially accounted for by the turn which modern literature has taken toward the purely psychiatric view of life, or the purely sociological. If all our miseries, our indignities, are born and bred within our minds, then all action, let alone the heroic action, is obviously impossible.

And if society alone is responsible for the cramping of our lives, then the protagonist must needs be so pure and faultless as to force us to deny his validity as a character. From neither of these views can tragedy derive, simply because neither represents a balanced concept of life. Above all else, tragedy requires the finest appreciation by the writer of cause and effect.

No tragedy can therefore come about when its author fears to question absolutely everything, when he regards any institution, habit or custom as being either everlasting, immutable or inevitable. In the tragic view the need of man to wholly realize himself is the only fixed star, and whatever it is that hedges his nature and lowers it is ripe for attack and examination. Which is not to say that tragedy must preach revolution.

The Greeks could probe the very heavenly origin of their ways and return to confirm the rightness of laws. And Job could face God in anger, demanding his right and end in submission. But for a moment everything is in suspension, nothing is accepted, and in this stretching and tearing apart of the cosmos, in the very action of the so doing, the character gains "size," the tragic stature which is spuriously attached to the royal or to the high born in our minds. The commonest of men may take on that stature to the extent of his willingness to throw all he has into the contest, the battle to secure his rightful place in his world.

There is a misconception of tragedy with which I have been struck in review after review, and in many conversations with writers and readers alike. It is the idea that tragedy is of necessity allied to pessimism. Even the dictionary says nothing more about the word than that it means a story with a sad or unhappy ending. This impression is so firmly fixed that I almost hesitate to claim that in truth tragedy implies more optimism in its author than does comedy, and that its final result ought to be the reinforcement of the onlooker's brightest opinions of the human animal.

For, if it is true to say that in essence the tragic hero is intent upon claiming his whole due as a personality, and if this struggle must be total and without reservation, then it automatically demonstrates the indestructible will of man to achieve his humanity.

The possibility of victory must be there in tragedy. Where pathos rules, where pathos is finally derived, a character has fought a battle he could not possibly have won. The pathetic is achieved when the protagonist is, by virtue of his witlessness, his insensitivity, or the very air he gives off, incapable of grappling with a much superior force.

Pathos truly is the mode for the pessimist. But tragedy requires a nicer balance between what is possible and what is impossible. And it is curious, although edifying, that the plays we revere, century after century, are the tragedies. In them, and in them alone, lies the belief — optimistic, if you will, in the perfectibility of man.

It is time, I think, that we who are without kings, took up this bright thread of our history and followed it to the only place it can possibly lead in our time — the heart and spirit of the average man.

FOR DISCUSSION

1. It seems paradoxical to argue that tragedy is more closely allied to optimism than to pessimism, but that's what Miller says. Can you explain his argument?

2. Is it true that mankind cherishes tragedy above all other forms of drama?

3. Why is the common man as fit a subject for tragedy as a king?

4. What social forces or attitudes have changed the earlier belief that only high-placed persons were fit subjects for tragedy?

5. Have you ever seen a movie that would fit Miller's conception of tragedy? Was *Gone with the Wind* a tragedy?

VOCABULARY: skepticism, circumspection, inherent, cosmos, inner dynamic, posit, metaphysical, immutable, pathetic, protagonist.

THEME TOPICS: Tragic elements in *Macbeth* (or any other Shakespearean play). "Life is a comedy to the man who thinks, a tragedy to the man who feels." Tragedy pits man against fate. The difference between pathos and tragedy. Tragedy, the highest form of drama.

The *Salesman's* Two Cases

JOHN HAGOPIAN

A careful study of *Death of a Salesman* in terms of Arthur Miller's own defense of it in various articles, prefaces, and interviews leads to the conclusion that the author himself does not understand his own accomplishment — and his confusion is shared by his critics. The fact of the matter is that not only is Miller's salesman suffering from schizophrenia, but the play itself is afflicted with that disease. Most plays, like most people, have multiple facets to their personalities, but these usually function more or less harmoniously within a single integrated being. The two personalities of Miller's play do, of course, inter-relate, but they are basically different genres — a dazzlingly experimental social drama is the dominant personality, but it detracts our attention from the more important and more conventionally-made drama of a moral struggle toward insight and honest personal commitment.

Shortly after the premier of *Death of a Salesman,* Arthur Miller defended his play in the *New York Times* from certain critical attacks by asserting that "the common man is as apt a subject for tragedy in its highest sense as the kings were. . . . The tragic feeling is evoked in us when we are in the presence of a character who is ready to lay down his life, if need be, to secure one thing — his sense of personal dignity." He elaborated his arguments in the introduction to *A View from the Bridge,* where he said that all good drama is essentially social drama, depicting man in a struggle to wrest from his society some recognition of his worth not as a customer, draftee, machine tender, ideologist, or whatever, but as a human being. Modern society refuses to grant him that recognition, and any determined effort to secure it is doomed to end tragically. "The reason *Death of a Salesman* . . . left such a strong impression was that it set forth unremittingly the picture of a man who was not even especially 'good' but whose situation made clear that at bottom

From *Modern Drama,* September, 1963. Reprinted by permission of the publisher.

we are alone, valueless, without even the elements of a human person, when once we fail to fit the patterns of [social] efficiency." The fullest discussion of the genesis, form, and meaning of all of Miller's plays to date is in his introduction to the *Collected Plays* where Miller takes his critics to task for misreading *Death of a Salesman* as an anti-capitalistic play or as a document of futility and pessimism. Perhaps Miller's most significant comment is that "Willy Loman has broken a law [of modern culture just as Oedipus had of Greek culture] without whose protection life is unsupportable if not incomprehensible to him and to many others; it is the law which says that a failure in society and in business has no right to live. . . . My attempt in the play was to counter this [law] with an opposing system which, so to speak, is in a race for Willy's faith, and it is the system of love which is the opposite of the law of success. It is embodied in Biff Loman, but by the time Willy can perceive his love it can serve only as an ironic comment upon the life he sacrificed for power and for success and its tokens."

Obviously, Miller focuses his attention on Willy Loman — Biff functions in a sub-plot designed to serve merely as an "ironic comment" on the main plot. But intention does not here square with achievement. Miller and his critics are in error in seeing the central character of the play in Willy Loman. The protagonist of a drama must be the one who struggles most for understanding, who faces the most crucial question, who achieves the most transforming insight, and whose motives, decisions, and actions most influence the total situation. By these criteria the main figure of *Death of a Salesman* is not Willy, whose understanding and values change not one bit from the beginning to the end; it is Biff Loman, who is seeking to "find himself" and does so in making an anguished choice between clear-cut alternatives — continued drifting or redeeming himself, achieving vitality at the sacrifice of his father and his father's values. Willy is simply a man to whom things happen and who responds with bewilderment and a desperate clinging to his old faith; Biff is a man who ultimately makes things happen, who responds to the great trauma in his life first with an emotional and moral paralysis and then with a determined effort to face the truth at whatever cost.

Probably the chief reason why audiences and critics have difficulty seeing this pattern of dramatic meaning is that Miller has experimented in drama with the two major innovations of modern fiction: stream-of-consciousness, and the controlling intelligence of a limited point of view. Since both techniques are used to construct Willy Loman, the dramatic pyrotechnics illuminate the salesman out of all proportion to his real dramatic, philosophical, and psychological importance. "The first image that occurred to me," says Miller, "was of an enormous face the height of the proscenium arch which would appear and then open up, and we would see the inside of a man's head. In fact, *The Inside of His Head* was the first title. . . . I wished to create a form which . . . would literally be the process of Willy Loman's way of mind." Even without the physical image of the huge head, Miller has succeeded in making the action of the play largely the stream-of-consciousness of Willy; through fluid stage setting and bold use of lighting the memories and hallucinations of Willy are rendered not as "flashbacks" to earlier events objectively seen but as happenings of the present in Willy's mind. But Miller has paid the price of having audiences respond emotionally to the medium itself rather than see through it to the magnificent drama which it contains. For it seems that Miller has created *Death of a Salesman* with artistic intuition rather than critical intelligence, despite his *ex post facto* suggestions to the contrary. For example, he says, "What was wanted . . . was not a mounting line of tension, nor a gradually narrowing cone of intensifying suspense, but a bloc, a single chord presented as such at the outset . . . to hold back nothing . . . even at the cost of suspense and climax." To be sure, in so far as Willy is not merely the medium but the subject of the drama, Miller has almost achieved his aim despite the fact that drama is a temporal, dynamic medium which must move forward. The very first image of Willy is of a man utterly defeated — "I'm tired to the death. I couldn't make it. I just couldn't make it, Linda," he says. And his death at the end of the play is merely confirmation of the fact established at the outset. However, in so far as Willy's mind is the frame, the controlling intelligence, the stream-of-consciousness within which is enacted the drama of Biff, there is a beautifully structured line of mounting tension. To a large degree, the movement of the play is exactly like that of Sophocles' *Oedipus;* the drama moves forward by accumulating significant moments of the past that gradually illuminate the central problem — the conflict between the father and his oldest son. Exactly what is that conflict? What brought it about? How will it be resolved? — these are the questions that are involved in the central movement. And although everyone in the play at some point or other faces that problem, it is Biff who acts to resolve it.

The very first dialogue of the play sets it up:

> WILLY. There's such an undercurrent in him. He became a moody man. . . .
> LINDA. . . . I think if he finds himself, then you'll both be happier and not fight any more.
>
> . . . .
>
> WILLY. Why did he come home? I would like to know what brought him home.
> LINDA. I don't know. I think he's still lost, Willy. I think he's very lost.

Biff is indeed lost, and he has come home to make one final effort to resolve his inner conflict; but at this stage, of course, we still do not know what the conflict is about. The dialogue suggests that it somehow has to do with his relations with his father, a notion confirmed in Biff's first dialogue with Happy:

> HAPPY. . . . What happened, Biff? Where's the old humor, the old confidence? (He shakes Biff's knee, Biff gets up and moves restlessly about the room.) What's the matter?

BIFF. Why does Dad mock me all the time? . . . / . . . Everything I say there's a twist of mockery on his face. I can't get near him.

. . . .

HAPPY. I think the fact that you're not settled, that you're still kind of up in the air . . .

BIFF. There's one or two other things depressing him, Happy.

HAPPY. What do you mean?

BIFF. Never mind. Just don't lay it all to me.

No suspense? No mounting line of tension? Only the most insensitive member of the audience would not at this point feel a rising curiosity focussed specifically on Biff's problem with his father. In the ensuing dialogue, Biff recapitulates his misery in trying to establish a foothold in the business world after leaving high school and the contrasting peace and content he experienced while working on a ranch in Texas: "There's nothing more inspiring or — beautiful than the sight of a mare and a new colt," an effective symbol of his urge toward vitality and creativity. Then why, as Willy had asked earlier, has he come home? Because his family is the arena of his unresolved conflict. Biff then listens in amazement and despair to his father's hallucinatory recapitulation of the idyllic past when he was still the idolized god of his sons, inculcating in them the false values he persisted in holding despite the fact that they did not work for him. That long scene ends with a revelation of Willy's immense feeling of guilt concerning his philandering during his lonely and unsuccessful treks to the markets of New England. No specific connection is made between that guilt and the father-son conflict, but again and again the first act thrusts relentlessly toward illumination of the conflict and an implicit connection is made.

When the neighbor, Charley (the chorus figure of the play), comes over to calm Willy after his raving hallucination, Willy says, "I can't understand it. He's going back to Texas again. . . . I got nothin' to give him, Charley"; and his kindly neighbor advises him to forget it, to release the boy, to let him live his own life according to his own code. Then, after Charley leaves and Willy decides to go for a walk, the two sons come down to discuss their father's plight with their mother and again the father-son issue is faced:

LINDA. When you write you're coming, he's all smiles. . . . And then the closer you come, the more shaky he gets. . . . He can't bring himself to open up to you. Why are you so hateful to each other? Why is that?

Biff is evasive and conciliatory, but the mother insists that the sons must have respect for their father, be concerned about his distraught and pitiable condition — "What happened to the love you had for him?"

BIFF. . . . I know he's a fake and he doesn't like anybody around who knows!

LINDA. Why a fake? In what way? What do you mean?

BIFF. Just don't lay it all at my feet. It's between me and him — that's all I have to say.

Again, the revelation of the cause of the conflict is avoided, but it is fore-shadowed when Linda, describing Willy's attempts at suicide, refers to a woman and Biff sharply interrupts with a tense question, "What woman?" before Linda can explain that she is referring to a woman who had witnessed Willy's deliberate smash-up in his car. Finally, this powerful dramatic line culminates at the end of the first act in a tremendous confrontation scene between father and son. The clash between their *social* values, which has been clear since the opening dialogue between Biff and Happy, is now openly faced, but the more powerful cause of discord, the *private*, secret anguish caused by the awareness of both father and son that Willy has be-trayed the love of his family, is only darkly suggested:

> BIFF. . . . They've laughed at Dad for years, and you know why? Because we don't belong in this nuthouse of a city! We should be mixing cement on some open plain, or — or carpenters . . .
>
> . . . .
>
> WILLY. Why do you always insult me?
>
> . . . .
>
> BIFF. Oh, Jesus, I'm going to sleep!
> WILLY. Don't curse in this house!
> BIFF. Since when did you get so clean?

But Biff succumbs to the forces of family reconciliation and reluctantly agrees to make an attempt to fulfill his father's dream for him. However, the first act ends ominously with Biff in the cellar holding the rubber tubing with which Willy has been planning to commit suicide, while Linda timidly asks the key question of the play: "Willy, dear, what has he got against you?"

Act II opens late the following morning with Willy announcing that he has "slept like a dead one" but feeling very optimistic. But the catastrophes begin to mount when, symbolically foreshadowing the climax of the play, the son of Willy's former boss (also his own godson) dismisses Willy from his job. In desperation Willy calls upon Charley to borrow money for the payment of his insurance premium, and in Charley's office the key question is again posed by Bernard, but this time much more narrowly focussed in time and place:

> WILLY. . . . There's something I don't understand. . . . His life ended after that Ebbets Field game. From the age of seventeen nothing good ever happened to him . . . / . . . Why did he lay down?
> BERNARD. . . . I got the idea he'd gone up to New England to see you. Did he have a talk with you then? . . . / . . . When he came back. . . . I knew he'd given up his life. What happened in Boston, Willy?

Willy is unable to face that question. At the restaurant where the victory banquet turns into a shambles when it is revealed that not only has Willy lost his job but that Biff was unable to get one, Willy interrupts Biff's attempts to explain with the outburst: "I'm not interested in stories about the past."

However, as inexorably as in Sophocles, the past must be faced. It rises in Willy's fantasies and collides head-on with the present that it has led to. As in Freudian psychotherapy, well-being can be restored only when the suppressed traumas of the past can be raised to consciousness and abreacted. The penultimate crisis of the play (and the answer to the intensely persistent question raised in the beginning: "What happened, Biff?") is reached when through Willy's consciousness we see enacted the shocking confrontation of the penitent son and the philandering father in a Boston hotel room fifteen years earlier. Biff's idol is shattered: "You fake! You phony little fake! You fake!" It is this discovery that had poisoned their relations and had rendered Biff unable to reconcile himself to his father's values. But neither had he the strength to reject his father, for that would mean cutting himself off from the strongest source of love he had ever known.

Now we are ready for the ambivalence to be resolved, and the final crisis occurs when Willy and Biff meet at home that evening. Biff announces to his mother "with absolute assurance, determination: 'We're gonna have an abrupt conversation, him and me.'" Biff does not intend to expose his father, as Willy fears, but he has resolved to break with him, to declare his independence, to assert his own identity and his own values: "I'm saying good-by to you, Pop . . . / . . . Today I realized something about myself. . . . To hell with whose fault it is or anything like that. Let's just wrap it up, heh?" But Willy cannot believe that rejection without hatred is possible and he provokes a scene that for emotional tension and dramatic illumination is one of the finest in modern drama. The discovery of the self and the honest assertion of it regardless of the consequences has always been the high point of the greatest tragedies. Here it has tragic consequence, but not for the protagonist; hence, *Death of a Salesman* is, in the highest sense as explained by Susanne Langer, a comedy. Because the forces that obstruct the development of vitality are grappled with and overthrown.

This fact is lost in the elaborate dramatic frame, Willy's consciousness, which calls excess attention to itself. The powerfully dynamic story of Biff is obscured and almost lost in the tidal waves of tragic feeling that wash over it. That is perhaps why there is so much critical controversy over whether or not *Death of a Salesman* is a tragedy. Even with Willy as protagonist, despite the immense pathos of his experience, there is a legitimate question. To be sure, *Hamlet, Samson Agonistes,* and other tragedies do open with the central characters already in a posture of defeat, but they at least achieve some insight and face their deaths with some degree of understanding. Willy Loman goes to his death still blindly committed to his false ideals. The fact that he does so out of an overwhelming love for his son and gratitude for the return of his son's love makes his gesture deeply pathetic, but hardly tragic. Within this frame of pathos is the experience of Biff in which we see an action that is serious, complete, and of sufficient magnitude, including a dynamic plot with ascending crises, epiphany, peripeteia, ethos, and dianoia.

Arthur Miller himself has been so preoccupied with his pathetic salesman that he does not realize that his own play does contain ethos (the moral decisions of a character) and dianoia (the ability of a character to say what is fitting in a given situation); he claims that *"Death of a Salesman* is a slippery play to categorize because nobody in it stops to make a speech objectively stating the great issues which I believe it embodies." What, then, are we to make of Biff's climactic speech which reveals that he has gained insight into himself, that he understands the issues involved in the conflict, and that he has made the morally and psychologically right decision?

> BIFF. No! Nobody's hanging himself, Willy! I ran down eleven flights with a pen in my hand today. And suddenly I stopped, you hear me? And in the middle of that office building, do you hear this? I stopped in the middle of that building and I saw — the sky. I saw the things that I love in this world. The work and the food and time to sit and smoke. And I looked at the pen and said to myself, what the hell am I grabbing this for? Why am I trying to become what I don't want to be? What am I doing in an office, making a contemptuous, begging fool of myself, when all I want is out there, waiting for me the minute I say I know who I am!

In his desperate fury to make his father understand, Biff seems on the verge of attacking him, but he breaks down sobbing, pleading for release from his father's phony dream. Willy, wild with relief at discovering that his son, far from hating him, truly loves him in spite of everything, relapses into his old dream: "That boy — that boy is going to be magnificent! . . . / . . . Can you imagine that magnificence with twenty thousand dollars in his pocket?" He rushes off to commit suicide, certain that with the insurance money Biff will "be ahead of Bernard again." But the dialogue of the "Requiem" shows that Biff is a new man, that he — and only he — truly understood his father: "He had the wrong dreams. All, all wrong . . . / . . . He never knew who he was . . . / . . . I know who I am."

There is, then, in *Death of a Salesman* a play within the play. Perhaps in the pre-Freudian era it was not possible for a drama to show a son resolving his Oedipus Complex by consigning his father to death without experiencing such tremendous guilt that the only possible consequence was tragedy. In Arthur Miller's play the son breaks away from the father image and in effect consigns him to death *without* the tragic consequences. However, for reasons impossible to determine here, Miller did not focus on that action, but rather on the pitiable father's fate. The result is a curious dramatic astigmatism.

The drama of Willy, daringly experimental in technique, has properly been described as social criticism; Harold Clurman calls it "a challenge to the American dream. . . . The death of Miller's salesman is symbolic of the breakdown of the whole concept of salesmanship inherent in our society." But Arthur Miller has denied that it is an anti-capitalistic play. "A play," he says, "cannot be equated with a political philosophy . . . / . . . provided, of course, that it is a play, which is to say a work of art." He says further, "The most decent man in *Death of a Salesman* is a capitalist (Charley) whose aims are not different from Willy Loman's. The great difference between them is that Charley is not a fanatic." Again, it must be concluded that Arthur Miller does not understand his own play. For one thing Charley's aims *regarding his son* are manifestly different from Willy's, but even on the socio-economic level Miller's remarks are misleading. To be sure, in its larger dimensions *Death of a Salesman* is not *primarily* concerned with politics or economics. Nevertheless, to the extent that it is concerned with these problems the play is clearly an indictment of the profit motive, of competitive salesmanship, and of planned obsolescence — three principal features of capitalistic society that distinguish it from other socio-economic systems. When Willy is cruelly deprived of his job after some forty years with the firm, Howard explains, "It's a business, kid, and everybody's gotta pull his own weight. . . . Business is business." And Willy howls in protest against planned obsolescence: "Once in my life I would like to own something outright before it's broken! I'm always in a race with the junkyard! I just finished paying for the car and it's on its last legs. The refrigerator consumes belts like a maniac. They time those things. They time them so when you finally paid for them, they're used up."

Miller has said also that the exponents of socialism cannot take heart from his work because "there is no such thing as a capitalist assembly line or dry-goods counter. . . . So long as modern man conceives of himself as valuable only because he fits into some niche in the machine-tending pattern, he will never know anything more than a pathetic doom." There is truth in this, and *Death of a Salesman* is broadly an indictment of all modern industrial society; nevertheless, in specifically attacking the profit motive, competitive salesmanship, and planned obsolescence, this play does specifically isolate the capitalistic form of modern society as its target.

This social problem drama of Willy Loman exists mainly in the outer frame of the play. In technique the inner drama is successfully integrated with the frame, but it is not so successfully integrated in content. That inner drama — Biff's drama — quite traditional in form and technique, has not been sufficiently appreciated as a uniquely American manifestation of the eternal, humanizing struggle of a man to achieve his own identity, even if it means the sacrifice of those he loves.

FOR DISCUSSION

1. The Willy-Biff relationship resembles the father-son relation in an earlier play by Miller, *All My Sons*. There the crime of the father is that during World War II, while manufacturing airplane engine parts, he allowed defective parts to be sent into the combat area rather than take a financial loss. As a result, a number of planes crashed. In the course of the play, the son exposes the father, the

father acknowledges the crime and kills himself. In *Death of a Salesman* there are several similarities and differences to be considered.

2. The traumatic event which has poisoned the relations of father and son for fifteen years is the son's discovery of the father's infidelity. By putting the scene on stage Miller tells the audience what happened fifteen years ago, but does he tell anyone else anything he did not already know? Is the event "raised to consciousness and abreacted" as Mr. Hagopian suggests? Is it relived by Biff?

3. Finally Biff declares his independence from his father's phony dream. How much of this declaration does Willy hear and understand? Does Willy go to his suicide really to provide money for Biff, or to show his love, or to expiate his guilt for his infidelity, or for other reasons?

THEME TOPICS: Guilt and punishment in literature and in the courts. Why does Biff steal? Social laws that are often broken.

Sophocles' Oedipus

BERNARD KNOX

Sophocles' Oedipus is not only the greatest creation of a major poet and the classic representative figure of his age: he is also one of the long series of tragic protagonists who stand as symbols of human aspiration and despair before the characteristic dilemma of Western civilization — the problem of man's true nature, his proper place in the universe.

In the earlier of the two Sophoclean plays which deal with the figure of Oedipus, this fundamental problem is raised at the very beginning of the prologue by the careful distinctions which the priest makes in defining his attitude toward Oedipus, the former savior of Thebes, its absolute ruler, and its last hope of rescue from the plague. "We beg your help," he says, "regarding you not as one equated to the gods, θεοῖσι . . οὐκ ἰσούμενον, but as first of men."

"Not equated to the gods, but first of men." The positive part of the statement at any rate is undeniably true. Oedipus is *tyrannos* of Thebes, its despotic ruler. The Greek word corresponds neither to Shelley's "Tyrant" nor to Yeats's "King": tyrannos is an absolute ruler, who may be a bad ruler, or a

From *Tragic Themes in Western Literature* (Yale University Press). Reprinted by permission of the author.

good one (as Oedipus clearly is), but in either case he is a ruler who has seized power, not inherited it. He is not a king, for a king succeeds only by birth; the tyrannos succeeds by brains, force, influence. "This absolute power, τυραννίς," says Oedipus in the play "is a prize won with masses and money." This title of Oedipus, tyrannos, is one of the most powerful ironies of the play, for, although Oedipus does not know it, he is not only tyrannos, the outsider who came to power in Thebes, he is also the legitimate king by birth, for he was born the son of Laius. Only when his identity is revealed can he properly be called king: and the chorus refers to him by this title for the first time in the great ode which it sings after Oedipus knows the truth.

But the word tyrannos has a larger significance. Oedipus, to quote that same choral ode, is a παράδειγμα, a paradigm, an example to all men; and the fact that he is tyrannos, self-made ruler, the proverbial Greek example of worldly success won by individual intelligence and exertion, makes him an appropriate symbol of civilized man, who was beginning to believe, in the 5th century B.C., that he could seize control of his environment and make his own destiny, become, in fact, equated to the gods. "Oedipus shot his arrow far beyond the range of others" — the choral ode again — "and accomplished the conquest of complete prosperity and happiness."

Oedipus became tyrannos by answering the riddle of the Sphinx. It was no easy riddle, and he answered it, as he proudly asserts, without help from prophets, from bird-signs, from gods; he answered it alone, with his intelligence. The answer won him a city and the hand of a queen. And the answer to the Sphinx's riddle was — Man. In Sophocles' own century the same answer had been proposed to a greater riddle. "Man," said Protagoras the sophist, "is the measure of all things."

Protagoras' famous statement is the epitome of the critical and optimistic spirit of the middle years of the 5th century; its implications are clear — man is the center of the universe, his intelligence can overcome all obstacles, he is master of his own destiny, tyrannos, self-made ruler who has the capacity to attain complete prosperity and happiness.

In an earlier Sophoclean play, *Antigone*, the chorus sings a hymn to this man the conqueror. "Many are the wonders and terrors, and nothing more wonderful and terrible than man." He has conquered the sea, "this creature goes beyond the white sea pressing forward as the swell crashes about him"; and he has conquered the land, "earth, highest of the gods . . . he wears away with the turning plough." He has mastered not only the elements, sea and land, but the birds, beasts, and fishes; "through knowledge and technique," sings the chorus, he is yoker of the horse, tamer of the bull. "And he has taught himself speech and thought swift as the wind and attitudes which enable him to live in communities and means to shelter himself from the frost and rain. Full of resources he faces the future, nothing will find him at a loss. Death, it is true, he will not avoid, yet he has thought out ways of escape from desperate diseases. His knowledge, ingenuity and technique are beyond anything that could have been foreseen." These lyrics describe the rise to power of anthropos tyrannos; so taught he seizes control of his environment, he is master of the elements, the animals, the arts and sciences of civilization. "Full of resources he faces the future" — an apt description of Oedipus at the beginning of our play.

And it is not the only phrase of this ode which is relevant; for Oedipus is connected by the terms he uses and which are used to and about him, with the whole range of human achievement which has raised man to his present level. All the items of this triumphant catalogue recur in the *Oedipus Tyrannos;* the images of the play define him as helmsman, conqueror of the sea, and ploughman, conquerer of the land, as hunter, master of speech and thought, inventor, legislator, physician. Oedipus is faced in the play with an intellectual problem, and as he marshals his intellectual resources to solve it, the language of the play suggests a comparison between Oedipus' methods in the play and the whole range of sciences and techniques which have brought man to mastery, made him tyrannos of the world.

Oedipus' problem is apparently simple: "Who is the murderer of Laius?" but as he pursues the answer the question changes shape. It becomes a different problem: "Who am I?" And the answer to this problem involves the gods as well as man. The answer to the question is not what he expected, it is in fact a reversal, that *peripeteia* which Aristotle speaks of in connection with this play. The state of Oedipus is reversed from "first of men" to "most accursed of men"; his attitude from the proud ἀρκτέον "I must rule" to the humble πειστέον, "I must obey." "Reversal," says Aristotle, "is a change of the action into the opposite," and one meaning of this much disputed phrase is that the action produces the opposite of the actor's intentions. So Oedipus curses the murderer of Laius and it turns out that he has cursed himself. But this reversal is not confined to the action; it is also the process of all the great images of the play which identify Oedipus as the inventive, critical spirit of his century. As the images unfold, the enquirer turns into the object of enquiry, the hunter into the prey, the doctor into the patient, the investigator into the criminal, the revealer into the thing revealed, the finder into the thing found, the savior into the thing saved ("I was saved, for some dreadful destiny"), the liberator into the thing released ("I released your feet from the bonds which pierced your ankles" says the Corinthian messenger), the accuser becomes the defendant, the ruler the subject, the teacher not only the pupil but also the object lesson, the example. A change of the action into its opposite, from active to passive.

And the two opening images of the *Antigone* ode recur with hideous effect. Oedipus the helmsman, who steers the ship of state, is seen, in Tiresias' words, as one who "steers his ship into a nameless anchorage," "who" in the chorus' words "shared the same great harbor with his father." And Oedipus the ploughman — "How," asks the chorus, "how could the furrows which your father ploughed bear you in silence for so long?"

This reversal is the movement of the play, parallel in the imagery and the action: it is the overthrow of the tyrannos, of man who seized power and thought himself "equated to the gods." The bold metaphor of the priest introduces another of the images which parallel in their development the reversal of the hero, and which suggest that Oedipus is a figure symbolic of human intelligence and achievement in general. He is not only helmsman, ploughman, inventor, legislator, liberator, revealer, doctor — he is also equator, mathematician, calculator; "equated" is a mathematical term, and it is only one of a whole complex of such terms which present Oedipus in yet a fresh aspect of man tyrannos. One of Oedipus' favorite words is "measure" and this is of course a significant metaphor: measure, mensuration, number, calculation — these are among the most important inventions which have brought man to power. Aeschylus' Prometheus, the mythical civilizer of human life, counts number among the foremost of his gifts to man, "And number, too, I invented, outstanding among clever devices." In the river valleys of the East generations of mensuration and calculation had brought man to an understanding of the movements of the stars and of time: in the histories of his friend Herodotus, Sophocles had read of the calculation and mensuration which had gone into the building of the pyramids. "Measure" — it is Protagoras' word: "Man is the measure of all things." In this play man's measure is taken, his true equation found. The play is full of equations, some of them incomplete, some false; the final equation shows man equated not to the gods but to himself, as Oedipus is finally equated to himself. For there are in the play not one Oedipus but two.

One is the magnificent figure set before us in the opening scenes, tyrannos, the man of wealth and power, first of men, the intellect and energy which drives on the search. The other is the object of the search, a shadowy figure who has violated the most fundamental human taboos, an incestuous parricide, "most accursed of men." And even before the one Oedipus finds the other, they are connected and equated in the name which they both bear, Oedipus. Oedipus — Swollen-foot; it emphasizes the physical blemish which scars the body of the splendid tyrannos, a defect which he tries to forget but which reminds us of the outcast child this tyrannos once was and the outcast man he is soon to be. The second half of the name πούς, "foot," recurs throughout the play, as a mocking phrase which recalls this other Oedipus. "The Sphinx forced us to look at what was at our feet," says Creon. Tiresias invokes "the dread-footed curse of your father and mother." And the choral odes echo and re-echo with this word. "Let the murderer of Laius set his foot in motion in flight." "The murderer is a man alone with forlorn foot." "The laws of Zeus are high-footed." "The man of pride plunges down into doom where he cannot use his foot."

These mocking repetitions of one-half the name invoke the unknown Oedipus who will be revealed: the equally emphatic repetition of the first half emphasizes the dominant attitude of the man before us. *Oidi* — "swell," but it is also *Oida,* "I know," and this word is often, too often, in Oedipus' mouth. His knowledge is what makes him tyrannos, confident and decisive; knowledge has made man what he is, master of the world. Οἶδα, "I know" — it runs through the play with the same mocking persistence as πούς, "foot," and sometimes reaches an extreme of macabre punning emphasis.

When the messenger, to take one example of many, comes to tell Oedipus that his father, Polybus, is dead, he enquires for Oedipus, who is in the palace, in the following words:

> "Strangers, from you might I learn where
> is the palace of the tyrannos Oedipus,
> best of all, where he is himself if you know where."

Here it is in the Greek:

> ἆ ρ' ἄν παρ' ὑμῶν ὦ ξένοι μάθοιμ' ὅπου (oimopou)
> τὰ τοῦ τυράννου δώματ' ἐστὶν Οἰδίπου (oidipou)
> μάλιστα δ' αὐτὸν εἴπατ' εἰ κάτισθ' ὅπου (isthopou)

Those punning rhyming line-endings, μάθοιμ' ὅπου, Οἰδίπου, κάτισθ' ὅπου, "learn where," "Oedipus," "know where," unparalleled elsewhere in Greek tragedy, are a striking example of the boldness with which Sophocles uses language: from the "sweet singer of Colonus" they are somewhat unexpected, they might almost have been written by the not-so-sweet singer of Trieste-Zürich-Paris.[1]

Οἶδα, the knowledge of the tyrannos, πούς, the swollen foot of Laius' son — in the hero's name the basic equation is already symbolically present, the equation which Oedipus will finally solve. But the priest in the prologue is speaking of a different equation, ἰσούμενον, "We beg your help, not as one equated to the gods. . . ." It is a warning, and the warning is needed. For although Oedipus in the opening scenes is a model of formal and verbal piety, the piety is skin-deep. And even before he declares his true religion, he can address the chorus, which has been praying to the gods, with godlike words. "What you pray for you will receive, if you will listen to and accept what I am about to say."

The priest goes on to suggest a better equation: he asks Oedipus to equate himself to the man he was when he saved Thebes from the Sphinx. "You saved us then, be now the equal of the man you were." This is the first statement of the theme, the double Oedipus; here there is a contrast implied between the present Oedipus who is failing to save his city from the plague and the successful Oedipus of the past who answered the riddle of the Sphinx. He must answer a riddle again, be his old self, but the answer to this riddle will not be as simple as the answer to the first. When it is found, he will be equated, not to the foreigner who saved the city and became tyrannos, but to the native-born king, the son of Laius and Jocasta.

[1] *I.e.,* James Joyce [editors' note].

Oedipus repeats the significant word, "equal," ὅστις ἐξ ἴσου νοσεῖ. "Sick as you are, not one of you has sickness equal to mine," and he adds a word of his own, his characteristic metaphor. He is impatient at Creon's absence. "Measuring the day against the time (ξυμμετρούμενον χρόνῳ), I am worried. . . ." And then as Creon approaches, "He is now commensurate with the range of our voices" — ξύμμετρος γὰρ ὡς κλύειν.

Here is Oedipus the equator and measurer, this is the method by which he will reach the truth: calculation of time and place, measurement and comparison of age and number and description — these are the techniques which will solve the equation, establish the identity of the murderer of Laius. The tightly organized and relentless process by which Oedipus finds his way to the truth is the operation of the human intellect in many aspects; it is the investigation of the officer of the law who identifies the criminal, the series of diagnoses of the physician who identifies the disease — it has even been compared by Freud to the process of psychoanalysis — and it is also the working out of a mathematical problem which will end with the establishment of a true equation.

The numerical nature of the problem is emphasized at once with Creon's entry. "One man of Laius' party escaped," says Creon, "he had only one thing to say." "What is it?" asks Oedipus. "One thing might find a way to learn many." The one thing is that Laius was killed not by one man but by many. This sounds like a problem in arithmetic, and Oedipus undertakes to solve it. But the chorus which now comes on stage has no such confidence: it sings of the plague with despair, but it makes this statement in terms of the same metaphor; it has its characteristic word which, like the priest and like Oedipus, it pronounces twice. The chorus' word is ἀνάριθμος, "numberless," "uncountable." "My sorrows are beyond the count of number," and later, "uncountable the deaths of which the city is dying." The plague is something beyond the power of "number . . . outstanding among clever devices."

The prologue and the first stasimon, besides presenting the customary exposition of the plot, present also the exposition of the metaphor. And with the entry of Tiresias, the development of the metaphor begins, its terrible potentialities are revealed. "Even though you are tyrannos," says the prophet at the height of his anger, "you and I must be made equal in one thing, at least, the chance for an equal reply," ἐξισωστέον τὸ γοῦν ἴσ ἀντιλέξαι. Tiresias is blind, and Oedipus will be made equal to him in this before the play is over. But there is more still. "There is a mass of evil of which you are unconscious which shall equate you to yourself and your children."

ἃ σ' ἐξισώσει σοί τε καὶ τοῖς σοῖς τέκνοις.

This is not the equation the priest desired to see, Oedipus present equated with Oedipus past, the deliverer from the Sphinx, but a more terrible equation reaching farther back into the past, Oedipus son of Polybus and Merope equated to Oedipus son of Laius and Jocasta; "equate you with your own children," for Oedipus is the brother of his own sons and daughters. In his closing words Tiresias explains this mysterious line, and connects it with the unknown murderer of Laius. "He will be revealed, a native Theban, one who in his relationship with his own children is both brother and father, with his mother both son and husband, with his father, both marriage-partner and murderer. Go inside and reckon this up, λογίζου, and if you find me mistaken in my reckoning, ἐψευσμένον, then say I have no head for prophecy."

Tiresias adopts the terms of Oedipus' own science and throws them in his face. But these new equations are beyond Oedipus' understanding, he dismisses them as the ravings of an unsuccessful conspirator with his back to the wall. Even the chorus, though disturbed, rejects the prophet's words and resolves to stand by Oedipus.

After Tiresias, Creon: after the prophet, the politician. In Tiresias, Oedipus faced a blind man who saw with unearthly sight; but Creon's vision, like that of Oedipus, is of this world. They are two of a kind, and Creon talks Oedipus' language. It is a quarrel between two calculators. "Hear an equal reply," says Creon, and "Long time might be measured since Laius' murder." "You and Jocasta rule in equality of power." And finally "Am I not a third party equated, ἰσοῦμαι, to you two?" Creon and Oedipus are not equal now, for Creon is at the mercy of Oedipus, begging for a hearing; but before the play is over Oedipus will be at the mercy of Creon, begging kindness for his daughters, and he then uses the same word. "Do not equate them with my misfortunes."

μηδ' ἐξισώσῃς τάσδε τοῖς ἐμοῖς κακοῖς

With Jocasta's intervention the enquiry changes direction. In her attempt to comfort Oedipus, whose only accuser is a prophet, she indicts prophecy in general, using as an example the unfulfilled prophecy about her own child, who was supposed to kill Laius. The child was abandoned on the mountainside and Laius was killed by robbers where three wagon roads meet. "Such were the definitions, διώρισαν, made by prophetic voices," and they were incorrect. But Oedipus is not, for the moment, interested in prophetic voices. "Where three wagon roads meet." He once killed a man at such a place and now in a series of swift questions he determines the relation of these two events. The place, the time, the description of the victim, the number in his party, five, all correspond exactly. His account of the circumstances includes Apollo's prophecy that he would kill his father and be his mother's mate. But this does not disturb him now. That prophecy has not been fulfilled, for his father and mother are in Corinth, where he will never go again. "I measure the distance to Corinth by the stars," ἄστροις . . . ἐκμετρούμενος. What does disturb him is that he may be the murderer of Laius, the cause of the plague, the object of his own solemn excommunication. But he has some slight ground for hope. There is a discrepancy in the two events. It is the same numerical distinction which was discussed before, whether Laius was killed by one man or many. Jocasta said robbers and Oedipus was alone. This distinction is now all-important, the key to the solution of the equation. Oedipus sends for the survivor who can confirm or deny the saving detail. "If he says the same number as you then I am not the murderer. For one cannot equal many."

οὐ γὰε γένοιτ' ἂν εἰς γε τοῖς πολλοῖς ἴσος

which may fairly be rendered, "In no circumstances can one be equal to more than one." Oedipus' guilt or innocence rests now on a mathematical axiom.

But a more fundamental equation has been brought into question, the relation of the oracles to reality. Here are two oracles, both the same, both unfulfilled; the same terrible destiny was predicted for Jocasta's son, who is dead, and for Oedipus, who has avoided it. One thing is clear to Jocasta. Whoever turns out to be Laius' murderer, the oracles are wrong. "From this day forward I would not, for all prophecy can say, turn my head this way or that." If the equation of the oracles with reality is a false equation, then religion is meaningless. Neither Jocasta nor Oedipus can allow the possibility that the oracles are right, and they accept the consequences, as they proceed to make clear. But the chorus cannot, and it now abandons Oedipus the calculator and turns instead to those "high-footed laws, which are the children of Olympus and not a creation of mortal man." It calls on Zeus to fulfill the oracles. "If these things do not coincide," ἁρμόσει, if the oracles do not equal reality, then "the divine order is overthrown," ἔρρει τὰ θεῖα. The situation and future of two individuals has become a test of divine power: if they are right, sings the chorus, "why reverence Apollo's Delphi, the center of the world? Why join the choral dance?" τί δεῖ με χορεύειν; and with this phrase the issue is brought out of the past into the present moment in the theater of Dionysus. For this song itself is also a dance, the choral stasimon which is the nucleus of tragedy and which reminds us that tragedy itself is an act of religious worship. If the oracles and the truth are not equated the performance of the play has no meaning, for tragedy is a religious ritual. This phrase is a tour de force which makes the validity of the performance itself depend on the dénouement of the play.

The oracles are now the central issue; the murder of Laius fades into the background. A messenger from Corinth brings news, news which will be greeted, he announces, "with an equal amount of sorrow and joy." "What is it," asks Jocasta, "which has such double power?" Polybus is dead. The sorrow equal to the joy will come later; for the moment there is only joy. The oracles are proved wrong again: Oedipus' father is dead. Oedipus can no more kill his father than the son of Laius killed his. "Oracles of the gods, where are you now?" Oedipus is caught up in Jocasta's exaltation, but it does not last. Only half his burden has been lifted from him. His mother still lives. He must still measure the distance to Corinth by the stars, still fear the future.

Both Jocasta and the messenger now try to relieve him of this last remaining fear. Jocasta makes her famous declaration in which she rejects fear, providence, divine and human alike, and indeed any idea of order or plan. Her declaration amounts almost to a rejection of the law of cause and effect: and it certainly attacks the basis of human calculation. For her, the calculation has gone far enough: it has produced an acceptable result; let it stop here. "Why should man fear?" she asks. "His life is governed by the operation of chance. Nothing can be accurately foreseen. The best rule is to live blindly, at random, εἰκῇ, as best one can." It is a statement which recognizes and accepts a meaningless universe. And Oedipus would agree, but for one thing. His mother lives. He must still fear.

Where Jocasta failed the messenger succeeds. He does it by destroying the equation on which Oedipus' life is based. And he uses familiar terms. "Polybus is no more your father than I, but equally so." Oedipus' question is indignant: "How can my father be equal to a nobody, to zero? τῷ μηδενί" The answer — "Polybus is not your father, neither am I." But that is as far as the Corinthian's knowledge goes; he was given the child Oedipus by another, a shepherd, one of Laius' men. And now the two separate equations begin to merge. "I think," says the chorus, "that that shepherd was the same man that you already sent for." The eyewitness to the death of Laius. He was sent for to say whether Laius was killed by one or many, but he will bring more important news. He will finally lift from Oedipus' shoulders the burden of fear he has carried since he left Delphi. Chance governs all. Oedipus' life history is the operation of chance; found by one shepherd, passed on to another, given to Polybus who was childless, brought up as heir to a kingdom, self-exiled from Corinth he came to Thebes a homeless wanderer, answered the riddle of the Sphinx, and won a city and the hand of a queen. And that same guiding chance will now reveal to him his real identity. Jocasta was right. Why should he fear?

But Jocasta has already seen the truth. Not chance, but the fulfillment of the oracle; the prophecy and the facts coincide (ἁρμόσει), as the chorus prayed they would. Jocasta is lost, but she tries to save Oedipus, to stop the enquiry. But nothing can stop him now. Her farewell to him expresses her agony and knowledge by its omissions: she recognizes but cannot formulate the dreadful equation which Tiresias stated. "ἰοὺ, ἰού, δύστηνε, Unfortunate. This is the only name I can call you." She cannot call him husband. The three-day-old child she sent out to die on the mountain-side has been restored to her, and she cannot call him son.

Oedipus hardly listens. He in his turn has scaled the same heights of confidence from which she has toppled, and he goes higher still. "I will know my origin, burst forth what will." He knows that it will be good. Chance governs the universe and Oedipus is her son. Not the son of Polybus, nor of any mortal man but the son of fortunate chance. In his exaltation he rises in imagination above human stature. "The months, my brothers, have defined, διώρισαν, my greatness and smallness"; he has waned and waxed like the moon, he is one of the forces of the universe, his family is time and space. It is a religious, a mystical conception; here is Oedipus' real religion, he is equal to the gods, the son of chance, the only real goddess. Why should he not establish his identity?

The solution is only a few steps ahead. The shepherd is brought on. "If I, who never met the man, may make an estimate (σταθμᾶσθαι), I think this is the shepherd who has been the object of our investigation (ζητοῦμεν). In age he is commensurate σύμμετρος with the Corinthian here." With this significant prologue he plunges into the final calculation.

The movement of the next sixty lines is the swift ease of the last stages of the mathematical proof: the end is half foreseen, the process an automatic sequence from one step to the next until Oedipus tyrannos and Oedipus the accursed, the knowledge and the swollen foot, are equated. "It all comes out clear," he cries. τὰ πάντ᾽ ἂν ἐξήκοι σαφῆς. The prophecy has been fulfilled. Oedipus knows himself for what he is. He is not the measurer but the thing measured, not the equator but the thing equated. He is the answer to the problem he tried to solve. The chorus sees in Oedipus a παράδειγμα, an example to mankind. In this self-recognition of Oedipus, man recognizes himself. Man measures himself and the result is not that man is the measure of all things. The chorus, which rejected number and all that it stood for, has learned to count; and states the result of the great calculation. "Generations of man that must die, I add up the total of your life and find it equal to zero." ἴσα καὶ τὸ μηδὲν ζώσας ἐναριθμῶ.

The overthrow of the tyrannos is complete. When Oedipus returns from the palace he is blind, and, by the terms of his own proclamation, an outcast. It is a terrible reversal, and it raises the question, "Is it deserved? How far is he responsible for what he has done? Were the actions for which he is now paying not predestined?" No. They were committed in ignorance, but they were not predestined, merely predicted. An essential distinction, as essential for Milton's Adam as for Sophocles' Oedipus. His will was free, his actions his own, but the pattern of his action is the same as that of the Delphic prophecy. The relation between the prophecy and Oedipus' actions is not that of cause and effect. It is the relation suggested by the metaphor, the relation of two independent entities which are equated.

Yet no man can look on Oedipus without sympathy. In his moment of exaltation — "I am the son of fortune" — he is man at his blindest, but he is also man at his most courageous and heroic: "Burst forth what will, I will know." And he has served, as the chorus says, to point a moral. He is a paradigm, a demonstration. True, Oedipus, the independent being, was a perfectly appropriate subject for the demonstration. But we cannot help feeling that the gods owe Oedipus a debt. Sophocles felt it too, and in his last years wrote the play which shows us the nature of the payment, *Oedipus at Colonus.*

This play deals with Oedipus' reward, and the reward is a strange one. How strange can be seen clearly if we compare Oedipus with another great figure who also served as the subject of a divine demonstration, Job. After his torment Job had it all made up to him. "The Lord gave Job twice as much as he had before. For he had 14,000 sheep, and 6,000 camels and 1,000 yoke of oxen and 1,000 she-asses. He had also 7 sons and 3 daughters. And after this lived Job an hundred and forty years, and saw his sons and his sons' sons, even four generations." This is the kind of reward we can understand — 14,000 sheep, 6,000 camels — Job, to use an irreverent comparison, hit the patriarchal jackpot. Oedipus' reward includes no camels or she-asses, no long life, in fact no life at all, his reward is death. But a death which Job could never imagine. For in death Oedipus becomes equated to the gods. The ironic phrase with which the first play began has here a literal fulfillment. Oedipus becomes something superhuman, a spirit which lives on in power in the affairs of men after the death of the body. His tomb is to be a holy place, for the city in whose territory his body lies will win a great victory on the field where Oedipus lies buried. By his choice of a burial place he thus influences history, becomes a presence to be feared by some and thanked by others. But it is not only in his grave that he will be powerful. In the last hours of his life he begins to assume the attributes of the divinity he is to become; the second play, *Oedipus at Colonus,* puts on stage the process of Oedipus' transition from human to divine.

"Equated to the gods." We have not seen the gods, but we know from the first play what they are. That play demonstrated that the gods have knowledge, full complete knowledge, the knowledge which Oedipus thought he had. He was proved ignorant; real knowledge is what distinguishes god from man. Since the gods have knowledge their action is confident and sure. They act with the swift decision which was characteristic of Oedipus but which was in him misplaced. Only a god can be sure, not a man. And their action is just. It is a justice based on perfect knowledge, is exact and appropriate, and therefore allows no room for forgiveness — but it can be angry. The gods can even mock the wrongdoer as Athene does Ajax, as the echoes of his name mocked Oedipus. This sure, full, angry justice is what Oedipus tried to administer to Tiresias, to Creon, but his justice was based on ignorance and was injustice. These attributes of divinity — knowledge, certainty, justice — are the qualities Oedipus thought he possessed — and that is why he was the perfect example of the inadequacy of human knowledge, certainty, and justice. But in the second play Oedipus is made equal to the gods, he assumes the attributes of divinity, the attributes he once thought his, he becomes what he once thought he was. This old Oedipus seems to be equal to the young, confident in his knowledge, fiercely angry in his administration of justice, utterly sure of himself — but this time he is justified. These are not the proper attitudes for a man, but Oedipus is turning into something more than man; now he knows surely, sees clearly, the gods give Oedipus back his eyes, but they are eyes of superhuman vision. Now in his transformation, as then, in his reversal, he serves still as an example. The rebirth of the young, confident Oedipus in the tired old man emphasizes the same lesson; it defines once more the limits of man and the power of gods, states again that the possession of knowledge, certainty, and justice is what distinguishes god from man.

The opening statement of Oedipus shows that as a man he has learned the lesson well. "I have learned acquiescence, taught by suffering and long time." As a man Oedipus has nothing more to learn. With this statement he comes to the end of a long road. The nearby city whose walls he cannot see is Athens, and here is the place of his reward, his grave, his home. The welcome he receives is to be ordered off by the first arrival; he has trespassed on holy ground, the grove of the Eumenides. He knows what this means, this is the resting place he was promised by Apollo, and he refuses to move. His statement recalls the tyrannos, a characteristic phrase: "In no circumstances will I leave this place." The terms of his prayer to the goddesses of the grave foreshadow his transition from body to spirit. "Pity this wretched ghost of Oedipus the man, this body that is not what it once was long ago."

As a body, as a man, he is a thing to be pitied; he is blind, feeble, ragged, dirty. But the transformation has already begun. The first comer spoke to him with pity, even condescension, but the chorus of citizens which now enters feels fear. "Dreadful to see, dreadful to hear." When they know his identity their fear changes to anger, but Oedipus defends his past. He sees himself as one who was ignorant, who suffered rather than acted. But now he is actor, not sufferer. He comes with knowledge, and power. "I come bringing advantage to this city."

He does not yet know what advantage. His daughter Ismene comes to tell him what it is, that his grave will be the site of a victory for the city that shelters him. And to tell him that his sons and Creon, all of whom despised and rejected him, now need him, and will come to beg his help. Oedipus has power over the future and can now reward his friends and punish his enemies. He chooses to reward Athens, to punish Creon and his own sons. He expresses his choice in terms which show a recognition of human limitations; Athens' reward, something which lies within his will, as an intention; his sons' punishment, something over which he has no sure control, as a wish. "May the issue of the battle between them lie in my hands. If that were to be, the one would not remain king, nor the other win the throne."

Theseus, the king of Athens, welcomes him generously, but when he learns that Thebes wants Oedipus back and that he refuses to go, Theseus reproaches the old man. "Anger is not what your misfortune calls for." And the answer is a fiery rebuke from a superior. "Wait till you hear what I say, before you reproach me." Oedipus tells Theseus that he brings victory over Thebes at some future time, and Theseus, the statesman, is confident that Athens will never be at war with Thebes. Oedipus reproaches him in his turn. Such confidence is misplaced. No man should be so sure of the future: "Only to the gods comes no old age or death. Everything else is dissolved by all-powerful time. The earth's strength decays, the body decays, faith dies, mistrust flowers and the wind of friendship changes between man and man, city and city." No man can be confident of the future. Man's knowledge is ignorance. It is the lesson Oedipus learned in his own person and he reads it to Theseus now with all the authority of his blind eyes and dreadful name — but he does not apply it to himself. For he goes on to predict the future. He hands down the law of human behavior to Theseus speaking already as a *daemon,* not one subject to the law but one who administers it. And with his confident prediction, his assumption of sure knowledge, goes anger, but not the old human anger of Oedipus tyrannos. As he speaks of Thebes' future defeat on the soil where he will be buried, the words take on an unearthly quality, a daemonic wrath.

ἵν' οὑμὸς εὕδων καὶ κεκρυμμένος νεκύς
ψυχρὸς ποτ' αὐτῶν θερμὸν αἷμα πίεται
εἰ Ζεὺς ἔτι Ζεὺς χὠ Διὸς Φοῖβος σαφής.

"There my sleeping and hidden corpse, cold though it be, will drink their warm blood, if Zeus is still Zeus and Apollo a true prophet." What before was wish and prayer is now prediction. But the prediction is qualified: "if Apollo be a true prophet." He does not yet speak in the authority of his own name. That will be the final stage.

And when it comes, he speaks face to face with the objects of his anger. Creon's condescending and hypocritical speech is met with a blast of fury that surpasses the anger he had to face long ago in Thebes. The final interview is a repetition of the first. In both Creon is condemned, in both with the same swift vindictive wrath, but this time the condemnation is just. Oedipus sees through to the heart of Creon, he knows what he is: and Creon proceeds to show the justice of Oedipus' rejection by revealing that he has already kidnapped Ismene, by kidnaping Antigone, and laying hands on Oedipus himself. Oedipus is helpless, and only the arrival of Theseus saves him. This is the man who is being equated to the gods, not the splendid tyrannos, the man of power, vigor, strength, but a blind old man, the extreme of physical weakness, who cannot even see, much less prevent, the violence that is done him.

Physical weakness, but a new height of spiritual strength. This Oedipus judges justly and exactly, knows fully, sees clearly — his power is power over the future, the defeat of Thebes, the death of his sons, the terrible reversal of Creon. One thing Creon says to Oedipus clarifies the nature of the process we are witnessing. "Has not time taught you wisdom?" Creon expected to find the Oedipus of the opening scene of the play, whom time had taught acquiescence, but he finds what seems to be the tyrannos he knew and feared. "You harm yourself now as you did then," he says, "giving way to that anger which has always been your defeat." He sees the old Oedipus as equal to the young. In one sense they are, but in a greater sense they are no more equal than man is equal to the gods.

With the next scene the whole story comes full circle. A suppliant begs Oedipus for help. Our last sight of Oedipus is like our first. This suppliant is Polynices, his son, and the comparison with the opening scene of the first play is emphasized by the repetitions of the priest's speech — words, phrases, even whole lines — which appear in Polynices' appeal to his father. It is a hypocritical speech which needs no refutation. It is met with a terrible indictment which sweeps from accusation through prophecy to a climax which, with its tightly packed explosive consonants resembles not so much human speech as a burst of daemonic anger:

θανεῖν κτανεῖν θ'ύφ' οὗπερ ἐξελήλασαι
τοιαῦτ' ἀρῶμαι καὶ καλῶ τὸ Ταρτάρου
στυγνὸν πατρῷον ἔρεβος ὥς σ' ἀποικίσῃ

"Kill and be killed by the brother who drove you out. This is my curse, I call on the hideous darkness of Tartarus where your fathers lie, to prepare a place for you. . . ." This is a superhuman anger welling from the outraged sense of justice not of a man but of the forces of the universe themselves.

Creon could still argue and resist, but to this speech no reply is possible. There can be no doubt of its authority. When Polynices discusses the speech with his sisters, the right word for it is found. Oedipus speaks with the voice of an oracle. "Will you go to Thebes and fulfill his prophecies? (μαντεύματα)" says Antigone. Oedipus who fought to disprove an oracle has become one himself. And his son now starts on the same road his father trod. "Let him prophesy. I do not have to fulfill it." Polynices leaves with a phrase that repeats his mother's denunciation of prophets. "All this is in the power of the divinity ἐν τῷ δαίμονι, it may turn out this way or that." In the power of a god — in the power of chance — whatever he means, he does not realize the sense in which the words are true. The daemon, the divinity, in whose power it lies is Oedipus himself.

Oedipus has stayed too long. Power such as this should not walk the earth in the shape of a man. The thunder and lightning summon him, and the gods reproach him for his delay. "You Oedipus, you, why do we hesitate to go? You have delayed too long."

ὦ οὗτος οὗτος Οἰδίπους τί μέλλομεν
χωρεῖν; πάλαι δὴ τἀπὸ σοῦ βραδύνεται.

These strange words are the only thing the gods say in either play. And as was to be expected of so long delayed and awful a statement, it is complete and final. The hesitation for which they reproach Oedipus is the last shred of his humanity, which he must now cast off. Where he is going vision is clear, knowledge certain, action instantaneous and effective; between the intention and the act there falls no shadow of hesitation or delay. The divine "we" — "Why do *we* hesitate to go" — completes and transcends the equation of Oedipus with the gods; his identity is merged with theirs. And in this last moment of his bodily life they call him by his name, *Oidipous,* the name which contains in itself the lesson of which not only his action and suffering but also his apotheosis serve as the great example — *oida* — that man's knowledge, which makes him master of the world, should never allow him to think that he is equated to the gods, should never allow him to forget the foot, *pous,* the reminder of his true measurement, his real identity.

FOR DISCUSSION

1. Compare the characterization given here of the tyrannos, "the proverbial Greek example of worldly success," and Uncle Ben in *Death of a Salesman.* Would it be true to say that Oedipus failed because he aimed too high? Would it be true to say that Willy Loman failed because he aimed too high?

2. In *Oedipus at Colonus* what similarities are there between the old Oedipus and the younger one? What differences are there?

3. Why would "justice based on perfect knowledge" allow "no room for forgiveness"?

VOCABULARY: paradigm, sophist, peripateia, mensuration, parricide, macabre, commensurate, daemonic, suppliant, apotheosis.

THEME TOPICS: Irony of outcome and irony of words. If we knew all, would we forgive all? Is Oedipus tyrannos over-confident?

Yeats's "Sailing to Byzantium"

ELDER OLSON

In *Sailing to Byzantium* an old man faces the problem of old age, of death, and of regeneration, and gives his decision. Old age, he tells us, excludes a man from the sensual joys of youth; the world appears to belong completely to the young, it is no place for the old; indeed, an old man is scarcely a man at all — he is an empty artifice, an effigy merely, of a man; he is a tattered coat upon a stick. This would be very bad, except that the young also are excluded from something; rapt in their sensuality, they are ignorant utterly of the world of the spirit. Hence if old age frees a man from sensual passion, he may rejoice in the liberation of the soul; he is admitted into the realm of the spirit; and his rejoicing will increase according as he realizes the magnificence of the soul. But the soul can best learn its own greatness from the great works of art; hence he turns to those great works, but in turning to them, he finds that these are by no means mere effigies, or monuments, but things which have souls also; these live in the noblest element of God's fire, free from all corruption; hence he prays for death, for release from his mortal body; and since the insouled monuments exhibit the possibility of the soul's existence in some other matter than flesh, he wishes reincarnation, not now in a mortal body, but in the immortal and changeless embodiment of art.

There are thus the following terms, one might say, from which the poem suspends: the condition of the young, who are spiritually passive although sensually active; the condition of the merely old, who are spiritually and physically impotent; the condition of the old, who, although physically impotent, are capable of spiritual activity; the condition of art considered as inanimate — i.e., the condition of things which are merely monuments; and finally the condition of art considered as animate — as of such things as artificial birds which have a human soul. The second term, impotent and unspiritual old age, is a privative, a repugnant state which causes the progression through the other various alternative terms, until its contrary is encountered. The first and third terms are clearly contraries of each other; taken together as animate nature they are further contrary to the fourth term, inanimate art. None of these terms represents a wholly desirable mode of existence; but the fifth term, which represents such a mode, amalgamates the positive ele-

From *The University Review*, Spring, 1942. Reprinted by permission of the publisher.

ments and eliminates the negative elements of both nature and art, and effects thus a resolution of the whole, for now the soul is present, as it would not be in art, nor is it passive, as it would be in the young and sensual mortal body, nor is it lodged in a "dying animal," as it would be in the body of the aged man; the soul is now free to act in its own supremacy and in full cognizance of its own excellence, and its embodiment is now incorruptible and secure from all the ills of flesh.

About these several oppositions the poem forms. The whole turns on the old man's realization, now that he is in the presence of the images of Byzantium, that these images have souls; there are consequently two major divisions which divide the poem precisely in half, the first two stanzas presenting art as inanimate, the second two, as animate; and that this is the case can be seen from such signs as that in the first half of the poem the images are stated as passive objects — they are twice called "monuments," they are merely objects of contemplation, they may be neglected or studied, visited or not visited, whereas in stanzas III and IV they are treated as gods which can be prayed to for life or death, as beings capable of motion from sphere to sphere, as instructors of the soul, as sages possessed of wisdom; and the curious shift in the manner of consideration is signalized by the subtle phrasing of the first two lines of stanza III: "O sages standing in God's holy fire / As in the gold mosaic of a wall." According to the first part, the images at Byzantium were images, and one should have expected at most some figurative apostrophe to them: "O images set in the gold mosaic of a wall, much as the sages stand in God's holy fire": but here the similitude is reversed, and lest there should be any error, the sages are besought to come from the holy fire and begin the tuition of the soul, the destruction of the flesh.

Within these two halves of the poem, further divisions may be found, coincident with the stanzaic divisions. Stanza I presents a rejection of passion, stanza II an acceptance of intellection; then, turning on the realization that art is insouled, stanza III presents a rejection of the corruptible embodiment, and stanza IV, an acceptance of the incorruptible. There is an alternation, thus, of negative and affirmative: out of passion into intellection, out of corruption into permanence, in clear balance, the proportion being I : II :: III : IV; and what orders these sections is their dialectical sequence. That is, passion must be condemned before the intellect can be esteemed; the intellect must operate before the images can be known to be insouled; the realization that the images are insouled precedes the realization that the body may be dispensed with; and the reincarnation of the soul in some changeless medium can be recognized as a possibility only through the prior recognition that the flesh is not the necessary matter of the soul. The parallel opposition of contraries constitutes a sharp demarcation; in stanza I a mortal bird of nature amid natural trees sings a brief song of sensual joy in praise of mortal things, of "whatever is begotten, born, and dies"; in stanza IV an immortal and artificial bird set in an artificial tree sings an eternal song of spiritual joy in praise of eternal things, of "what is past, or passing, or to come"; and similarly, in stanza II a living thing is found to be an inanimate artifice, "a tattered coat upon a stick," incapable of motion, speech, sense or knowledge whereas in stanza III what had appeared to be inanimate artifice is found to possess a soul, and hence to be capable of all these. A certain artificial symmetry in the argument serves to distinguish these parts even further: stanzas I and IV begin with the conclusions of their respective arguments, whereas II and III end with their proper conclusions, and I is dependent upon II for the substantiation of its premises, as IV is dependent upon III.

This much indication of the principal organization of the work permits the explication, in terms of this, of the more elementary proportions. The first line of stanza I presents immediately, in its most simple statement, the condition which is the genesis of the whole structure: "That is no country for old men"; old men are shut out from something, and the remainder of the first six lines indicates precisely what it is from which they are excluded. The young are given over to sensual delight, in which old men can no longer participate. But a wall, if it shuts out, also shuts in; if the old are excluded from something, so are the young; lines 7 and 8, consequently, exhibit a second sense in which "That is no country for old men," for the young neglect all intellectual things. Further, the use of "that" implies a possible "this"; that is, there is a country for the old as for the young; and, again, the use of "that" implies that the separation from the country of the young is already complete. The occupation of the young is shrewdly stated: at first sight the human lovers "in one another's arms" have, like the birds at their song, apparently a romantic and sentimental aura; but the curious interpolation of "Those dying generations" in the description of the birds foreshadows the significance they are soon to have; and the phrases immediately following remove all sentimentality: "the salmon-falls, the mackerel-crowded seas" intend the ascent of salmon to the head-waters, the descent of mackerel to the deep seas in the spawning season, and the ironic intention is clear: all — the human lovers, the birds, the fish, do but spawn, but copulate, and this is their whole being; and if the parallel statement does not make this sufficiently evident, the summation of all in terms merely of animal genera — "fish, flesh, or fowl" — is unmistakable. The country of the young, then, is in its air, in its waters, and on its earth, from head-waters to ocean, wholly given over to sensuality; its inhabitants "commend all summer long" anything whatsoever, so long as it be mortal and animal — they commend "whatever is begotten, born, and dies"; and while they "commend" because they have great joy, that which they praise, they who praise, and their praise itself are ephemeral, for these mortals praise the things of mortality, and their commendation, like their joy, lasts but a summer, a mating season. The concluding lines of the stanza remove all ambiguity, and cancel all possibility of a return to such a country; even if the old man could, he would not return to a land where "caught in that sensual music, all neglect / Monuments of unageing intellect." The young are "caught," they are really passive and incapable of free action; and they neglect those things which are unageing.

Merely to end here, however, with a condemnation of youthful sensuality would be unsatisfactory; as the second stanza expounds, old age itself is no solution; the old man cannot justly say, like Sophocles when he was asked whether he regretted the loss of youth and love, "Peace; most gladly have I escaped the thing of which you speak; I feel as if I had escaped from a mad and furious master"; for merely to be old is merely to be in a state of privation, it is to be "a paltry thing / A tattered coat upon a stick," it is to be the merest scarecrow, the merest fiction and semblance of a man, an inanimate rag upon a dead stick. A man merely old, then, is worse off than youth; if the souls of the young are captive, the old have, in this sense at least, no souls at all. Something positive must be added; and if the soul can wax and grow strong as the body wanes, then every step in the dissolution of the body — "every tatter in its mortal dress" — is cause for a further augmentation of joy. But this can occur only if the soul can rejoice in its own power and magnificence; this rejoicing is possible only if the soul knows of its own magnificence, and this knowledge is possible only through the contemplation of monuments which recall that magnificence. The soul of the aged must be strong to seek that which youth neglects. Hence the old must seek Byzantium; that is the country of the old; it is reached by sailing the seas, by breaking utterly with the country of the young; all passion must be left behind, the soul must be free to study the emblems of unchanging things.

Here the soul should be filled with joy; it should, by merely "studying," commend changeless things with song, as youth commends the changing with song; it would seem that the problem has been resolved, and the poem hence must end; but the contemplation of the monuments teaches first of all that these are no mere monuments but living things, and that the soul cannot grow into likeness with these beings of immortal embodiment unless it cast off its mortal body utterly. Nor is joy possible until the body be dissolved; the heart is still sick with the impossible desires of the flesh, it is still ignorant of its circumstances, and no song is possible to the soul while even a remnant of passion remains. Hence the old man prays to the sages who really stand in God's holy fire and have merely the semblance of images in gold mosaic; let them descend, "perning in a gyre," that is, moving in the circular motion which alone is possible to eternal things, let them consume with holy fire the heart which is the last seat of passion and ignorance, let them instruct the soul, let them gather it into the artifice of eternity and make the old man like themselves; even Byzantium, so long as the flesh be present, is no country for old men.

What it is to be like these, the soul, as yet uninstructed, can only conjecture; at any rate, with the destruction of the flesh it will be free of its ills; and if, as in Plato's myth of Er, the soul after death is free to choose some new embodiment, it will never again elect the flesh which is so quickly corruptible and which enslaves it to passion; it will choose some such form of art as that of the artificial birds in Theophilus' garden, it will be of incorruptible and passionless gold; and it will dwell among leaves and boughs which are also of incorruptible and passionless metal. And now all sources of conflict are resolved in this last: the old has become the ageless; impotency has been exchanged for a higher power; the soul is free of passion and free for its joy, and it sings as youth once sang, but now of "What is past, and passing, and to come" — of the divisions of Eternity — rather than of "Whatever is begotten, born, and dies" — of the divisions of mortal time. And it has here its country, its proper and permanent habitation.

FOR DISCUSSION

1. What interpretations advanced by the author had not occurred to you as you studied the poem?

2. Do you find evidence to support the author's interpretations, or do some of them seem to you to be without foundation?

VOCABULARY: artifice, rapt, privative, apostrophe, dialectical, insoul, genera, ephemeral, privation.

THEME TOPICS: Squeezing a poem too hard. The over-all plan of a poem.

Three Poems by Dylan Thomas

CLARK EMERY

In My Craft or Sullen Art

It is not a fit audience nor are they a few to whom Thomas proclaims his allegiance. Nor, as he conceives them, are they particularly responsive. Small wonder that the epithet *sullen,* with its connotations of loneliness and moroseness and unrewardedness (cf. Skeat — "a portion served out to a religious person"), darkens this poem.

Is the poem, then, a complaint? or a realistic acceptance? or, in some odd way, a manifesto? It is something of each. The self-righteousness of his divorce from fame, money, popularity, approval of the elite is not without its tincture of self-pitying braggadocio. He may not exactly be all alone beweeping his outcast state, yet neither is there a sense in the poem of his arising from sullen earth to sing hymns. A sense of the highness of his calling rever-

From *The World of Dylan Thomas.* Reprinted by permission of the University of Miami Press.

berates far more thrillingly through "Author's Prologue" than through the present poem. And no one, remembering his fire-horse eagerness when an audience offered, can view with other than irony his strictures against "the strut and trade of charms/On the ivory stages." As Caitlin says: "Nobody ever needed encouragement less, and [in America] he was drowned in it. He gave to those wide-open-beaked readings the concentrated artillery of his flesh and blood, and, above all, his breath." His small-boy vanity shows in the false modesty with which he greeted Brinnin's encomium: "When I had finished reading, Dylan said, as if he were quoting a newspaper headline: 'Randy-dandy, Curly-girly Poet Leaps into Sea from Overdose of Praise,' and made as if to throw himself over the sea wall."

Still, with all his vanity, posturing, attention-demanding, when he went to work, he did so with a seriousness and dignity that made him a different person — one willing to suffer the isolation, uncertainty, tension, and self-mutilation required of the precisionist working in imprecisions and willing to do so with or without profit.

It is as a manifesto, however, that the poem is most interesting. D. R. Howard has suggested that the poem is intended as an answer to Yeats's "Sailing to Byzantium."

> In that poem, Yeats divorces himself from "the young in one another's arms" in order to pursue "monuments of unaging intellect," the possibility of permanence in a world of flux. Thomas, on the other hand, takes the lovers as the central thing to his art, and the phrase "sullen art" may be a reply to Yeats' demand that "soul clap its hands and sing."

The suggestion has merit. Nothing could be more alien to Thomas's spirit than to deny the flesh, love, and lovers for a mechanical singing bird. Nothing more entrances his interest than "those dying generations" which were the object of Yeats's irony. And his sympathy is never with Carlylean heroes past or present, but with "the scorned — the rejected — the men hemmed in with the spears." . . . .

The parallel between Keats and Thomas is close. Both were precocious young men; both extraordinarily sensuous; both outsiders — the one Cockney, the other Welsh; both were sensitive about their intellectual deficiencies; neither was, therefore, ever free from an uneasiness — Keats in the company of Wordsworth or Shelley, Thomas with Eliot and his compeers; each felt a falling-off of his powers; each could therefore speak without a false humility of having writ in water. Keats, more burningly ambitious than Thomas, made his effort, with *Hyperion,* to join the immortals. He knew he had failed. Thomas, perhaps more self-aware, certainly the rocked boy of his age, tried neither the epic nor the tragic vein. He did not hope for the intellectual aristocracy in his audience and was distinctly uncomfortable when their representatives appeared. His aim was lower. Yet it was high enough to justify W. S. Merwin's statement:

... he writes his poems 'Not for ambition or bread,' nor for public acclaim nor for the edification of the self-righteous, nor for the dead, but for the lovers ... If the act of love is conceived as the central act of creation, where love, in joy and then in pain and then in joy, overcomes death, it is clear why he should have felt that his poems were so directed.

The Force That Through the Green Fuse

This is the poem that started Thomas on his way. As Empson says, "What hit the town of London was the child Dylan publishing *The force that through the green fuse* as a prize poem in the *Sunday Referee,* and from that day he was a famous poet; I think the incident does some credit to the town, making it look less clumsy than you would think."

One of Thomas's least obscure poems, it could not have cost its earliest readers much effort to come to an understanding of its general meaning. G. S. Fraser has expressed it as well as any: "The forces, he is saying, that control the growth and decay, the beauty and terror of human life are not merely similar to, but are the very same forces as we see at work in outer nature." W. S. Merwin stresses Thomas's outgoing emotion: ". . . the doom within life is described again, but described because of emotion for things mortal, and the compassion makes the poet at once wish to be able to communicate with all other things that are doomed, to tell them he understands their plight because his own is similar, and makes him feel the depth to which he is inarticulate and painfully unable to do so."

Elizabeth Drew has been utterly defeated by the lines

> And I am dumb to tell a weather's wind
> How time has ticked a heaven round the stars.

"Is he," she asks, "describing love as a *seeming* absolute, 'A heaven round the stars,' and telling lovers that time and the seasons really control it too? It, too, is nothing but *process*?" But when the poem was published, the lines read

> And I am dumb to tell the timeless clouds
> That time is all.

The earliest readers were not confronted by a time-ticked heaven and did not suffer Professor Drew's uncertainty.

However, supposing the general idea of the poem to have been immediately comprehensible, would those earliest readers have been stymied by particular lines? Or, if not stymied, perhaps irritated by what might seem to them metaphorical irresponsibility? Imagine a conversation with a determined rationalist — such a one as wonders why Burns so emphasizes the redness of his "luv," who thinks of insecticide when he reads "There is a garden in her face," and who considers leaving a kiss within a cup both absurd and unhygienic.

The opening image will provoke his scorn. The flower, he will say, is the explosion. Agreed? And the stem is the fuse, and the force is the combustible in the fuse that produces the explosion. Now — according to the poem, the force is greater than the flower, and it is supposed to continue its operations after the destruction of the flower. But (and he gestures emphatically) the combustible in the fuse is never as powerful as the explosive charge it ignites. That is, the force is less than the rose. And both the combustible and the fuse are destroyed *before* the explosion occurs. Is this the case with Thomas's force and stem? It is not. Ergo, the metaphor is absurd.

Nor will he stop there. A condescending tolerance will move him to pass the imprecision of the metaphor. But he will transfer his scorn to the second of the poem's basic themes. To the first he has no objection: that that (whatever it is) which creates life and compels its maturation, ultimately destroys it. Well and good. A platitude, of course; but after all, is there anything whereof it may be said, see, this is new? But why should Thomas want to go about discussing the matter with roses, arteries, and the winds? If people who talk to themselves are suspect, what about those who talk to their blood vessels? Who would not think them "dumb" in the vulgar sense of the word?

If, thrown off balance by this attack, you mutter something about powerful emotion, expressed in vivid images and given compulsive power by dynamic verbs, and tightly packed into paralleling stanzas structured to offer statement, counter-statement, and refrain — he will catch you up short.

Emotion? he will query gently, and, musingly, Integrity of emotion? And, decisively, No. No poet who plays with words as Thomas does feels intensely. He is too busy thinking all the time, too much engaged with his dictionary. Consider, and he opens the book, the triple play on "mouth" in the second stanza. The triple-entendre is puerile — and it has an ugly sound. He is more clever when, life waning, he has the blood wax, but cleverness cancels passion out.

But that third stanza: carrying the sucking mouth of the second stanza through whirlpool and quicksand and lime-pit to the leeching lips of the fourth; playing the live sand that suffocates against the dead clay that burns; concatenating whirl — lasso — shroud — rope; obliquely relating sails to the lime that whitens them, as it whitens the bones of the man who had sailed, windless, through space; relating the shroud sail both to the leech (the edge of a sail) and to the last stanza's sheet. This man is not merely three sheets but three shrouds and three leeches to the wind.

And he shifts attack to the fourth stanza. With a quiet reasonableness.

There has been, he will start, no indication that the force in this poem is time. If you were philosophical you might think of it as a generalized *élan vital;* if you were religious, it would be God. (Here, though he is a professed free-thinker, he shows off by quoting some possible parallel passages from Books 10, 12, 14, 23, 24, and 28 of *Job.*) But, he resumes, notice that Time in leeching to the fountain head is the equivalent of the mouth that sucks the mountain stream. However, Time is not a force; it is that within which the force works, merely the period during which a process continues. No one ever says that God is Time — though Yeats was thinking as muddily as Thomas when he wrote

> The stallion Eternity
> Mounted the mare of Time
> 'Gat the foal of the world.

But a great many people do say that God is Love. Yet here what do we find? that Love is blood, blood collected in a pool, as in a black eye, the pressure of which is eased by the suction of Time. This blood is, of course, at the "fountain head," which must be the heart. But if it is there, and not under a contusion, can it be said to drip and gather? And how can blood fallen from the heart "calm her sores"? Except in death. But to this point, death has been the destroyer; now in relieving the pain of love it becomes the healer. There's an inconsistency here.

And then *Hirudo medicinalis* becomes an arachnid (order *Acardida*) — the blood-sucking tick — and then a clock, with a heart-like audible beat. Now how about that heaven that gets ticked around the stars? Are we considering "man's small place in the well-integrated, clockwork universe?" Or "the ecstasy of love 'ticking a heaven round the stars'"? The poet says Time does the ticking. Common sense says that man, hating time, has imagined the idea of eternity, thus in a way ticking off time. And perhaps this is what Thomas meant; but in his cleverness he didn't say so.

But you know, he says, relenting, Thomas *is* clever. You remember your muttering about statement and counter-statement. Do you realize that the whole poem is the counter-statement to its counter-statement? It's like this: In each of the first three stanzas the statement is that "the force" generates life; the counter-statement is that the same force destroys. Now since the refrain refers always to a helplessness, increasing the effect of the negative counter-statement, the pervasive tone of the poem is negative. And the conclusion scarely seems a happy one:

> And I am dumb to tell the lover's tomb
> How at my sheet goes the same crooked worm.

But it really is, because this particular crooked worm at the sheet bears Time-defeating sperm. We have been subtly led from compassion (for the hanging Christ-figure), to love, to that good joke on Time that, because of Death man has created an anti-Time (heart-beat quelling clock-tick), and finally to the idea of the infinite continuation of life-cycles. The poem itself is a perfect circle, *crooked* in the last line linking with *crooked* in the first. And as for the poet's being dumb — the poem is his own refutation. A really beautiful job!

And one is dumb to tell the determined rationalist, now reading the poem aloud á la Thomas, that in poetry absurdities don't matter when the words fall right.

Fern Hill

Nothing of the Wordsworthian mighty prophet, seer blest, best philosopher appears in this description of Thomas as a child, nor does the poem suggest that like Traherne at age four ("sitting in a little obscure room in my father's poor house") Thomas reasoned: "If there be a God, certainly he must be infinite in goodness." The poem makes no effort to articulate the fervors of Christian mysticism, nor to probe behind childhood's simple creed of delight and liberty to ascertain the nature of the "master-light of all our seeing."

Without either religious or philosophic underpinning, and written with no ostensible purpose save to evoke the delight and liberty of childhood, it may perhaps seem a less substantial work than Wordsworth's or Traherne's, a local color piece rather than a landscape of the soul. But it does succeed in that evocation: it is dramatic where Traherne is exclamatory; it is real, putting the child — and the reader — in nature whereas Traherne puts him in his *idea* of nature, a kind of jewel-box; it is objective, the older Thomas and his problems removed from the poem as Wordsworth is not; and it has a delicate rightness of touch that the heavy-handed Wordsworth ("Behold the child among his newborn blisses," *et seq.*) cannot match.

All three poets are concerned with a loss, the forfeiture of something peculiar to childhood. What may make the loss seem inconsequential in Thomas is that it is not a loss within an ideational context which, understood in its relation to that context, is recognized as other than loss. Traherne can praise God for the burning, ardent desire that destroyed his childish innocence. And Wordsworth, having relinquished only one delight, gained more and profounder joys. In each case, the deprivation is philosophically justified, like the *felix culpa* of Christian ideology.

In "Fern Hill," childhood was and childhood ended — because time passed. God does not figure; there are no intimations of immortality or parallelings of Platonic epistemology; it is not custom or society which eclipses the first light which shined on him in his infancy. The poem has only to do with a natural course of events. There is not even, implicitly or explicitly, a hinting of the necessary complementary relationships of innocence and experience, as in Blake.

Yet, for all that, the poem does not mildly impinge upon or glance off the reader's consciousness. It has the striking-force of drama, not of lyricism. And analysis shows that every stanza, in tiny hints of things to come unrecognized by the sacrificial victim, points to the inevitable reversal of fortune. Time throughout is the omnipotent antagonist; the hero adopts a variety of *personae:* the Prince; the Shepherd; the Runner; and Adam.

The poem opens with a subtle, unemphasized opposition. The boy is playing about the house and under the apple trees as "happy as the grass was green" — that is, as happy as the day was long. And the rest of the stanza describes a daytime scene. But the line immediately succeeding "happy as the grass was green" skips ahead to the time of an end of playing — "The night above the dingle starry." The line is quite out of place: this is not a nocturnal stanza. But the amusing accent of *dingle* and the affirmative connotation of *starry* so take the darkness out of *night* that one scarcely realizes that an incongruity has been perpetrated. It is further concealed by its being narrowly hemmed in by *green* and *golden*. Yet the darkness of that night — under that grass so green — remains.

The antagonist is introduced as a permissive avuncular sort, letting the young dauphin have and go his ways. But only within limits. In revising the old formula to *"once below a time,"* Thomas has stated exactly the relative positions of life and time. But Thomas's pleasant ingenuity here and the phrase's reminder of "happy as the grass was green" distract attention from the serious, literal meaning and keep us in a world of timeless make-believe.

Thomas employs equal finesse and with the same result in the last line: "Down the rivers of the windfall light." The basic metaphor, rivers of light, is strong in its suggestion of an unceasing flow. The contradictory significance of the odd epithet *windfall* almost escapes attention. The temptation is to relate it to "easy under the apple boughs." Light thus is that which comes easily, naturally, and as a kind of largesse. The concept of a decay and end of light has little or no initial impact.

In the second stanza, Thomas is overt enough in the phrase "the sun that is young once only." But in "And the sabbath rang slowly," he is at his tricks again. On the one hand there is the idea that every day is a holiday and a holy day, as long as one of those Victorian Sunday afternoons which never seemed to end. These days were not, however, Sundays but sun's days, and they died with the light of the dying sun.

This idea is made explicit in the third stanza in "All the sun long it was running. . . ." And in this phrase is the next contradiction — between *long* and *running*. It is not only Thomas who is running but also the horses of the day. Only barely hinted at, behind all the lovely activity of the running, there is the quiet looking up from the grave. Runners do not look upward; but Thomas sees high hayfields and smoke from the chimneys. And there is a oneness, an assimilation of himself into the four elements:

> it was air
> And playing, lovely and watery
> And fire green as grass.

One cannot avoid thinking of Housman's athletes and brook-leapers.

In the second half of the stanza, the child is actually lying down and looking up. His movement does not cease — he *rides* to sleep. But it is a less dramatic movement than that of the farm about him, which flies into space, and of the horses, which transform into *eques noctis*.

This diminishment in the darkness foretokens the change-to-come from child's-eye view of the farm to man's-eye view, a change which amounts to a reversal of a telescope. When Brinnin visited Thomas in 1953, they went to Fern Hill. "It all seemed much smaller and emptier than he remembered,

Dylan said. . . ." Shriveled and colorless were words he found apt to describe what had once been "Adam and maiden."

For the child, the farm so fabulously wafted away, fabulously returns, like the Prodigal, or Adam restored to the Garden (his exclusion a bad dream), or Peter waking to find himself unforsworn. But merely to name the Prodigal, and Adam, and Peter is to bespeak the inevitable loss of simplicity, of innocence, of faith. Even this fourth stanza, so wondrously "white with the dew," has its hints of mortality. They are not emphatically expressed, to be noted and filed away by the intellect; they are only hints in the atmosphere, causing chills at the spine like those premonitions of winter ineffably evident on even the hottest Indian Summer day.

What Thomas has achieved is to create a child's world from the viewpoint of the child who has never lost it. Wordsworth and Traherne speak from a remove, as adults, the sense of loss (and recognition of compensatory gain) strong upon them; theirs is a re-creation, not a creation; they are not in the child's world but looking back and expounding upon it. Thomas does not, until his final stanza, express his tragic point at all, but such is his skill that it was felt, if not understood, before the completion of his opening sentence.

FOR DISCUSSION

1. In his discussion of the second poem, does Emery mean to give the impression that Thomas is metaphorically irresponsible? Do you think he is? Does Emery perhaps mean, in the last sentence of the discussion, that "absurdities don't matter when the words fall right"?

VOCABULARY: manifesto, braggadocio, encomium, stymied, dingle, avuncular, largesse, unforsworn.

The Posthumous Life of Dylan Thomas

ALFRED KAZIN

Dylan Thomas's posthumous life began before he died. Before he died, before he lay for days in a coma in St. Vincent's Hospital, New York, while the literati, literary hostesses, patrons, and others milled around the hospital

From *The Atlantic Monthly*, October, 1957. Reprinted by permission of the author.

— one lady even came into his room and stared at him for half an hour while he lay trussed up like an animal in an oxygen tent, with tubes in his mouth and nose — anyone up and down the broad literary-academic acreage of this country who heard him read, or watched him drink, could have said to himself, more usually herself, "That man is great, that man is disturbing, nothing so exciting has happened to me since I passed my Ph.D. orals. I am going to remember this, he will soon be dead."

He will soon be dead. The legend of the poet-dying-young is based not merely on the opposition between poetic idealism and a materialistic society documented by Chatterton, Keats, Shelley, Hart Crane, but on the romantic faith that true poetry is of a shattering intensity that destroys the poet even as it brings out of him, in letters of fire, the poetry itself. And the expectation is superstitious. What is peculiarly dear to us, what really transports and charms us, what brings new life to us from the hero, the poet, the great man — this, by an automatic human discount, is vulnerable and frail. But beyond these general considerations was the overwhelming single consideration of Dylan Thomas, who seemed not only more gifted, more eloquent, more joyous than any other poet of his generation, but who was peculiarly available to all and everyone, so utterly without pose and literary pomp — he was always ragging his own poetry and, as he beerily filled out, the little barrel figure he made — that alive he was already "Dylan" to every casual pub-mate and literary pick-me-up, with the impending appeal, winsome and rakish, of a Frank Sinatra.

It was this combination of genius and plainness, of force and sweetness, that made so many people write him off from the living before he was dead. He had an old-fashioned "big" gift that made people identify him with the "big" tragedies of old-fashioned poets. Just as many people in England and America who had no contact with advanced poetry read him with a puzzled but obstinate sense that he was important, while foreigners in Germany and Sweden, puzzling out his poems, would say with a sigh, *"This* is a poet," so they knew, they all knew, that he would "die soon." For beyond everything else — beyond the fact that he was endlessly available, that he conducted his life in public, so that everyone knew whom he loved and whom he drank with and how he had turned over a table full of food and drink at Sweet Thing College — lay the overwhelming fact that he was so obviously not in control of his life and did not pretend to be. Perhaps no one is in control any more and it is only in America that people still pretend to be. But the ruling fiction in government and philosophy and education, and even among writers, is that we must all know exactly where we are going

---

And furthermore, my son, be admonished: of making many books there is no end; and much study is a weariness of the flesh.

ECCLESIASTES

and how to get there. As *Time* once noted admiringly about a surburban housewife, "she had life by the tail."

It was just the other way with Dylan Thomas. And it was because in an age full of supremely careful people searching for the "security" of personal happiness Dylan lived without sense, without a bank account, without an analyst, that he provoked the most tremendous astonishment and affection from people who had understandably forgotten what an enormous personal force can lie behind poetry. But he also aroused a certain fear, a fear for him and just as strong a fear of him, of all he could do to people's arrangements and engagements, and this often took the form of wishing "justice" to be done to him. He was so *outrageous,* as a student once complained, that in certain quarters his death aroused moral approval. And this belief in punishment, in righteous wrath against the outrager, was something that Dylan himself felt. When he first got the d.t.'s near the end of his life, he said that he had seen "the gates of hell." With his background in the shabby-genteel and the Nonconformist Welsh conscience; with his all-too-schoolteachery father and profoundly influential mother (to whom he paid dutiful daily visits at home), he not only felt at the end that he was in hell but that he deserved to be.

Of course he felt this — nobody brought up in our Hebraic-Anglo-Saxon-Puritan tradition ever sins carelessly, is ever totally apart from the sense of "sin." But the essential fact remains that Dylan Thomas didn't yield to that peculiarly American and modern folly of imagining that one can morally insure one's destiny. As a poet and as a very canny observer in several countries, he felt that life in the twentieth century is peculiarily chaotic and measureless, full of desperate private rebellions and self-blame in a society which less and less gives most people any ideal to be faithful to. He felt that metaphysically we have no knowledge and no certainty — he said that his poems had been written "in praise of God by a man who doesn't believe in God" — and that only "the force that through the green fuse drives the flower," the life process from love to death, is real.

And since he lived what he believed, or rather what he didn't believe, it was quite clear, oh terribly clear long before his death! that Dylan Thomas was wonderful but extreme, and that he would die soon. It was not merely that he behaved badly, that he turned over the plate of canapés at one place and addressed ribald remarks to the pretty young dean of women at another. What made him outrageous to some — and exactly as challenging to others — was that he had, in the provocative sense, no hope.

He had no hope. I don't pretend to know exactly why this was, and it's too easy to say, as so many have, that he drank in order to recover the first excitement of his lyrical gift. I think that fundamentally his lack of hope came from the lack of ideas suitable to the boldness of his temperament and vocation. He had no philosophy or belief that could express for him, that could work for him, that could even explain the burden of love and terror before the natural world that is the subject of all his poetry. He was almost the pure type of the romantic artist in our world, determined to write only "happy" poems that would show life as joy. But he was unable or unwilling to bridge the gap between the splendor of his solitary conception and the deadness of the world without the poet's light on it. All of Thomas' poetry shows the profound romantic need to intensify existence, to make it all come alive as it is in personal consciousness. But where so many great poets — Blake, Wordsworth, Keats, even Whitman — have recognized that their task is not to lose their new vision to the commonplace world but to explain and to unite it to human existence, Thomas felt absurd and histrionic, acted like a man who in his heart thought himself a fake.

He was too humble. It is a strange thing to remember of anyone whose gift was so personal and sweeping, but he regarded his own gift as slightly absurd; he sheltered it, wouldn't have his poems discussed, because he couldn't admit that poetry *is* thought, and that what he said in his poems many of his contemporaries really believed and were most deeply grateful to a poet for saying again. He was left with his fantastic linguistic gift as if it were something to read from, to entertain with, but not, in the artistic sense, to practice as a criticism of life.

But then, how could he have felt this in our age? The great romantic manifestoes were charters of human liberation by poets who identified themselves with new classes and revolutionary new ideas in society. In the gray drab British welfare state, Dylan Thomas felt like a "spiv," a juvenile delinquent. Being an utterly accessible and friendly and idle-feeling man, he couldn't help seeing himself as a faintly comic version of that universally respected legend, "The Poet." The public entertainer in him exploited the miseries of that humble bloke, that rumpled and tired Welshman, Dylan Thomas, who had no trouble enjoying his gift but who sometimes looked on it as something that had oddly been given *him* — he couldn't say just why! About other poets he could be utterly conventional in his admiration; his BBC talks on poets of Welsh background are banal. He even read the poetry of others with steadier power than he did his own. But if he was more reserved with people and perceptive about them than anyone watching him would have guessed, he was, about himself, without hope in the sense that he had nothing with which to explain and to justify the utter naturalness and human application of his poetry.

He believed in himself as a poet, there is no question about that; what he didn't believe in was what it was peculiarly the task of someone with *his* genius to believe in: that his poetry gave us truth about life and was a judgment on all of us, not just on himself. When people say that he drank in order to recapture the old ecstasy, his first excitement, they forget that his problem was not merely to recover this ecstasy, which understandably flagged, but to believe in it. Only this would have shown that he was in fact as great as others knew he was.

But guessing at his vulnerability, people foresaw his early death; and observing his abandon, they mistook his hopelessness for confusion. Obviously no poet of such fierce perception can tidily put his life away when he is not writing. The poet lives the truth he has to write, and when he is not writing he may live it in a chaos of unorganized sensations, of an excitement throwing itself upon life, that can bound back and destroy him. And Dylan Thomas's lack of "hope," in the specific sense in which I have tried to state it, should not obscure the central fact that as a poet he was the very opposite of the anxious salvation-seekers who are so dear to contemporary poetry. The tremendous vogue of Thomas's poetry stems from the fact that after the era of would-be "hard," pseudo-Christian verse of T. S. Eliot's followers and the self-conscious ironies of Auden, Thomas brought back to poetry resonance of feeling, the connection with nature, love, and death which is the peculiar power of poetry and which Rilke defined as "the past that breaks out in our hearts."

The deepest side of such poetry — and of such an attitude to poetry — is not merely that it rests on images which are to be accepted literally in their unmediated force, but that it represents an attitude toward life itself which is the opposite of control, complacency, and deliberation. In Thomas's poetry, life speaks *through* us:

> The force that drives the water through the rocks
> Drives my red blood;

man is an instrument of the energy that is divine; he is not, to use the American idiom, "structuring" life to make all things neatly realizable and containable. Ours is an irreverent culture. In the work of Thomas — and of Thomas's beloved Whitman — life, in the final vision, attains not a definite character but the quality of a worshiped and awesome natural force. It becomes a great fire, beyond man's ability to put it out, but to which he is glad, at most, to get near, still nearer, so as to be able to get down in words a breath of this radiant flame.

Obviously, then, Dylan Thomas represented for many Americans a rare touch of greatness, a relief from the ever-pressing success story. He embodied, without a word said to this effect outside his poetry, the pure romantic vision that is still admired in America underneath the automatic responses of our culture. No matter how fussily detailed and self-conscious our lives become, there is in our fundamental classlessness and our physical restlessness freedom from the frigid respectability that can be so depressing a feature of middle-class life in Britain. And Dylan was so friendly, in this respect so much like an American, so easy to call by his first name! He encountered a welcome here which not only made him feel as if he were free-floating in a sky made up of unlimited parties, girls, and liquor, but which, in the heady, inflated, overprosperous, overstimulated atmosphere of America since the war, must have made him, with his peculiarly heightened capacities for life, feel that he had been sent spinning out of the damp, dark wrappings of seaside life in Wales and hack work in London. The more uncontrolled he felt about life, the more he fell upon American parties, American excitement, American adulation, as if everything came from a rich, infatuated, always indulgent mistress. He drank here not like an alcoholic who enjoys his liquor, but like a fat boy gobbling down chocolate bars who can't believe that they make him fat. Inevitably, his death here made it seem to many glumly envious and depressed Britons at home as if Dylan Thomas had died of America as well as in America, and as soon as the news of his death at thirty-nine reached London, the word went out from his old literary pals that "America killed Dylan Thomas."

In a sense it was true. Just as many Americans die of the American way of life, of the American pace, of American traffic, so Dylan Thomas's end was certainly speeded by that unlimited supply of hard liquor without which nobody dares entertain any more, and which is not only more difficult to obtain in Britain, on British incomes, but which became to Dylan what poetry might have been if, in his own rueful words, he hadn't been flying over America "like a damp, ranting bird."

But it is also true that since the war a great many Britishers haven't needed to find in Dylan Thomas's death a reason for being exasperated with America: they already have so many. Any American who follows the British literary and highbrow press becomes hardened to the bitter and sometimes hysterical jealousy of this country — particularly from Marxists who can't bear to admit how much, in different fashions, Russia and the gray British welfare state have let them down — but it is ironic that Dylan Thomas's death should be blamed entirely on America. Like so many romantic writers, he felt a natural affinity with this country, while in Britain, being utterly outside the "Establishment," he was regarded with a certain loving contempt by some of the snobs who so righteously gnashed their teeth after his death. Nevertheless, Thomas's death was a terrible loss to his own people, to his own kind, and it is really because the mediocrity of literature today is less cleverly concealed in Britain than it is in this country that the death hit so hard.

The posthumous life of Dylan Thomas as a legend and a symbol — the last romantic poet in a conformist society, the Welsh lyric singer corrupted by the American fleshpots — became really intense when the personal rivalries between those who had loved Dylan came out into the open. Now that he was dead, many people felt an enrichment of their lives through their retrospective share in him. The fact is that Dylan Thomas was a peculiarly lovable as well as magnetically gifted person, that he inspired a great many

Writers, like teeth, are divided into incisors and grinders.

WALTER BAGEHOT

gifted people with the sense of an unusual radiance in their lives. And just as the many elegies after his death addressed him with an intimacy that is inconceivable in relation to any other famous poet of our time, so the extraordinary agitation he inspired lives on after him in the fascinated reportage of every detail of his life by people who obviously preferred Dylan drunk to anyone sober.

John Malcolm Brinnin's *Dylan Thomas in America* was, of course, the principal tool in shaping the posthumous legend of Dylan Thomas. And it is a mark of Thomas's fantastic vitality in death that a great many people who don't read his poetry, but who very properly see his life as a symbol of it, have found in Brinnin's book the documented record of what they regard as the very poetry of excess. They love this excess because it gives them a touch of the old romantic heedlessness and abandon, the price of which they do not have to pay, and which, as they read in Brinnin the account of Thomas's terrible last days, makes them shudder at an end so violently consistent with his life.

It is no accident that in our period the unconscious protest of so many young people against an overregulated but vacuous society is embodied in the admiration of recklessness which one sees in the cult of the young movie actor, James Dean, who died speeding; and that among a great many of the young intellectuals there is a similar cult of "Dylan," whose extraordinary records are fancied by the same people who admire the new jazz and hot rods. In colleges all over the country, listening to Dylan's voice as, "crooning" his poems, he still tries to catch his breath between lines, young people get from him the same suggestion of pure feeling that they get from good jazz. The California poet, Kenneth Rexroth, has linked as heroes of "the beat generation" "two great dead juvenile delinquents — the great saxophonist Charlie Parker, and Dylan," and insists that "if the word deliberate means anything, both of them certainly destroyed themselves . . .

"Both of them," Rexroth has written, "were overcome by the horror of the world in which they found themselves, because at last they could no longer overcome that world with the weapon of a purely lyrical art. . . . Both of them did communicate one central theme: Against the ruin of the world, there is only one defense — the creative act. . . . Dylan Thomas's verse had to find endurance in a world of burning cities and burning Jews. He was able to find meaning in his art as long as it was the answer to air raids and gas ovens. As the world began to take on the guise of an immense air raid or gas oven, I believe his art became meaningless to him." And in a violent but deeply moving elegy to Thomas, "Thou Shalt Not Kill," Rexroth attributes the poet's death to the superficiality of his contemporaries:

> Who killed the bright-headed bird?
> You did, you son of a bitch.
> You drowned him in your cocktail brain.
> He fell down and died in your synthetic heart.

The bitterness in these lines is by no means unusual. All over the country, often in isolated places, there are people, more especially young people, who look on Thomas as a rebel against mass society and a victim of the organization man. It is in America, at the antennae of the modern age, where the full force of technological culture is felt, that the cult of Dylan Thomas has reached its peak — documented, too often, from the remorseless day-by-day record of Thomas the drunk and the wastrel which Brinnin put down with so much fervor and unconscious resentment against the elusiveness of this magnetic figure. So closely do people feel related to Thomas that there are endless arguments still about Brinnin's book, for people tend to identify with Thomas to the point where they resent its itemization of his "lapses." When Brinnin admitted that he could not really account for Thomas's more extreme behavior, he meant that he did not want to and was punishing him for being so unmanageable. But to the "ardents," Thomas's life in itself, not in relation to them, has a heroic significance quite the opposite of the continuous disintegration that Brinnin leaves us with.

It was in protest against this impression that Dylan's widow, Caitlin Thomas, offered a brief foreword to Brinnin's book. And now that her own memoir, *Leftover Life to Kill*, has finally been written, a most important word from the most intimate source of all has been said. In his posthumous life Dylan Thomas really speaks now, through his widow. Caitlin Thomas's book is not the "answer" to Brinnin — the mere justification of her husband — that had been expected. It is better than that. It is an amazing duplication of Thomas's own strength and recklessness and abandon by a woman who obviously was the only person with a spirit equal to his and who consequently fought him and hated him and loved him to the point where their conflicting intensities almost killed each other. The only thing I don't admire in Mrs. Thomas's book is the self-pity in the title and a would-be pathos, at the end as at the beginning; but the self-pity is utterly shown up and exploded by the fierce emotional charge of the book and a powerful style which, once she gets control of it, gives one the same pleasant Celtic resonance from her careening Irish sentences that one gets from his tipsy Welsh ones.

The people who will be shocked by Caitlin Thomas's book would be shocked by Dylan Thomas if he were alive. A posthumous life is easy to take, for us who deal with it as symbol; Caitlin Thomas is so much alive that her book, which is as much about herself as about Dylan, never explains Dylan's directness and eloquence so much as when, with amusing honesty and perfect tenderness, she recounts her life on the Isle of Elba with a young Italian miner, surrounded by the violently hostile respectable.

There is about her, as about Dylan, a perfect genius for trouble. She is a born rebel who in today's situation doesn't know what to rebel against. She has her husband's instinct for extreme and desperate situations. But reading the account of her dismal life in Wales after Dylan's death, and of her flight to Elba with her five-year-old son, I could not help feeling that, given her temperament, she behaved with exemplary courage and humanity. What makes the book so remarkable is that, time and again, whether she is writing about Dylan, or herself, or her children, one hears the boisterous Thomas lilt, the authentic note, the lyrical cry from the heart that gives his style its force. And most unexpected and revealing, she makes it clear that in her, as in Dylan, is the fatal mixture, with her powerful temperament, of that intellectual frailty, that excessive availability and need to be loved, which so many pettier types have known how to protect themselves from.

The tragedy of Caitlin Thomas is not what she says it is — not entirely a matter of the tempestuous life with a genius as erratic as herself or of the subsequent loss which, frightful as it is, has obviously given her back to herself. The tragedy is in the excessive vulnerability, the constant readiness to be hit in the face which, in a person with her insurrectionary heart, cripples her at the very moment that she can rise to her full strength. She tells us that she had a passion for solitary dancing à la Isadora Duncan, where she could feel the "flowing" — but "as soon as I spotted the 'glance' of an audience, I was finished: the brain on the alert, all suspicion again, put the pincers on, and the capricious flow stopped abruptly. . . .

"That was one reason, now I come to think of it, why Dylan found it so annoying: it is the direct opposite of words. . . . It may be one of the substances that poetry is made of; that words are formed from; but its ele-mental — right back, through the encumbering ages, to the creation, the planets, the dinosaurs; the skeletons and protoplasm — force is, above any other point of supremacy, *wordless.* . . ."

Actually, her sense of what art means to her — this elemental force, right back through the encumbering ages — is exactly what makes her husband's poetry so vivid. In her, as in him, there is this same exciting and disturbing combination of force without hope — without a meaning she can assign to her experience that would relieve her from emotional suffering. Her rule of life, she says, is "always be ready to clasp the impending disasters," and I believe her. So that despite the essential modesty that seems to me the key to the tragedy of Dylan Thomas and the long-delayed emergence of his wife, it is this elemental force for which one remains grateful in reading her book. It is so much rarer than a "defense" of Dylan Thomas — who needs none.

✿ INDEX